EU Law

GERARD CONWAY

Routledge
Taylor & Francis Group

LONDON AND NEW YORK

First published 2015
by Routledge
2 Park Square, Milton Park, Abingdon, Oxon, OX14 4RN

and by Routledge
711 Third Avenue, New York, NY 10017

*Routledge is an imprint of the Taylor & Francis Group,
an informa business*

© 2015 Gerard Conway

British Library Cataloguing in Publication Data
A catalogue record for this book is available from the British Library

Library of Congress Cataloging-in-Publication Data
A catalog record for this title has been requested

ISBN: 978-0-415-81632-8 (hbk)
ISBN: 978-0-415-81631-1 (pbk)
ISBN: 978-1-315-70825-6 (ebk)

Typeset in Avenir, Bell and Bembo
by Apex CoVantage, LLC
Printed in Great Britain by Ashford Colour Press Ltd.

DEDICATION
To my parents and family

OUTLINE CONTENTS

DETAILED CONTENTS

PREFACE

EU law is often seen by law students as amongst the most difficult of the core undergraduate subjects in a law degree. Undoubtedly, EU law possesses a complexity beyond that of national law. While to some extent this reflects the fact that it is a legal system catering to 28 different Member States, there are also instances of seemingly unnecessary complexity, such as the parallel existence of the basic treaties of the Treaty on European Union and Treaty on the Functioning of the European Union, without a very clear division of content between them (following on from the original complexity of three distinct treaties and communities with the European Coal and Steel Community Treaty 1951, European Atomic Energy Community Treaty 1957 and the European Economic Community Treaty 1957[1]); sometimes unnecessary differentiation in the forms of legislative instruments and what might be called quasi-legislative instruments;[2] and overlap with the Council of Europe system.

This textbook seeks to highlight the distinctive features of EU law and its relationship with both national and international law. Arguably, the EU can only be fully understood in the context of the background of public international law, from which the EU originated. However, to some extent the EU has transcended international law, albeit that important aspects of the EU still reflect public international principles. It would certainly help law students to understand the EU if they first had to study public international law, which would provide a better understanding of how EU law more radically impacts on national law; this textbook seeks to do so within the limits of the space available.

As well as adopting a more contextual approach to EU law relative to principles of national law and of public international law, this textbook adopts a series of pedagogical features designed to help with the practicalities of getting to grips with EU law. Thus, basic learning points, more developed explanations of particular points and critical analysis are all highlighted in each chapter. Each chapter also contains a glossary to explain technical terms, one of the aspects of EU law that can make it seem inaccessible, although this is true of law in general as a discipline.

This book originated from an invitation by Dr Stefan Fafinski and Dr Emily Finch, who were at the time editors of the *Spotlights* series, to be an author for it. There already exists a wide range of textbooks in English on EU law. A number of these are excellent,

---

1   The adoption of the Merger Treaty in 1965, recognising the practical reality that the three treaties and communities in substance amount to a joint or fused entity did not change the legal complexity, as the three treaties remained operative.

2   The standard instruments of secondary legislation in the EU (regulations, directives and decisions under Article 288 TFEU, roughly equivalent to Acts of Parliament in a national system) are distinguished on the basis of their level of detail or the need for national implementing legislation and their addressees, whereas in a national system, differences in the level of detail and addressees are also found, but without differentiating the types of instruments used in this way. Although the Lisbon Treaty reduced the number of legal instruments, dropping the separate legal instruments in the former second and third pillars, it has, for example, introduced a confusing distinction between non-legislative delegated and non-legislative implementing acts in Articles 290–291 TFEU.

including *EU Law* by Alina Kaczorowska, also with Routledge. This book is distinctive in how it relates EU law more fully to national legal systems and to the international legal system, while also taking a critical – but not carping! – perspective on the subject. Owing to the detail and breadth of EU law, there is a temptation to produce a text that covers a wide range of detail, but tends towards description, rather than more contextual and crucial discussion. This book could not cover all topics of EU law – some aspects are only very briefly referred to (e.g. state aids under competition law and criminal law, while intellectual property and visa and asylum law are not included), although the book does seek both to put EU law in its broader context and to cover the essential elements of the subject.

I would like to express my thanks in particular to a number of people. First, I would like to thank especially Fiona Briden and her editorial team at Routledge. Fiona shepherded the process from the outset, and her care and sound judgement were very helpful at various points in addressing any difficulties and in bringing the process of writing the text to a successful conclusion. Damian Mitchell and then Emily Wells were both very helpful in dealing with the submission of different chapters and passing on reviewer feedback, and all three showed much patience in my various requests to extend submission deadlines (or when I missed the deadline without any prior request). Relative to their contributions, Fiona and her team deserve more than a mention in the preface. The process of text review was very helpful and brought about some notable improvements in some chapters, and I would like to thank the anonymous reviewers for their work. I am very grateful to Nicola Prior and Hazel Sharkey for their careful work in the final stages, as well as to Emily Wells for her work on the Web site. Dr Leanne O'Leary and Dr Jurgita Malinauskaite read over parts and provided very helpful advice. Finally, I would like to thank my family, in particular my parents, for support and encouragement during the lengthy process of writing the book.

This book was mostly completed by late 2014. It has been possible to include some more recent developments only quite briefly. Amongst the most recent developments that have been included to some extent, but not as fully as may be deserved, are the judgments of the Court of Justice in *Dano*[3] and *Opinion 2/2013 on Accession of the EU to the ECHR*.[4] These are more fully dealt with on the book's accompanying Web site.

A brief note on terminology. Terminological overlaps frequently and understandably cause confusion in EU law and the study of European cooperation. In particular, the EU and Council of Europe – which are two distinct, regional international organisations for cooperation amongst European states – can be easily confused. This is especially so because two of the institutions or organs of the EU – the 'European Council' (meeting of national heads of government of EU Member States) and 'the Council' (meeting of national ministers of EU Member States) – have similar names to each other and to the Council of Europe. For clarity, the 'Council' is usually described in this text as 'the Council (of Ministers)', though technically, 'the Council' alone is the correct title (see especially Chapter 4).

....

3   Case C-333/13, *Elisabeta Dano, Florin Dano v. Jobcenter Leipzig*, 11th November 2014.
4   Opinion 2/13 on EU accession to ECHR, 18th December 2014.

GUIDE TO THE SPOTLIGHTS SERIES

The Routledge Spotlights series is an exciting new textbook series that has been carefully developed to help give you a head start in your assessments. We've listened to lecturers and examiners to identify what it takes to succeed as a law student and we've used that to develop a brand new series of textbooks that combines detailed coverage of the law, together with carefully-selected features designed to help you translate that knowledge into assessment success.

AS YOU READ

sections at the start of each chapter introduce you to the key questions and concepts that will be covered within the chapter to help you to focus your reading.

AS YOU REA

The key questio

— What was '
  (EU)?

KEY LEARNING POINTS

throughout each chapter highlight important principles and definitions to aid understanding and consolidate your learning.

KEY LEAR

SCOPE OF '
The Treaty of
It intended
energy '

EXPLAINING THE LAW

brings the subject to life through the use of practical examples to provide valuable context to your learning.

EXPLAININ

THREE CO
Although it
commur

ANALYSING THE LAW

invites you to consider your own response to legal dilemmas and debates. Critical thinking is key to assessment success and, with this feature, our authors invite you to critique the law or evaluate conflicting arguments in a debate.

ANALYSING

WHY COAL A
The first area o'
was that thes'
cooperatic

APPLYING THE LAW

Problem questions will form a large part of your assessment and Applying the Law allows you to develop your problem-solving skills by showing how the law can be applied to a given situation. Learn how to interpret the law and apply it to any problem question.

APPLYING

ANSWERIN
AND 110 ᵀ
A probler

KEY CASES

Using legal authority correctly is essential for assessment success. Key Cases provide insight and analysis of the most important cases and judgments.

KEY CASE

In a recent ju
the distincti
No 528/2

MAKING CONNECTIONS

will help you impress examiners, showing you how a topic fits into the bigger picture, not just of the wider subject but also across the legal curriculum.

MAKING CC
+ + + + + + + +
THE EU CH
There is a l?
Article 5ᵉ

POINTS TO REVIEW

bring together all of the principles and themes for the chapter, helping to reinforce your learning.

POINTS TO ᵢ

–   This chapter

–   The EU wᵀ
    hoᵤᵤ

TAKING IT FURTHER

Reading widely impresses examiners! Taking it Further provides annotated lists of journal articles, book chapters and useful websites for further reading, which have been carefully selected to help you to demonstrate an enhanced understanding of the topic.

TAKING THIₙ

A Maddox 'A nₑ
Science Reviev

LEGAL VOCABULARY

Studying law brings with it the need to master the Legal Vocabulary unique to that subject. New terms are defined throughout and key vocabulary is listed in an end-of-chapter glossary.

Anti-trust is thₑ
for historical reₐ
law. The reason
century, corpor⁻
shares in othe
meₐₙₛ

GUIDE TO THE WEBSITE

LEGAL EXERCISES

to test knowledge and promote critical thinking, including exam/coursework questions and thinking points for further study and reflection.

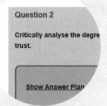

MULTIPLE CHOICE QUESTIONS

for self-testing, helping you to diagnose where you might feel less confident about your knowledge so you can direct your revision time in the right direction.

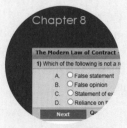

REVISION ADVICE AND STUDY TIP PODCASTS

will help you to improve your performance and raise your grades.

KEY CASE FLASHCARDS

will help you to revise and remember the key cases and the legal principles they illustrate.

UPDATES

on cases and legislation will help you to stay on top of all the most important recent legal developments in the subject area.

TABLE OF CASES

GENERAL COURT/COURT OF FIRST INSTANCE

INTERNATIONAL COURT OF JUSTICE

TABLE OF LEGISLATION

NATIONAL LEGISLATION

INTERNATIONAL TREATIES AND SOURCES

Part 1

INSTITUTIONAL AND CONSTITUTIONAL CONTEXT

CHAPTERS IN THIS PART:

1

CHAPTER 1
THE ORIGINS OF THE EU AND INTRODUCTION

This chapter briefly surveys the development of what is now the EU and summarises the content of the book. The original treaties were the European Coal and Steel Community (ECSC) Treaty, the European Atomic Energy Community (EURATOM) Treaty and the European Economic Community (EEC) Treaty. EU competences have expanded beyond the core ideas of a free trade area or common market (now called internal market), including the failure of the Treaty establishing a Constitution and the subsequent passing of the Lisbon Treaty, and the adoption by 25 of the (then) 27 Member States of the 'Fiscal Compact' in 2011 and European Stability Mechanism (ESM) Treaty in 2012. Other sections briefly explain the way in which the EU is financed and identify the different central institutions of the EU. Finally, the chapter looks at some theories of integration that seek to offer an overall perspective of the underlying process of integration: what drives integrations, which actors or players in the process have the most influence? Is it the Member States or the central EU institutions that really drive the process forward or is it a combination of both? Can an overall pattern be observed? Finally, the chapter provides a summary of the other chapters in the book.

In this chapter, some of the key terminology of EU studies will be introduced. One of the difficulties of EU law is that its terminology can be somewhat complex and hard to understand; it is important to begin to master the terms commonly used by EU lawyers and EU specialists. The glossary at the end will help you do this.

AS YOU READ . . .

The key questions that will be answered in this chapter are as follows:

– What was the motivation behind the creation of what is now the European Union (EU)? Was there a single motivation or several?

– What does the 'common market' or 'internal market' mean?

- The term 'EU' is now used, but originally there were three interconnected 'Communities' rather than a single 'Union'. How and why was this so? What is the reason for and significance of the change to 'EU'?

- What are the main institutions of the EU?

- In what way can the EU be described as 'constitutional' and how is this significant?

- What are the main theories seeking to explain the EU overall as a political (and legal) phenomenon?

1.1 THE ORIGIN OF THE EUROPEAN UNION AND THE THREE 'COMMUNITIES'

The European Union (EU), as we now know it, first began life as three separate legal Communities in the 1950s. First, six countries set up a Community to cooperate in the area of coal and steel. They formed the European Coal and Steel Community (ECSC) in 1951 by adopting the European Coal and Steel Community Treaty (also known as the Treaty of Paris, where it was signed). Then two further 'Communities' followed in 1957, one in the area of atomic energy and the other a more general 'economic Community', but which used more or less identical institutions and methods.

The reason coal and steel were the first areas of cooperation was because these materials were central to military capacity, and an underlying idea was to ensure economic cooperation instead of rivalry in these areas in the hope that this would translate into peaceful coexistence and the avoidance of the military conflicts such as the First and Second World Wars. The adoption of the European Atomic Energy Community Treaty (EURATOM) followed the same logic, in a field at the time that seemed set to dominate future industry.

ANALYSING THE LAW

WHY COAL AND STEEL?
The first area of cooperation was the coal and steel industries. A rationale for this was that these were the industries most important to military strength and thus, cooperation here would reduce the militaristic rivalries of the past.

The third Community and, in practice, the most important because it was more wide-ranging, was the European Economic Community Treaty (or EEC Treaty), also known as the Treaty of Rome. It was signed in Rome in 1957.

SCOPE OF THE EUROPEAN ECONOMIC COMMUNITY

The Treaty of Rome or EEC Treaty was concerned with economics more generally. It intended to create a common market not just in coal and steel and atomic energy, but in economic goods generally. However, it was not concerned with government spending; this remains to this day for national governments. Nonetheless, the idea of free trade is very broad and can encompass many aspects of the competences of Member States, as we will see further later.

The institutions and legal means for the three Communities were largely the same. The general idea was to establish a common market in economic goods and materials. Two cardinal principles were contained in the project:

1. free movement of economic goods (free movement of workers, free movement of goods, free movement of services and free movement of capital) and
2. undistorted or open competition in a common market (later termed the 'single market' and now the 'internal market'), joining up the economies of the Member States.

Free movement of goods meant that there were to be no taxes and no numerical restrictions (quotas) or equivalent restrictions imposed on goods from one Member State being exported to another Member State. In addition to free movement and undistorted competition, there was to be a Common Customs Union.

A COMMON CUSTOMS UNION

A Common Customs Union means that a single set of customs rules would apply to goods being imported into any of the Member States from any other countries not in the Communities. For example, the level of customs duties on cars imported into an EU country from the US would be the same, whichever was the EU country.

It would have been simpler for there to be one single Community; that was not the legal path first chosen, although the reasons for this are not very obvious.

THREE COMMUNITIES

Although it would have been simpler formally and fully to merge the three communities, in practice, the three functioned as if they were part of the same entity. This was later recognised in 1965 when a 'Merger Treaty' was adopted formally joining the three Communities up, although maintaining their legally

distinct identities – so the expression 'the Communities' continued to be used.
Some minor difference existed between the three (e.g. some special provisions
applied to EURATOM), but in substance the three constituted a single entity.

However, the three separate treaties still existed and the term 'Communities' was used up
until the Maastricht Treaty in 1992.[1] Today, there is just a single 'Union', although it is
still governed by two different treaties, which we will discuss further below.

As noted in the text box above, an important point to remember is that, although
the Treaty of Rome or EEC Treaty was more general than the others in setting up a
community concerned with all economic goods, this did not mean that all economic
matters were now to be dealt with by the EEC and not by the Member States. Very
important economic matters remained within the competence of each Member State,
i.e. each Member State could adopt its own rules in very important economic matters,
including in all manner of personal and corporate taxation, government spending and
budgeting, currency and money supply. It was only later, in the 1980s, that some of
the Member States decided to adopt a common currency, which replaced the national
currencies in the Member States on 1 January 2002.

EXPLAINING THE LAW

THE FOUNDING MEMBER STATES

The first countries to enter into the new agreement for European cooperation
were Belgium, France, West Germany, Italy, Luxembourg and the Netherlands.
The United Kingdom was not one of the founding Member States. Winston
Churchill, for example, saw the European Communities mainly as a way for
continental countries to cooperate and help avoid future wars. Churchill expressed
his views in the inter-war period, in response to the proposal of French foreign
minister Aristide Briand for a federal Europe,[2] but even then his later approach can
be seen: 'We have our own dream and our own task. We are with Europe but not
of it. We are linked, but not comprised. We are interested and associated, but not
absorbed'.[3] The United Kingdom first applied to join in the 1960s, but its entry was
blocked by President de Gaulle of France. It eventually joined in 1973.

....

1   The European Coal and Steel Community Treaty expired in 2001; see further ch 2.
2   A Briand *Memorandum on the Organization of a System of Federal European Union* (France Ministry of Foreign
    Affairs 1 May 1930).
3   'The United States of Europe' *Saturday Evening Post* (15 February 1930); W Lipgens, W Loth (eds) *Documents on
    the History of European Integration* (de Gruyter 1988) 662–63, citing R Coudenhove-Kalergi *An Idea Conquers the
    World* (Hutchinson 1953) 162 ff; R V Harrison *Winston Churchill and European Integration* (PhD thesis University
    of Aberdeen 1985).

KEY LEARNING POINT

HOW DOES THE EU FINANCE ITSELF?

Since 1971, as a result of legislation adopted by the Council,[4] the Communities developed a system of their own resourcing. This consisted of various levies automatically paid on certain goods sold in the Member States or imported into the Member States. Since 1968, the Common Customs Union has been agreed by the Member States, which means that they have agreed common tariffs (a 'common customs tariff'[5]) for goods coming from third countries, although there can be agreed exceptions. Money from the common customs tariff goes directly to the Union budget. In addition, the EU receives automatically and directly a percentage of value added tax and of agricultural levies.[6] These three sources of income are together what give the EU institutions a degree of financial independence, although they are still reliant on annual contributions from the Member States. This money automatically collected from levies and VAT allows the EU institutions to be more assertive politically against the Member States, while the annual levy on each Member State still makes up the greatest share of the budget.

Under Article 314 TFEU, the annual budget must be agreed between the Council (of Ministers) and European Parliament.[7]

1.2 OVERVIEW OF TREATY CHANGE

We will examine in more detail in Chapter 3 the evolution of changes to the basic treaties founding the EU, but this section offers a very brief overview. As noted above, the founding treaties were the ECSC Treaty 1951 and the EURATOM and EEC treaties of 1957. Following the Merger Treaty 1965 (which was a consolidating, rather than a reforming measure), the next major change was the Single European Act 1986 (SEA).

---

4   Decision of 21 April 1970, OJ L 94 28.10.1970 p. 19. This decision can only be changed unanimously by the Member States, rendering it more or less permanent. Subsequent legislation has been passed on the details of this system, but not changing it fundamentally.

5   Now set out in e.g. art 28(1) TFEU, which states: 'The Union shall comprise a customs union . . . and the adoption of a common customs tariff in their relations with third countries'. Under art 31 TFEU, the common customs tariff is set by the Council (of Ministers) on a proposal from the Commission. Note that the European Parliament is not involved.

6   Article 311 TFEU provides that: 'The Council [of Ministers, i.e. the Member States], acting in accordance with a special legislative procedure, shall unanimously and after consulting the European Parliament adopt a decision laying down the provisions relating to the system of own resources of the Union'.

7   The Commission publishes a very detailed handbook on the system of financing of the EU. See *European Union Public Finance* (4th edn 2008) http://ec.europa.eu/budget/library/biblio/publications/public_fin/EU_pub_fin_ en.pdf#page=235 (last accessed 18 January 2015).

Since the SEA was adopted, there have been new treaties every five or six years. In the following, each treaty change is briefly summarised. In addition to the treaties below, there has been an 'Accession Treaty' signed each time a new Member State joined. It need only be noted here that these accession treaties do not change EU law, but made the necessary changes (e.g. to the detail of voting procedures in the Council (of Ministers)) to permit a new Member State and reflect that the number of countries had increased. The most recent Accession Treaty at the time of writing was agreed in 2012 to allow Croatia to join in 2013.

KEY LEARNING POINT

THE ROLE OF TREATIES IN DEVELOPING EU LAW
Major changes to EU law must be agreed by the Member States. They do so in the form of treaties. Treaties are the main way in which international law is developed. They are like contracts between countries. We will look at this in more detail in Chapters 2 and 3.

A BRIEF SUMMARY OF THE MAIN TREATIES[8]

Treaty	What the treaty did
European Coal and Steel Community Treaty (ECSC) 1951 (Treaty of Paris)	– Set up a common market in coal and steel – Established the main institutions – 'Prototype treaty'
European Atomic Energy Community Treaty 1957 (EURATOM)	– Set up a common market in atomic energy – Similar institutions to ECSC
European Economic Community Treaty 1957 (EEC Treaty)	– Set up a common market in all economic goods – Similar institutions to ECSC
Merger Treaty 1965	– Formally merged the institutions operating under the three Communities – Legally, the three Communities remained distinct, hence the term 'Communities' remained

8   This is only a summary, to give a flavour of the main changes each treaty introduced.

Single European Act 1986	– The first treaty revision – Despite use of the term 'Act', this is a treaty – Extended use of Qualified Majority voting in Council (of Ministers) – Increased role of European Parliament – Expanded competences, e.g. to consumer protection, the environment – Provided a legal basis for Economic and Monetary Union (EMU) – Established the Court of First Instance
Treaty of Maastricht 1992	– Introduced Pillar structure to include new intergovernmental competences in criminal justice, visa and asylum matters, foreign policy – Extended use of qualified majority voting in Council (of Ministers) – Increased role of European Parliament by introducing co-decision procedure – Introduced general principles of subsidiarity and conferral – Further extended competences, including through Social Policy Annex – Changed EEC Treaty to European Community Treaty (EC Treaty, now the First Pillar) and introduced the term 'European Union' to describe the three Pillars together
Treaty of Amsterdam 1997	– Transferred visa and asylum (including immigration) to the Community/supranational Pillar – Established treaty framework for enhanced cooperation
Treaty of Nice 2001	– Facilitated enlargement – Further extended use of qualified majority voting in Council (of Ministers) – Further increased role of the European Parliament – Provided for further enhanced cooperation – Dealt with expiry of ECSC Treaty

Treaty of Lisbon 2009	– Mostly incorporated criminal justice elements into supranational framework
	– Categorised and extended EU competences
	– Incorporated EU Charter on Fundamental Rights and provided for EU to accede to ECHR
	– Increased role of European Parliament by establishing co-decision procedure as the ordinary legislative procedure and extending its use
	– Dropped the term 'Community' and dropped the Pillar structure

Two further treaties have since been adopted, but they do not include all the Member States, the UK having vetoed an EU–wide treaty.[9] These two treaties were adopted mainly to deal with the economic crisis in the Eurozone, although they also involve a more general attempt to transfer competences to the EU, at least for Eurozone Member States. The two treaties are the Treaty on Stability, Coordination and Governance in the Economic and Monetary Union (or Fiscal Compact) 2011 and the Treaty establishing the European Stability Mechanism 2012. We will look at these treaties in more detail in Chapter 3.

1.3 AN OVERVIEW OF THE MAIN INSTITUTIONS OF THE EU

This section briefly identifies the main institutions of the EU. In Chapter 4, we will look more closely at how these are similar to or differ from national institutions, as this makes the organisation of the EU institutions easier to understand. As with any government system, the institutions can be divided broadly into a legislature (law-making body), executive (the body applying laws) and judiciary (the body adjudicating on disputes about the law).

The *main* institutions of the EU (there are a number of others, such as the Committee of the Regions and Social and Economic Committee, but these have mainly consultative roles) are the following.

....

9   The Czech Republic ultimately decided not to adopt the Fiscal Compact either.

EXPLAINING THE LAW

IDENTIFYING THE LEGISLATURE, EXECUTIVE AND JUDICIARY OF THE EU

Legislature	Executive	Judiciary
Commission (right of initiative)	Commission	ECJ/CJEU
+	+	+
Council (of Ministers)	Member States	General Court
+	+	
European Parliament	Specialised agencies	
	+	
	European Council	

European Council: This is a body consisting of all of the heads of government – usually prime ministers, although, e.g. in France, the president is the head of government – and it decides the broad policy of the EU, although it has some quasi-legislative powers.

Council (of Ministers): This consists of government ministers with the same responsibility from each Member State meeting and acting together (e.g. all ministers for finance from the Member States). The Council deals with more specific matters in the different areas of cooperation than does the European Council. It is also the main authority with power to make laws (for a long time, only the Council could adopt legislation, but now it usually must act with the approval of the European Parliament).

Presidency: For a period of six months, one Member State will hold the Presidency of the Council (of Ministers). The president acts as chairperson and the presidency involves organising meetings of the Council (of Ministers) for the six-month period and liaising between the Member States for the conduct of EU business.

European Parliament (EP): The European Parliament consists of representatives from all Member States who are directly elected. It was originally an appointed body: national parliamentarians were chosen by each Member State to sit on it, but it has been directly elected since 1979. It does not have as much power as a parliament in a national system; it must cooperate with the European Commission and Council (of Ministers) in the passing of laws. In effect it is one chamber of the EU legislature, the Council (of Ministers) being the other chamber.

European Commission: This is the executive part of the EU. This means it has the main responsibility for making sure decisions adopted by the other institutions are put into effect. It also has the central role in proposing new policies and laws, called the right of initiative (normally only the Commission may propose new laws). One of the vice-presidents of the Commission is responsible for coordinating EU foreign policy and is known as the High Representative for Foreign Affairs and Security Policy.[10]

European Court of Justice (ECJ) or *Court of Justice of the European Union* (CJEU): This is the Court of the EU and decides legal disputes concerning the laws of the EU. Member States must accept its decisions and put them into effect. The ECJ has played a central role in increasing integration.

General Court: Prior to the Lisbon Treaty, this was known as the Court of First Instance (CFI). It was established in 1988 initially to assist the ECJ, but it has since become more important and has jurisdiction over a wide variety of cases, although some cases must still be brought directly before the Court of Justice. Some of its decisions may be appealed to the ECJ on a point of law.

Court of Auditors: This is not really a court as we normally understand; rather, it is a regulatory body that makes sure the EU and its institutions spend money properly. It acts as an auditor for the EU, just as accountants act as auditors for companies. It was created in 1975.

European Central Bank (ECB): This is responsible for monetary policy, which includes the single currency (Euro) and bank interest rates, but only for Member States that have adopted the Euro. The ECB was created on 1 June 1998, resulting from the Treaty of Maastricht.

Committee of Permanent Representatives (COREPER): This consists of the permanent ambassadors of each country/Member State to the EU. It does the preparatory work for the Council (of Ministers)' meetings.

1.4 CHAPTER SUMMARIES

1.4.1 PART 1 – INSTITUTIONAL AND CONSTITUTIONAL CONTEXT

Chapter 2 examines the EU in the context of international law generally. It summarises the main features and historical development of the international legal system and the 'Westphalian' principle of state sovereignty and then explains what distinguishes the EU from general public international law. It also explains the relationship between the EU system and the Council of Europe system (including the European Convention on Human Rights).

....

10 The high representative also chairs meetings of the Council (of Ministers) consisting of foreign ministers of the Member States.

Chapter 3 examines the evolution of the EU through treaty-making, from the Treaty of Rome in 1957 to the Treaty of Lisbon, which came into effect on 1 December 2009. It outlines the successive stages of treaty development, beginning with the first major revision of the Single European Act 1986 and the frequent treaty revision since then, including the failed Treaty establishing a Constitution for Europe.

Chapter 4 examines the institutional working of the EU: institutions and law-making. It overviews the workings of the principal EU institutions, focusing on the European Council, the Council (of Ministers), COREPER, the European Parliament, and the European Central Bank. It also explains the law-making process in the EU and analyses the horizontal separation of powers between the EU institutions.

Chapter 5 surveys the special role of the Court of Justice in the EU. It outlines the central role played by the ECJ as a 'motor of integration', through the development of doctrines of supremacy, direct effect, parallelism, fundamental rights and expansive interpretation of competences and analyses the academic debate on the role of the Court and of its methods of interpretation. In addition, it explains the main different types of procedure before the ECJ.

Chapter 6 assesses the interaction of EU law with national law. It examines the reception of the supremacy doctrine in national constitutional law (including resistance to an absolute supremacy principle), and the doctrines of direct effect and indirect effect. Further, it explains the doctrine of state liability.

Chapter 7 overviews the issue of competences of the EU relative to the competences of the Member States. It looks at the different categories of competence in EU law (exclusive, shared, concurrent) and the principle of conferral, the role of the EU in external relations (both the general law of external relations and the Common Foreign and Security Policy), and the Area of Freedom, Security and Justice (encompassing asylum, visa, immigration and criminal justice). In addition, it looks at the yellow card system, introduced by the Treaty of Lisbon, relating to national parliaments. Finally, it assesses in some detail the way in which competence is addressed in the legal reasoning of the ECJ, which is at least as important as anything the treaties say on competence, including the way in which the principle of subsidiarity is applied by the Court.

Chapter 8, the final chapter in Part 1, looks at fundamental rights and the concept of citizenship in EU law. It outlines the historical development by the ECJ of an embryonic fundamental rights jurisdiction, the emergence of the concept of citizenship in the treaties and its treatment in the case law of the ECJ (including the gradual drawing out by the ECJ of financial implications for the Member States), the adoption of the EU Charter of Fundamental Rights and the relationship between EU law and the European Convention on Human Rights (ECHR) (which will be much more important when the EU accedes to the ECHR, as provided for in Article 6 TEU).

1.4.2 PART 2 – SUBSTANTIVE LAW

Chapter 9 examines the free movement of goods, the first of the four free movement principles, focusing on taxes and customs duties. It examines the prohibition on customs duties and discriminatory and protective internal taxation on goods between Member States and the common customs tariff, including exceptions and derogations.

Chapter 10 looks at the second aspect of free movement of goods, the prohibitions on quantitative restrictions and measures having equivalent effect (MEQRs), including case law on non-discriminatory obstacles and mutual recognition (the *Cassis de Dijon* and *Dassonville* lines of case law) and the exceptions and derogations therefrom.

Chapter 11 examines one of the two main categories of free movement of persons, namely, the free movement of workers. It surveys the development of the law on free movement of workers, including statutory regulation of the conditions of free movement, as well as the exceptions and derogations to free movement.

Chapter 12 surveys the free movement of establishment and services, covering the free movement of employers (such as companies) and the self-employed on a long-term (establishment) or short-term (services) basis. This includes the principle of mutual recognition in this area, and exceptions and derogations.

Chapter 13 looks at the free movement of capital and payments, explaining its relationship to the other free movement principles, the scope of its coverage and of the exceptions and derogations to it.

Chapter 14 introduces the second major element of the common or (as it is now known) internal market, apart from free movement, namely, competition law. It overviews the rationale of competition law and surveys procedural aspects of enforcement of EU competition law, including decentralisation of enforcement.

Chapter 15 examines the regulation of cartels or the prohibition on concerted practices and similar behaviours amongst different businesses in the marketplace, under Article 101 TFEU, the first of two main treaty provisions on practices prohibited as anti-competitive.

Chapter 16 surveys the second main treaty prohibition on anti-competitive practices, the abuse of a dominant position under Article 102 TFEU.

Chapter 17 overviews the process of Economic and Monetary Union (EMU). It outlines the development of EMU and the Eurozone, explaining its constitutional context, as well as the special position of the UK and non-Eurozone members. Finally, it looks at the implications and fall-out from the crisis in the Eurozone at treaty, legislative and political levels.

Chapter 18 looks at 'Social Europe', the competence of the EU in social aspects of employment. It examines some of the key features of what is a wide field, including sex equality law, the development of a broader equality principle, the Working Time Directive and indirect social competences arising from the internal market principles.

1.5 AN OVERVIEW OF SOME THEORIES OF INTEGRATION

A number of political science theories have tried to explain the overall pattern of the evolution and development of the EU, to try to understand what factors are most important in encouraging the process of integration. The two main theories are neo-functionalism and liberal inter-governmentalism.

1.5.1 NEO-FUNCTIONALISM

The first and probably the most influential is the theory of neo-functionalism.

KEY LEARNING POINT

NEO-FUNCTIONALISM

This emphasises the functions of individual institutions and how their self-interest encourages them to expand their roles and competences. Often, the institutions can be understood as acting together to increase integration and, correspondingly, reduce the scope of competence or sovereignty still remaining with the Member States. The first influential neo-functionalist writer was the US academic Ernst Haas. The idea that political institutions act in their own self-interest is an important one in political theory generally.

An important idea in neo-functionalist thinking is that of spillover. Spillover conveys the idea that one area of competence for the EU will drag in other areas eventually.[11] While the original idea was for a common market, i.e. essentially a free trade area, this has drawn in other aspects of economics, such as the idea of a single

---

11 E Haas *Beyond the Nation State: Functionalism and International Organization* (Stanford University Press 1964) 48. See also A-M Burley, W Mattli 'Europe before the Court: a political theory of integration' (1993) 47(1) *International Organization* 41–76 at 55 ff; A Stone Sweet *The Judicial Construction of Europe* (Oxford University Press 2004) 74–75, 109–45, 243; G de Búrca 'Rethinking law in neo-functionalist theory' (2005) 12(1) *Journal of European Public Policy* 310–26 at 317. Later Haas acknowledged that neo-functionalism did not provide a complete theory of European integration, but he did not step back from its basic principles of the motivation of self-interest and the impact of spillover: see E Haas *The Obsolescence of Regional Integration Theory* (Institute of International Studies Berkeley 1975).

currency[12] (the idea of spillover is useful for understanding EU competences at the level of legal reasoning, which we will look at in Chapter 7 in more detail).

Neo-functionalists tended to view legitimacy of European cooperation in terms of outcomes, such as peace and prosperity, rather than in terms of process, i.e. the extent to which it was democratically driven.[13] Haas's emphasis on discrete actors seeking to advance their own interest was more consistent with a relatively low-profile organisation that did not capture the public interest in a sustained way because of its relatively narrow focus of activity. With the movement beyond the pure common market to a more political integration and the growing perception amongst European citizens that the process of integration affects their daily lives, this emphasis on specific interests acting outside of daily political life at a national level is less suitable for explaining the present dynamic of integration. The move toward political integration, to the extent that it has occurred, has engaged ordinary citizens.[14] Neo-functionalism can provide a good understanding of élite actors at a descriptive level, but is not so suitable for justifying the role of institutions in the process of integration as it advances.

1.5.2 INTER-GOVERNMENTALISM

A theory that competes with neo-functionalism is liberal inter-governmentalism.

> KEY LEARNING POINT
>
> **INTER-GOVERNMENTALISM**
> Under this theory, the big Member States are seen as most important forces or influences in the integration process. This contrasts with neo-functionalism, which sees the institutions as having a more central role. Liberal inter-governmentalism (most associated with the work of Andrew Moravcsik) emphasises the state as a rational actor, with the costs and benefits of economic interdependence as the most important motivation in state behaviour. Integration is favoured if the economic benefits outweigh the costs.

In this way, integration is understood as a process of demand and supply. The reason for pooling sovereignty in the manner of the Community institutions was this concern with economic efficiency:

> For individual Member States carrying out such a cost-benefit calculation, the decision to delegate or pool sovereignty signals the willingness of national

----

12 There were different understandings of the common market in the 1950s, the UK understanding being in the more limited vein of a free trade area, whilst others had a more ambitious idea of economic union: see e.g. H Singh Chopra *De Gaulle and European Unity* (Shakti Halik Abhinav Publications 1974) 185–188.

13 P Craig 'The nature of the Community: integration, democracy and legitimacy' in P Craig, G de Búrca (eds) *The Evolution of EU Law* (Oxford University Press 1999) 7.

14 A development that Haas himself described as 'turbulence': see E Haas 'Turbulent fields and the theory of regional integration' (1976) 30(2) *International Organization* 173–212.

governments to accept an increased risk of being outvoted or overruled on any individual issue in exchange for more efficient collective decision-making on average.[15]

In addition, Moravcsik suggests national governments can be motivated to support integration as a way of overcoming opposition to their own policies, as government policies can seem more necessary when linked to integration. One of the apparent difficulties liberal inter-governmentalism faces is explaining the law-creating role of the ECJ. On the role of the Court, Moravcsik acknowledges it as hard to explain for inter-governmentalists, given the overall emphasis he places on the role of the Member States.[16]

It is difficult to evaluate theories of political behaviour or to 'prove' one as more correct.[17] Neo-functionalism, however, captures a long-standing insight, namely, that political actors act in their own self-interest and to advance their own power. For example, this insight is behind traditional separation of powers thinking. Liberal inter-governmentalism has difficulties explaining integration beyond economic matters, although an understanding of the pre-eminent role of élites in some political cultures helps explaining acceptance of the ECJ role in that political élites in the dominant Member States (Germany and France) favoured an ideology of integration.[18] Since neo-functionalism tends to explain integration in terms of a confluence or combination of various élite interests, it also has at least some difficulty explaining the quite remarkable extent of the role of the ECJ.[19]

EXPLAINING THE LAW

'FOUNDING FATHERS'? THE ROLE OF ROBERT SCHUMAN AND JEAN MONNET IN FOUNDING THE EUROPEAN COMMUNITIES

We have just looked at some theories that suggest general causes – the self-interest of supranational institutions or economic efficiency – as explanations of the pace and development of integration. Individuals can also be influential

....

15 A Moravcsik 'Preferences and power in the European Community: a liberal inter-governmentalist approach' (1991) 31(4) *Journal of Common Market Studies* 473–523 at 509. More recently see A Moravcsik 'The European constitutional compromise and neo-functionalist legacy' (2005) 12(2) *Journal of European Public Policy* 349–86, arguing that the EU has reached a constitutional maturity that supersedes a neo-functionalist view of the supra-national institutions moving consistently toward 'ever-closer Union'.

16 Moravcsik (n 15) 513–14.

17 See further P Pierson 'The path to European integration: a historical institutionalist analysis' (1996) 29(2) *Comparative Political Studies* 123–63; A Stone, J Caporasa 'From free trade to supranational polity: the European court and integration' Centre for German and European Studies Working Paper No 245 (University of California Berkeley 1996); M Pollack 'Delegation, agency, and agenda setting in the European Community' (1997) 51(1) *International Organizations* 99–134.

18 R Hirschl 'Preserving hegemony? Assessing the political origins of the EU constitution' (2005) 3(2–3) *International Journal of Constitutional Law* 269–91.

19 P C Schmitter 'Ernst B. Haas and the legacy of neo-functionalism' (2005) 12(2) *Journal of European Public Policy* 255–77 at 267.

in political developments, or at least individuals who are effective leaders of broader groups or interests. In the EU, the term 'Founding Fathers', borrowed from US constitutional history, is used to describe some of the most influential individuals behind European integration. Although the term 'Founding Fathers' is used to describe several people who had important roles in the founding of the European Communities, amongst the most frequently noted as founding fathers are Robert Schuman and Jean Monnet.

Robert Schuman (1886–1963), from Luxembourg, was a French prime minister briefly (1947–1948), and also finance minister and foreign minister, in the period immediately after the Second World War. He advocated European integration as a response to the Second World War. At the time of the ECSC Treaty, he was French foreign minister (he occupied this position from 1948–1953). The Schuman Declaration of 1950, drafted by Schuman and a number of others, set out a plan for integration advocated by Schuman on behalf of the French Government. He later served as president of the European Parliament (1958–1960).

Jean Monnet (1888–1979) was a French business figure and sometime civil servant and diplomat. In the 1920s and 1930s, he was involved in the League of Nations and international financing. He was an early advocate of Anglo-French economic cooperation. After the Second World War, he was very involved in French economic reconstruction. He helped draft the Schuman declaration. He became the first President of the High Authority of the ECSC. In 1954, he resigned from this position, and in 1955 Monnet established the Action Committee for the United States of Europe,[20] demonstrating that the early figures involved in European integration did not see it just in economic terms. This Committee, in which politicians and trade unionists from across Europe were involved, was influential in subsequent integration moves in the 1950s, leading to the EURATOM and EEC treaties.

Schuman and Monnet were not, however, the first to propose the idea of a federal-like system in Europe. In 1923, in a book entitled *Pan-Europa*,[21] the Austrian aristocrat Richard von Coudenhove-Kalergi (1894–1972) and, in 1929, the French minister Aristide Briand (1862–1932), in a speech to the League of Nations, both proposed a similar idea. During the Second World War, the ministers for armaments and the economy in the Nazi government, Albert Speer, also suggested the creation of a single market in Europe.[22]

---

20 For information, see this link from the website of the Centre Virtuel de la Connaissance sur l'Europ http://www.cvce.eu/viewer/-/content/72da058e-e766–415e-ad6e-49bec4853946/en (last accessed 18 January 2015).
21 Pan-Europa Verlag 1923.
22 G Sereny *Albert Speer: His Battle with Truth* (Pan Macmillan 1996) 386–87; J Keegan 'From Albert Speer to Jacques Delors' in P Gowan, P Anderson (eds) *The Question of Europe* (Verso 1997).

1.6 THE EU AS A 'CONSTITUTIONAL' ENTITY

We have seen above, briefly, that the proposed Treaty establishing a Constitution for Europe was not adopted in the end. Does this mean that the EU does not have a constitutional character? Not necessarily. 'Constitutional' means something fundamental in a legal system. Constitutions generally set out the most important aspects of a legal system: how the legal system is to work or the rules about the rules. In addition, a constitution will often set out limits to the power of a government, including through the idea of individual rights governing the relationship between the state and the individual.

ANALYSING THE LAW

THE CONSTITUTIONAL CHARACTER OF THE EU
When we consider how important the impact of EU law is in national law, we can see that the EU treaties are 'constitutional' in nature. Indeed, the ECJ has described them in this way.[23] Most importantly, the doctrine of supremacy of EU law over national law means that in each Member State, part of its national constitution is governed by EU law. National courts must generally apply EU law when there is a conflict with national law, and EU fundamental rights apply within EU law. Thus, even though the issue is too politically sensitive to allow the EU Treaties to be formally called a constitution, they still have a constitutional meaning and impact. Nonetheless, many of the constitutional and supreme courts of the Member States have not accepted that EU law ultimately has supremacy over national constitutional law, as we will see further in Chapter 6.

1.7 CONCLUSION

In this chapter, the origin and development of the EU have been briefly overviewed. The EU began in the 1950s as three legally distinct Communities – the ECSC, EURATOM and the EEC. The three Communities used similar institutions and were all concerned with the idea of a common market. The immediate motivation for the creation of these three Communities was to substitute economic cooperation for nationalistic rivalries. The first expansion of competences occurred with the SEA 1986.

The Communities were later renamed the European Community (EC) in 1992 by the Treaty of Maastricht, reflecting a move beyond mere economic integration. This was also when the term 'European Union' or EU was introduced to describe both the EC and new inter-governmental areas of cooperation. The EU continues to expand its competences, but how far political integration should proceed is controversial. A proposed Treaty establishing a Constitution for Europe failed to be ratified, although

---

23 Case 294/83 *Parti Écologiste 'Les Verts' v European Parliament* [1986] ECR 1339 para 23.

much of its content (albeit with less constitutional symbolism) was later included in the Treaty of Lisbon.

The crisis in the Eurozone and the increasing scepticism in the UK towards the EU dominate political debate about the future of the organisation. Some suggest that the EU will have to accept a 'multi-speed Europe', i.e. with some Member States integrating more than others. This is already the case to some extent, given that 10 Member States do not use the Euro currency.

POINTS TO REVIEW

– This chapter is designed to give you an overview of the background to the EU.

– The EU was founded as three separate organisations in the 1950s, which even then, however, used common or almost identical institutions.

– The three founding treaties were the ECSC Treaty 1951 (also known as the Treaty of Paris), the EURATOM Treaty 1957 and the EEC Treaty 1957 (also known as the Treaty of Rome).

– They used similar institutions and aimed to create a common market, the EEC Treaty doing so across all areas of economic activity. The Merger Treaty recognised this and formally merged or joined the institutions of the three, although this had happened in practice to some extent.

– The impact of EU law in national law means it can be considered constitutional in nature, i.e. its impact is fundamental. This is despite failure of the Treaty establishing a Constitution for Europe gaining democratic endorsement. What exact impact it should have is controversial, however, as we will see in Chapter 6.

– Political science theories of integration identify different influences as most important in the development of EU law. Neo-functionalist theory suggests the actions of central EU institutions have the most influence. Liberal inter-governmentalism suggests the views of the bigger Member States are most important. In either case, the smaller Member States have a lesser influence.

CHAPTER GLOSSARY

Common Customs Union refers to a common system of customs duties applied by all EU Member States to goods coming into the EU from states outside the EU.

Common market/single market/internal market all refer to the same basic idea of an economic market with common rules for all the Member States of the EU.

The two key principles are the principle of free movement of goods, workers, services and capital and the principle of freedom of competition between all the Member States. The term 'internal market' is sometimes considered to have a more particular meaning of referring only to the relations between Member States, not including the Common Customs Union concerning common relations with states outside the EU.

Competence is a legal concept that means the authority or power of a body or person to make legally binding decisions.

Council (of Ministers) is an organ of the EU. It consists of ministers of the Member States meeting in a particular area. Its composition varies depending on which area of concern it is dealing with.

Enhanced cooperation refers to the possibility of some, but not all, of the Member States agreeing to cooperate or integrate further. It is also sometimes called flexible cooperation or variable geometry.

EURATOM is one of the three founding organisations or Communities of what is now the EU. It was concerned with establishing a common market in the area of atomic energy only.

European Coal and Steel Community (ECSC) was the founding organisation or Community of what is now the EU. It could be considered a 'prototype' for the other two founding treaties, the EURATOM Treaty and the EEC Treaty, and it was concerned with establishing a common market in only the areas of coal and steel.

European Commission is the central executive body of the EU. It could be compared to a civil service, but it has a more important role as it has the sole right of initiative in the EU legislative process. This means that only it can propose new laws, although there are exceptions to this.

European Council is the meeting of the heads of government of the Member States of the EU. It should not be confused with the Council (of Ministers).

European Court of Auditors is not a court of law, but instead is the auditing institution of the EU. It carries out audits of how the EU institutions spend their budgets. It is based in Luxembourg.

European Court of Justice (ECJ) or Court of Justice of the European Union (CJEU) is the highest court in the judicial structure of the EU legal system. It hears actions referred to it by courts of the Member States on points of EU law and actions brought by individuals against acts of the institutions of the EU. It is based in Luxembourg.

European Economic Community (EEC) is the term used to describe the most important and broadest in scope of the three founding treaties of the EU. It established a common market in goods, workers, services and capital. It is also known as the Treaty of Rome, where it was signed in 1957.

European Parliament refers to the parliamentary assembly of the EU. It was first called the 'Common Assembly' under the ECSC Treaty. It was originally appointed from national parliamentarians, but since 1979 has been directly elected.

It exercises joint legislative power with the Council (of Ministers) in most areas of EU competence.

General Court refers to the court of first instance in the EU judicial system. It used to be called the Court of First Instance.

Inter-institutional means between the EU institutions (rather than, for example, the relations between the institutions or an institution and the Member States).

Justice and Home Affairs refers to two areas of EU cooperation taken together, especially in the period from 1992–1998 (after the adoption of the Treaty of Maastricht and before the adoption of the Treaty of Amsterdam): asylum, visa and immigration matters and criminal justice matters.

Liberal inter-governmentalism refers to a theory of European integration that emphasises the importance of the bigger EU Member States in the process of integration.

Multi-speed Europe refers to the phenomenon of some Member States of the EU pushing ahead with more

integration than others. The Euro currency is an example.

Neo-functionalism refers to a theory from political science that understands the evolution of the EU as a result of the self-interest of the EU institutions as political actors working in tandem to expand integration.

Ordinary legislative procedure refers to the standard method of adopting legislation in the EU. It involves joint decision-making power between the Council (of Ministers) and the European Parliament voting on a proposal made by the European Commission.

Right of initiative refers to the exclusive right under the EU treaties of the European Commission to make legislative proposals.

'The Communities' is the term used to describe the three original organisations of Communities that made up what is today called the EU. These three are the ECSC, the EURATOM and the EEC Community.

Variable geometry is an alternative term for enhanced or flexible cooperation.

TAKING THINGS FURTHER

A Maddox 'A note on the meaning of constitution' (1982) 76(4) *American Political Science Review* 805–809 This article provides a very clear explanation of the meaning of the term 'Constitution' in Western legal history. It will provide useful background reading as you consider what aspects of the EU are 'constitutional'.

H Su 'Jean Monnet's grand design for Europe and its criticism' (2009) 15(2) *Journal of the History of European Integration* 29–46 This article offers an historical account of the thinking of one of the founding fathers of the EU, Jean Monnet. It is interesting as it explains how the rationale for founding the EU was not simply the preservation of peace, but to centralise power in a federal structure for Europe comparable to the USA that was intended to give Europe a more powerful voice on the global stage.

P Craig, G de Búrca *The Evolution of EU Law* (2nd edn Oxford University Press 2011) This book provides an analytical overview of the process of integration. It assumes a general knowledge of EU law and includes chapters by leading authors on different aspects or themes of EU studies. For example, it includes discussion of the theories of neo-functionalism and inter-governmentalism.

H Schulz-Forberg, B Stråth *The Political History of European Integration: The Hypocrisy of Democracy-Through-Market* (Routledge 2012) This book provides a critical analysis of how the goal of economic integration is in tension with the democractic legitimacy of the European Union. It argues that as the process unfolds, increasingly it is accompanied by social disintegration.

2

CHAPTER 2
THE EU IN INTERNATIONAL LAW

The EU legal system is often considered to be different to international law and to constitute its own, distinct legal system. Nonetheless, the EU was created by international law treaties. However, it has several, very important distinct features that differentiate it from 'ordinary' international law. The term 'supranationalism' is often used to describe these distinct features, and what this term captures is the idea that the EU involves giving up authority to an institution or body beyond the nation state in a way that goes further than the degree of cooperation typical of international law. In contrast, the term 'inter-governmental' is used to describe the kind of cooperation typical of international law where individual state sovereignty remains decisive. This chapter will enable you to understand how the EU is both a product of international law, while also being different to it in several ways. One of the complexities of this topic is the interaction of the EU legal system with the Council of Europe system.

AS YOU READ . . .

The key questions that will be answered in this chapter are as follows:

– How can the origin of the EU be understood in the context of public international law?

– What are the key rules governing the relationships between states in international law? How did they develop?

– How is the EU similar to and different from 'normal' international law cooperation?

– How does the EU legal system interact with the Council of Europe system?

– In particular, what is the relationship between EU law and the European Convention on Human Rights or ECHR (the ECHR is part of the Council of Europe system)?

– Can the Member States withdraw from the EU? How does the issue of withdrawal affect the legal character of the EU in terms of international law?

2.1 THE ORIGIN AND FEATURES OF INTERNATIONAL LAW AND COOPERATION BETWEEN STATES

International law governs legal relationships across jurisdictions and borders. In the past, it was understood as primarily concerned with relationships between states, but it now increasingly involves individuals, non–governmental organisations and international institutions, and also increasingly impacts on national legal systems. For example, individuals are increasingly affected by international human rights law. International law has a long history in the Western world, with the basic elements of a body of international law developing in Ancient Greece and Rome. Although the beginnings of international law can be found in various civilisations of antiquity, this chapter will focus on its Western origins, which have over time been a dominant influence, and especially of course in Europe.

'Modern' principles of international law, in which states are the key unit of sovereignty or power, emerged in a clear form in the 1600s in Europe. It is within the framework of international law that the EU originated and is best understood. The first and many subsequent steps in the creation of the EU legal system were by means of one of the sources of international law: treaties between the Member States. It is traditional for EU lawyers to consider EU law to be quite separate to international law or at least as sufficiently separate that international law is not really addressed, except for specialist audiences. This, however, can be somewhat mistaken, as it prevents a full understanding of the hybrid character of the EU – developed from international law, yet with distinct features in which individual states have given up or lost some of their powers.

KEY LEARNING POINT

THE FOUNDING TREATIES OF THE EU AS BASED ON INTERNATIONAL LAW

The founding treaties of the EU – the European Coal and Steel Community Treaty (ECSC Treaty), the European Atomic Energy Community Treaty (EURATOM Treaty) and the European Economic Community Treaty (EEC Treaty) – were adopted by the Member States according to the ordinary rules of treaty-making in international law. Subsequent amendments to these treaties, the most recent of which is the Treaty of Lisbon, also follow the standard rules of treaty-making in international law.

This approach of disconnecting the EU from international law makes it harder to understand the significance of EU law in national law compared, say, with the impact of the European Convention on Human Rights (ECHR). This chapter seeks to explain the international law background to the emergence of the EU and how EU law is both a product of public international law, while also being different from it in some key respects. In particular, this will make it easier to see how EU law is different from, but also relates to, the ECHR.

2.2 DEFINING INTERNATIONAL LAW

In the previous section, international law has been defined as the legal rules governing transactions and government activity across jurisdictions and borders. One useful definition is:

> International law may be defined as that body of law which is composed for its greater part of the principles and rules of conduct which states feel themselves bound to observe and, therefore, do commonly observe in their relations with each other, and which includes also:
>
> (a) the rules of law relating to the functioning of international institutions or organisations, their relations with each other, and their relations with states and individuals; and
> (b) certain rules of law relating to individuals and non-states so far as the rights or duties of such individuals and non-state entities are the concern of the international community.
>
> I Shearer *Starke's International Law* (11th edn Butterworths London 1994) 3

Two categories of international law can be identified: (a) public international law and (b) private international law. Public international law is concerned, in the first instance, with the relationships *between states* and the *legal duties owed by states to individuals*, whereas private international law is concerned primarily with relationships between *individuals* and other non-state legal persons (such as companies) across borders. EU law started from public international law. The EU was created according to the 'rules of change' (i.e. the rules governing how law changes)[1] in public international law: it was created by international treaties. Originally, it was not clear from the wording of the Community treaties that the EU as it is now was meant to be very different to other international law.[2] A key role was played here by the European Court of Justice (ECJ or CJEU), which creatively interpreted key features of the text to create important new doctrines that did in fact make (then) Community law (now Union law) different to other international law.

....

1   The distinction between primary, i.e. substantive rules, and secondary rules, i.e. rules about the rules (how rules change, how disputes about the rule are judged or resolved, how a legal rule is recognised) is attributable to Herbert Hart *The Concept of Law* (2nd edn Clarendon Press 1994) 80–81.

2   Stone Sweet argues that the treaties at the founding represented 'international law plus', i.e. standard international law cooperation with the added feature of compulsory ECJ jurisdiction and the particular role of the Commission as initiator of legislative proposals. See A Stone Sweet 'The juridical coup d'état and the problem of authority' (2007) 8(10) *German Law Journal* 915–28. For further critique and discussion see T Hartley 'International law and the law of the European Union: a reassessment' (2001) 72 *British Yearbook of International Law* 1–35.

THE ESSENTIAL DIFFERENCE BETWEEN EU AND INTERNATIONAL LAW

The key difference of EU law compared to the rest of international law is in the degree of sovereignty or power that the Member States have given up as a consequence of joining the EU. The Court of Justice played the most important role in this development through its case law on direct effect and supremacy.

The EU is just one of many international organisations. Quite literally, hundreds of international organisations exist, ranging from the Universal Postal Union (the first modern international legal organisation, founded in 1874) to the United Nations (UN) (the largest international organisation, founded in 1945 at the end of the Second World War). However, none involves quite the degree of sharing of sovereignty among central institutions as does the EU. The EU has developed in this way to some extent because of the role those central institutions themselves have played in developing their own powers (this is especially true of the European Court of Justice or ECJ); to some extent, the institutions have been able to expand their own powers (or very broadly interpreted their powers),[3] albeit in a slow, evolutionary way. The Member States have tended to accept this, while also deciding themselves to confer more powers.

EXPLAINING THE LAW

HOW DOES THE EU INVOLVE MORE POWERS BEING GIVEN UP BY MEMBER STATES?

As you read this chapter, it will be useful to keep in mind that there are specific characteristics of the EU that give it greater power over the Member States than is normal in international law:

- Member States agree to accept *EU laws being passed by (qualified) majority voting amongst their representatives* (normally in international law organisations, states can opt in and opt out as they wish to any laws the organisation adopts). This was something agreed to by the Member States in the treaties
- Member States have agreed to allow a *directly elected international body*, i.e. the European Parliament, *have a say in passing EU laws* (normally only ministers of a state can agree to bind a state)
- The *impact of EU law is stronger in national law* than is the impact of international law: (a) if there is a conflict between national law and EU law, EU law prevails in national courts under the doctrine of supremacy developed by the Court of Justice (although this is subject to qualified acceptance by some

---

3   The tendency of the EU institutions, and especially of the ECJ, to interpret implied powers expansively is much more marked than is the case with other international institutions.

of the highest courts of the Member States); and (b) individuals are allowed
to invoke EU law in a national court (normally, concerning international law,
neither (a) nor (b) is the case)

– Member States accepted the *compulsory jurisdiction of an international court*
in all disputes involving EU law (it is more typical for states only to accept the
jurisdiction of their own courts or to accept jurisdiction of an international
court or tribunal in a more limited way[4]).

The next section will survey how international law developed in the Western world.
This will help you see that the issues dealt with in EU law – how states are to legally
regulate their relationships with each other and how the resulting rules have an effect
in the legal system of each state – are not new issues. The same issues have recurred
throughout history. What is different about the EU is to how they are dealt with.
However, the EU is not completely different to international law, as we will see. This is
not of course a comprehensive overview of the development of international law, but it
should help to explain the broader context of legal relationships between states.

2.3 THE EVOLUTION OF INTERNATIONAL LAW

2.3.1 THE BEGINNINGS OF MODERN INTERNATIONAL LAW IN THE WESTERN WORLD: THE GREEKS AND ROMANS[5]

Ancient Greece (circa 1100 BC to 146 AD) had few relations with its neighbours, but
because ancient Greece consisted of a series of cities independent from one another,
certain rules grew up as to how the cities should relate to each other (rules that were
facilitated by their common Greek identity and culture). The Greeks did not have the
concept of a state in the modern sense that is now central to international law, but their
use of the term *polis* to describe the political organisation of cities comes close to the
modern understanding (note also the modern term 'polity' derived from *polis*). These
rules included: war should be avoided, war should only be commenced by a declaration,
the obligation not to harm heralds or messengers, the entitlement of soldiers killed in
battle to a burial, the right of refuge in a temple, a prohibition on the killing of prisoners
(they could be ransomed or exchanged or at worst be enslaved), and an exemption of

....

4   Under the Statute of the International Court of Justice (ICJ), states may opt to accept its jurisdiction in all
    cases or in some cases, under art 36(2). The World Trade Organization (WTO) involves a degree of compulsory
    dispute settlement, but the judicial organ is less powerful than in the EU.

5   See generally J M Kelly *A Short History of Western Legal Theory* (Oxford University Press Oxford 1994) 77–78,
    156–58, 199–202, 299–300, 345–47, 451–54; W G Grewe *The Epochs of International Law* (M Byers (ed) Walter
    de Gruyter 2000). The focus of this chapter is on Western international law, but varieties of international law
    existed in antiquity in China and Persia, for example.

priests and seers from the use of force in war. Although the Greeks considered these obligations to be religious ones and so sometimes they are not considered 'law', they involve a set of rules for the proper conduct of relations that were generally followed between the Greek cities. In regulating both the manner of going to war and the conduct of war, as well as communication between cities, these rules can be seen as an early form of what are key elements in modern international law: the law on the permissible use of warfare (*jud ad bellum*), the law on the permissible conduct of warfare (*jus in bello*) and diplomatic law.

KEY LEARNING POINT

INTERNATIONAL LAW ON THE USE OF FORCE AND WAR IN THE CONTEXT OF THE EU

The use of force between countries is governed by international law, not by EU law. Article 347 TFEU provides only that the Member States must consult each other in the context of such issues affecting the internal market with a view to taking together the steps needed to prevent the functioning of the internal market being affected. This applies when the Member States take measures in the event of serious internal disturbances affecting the maintenance of law and order, in the event of war, serious international tension constituting a threat of war, or in order to carry out obligations it has accepted for the purpose of maintaining peace and international security.

Rules governing the use of force are an important part of international law. But on a more day-to-day basis, a key issue since the beginnings of international law is differences in treatment of foreigners and local citizens. There existed tensions in Ancient Greece between different understandings of foreigners.

ANALYSING THE LAW

THE TREATMENT OF FOREIGNERS IN A DOMESTIC LEGAL SYSTEM

As we will see in later chapters, a key feature of EU law is how, in many respects, Member States agree to treat each other's citizens in the same way as they do their own citizens when citizens move from one Member State to another. How open or receptive a legal system should be to foreigners is not a new problem, and different attitudes to it can be seen in Ancient Greece and Rome.

Sparta was, compared to Athens, a more nationalistic, even chauvinistic, city state. This difference was part of the reason Sparta went to war with Athens (simple power rivalry was also present, and Sparta did cooperate with others in the war against Athens).[6] The

....

6   The Peloponnesian War took place between Athens and Sparta from 431–404 BC.

tension, therefore, between a 'nationalism' as we now call it and a more open attitude to outsiders was found in Ancient Greece too. In the EU today, Member States still struggle to strike a good balance between the two concerns of preserving a nation's political and community identity and cooperating with and welcoming 'outsiders'.

The Romans (c. 900 BC to c. 450 AD) further developed an understanding of the relationship between different peoples that could be considered an early type of international law. In particular, the Romans expanded on the rules governing warfare and on the application of a set of legal rules to non-Romans. The Romans during a certain period had a special priesthood called the '*fetiales*', whose function was to regulate relationships with other peoples and the rules related to matters of conflict, such as declarations of war and peace agreements/treaties. This body of law, *ius fetiale*, seems to have been understood to apply to all peoples. The Romans developed a doctrine of a *just war*. Cicero made reference to a law of war (*ius bellicum*), which, for example, included the principle that the terms of an oath or agreement with an enemy must be observed. Cicero referred to an enemy in this context as 'open and organized', in a way that could be related to the modern notion of 'a state' and which Cicero (106–43 BC) contrasted with pirates.[7]

KEY LEARNING POINT

RECIPROCITY IN THE BEHAVIOUR OF STATES

The development of a doctrine of a just war implicitly recognises that the sovereignty of another political power cannot simply be violated at will. Implicit in this is a recognition of the sovereignty of another political power as deserving recognition, which implies a concept of reciprocity of political recognition. These can be considered foundational ideas in modern international law also.

More generally, Roman law distinguished between the treatment to be given to foreigners when there was an agreement or treaty with their government and when there was no such agreement or treaty; in the latter case, people or property from other peoples were not entitled to legal protection and could be seized and enslaved (although ambassadors were always inviolable). But if a treaty of agreement or friendship existed, foreigners were entitled to legal protection. The use of treaties or agreements in this way between peoples is of course a key feature of international law today, where treaties are one of the primary sources of law. The rules governing these foreign people developed into a system of its own called *ius gentium*, in contrast with the *ius civile* that applied to the Romans themselves. Often treaties contained a clause that conflicts in future were to be solved by arbitration (*recuperatores*).[8]

---

7   Cicero *De officiis* Book III, chapter XXIX (44 BC).

8   *Ius genetium* and *ius fetiale* together make up what today would be regarded as a single category of international law, but in Rome it seems the two bodies of legal rules were often considered distinct. See H Nettleship *Contributions to Latin Lexicography* (1889, republished by Cambridge University Press Cambridge 2010) 504–506.

EXPLAINING THE LAW

AGREEMENTS GIVING MORE RIGHTS TO PARTICULAR FOREIGNERS

The Roman law concept of *ius gentium* granted certain rights to foreigners with whom Rome concluded a treaty or agreement of friendship. Foreigners from states or cities with whom Rome did not have such a treaty enjoyed few rights, while those foreigners who could benefit from the *ius gentium* still did not enjoy the same level of rights as Roman citizens benefiting from the *ius civile*. The distinction in the legal treatment between a state's own citizens and citizens from outside is of course a feature of contemporary national and international law.

Few if any contemporary states grant all the same rights to foreigners as they do to their own citizens. As in the Roman era, states commonly do grant certain rights to citizens from other countries with whom treaties have been concluded. This is especially the case with EU law: one of the distinguishing features of EU law is just how much rights citizens of the Member States gain in other Member States as a result of EU membership. In some matters, EU law requires EU Member States to treat citizens from other Member States in the same way as citizens from their own Member States. This mainly applies to 'economic actors': workers and the self-employed. In the EU, this is called 'free movement of workers' and 'free movement of services'. However, the requirement of equal treatment is largely confined to EU citizens who are employed or self-employed in another Member State, although there has been some development of this, including for the family members of EU citizens exercising freedom of movement. We will look at this in more detail in Chapters 8, 10 & 11.

2.3.2 THE MIDDLE AGES (C. 450 AD TO 1450 AD)

After the fall of the Roman Empire, political and cultural life in Europe is often considered to have entered a period of decline. Instead of the single, organised, universal jurisdiction of the Roman political system over most of the then known (Western) world, political power became fragmented between smaller local territories, with little development of political theory. In the Middle Ages, a feudal system developed with a pyramidal structure in society marked by reciprocal duties between lords and their vassals. Vassals were very much subject to the political power of this local lord, not to a general political system.

Reflecting this relative lack of organised political power as compared to the Roman period, no systematic development of a field of international law occurred during this time. However, some rules on trading developed (e.g. French *Rolls of Orléon*, English

Black Book of the Admiralty, Spanish *Consolato del Mare*[9]). Other practices between
political powers also developed, including the role of the papacy as a mediator between
warring or fighting powers, the conclusion of treaties and the use of ambassadors as
representatives sent to other powers.

EXPLAINING THE LAW

LIMITED NATURE OF INTERNATIONAL LAW IN VARIOUS CUSTOMS OF THE MEDIEVAL PERIOD

During the Medieval period, there was no systematic international law. Some
customary rules concerning trade developed and the papacy had an important
role as a mediator between political powers in conflict (and sometimes claimed
ultimate moral authority itself to decide what political powers should do).

The consolidation of political power into centralised nation states had not yet emerged.
Some consolidation of political power and the process of emergence of nation states
began, for example, with the emergence of England and French centralised power from
800–1000 AD. The emergence, however, of the Holy Roman Empire (in 962 AD under
the first Holy Roman emperor, Otto I) meant that there was not much need to *theorise*
the relationship between individual political states or powers. The Holy Roman Empire
was conceived of, in effect, as successor or replacement of the universal political power
of the Roman Empire. The idea of the Holy Roman Empire as a universal power was
never really a political reality, with many local lords and smaller kingdoms being in fact
independent, but its theoretical power reduced the practical need to develop principles
of international law. The Holy Roman Empire only really had control over central
Europe for a sustained period of time. The emergence of the modern nation state, from
1200 AD onwards, and their de facto independence resulted in a plurality of states or
political powers, and this was a key factor in the emergence of modern international law.

KEY LEARNING POINT

THE EMERGENCE OF NATION STATES

Although the ideology of the 'nation state' reached its height in the nineteenth
and twentieth centuries, the emergence of ethnically homogeneous states
became apparent during the later Medieval period and the early modern period
(1200–1700 AD). The nation state was a political, self-governing unit in which most
of the peoples belonging to it shared the same cultural identity, speaking the
same language and following similar traditions.

....

9   The exact origins of the *Consolato del Mare* are debated; it appears to have been a mixture of customary laws from
various sources in the Mediterranean adopted especially in Aragon and Barcelona (in modern-day Spain) and
Pisa (in modern-day Italy), but also recognised more widely. See e.g. D A Azuni *The Maritime Law of Europe* (first
published in Italian 1795–1796, Lawbook Exchange Ltd 2006) 326–72. See also e.g. T J Schoenbaum *Admiralty
and Maritime Law* (West Publishing Co 2001) 11. A version called the *Consulat del Mar* was adopted in Barcelona.

EXPLAINING THE LAW

THE HOLY ROMAN EMPIRE, NATION STATES AND INTERNATIONAL LAW

The Holy Roman Empire existed from 962–1806 AD. In theory, it replaced the Roman Empire as a universal form of government in Europe, i.e. in theory it was the highest political authority for all of Europe. This, however, was never a reality. The Holy Roman Empire was strongest in central Europe, but did not have much control over the rest of Europe for a sustained period of time. Nation states in Europe, as we now know them, started to emerge from 900–1000 AD onwards. England became a unified state in 927 AD. Scotland emerged around this period also. France emerged earlier as the centre of the Frankish Empire under Charlemagne, which was a forerunner to the Holy Roman Empire, but the modern state was more or less established by the late 900s. The emergence of various nation states, which became more and more powerful from 1000 AD onwards, made it necessary to have rules governing their relations with each other.[10]

2.3.3 EARLY MODERN EUROPE (1450 AD–1600 AD) AND THE EMERGENCE OF THE WESTPHALIAN SYSTEM

By the 1500s, a clear concept emerged of an international law or body of legal rules applicable to relationships between states. Amongst the historical factors that prompted this, apart from the emergence of nation states, was the discovery of new lands and peoples by explorers. These developments meant a need to theorise and develop practical rules on the relationship between colonising powers and the colonised territories, especially given the extent of British and French colonisation in North America and Spanish and Portuguese colonisation in South America.

KEY LEARNING POINT

FRANCISCO DE VITORIA AND THE EMERGENCE OF MODERN INTERNATIONAL LAW

The phrase from Roman law *ius gentium* was now modified by Francisco de Vitoria (1492–1546 AD), sometimes described as the father of international law, to mean rules applicable to and between all peoples and nations (rather than

---

10 This period also saw the further development of theories of a just war, which implies a struggle between political powers more or less equivalent to each other (rather than all being subject to an emperor), developing from Saint Augustine (354–430 AD), especially by Saint Thomas Aquinas (1225–1274 AD).

the law applicable to foreigners, as it meant in the Roman Empire). Amongst the principles he considered to be part of it were:

- to travel
- to trade peacefully
- to settle and own land settled on
- not to be despoiled of land owned
- that a war to conquer territory was not justified by a refusal of its people of princes to accept Christianity.[11]

All these principles remain recognised today and, indeed, the EU is distinct in the very full extent to which it recognises the rights of citizens of the Member States to travel and trade in each other's territories. Vitoria's approach is to understand international law in universal terms, as inhering in it certain principles independently of specific treaties of friendship.

By the late 1500s, Alberico Gentili (1552–1608 AD) wrote the first treatise on the subject of embassies, entitled *De legationibus* (1585), reflecting the establishment by that time of well recognised principles of diplomatic law.

EXPLAINING THE LAW

THE EXTERNAL ACTION SERVICE OF THE EU

Initially, what is now the EU had no diplomatic officials of its own. Relations with third countries were understood to remain primarily within the competence of the Member States, acting individually if they wished. A key development that changed this was the development by the Court of Justice of the doctrine of 'parallelism': under this doctrine, when the Member States have adopted common policies internally within the Union, the EU automatically acquires an exclusive competence to engage in external relations with third states.[12] The logical conclusion of this doctrine would be that the EU would have its own diplomats and embassies. This developed informally at first, but was confirmed at treaty level by the Treaty of Lisbon, which established an external relations service for the EU in Article 27 TEU. It was formed from the external relations departments of the Commission and of the Council, which had been developed at an administrative level prior to the Lisbon Treaty.

11 *Relectio de Indis et de Ivre Belli* (1557 AD in the original, 1917 in the English translation by the Carnegie Institute).
12 *Commission v Council (European Road Transport Agreement) (ERTA)* [1971] ECR 263. The adoption of common policies at EU level pre-empts Member State competence to conduct external relations regarding those policies. Thus, for example, the EU represents the interests of the Member States at the World Trade Organization.

Among the first to make explicit the idea of international law was Richard Hooker (1554–1600 AD) in *Laws of Ecclesiastical Polity* (1594 AD) who referred to a distinct category of law 'which toucheth all such several bodies politic, so far forth as one of them hath public commerce with another', consisting of primary rules governing embassies, foreigners' rights and trade, and secondary rules governing conduct when normal relations broke down, i.e. war.[13] Francisco de Suárez (1548–1617 AD) gave the first full articulation of the idea of international law:

> No matter how many diverse peoples and kingdoms the human race may be divided into, it always has a certain unity, not merely as a species but even a sort of political or moral unity, which is indicated by the natural precept of mutual love and mercy which extends to foreigner, even to foreigners of any nation. No matter how a sovereign state, commonwealth or kingdom may be in itself a perfect society with its own members, each one is also, in a sense, as seen from the point of view of the human race, a member of the universal community; for states standing alone are not so self-sufficient that they never require some mutual help, association and intercourse … They therefore need some law to direct and order rightly this type of intercourse and association … and so certain specific laws could be introduced through the usage of the nations.[14]

Hugo de Groot (more often known as Grotius) (1583–1645 AD) is considered perhaps the most important founder of modern international law, mainly through *De iure belli et pacis* (1625) ('On the law of war and peace'). Grotius based his thinking on the idea of a natural law that had validity irrespective of whether one believed in God or not (his *etsi daremus* formula – 'even if we were to concede the non-existence of God', Grotius identifying himself as being a Christian). He started with the belief, also found as far back as the thought of Aristotle, that men are by nature sociable and have an impelling desire for society, which calls forth the need for a social order.

KEY LEARNING POINT

GROTIUS AND THE SOURCES OF INTERNATIONAL LAW

Although endorsing natural law in theory, Grotius also placed much emphasis on voluntary agreement and custom of states (*ius voluntarium*) (which can be associated with positivism in contrast to the idea of natural law[15]). *Ius voluntarium* encompassed both:

1. treaties and
2. customary practice.

13 *Laws of Ecclesiastical Polity* (1594 AD) 1. 10.
14 *De legibus ac Deo Legislatore* (1612) 2.19.8.
15 Natural law refers to the idea of timeless, universally valid moral principles that must inform the content of valid actual or 'positive' laws.

Treaties and custom have come to be seen as the main sources of international law today. As we will see in Chapter 3, treaties play a very important role in EU law, but customary law does not.

Among the principles Grotius argued for were:

- against theft or depriving others of their rightful property
- in favour of restitution where property is wrongfully seized
- and the importance of following rules apparent from settled custom and practice (so not all rules stemmed from natural law, there was a voluntary law or *ius voluntarium*).

EXPLAINING THE LAW

THE WESTPHALIAN SYSTEM OF RELATIONS BETWEEN STATES

The Peace Treaty of Westphalia of 1648 (AD), which brought to an end the Thirty Years' War in the Holy Roman Empire and the Eighty Years' War between Spain and its province of the Netherlands, is seen as a decisive moment in the emergence of the states as the most important actor in international law. The agreements at Osnabrück and Münster resulted from a congress at which participants were organised mostly according to their states or kingdoms/ principalities, whereas previously such peace agreements were seen as regulations of the Holy Roman Empire, rather than agreements between sovereign equals. The peace settlement recognised states as the decisive unit of authority, for example, confirming the principle in the Peace of Augsburg 1555 that the monarch of each state should decide its religion and clarifying the boundaries between states. Even today, the term 'Westphalian' is used to convey the idea of states as the decisive site of sovereignty or power: the most important source of international law is what is agreed by states through treaties or conventions, essentially, contracts between states.[16] One of the fundamental characteristics of the EU is its tendency to reduce the power of states in favour of a supranational entity, with some supporters of integration believing ultimately in the idea of a federal 'United States of Europe'.

2.3.4 FROM THE EMERGENCE OF THE WESTPHALIAN SYSTEM TO THE MODERN ERA

The above has offered a sketched history of international law. Although experts in this field would no doubt consider it incomplete and would wish to say much more, the most fundamental elements have been identified to help understand that states are decisive

---

16 See http://avalon.law.yale.edu/17th_century/westphal.asphttp://avalon.law.yale.edu/17th_century/westphal.asp (last accessed 18 January 2015).

units of sovereignty in international law and relations today. The Treaty of Westphalia is widely accepted as a key moment in this development.

ANALYSING THE LAW

STATES AND THE EMERGENCE OF INTERNATIONAL ORGANISATIONS

The dominance of states arguably continues to this day, although international organisations are now increasingly important. The future of the international legal system may well be dominated by tension between the continuing power of states and increasing power of international organisations.

A predecessor of such international bodies might be seen in the 'Congress System' or 'Concert of Europe' of European diplomacy. The Congress System prevailed in much of the nineteenth century following the defeat of Napoleon in 1815, and beginning with the Congress of Vienna in that year to decide the map of Europe following 25 years of conflict on the continent after the French Revolution and the rise of the French Napoleonic Empire, which had conquered much of the continent of Europe during that time. Under the Congress system, the major European powers met to resolve disputes both in Europe and overseas as European powers competed to expand their colonial empires.

KEY LEARNING POINT

THE EMERGENCE OF INTERNATIONAL ORGANISATIONS

The first modern international organisation was the Universal Postal Union in 1874, which regulated the development of the new international system of postage, following the development of the system of postal stamps from 1840. Now, hundreds of these organisations exist, most notably the UN, the World Trade Organization (WTO) and, perhaps, the EU. The UN is a worldwide body with global competence, primarily, to maintain peace and security.

The predecessor of the UN was the League of Nations, which was created following the First World War in an attempt to provide a permanent world-wide forum for the peaceful resolution of disputes, as opposed to the informal congress system and bilateral diplomacy between states, which had become discredited for failing to prevent the First World War. However, the League of Nations failed in its mandate to achieve peace in the world, not least because the United States refused to join it, but also because it lacked effective enforcement powers. The strongest powers it possessed for dealing with states that threatened peace and security were economic sanctions, which were ineffective in practice.

The weakness of the League of Nations became obvious during the 1930s, especially when it failed to prevent militaristic expansion by Germany and Italy in Europe and Japan in Asia. Its failures ultimately contributed to the outbreak of the Second World War. However, lessons were at least learned for the period after the Second World War, when the UN was created as a successor to the League, but with stronger powers, including the sanctioning of military force by UN members in response to threats to peace and security from individual or groups of countries.

The League of Nations was dissolved in April 1946, shortly after the UN was created in October 1945. A number of organs of the League of Nations were transferred to the UN, including the Permanent Court of International Justice (PCIJ), renamed the International Court of Justice (ICJ).

During the nineteenth and twentieth centuries, another important development was the process of decolonisation, which began in North America in the late eighteenth century, continued in South America in the nineteenth century (while the reverse process of colonisation was occurring in Africa and Asia), and decolonisation spread to Africa and Asia in the twentieth century. This did not have dramatic effects on international law, but the main new principle or doctrine to emerge was *uti possidetis*, namely, that newly decolonised territories in general should comply with the same borders as during colonisation.

This principle served a practical purpose of preventing endless historical disputes about the ownership of land. *Uti possidetis juris* might become relevant in an EU context if part of the territories of EU Member States secede and become independent, which is at least a possibility in the case of the UK concerning Scotland and in the case of Spain concerning the Basque and Catalan regions.

2.3.5 SOURCES OF INTERNATIONAL LAW

One of the most important issues in international law is the question of sources of international law.[17]

KEY LEARNING POINT

THE IMPORTANCE OF SOURCES IN INTERNATIONAL LAW

As there is no single, general legislative authority in international law, the question of sources of law takes on added importance. The sources of international law reflect the central role of states in the international legal system that emerged with the Treaty of Westphalia. The sources are set out in Article 38(11) of the Statute of the International Court of Justice (ICJ), and the two most important sources are (i) treaties agreed by states and (ii) customary practices of states.

---

17 See recently e.g. J D'Aspremont *Formalism and the Sources of International Law* (Oxford University Press 2011).

The authoritative statement of the sources in international law is generally taken to be Article 38 of the Statute of the International Court of Justice (ICJ), the highest judicial organ of the United Nations (UN), which is the same as Article 38 of the Statute of its predecessor court under the League of Nations, the Permanent Court of International Justice (PCIJ) (see further below).

2.3.5.1 THE MAIN SOURCES

The classical statement of the sources is Article 38(1) of the Statute of the ICJ:

> 1. The Court, whose function is to decide in accordance with international law such disputes as are submitted to it, shall apply:
>
>> a. *international conventions*, whether general or particular, establishing rules expressly recognized by the contesting states;
>>
>> b. *international custom*, as evidence of a general practice accepted as law;
>>
>> c. the *general principles of law* recognized by civilized nations;
>>
>> d. subject to the provisions of Article 59, *judicial decisions* and the *teachings of the most highly qualified publicists* of the various nations, as subsidiary means for the determination of rules of law.
>
> 2. This provision shall not prejudice the power of the Court to decide a case *ex aequo et bono*, if the parties agree thereto.

The most important sources are treaties and custom, but general principles are also important. Case law is of importance in clarifying international law (especially case law of the ICJ), but it does not have the dramatic law-making role it has in the EU. Doctrine is the source least relied upon, but it has an important background role in informing legal argument and debate; its exact influence on international law and practice is hard to measure.

2.3.5.1.1 INTERNATIONAL CONVENTIONS (ALSO CALLED TREATIES OR AGREEMENTS)

KEY LEARNING POINT

TREATIES AND CONVENTIONS AS SOURCES OF INTERNATIONAL LAW
This is probably the most important and clearest of sources. These are in effect contracts between states. They can be bilateral, i.e. between just two countries, or multilateral, i.e. between more than two countries. There are hundreds of these treaties, amongst the most notable of which are the UN Charter and founding treaties of the EU, which are examples of multilateral treaties.

Since the middle of the nineteenth century, many multilateral treaties have been signed to regulate matters of concern to states in general. Some of these multilateral treaties establish intergovernmental organisations, i.e. organisations consisting of representatives of several or many governments. Among the first of these was the Universal Postal Union, established by the Treaty Concerning the Formation of a General Postal Union, Berne, 9 October 1874.[18] The treaties founding the EU are such multilateral treaties.

2.3.5.1.2 CUSTOM

> KEY LEARNING POINT
> ....
>
> **CUSTOM AS SOURCES OF INTERNATIONAL LAW**
> This is a somewhat paradoxical or ambiguous concept despite being one of the main sources. There are two elements to any claimed rule of customary international law:
>
> 1. practice by states consistent with the claimed rule (state practice)
> 2. a belief by states that the rule is one that should be followed as a matter of law (*opinio juris*).

Both state practice and supporting *opinio juris* are necessary before a rule can be considered custom. So it arises that at some point a settled practice by states will crystallise into a customary rule because the opinion or belief has developed among states that it is a legal binding rule. It can be difficult, however, to pinpoint the exact moment that that happens; there may not be one such moment. Rather, it is a gradual process.

A further aspect of custom illustrates again the key role that state sovereignty has in international law. Under the persistent objector test, a state can exempt itself from a rule of custom if it clearly and consistently states its rejection of it.[19] Thus, a rule of custom cannot be imposed upon a state, although it may be politically and practically difficult to object persistently in this way.

2.3.5.1.3 GENERAL PRINCIPLES
The exact meaning of the concept of 'general principles' in Article 38(1)(c) has been somewhat debated; some theorists thought it was a reference to natural law, others thought it was almost redundant and simply referred to custom and treaties in a general way. Most international lawyers considered that 'general principles' are a separate category.

....

18 Recorded in C Bevans *Treaties and Other International Agreements of the United States of America 1776–1949* http:// avalon.law.yale.edu/19th_century/usmu010.asp (last accessed 18 January 2015).

19 See generally T Stein 'The approach of a different drummer: the principle of persistent objection in international law' (1985) 26 *Harvard International Law Journal* 457–82; D Bederman 'Acquiescence, objection and the death of customary international law' (2010) 21 *Duke Journal of Comparative and International Law* 31–45. For authority from the ICJ see e.g. *Colombia v Peru* (Asylum) [1950] ICJ Rep 266 at 277–78. States may not derogate from *jus cogens* norms through persistent objection.

| KEY LEARNING POINT |

GENERAL PRINCIPLES AS SOURCES OF INTERNATIONAL LAW COMPARED WITH EU LAW

Being distinct from treaties and custom as sources of international law means general principles do not need to be specifically found in a treaty (although they are likely to be in practice) nor do they rely on proof of state practice and the accompanying *opinio juris* needed for a rule to be recognised as a customary one. They can be considered principles that are inherent in a legal system. As a matter of legal theory, general principles can give the judiciary an important role: the more important the role of general principles, the more powerful the judiciary, since it is the judiciary and not states that determine the existence and content of general principles.

In international law, general principles can be considered systemic rules. A key general principle is *pacta sunt servanda*, which is that 'every treaty in force is binding upon the parties to it and must be performed by them in good faith' (Article 26 of the Vienna Convention on the Law of Treaties). A related general principle is *clausula rebus sic stantibus*, which is that states may be relieved of the obligation to obey a treaty following a compelling change of circumstances.[20]

The above general principles of international law could also be assumed to be accepted within EU law, but general principles in EU law have a more prominent role. This is partly because the Court of Justice has excluded fall-back on international law rules and principles where there is a gap in the EU system,[21] and related to this, has developed a number of general principles or concepts related to its pro-integration teleological approach to interpretation: the effectiveness or *effet utile* of EU law, the equivalence of national procedural enforcement of EU law relative to enforcement of national law, proportionality, legal certainty and fundamental rights. Identifying fundamental rights as within general principles is important because of the breadth of the concept. To some extent, the EU legislature has caught up through the adoption of the EU Charter of Fundamental Rights (see Chapter 8).

The category is not that frequently invoked by the ICJ, and the principles of legal liability and reparation for a breach of international obligation is perhaps the main area in which it is invoked, e.g. *Chorzow Factory* case, where the Permanent Court of International Justice (PCIJ, predecessor of the ICJ) stated that a party cannot take advantage of its own wrong was a principle 'generally accepted in the jurisprudence of international arbitration, as well as by municipal courts' and the PCIJ stated 'it is a general conception of law that every violation of an engagement involves an obligation to make reparation'.[22] Harris notes that the ICJ frequently equates general principles

20 See art 62 of the Vienna Convention on the Law of Treaties, 23 May 1969, 1155 *UNTS* 331, 8 *ILM* 679, entered into force 27 January 1980, and the ICJ judgment in *United Kingdom v Iceland* (Fisheries Jurisdiction) [1973] ICJ Rep 3.
21 Hartley (n 2) 12 and the references therein.
22 (1927) A/9 at 31.

with equity, which tends to overlap with Article 38(2), but without the requirement for the agreement of the parties set out in the latter provision.[23]

In this respect, the category can be open to some criticism on the grounds of its potential vagueness and the discretion this appears to give to the judiciary, a point noted by Bobbio regarding the role of general or systemic principles in legal reasoning in general.[24] This is true to an extent of all legal systems: general principles provide the judiciary with a degree of autonomy from the law-maker,[25] in that they do not require a legislative basis.

2.3.5.1.4 OTHER SOURCES

Two other sources informally have become important, although technically they are evidence of the other sources, rather than independent sources themselves:

a. resolutions of the General Assembly of the UN
b. resolutions of the UN Security Council, which come into a special category relating to the responsibility of the UN for maintaining world peace
c. draft codes prepared by the International Law Commission, which is a body that is part of the UN system with responsibility for studying and assisting with the development of international law.

2.3.5.2 HIERARCHY OF THE SOURCES AND OVERALL COMMENT ON THE SOURCES

Most conceptually and practically difficult are general principles. General principles can be problematic because of their vagueness and the potential scope of judicial autonomy from the law-maker, although this does not appear to have become a problem to date in general public international law. Custom is sometimes difficult to apply as a source because of its inherent ambiguity.

EXPLAINING THE LAW

WHEN PRACTICES 'CRYSTALLISE' INTO CUSTOMARY RULES

A rule is a rule of custom because it is considered a binding rule of custom, but there must have been some point at which a mere practice evolved into a binding rule. Identifying evidence of a rule of custom, both state practice and *opinio juris*, is an important skill for international lawyers and involves a more refined search and study of sources than is typical in a national system. Pinpointing that moment can be difficult. In EU, there is equivalent of customary law; in this respect, EU law is more like a national legal system.

---

23 D Harris *Cases and Materials on International Law* (5th edn Sweet & Maxwell 1998) 51–52.
24 N Bobbio, 'Des Critères pour résoudre les antinomies' in C Perelman (ed) *Les Antinomies en Droit* (Bruylant Bruxelles 1965) 240–41.
25 J Ghestin, G Goubeaux and M Fabre-Magnan *Traité de droit civil: Introduction générale sous la direction de Jacques Ghestin* (4th edn, Paris: Librairie Générale de Droit et de Jurisprudence E.J.A., 1994) 470.

There is not a strict hierarchy of the sources in international law, and the drafters of the Statutes of the PCIJ and ICJ deliberately omitted any express statement of which was most important.

KEY LEARNING POINT
....

AN INFORMAL HIERARCHY OF THE SOURCES OF INTERNATIONAL LAW

Although there is no formal hierarchy in international law, informally treaties tend to generally have the highest status, following by general principles, followed by custom.[26] The relationship between treaty law and customary law is somewhat complex. In general, they can coexist if they relate to the same subject matter.[27] However, it also seems that logically treaties can deliberately abrogate custom, treaties being a more deliberate expression of state consent, but the intention would need to be made explicit.

General principles can be considered more important than custom in that they are inherent in the international legal system, although the material scope of custom is broader, i.e. many more matters are regulated by custom than general principles. The concept of *jus cogens* or peremptory norms has more recently developed and which could be characterised as the highest source of international law. Saying it is the highest source means that if *jus cogens* is in conflict with any other source, *jus cogens* prevails.

Jus cogens refers to 'peremptory norms of international law' and is referred to in the Vienna Convention on the Law of Treaties,[28] Article 53 of which states that any treaty that conflicts with *jus cogens* will be void. This concept could be compared with the more classical idea of natural law: that there are certain principles of humanity that are so fundamental that they are binding in all places and at all times and do not permit of exception or derogation. However, there is not much agreement on what rules or principles deserve the status of *jus cogens* beyond the prohibitions on slavery and genocide. In ordinary circumstances, therefore, *jus cogens* does not impact on a day-to-day basis on the hierarchy of norms to restrict state sovereignty expressed through treaty making.

....

26 See generally M Koskenniemi 'Hierarchy in international law: a sketch' (1997) 8(4) *European Journal of International Law* 566–82.

27 *Military and Paramilitary Activities in and against Nicaragua* (Merits) [1986] ICJ Rep 114. See B Bing Jia 'The relations between treaties and custom' (1969) 9(1) *Chinese Journal of International Law* 81–109.

28 The relationship between *jus cogens* and the concept of *erga omnes* obligations in international law is not altogether clear. *Erga omnes* obligations are obligations that bind all states, not just parties to a treaty. *Jus cogens* are of their nature *erga omnes* obligations, but *erga omnes* obligations are a broader category and, for example, could include general principles of international law and some universal rules of custom.

EXPLAINING THE LAW

COMPARING THE SOURCES OF EU AND OF INTERNATIONAL LAW

One way in which the EU differs importantly from international law is in its sources.

International law	EU law
Treaties	Treaties
Custom	*No customary law in the EU*
General principles	Much more important in EU law, a much broader category, and this gives the EU judiciary more power as general principles are independent of the legislature
Jus cogens *(peremptory norms)***	It is not clear if the ECJ accepts these as a higher source of law than EU law
Doctrine and *case law*	Case law only, but much more important in EU law. The ECJ has developed key constitutional doctrines in its case law
UN Security Council Resolutions	Binding in international law, but subordinate to EU law (*Kadi*[29] case)
Acts of international organisations	Secondary legislation (regulations, directives, decisions) passed by the EU institutions: much more important in EU law

....

** It is not fully clear whether *jus cogens* are best categorised as general principles or customary rules, but most international lawyers consider them the highest source of international law

---

Comparing the sources overall, in EU law, the central EU institutions have much more power than do institutions in international law.

2.4 DISPUTE SETTLEMENT, ENFORCEMENT AND THE LAW OF STATE RESPONSIBILITY

In contemporary international law, the major exception to the principle of state sovereignty is the enforcement power of the United Nations (UN) Security Council to maintain peace and security in the international community, under Chapter VII of the UN Charter.

....

29 Joined Cases C–402 & 415/05P *Kadi and Al Barakaat International Foundation v Council & Commission* [2008] ECR I–6351. See further ch 8 below.

THE SPECIAL ROLE OF THE UN SECURITY COUNCIL IN ENFORCING PEACE AND SECURITY

In general, the UN Security Council has the sole competence to authorise the use of force unless states are acting in self-defence.[30]

The UN is in effect the successor of the largely ineffective League of Nations, established after the First World War in an attempt to regulate the use of force in international relations, i.e. to transcend the principle of state sovereignty in order to avoid war. The UN Charter itself is in the form of a treaty, albeit a treaty of a special character in international law, being the closest thing to a general constitutional document in the international legal system. The enforcement power of the UN Security Council under Chapter VII[31] is quite exceptional, however. Although other international organisations have become increasingly important since the late 1800s, their rules still reflect the importance of state sovereignty. It is in this general respect that the EU is exceptional to the extent that it involves law-making by an international institution.[32]

THE INTERNATIONAL LAW OF STATE RESPONSIBILITY

Outside of the special role of the UN Security Council in matters of peace and security, the question of the enforcement of international law is dealt with by the law of state responsibility. Essentially, this amounts to a system of regulated self-help.

There is no centralised enforcement mechanism in the international legal system (i.e. apart from the special role the United Nations (UN) has in relation to the use of force in international law). The ICJ is a general international court that may hear any case for which the states parties agree to ICJ jurisdiction, but many states are unwilling or reluctant to accept this jurisdiction fully and, even when they do, they may not fully respect the judgments of the ICJ.

Although it is a principal organ of the UN, the ICJ has no enforcement power and generally cannot direct the Security Council (although there is some debate about judicial review of Security Council resolutions). As a result, the enforcement of international legal obligations is often a matter of self-help by states. Quite detailed rules

---

30 Although over the last 20 years it has become debated whether states can use force unilaterally for the purpose of humanitarian intervention.
31 Chapter VII of the UN Charter, 59 Stat 1031; TS No 993, deals with action regarding threats to the peace, breaches of the peace and acts of aggression. It gives to the Security Council sole competence to determine the existence of a threat to or breach of the peace or of an act of aggression (art 39), although it preserves the right of states to act in self-defence (art 51). Article 53 under Chapter VIII allows the Security Council to act through regional organisations when engaging in enforcement action.
32 On the latter topic generally in international law, see J E Alvarez *International Organizations as Law Makers* (Oxford University Press 2005).

about this self-help have developed. They allow individual states to take measures to protect their own interests and repair any breach of an international obligation owed to them. These rules are referred to as the international law of state responsibility.[33]

The rules of state responsibility have been semi-codified by the International Law Commission in its (Draft) Articles on State Responsibility (DASR) 2001,[34] and the DASR are mostly considered to be authoritative statements of the relevant rules.

EXPLAINING THE LAW
_____

UNDERSTANDING STATE RESPONSIBILITY

State responsibility arises *anytime there is a breach of an international legal obligation*, whether the source of law in general is a treaty, customary law, or a general principle of law. Most usually it relates to an obligation owed by one state to another state. The principle of state responsibility itself can be considered a general principle of international law. State responsibility is the corollary of the idea of a legal right or of an obligation: without some system of responsibility for their breach, legal rights and obligations would lack substance.[35]

As in national systems, some problems arise about the mental element of an infraction of the law, i.e. of international wrongs (fault or culpability). In general, it is enough that a state or an agent of a state brought about or caused the international wrong, without the need to prove the mental states of specific actors. The practice of international courts and tribunals varies somewhat, but the tendency is to treat knowledge by states as something that can be inferred automatically, while still accepting the basic principle that there must be some wrongful knowledge or *dolus*, e.g. in the *Corfu Channel* case, the ICJ held that the Albanian Government had violated 'every State's obligation not to allow knowingly its territory to be used for acts contrary to the rights of other States'.[36]

A further, related issue to fault or culpability is the extent to which states are liable for the actions of all their agents or officials, i.e. whose actions are attributable to a state for

---

33 On a terminological note, the term 'state liability' is sometimes used in international law in contrast to the term 'state responsibility'. State liability refers to a duty to compensate arising from conduct that is *itself not unlawful*, with state responsibility being used to refer to a duty of reparation resulting from conduct that is a breach of international law. An example of state liability is a duty by one country to compensate another country due to pollution, when the polluting activity is itself not unlawful. The responsibility–liability distinction is not always followed in international law writing.

34 Annex to General Assembly Resolution 56/83 of 12 December 2001 and corrected by document A/56/49 (Vol I)/Corr.4 http://legal.un.org/ilc/texts/instruments/english/draft%20articles/9_6_2001.pdf (last accessed 18 January 2015).

35 *Spanish Zone of Morocco Claims* (French text) RIAA ii.615 at 641 (Judge Huber); *Chorzów Factory* (Indemnity) [1928] PCIJ Rep Ser A No 17 at 29.

36 [1949] ICJ Rep 4.

the purposes of state responsibility. Article 4 DASR states that the action of any organ of a state can be attributed to it, while Article 8 DASR further provides that the conduct of any person or entity acting on the instructions of, or under the direction or control of, that state in carrying out the conduct, is also attributable to the state.[37]

The next practical issue is the consequences of an international wrong. Article 30 DASR provides for an obligation to desist, i.e. that the offending state must cease to perform the wrong and must give guarantees of a non-repetition. Article 31 DASR provides for reparation, stating that the responsible state is under an obligation to make full reparation for the injury caused by the internationally wrongful act. In general, state responsibility gives rise to the right of a state suffering a breach to engage in countermeasures.[38]

KEY LEARNING POINT
....

SELF-HELP BY STATES IS NOT GENERALLY FOUND IN THE EU SYSTEM

This method of self-help is a key distinguishing feature between national systems and international law *and* between EU law and international law.

Countermeasures generally involve a right to suspend the performance of obligations that would otherwise be owed to the offending state, and the main rules are set out in Articles 49–54 DASR. Countermeasures must:

— not violate certain rules, including those relating to the use of force under the UN Charter, obligations of a humanitarian character prohibiting reprisals, *jus cogens* (Article 50 DASR)
— be proportionate (Article 51 DASR)
— be notified to the offending state and the opportunity given to the latter to negotiate to resolve the breach (Article 52 DASR).[39]

....

37 Article 6 DASR provides that the conduct of organs placed at the disposal of a state by another state are attributable to the first state; arts 18–19 provide detailed rules on how states can be liable when they are acting along with another state engaging in an international wrong. Article 7 DASR provides in effect that even *ultra vires* decisions of officials are attributable to the state.

38 The term 'reprisals' is used to describe self-help measures that are unlawful.

39 A final point concerns defences or circumstances precluding wrongfulness. A number of defences are available, as set out in the DASR, which justify what would otherwise be an international wrong: *force majeure* (art 23 DASR); distress (art 24 DASR); necessity (art 25 DASR); compliance with peremptory norms/*jus cogens* (art 26 DASR). Be careful not to confuse these justifying factors under the general law of state responsibility with the specific defences available to states, for breaches of a treaty obligation, under the Vienna Convention on the Law of Treaties (VCLT), which is available at the following link http://untreaty.un.org/ilc/texts/instruments/english/conventions/1_1_1969.pdf (last accessed 18 January 2015). The defences available under the VCLT include: a manifest violation of a fundamental rule of internal law where it is objectively evident to any state conducting itself in the matter in accordance with normal practice and in good faith (art 46 VCLT); error (art 48 VCLT); fraud (art 49 VCLT); corruption of a representative of a state (art 51 VCLT); coercion by a state

| KEY LEARNING POINT

EU LAW HAS ITS OWN SYSTEM OF STATE LIABILITY

One of the distinguishing features of EU law compared to public international law generally is in this area of state responsibility, or state liability as it is referred to in EU law. EU law has developed its own system of liability.

The EU rules largely displace the system described above that applies to public international law generally. Generally speaking (although ultimately not always, as noted below), EU law reduces the element of self-help that unilaterally can be taken by states. The ECJ has held that: 'Above all, it must be pointed out that in no circumstances may the Member State rely on similar infringements by other Member States in order to escape their own obligations under the provisions of the Treaty'.[40] In international law, a state suffering a breach of a duty owed to it by another state may suspend its own duties under treaties towards the offending state; this is not generally permitted in EU law. When one EU Member State breaches EU law obligations to another Member State, the enforcement procedure under Articles 258–259 TFEU applies (see further Chapter 5):

1. The European Commission engages in discussions with both Member States.
2. If there is no solution, either the Member State or the European Commission can bring a case before the ECJ.
3. ECJ jurisdiction is compulsory.
4. If a Member State failed to comply with an adverse ECJ judgment, it can be subject to a second action and a fine under Article 260 TFEU;
5. If a Member State continually fails to abide by an ECJ judgment, it may have some of its rights under the EU treaties suspended by the Council (of Ministers) (under Article 7 TEU), a procedure that has never been used to date.

In this way, breaches of EU law are subject to special rules of the EU treaties (although arguably, public international law still has a potential application as a last resort, in the event of a failure of the EU's own rules).[41] Member States cannot in general 'help themselves' through countermeasures.

by the threat or use of force (art 52 VCLT); violation of *jus cogens* (art 53 VCLT); implied right to withdraw or denounce given nature of treaty (art 56 VCLT).

40 Joined Cases 142 and 143/80 *Amministrazione delle Finanze dello Stato v Essevi* [1981] ECR 1413 at 1431.

41 See G Conway 'Breaches of EC law and the international responsibility of Member States' (2002) 13(3) *European Journal of International Law* 679–95; B Simma, D Pulkowski 'Of planets and the universe' (2006) 17(3) *European Journal of International Law* 483–529.

EXPLAINING THE LAW

COMPARING STATE RESPONSIBILITY AND SELF-HELP IN INTERNATIONAL LAW TO ENFORCEMENT IN EU LAW[42]

Under international law, outside of the special role of the United Nations Security Council in the use of force by states, there is no centralised enforcement of international law. Breaches of international law are dealt with through rules governing state responsibility. These allow for self-help by states, i.e. states who suffer a breach of international law by another state, are allowed to take countermeasures in response.

International Law	EU Law
Diplomacy	Diplomacy
Courts if both states agree	Enforcement role of European Commission
Countermeasures	Compulsory jurisdiction of ECJ
	Article 7 TEU suspension of rights

KEY LEARNING POINT

IN DISPUTE SETTLEMENT IN THE EU, THE EU INSTITUTIONS HAVE MORE POWER THAN INDIVIDUAL STATES

EU law gives more power to the EU institutions compared to international institutions in international law: in the EU, the European Commission, the ECJ and the Council (of Ministers) all have an important role to play, in sequence one after the other, as set out by EU law.

2.5 PENETRATION OF INTERNATIONAL LAW INTO NATIONAL LAW: MONISM AND DUALISM

Primarily in the context of treaties, a basic distinction exists as to how national legal systems interact with international law:

---

42 For detailed recent discussion comparing state liability in EU law with state responsibility in international law see A Vaitkevičiūtė 'The relationship between Member State liability in damages for breach of the European Union law and state responsibility for breach of international law' (2012) 19(1) *Jurisprudencija* 71–86.

KEY LEARNING POINT

HOW INTERNATIONAL TREATIES BECOME A PART OF NATIONAL LAW

(1) *Monism*: once a treaty has been signed/ratified by the government (i.e. the executive, e.g. foreign minister), the treaty is automatically a part of national law. This approach treats national law and international law as part of the one legal system and requires just one step for a treaty to have effect in national law.
(2) *Dualism*: under this approach, the national legal system and the international legal system are considered separate systems. Two steps needed for an international treaty to be part of national law:

  i. signature and ratification by the government/executive
 ii. incorporation by Parliament.

Most common law countries, including the UK, are dualist. Incorporation is usually by an Act of Parliament, e.g. the European Convention on Human Rights 1950 was incorporated into UK law by the Human Rights Act 1998, although the UK Government signed and ratified it in 1951.[43] Many systems that are dualist are more receptive to other sources of international law than treaties, such as custom and general principles. For example, customary international law and general principles of law are part of the common law;[44] they are, however, thus subordinated to any treaty rule incorporated at statutory level.

KEY LEARNING POINT

TWO VERSIONS OF MONISM
Two versions of monism can be distinguished:

(1) *Strong monism*: once the government/executive signs and ratifies, the international treaty is part of domestic/national law *and* has the same standing or a higher standing than constitutional law, e.g. the Fourth French Republic (1948–1958), the Netherlands.
(2) *Weak monism*: once the government/executive signs and ratifies, the international treaty is part of domestic/national law, but has the same status as an ordinary statute, e.g. Fifth French Republic (1958 to date).

43 In the UK: as a matter of practice that has developed into a constitutional convention, the government lays a treaty before Parliament 21 days before ratifying so Parliament can discuss it and object to it if it wishes. This is known as the Ponsonby rule. This has now been regulated by statute, the Constitutional Reform and Governance Act 2010 s 20 of which sets three preconditions that the government/executive must meet before ratifying a treaty:
    (a) it must lay a copy of the Treaty before Parliament
    (b) the treaty must be published 'in a way that a Minister of the Crown considers appropriate' and
    (c) the government must wait for 21 days to elapse after the treaty has been laid, without either House voting against ratification.
44 See e.g. *Thakrar v Secretary of State for the Home Department* [1974] 2 All ER 261 (UK); *Government of Canada v Employment Appeals Tribunal* [1992] 2 IR 484 (Ireland).

There are not two versions of dualism, since it is inherent in dualism that national law will determine in each particular case at what level incorporation occurs within the hierarchy of national sources.

EXPLAINING THE LAW
***

THE EU TREATIES AND DUALISM, EU SECONDARY LEGISLATION AND MONISM

Even countries that are monist normally as regards international treaties, usually require some kind of incorporation of EU treaties, by either legislation or constitutional amendment. This is because of the constitutional importance of the EU Treaties.

However, one of the important effects of the doctrine of direct effect developed by the Court of Justice is that they make all EU Member States monist as to how they receive in national law 'ordinary EU laws' (regulations, directives, decisions).

2.5.1 SUMMARY OF THE CONTINUING 'WESTPHALIAN' CHARACTER OF INTERNATIONAL LAW

- *Apart from UN Security Council resolutions in enforcing peace and security and the limited category of* jus cogens, *states cannot in general have international law imposed on them.* States must consent to be bound by any treaty as a voluntary party to the treaty, and states may exempt themselves from customary international law through the operation of the persistent objector test.[45] General principles of law do appear to bind states irrespective of consent, especially the laws on state responsibility empowering other states to take countermeasures. However, general principles are usually rules about substantive rules (they are usually what Hart called secondary rules), and state responsibility only arises where a state has consented to be bound in the first place to a substantive treaty rule or substantive rule of custom.
- *States cannot be forced to submit to the jurisdiction of an international court or tribunal.* The only court with a general jurisdiction in the international legal system is the International Court of Justice/ICJ, whose jurisdiction states must individually accept.
- *How states accept international law in their own legal system is a matter for each legal system* (although states may not in general plead national law as a defence in international law for not complying with international law[46]), i.e. whether to accept monism or dualism.
- *A principle of the formal equality of states is reflected in international law.* Thus, there is usually no weighted voting in international institutions and each state has an

---

45 See above note 19.

46 Article 27 Vienna Convention on the Law of Treaties states that: 'A party may not invoke the provisions of its internal law as justification for its failure to perform a treaty', although art 47 provides that while a state may not generally invoke the fact that its consent to be bound by a treaty has been expressed in violation of a provision of its internal law regarding competence to conclude treaties as invalidating its consent, it may do so if that violation was manifest and concerned a rule of its internal law of fundamental importance.

equal vote, regardless of its size. Some notable exceptions to this exist, especially concerning the power of veto of permanent members of the UN Security Council.

- *In the absence of an international enforcement body or police force (apart from the role of the UN Security Council), even where a state does accept the jurisdiction of a court or tribunal, enforcement of a judgment is ultimately a matter of self-help through the law of state responsibility.* Self-help is not found in national legal systems or (generally speaking) in the EU.
- *International law is mediated through national executives, who thus have control over how the national system interacts with international law.* However, executives are subject to ultimate control by Parliament.

2.6 OVERVIEWING THE DISTINCTIVE CHARACTERISTICS OF THE EU RELATIVE TO INTERNATIONAL LAW

It is much easier to understand the legal nature and character of the EU in the context of the above outline of the central features of general public international law. Comparison has been made between the two systems, and this section overviews this issue. Being founded upon a series of agreements in the form of treaties between Member States, the EU is a product of international law. Treaty change at EU level follows the rules on treaty-making of international law.[47] Nonetheless, overall, the EU has evolved a series of legal characteristics. Taken together, these characteristics make a unique system within international law to the extent that states have given up their sovereignty to centralised institutions that can 'overcome' state resistance to acceptance.

EXPLAINING THE LAW

DIFFERENTIATING THE EU FROM ORDINARY INTERNATIONAL LAW
The ECJ from its early period deliberately followed a strategy of differentiating EU law from general public international law.[48] This made it more plausible to accept some of the remarkable doctrines developed by the ECJ, especially the doctrines of the supremacy and direct effect of EU law. This approach of treating EU law as different to international law can be seen in two of the leading early cases of the ECJ, *Costa v ENEL* on the supremacy doctrine and *Van Gend en Loos* on direct effect. It is important to remember, however, that this entire approach is a product of the case law of the ECJ and was not authored by the founding Member States.

....

47 See art 48 TEU.

48 By 'general public international law' here is meant the overall rules of the international legal system, rather than the specific category or source of general principles of public international law. I am grateful to Prof. Roda Mushkat for suggesting this clarification.

In *Costa v ENEL*, the ECJ established the doctrine of the supremacy of EU law over national law and, in *Van Gend en Loos*, the ECJ established the direct effect of EU law in national legal systems. Direct effect meant that EU law could be invoked by an individual in a national court, and it did not need implementing national legislation for this to happen, i.e. direct effect creates a kind of monism for EU law. In *Van Gend en Loos*, the ECJ observed that the 'Community constitutes a new legal order of international law'.[49]

More explicitly, in *Costa v ENEL* the Court asserted that: 'By contrast with ordinary international treaties, the EEC treaty has created its own legal system'.[50] This strategy of differentiation has continued down to the present. In the recent *Kadi* case, the ECJ dealt with the compatibility of UN sanctions against individuals, part of the fight against terrorism, with EU law. The ECJ asserted the autonomy of the EU system from general public international law and concluded that it could review the compatibility of the sanctions, which were adopted under Chapter VII of the UN Charter, with fundamental rights.[51]

The main features of the EU legal system that are different to general public international law can be summarised as follows:

| KEY LEARNING POINT

WHAT IS DIFFERENT ABOUT THE EU COMPARED WITH INTERNATIONAL LAW

-   more clearly hierarchical law-making in EU law
-   inequality in the voting status of states in the adoption of EU laws and the weakening of the state consent principle through majority voting
-   law-making role for a directly elected parliamentary assembly
-   manner of the penetration of EU law in national law and the doctrines of supremacy and direct effect
-   compulsory jurisdiction of a general court
-   the extent of the law-making role of the ECJ
-   the representation of the EU in external relations in place of the former power of Member States in matters governed by common EU rules.

We will now look at each of these briefly in more detail:

-   *More clearly hierarchical law-making.* In EU law, there is a much stronger hierarchy of the sources of law, while the law-making process is formalised to the extent

---

49 Case 6/64 *Costa v ENEL* [1963] ECR 585 at 593.
50 Case 26/62 *Van Gend en Loos v Nederlandse Administratie der Belastingen* [1963] ECR 1 at 12.
51 See *Kadi and Al Barakaat International Foundation v Council* (n 29). To an extent, this reasoning is circular: what differentiated the then European Economic Community (EEC) system from general public international law was to a large extent the very case law of the ECJ.

that customary law is not a source. The founding treaties, and those subsequent treaties that have amended them, are in effect a constitution.[52] Ordinary EU laws – regulations, directives and decisions – are the equivalent of Acts of Parliament in a national system. Owing to the expansive or creative approach to interpretation of the ECJ, general principles of EU law are also a very important source of EU law, more so than is the case in international law (the judiciary are generally less 'activist' in the international legal system).

– *Inequality in the voting status of states in the adoption of EU laws and the weakening of the state consent principle through majority voting.* Member States of the EU can be outvoted in the process of making 'ordinary' EU laws, i.e. the day-to-day legal instruments of the EU (rather than founding treaties, which are still subject to a unanimity rule). Regulations, directives and decisions are usually subject to majority voting amongst the Member States and agreement by the European Parliament. The ordinary legislative procedure thus involves joint law-making by the Council (of Ministers) and by the European Parliament (comparable with the functioning of a bicameral legislature in a federal system such as Germany). Qualified majority voting provides for a weighting of votes to some extent proportionate to population size. In contrast, in international law, the principle of equality of states excludes such a proportionate weighting of a state's vote, although in practice, of course, states do not enjoy the same actual political power as each other in international relations. When voting under the ordinary legislative procedure,[53] the Council (of Ministers) votes by a majority, which is ordinarily, when all Member States are voting, defined as at least 72 per cent of the members of the Council, representing Member States comprising at least 65 per cent of the population of the Union.[54]

KEY LEARNING POINT

....

THE EU IS USUALLY MONIST REGARDING INTERNATIONAL LAW IN THE EU LEGAL ORDER

Although the Court of Justice has been keen to differentiate the EU from the general system of public international law, the EU itself does adopt a monist approach in some instance to international law. For example, when the EU becomes a party to an international treaty, the Court of Justice applies a monist approach to the treaty having legal effect in the EU legal order (so it is not

....

52 In Case 294/83 *Parti écologiste 'Les Verts' v European Parliament* [1986] ECR 1357 at para 23, the ECJ referred to the European Economic Community Treaty (EEC Treaty) as a 'constitutional charter'.

53 In the EU, majority voting takes place in the Council (of Ministers), which is in effect the upper chamber of a bicameral parliament in the EU under the ordinary legislative procedure. Under the ordinary procedure, both the Council (of Ministers), consisting of representatives of Member State governments, and the directly elected European Parliament, jointly pass new laws.

54 Article 238(2) TFEU.

necessary usually to pass secondary legislation to incorporate it).[55] However, the
Court's approach is variable. In *Kadi*, the Court held that the effect of Security
Council resolutions in EU law would depend on their compatibility with the
fundamental principles of the EU.[56]

- *Law-making role for a directly elected parliamentary assembly.* In international
  law, it is the national executive that represents each state. The process of law-
  making, through treaties or conventions, is thus between national executives at the
  international level, although of course each one will be subject to some ultimate
  parliamentary control in its system. In contrast, EU law now gives a more or less co-
  equal role with national executives to a directly elected parliamentary assembly, i.e.
  the European Parliament. Each Member State elects a number of members of the
  European Parliament, according to its population size (in this latter respect again a
  departure from the formal equality of sovereign states).
- *Manner of the penetration of EU law in national law and the doctrines of supremacy
  and direct effect.* Through operation of the doctrines of direct effect and the
  supremacy of EU law, in effect, a system of strong monism applies to ordinary
  EU laws (apart from the founding treaties and amendments to them) in every
  Member State. Each Member State does not have a choice of opting out of this
  approach. Direct effect means that individuals in the Member States can invoke EU
  law against their own governments and sometimes other citizens. This contrasts
  with the traditional situation with regard to public international law, under which
  only states could invoke international law in a court: only states could be 'subjects
  of international law'. Although there has been a departure from this traditional
  approach in international law itself with the development of international human
  rights law, in EU law the idea that only states could be subjects has been dispensed
  with for most EU laws. The combination of the doctrines of direct effect and of the
  supremacy of EU law over national law has had a radical effect on national legal
  systems. The ultimate supremacy of EU law over national law has been disputed by
  the supreme or constitutional courts of some Member States (we will look at this
  further in Chapter 6). However, in practice, EU law prevails on a day-to-day basis in
  the national courts of the Member States when invoked by national citizens against
  their own national law.
- *Compulsory jurisdiction of a general court.* In international law, generally speaking,
  adjudication by courts and tribunals is generally subject to the consent of states in

....

55 See D McGoldrick 'EU law and international law: the interface for the new millennium' in I Cameron, A
   Simoni (eds) *Dealing with Integration Vol 2* (Iustus Förlag 1998) 133. McGoldrick comments that the test for direct
   effect of international treaties to which the EU is a party appears to be the same as for direct effect generally –
   clear, precise and unconditional. Timmermans suggests that the test for direct effect of treaties is stricter and also
   depends on the system and context of the treaty relationship, citing Case 104/81 *Hauptzollamt Mainz v Kupfer-
   berg & Cie KG* [1982] ECR I–3641 and Case C–469/93 *Chiquita Italia* [1995] ECR I–4558. See C Timmermans
   'The international lawyer and the EU' in C Wickremasinghe (ed) *The International Lawyer as Practitioner* (BIICL
   2000) 95.
56 *Kadi and al Barakaat International Foundation v Council* (n 29).

individual disputes. If a state refused to accept a method of judicial or quasi-judicial settlement of disputes (arbitration or a court procedure), then the resolution of a dispute falls within the self-help principles of state responsibility. In contrast, in EU law, Member States must accept the jurisdiction of the ECJ over most of the large body of EU rules. Although there are some exceptions and some Member States have negotiated opt-outs from ECJ jurisdiction, for example, concerning the criminal law matters, in general, compulsory jurisdiction applies.[57]

– *The extent of the law-making role of the ECJ.* It has by now been well noted that the ECJ has played a remarkable role in EU law as a 'motor of integration' (this point is further discussed in Chapter 5).[58] It has originated many of the key constitutional doctrines of the EU, without explicit Treaty support at the time of its judgments, including supremacy, parallelism in external relations, fundamental rights and an expansive approach to the interpretation of EU competences. The ECJ is untypical of international courts in general,[59] in that it inverts the normal order of priority in international law on the methods of interpretation. Whereas Article 31 of the Vienna Convention on the Law of Treaties accord the text priority as governing interpretation, followed by object and purpose, the ECJ has inverted this by treating the text as secondary to object and purpose.[60] Moreover, the ECJ interprets object and purpose at a high level of generality, again a point of departure from the practice of international courts and tribunals. For the ECJ, object and purpose are to be stated at a systemic level of generality, meaning specific rules are interpreted as having as their object and purpose the overall goal of enhancing integration amongst the Member States (i.e. the ECJ tends not to emphasise the more local object and purpose of specific rules as evidenced by the text).

– *The representation of the EU in external relations in place of the former power of Member States, in matters governed by* common *EU rules.* One of the most significant interventions of the ECJ in the development of the European Economic Community was its statement of what is known as parallelism: the principle or rule that when the EU has adopted common internal rules on a matter, the EU has a parallel competence to adopt rules with outside countries and/or organisation and, most importantly, this takes over and eliminates Member State competence.[61] Thus, as the internal competence of the EU grows, so does its external competence. The

....

57 Prior to the Treaty of Lisbon, under art 35 TEU, consistent with the normal approach in international law, Member States had the option of accepting or not ECJ jurisdiction over the then (intergovernmental) third pillar.

58 H Rasmussen *On Law and Policy of the European Court of Justice* (Kluwer 1986); G Conway *The Limits of Legal Reasoning and the European Court of Justice* (Cambridge University Press 2012).

59 M Sørensen 'Autonomous legal orders: some considerations relating to a systems analysis of international organisations in the world legal order' (1983) 32(3) *International and Comparative Law Quarterly* 559–76 at 573; B Simma 'Self-contained regimes' (1985) 16 *Netherlands Yearbook of International Law* 111–36 at 125; C-D Ehlermann 'Some personal experiences as member of the appellate body of the WTO' (2002) Robert Schuman Centre Policy Paper No 02/9 paras 42–47.

60 Comment by Professor Francis Snyder, 6th International Workshop for Young Scholars (WISH): Evolution of the Community Courts, University College Dublin (16 November 2007).

61 Case 22/70 *Commission v Council (ERTA)* (n 12); *Opinion 2/91 Re Convention No 170 International Labour Organisation on Safety in the Use of Chemicals at Work* [1993] ECR I–1061.

logical consequence of such a doctrine is the development of a corresponding EU diplomatic service. This is something that the Treaty of Lisbon has consolidated as an EU competence through the new role of a High Representative of the Union for Foreign Affairs and Security Policy, who will head a new consolidated external action service.[62] We will look at this further in Chapter 4.

- *Special rules on state liability through reducing the role of unilateral countermeasures or self-help.* The EU has developed its own system of the liability of Member States for breaching EU law, and we have looked briefly at the main differences between this and the international law of state responsibility. Again, the ECJ played a decisive role by developing a doctrine of state liability granting a right of damages to individual citizens where a Member State failed to implement EU law properly.[63] One commentator, writing in 1985, listed four features of the EU's own regime of liability: (1) proceedings before the ECJ; (2) deliberation before the Council (of Ministers); (3) secondary legislation dealing with a breach of treaty obligations and its competences; and (4) the direct effect of Union law before national courts.[64] Since that time, the EU augmented its own system of liability through the development of a more specific doctrine of state liability in damages payable by Member States to individuals affected by non-implementation of EU law (beginning with the judgments in *Francovich* and *Brasserie du Pêcheur*[65]), by providing for a procedure for fining states that refused to comply with a judgment of the ECJ[66] and, ultimately, by providing for the suspension of a Member State that committed a fundamental violation of EU law.[67] However, even suspension of a Member State's rights under EU law may not be a satisfactory remedy if one Member State persists in disobeying EU law. In fact, the other Member States' obligations would not be suspended towards it, under the procedure in Article 7 TEU. In this situation, EU law currently has no special rules and fall-back on countermeasures may be justified.[68] This, however, would be an entirely exceptional and out-of-the-ordinary situation. In general, EU law has its own special regime of state liability, distinct from the general rules on state responsibility in international law.

KEY LEARNING POINT

INTER-GOVERNMENTALISM VERSUS SUPRANATIONALISM

Compared with cooperation between states in general in international law and relations, the EU involves a greater transfer of sovereignty towards international/centralised institutions above the state. The term 'supranationalism' is used

---

62 Article 18 TEU and Part V TFEU.
63 For clarity, it can be helpful to distinguish here between state liability as a general concept and the specific doctrine of state liability entailing a remedy in damages.
64 Simma (n 59) 125.
65 Joined Cases C–6/90 and 9/90 *Francovich and Bonifaci v Italy* [1991] ECR I–5357; Joined Cases C–46/93 and C–48/93 *Brasserie du Pêcheur v Germany and Factortame v UK* [1996] ECR I–1029.
66 Article 228 ECT, now art 260 TFEU.
67 Article 7 TEU.
68 Conway (n 41); Simma and Pulkowski (n 41).

> to describe this different type legal cooperation or integration, in contrast to more typical international law cooperation where individual state consent is decisive. Specifically, what the supranationalism of the EU involves is the main distinct features just discussed: (1) the supremacy of EU law over national law; (2) the doctrine of direct effect whereby there is direct adoption or implementation of EU law without needing national legislation for individuals to invoke EU law in national courts; (3) compulsory jurisdiction of a transnational court; (4) outvoting of individual states in the law-making process; and (5) a directly elected transnational parliament with a law-making role.

2.7 WITHDRAWAL FROM THE EU

The original treaties did not deal with the question of withdrawal from the Communities, what is now the EU. In *Costa v ENEL*, the Court of Justice described the transfer of sovereignty to the Community structure in the founding treaties to be permanent:

> The transfer by the States from their domestic legal systems to the Community legal system of the rights and obligations arising under the Treaty carries with a permanent limitation of their sovereign rights, against which a subsequent unilateral act incompatible with the concept of Community cannot prevail.[69]

Thus, any attempt to withdraw would seem contrary to then Community law, at least according to the Court. Interestingly, the Court did not situate its statement within the context of the applicable international law rules on withdrawal from or denunciation of a treaty. These rules were later set out in the Vienna Convention on the Law of Treaties (which for the most part codified customary rules on treaty-making). This is something of a grey area. Article 56 of the Vienna Convention states:

1. A treaty which contains no provision regarding its termination and which does not provide for denunciation or withdrawal is not subject to denunciation or withdrawal unless: (a) it is established that the parties intended to admit of denunciation or withdrawal; or (b) a right of denunciation or withdrawal may be implied by the nature of the treaty.
2. A party shall not give less than 12 months' notice of its intention to denounce or withdraw from a treaty under paragraph 1.

In *Costa v ENEL*, the Court of Justice did not seek to establish the intentions of the Member States, nor did it analyse the nature of the treaty in depth; it simply asserted the performance of a permanent transfer of sovereignty. This raises the question of the relationship of

....

69 *Costa v ENEL* (n 49) 594.

the EU system at its origin with general public international law, an issue very clearly analysed by Hartley.[70] Hartley notes how the Court of Justice had described by the mid-1980s the treaties as a 'constitutional charter'.[71] He outlines two different meanings the term constitution could have: (a) a quite general sense of the treaties setting out the rules governing the organisation of the Communities (the way a founding document for any organisation or association contains its governing rules); or (b) a stronger sense of the constitution, according to which the treaties are a self-sustaining basis for the Communities.

In the stronger sense, the treaties could be compared to the Constitution of the United States of America, which is something that is not based on a prior legal rule or norm itself, the way legal rules generally are, but is a new, self-sustaining act of legality that is the product, not of a prior legal rule, but of political and historical circumstances.[72] This stronger sense of the term constitution would suggest the EU is independent of the Member States, that the Member States are no longer 'masters of the treaties'. This would support the Court of Justice's suggestion in *Costa v ENEL* that withdrawal is not possible.

Contrary to this, however, is the absence of any clear line of reasoning in the judgment in that case as to why this is so. It really was merely an assertion, and the founding treaties themselves never purported to achieve such a substantial shift in sovereignty; they are ordinary treaties deriving their validity from the signatory Member States. The continuing importance of national identity and national political loyalty and the principle of democracy also count against the view of a radical change.[73]

This debate has now been put to rest by Article 50 TEU, included by the Treaty of Lisbon, which expressly provides that the Member States may withdraw. Prior to the Treaty of Lisbon, no Member State had sought to withdraw. The closest to this was the secession of Greenland from being fully under the rule of Member State Denmark. Greenland was granted internal self-rule within Denmark and, in a referendum in 1982, voted in favour of leaving the Community. The Danish Government, which still dealt with foreign affairs for Greenland, negotiated with the other Member States.

These changes led to amendments to the Community treaties, which took effect in 1985. This is different to withdrawal of an existing Member State in that Greenland never joined as a separate state; withdrawal from the European Union was not made by Greenland itself, but by Denmark on its behalf, which renegotiated the application of the treaties to its territory.[74]

---

70 Hartley (n 2).

71 *Parti écologiste 'Les Verts' v European Parliament* (n 52) para 23.

72 Hartley (n 2) 4–5.

73 Ibid 6–10.

74 C Reider 'The withdrawal clause of the EU Treaty in light of EU citizenship: between disintegration and integration' (2013) 37 *Fordham Journal of International Law* 147–174 at 149; Treaty amending, with regard to Greenland, the Treaties establishing the European Community, OJ No L 29 01.02.1985 p. 1.

2.8 DISTINGUISHING THE EU FROM THE COUNCIL OF EUROPE

2.8.1 INTRODUCTION

Both these organisations, the Council of Europe and the EU, were set up after the Second World War (1939–1945) to encourage cooperation between European countries.

> ▌KEY LEARNING POINT
>
> **COMPARING AND CONTRASTING THE COUNCIL OF EUROPE AND THE EU**
> The Council of Europe and the EU differ in both (1) the areas with which they are primarily concerned to specialise and cooperate in and, especially, (2) the legal mechanisms of cooperation. The focus of the Council of Europe has been the promotion of human rights and democracy. The EU was originally concerned with the essentially economic issue of a common market. The key difference in the mechanism of cooperation is that the Council of Europe is typical of public international law. It has none of the distinct 'supranational' characteristics of the EU outlined above. The cooperation within the Council of Europe system is 'intergovernmental', not 'supranational'.

As the EU has expanded its competence (through both the case law of the ECJ and treaty amendment), there is increasing potential for duplication and overlap. The Council of Europe has adopted over 200 treaties or conventions on various matters, some of which are concerned with social matters and criminal justice. In the criminal justice sphere, for example, the Council of Europe Treaty on Extradition 1957[75] has been important. However, undoubtedly, the most important Council of Europe legal instrument has been the European Convention on Human Rights (ECHR).[76]

The general aims and objectives of the Council of Europe are set out in Article 1 of the Statute of the Council of Europe 1949:[77]

    a   The aim of the Council of Europe is to achieve a greater unity between its members for the purpose of safeguarding and realising the ideals and principles which are their common heritage and facilitating their economic and social progress.

    b   This aim shall be pursued through the organs of the Council by discussion of questions of common concern and by agreements and common action in economic, social, cultural, scientific, legal and administrative matters and in the maintenance and further realisation of human rights and fundamental freedoms.

75 ETS no 24.

76 Ibid no 5.

77 Ibid no 1.

c   Participation in the Council of Europe shall not affect the collaboration of
    its members in the work of the United Nations and of other international
    organisations or unions to which they are parties.

d   Matters relating to national defence do not fall within the scope of the Council
    of Europe.

The relatively modest and limited role of the Council of Europe is reflected in the
statement in Article 1(c) that involvement in the Council of Europe shall not affect
the collaboration of its members in the work of the UN and of other international
organisations or unions to which they are parties. Its role is seen as secondary and in
the background. However, owing to the influence and status achieved by the ECHR
and, in particular, due to the provision in the Treaty of Lisbon for the EU to accede to
the ECHR, this aspect of the Council of Europe is of more significance than Article
1(c) may suggest. It is even possible now to think of a hierarchical relationship between
the European Court of Human Rights (ECtHR) and the ECJ, with the ECtHR in the
position (after accession by the EU) of enjoying a higher rank, at least in the field of
human rights norms. Despite the Treaty provisions for EU accession to the ECHR, the
ECJ appeared to rule out accepting that its judgments could be appealed in some way to
the European Court of Human Rights.[78]

> ### KEY LEARNING POINT
>
> #### UNLIKE THE EU THE COUNCIL OF EUROPE IS INTER-GOVERNMENTAL AND TYPICAL OF PUBLIC INTERNATIONAL LAW
>
> In EU cooperation, *countries give up more of their sovereignty* to the institutions
> of the EU, in all the ways outlined in the previous section e.g. they may be
> outvoted (so a unanimity rule does not always apply, whereas it does always
> apply in the Council of Europe), compulsory (not optional) jurisdiction of a
> transnational court applies, supremacy and direct effect of laws mean EU law
> penetrates national law. This is not so with cooperation in the Council of Europe,
> which is always on a voluntary basis. Its legal instruments are ordinary treaties or
> conventions of international law, to which the principle of state consent applies.
> The EU has its own special legal instruments, which are more like laws at a
> national level.

There are many hundreds of EU laws. Laws passed by the EU automatically become
part of national law and have, generally speaking, precedence/supremacy over national
law if there is a conflict between the EU law and a national law. In contrast, whether
treaties and conventions agreed as part of the Council of Europe become a part of
national law is a matter for each country. If there is a conflict between a Council of
Europe measure and a national law, usually the national law has priority or supremacy.[79]

---

78 Opinion 2/13 on EU accession to ECHR, 18th December 2014 (see further Chapter 8).
79 See e.g., s 4 of the Human Rights Act 1998 in the UK; where there is a conflict between UK statutory law and
   the ECHR, the UK Act prevails.

2.8.2 COMPARISON OF COMPETENCES

The potential for overlap between these two entities has always existed. Although the focus of Council of Europe activity has been human rights and the rule of law and democracy and the focus of EU activity has been the establishment of a common market, the Council of Europe's formal statement of competences makes a general reference to 'social and economic matters'. The Council of Europe has always had some involvement in matters outside 'pure' human rights and rule of law concerns, while the EU has greatly expanded its competences beyond core common market activities. The potential for duplication and overlap is increased by the passing of the Treaty of Lisbon, which considerably extends EU competences. The possibility of overlap, duplication and unnecessary complexity is also increased by the similar terminology that is used to denote the respective institutional frameworks of the organisations.[80]

The need for some kind of cooperation between emerging organisations for European cooperation[81] was reflected in specific provisions of the founding treaties of the EU, especially of the European Coal and Steel Community (ECSC) Treaty. Article 49 ECSC Treaty provided that the relations between the Council of Europe and the ECSC institutions would be assured under the terms of an annexed Protocol. The treaties establishing the European Economic Community (EEC) and the European Atomic Energy Community (EURATOM) both provided for 'all appropriate forms of cooperation with the Council of Europe' (Article 230 EEC Treaty, now Article 220 TFEU and Article 200 EURATOM Treaty).

In 1959, 1987 and 1996, an exchange of letters between the two organisations reiterated the need for dialogue, consultation and representation to each other's institutions. It was not until 2007 that a formal memorandum of understanding was adopted between them. However, no systematic coordination between the EU and Council of Europe has been established. The first and one of the few academic commentators to examine in depth the general issue of interaction and overlap between the two European frameworks of cooperation and particularly of law-making,[82] published in 1978, identified the possibility of overlap in the following areas: free movement of

....

80 For example, the Council of Europe itself is often confused with two organs of the EU, namely, the European Council (meeting of heads of government of the Member States of the EU) and the Council (of Ministers) (meetings of ministers of the Member States of the EU). Formerly, the European Commission on Human Rights (abolished by Protocol 11, ETS no 155, to the European Convention on Human Rights, ETS no 5) was sometimes confused with the European Commission of what is now the EU.

81 See T Joris, J Vandenberghe 'The Council of Europe and the European Union: natural partners or uneasy bedfellows?' (2008–2009) 15(1) *Columbia Journal of European Law* 1–41 at 8–17.

82 The law-making role of the two entities can be distinguished from their provision of technical expertise. They sometimes cooperate in providing technical expertise. For an overview of such joint 'technical assistance' projects see http://www.jp.coe.int/Default.asp (last accessed 18 January 2015). The question of overlap and interaction in the context of human rights has been addressed to a greater extent in the secondary literature: S Douglas-Scott 'A tale of two courts: Luxembourg, Strasbourg and the growing European Human Rights *acquis*' (2006) 43 *Common Market Law Review* 629–65.

persons, social security, human rights, migration, products liability and environmental protection.[83] To this list can now be added human rights and criminal law.

ANALYSING THE LAW

COMPETENCE OVERLAP

To date, the different impact of the two bodies of law, originating in the EU and the Council of Europe, in national law reduces the problem of overlap and conflict, since EU law will generally be supreme. Despite its potential for broad competences, the Council of Europe tends to focus in practice on human rights. It is in the sphere of human rights that a problem of overlap and conflict between the EU and Council of Europe is most likely. This is because the EU has its own Charter of Fundamental Rights and especially as EU law now provides that the EU is to accede to the ECHR. We will examine this further in Chapter 8. More generally, the overlap in competences can be taken as a good example of a tendency for legal cooperation at European level to be unnecessarily complex and lacking in transparency. This tends to undermine the legitimacy of European cooperation and unnecessarily so.

2.8.3 INSTITUTIONAL DIFFERENTIATION

The institutions of the EU and of the Council of Europe are entirely separate.

KEY LEARNING POINT

DISTINGUISHING THE COUNCIL OF EUROPE FROM THE EUROPEAN COUNCIL

Unfortunately, due to terminological similarity, two of the organs of the EU, the EU's Council (of Ministers) and the EU's European Council, are often confused with the Council of Europe itself.

Conversely, it is sometimes assumed that the main legal instrument of the Council of Europe, the ECHR, originated in the EU legal system, which is not the case. Although the ECHR can and does influence EU law and although the EU is going to accede to the ECHR, the ECHR is autonomous from EU law.

---

83 F E Dowrick 'Overlapping European laws' (1978) 27(3) *International & Comparative Law Quarterly* 629–60 at 631–38; more recently see e.g., T Joris and J Vandenderghe, 'The Council of Europe and the European Union: Natural Partners or Uneasy Bed Fellows?' (2008–2009) 15 *Columbia Journal of European Law* 1–41.

THE MAIN INSTITUTIONS OF THE COUNCIL OF EUROPE

The main institutions or organs of the Council of Europe are as follows:

– Committee of Ministers
– Parliamentary Assembly
– Congress of local and regional authorities
– Secretariat
– European Court of Human Rights.[84]

We will now look at each of these briefly in a bit more detail:

The Committee (of Ministers) is the Council of Europe's decision-making body, composed of the foreign ministers of all the Member States or their Strasbourg-based deputies (ambassadors/permanent representatives). It is a traditional, intergovernmental forum of international law in that each country is represented by its executive, usually the foreign minister. The Committee of Ministers has the law-making function in the Council of Europe: it is a forum within which the contracting/Member States agree ordinary international treaties and conventions.

The Parliamentary Assembly debates and scrutinises areas of concern of the Council of Europe. It is not directly elected, it consists of appointed members; each country appoints its own members. Furthermore, it does not make laws. This is reflected in its original title, which was 'Consultative Assembly'. Usually, the appointees are members of national parliaments, so in practice it does have something of a parliamentary character. Its functions include electing the judges of the European Court of Human Rights[85] as well as electing, upon recommendation of the Council (of Ministers), the Secretary General and Deputy Secretary General of the Council of Europe[86] and its own Secretary General.[87] It also conducts debates and issues opinions.

The Congress of local and regional authorities is meant to represent Europe's regions and municipalities, and is composed of a chamber of local authorities and a chamber of regions. The Congress also performs a function of examining local democracy in Europe, by producing 'monitoring reports' on the situation in each Member State. It monitors local and regional election and their standards. It is somewhat comparable to

---

84 The Council of Europe also has a Human Rights Commissioner, whose function is to monitor and advise Member States on human rights issues. The Office of Human Rights Commissioner was created in 1999 by resolution of the Committee of Ministers.
85 Article 22 of the ECHR.
86 Article 36(b) of the Statute of the Council of Europe.
87 Rule 65 of the Rules of Procedure of the Assembly.

the role played by the Committee of the Regions in the EU:[88] both are essentially just consultative bodies.

There is also an 1800-strong secretariat recruited from Member States, which is headed by a Secretary General. The Secretary General is responsible to the Committee of Ministers.[89] The officials work for the Council of Europe and not for their country of origin, they are not meant to act as representatives for their countries.[90]

The European Court of Human Rights is probably the best known institution of the Council of Europe, but is one of its more specialised organs. The Council of Europe has adopted about 200 conventions or treaties, and the ECHR, which established the ECtHR, is just one of them. The ECtHR has jurisdiction only over the ECHR and its Protocols, not over any other Council of Europe law. The Court is composed of a number of judges equal to that of the contracting states. Judges are elected by the Parliamentary Assembly of the Council of Europe, which votes on a shortlist of three candidates put forward by governments. Although the term of office is six years, judges may be re-elected. Judges sit on the Court in their individual capacity and do not represent any Member State. The appointment of judges and organisation of the Court are dealt with in Section II of the ECHR.

EXPLAINING THE LAW

THE COUNCIL OF EUROPE AND THE EU ARE SEPARATE

The Council of Europe is a separate organisation to the EU. Do not confuse two of the organs of the EU, the Council (of Ministers) and the European Council, with the Council of Europe. Cooperation in the Council of Europe is different to cooperation in the EU. Cooperation in the Council of Europe is intergovernmental and typical of international law, whereas cooperation in the EU is supranational and substantially different to most international law. Even when the EU accedes to the ECHR (in much the same way as a country would accede to it, although the EU is obviously not a country), which is the most important law under the Council of Europe system, the two organisations will remain separate.

KEY LEARNING POINT

THE EUROPEAN COURT OF HUMAN RIGHTS

The European Court of Human Rights is not a part of the EU legal system, it is a part of the Council of Europe legal system and it has jurisdiction only over the European Convention on Human Rights (ECHR). Part II of the ECHR created the European Court of Human Rights.

88 The EU has a Committee of the Regions, which has a purely advisory role (see arts 300, 305–307 TFEU).
89 Article 37(b) of the Statute of the Council of Europe.
90 Ibid art 36(f).

2.8.4 TERMINOLOGICAL SIMILARITY BETWEEN THE EU AND COUNCIL OF EUROPE

Main Institutions of the EU	Main Institutions of Council of Europe
(most in Brussels):	*(based in Strasbourg):*
European Council	*No equivalent in Council of*
(heads of government)	*Europe*
Council (of Ministers)	*Committee of Ministers*
(ministers meeting)	(ministers meeting)
European Parliament	*Parliamentary Assembly*
(directly elected)	(appointed)
European Commission	*Secretariat*
(EU civil service)	
European Court of Justice	*European Court of Human*
(in Luxembourg, general jurisdiction)	*Rights* (specialised jurisdiction, only over ECHR)

2.9 CONCLUSION

Having worked through this chapter, you should have a solid understanding of the distinct or special nature of the EU compared to typical or 'normal' cooperation between states in international law and relations (the final section draws your attention in summary form to key points and terminology from this chapter and guides you towards some further reading that will help you to understand the distinct nature of the EU).

The issues that are dealt with by international law have existed since different political entities existed side-by-side. Modern international law emerged in the 1500s–1600s, whereby states in the modern sense (usually nation states) emerged, having a strong central government and clear identity. The EU has started the way any other international organisation does, namely through the adoption by sovereign countries of a founding treaty or treaties.

These treaties contained some novel features – the role of the Commission as initiator of legislative proposals, provision for majority voting amongst state representatives and compulsory jurisdiction of a transnational court. However, what transformed the EU into something clearly different from other international organisations was the role of the Court of Justice in attributing the doctrines of supremacy and direct effect, both marked departures from 'normal' public international law where states determined the impact of international law in their own legal system.

Nonetheless, ultimately the Member States remain 'masters of the treaties' in the sense that each can now decide to withdraw from the EU. In practice, this is quite an extreme option, although it is increasingly under consideration in the UK at the time of writing. On a day-to-day basis, the reality of a pooling of sovereignty much more than is normally the case in international law exists in the EU.

POINTS TO REVIEW

Looking back to the key points that were identified at the beginning of this chapter, you should now see how the questions posed could be answered.

– The EU originated as a legal system in the form of three Communities created in the 1950s through the normal method of law-making in international law between states, i.e. the adoption of treaties: the European Coal and Steel Community (ECSC) Treaty 1951, the European Atomic Energy Community Treaty (EURATOM) 1957, the European Economic Community (EEC) Treaty 1957.

– Key principles governing the relationships between states in international law are the formal equality of states and the role of states as the decisive units of sovereignty and in the law-making process. Concerning the two main sources of international law, treaties/conventions and custom, the consent of a state is necessary for it to be bound. Similarly, states must consent to being sued before a court or brought before an arbitral tribunal. When international law is broken, apart from the special case of the use of force outside of the context of immediate self-defence (which is governed by the UN Security Council), states are permitted to engage in self-help as a remedy by taking countermeasures when a state that has broken international law. Further, it is a matter for each state to decide how international law has effect in the state's legal system.

– The EU is similar to other international organisations in that it was created by international treaties, but it is different from 'normal' international law cooperation in the degree of sovereignty states give up once they join the EU. After joining, the consent of a state is no longer decisive in every case of law-making as states can generally be outvoted in the making of laws, the European Court of Justice (ECJ) has compulsory jurisdiction and the way in which EU law penetrates national law is mostly governed by EU law and not by national law.

– The EU and the Council of Europe are separate international/regional organisations with their own, distinct legal systems. The Council of Europe adopts law in the ordinary manner of international law, whereas most EU laws (apart from the founding treaties of the EU) – regulations, directives and decisions – are adopted by the EU's own rules. The ECJ is the court of the EU and sits in Luxembourg. The European Court of Human Rights is a specialised court set up by the Council of Europe to adjudicate on the most important legal instrument adopted by the

Council of Europe, namely the European Convention on Human Rights, and it sits in Strasbourg.

– Presently, the ECHR is not a part of EU law, although the ECJ refers to it as a source. Under the Treaty of Lisbon, the EU is to become a party to the ECHR. We will look at this in more detail in Chapter 8, although the process of EU accession to the ECHR is turning out to be slow.

CHAPTER GLOSSARY

Compulsory jurisdiction refers to a legal requirement that a state accept the jurisdiction of a court to resolve a legal dispute, whether or not the state wishes to in a particular case.

Conventions/Treaties are the main source of international law. They are like contracts between states.

Council of Europe is an organisation of 47 states in Europe primarily concerned with promoting human rights and democracy. It is typical of international law in that the degree and extent of participation of states is always a matter for each individual state. The Council of Europe should not be confused with the European Council or the Council (of Ministers), which are organs of the EU.

Council (of Ministers) is one of the organs of the EU. It consists of ministers of the Member States meeting together (its composition varies depending on what issue it is discussing, e.g. it may be finance ministers meeting or environmental ministers meeting etc).

Customary law is the second main source of international law, it consists of (1) state practice that is (2) believed to be binding (this second element is referred to as *opinio juris*).

Direct effect refers to the possibility for individual citizens to invoke EU law in national courts.

Dualism is one of the two ways in which national legal systems interact with international law (the other is monism). Under a dualist approach, for an international treaty or convention to become a part of national law, two steps are needed: signature/ratification by the executive/government and incorporation by parliament.

European Council is an organ of the EU consisting of a meeting of the heads of government of the Member States of the EU.

European Court of Human Rights (ECtHR) is a specialised court set up by the Council of Europe to adjudicate on the most important legal instrument adopted by the Council of Europe, namely, the European Convention on Human Rights.

European Court of Justice (ECJ) is the highest court of the EU. It has a general jurisdiction over EU law. It sits in Luxembourg and is not to be confused with the European Court of Human Rights.

General principles is one of the sources of international law. As a source of law, it consists of principles that are part of the system of law, e.g. that a wrong must be compensated. It consists of principles common to legal systems. General principles are also a source of EU law. However, in EU law it is a much broader category. For example, in EU law, it includes human rights law. Expanding the category of general principles gives the judiciary more power, since general principles are independent of the legislature, i.e. they are considered just to be part of the legal system.

Intergovernmental refers to the kind of voluntary cooperation in which state sovereignty remains intact, which is typical of international law.

International Court of Justice is an organ of the United Nations and is the highest international court. It can deal with international law disputes submitted to it by states (it also has an advisory jurisdiction concerning issues referred to it by several of the UN organs). Its jurisdiction must be accepted by individual states.

International law is the body of law governing relations between states and across national borders. There are two categories: public and private. Public international law is concerned with the relationships between states and the legal obligations on states, private international law is concerned with the legal relationships between individuals across national borders.

Monism is one of the two ways in which national legal systems interact with international law (the other is dualism). Monism means a treaty is incorporated automatically in national law once ratified by the executive of that state.

Natural law refers to the idea of timeless, universally valid moral principles that must inform valid actual or 'positive' laws.

Opinio juris refers to the second element required for a customary rule of international law. It is a belief that a practice by states is binding.

State sovereignty refers to the idea that states retain authority to determine their own legal relationships in international law.

Supranational is the term used to describe the distinctive legal nature of the EU compared with typical international law in that in EU law Member States surrender part of their sovereignty to EU institutions.

Treaties are agreements between states. They are one of the main sources of international law and might be described as 'contracts between states'. The term 'convention' is a synonym for 'treaty'.

United Nations (UN) is an international organisation and is the highest legal authority in the international legal system, and almost all countries are members of it. It has special responsibility regarding the use of force. Outside of a situation of self-defence by a state, the use of force in international law must be authorised by the UN Security Council.

UN Security Council is a principal organ of the UN with special responsibility concerning the use of force and the maintenance of peace in the international legal system.

Uti possidetis juris is a principle of international law that newly independent territories should comply with the borders existing prior to independence. It is especially relevant to decolonisation.

Westphalian refers to the idea that states are the decisive unit of legal sovereignty and authority in international law. The term derives from the Treaty of Westphalia 1648.

TAKING THINGS FURTHER

J M Kelly *A Short History of Western Legal Theory* (Oxford University Press 1994) 77–78, 156–58, 199–202, 299–300, 345–47, 451–54 Offers an excellent overview of some of the key developments in the emergence and evolution of international law through history.

E Denza 'Two legal orders: divergent or convergent?' (1999) 48(2) *International & Comparative Law Quarterly* 257–84 This compares the legal system of the EU with international law as the EU had developed to that time, discussing the issue of whether EU law was to be regarded as a particularly effective system of regional international law, or had it been created as, or mutated into, an entirely new species of law. It concludes that inter-governmentalism and supranationalism are both useful approaches.

F E Dowrick 'Overlapping European laws' (1978) 27(3) *International & Comparative Law Quarterly* 629–60 Although an old article, offers a very clear and critical explanation of the relationship between the then European Economic Community and the Council of Europe (one of the few articles to address this topic).

T Hartley 'International law and the law of the European Union: a reassessment' (2001) 72 *British Yearbook of International Law* 1–35 Offers a critical perspective on the orthodox position that the EU is to be distinguished from and differentiated from international law.

S Neff 'A short history of international law' in M Evans (ed) *International Law* (2006) 31–58 This provides an overview in one chapter of the history of international law.

B Simma, D Pulkowski 'Of planets and the universe: self-contained regimes in international law' (2006) 17(3) *European Journal of International Law* 483–529 Explains the relationship between EU law on state liability and the international law of state responsibility and puts the issue in the context of public international law generally.

3

CHAPTER 3
EVOLUTION AND DEVELOPMENT OF THE EU: FROM ROME IN 1957 TO LISBON IN 2009

This chapter overviews the development of the EU through treaty revision since the 1950s. The title of the chapter may suggest that the EU began in 1957 with the Treaty of Rome but, as we saw in Chapter 1, the European Coal and Steel Community Treaty of 1951 was the prototype for what is now, after much development, the EU. However, Rome is chosen in the title because for many, the Treaty of Rome signifies the real beginning of the EU: the attempt to create a general common market, beyond specific sectors such as coal and steel or atomic energy. An important point to bear in mind is that treaty change is by no means the only way the EU has developed: the Court of Justice has played a key role through its case law. However, we will look at the role of the ECJ in another chapter. We will begin this chapter with an overview of the ECSC Treaty 1951 and proceed chronologically to overview all the other treaty developments, which will include the two most recent treaties adopted since the Treaty of Lisbon: the so-called Fiscal Compact of 2011 and the European Stability Mechanism Treaty 2012. These latter two are curiosities from a legal point of view, because they are not fully within the EU legal framework. However, the adoption of these two treaties perhaps says much about the problems and prospects of the EU.

AS YOU READ . . .

The key questions that will be answered in this chapter are as follows:

– How are treaties adopted by the EU, including the role of flexible cooperation?

– What were the central features of the founding treaty, the European Coal and Steel Community (ECSC) Treaty of 1951?

– In what way did the three founding treaties – the ECSC Treaty, the European Atomic Energy Community Treaty, and the European Economic Community (EEC) Treaty – share common features?

- What were the main changes introduced, and what was the political background to, the next major treaty change following the founding treaties, the Single European Act 1986 (this will include discussing European Monetary Union or EMU)?

- In what way did the next major treaty revision, the Treaty of Maastricht of 1992, introduce, as one commentator described it, a 'Europe of bits and pieces'?

- What were the key features of the failed Treaty establishing a Constitution for Europe of 2004 and how much of it was enacted in the Treaty of Lisbon of 2009?

- In what ways are the two most recent treaties, the so-called Fiscal Compact of 2011 and the European Stability Mechanism Treaty of 2012, different from other EU treaties and what does the difference suggest about the problems and prospects of European cooperation and integration in its current form?

3.1 INTRODUCTION

We have seen how, in the 1950s, six countries in Europe set up a Community to cooperate in the area of coal and steel, adopting the ECSC Treaty in 1951. This was followed by two further 'Communities' in 1957, one in the area of atomic energy and the other a more general 'economic Community'. All three Communities – ECSC, European Atomic Energy Community (EURATOM) and European Economic Community (EEC) – used very similar institution and methods, despite the existence of three separate treaties.

In this chapter, we will look more closely at the process of treaty adoption, which has continued right up to the present day as the main way in which the treaties are amended and developed (although the European Court of Justice or ECJ has often engaged in de facto treaty development through creative interpretation). The chapter looks at each treaty chronologically. More attention is paid to the most recent, general treaty amendment, by the Lisbon Treaty, which came into effect in 2009. In addition, we will examine in more detail the founding treaties, as well as the most major revisions by other treaties, the Single European Act 1986 (SEA) and the Treaty of Maastricht 1992.

Finally, we will also look at the two inter-governmental treaties adopted most recently (in 2011 and 2012). These latter two treaties were part of efforts to deal with crisis of the Eurozone.

First, we will look briefly at the general rules governing treaty-making in public international law.

The ECJ and integration enthusiasts have often been at pains to distinguish EU law from general public international law. The reason for this is the idea that we should move beyond considering states as the decisive unit of power or sovereignty, as we have seen in Chapter 2. In a 'supranational' way of thinking, states will eventually be overcome in importance by centralised, transnational institutions.

KEY LEARNING POINT

THE TREATIES ARE ADOPTED ACCORDING TO STANDARD RULES OF INTERNATIONAL LAW?

Remember from Chapter 2 that, although many EU specialists and the EU institutions like to differentiate the EU from 'normal' international law, the process of treaty-adoption and treaty-change follows the standard rules in international law. In public international law states, not international institutions, have the most power in the adoption of treaties.

In this regard, there is a debate in the academic literature about who are 'the masters of the treaties'. Given the exclusive role assigned to the Member States in treaty-making, it would be natural to assume that the Member States are the masters. Nonetheless, the interpretative methods of the ECJ supported by the other institutions, especially the European Commission, mean that the EU law often results in requirements that the Member States did not intend when adopting the treaties.

ANALYSING THE LAW

ARE THE MEMBER STATES, AND SHOULD THEY BE, 'MASTERS OF THE TREATIES'?

The justification for seeing the Member States as 'masters of the treaties' is the political authority of states as representing the democratic expression of their peoples. The Member States have political legitimacy in this way because their peoples identify with them. People recognise and accept the legitimacy of the power and authority of their governments as a result of a long and often violent struggle to secure democracy in Europe, usually along national lines. Political legitimacy in Europe to date has worked largely along the lines of the nation state. Although many Europeans see that the EU can play a useful role, it appears they do not see it as an alternative to the Member States. As Weiler has expressed this, there is no *demos* in the EU: no shared sense of political identity across the Member States that allows the peoples of Europe to connect with government at the supranational level.[1] It remains to be seen whether a Europe-wide *demos* or shared sense of political identity will ever develop.

---

1   J H H Weiler 'The state *"über alles"*; *Demos, Telos,* and the German Maastricht decision' *NYU Jean Monnet Working Paper No 6/1995* (1995).

3.2 TREATY-MAKING IN INTERNATIONAL LAW AND THE EU, INCLUDING ENHANCED COOPERATION

Treaty-making in international law is governed by the Vienna Convention on the Law of Treaties of 1969 (VCLT).[2] Under Article 9(1) VCLT, treaties may be concluded by participating states upon consent of a duly authorised representative of the state. In the EU, it is generally the foreign ministers and prime ministers who are authorised to consent on behalf of each Member State. Under Article 9(2) VCLT, the adoption of the text of a treaty at an international conference takes place by the vote of two-thirds of the states, unless by the same majority they shall decide to apply a different rule (although it is still up to each country individually to decide whether to ratify the treaty). In the EU, there is a different rule, which is that unanimity is needed for treaty amendments to be adopted.[3]

Beginning with the Treaty of Amsterdam in 1997, general provision was made in the EU treaties themselves for some Member States to move toward further integration if they wished, without other Member States participating. This is called flexible or enhanced cooperation (the TEU uses the expression 'enhanced cooperation') and sometimes in the jargon of EU studies 'variable geometry' or 'differentiation/differentiated cooperation'.[4] It is permitted when at least nine Member States agree.[5]

Generally, when the flexibility clauses are invoked, the Member States concerned do not adopt a treaty, rather they adopt secondary legislation. However, in 2011 and 2012, two treaties were adopted outside of the framework of the existing treaties, although the two new treaties, the so-called Fiscal Compact and the European Stability Mechanism (ESM) Treaty, make some use of the EU institutions in the normal way. The reason for the adoption of these two treaties in this way was that the UK, in particular, and also the Czech Republic, refused to ratify the more important of the two treaties, the so-called Fiscal Compact.

KEY LEARNING POINT

ENHANCED COOPERATION
The general provision on flexible or enhanced cooperation is now dealt with in Article 20 TEU, with the detail set out in Articles 326–334 TFEU. At least nine Member States must agree and the resulting cooperation must be compatible with EU law and not impact on the competences of the Member States not participating (Articles 326–327 TFEU).

2   23 May 1969, 1155 *UNTS* 331, 8 *ILM* 679 (1969) entered into force on 27 January 1980.
3   See art 48 TEU.
4   For a thorough dicussion of the background see e.g. C–D Ehlermann 'Differentiation, flexibility, closer coopera-tion: the new provisions of the Amsterdam Treaty' (1998) 4(3) *European Law Journal* 246–70.
5   Article 20(2) TEU.

The first basic principle of enhanced or flexible cooperation is that the Member States which intend to establish closer cooperation among themselves may make use of the institutions, procedures and mechanisms laid down by the treaties, as long as the resulting cooperation meets certain conditions. The most important of these conditions is that the cooperation agreed must be compatible with the *acquis communautaire*, i.e. the body of existing EU law.[6]

The issue with the Fiscal Compact was that it was of a constitutional nature, so it could not be adopted under the ordinary provisions for flexible cooperation, but at the same time it could not be adopted as an amendment to the existing treaties because two Member States refused to agree to it.

ANALYSING THE LAW

WHY IS PROVISION FOR ENHANCED COOPERATION NEEDED?

It might be asked why Member States could not simply cooperate in international law in the normal way, why was provision for enhanced cooperation needed? One reason is that the doctrines of parallelism and of pre-emption of Member States' external competences, developed by the ECJ, means that the Member States lose the legal capacity to operate outside the treaties in international matters once a matter has been addressed within the treaty framework by the development of internal common policies. Cooperation outside the treaties then becomes legally doubtful, according to the interpretative method of the ECJ. We will look at the doctrine of pre-emption more fully in Chapter 7. Further, regulation of enhanced cooperation in the EU treaties is needed to avoid a conflict of norms, i.e. a conflict between existing EU law (the *acquis communautaire*) and the new rules agreed between some of the Member States through enhanced cooperation.

The provisions on enhanced cooperation demonstrate that a one-size-fits-all approach to further cooperation and integration is not legally necessary. It creates a more flexible EU, in which individual and smaller Member States, perhaps in a minority, are in a better position to resist political pressure to accept unwanted further integration while, equally, those that do want to integrate further are not held up.

Finally, there are two stages to the adoption of EU treaties; the adoption at European level and incorporation at national level. This is the same as with any international treaties, and we have seen in Chapter 2 the two main different approaches among national systems to this issue: monism and dualism. A difference, however, with the EU treaties is that because of their constitutional significance, countries sometimes have

....

6   Articles 326–27 TFEU.

more onerous requirements than for 'ordinary' international treaties: in this respect, generally the Member States are dualist when it comes to the EU treaties.

> **KEY LEARNING POINT**
> ....
>
> **STAGES OF EU TREATY ADOPTION**
> It is important to note that there are two stages to the adoption of EU treaties:
> (i) signature at international level (usually by the foreign minister or prime
> minister); and (ii) adoption at national level by all of the Member States. Because
> of the importance of the EU, the Member States generally are required to
> alter their constitutions to reflect a new treaty. This often proves difficult, as
> government leaders in the past tended to be more in favour of EU integration
> than their populations, and some Member States, such as Ireland, require a
> popular referendum on any significant new EU treaty. In the UK, the European
> Union Act 2011, in s.18, requires a referendum for any future transfer of more
> power to the EU.

Thus, for example, the Netherlands has a very strong version of monism when it comes to international treaties being incorporated into national law: once they are ratified at international level, they are automatically binding in national law and even have superiority over national constitutional law.[7] However, for the Treaty establishing a Constitution for Europe, the Netherlands held a referendum in which the treaty was rejected. The Netherlands did not hold a referendum on the Lisbon Treaty; it was ratified by Parliament.

3.3 CHRONOLOGICAL SUMMARY OF THE TREATIES

3.3.1 EUROPEAN COAL AND STEEL COMMUNITY TREATY 1951 (ECSC)

Also known as the Treaty of Paris, this was the first and founding treaty of what is now the EU. It set up the institutions as they now are:

- a centralised executive called a *High Authority*, independent of the Member States and whose responsibility was to enforce Community policies.[8] Unlike the European Commission under the EEC Treaty, it did not have an exclusive right to initiate

....

7   See art 91 of the Constitution of the Netherlands. However, a treaty that conflicts with the Constitution requires a two-thirds majority approving it in both Houses of the Parliament of the Netherlands.
8   Article 8 ECSC Treaty stated that the High Authority 'shall be responsible for assuring the fulfilment of the purposes stated in the present Treaty under the terms thereof'.
9   Article 26 ECSC Treaty.

or propose new laws,[9] but it did have a general authority to pass legally binding decisions.[10] The High Authority was later merged, by the Merger Treaty, with what was the equivalent organ of the EEC Treaty, the European Commission[11]

– a *Council (of Ministers)*,[12] consisting of representatives of the Member States, which was meant to balance the centralisation of power in the High Authority, and which passed ECSC measures. Interestingly, the ECSC Treaty did not describe measures adopted by the institutions as laws, perhaps this was due to the sensitivity of giving a law-making function to supranational bodies[13]
– a *Court of Justice*, to rule on legal disputes[14] and
– a *Common Assembly*[15] (consisting of national representatives appointed from among the Parliaments of the first Member States). The Common Assembly did not have the power to pass legislation, but it did have the power by a two-thirds majority of its members to censure and require the resignation of the members of the High Authority.[16]

The overall purpose was to establish a common market in coal and steel only. Thus, it enshrined the principles of freedom of competition[17] and freedom of movement[18] and created a basis for common customs rules applied to these products from countries outside the ECSC.[19] The ECSC was empowered to engage in international relations with powers equivalent to a state, but notably, these powers were not exclusive, i.e. they did prevent the Member States exercising international or external powers, such as making treaties with third countries etc.[20] The High Authority was provided with a range of powers, including:

– it could make investments and provide financial assistance[21]
– establish production quotas[22]
– provide proposals to the Council to determine consumption priorities and
– determine the allocation of the coal and steel resources of the Community among the industries subject to its jurisdiction, exports, and other consumption.[23]

....

10 Article 15 ECSC Treaty stated that when decisions and recommendations of the High Authority are individual in character, they shall be binding on the interested party upon their notification to him and, in other cases, they shall take effect automatically upon publication.
11 See arts 8–19 of the ECSC Treaty.
12 Ibid arts 26–30.
13 Ibid art 28.
14 Ibid arts 31–45.
15 Ibid arts 8–19.
16 Ibid art 24. The Common Assembly and now the European Parliament of the EU should not be confused with the Parliamentary Assembly of the Council of Europe, see further ch 2 above.
17 Articles 60–67 ECSC Treaty.
18 Ibid arts 68–70.
19 Ibid arts 72–73.
20 Ibid arts 71–75.
21 Ibid arts 54–56.
22 Ibid art 58.
23 Ibid art 59.

The ECSC Treaty was the prototype of the two later Communities, the European Economic Community (EEC) and European Atomic Energy Community (EURATOM). Under its own provisions, the ECSC Treaty was to expire after 50 years.[24] When 50 years had passed, its powers were simply fully merged into the European Community (coal and steel fall within the free movement of goods), which was in any case how things worked in practice from the late 1950s onwards.[25]

3.3.2 EUROPEAN ATOMIC ENERGY COMMUNITY TREATY 1957 (EURATOM)

This treaty adopted more or less the same structure as the ECSC Treaty.

EXPLAINING THE LAW

THE EURATOM LARGELY FOLLOWED THE ECSC TREATY MODEL

In essence, the EURATOM Treaty applied the ECSC Treaty model to the creation of a common market in atomic energy, instead of a common market in coal and steel. Some provisions were particular to the subject matter of atomic energy, but the institutions it created were similar to the ECSC Treaty. A difference of terminology was that the central executive body it created that was independent of the Member States was called the European Commission instead of the High Authority as under the ECSC. In EURATOM, the Commission was complemented by a EURATOM Supplies Agency and a EURATOM Safeguards Office.

As well as the European Commission, it created a European Parliament, a Council (of Ministers), and a Court of Justice.[26]

Believing that civil nuclear power was the key energy technology of the future, the founding fathers of the European Communities shared a 'functionalist' belief that by obliging collaboration over the development of this technology between the Member States, via the EURATOM Treaty, then political integration would more likely follow. Article 1 EURATOM relates atomic energy to broader goals: 'to contribute to the raising of the standard of living in the Member States and to the development of relations with the other countries by creating the conditions necessary for the speedy establishment and growth of nuclear industries'.

....

24 Ibid art 97.
25 Council Decision 2002/595/EC on the consequences of the expiry of the Treaty establishing the European Coal and Steel Community (ECSC) on the international agreements concluded by the ECSC OJ L 194 23.07.2002 p. 35.
26 Article 3 EURATOM.

The treaty aimed to give considerable centralised powers to the institutions responsible for its implementation. Thus, the EURATOM Supplies Agency[27] would own and control the supply of all fissile materials in the Community, and the Commission would control the distribution of patent rights and production licences for a series of reactor designs and fuel cycle technologies to be developed by the Joint Nuclear Research Centre (JNRC). Provisions for research (Article 7) and international agreements (Article 101) were important features of the treaty: research was required to establish nuclear capability, and international agreements were required to gain access to fissile materials and technologies.[28] Article 2 set out the tasks more specifically, in that EURATOM is to:

– promote research and ensure the dissemination of technical information
– establish uniform safety standards to protect the health of workers and of the general public and ensure that they are applied
– facilitate investment
– ensure that all users in the Community receive a regular and equitable supply of ores and nuclear fuels
– make certain, by appropriate supervision, that nuclear materials are not diverted to purposes other than those for which they are intended
– exercise the right of ownership conferred upon it with respect to special fissile materials
– ensure wide commercial outlets and access to the best technical facilities by the creation of a common market in specialised materials and equipment, by the free movement of capital for investment in the field of nuclear energy and by freedom of employment for specialists within the Community
– establish with other countries and international organisations such relations as will foster progress in the peaceful uses of nuclear energy.

Article 2(g) refers to the concepts of common market (dealt with in detail in Articles 92–100) and free movement, which are central to the ECSC Treaty and the EEC Treaty.

EXPLAINING THE LAW

THE CONTEXT OF AND MOTIVATION FOR EURATOM

The context of the creation of EURATOM was the dramatic effect on world consciousness of the power of nuclear energy following the dropping of atomic bombs at the end of the Second World War. Jean Monnet, who was instrumental in the adoption of EURATOM, saw nuclear energy as a key energy source for the future and thus saw EURATOM as central to the idea of an integrated or united Europe. Overall, EURATOM has not lived up to this expectation. Nuclear energy arouses markedly different opinions amongst the Member States, not least due

---

27 http://ec.europa.eu/euratom/index.html (last accessed 18 January 2015).
28 European Parliament Research Directorate/M O'Driscoll and G Lake 'The European Parliament and the EUR-ATOM Treaty: past, present and future' Energy and Research Series Working Paper ENER 114 (2001) i.

to nuclear accidents such as at Chernobyl, and there has been a reluctance to develop EURATOM.[29]

As a result, EURATOM has never been substantively amended. Minor adjustments have been made by the Merger Treaty 1965 and to keep pace with the other treaty changes.[30] Consequently, a key difference between EURATOM and the EU treaties relates to the role of the European Parliament: under EURATOM it is only consulted, apart from in the budgetary procedure, where it must consent.[31]

Unlike the ECSC Treaty, the EURATOM Treaty provided for the adoption of legislation at Community level under Article 161 EURATOM Treaty. This is the same as the equivalent provision under the EEC Treaty, which we will look at further below.

Legal disputes relating to EURATOM do occasionally arise, the most recent major decision being *Oberösterreich v ČEZ as (Temelín)*.[32] This case concerned a dispute between Austria and the Czech Republic over the health impact on Austrian territory of a Czech nuclear facility close to the Czech border with Austria. Austria had adopted national legislation that permitted injunctions to be issued against nuclear facilities authorised by a foreign authority, whereas nuclear facilities authorised by Austrian authorities could only be the subject of a compensation claim. In a preliminary reference procedure, the ECJ held that the Austrian rule was contrary to EURATOM, because of the discrimination on nationality grounds and, moreover, it held this could not be justified on public health grounds since the Czech nuclear facility satisfied EURATOM standards.

ANALYSING THE LAW

CRITIQUING THE JUDGMENT IN *TEMELÍN*
The ECJ judgment in *Temelín* has been criticised for ignoring the separateness of EURATOM to the other treaties: EURATOM did not contain the same non-discrimination principles as was then in Article 12 EC Treaty,[33] but the ECJ decided that non-discrimination was a general principle of Community law that could be applied across all treaties.[34] The ECJ therefore ignored EURATOM as a

---

29 O'Driscoll and Lake (n 28); S Wolf 'EURATOM, the European Court of Justice, and the limits of nuclear integration' (2011) 12(8) *German Law Journal* 1637–58 at 1637–39.
30 The Treaty of Lisbon also just made minor amendments to EURATOM, largely to reflect the amendments it made to the TEU and ECT.
31 Article 177 EURATOM.
32 Case C–115/08 [2009] ECR I–10265.
33 Articles 92–99 EURATOM contain some specialised rules on non-discrimination, but there is no general principle to this effect.
34 Case C–115/08, para 90.

lex specialis that should have been applied over and above the EC Treaty,[35] whilst its conclusion that the Austrian rule could not be justified on health grounds has also been doubted.[36] In addition, the ECJ judgment in *Temelín* seemed to go further than previous case law in suggesting that the EURATOM had an exclusive competence in nuclear safety standards and that Member States could not adopt more stringent standards.[37]

3.3.3 EUROPEAN ECONOMIC COMMUNITY TREATY 1957 (EECT/ECT) (NOW KNOWN AS THE TREATY ON THE FUNCTIONING OF THE EUROPEAN UNION OR TFEU)

EXPLAINING THE LAW
_____

THE EEC LARGELY FOLLOWED THE ECSC AND EURATOM TREATY MODELS

This treaty adopted a very similar structure as the EURATOM Treaty, but instead applied it to create a common market in all types of economic goods. Thus, it is the most wide-ranging and important of the founding treaties. It sought to establish a common market for all economic goods – physical goods, workers, services, and capital. It did this by establishing freedom of movement for each of these types of goods, as well as the principle of freedom of (or undistorted) competition between these goods across the Community.[38]

Further, a common customs union with outside countries was also created,[39] and a common agricultural policy and common transport policy were envisaged.[40]

Some provisions were quite broadly framed, however, and hinted at the idea of fuller economic and political integration that developed later, beyond the creation of a common market. For example, Article 1 stated:

> It shall be the aim of the Community, by establishing a Common Market and progressively approximating the economic policies of Member States, to promote throughout the Community a harmonious development of economic activities, a

....

35 Wolf (n 29) 1645.

36 Ibid 1647 ff.

37 Ibid, contrasting the ECJ judgment in Case C–376/90 *Commission v Belgium* [1992] ECR I–6153. We have seen above that art 2(b) EURATOM refers to uniform safety standards, but this does not necessarily exclude more stringent standards adopted by individual Member States.

38 Article 3 of the EEC Treaty.

39 Ibid arts 9, 12–29.

40 Ibid art 3.

continuous and balanced expansion, an increased stability, an accelerated raising of
the standard of living and closer relations between its Member States.

The final expression, 'closer relations between its Member States', is more general than
merely the idea of a common market.

Individual provisions established:

- freedom of movement of goods (Articles 9, 12 and 16 EEC Treaty on customs
  duties, Article 95 EEC Treaty on internal taxation and Articles 30–37 EEC Treaty on
  quantitative restrictions)
- freedom of movement of workers (Articles 48–51 EEC Treaty)
- freedom of movement of services and establishment (Articles 52–66 EEC Treaty)
- freedom of movement of capital and payments (Articles 67–73 EEC Treaty).

A central principle was that of non-discrimination on grounds of nationality in the exercise
of the four freedoms: thus Member States were to apply the same rules to goods, workers,
services, and capital from other Member States as to those from their own Member State.[41]

The main provisions on competition prohibited concerted practices designed to achieve
certain restrictions on competition (Article 85 EEC Treaty) and the abuse of a dominant
position in a given market (Article 86 EEC Treaty).

To support these objectives, it established the institutions of:

- a central executive body that was independent of the Member States (as with
  EURATOM, this body was called the *European Commission* instead of the High
  Authority as under the ECSC Treaty)[42]
- a *Council (of Ministers)*[43]
- a *Common Assembly* (appointed from national parliamentarians, from which the
  current European Parliament developed)[44] and
- a *Court of Justice*.[45]

EXPLAINING THE LAW

COMPARING THE ECSC TREATY AND THE EEC TREATY
Some important differences existed with the ECSC structure, especially regarding
(a) the role of the European Commission of the ECSC compared to the High

....

41 Ibid art 7.
42 Ibid arts 137–44.
43 Ibid arts 145–54.
44 Ibid arts 137–44.
45 Ibid arts 164–88.

Authority of the ECSC and regarding (b) law-making. Under the EEC Treaty, the European Commission was generally given an exclusive right of legislative initiative throughout the treaty (i.e. the Member States could not propose EEC secondary legislation[46]), while the Council (of Ministers) had sole general legislative power. The ECSC did not provide for any legislative power. The Commission could propose to the Council (of Ministers) certain policies be adopted, the exercise of these policies would have been a matter of normal implementation of foreign relations by the Member States, rather than being in the form of Community legislation.

The Common Assembly (later renamed the European Parliament as under the EURATOM Treaty) had only a consultative role in law-making under the EEC Treaty.[47]

On law-making, the status of measures adopted was clearly stated in the EEC Treaty (and EURATOM Treaty) to be in the form of legislation. Four types of legislative measure could be adopted as secondary legislation:

– Regulations, which were directly applicable in the Member States (they did not need national implementing legislation) and were of general application (they were not directed at individuals or a narrow category)
– Directives, which were binding as to their results, but left their implementation to the Member States
– Decisions, which were similar to Regulations, but instead were directed at individuals
– Recommendations, which were not legally binding, but advisory only or a type of 'soft law'.[48]

Finally, it is worth noting now that the EEC Treaty and ECSC Treaty were frequently amended, though not until the 1980s onwards. However, it is important to note also that, independently of the process of treaty amendment or revision, substantial development of EEC law occurred through creative interpretation in the case law of the ECJ.

....

46 Ibid art 226. They could propose revisions of the treaty.
47 A difference with the current institutions is the role of the Court of Auditors. Under the original Community treaties, there was no Court of Auditors; instead art 206 EEC Treaty, for example, provided for a committee of auditors. The Court of Auditors was established by the Treaty of Brussels of 22 July 1975 (OJ L 359 31.12.77 p. 1) and started functioning as an external Community audit body in 1977, based in Luxembourg. It became a full institution on 1 November 1993 with the entry into force of the Treaty of Maastricht.
48 Article 189 EEC Treaty. The EURATOM Treaty equivalent is art 161.

EXPLAINING THE LAW

CHANGES OF NAME AND OF SUBSTANCE OF THE EEC TREATY

(1) Changes of name: The EEC Treaty was renamed the European Community Treaty (ECT) by the Treaty of Maastricht and was further renamed the Treaty on the Functioning of the European Union (TFEU) by the Treaty of Lisbon.
(2) Among the important substantive changes introduced since 1957, which we will look at further below, are:
  – the granting of a much stronger legislative role to the European Parliament, first by the SEA and then by the Treaty of Maastricht and subsequent treaties (under the EEC Treaty 1957, the European Parliament only had a consultative role in the process of adopting laws)
  – the expansion of competences beyond purely economic matters
  – the strengthening of the legal structure through important new 'constitutional' doctrines first developed by the ECJ in its case law, including the doctrines of supremacy, direct effect, and parallelism and pre-emption in external matters.

We will look at the EEC Treaty in further detail below (as it now is following much amendment) when we examine the Treaty of Lisbon. The Treaty of Lisbon is the most recent general amendment to the EEC Treaty.[49]

3.3.4 MERGER TREATY 1965

This treaty formally merged the institutions established under the three founding treaties. This had already happened with the Common Assembly, which in 1958, as a result of the EURATOM Treaty and EEC Treaty, was renamed the European Parliamentary Assembly. Similarly, the same Court of Justice had always been used for all three Communities. To an extent, therefore, the Merger Treaty was merely recognising what had already happened. However, one practical change that resulted was that the High Authority of the ECSC was merged into the European Commission. The separate existence of the treaties and the terminology of the Communities remained even after the Merger Treaty.

3.3.5 SINGLE EUROPEAN ACT 1986 (SEA)

Despite being called an 'Act', this was in fact a treaty just like the previous ones. The SEA entered into force in July 1987 having been signed the previous year by the then nine Member States (UK, Ireland and Greece had joined the original six since the 1950s).

....

49 The most recent revision to the EEC Treaty (now the TFEU) was the Accession Treaty of Croatia, but this only made minor amendments solely for allowing Croatia to join (see further below).

THE 'EMPTY CHAIR CRISIS', MAJORITY VOTING IN THE COUNCIL (OF MINISTERS), AND THE SEA AS THE FIRST MAJOR AMENDMENT

The SEA was the first major amendment of the Treaty establishing the EEC Treaty.[50] The lack of amendment up until then was a result of the previous reluctance of the Member States to integrate further, especially the reluctance of France to integrate further in the 1960s under General de Gaulle.[51] In 1965, there occurred what is called the 'Empty Chair Crisis' in the Council (of Ministers). France under President de Gaulle objected to proposals being developed by European Commission President Walter Hallstein to give the European Parliament more power and to reduce national vetoes in the Council (of Ministers). France decided to refuse to send its ministers to the Council when France occupied the EEC Presidency. Thus, the Council had no chairperson. Eventually, a compromise was agreed whereby Member States were informally to be allowed to veto proposals, even where majority voting applied under the treaties, when important national interests were affected. This compromise was known as the 'Luxembourg Accord' and it resulted in a de facto veto for each Member State. It was only with the adoption of the SEA in 1986 that majority voting was reasserted, although not in all matters.

One of the other significant consequences of the SEA was a constitutional challenge in Ireland to the ratification of the treaty by the government. The Irish Government proposed to implement the treaty by legislation, but the Irish Supreme Court in *Crotty v An Taoiseach*[52] held that any alienation of sovereignty required a constitutional referendum. The referendum subsequently held in Ireland was passed, but the decision of the Irish Supreme Court was to have important consequences for later treaty revisions, two of which were rejected by referenda in Ireland.

The SEA was adopted by an inter-governmental conference consisting of the authorised representatives of the Member States (their respective foreign ministers and heads of government). It consists of a preamble and four titles and also a series of declarations. The preamble states the fundamental goals of the treaty to transform their relations

---

50 Generally see e.g. C-D Ehlermann 'The internal market following the Single European Act' (1987) 24(3) *Common Market Law Review* 361–409.

51 General de Gaulle was first president of the Fifth French Republic from 1959–1969. He vetoed UK entry to the Communities.

52 [1987] IR 713. See G W Hogan 'The Supreme Court and the Single European Act' (1987) 22(1) *Irish Jurist* 55–70; J Temple Lang 'The Irish court case which delayed the Single European Act: *Crotty v An Taoiseach and Others*' (1987) 24(4) *Common Market Law Review* 709–718.

through further integration with a view to creating a European Union. However, the degree of integration involved is not identified clearly in the preamble.[53]

The SEA was most concerned with furthering economic integration and the completion of the single market,[54] including by launching European Economic and Monetary Union (EMU). However, it also contained a title (Title III) on political cooperation,[55] which was later to develop into the Common Foreign and Security Policy. Title I concerned some general provisions applicable across the titles. Title II contained the main provisions amending the ECSC Treaty, Chapter I of Title II, and EEC Treaty, Chapter II of Title II. Echoing later developments, Subsection IV of the latter inserted Title V in the EEC Treaty dealing with economic and social cohesion. Article 130b, for example, referred in a general way to the coordination of economic policy by the Member States, which remains an outstanding issue today as we will see below in looking at the Fiscal Compact 2011 and ESM Treaty 2012.

Title V was mainly concerned with various Community funds for promoting economic and social development (European Agricultural Guidance and Guarantee Fund, Guidance Section, European Social Fund, European Regional Development Fund). Subsection V inserted Title VI in the EEC Treaty, which dealt with research and technological development. Subsection VI dealt with environmental provisions.

The following is a summary of the most important provisions of the SEA. On institutions and law-making and on competences:

– It increased the number of cases in which the Council could decide by *qualified majority voting* instead of unanimity. Unanimity was no longer required for measures designed to establish the Single Market,[56] with the exception of measures concerning taxation,[57] the free movement of persons, and the rights and interests of employed persons.[58]
– It established a new *cooperation procedure for passing legislation* between the Council and the European Parliament for adopting legislation, which enabled the Parliament to require unanimity in the Council.[59] Article 6 SEA stated that the cooperation procedure was to be used for legislation on discrimination on grounds of nationality (Article 7 EEC Treaty), free movement of workers (Article 49), freedom of establishment (Articles 54(2), second sentence of 56(2), 57 with the exception of the second sentence of paragraph 2), the functioning of the internal

---

53 For example it refers to 'the results achieved in the fields of economic *integration* and political co-*operation*' (emphasis added), using the softer expression of cooperation for political decision-making, 'cooperation' being a looser, less loaded term than 'integration'.
54 Articles 13 and 14 SEA inserting arts 8a and 8b EEC Treaty.
55 Title III had just one, rather long, art 30 SEA.
56 Article 14 SEA inserting art 14b EEC Treaty and art 16(3) SEA amending art 59 EEC Treaty on services.
57 Article 17 SEA inserting art 99 EEC Treaty and art 18 SEA inserting art 100a(2) EEC Treaty.
58 Article 18 SEA inserting art 100a(2) EEC Treaty.
59 Article 7 SEA inserting art 149 EEC Treaty.

market (Articles 100a, 100b), health and safety of workers (Article 118a), economic and social cohesion (Article 130e), and research and technology (Article 130q(2)).

– It further *increased the power of the European Parliament* by requiring its consent for an association agreement with a non-EU Member State.[60]

– It provided treaty recognition for the first time of the *European Council* (meetings of the heads of government of the EU Member States), but without specifying its competences.

– It established the *Court of First Instance*[61] (now known since the Treaty of Lisbon as the General Court), to act as a lower court in the judicial system of the Community in order to relieve the workload of the ECJ.

– On *implementing powers*, the SEA provided as a general rule, that the Council confer on the Commission implementing powers for legislation, but that the Council could reserve the right to directly exercise implementing powers in specific cases.[62]

– It inserted provisions on *monetary capacity*,[63] but convergence of economic and (to a lesser extent) monetary policy already belonged to an extent in the framework of existing powers, especially regarding free movement of capital and payments. Article 105(2) EEC Treaty had already provided that in order to promote the co-ordination of the policies of Member States in monetary matters to the full extent necessary for the functioning of the Common Market, a Monetary Committee with consultative status was to be established, whose tasks were to review the economic and monetary conditions of the Member States and advise them and the Community institutions in this area. For example, the SEA formally recognised at treaty level the European Monetary System (EMS) and European Currency Unit (ECU), which sought to maintain fixed exchange rates between the Member States. The EMS and ECU were formalised by initiative of the European Monetary System in 1979, but had already been developed outside or parallel to the framework of the treaties since 1972.[64]

– The SEA adopted a Community policy of *economic and social cohesion* to redress an imbalance created by the effects of the single market on less developed Member States through creating the European Agriculture Guidance and Guarantee Fund (EAGGF) and the European Regional Development Fund (ERDF).[65]

– A Community competence was established in *research* 'to strengthen the scientific and technological basis of European industry and to encourage it to become more competitive at international level', with multi-annual research programmes to be approved unanimously by the Council.[66]

....

60 Article 8 SEA amending art 237 EEC Treaty and art 9 SEA, amending art 238 EEC Treaty.

61 Articles 4 and 11 SEA inserting art 32d and 168a EEC Treaty respectively.

62 Article 10 SEA amending art 145 of the EEC Treaty.

63 Article 20 SEA inserting Chapter 1 in Title III, Part 2 EEC Treaty and art 10.

64 See G Zis 'European Monetary System 1979–1984: an assessment' (1984) 23(1) *Journal of Common Market Studies* 45–72.

65 Article 23 SEA inserting Title V of Chapter and art 130a–e EEC Treaty.

66 Article 24 SEA inserting art 130(F)–(Q) of the EEC Treaty.

– A Community competence in *environmental matters* was affirmed by the SEA, inserting three new articles into the EEC Treaty permitting the Community 'to preserve, protect and improve the quality of the environment, to contribute towards protecting human health, and to ensure a prudent and rational utilization of natural resources'.[67] In these provisions on environmental law, the SEA here introduced the principle of subsidiarity (later adopted more generally at the Treaty of Maastricht), stating that the Community can only intervene in environmental matters when this action can be attained better at Community level than at the level of the individual Member States. This principle was to achieve greater importance with the Treaty of Maastricht in 1992.

KEY LEARNING POINT
....

THE MAIN FEATURES OF THE SEA 1986
The main changes to the EEC Treaty introduced by the SEA were:

– greater use of majority voting in the Council (of Ministers)
– the adoption of the cooperation procedure in passing legislation, giving the European Parliament the power to force unanimity in the Council (of Ministers)
– the creation of the Court of First Instance
– expanded or confirmed more fully competence in economic and monetary union, economic and social cohesion, research and technological development, and environmental policy.

3.3.6 TREATY OF MAASTRICHT 1992 (TOM)

This treaty confirmed the continuation and completion of the common market, now renamed the single market, and of EMU, as well adding to new areas of cooperation, albeit a more flexible and looser form of cooperation: in *foreign policy* and in what was called *justice and home affairs* (JHA). More specifically, the following are the main features of the Treaty of Maastricht:

– It renamed the EEC Treaty as the European Community Treaty or ECT (i.e. the word 'economic' was dropped from its title) to reflect the move from purely economic cooperation, but it also confirmed EMU as an objective of the EC.[68]
– With the addition of cooperation in foreign policy and JHA, a new Treaty called the Treaty on European Union (TEU) was launched alongside the ECT, with the EC and the two new areas of competence now being given a new overall title of 'European Union' or EU.[69] The term 'pillars' was introduced here to describe the ECT, where the supranational method of cooperation was to be used, and the two new areas of foreign policy (now called the 'Common Foreign and Security Policy' or CFSP) and JHA, where an inter-governmental method was used.

....

67 Article 25 SEA inserting arts 130R, 130S and 130T of the EEC Treaty.
68 Article G(B)(2) ToM amending the EEC Treaty and art 2 ECT.
69 Article A TEU (this was a new provision, rather than an amending one).

KEY LEARNING POINT

THE STRUCTURE OF THE TREATY OF MAASTRICHT

The Treaty of Maastricht created two separate new treaties:

European Community Treaty (ECT) (this was created from and replaced the EEC
   Treaty) = first pillar

Treaty on European Union (TEU) → Contained the second and third pillars, as well
   as general provisions affecting both the TEU and the ECT.

KEY LEARNING POINT

THE LEGAL INSTRUMENTS SPECIFIC TO THE INTERGOVERNMENTAL PILLARS ESTABLISHED BY THE TREATY OF MAASTRICHT

The two inter-governmental pillars of the Treaty of Maastricht were:

– the second pillar on Common Foreign and Security Policy (CFSP) (Title V,
   Articles J.1–J.11 TEU)
– the third pillar on Justice and Home Affairs (JHA) (Title VI, Articles K, K.1–K.9,
   TEU).

The second and third pillars had their own legal instruments, distinct from the
pre-existing legislative instruments (regulations, directives and decisions) under
the first pillar. Under the second pillar, these were called *Common Positions*
(Article J.2) and *Joint Actions* (Article J.3). Under the third pillar, these were
called *Joint Positions*, *Joint Actions* and *Conventions* (Article K.2).** The Treaty
of Amsterdam later established framework decisions as a third pillar legal
instrument (Article K.6(b)(2), as inserted by the Treaty of Amsterdam).

The exact status of these legal instruments under the second and third pillars
was not made clear. They are probably best compared to international treaties
or conventions, in so far as they are legally binding, in that the compulsory
jurisdiction of the ECJ and the doctrines of supremacy and direct effect of EU
law did not apply to them. For example, Article K.2 stated that conventions
under the third pillar were to be proposed by the Council and adopted by the
Member States in accordance with their respective constitutional requirements.
The second pillar/CFSP instruments and the other two third pillar instruments did
not seem to be expressed in binding legal terms and could be considered merely
formalised policy positions. These distinct instruments were abolished by the
Treaty of Lisbon.

*** The Article references refer to those established at the Treaty of Maastricht; these were
altered later by subsequent treaties. For example, the Treaty of Amsterdam amended the
sequence of articles so that Joint Actions under the second pillar/CFSP were dealt with
under Article J.4 and the legal instruments under the third pillar were dealt with under
Article K.6.*

The division between the two inter-governmental pillars and the first or 'Community' pillar was not watertight. This was because, under the case law of the ECJ, many matters now in the first or Community pillar had a foreign or external aspect governed by the supranational method. So not all 'foreign policy' was in the new second pillar (the CFSP). Further, at least one provision of the first or Community pillar (ECT) dealt with visas (which were mostly dealt with under the third pillar), Article 100a concerning Community competence to decide the third countries whose nationals must be in possession of a visa when crossing the external borders of the Member States.[70] We will look at the overlap between the general law of external relations and the CFSP in Chapter 7.

The following are main specific provisions of the Treaty of Maastricht on the first pillar:

–   Article 3 ECT was amended to *add additional competences* in the areas of *health protection, education, culture, development cooperation, consumer protection, energy civil protection, tourism.*[71] These competences were not exclusive, rather the EU was given some partial competence in these areas, while the Member States also kept some competence.
–   Article 3a was inserted into the ECT to *confirm EMU and establishment of a single currency as part of EMU.*[72] To support the creation of the single currency, the European Central Bank (ECB) and European System of Central Banks were established.[73] In addition, provisions on coordinating economic policy were inserted as Articles 102–109m ECT.[74] Amongst these measures was provision for oversight by the European Commission and Council (of Ministers) of the budget policies of the Member States in order to avoid excessive borrowing (we will look at this again in Chapter 17). This was to lay the basis for the single currency, so that some Member States would not cause economic problems for the others by defaulting on excess debt.

EXPLAINING THE LAW

THE PROVISIONS OF THE TREATY OF MAASTRICHT ON BUDGETARY OVERSIGHT

It is worth looking at an excerpt of these provisions of the ToM on budgetary oversight, as these have become the focus of the most recent EU reforms and the centre of public debate on the role of the EU in the financial crisis. The provisions in the ToM were not legally binding, the Council (of Ministers) was to exercise political oversight. A key change to this with Fiscal Compact of 2011 is to give the ECJ a prominent role in policing a legally binding prohibition on budget

70 Article G(D)(23) ToM.
71 Ibid art G(B)(3).
72 Ibid art G(B)(4).
73 Ibid art G(B)(7).
74 Ibid art G(D)(25).

deficits and to require implementation in national law. Secondary legislation – the so-called six-pack and two-pack – were adopted prior to the Fiscal Compact and ESM Treaty. We will return to this at the end of the chapter. Here are the relevant parts of the ToM on budget deficits:

Article 103: *1. Member States shall regard their economic policies as a matter of common concern and shall co-ordinate them within the Council, in accordance with the provisions of Article 102a.*

2. The Council shall, acting by a qualified majority on a recommendation from the Commission, formulate a draft for the broad guidelines of the economic policies of the Member States and of the Community, and shall report its findings to the European Council.

The European Council shall, acting on the basis of the report from the Council, discuss a conclusion on the broad guidelines of the economic policies of the Member States and of the Community. On the basis of this conclusion, the Council shall, acting by a qualified majority, adopt a recommendation setting out these broad guidelines. The Council shall inform the European Parliament of its recommendation.

3. In order to ensure closer co-ordination of economic policies and sustained convergence of the economic performances of the Member States, the Council shall, on the basis of reports submitted by the Commission, monitor economic developments in each of the Member States and in the Community as well as the consistency of economic policies with the broad guidelines referred to in paragraph 2, and regularly carry out an overall assessment. For the purpose of this multilateral surveillance, Member States shall forward information to the Commission about important measures taken by them in the field of their economic policy and such other information as they deem necessary.

4. Where it is established, under the procedure referred to in paragraph 3, that the economic policies of a Member State are not consistent with the broad guidelines referred to in paragraph 2 or that they risk jeopardizing the proper functioning of economic and monetary union, the Council may, acting by a qualified majority on a recommendation from the Commission, make the necessary recommendations to the Member State concerned. The Council may, acting by a qualified majority on a proposal from the Commission, decide to make its recommendations public. The President of the Council and the Commission shall report to the European Parliament on the results of multilateral surveillance. The President of the Council may be invited to appear before the competent Committee of the European Parliament if the Council has made its recommendations public.

5. The Council, acting in accordance with the procedure referred to in Article 189c, may adopt detailed rules for the multilateral surveillance procedure referred to in paragraphs 3 and 4 of this Article.

Article 104c established a means of reviewing government deficits, but the enforcement was for the Council: *1. Member States shall avoid excessive government deficits.*

2. The Commission shall monitor the development of the budgetary situation and of the stock of government debt in the Member States with a view to identifying gross errors. In particular it shall examine compliance with budgetary discipline on the basis of the following two criteria:

(a) whether the ratio of the planned or actual government deficit to gross domestic product exceeds a reference value, unless:

– either the ratio has declined substantially and continuously and reached a level that comes close to the reference value;

– or, alternatively, the excess over the reference value is only exceptional and temporary and the ratio remains close to the reference value;

(b) whether the ratio of government debt to gross domestic product exceeds a reference value, unless the ratio is sufficiently diminishing and approaching the reference value at a satisfactory pace.

The reference values are specified in the Protocol on the excessive deficit procedure annexed to this Treaty . . .

– *Citizenship of the EU* was established (by inserting Part 2 Articles 8 and 8a–e into the ECT).[75] It is not obvious why the concept of citizenship of the *Union* was introduced into the ECT, rather than in the TEU. However, the concept was largely symbolic and did not create of itself very substantial new rights at that stage; rather, it provided a framework or concept for articulating the idea of the right of citizens in the EU under EU law. Later, the ECJ gradually started to use the citizenship provisions to create small entitlements in EU law, which we will look at further in Chapter 8. The Council was empowered to adopt legislation setting out the rights, established in the treaties, of citizens to move and reside freely in other Member States, on a proposal from the Commission and with the assent of the European Parliament (Article 8a ECT), although the Parliament was to be only consulted on legislation specifying how the right to vote in a host Member State was to be exercised (Article 8b ECT) and on legislation strengthening treaty rights (Article 8e ECT).

– Further provision was made for *completing the internal or single market* (especially in free movement/establishment).[76]

....

75 Ibid art G(C).

76 Ibid art G(D)(10–17), making various amendments/additions to the ECT, including art 54(2) on establishment, art 57 on mutual recognition of educational qualifications, and inserting arts 73a–h regarding capital and payments.

– The *European Parliament* was given a joint legislative role with the Council (of Ministers), under Article 189b ECT. This substantially strengthened the Parliament's role. *Co-decision* required the consent of the European Parliament. It was different from a simple requirement for the assent of Parliament under the 'assent procedure' in that, with co-decision, a conciliation procedure existed to reconcile differing views in the Council and the Parliament. Co-decision largely replaced the cooperation procedure introduced under the SEA, although the cooperation procedure was only fully abolished at the Treaty of Lisbon. Among the broad range of areas where co-decision now applied under the Treaty of Maastricht were the important general provision on the internal market;[77] free movement of workers;[78] freedom of establishment;[79] education, vocational training and youth;[80] culture;[81] public health;[82] consumer protection;[83] transport and telecommunications;[84] and research and technology.[85] We will look in more detail at the different legislative procedures, their history and current operation, in Chapter 4.

– The *principle of subsidiarity* introduced for environmental matters was now upgraded to a principle applicable across EU law. It was complemented by a newly created principle of conferral, under which the EU institutions only had powers as specifically conferred by the treaties. Subsidiarity and the principle of conferral together were meant to reduce concerns that the EU was overstepping its role and intruding on competences that were meant to be for the Member States.

ANALYSING THE LAW

WHY WERE PRINCIPLES OF SUBSIDIARITY AND CONFERRAL INTRODUCED BY THE TREATY OF MAASTRICHT?

We have seen how the Treaty of Maastricht introduced the principles of conferral (the EU has only those powers specifically given to it in the treaties) and subsidiarity (the EU should only take action if it can do this more effectively than the Member States). These two principles are concerned first with defining EU competences and second with their effective exercise. They reflected concerns that the EU was exercising competences that it should not have been exercising or that could be better exercised by the Member States. We will look at whether they have been successful in Chapter 7 on competences.

....

77 Article 100a(1) ECT as inserted by art G(D)(22) ToM.
78 Article 49 ECT as amended by art G(D)(10) ToM.
79 Article 54(2) ECT as amended by art G(D)(11) ToM.
80 Article 126(4) ECT as amended by art G(D)(36) ToM.
81 Article 128(5) ECT as amended by art G(D)(37) ToM.
82 Article 129(4) ECT as amended by art G(D)(38) ToM.
83 Article 129(a)(2) ECT as amended by art G(D)(38) ToM.
84 Article 129(c)(1) ECT as amended by art G(D)(38) ToM.
85 Article 130(i)(1) ECT as amended by art G(D)(38) ToM.

- The Treaty of Maastricht adopted a somewhat controversial social policy annex or protocol, with the UK being given an opt-out (the UK later decided to opt in, in 1997). The Social Policy Protocol *was* concerned with employment and industrial relations and provided the first substantial legal basis for EC legislation in this area. The Protocol required the Commission to consult management and workers in the development of Community law on social policy and allowed for qualified majority voting in the Council (of Ministers). We will look at this more in Chapter 18 on 'Social Europe'.

KEY LEARNING POINT

SUMMARISING THE TREATY OF MAASTRICHT

Along with the SEA, the Treaty of Maastricht is the most important of the treaties amending the original treaties. The later treaties – Amsterdam 1997, Nice 2001, and even Lisbon 2009 – were all more evolutionary, whereas the Treaty of Maastricht was more radical. The key changes introduced by the Treaty of Maastricht were:

- the creation of the pillar structure: everything involved in cooperation up to this date was put in the first pillar and relabelled the European Community Treaty or ECT, instead of European Economic Community Treaty as it had been up to then, and new and more informal 'pillars' relating to cooperation in foreign policy and in criminal law and home affairs were added, with an overarching treaty called the Treaty on European Union or TEU
- a new legislative procedure of co-decision was established, with the European Parliament and Council (of Ministers) being given a more or less equal role in adopting EU legislation and applied this to most areas of EU competence
- EU citizenship was created
- the general principles of subsidiarity and conferral were established
- a social policy with UK opt-out was established
- competences to include partial EU competences in health protection, education, culture, development cooperation, consumer protection, energy civil protection and tourism were expanded.

The Treaty of Maastricht was politically controversial at the time of its adoption. The pillar structure was adopted largely under UK influence, as it provided a looser, inter-governmental form of cooperation. The Conservative UK Government of Prime Minister John Major, who had a small parliamentary majority, had considerable difficulty ensuring it passed through the House of Commons.[86] In Germany, the treaty was challenged before the Federal Constitutional Court, which issued a judgment permitting Germany to adopt the treaty, but qualifying German

....

86 European Communities (Amendment) Act 1993.

acceptance of the supremacy doctrine of EU law.[87] We will look at this in more detail in Chapter 6.

3.3.7 TREATY OF AMSTERDAM 1997 (TOA)

As noted above, the Treaty of Amsterdam, which was adopted only a few years after the Treaty of Maastricht, was an evolution and much less far-reaching than the Treaty of Maastricht. We will not look at it in as much detail. When the Treaty of Amsterdam was being negotiated, quite a wide range of reforms to the EU institutions were discussed, including: 1. an adjustment of the countries' vote weights in the Council for qualified majority voting; 2. a limit on the number of Commissioners; 3. an extension of qualified majority voting in the Council; and 4. a further increase in the Parliament's powers.

However, opposition from small countries meant that it did not adjust the vote weights of each Member State in the Council to better reflect population sizes (as this would have reduced the votes of the smaller Member States) and similarly it did not limit the number of Commissioners (each Member State could still appoint one Commissioner). The main reforms of the Treaty of Amsterdam were:

- to extend qualified majority voting in the Council (of Ministers)[88]
- to increase the European Parliament's powers by providing for a wider application of the co-decision procedure[89]
- to simplify (somewhat) the co-decision procedure[90]
- to transfer of visa, asylum, and immigration from the inter-governmental third pillar to the supranational first pillar (with some transitional provisions)[91]
- to provide a general competence to deal with various forms of discrimination[92]
- to establish a High Representative for the CFSP[93]
- to introduce a system of sanctions for breaches of fundamental principles of EU law.[94]

....

87 *Brunner v European Union Treaty* [1994] CMLR 57.

88 Including some aspects of implementation of the CFSP (art J.13 TEU inserted by art 1(10) TEU); employment *incentive* (art 109r ECT as inserted by art 2(19) ToA); social exclusion (art 118(2) EEC Treaty as amended by art 2(22) ToA); and public health (art 129 ECT as amended by art 2(26) ToA).

89 Including in the areas of discrimination (art 6 ECT as amended by art 2(6) ToA); visa, asylum, and immigration (art 73i-I TEU as inserted by art 2(15) ToA); the development of guidelines on employment (art 109q TEU as inserted by art 2(15) ToA); and the adoption of programmes in research and technology (art 130o TEU as amended by art 2(33) ToA).

90 For example by allowing a legislative draft to be adopted at the first reading by both the Council (of Ministers) and the European Parliament if they agreed to it (art 189b ECT as amended by art 2(44) ToA).

91 Title IIIa, arts 73i–73q ECT inserted by art 2(15) ToA.

92 Article 6a ECT inserted by art 2(7) ToA.

93 The High Representative for the CFSP was to be the Secretary General of the Council (of Ministers), under art J.8(3) TEU, as inserted by art 1(10) ToA.

94 Article F.1 TEU, as inserted by art 1(9) ToA.

Related to the idea of an opt-out from the Social Policy Protocol by the Treaty of Maastricht, the Treaty of Amsterdam established a general framework for *enhanced cooperation*.[95] This allowed some Member States to push ahead with further integration and others to not participate in this. Previously, the general approach had been that all Member States should move ahead together or not at all.

EXPLAINING THE LAW

ENHANCED COOPERATION AND THE SCHENGEN SYSTEM

Some Member States had already began such cooperation through the Schengen system, whereby they relaxed border controls with each other, while also developing a security information system to counter-balance this reduction in border security. The UK and Ireland did not participate in Schengen. The Treaty of Amsterdam later incorporated the Schengen system or *acquis* into the EU under the framework of enhanced cooperation, with its detailed provision being appended to the EU Treaty as a Protocol. However, in practice, in monetary matters with the EMS and ECU, a degree of enhanced cooperation had already been practised since the 1970s.

3.3.8 TREATY OF NICE 2001

Even more so than the Treaty of Amsterdam, the Treaty of Nice was an updating of some provisions, rather than a far-reaching overhaul. It dealt with enlargement as a result of countries in Eastern Europe joining or applying to join. However, it continued a pattern of increasing the use of co-decision by the Council (of Ministers) and European Parliament as a legislative procedure. This made it by far the most common legislative procedure. The Treaty of Nice also increased the use of majority voting in the Council (of Ministers). The following is a brief summary of the main changes made by the Treaty of Nice:

- agreed institutional changes necessary for enlargement, including changes to weighting of votes in the Council (of Ministers)[96]
- dealt with the expiry of the ECSC Treaty by incorporating it into the ECT[97]
- reformed aspects of the jurisdiction and procedure of the ECJ and CFI[98]

---

95 Articles K.15–K.17 TEU inserted by art 1(12) ToA and art 5a ECT as inserted by art 2(5) ToA.

96 Treaty of Nice Protocol on the enlargement of the European Union.

97 Treaty of Nice Protocol on the financial consequences of the expiry of the ECSC Treaty.

98 Article 225 ECT as amended by art 2(31) ToN; art 229 and 230 ECT inserted by art 2(33) and 2(34) ToN respectively; art 140a ECT as amended by art 3(13) ToN; and Protocol on the Statute of the Court of Justice.

- extended co-decision as a legislative method[99]
- increased the use of qualified majority voting in the Council (of Ministers)[100] and
- added further provisions on enhanced cooperation.[101]

3.3.9 TREATY ESTABLISHING A CONSTITUTION FOR EUROPE 2004

This was the most ambitious EU treaty to date (although it was ultimately not ratified), mainly because of its symbolism, rather than concrete changes it proposed. It would have formalised the idea of the EU as a constitutional entity. The Constitutional Treaty, in Article I-8, seemed to adopt symbols that were reminiscent of a state, including a flag, and a national day:

- the flag of the Union, which is a circle of 12 gold stars on a blue background
- the anthem of the Union, which is based on the 'Ode to Joy' from the Ninth Symphony by Ludwig van Beethoven
- the motto of the Union, which is 'United in diversity'
- the currency of the Union, which is the Euro
- 9 May, which is celebrated throughout the Union as Europe Day, in memory of the 1950 declaration by Robert Schuman, who initiated the European integration project.

Informally, the EU already reflected many of the provisions of the Treaty establishing a Constitution, as we shall discuss at the end of the chapter. However, in its symbolism and in openly and in explicitly stating the supremacy doctrine of EU law over national law, the EU would have been symbolising transcendence over the Member States. The treaties had not been explicit about supremacy to date, despite rhetoric from the ECJ over the years in its case law. The treaty provision on supremacy, Article I-6, stated:

> The Constitution and law adopted by the institutions of the Union in exercising competences conferred on it shall have primacy over the law of the Member States.

Taken together, these provisions could be taken to suggest the EU was in a way 'taking over' from the role of the Member States as the source of political identity of EU citizens. Similarly, a proposed Minister for Foreign Affairs[102] 'wantonly encourag[ed] comparison to national systems'.[103] The treaty was rejected by voters in both France and the Netherlands and, with this lack of popular support, had to be abandoned.

....

99 For example concerning Council–Commission cooperation under art 161 ECT as amended by art 2(14) ToN; economic, financial and technical cooperation with third countries under art 181a ECT as inserted by art 2(16) ToN.

100 For example concerning some social matters under art 137 TEU as amended by art 2(9) ToN.

101 Articles 27a–e TEU inserted by art 1(6) ToN, arts 40, 40a, 40b TEU inserted by art 1(9) ToN, art 43 TEU as amended by art 1(11) ToN, arts 43a and 43b inserted by art 1(12) ToN, arts 44 and 44a TEU as inserted by art 1(13) ToN, arts 11 and 11a inserted by art 29(10) ToN.

102 Articles III-292 and III-293 of the Treaty establishing a Constitution for Europe.

103 M Dougan 'The Treaty of Lisbon 2007: winning minds, not hearts' (2008) 45 *Common Market Law Review* 617–703 at 622.

WHY WAS THE TREATY ESTABLISHING A CONSTITUTION FOR EUROPE NOT ADOPTED?

The immediate reason why the Treaty establishing a Constitution for Europe was not adopted was that it has been rejected by voters in France and the Netherlands. However, this rejection perhaps points to a broader phenomenon of the European integration 'project': it is very much a project and ambition of political (and especially legal) élites, but it has not (or not yet at least, and there seems little sign of this changing) achieved much popular support in many Member States, although it tends to attract strong support in Germany. In Member States where referenda are needed for constitutional change, amending treaties to the founding treaties have more often than not been rejected. However, pressure from the other Member States can 'persuade' electorates to change their position in a second referendum, although this is generally only after opt-outs and concessions have been granted to the Member States to reflect voter concerns, Ireland being the main example (the Irish electorate rejected both the Treaty of Nice and the Treaty of Lisbon in the first referendum held on these treaties).

3.3.10 TREATY OF LISBON 2009

3.3.10.1 INTRODUCTION

Adopted in 2006, this finally came into effect at the end of 2009. It did not dramatically change the EU, but did contain some significant reforms, especially the incorporation of the third pillar (cooperation in criminal matters) into the 'supranational' or 'Community method' (although with significant inter-governmental elements remaining). It incorporated the EU Charter of Fundamental Rights fully into EU law, whilst also providing for the EU to become a party to the ECHR. Notably, it contains a weaker statement of the supremacy principle than the failed Treaty establishing a Constitution. However, the majority of the failed Treaty establishing a Constitution was ratified as part of the Lisbon Treaty.[104]

One significant terminological change was to the 'European Community Treaty'. This was renamed the 'Treaty on the Functioning of the European Union' or TFEU. This retained two treaties as the constitutional basis of the EU: the TEU and TFEU. As the Treaty of Lisbon was the most recent general treaty, we will look at this in more detail than the previous ones, under these headings: (a) general constitutional principles, (b) institutions, (c) law-making or legislation, (d) competences, (e) the Area of Freedom, Security and Justice, and (f) the UK opt-outs.

....

104 Ibid 700–701.

3.3.10.2 GENERAL CONSTITUTIONAL PRINCIPLES

The Treaty of Lisbon is *somewhat disorganised* in its presentation of general constitutional principles. Some are in the TEU and some are in the TFEU. This is also reflected in the organisation or naming of different sections of the two treaties. Whereas the term 'Title' is used to divide up the TEU into different sections, the TFEU contains sections called both 'Titles' and 'Parts'. The TEU includes the Union's objectives (Article 5 TEU); the principle of conferral (indicating the limits of EU competences) (Article 5 TEU); respect for fundamental rights (Title 1), democratic principles upon which the Union is founded (Title II); the general provisions on external action and specific provisions on the CFSP (Title V) (bulk of TEU) (although some aspects of external action are in the TFEU);[105] and final provisions, dealing with legal personality, amendments of the treaties, accession to/withdrawal from the Union (Title VI).

The TFEU contains the principles of sex equality, data protection, protection of the environment (Part One); non-discrimination and Union citizenship (Part Two); substantive provisions on Union policies and internal actions (Part Three); association of overseas countries and territories (Part Four); external action by the Union (other than the CFSP) (Part Five); and more detailed provisions on the functioning of the Union's institutions, arrangements governing finances, detailed rules on enhanced cooperation (Part Six).

KEY LEARNING POINT

ORGANISATION OF THE TREATY OF LISBON

The Treaty of Lisbon does not achieve a very clear organisation of constitutional principles: some are in the TEU and some are in the TFEU.

An important difference as to constitutional principles concerns the doctrine of supremacy. An express *supremacy/primacy* clause is not included in the Lisbon Treaty as compared to the Constitutional Treaty. Instead, the Treaty of Lisbon refers to case law of the ECJ and to the Council Legal Service's opinion on supremacy of *Community* law in Declaration No. 17 annexed to the Final Act. In other words, supremacy is almost smuggled into the treaty. It seems that this may have been to avoid the problem of national rejections of the Constitutional Treaty for ceding too much sovereignty. The way in which the Lisbon Treaty does this, however, leaves room for doubt as to the exact scope of the supremacy doctrine. This is because the reference in Declaration No. 17 refers to EC law, i.e. to the first pillar pre-Lisbon, leaving open the question as to what extent supremacy applies to the CFSP and criminal law cooperation under the Lisbon Treaty.

---

105 Remember that 'external action' differs from, although it can overlap with, the Common Foreign and Security Policy. The expression 'external action' refers to the competence of the EU to exercise foreign relations where common policies have been adopted internally by the Member States, e.g. external aspects of the Common Commercial Policy.

KEY LEARNING POINT

THE DOCTRINE OF THE SUPREMACY OF EU LAW AND
THE LISBON TREATY

An express *supremacy/primacy* clause is not included in the Lisbon Treaty as compared to the Constitutional Treaty. Instead, the Treaty of Lisbon refers to case law of the ECJ and to the Council Legal Service's opinion on supremacy of *Community* law in Declaration No. 17 annexed to the Final Act.

3.3.10.3 INSTITUTIONS

The Treaty of Lisbon did not make major changes to the institutions. These are the main changes:

- The *European Council* (Article 15 TEU) has the same essential role as before of defining general political and policy objectives, but it is given some 'quasi-legislative powers',[106] such as deciding the future composition of the European Parliament and of the Commission relative to the size of the Member States.[107] The rotating presidency is brought to an end, with a new role of President elected by the European Council for 2.5 years (Article 15 TEU).[108] The President has no independent powers, but has a role as a coordinator and spokesperson.
- The *Council (of Ministers)* (Article 16 TEU) will have two configurations, General Affairs and Foreign Affairs, with a presidency rotated amongst the Member States every six months as had been the case before. It retains its central legislative role through the co-decision procedure, re-named the 'ordinary legislative procedure'.
- The *European Parliament*'s role remains the same.
- The *European Commission*'s role remains the same also,[109] but a new position of High Representative for Foreign Affairs is created (Article 18 TEU), which takes over from the role of the Commissioner for External Relations and the previous High Representative for the Common Foreign and Security Policy. The High Representative for Foreign Affairs is to sit in both the Council (of Ministers) as chairperson for both general external relations and the CFSP matters,[110] but is also to be a Vice-President of the Commission[111] and is to take part in the work of the European Council.[112] However, the role is a coordinating one only, although the High Representative does have a right to propose new policies.

....

106 See Dougan (n 103) 626–27.
107 See art 14(2) TEU regarding the European Parliament and arts 17(5) TEU and 244 TFEU regarding the Commission.
108 Article 15 TEU.
109 Following a referendum in Ireland on the Lisbon Treaty, it was agreed that each Member State could appoint (at least) one Commissioner, a practice that the Treaty of Lisbon proposed to end in favour of a system of rotation, but subject to decision by the European Council (art 17(5) TEU).
110 Ibid art 18(3).
111 Ibid art 18(4).
112 Ibid art 15(2).

3.3.10.4 LAW-MAKING

Law-making covers all of the activities of the EU except the CFSP. In the CFSP, it seems that decisions are taken at the level of policy, not at the level of legislation (this is also generally the case in national systems, when it comes to foreign policy).

> KEY LEARNING POINT
> ....
>
> **LEGISLATIVE BASES AFTER THE TREATY OF LISBON**
> Under the Treaty of Lisbon, no legislative bases are in the TEU; all are in the TFEU.

The TEU contains general provisions on enhanced cooperation (Title IV), while the details of how these will work are in the TFEU (Part Six).

> **EXPLAINING** THE LAW
> _____
>
> **THE LISBON TREATY AND THE LEGISLATIVE PROCESS**
> The Treaty of Lisbon did not introduce dramatic changes to law-making here. It re-named co-decision as the *ordinary legislative method*. It abolished the peculiar legal instruments under the existing second pillar to be replaced by 'decisions', which will become a generic legal instrument for the EU, but which should be considered distinct when arising under CFSP.[113] Generally speaking, national governments do not 'enact' foreign policy by legislation, and it seems there is no reason why the EU should be different. There is perhaps scope for doubt about this and it awaits ECJ interpretation. The distinct legal instruments under the existing third pillar were also abolished.

The following are among the main changes to law-making made by the Treaty of Lisbon:

- The separate second and third pillar instruments were abolished in favour of unified instruments for Union as a whole.
- The Commission retains the right of initiative except when the treaties state otherwise.[114] This provision for exceptions is an innovation, the main example is regarding police and judicial cooperation in criminal matters, when one quarter of the Member States may initiate.[115]
- A new right of popular initiative is established, whereby if 1 million citizens sign a petition, a new law may be proposed (Article 11(4) TEU).
- The co-decision procedure is renamed the ordinary legislative procedure (Article 294 TFEU).

....

113 Dougan (n 103) 624.
114 Article 17(2) TEU and art 289 TFEU.
115 Article 76 TFEU. See also art 289(4) TFEU.

EXPLAINING THE LAW

ESTABLISHING THE ORDINARY LEGISLATIVE PROCEDURE

As well as renaming the co-decision procedure the ordinary procedure, the Treaty of Lisbon extended its application to, e.g. agricultural policy,[116] the common commercial policy;[117] and across all of the Area of Freedom, Security and Justice.[118] Even before the Treaty of Lisbon, the co-decision procedure was the most common, and since the Treaty of Maastricht, when it was introduced, each treaty extended its use. Since the Treaty of Lisbon, the ordinary procedure, as its name suggests, is used in the large majority of the treaty. The ordinary procedure established the Council (of Ministers) and the European Parliament as equal in law-making, in effect, creating a bicameral legislature. We will look at this further in Chapter 4. Exceptions to the ordinary legislative procedure are called *special legislative procedures*.

– *Special legislative procedures* are any method of passing legislation other than the ordinary legislative method. Generally, these procedures require unanimity in the Council (of Ministers), instead of qualified majority voting, and either just consultation or straightforward assent by the European Parliament (like the pre-existing consultation and assent procedures for passing legislation). Provision is made for some of these special procedures to transition to the ordinary legislative method, under what are called '*passarelle* clauses' (there is a general *passarelle* clause in Article 48(7) TEU). The general *passarelle* clause requires unanimity in the Council (of Ministers), the consent of the European Parliament, and a provision is also made for a veto by national parliaments. In some provisions, 'emergency breaks' are established, whereby Member States can exercise a veto where fundamental national interests are affected (e.g. Article 48 TFEU re social security system). We will look at this in more detail in Chapter 4.
– What is in some respects a somewhat confusing *distinction is drawn between legislative and non-legislative acts.*[119] We will also look at this in more detail in Chapter 4.

3.3.10.5 COMPETENCES

For the most part, competences are not greatly changed by the Treaty of Lisbon. The principle of conferral is retained (Article 5(1) TEU). However, there is an attempt to define different categories of competence, depending on the degree of competence

....

116 Article 43 TFEU, previously subject to cooperation procedure, see art 37 ECT.
117 Article 207 TFEU, previously the European Parliament was uninvolved under art 133 ECT.
118 Title V TFEU.
119 Ibid art 290.

transferred to the EU or, conversely, retained by the Member States. Articles 2–6 TFEU define for the first time meaning of exclusive, shared and supporting competences, with indicative lists. This generally does not change competences compared to the situation prior to the Treaty of Lisbon, but it does attempt to be more systematic about competences. There are some new competences, such as complementary competence regarding space[120] and complementary competence regarding sport.[121] We will look at this in more detail in Chapter 7.

One significant innovation concerns the principle of subsidiarity, which is retained in Article 4(2) TFEU, but strengthened in how it is applied. A Protocol on the application of subsidiarity and proportionality establishes a system whereby national parliaments are notified of EU legislative proposals and can ask for their re-consideration.[122] Notably, national parliaments were not given a veto. Although it is praiseworthy as an attempt to enhance the legitimacy of EU law-making by connecting it more with national political authority, it remains to be seen how this works in practice. We will also look at this further in Chapter 7.

3.3.10.6 AREA OF FREEDOM, SECURITY AND JUSTICE

KEY LEARNING POINT

OVERLAPPING TERMINOLOGY CONCERNING THE AREA OF FREEDOM, SECURITY AND JUSTICE

It has often been observed that the EU legal and political system is notably complex. One aspect where this is certainly true concerns somewhat overlapping and confusing terminology. An example is the terminology on the Area of Freedom, Security and Justice (AFSJ). This term is used to describe what used to be more commonly known as Justice and Home Affairs (JHA). The term JHA was introduced at Maastricht to describe the then third pillar, which consisted of two aspects: (i) criminal justice cooperation; and (ii) cooperation in the area of visa, asylum and immigration. At the Treaty of Amsterdam, the second aspect of JHA – visa, asylum and immigration – was transferred to the first pillar. This meant that the term JHA now covered the third pillar and an aspect of the first pillar. The term JHA was later superseded by AFSJ, although the term JHA is sometimes used still by the institutions.

Under the Treaty of Lisbon, Title VI TEU was amalgamated with Title IV ECT on border checks, asylum, immigration, and judicial cooperation in civil matters to create Title IV TFEU.

---

120 Ibid art 189.
121 Ibid art 12.
122 See arts 4–6 of the Protocol.

EXPLAINING THE LAW

THIRD PILLAR WAS MADE (MOSTLY) SUPRANATIONAL AT THE TREATY OF LISBON

One of the key changes made by the Treaty of Lisbon was to make the third pillar a part of the standard, supranational framework of the treaties. This means that the ordinary legislative procedure now applies to criminal justice, as does compulsory jurisdiction of the ECJ. However, some elements of inter-governmentalism remain concerning criminal justice. A special legislative procedure would apply to certain competences (e.g. on default powers to facilitate free movement[123] and cooperation between national law enforcement agencies[124]). Further, where the ordinary legislative procedure does apply, there is provision for an emergency break mechanism regarding judicial cooperation in criminal matters and the definition of criminal offences and sanctions.[125] Note also that most aspects of criminal law are still within national and not EU competence.

Article 276 TFEU excludes the jurisdiction of the ECJ from national criminal justice agencies.

Article 86 TFEU contains a legal basis for a potentially far-reaching Office of a European Public Prosecutor, with competence to prosecute in the courts of the Member States crimes against the financial interests of the EU (and its competence could be extended to cover cross-border crimes of a serious nature). However, unanimity is required to establish this Office, although provision is made for enhanced cooperation.

3.3.10.7 UK OPT-OUTS

An opt-in and opt-out system for the UK and Ireland regarding the Schengen system is extended by the Treaty of Lisbon to the AFSJ as a whole, under Articles 5(3)–(5) of the Schengen Protocol. This is interesting, as it is an example of a loosening of competences by the EU, rather than a strengthening of it.

The primary UK opt-out remains, of course, from the single currency. Article 5(2) TFEU, for example, notes that specific provisions shall apply to those Member States whose currency is the Euro. Articles 136–138 TFEU contains provisions specific to just those countries that use the Euro, while Article 282(4) TFEU notes that those Member States whose currency is not the Euro, and their central banks, shall retain their powers in monetary matters.

....

123 Article 77(3) TFEU, involving consultation only with the European Parliament.
124 Ibid art 87(3), involving consultation with the European Parliament, other than regarding the Schengen *acquis*.
125 Ibid arts 82(3) and 88(3), respectively.

3.3.11 TREATY ON STABILITY, COORDINATION AND GOVERNANCE IN THE ECONOMIC AND MONETARY UNION (OR 'FISCAL COMPACT') 2012

This treaty[126] is different to all the other treaties above in that, technically, it is not an 'EU treaty' because it has not been ratified by all the Member States.

KEY LEARNING POINT

NOT ALL 27 MEMBER STATES RATIFIED THE FISCAL COMPACT (FC)
Only 25 of the (then) 27 Member States were willing to ratify it, the UK and the Czech Republic opting out. For that reason, it is not fully an EU treaty, although it makes use of the institutions of the EU.

It is designed to tighten fiscal coordination and spending restraint in the Member States of the Eurozone, that is, to prevent Eurozone countries having large budget deficits. This had already been agreed at the Treaty of Maastricht in the Stability and Growth Pact, as we will see in Chapter 17, but enforcement was weak. The most significant provisions prevent Member States having a budget deficit and from allowing their national debt to exceed 60 per cent of GDP. Although outside the framework of the treaties, it has a very significant element of supranationalism in the role given to the ECJ to police compliance with the treaty and it requires national implementation at constitutional level.

Article 8 states that the ECJ shall have jurisdiction in two situations: (i) if a Member State ('Contracting party') believes another Member State has failed to comply with Article 3(2), it may bring a proceeding, in which case the ECJ may order compliance; (ii) if a Member State believes another Member State has failed to comply with an ECJ judgment under paragraph 1, it may bring a further proceeding, in which case the ECJ may impose a fine, as under Article 260 TFEU, of not more than 1 per cent of GDP. Normally, it seems the Commission will have initiated a report, but this is not necessary for a Member State to bring a case under either paragraph.

Article 3 FC is concerned with budget balances and surpluses: essentially a balance or surplus must be achieved. Article 3(2) FC is the implementing provision:

– it mandates the establishment of a 'correction mechanism' if the target is not reached
– it refers to an independent monitoring system at national level, but also states that the prerogative of national Parliaments is to be fully respected.

A key issue here is what criteria are the ECJ to use to determine an acceptable national implementation of a correction mechanism? Some are set out explicitly in the treaty:

– It is stated that the FC shall not encroach on Union competence, and that the TEU and TFEU have primacy (Article 2(2) FC and Article 3(1) FC). This is a conflict of

---

126 Treaty on Stability, Coordination and Governance in the Economic and Monetary Union, Brussels, 2nd March 2011.

norms rule. Without this rule, if the FC did extend the TEU and/or TFEU, the effect would be to bind the UK and the Czech Republic to a treaty they did not agree to. This creates an interesting situation: to give the FC wider impact, the ECJ would have to define the TEU and TFEU more narrowly. This the ECJ rarely does; its consistent tendency is to do exactly the opposite.

- A technical criterion is provided that appears to depend on economic expertise in setting an objective for national budget deficits. The rule under Article 3(1)(a) FC requiring a balance or surplus shall be deemed to be respected if the annual structural balance of the general government is at its country-specific medium-term objective, as defined in the revised Stability and Growth Pact, with a lower limit of a structural deficit of 0.5 per cent of the GDP at market prices (Article 3(1)(b) FC).

EXPLAINING THE LAW

JURISDICTION OF THE ECJ UNDER THE FISCAL COMPACT

- if the annual deficit of a Member State is greater than 1 per cent or 0.5 per cent of GDP at market prices (Article 3(1)(d) FC)
- if overall national debt of a Member State is greater than 60 per cent of GDP, the Member State must reduce it at a rate of 1/20 a year (Article 4 FC).

It is not as clear if the ECJ has jurisdiction to determine if compliance has been achieved with the Article 5 FC partnership programme as determined by EU law.[127] Article 8 FC, which confers ECJ jurisdictions, only refers to Article 3(2). However, Article 3(2) refers to Article 3(1), which refers to the maximum budget deficit rule, and the correction programme in Article 5 relates to the latter. So the ECJ could well decide, on a broad reading, that it has jurisdiction over Article 5 also.

Article 5 applies when a State fails to comply with the overall national deficit ceiling of 60 per cent of GDP.

Another point of much potential importance is that there is provision for the correction mechanism for current budget deficits under Article 3 to apply in an anticipatory way, i.e., under Article 3(1)(e) FC in the event of significant observed deviations from the medium-term objective for the current budget deficit or the *adjustment path* towards it. Depending on how broadly this was interpreted, considerable scope exists for EU intrusion in the fiscal policies of the Member States. A 'get-out clause' for exceptional circumstances is provided for the Member States where there is an unusual event outside of their control, so long as the exception does not endanger medium–term fiscal stability (Article 3(3)(b)).

....

127 Article 126 TFEU deals with the avoidance of government deficits and the role of the Commission and Council (of Ministers) in monitoring this.

ANALYSING THE LAW

HOW THE ECJ MIGHT EXERCISE ITS JURISDICTION UNDER THE FISCAL COMPACT

It remains to be seen how the ECJ will approach its jurisdiction. The ECJ is not a court that generally takes a modest view of its own function. It could adopt a narrow approach, where it would defer to economic expertise and only intervene in cases of a manifest breach, but the potential is there for the ECJ to adopt a broader supervisory role in economic matters that it does not seem especially suited to as a court. Amongst the specific possible consequences of a broad interpretation by the ECJ are:

- The reference to national Parliaments (in Article 3(2) FC), would be interpreted as *not* preserving their competences, as the ECJ could argue that the extent of national parliaments' powers depends on the interpretation of the competences of the EU institutions first. For example, the preamble *and its reference to the idea of an ever-closer economic union could be taken to negate preservation* through interpretation based on a high level of generality.
- The exceptional circumstances rule could be minimised so as to make little practical difference.
- The ECJ could decide Article 5 FC partnership programme does not go far enough and require specific measures of an economic nature to fulfil it.

Despite this potentially very significant role for the ECJ under the Fiscal Compact, inter-governmental elements are still prominent:

- The preamble refers to a desire to make more use of enhanced cooperation, suggestive of a looser public international law approach (not one strict supranational style fits all).
- The Commission has reduced enforcement power in one important respect: it has no standing to bring an enforcement action. Only other contracting Member States can sue, and it is likely to be highly sensitive politically to sue. On the other hand, the extent of Commission powers regarding the budget deficit correction procedure (e.g. under Article 5) is significant.
- Article 7 FC has a potentially very significant saving clause allowing Member States to evade European Commission proposals. It states:

This obligation [to comply with European Commission proposals] shall not apply where it is established among the Contracting Parties whose currency is the Euro that a qualified majority of them . . . is opposed to the decision proposed or recommended.

So the Member States can reverse a Commission decision. Depending on how much use was made of Article 7 FC, inter-governmentalism could be increased, reducing the powers of the EU institutions.

EXPLAINING THE LAW

COMPARING BUDGET SUPERVISION UNDER THE MAASTRICHT TREATY AND UNDER THE FISCAL COMPACT

Compared to the Treaty of Maastricht, the Fiscal Compact gives the ECJ a much more important role in supervising if the Member States are sticking to the budget rules. Under the Treaty of Maastricht, the ECJ has no role in this. It is unusual for a court to have close supervisory powers of budgetary matters. In addition, the Fiscal Compact requires much tighter and more binding national implementation.

3.3.12 TREATY ESTABLISHING THE EUROPEAN STABILITY MECHANISM 2012 (ESM)

The ESM Treaty is designed to provide a safety fund to help members of the Eurozone in financial difficulty, e.g. who are in danger of defaulting on their national debts. It supplements the Fiscal Compact (FC). It will function somewhat like the International Monetary Fund,[128] except it is particular to the Eurozone countries. It complements the Fiscal Compact and will only be ratified by those Member States that are in the Eurozone,[129] although all the then 27 Member States ratified the amendment to the TFEU that put the ESM Treaty into effect.

The ESM Treaty will help finance 'bailouts' of Eurozone countries in danger of defaulting; the rationale is that a default by one Eurozone country would undermine confidence in the Euro overall and, therefore, threaten the stability of all Eurozone members. It came into force when Member States representing 90 per cent of its capital have ratified it,[130] in September 2012. The fund is to obtain its capital by proportionate contributions from the Member States.[131]

Although it is an inter-governmental treaty, there are some notable elements of supranationalism. In particular, the Board of Governors of the ESM has considerable powers in some circumstances, including that:

-   It may amend the treaty to accommodate new Member States.[132]
-   It may require an increase in capital from the Member States and is to review the total capital per Member State at least every 5 years.[133]

....

128 Recital (8) ESM Treaty.
129 Ibid recital (7).
130 Ibid art 48. The ESM Treaty required the European Council to exercise its power to amend Article 136 TFEU: see European Council Decision of 25 March 2011 amending Article 136 of the Treaty on the Functioning of the European Union with regard to a stability mechanism for Member States whose currency is the Euro, OL 91, 06.04.2011 p. 1.
131 Ibid arts 2(3) and 8(5).
132 Ibid art 7(4).
133 Ibid art 10(1).

THE DISTINCT NATURE OF THE FISCAL COMPACT AND THE ESM TREATY

The Fiscal Compact and the ESM Treaty are different to the other treaties in one very important way: they have not been ratified by all the EU Member States. They are thus referred to as 'inter-governmental' treaties: inter-governmental means that they were adopted by the Member States simply as States in international law, not as Member of the EU. In discussion of the EU, it is sometimes forgotten that there is an alternative to cooperation through the methods and institutions of the EU: that is, normal cooperation in international law through treaty-making. However, the two treaties are clearly related to EU law and the Fiscal Compact sets out an objective of being integrated into EU law. The two treaties make partial use of the normal institutional methods of the EU. The Fiscal Compact, in particular, gives an important role to the ECJ. We look at this in more detail in Chapter 3.

In November 2012, the ECJ addressed the issue of the competence of the EU to conclude the ESM Treaty, following a preliminary reference from the Supreme Court of Ireland.[134] The ESM Treaty had been implemented under Article 136 TFEU, which provides for measures to be adopted that are specific to the Member States who use the Euro as their currency. Specifically, those Member States on the basis of the simplified revision procedure under Article 48(6) TEU, which allows for simplified revision of Part III TFEU on internal Union policies and the internal market, inserted an Article 136(3) TFEU relating to the establishment of a stability mechanism.

The ECJ concluded that the revision did fall within Part Three TFEU on internal policy, and not under Part One TFEU on monetary policy (this is somewhat debatable, and we will look at this again in Chapter 7 on competence). Further, the ECJ held that the insertion of Article 136(3) did not increase EU competences, since the Member States could have done the same thing prior to the TFEU. In effect, here, the ECJ seems to see simplified revision as a type of enhanced cooperation.

CONFUSION AND COMPLEXITY IN TREATY RENUMBERING

One of the more confusing aspects of EU law is the constant renumbering, and the use of different or inconsistent styles or patterns of designating individual treaty articles (a mixture of letters and numbers can sometimes be used, as well as different ways in each treaty of indicating sub-headings: the SEA is especially

---

134 Case C–370/12 *Pringle v Government of Ireland* (27 November 2012, not yet reported).

inaccessible on this point). An example is given above concerning the special legal instruments that existed under the third pillar. In addition, each revising treaty itself is merely amending treaty for the other treaties, meaning each amendment entails two sets of numbering (the amending article of the amending treaty, e.g. Maastricht or Amsterdam, and the amended article of the founding treaties, e.g. of EURATOM, the TFEU or TEU as they now are after amendment).

NB In the summaries of each treaty above, the numbers of articles at the time of that treaty are given. For current numberings of the TEU and TFEU articles, see, as well as the section above on the Treaty of Lisbon, the other chapters of the book.

3.4 ACCESSION TREATIES

A final treaty issue to mention more briefly is the use of accession treaties to make the legal changes necessary for a new Member State to join the EU. Accession treaties are now governed by Article 49 TEU. This includes making minor adjustments to the institutions, for example, to the Council (of Ministers) and the system of weighted voting. They require unanimous consent of the Member States and the assent of the European Parliament. They are not politically problematic in practice and do not require significant constitutional amendments in the other Member States. The most recent has been the Accession Treaty for Croatia, ratified in 2012, to enable Croatia to join in 2013.

KEY LEARNING POINT

A CHRONOLOGY OF ACCESSION TREATIES

Treaties of Accession	Date of signature	Entry into force	Official Journal
Treaty of Accession of the United Kingdom, Ireland and Denmark	22.1.1972	1.1.1973	OJ L73 of 27.3.1972 at 5
Treaty of Accession of Greece	28.5.1979	1.1.1981	OJ L291 of 19.11.1979 at 17
Treaty of Accession of Spain and Portugal	12.6.1985	1.1.1986	OJ L302 of 15.11.1985

Treaty of Accession of Austria, Finland and Sweden	24.6.1994	1.1.1995	OJ C 241 of 29.8.1994
Treaty of Accession of the ten new Member States	16.4.2003	1.5.2004	OJ L236 of 23.9.2003
Treaty of Accession of Bulgaria and Romania	25.4.2005	1.1.2007	OJ L157 of 21.6.2005

And most recently . . .

Treaty of Accession of Croatia	05.12.2011	1.7.2013	OJ L112 of 24.04.2012

3.5 CONCLUSION

The three founding Communities have been amended both in form and substance. There are now two treaties: TEU and TFEU. The competences of the EU, as the Communities combined have been re-named, have gone well beyond the core idea of a common market to include a wide range of associated competences in matters of cross-border concern. This cooperation includes areas very sensitive from the point of view of national sovereignty, especially some aspects of criminal justice and foreign and security policy. The scope of supranationalism has been extended and it has taken over from inter-governmentalism – to some extent, but by no means completely – in important areas: co-decision between the European Parliament and the Council (of Ministers) is now the norm in the form of the ordinary legislative procedure.

Criminal justice retains important elements of inter-governmentalism, and the CFSP is still almost wholly inter-governmental. Competence in criminal justice is still very much subsidiary to the competence and sovereignty of the Member States in this field. Ratification difficulties with EU treaties show that the EU has an on-going legitimacy challenge. It remains to be seen how and if this will ever be overcome to achieve the degree of integration advocates of the Treaty establishing a Constitution unsuccessfully tried to achieve. One frequent criticism made of the EU, its notable complexity, is certainly present in the cumbersome renumbering and rearrangements in treaty revisions.

POINTS TO REVIEW

– The EU was founded as three separate organisations in the 1950s, which even then, however, used common or almost identical institutions.

–   The three founding treaties were the European Coal and Steel Community (ECSC)
    Treaty 1951 (also known as the Treaty of Paris), the European Atomic Energy
    Community (EURATOM) Treaty 1957, and the European Economic Community
    (EEC) Treaty 1957 (also known as the Treaty of Rome). Their similarity was
    recognised by the Merger Treaty 1965, which established that generally each
    Community was to use the same institutions.

–   Following disputes over the powers of the institutions of the Communities relative
    to the powers kept by the Member States, the next treaty reform was not until 1986
    with the Single European Act (SEA). Amongst its major elements, it extended areas
    of competence beyond purely economic matters, launched Economic and Monetary
    Union (EMU), increased the legislative role of the European Parliament through a
    cooperation procedure, and re-established end extended the use of qualified majority
    voting in the Council (of Ministers).

–   The Treaty of Maastricht 1992 represented a further major reform, including by
    introducing the Pillar structure and new inter-governmental areas of cooperation
    in the Common Foreign and Security Policy (CFSP) and Justice and Home
    Affairs (JHA) (criminal justice and visa, asylum, and immigration), establishing the
    legislative method of co-decision, increasing the use of qualified majority voting by
    the Council (of Ministers), and articulating the general principles of conferral and
    subsidiarity.

–   The next two treaty revisions, by the Treaty of Amsterdam 1997 and the Treaty of
    Nice 2001, were evolutions, rather than extensive reforms. They both extended the
    use of co-decision as a legislative method and increased the use of qualified majority
    voting in the Council (of Ministers). The Treaty of Amsterdam formalised the use
    of enhanced cooperation; transferred visa, asylum, and immigration issues to the
    first pillar; and strengthened EMU. The Treaty of Nice mainly made provision for
    enlargement.

–   The Treaty establishing a Constitution for Europe 2004 proved to be too ambitious a
    project of integration to gain democratic acceptance and had to be abandoned due to a
    lack of popular support, despite its careful propagation by political élites. However, much
    of it was re-enacted by the Treaty of Lisbon, which was eventually ratified in 2009.

–   The Treaty of Lisbon, amongst its most significant reforms, established co-decision
    as the ordinary legislative procedure and further extended its use, extended
    qualified majority voting in the Council (of Ministers), subjected criminal justice
    to the supranational method (although not fully, including as a result of opt-outs
    for Ireland and the UK), abolished the pillar structure, whilst also retaining the
    inter-governmental character of the CFSP and inter-governmental elements in
    criminal justice, introduced a warning system for national parliaments concerning
    subsidiarity, and established the posts of President of the European Council and High
    Representative for Foreign Affairs.

— The two most recent treaties, the Fiscal Compact (FC) 2012 and European Stability Mechanism (ESM) Treaty 2012, were designed to deal with the crisis of excess debt among some Eurozone Member States. They try to do this through strengthening supranational control over national fiscal policy in Eurozone Member States. The FC establishes as legally binding and subject to ECJ jurisdiction a balanced budget rule and maximum limit of 60 per cent of GDP as a national debt. The ESM Treaty provides for a loan or bailout facility for Eurozone countries that have excess debts. The UK and the Czech Republic refused to endorse this transfer of sovereignty. As a result, the first of two treaties, the Fiscal Compact, had to be ratified as an international treaty outside the EU framework, albeit using elements of EU institutions.

CHAPTER GLOSSARY

Accession Treaty is a treaty ratified by all EU Member States making the legal changes necessary for admission of a new Member State to the EU. An Accession Treaty, for example, modifies the weighting of votes in the Council (of Ministers) for the purpose of qualified majority voting and makes other changes to the institutions to accommodate the new Member State.

Acquis Communautaire is a term used prior to the Lisbon Treaty to describe the overall body of binding EU law.

Area of Freedom, Security and Justice tends to be used to describe what used to be referred to as Justice and Home Affairs (see below).

Common Foreign and Security Policy (CFSP) refers to cooperation in the area of foreign policy and defence in the EU. Cooperation in these areas is still wholly inter-governmental.

'Empty chair crisis' refers to the refusal by France for a period from 1965–1966 to take up its role as chairman of the Council (of Ministers), owing to French President de Gaulle's opposition to European Commission attempts to increase integration. It resulted in the Luxembourg Accord.

Enhanced cooperation refers to the legal possibility for some Member States to move ahead with increased integration, even if some of the Member States decided not to be included. A general provision for enhanced cooperation was introduced by the Treaty of Amsterdam and has been amended since.

European Monetary Union (EMU) refers to the adoption of a single currency by EU Member States.

Justice and Home Affairs (JHA) refers to the third pillar between the Treaty of Maastricht and Amsterdam. It describes two areas of EU cooperation: (i) criminal justice and (ii) asylum, visa, and immigration. Although the term is sometimes still used, it has been largely replaced by the term 'Area of Freedom, Security and Justice' (AFSJ). The second elements transferred to the First Pillar at the Treaty of Amsterdam.

Lex specialis is a principle of legal interpretation and norm conflict resolution that more specific provisions should prevail over more general provisions. It is relevant in this chapter, for example, in relating the EURATOM Treaty to what is now the TFEU.

Luxembourg Accord refers to a political agreement by the Member States following the Empty Chair Crisis to permit use of a veto by a Member State where its national interests were sufficiently affected, even where the treaties provided for majority voting in the Council.

Masters of the treaties is a term used to describe the idea of the exercise of control over the pace of treaty change. A degree of debate has occurred as to the relative degree of control of the Member States relative to the EU institutions over treaty change.

'Pillars' is the term used to describe the three divisions of the EU instituted by the Treaty of Maastricht. The first pillar consisted of the European Community Treaty. The second pillar consisted of the Common Foreign and Security Policy (CFSP). The third pillar consisted of Justice and Home Affairs (JHA) and later specifically (after the Treaty of Amsterdam) criminal justice matters. The legal character of the first pillar was supranational, whereas the legal character of the second and third pillars was inter-governmental. The term 'pillar' was abandoned by the Treaty of Lisbon.

Qualified Majority Voting refers to the voting method most commonly used in the Council (of Ministers), whereby the Member States have weighted votes related to (but not fully proportionately) population size.

Schengen refers to enhanced cooperation in the area of border controls and the exchange of security information.

Single European Act 1986 refers to the first major treaty revision after the founding treaties of the 1950s. It was a treaty, despite the use of the term 'Act' in its title.

Soft law is an expression referring to legal sources that are not legally binding, but that may have some legal influence or influence on the behaviour of legal actors.

Variable geometry is another term, sometimes used in academic literature, for 'enhanced cooperation'.

TAKING THINGS FURTHER

D Curtin 'The constitutional structure of the Union: a Europe of bits and pieces' (1993) 30(1) *Common Market Law Review* 17–69 This article discusses the nature of the EU as a constitutional system following the increased role of inter-governmentalism following the Treaty of Maastricht.

B de Witte 'Rule of change in international law: how special is the EC?' (1994) 25 *Netherlands Yearbook of International Law* 299–333 This article provides an explanation of how the adoption of new treaties by the EU Member States relies on the normal process of treaty adoption in public international law.

T F Cusack 'A tale of two treaties: an assessment of the EURATOM Treaty in relation to the EEC Treaty' (2003) 40(1) *Common Market Law Review* 117–42 This article discusses the relationship between the EEC Treaty (later the EC Treaty and now the TFEU) and the EURATOM Treaty. It includes discussion of the idea of EURATOM as *lex specialis*.

J Shaw 'Flexibility in a reorganised and simplified treaty' (2003) 40(2) *Common Market Law Review* 279–311 This article discusses the role of enhanced cooperation and relates it to the idea of simplifying the overly complex presentation of legal provisions in the EU treaties.

4

CHAPTER 4
THE INSTITUTIONAL WORKING OF THE EU: INSTITUTIONS AND LAW-MAKING

This chapter examines the different institutions of the EU, including how laws are made, explaining legislation in the context of the overall role of the EU institutions. It focuses on the European Council, the Council, the European Commission, the Court of Justice of the EU, the Court of Auditors and the European Central Bank. It explains the different types of legislation and the different ways legislation can be passed. Finally, it analyses the 'horizontal' separation of powers between the EU institutions, i.e. how the institutions interact at EU level. It is a common tendency to consider the EU to be distinct from national contexts on this point: a traditional separation of powers analysis has been substituted in the EU by the concept of 'institutional balance'. The chapter concludes that a separation of powers analysis is preferable to the vaguer idea of institutional balance.

AS YOU READ . . .

The key questions that will be answered in this chapter are as follows:

— What are the main institutions making up the EU legal system?

— How are laws made in the EU? What is the role of each of the institutions in the law-making process and which have the most power in the process?

— What are the main differences between ordinary legislative method and the special methods? What are the reasons for the adoption of special legislative methods?

— What is the role of non-legislative acts or 'quasi-legislation' in the EU system? What role does comitology play regarding implementing non-legislative acts?

— What are the main ways in which the EU institutions interact with each other?

— What is the overall horizontal separation of powers in the EU?

4.1 INTRODUCTION

Law-making is a key aspect of any legal system. As noted in Chapter 3, law-making can occur in all of the activities of the EU except the Common Foreign and Security Policy (CFSP). Decisions in the EU are not always made by legislation. Just as at national level, some decisions are made on a largely administrative basis, not by a binding legal instrument. Generally speaking, however, any acts by institutions in a legal system will need to have some legal basis. The civil service make many decisions that are not set out in legislation, but the authority of the civil service to make those decisions is usually set out in a prior legal source (usually legislation, although in the United Kingdom, the royal prerogative is also important here). The EU has its own institutions with legal authority to carry out certain activities. These institutions include a legislature.

In this chapter, we will look, first, at the institutions of the EU and their powers and, second, at how legislation or law-making occurs. Law-making in the EU is somewhat more complicated than at national level, but fundamentally it is a similar process. Many of the institutions of the EU are also a variation on the institutions of government found in states.

> KEY LEARNING POINTS
> ....
>
> **SOME GENERAL POINTS TO HIGHLIGHT**
> – EU law is *complicated* compared to national law, e.g. in a national system, there is usually one way of passing legislation, whereas in the EU there are several different ways of passing several different types of legislation. However, the Lisbon Treaty has gone some way to simplifying this part of how the EU works.
> – Do not mix up the EU or any of its organs/institutions with the Council of Europe (revise Chapter 2, especially the final part).
> – Remember that in EU law, the term 'primary legislation' refers to the founding and amending treaties agreed by the Member States. Primary legislation in the EU can be compared to a constitution in a national system. The term 'secondary legislation' refers to legislative acts of the institutions: secondary legislation in the EU can be compared to Acts of Parliament in a national system.

4.2 THE MAIN INSTITUTIONS OF THE EU

The *main* institutions of the EU are outlined in this section. The focus is on the primary institutions established by the treaties. There exists quite a range of specialist bodies and agencies established usually by secondary legislation, but also some by the treaties (of the latter, e.g. Committee of the Regions and Social and Economic Committee), which have mainly consultative or quite narrow roles.

4.2.1 THE EUROPEAN COUNCIL

This body consists of all of the heads of government, along with the president of the European Commission.[1] Usually, the head of government is the prime minister. However, e.g. in France, the president is the head of government. The European Council decides the broad policy direction of the EU.[2]

> KEY LEARNING POINT
>
> **FUNCTION OF THE EUROPEAN COUNCIL**
> The non-legislative role of the European Council is clear from Article 68 TFEU, which states that: 'The European Council shall define the strategic guidelines for legislative and operational planning'.

In the past, whichever Member State held the presidency of the EU also chaired or presided over the European Council. Since the Treaty of Lisbon, the European Council has a permanent chairperson, who is appointed by the European Council itself for a term of 2.5 years.[3] The first such appointed president of the European Council was Herman Van Rompuy, at the time prime minister of Belgium, who was appointed in November 2009 and took up the position on 1 January 2010. The second president, after Herman Van Rompuy's appointment was renewed for a second term, is Donald Tusk, former prime minister of Poland, who began his term of office on 1 December 2014 following his appointment in August 2014.

Somewhat surprisingly, the European Council was not one of the original institutions of the Communities when founded in the 1950s. The founding treaties seemed to view the presidency of the Commission as the 'leader' of the (then) Community institutions.

EXPLAINING THE LAW

LEGITIMACY OF THE EUROPEAN COUNCIL RELATIVE TO THE EUROPEAN COMMISSION
It could be said that the president of the Commission and the Commissioners are appointed, rather than elected, whereas the European Council consists of nationally elected heads of government (most prime ministers are elected by Parliament when they command a majority of support in Parliament). On this basis, the European Council, therefore, has more democratic legitimacy than the Commission. However, the president of the Commission has a degree of

---

1 Article 15(2) TEU. The High Representative of the EU for Foreign Affairs and Security Policy also takes part in the work of the European Council.
2 Ibid art 15(1).
3 Ibid art 15(5).

democratic legitimacy in that he or she is appointed by the European Council, acting by a qualified majority and taking into account the elections to the European Parliament, and the European Council's choice must be approved by the European Parliament (albeit that there is not the same degree of connection with electorates as is the case with nationally elected political figures). In the most recent election, Jean-Claude Juncker was nominated and was appointed as President of the European Commission by the European Council, albeit the issue was put to a vote and the UK and Hungary voted against the appointment. He had the support of the European People's Party, the largest political group in the Parliament.

Although the role of the European Council is not to legislate, but to set the broad policy direction of the EU, in some matters it has powers that might be described as 'quasi-legislative'.[4]

EXPLAINING THE LAW

QUASI-LEGISLATIVE POWERS OF THE EUROPEAN COUNCIL

The European Council has a number of powers that can be described as quasi-legislative:

– In certain matters, the European Council is given a role in the ordinary legislative procedure to try to achieve consensus amongst the Member States when one Member State believes its fundamental interests might be affected by legislation (the ordinary legislative procedure is suspended allowing this to happen). The European Council has the option to refer the matter back to the Council (of Ministers), in which case the ordinary legislative procedure will resume, or it can decide to terminate the procedure or can ask the Commission to submit a new proposal.[5]
– Other powers of the European Council that might be considered quasi-legislative include the power to decide on the configuration of the Council (of Ministers) and on the system of rotating presidencies (Article 236 TFEU, deciding by qualified majority voting), the number of Members of the European Parliament to be allocated to each Member (Article 14(2) TEU, deciding by unanimity and with the consent of the European Parliament) and similarly as regards the number of Commissioners for each Member State (but without needing the consent of the European Parliament) (Article 17(5) and Article 244 TFEU, deciding by unanimity).

....

4   M Dougan 'The Treaty of Lisbon 2007: winning minds, not hearts' (2008) 45 *Common Market Law Review* 617–703 at 626.
5   See e.g. art 45 TFEU on free movement of workers and art 87(3) on police cooperation.

Usually, the European Council reaches decisions by consensus (Article 15(4) TEU), but some provisions require unanimity[6] and QMV.[7] The term 'consensus' is not defined in the treaties. In practice, it amounts to the same thing as unanimity, since determined opposition by one Member State is enough to prevent consensus.

> KEY LEARNING POINT
>
> ....
>
> **SUMMARISING THE OVERALL ROLE OF THE EUROPEAN COUNCIL**
> Article 15(1) TEU well describes the role of the European Council, which consists
> of the heads of government of the Member States (usually prime ministers): 'The
> European Council shall provide the Union with the necessary impetus for its
> development and shall define the general policy directions and priorities thereof.
> It shall not have a legislative function'. Although it does not have a legislative
> function, as noted above, it has what might be described as a quasi-legislative
> function in a small number of matters.

4.2.2 THE COUNCIL (OF MINISTERS)

The Council (of Ministers) consists of government ministers from each Member State, with the same responsibility, acting collectively at EU level, e.g. all ministers for finance and/or trade making decisions regarding the internal market (i.e. its membership varies between types of minister depending on which area of cooperation is being deal with). The primary purpose of the Council (of Ministers) is to participate in passing legislation. Compared to the European Council, the Council (of Ministers) deals with more specific matters in the different areas of EU cooperation. The term 'the Council' is used in the Treaty, but in this textbook, the term 'Council (of Ministers)' is generally used, as it helps to distinguish the Council from the European Council and Council of Europe.

> KEY LEARNING POINT
>
> ....
>
> **FUNCTION OF THE COUNCIL (OF MINISTERS)**
> The primary function of the Council (of Ministers) is to legislate, usually with the
> agreement of a majority of the European Parliament under the ordinary legislative
> procedure (see further below).

As we saw in Chapter 2, gradually the European Parliament was given more legislative power: now, generally speaking, the Council (of Ministers) and the European Parliament together make up the legislature in the EU (and this arrangement could be compared to a bicameral legislature in a national context). In addition to legislating, the Council (of Ministers) is involved in passing the budget with the European Parliament (see further below).

....

6   See e.g. arts 14(2) TEU (above), 17(5) TEU (above), 42 TEU (on the adoption of a common defence policy) and
    art 86(4) TFEU (extension of the competence of a European Public Prosecutor).
7   See e.g. arts 15(5) TEU (on the election of President of the European Council), 17(7) TEU (on the appointment
    of President of the European Commission), 18(1) TEU (on the appointment of High Representative of the EU on
    Foreign Affairs and Security Policy) and art 236 TFEU (on deciding configurations of the Council (of Ministers)) .

KEY LEARNING POINT

ORGANISATION OF THE COUNCIL

The Treaty of Lisbon developed and reformed the Council (of Ministers) in several respects, as well as expanding the use of qualified majority voting. The Council sits in two configurations: 1. General Affairs and 2. Foreign Affairs, but there are currently eight other configurations in use.[8]

The Treaty of Lisbon developed and reformed the Council (of Ministers) in several respects. When dealing with foreign affairs, i.e. when it sits in the Foreign Affairs configuration, the High Representative of the Union for Foreign Affairs and Security Policy attends meetings and votes. However, when sitting in the Foreign Affairs configuration, the Council has no legislative power.[9] As in national systems, foreign affairs is not generally dealt with through legislation (however, foreign affairs can sometimes overlap with other legislative competences see further Chapter 7).

KEY LEARNING POINT

VOTING IN THE COUNCIL

In its decision-making, the Council (of Ministers) is to act by qualified majority voting, unless the treaty specifies otherwise.[10] The basic idea of QMV is that Member States with larger populations have a greater weighting attached to their vote (although not directly proportionate to population size). The details of this are complex in some respects, mainly due to the Ioannina Compromise. The Ioannina Compromise refers to modification of the ordinary legislative procedure whereby the legislative process can be delayed to consider more fully the objections of some Member States (see next).

In its decision-making, the Council (of Ministers) is to act by qualified majority voting, unless the treaty specifies otherwise.[11] The Ioannina Compromise was intended to protect the interests of dissenting countries, especially where a qualified majority made up by the other Member States is slim. As of 1 November 2014, under Article 16(4) TEU, a qualified majority must reach 15 Member States and 55 per cent overall of Members of the Council and must reach 65 per cent of the population

8 Article 16(6) TEU. For information on configurations other than General Affairs and Foreign Affairs, there are eight other configurations currently used, see <http://www.consilium.europa.eu/en/council-eu/configurations/> (last accessed 14 March 2015).

9 Ibid art 24(1).

10 Ibid art 16(3).

11 Ibid.

of the EU. At least four Council members are needed to constitute a blocking minority.[12]

Three periods apply for the purpose of QMV:

1. Until 31 October 2014, the previous arrangement under Article 205 ECT applies.[13] This involves a 'triple threshold' established by the Treaty of Nice, requiring (i) a weighted majority of votes from (ii) a simple majority of Member States (iii) representing at least 62 per cent of the actual Union population.
2. From 1 November 2014 until 31 March 2017, a different process or triple threshold of QMV applies under Article 16(4) TEU (as mentioned above this involves (i) at least 55 per cent of Member States, (ii) comprising at least 15 countries, (iii) representing at least 65 per cent of the actual Union population). In addition, a blocking minority must include at least four Member States, which is to prevent larger Member States being able (due to their larger populations) to dominate the smaller Member States.[14] However, during this period, any Member State may instead request that the vote be taken under the previous Article 205 ECT procedure.[15]
3. From 1 April 2017, the new process of QMV contained in Article 16(4) TEU only will apply.

Transitional voting provisions also apply from 2014–2017 under the Ioannina Compromise: this allows countries representing at least three-quarters of the population of the Union, or at least three-quarters of the number of Member States required to constitute a blocking minority (a blocking minority means four Member States or more,[16] so three-quarters of this means three Member States or, where not all Member States participate, at least the minimum number of Council Member States representing more than 35 per cent of the population of the participating Member States, plus one more Member State[17]) to oppose the vote by QMV of the Council.

The effect is to require the Council to try to find a solution to disagreement within a 'reasonable space of time', which is not defined. The majority may still adopt the measure after the reasonable space of time has ended. From 1 April 2017, when the new rule of qualified majority voting becomes compulsory, the activating percentage of the Ioannina compromise will be reduced to at least 55 per cent of the population of the EU or at least the same percentage of the number of Member States required to constitute a blocking minority.[18]

....

12 Ibid art 16(4).
13 Ibid art 16(5) and art 3(3) of the Protocol on Transitional Provisions.
14 Dougan (n 4) 632.
15 Article 16(5) TEU and art 3(2) of the Protocol on Transitional Provisions. Article 238(3) TFEU applies a variation of this formula where not all members of the Council participate.
16 See the second paragraph of art 16(4).
17 Article 238(3)(a) TFEU.
18 Declaration No 7 annexed to the Final Act of the Treaty of Lisbon. See also the summary at http://europa.eu/legislation_summaries/glossary/ioannina_compromise_en.htm (last accessed 18 January 2015).

THE OVERALL ROLE OF THE COUNCIL

Article 16(1) TEU describes the role of the Council, which consists of ministerial representatives of the Member States: 'The Council shall, jointly with the European Parliament, exercise legislative and budgetary functions. It shall carry out its policy-making and coordinating functions as laid down in the Treaties'.

According to one study, the operation of QMV in practice usually means that 74 per cent of the votes taken are needed. Quite often, the Council prefers to act by consensus, and so does not go through the procedure.[19] To understand the underlying reality, as opposed to the on-the-surface legal form, one might need to resort to group or social psychology. For example, it may be that where consensus is the expectation, peer pressure pushes Member States into agreeing to something they do not really agree with in principle.

Of all the Member States, the UK votes no the most often, followed by Germany, which votes no roughly half the times the UK does, while France and Lithuania very rarely vote no.[20]

4.2.3 THE COMMITTEE OF PERMANENT REPRESENTATIVES (COREPER)

This consists of the permanent ambassadors of each country/Member State to the EU. Its role is recognised at treaty level in Article 16(7) TEU. It does the preparatory work for Council (of Ministers) meetings. In practice, it is quite important, since the Council (of Ministers) can only meet infrequently, whereas COREPER is a more permanent, ongoing body of officials.[21]

COREPER

Under Article 16(7) TEU, COREPER has the task of preparing meetings of the Council (of Ministers). It consists of national officials at ambassador level.

4.2.4 THE PRESIDENCY OF THE COUNCIL (OF MINISTERS)

For a period of six months, one Member State will hold the presidency of the Council (of Ministers).[22] The president acts as chairperson and involves organising meetings of both councils for the six-month period, liaising between the Member States for the

---

19 V Miller 'Voting behaviour in the EU Council' House of Commons Research Note SN/IA/6646 (2013).

20 Ibid 14.

21 This raises a debate about whether national ministers still effectively control the Council: see e.g. F Häge 'Who decides in the Council of the European Union?' (2008) 46(3) *Journal of Common Market Studies* 533–58.

22 See art 16(9) TEU. The European Council may amend the configuration of the Presidency of the Council (of Ministers), under art 236 TFEU.

conduct of EU business. Previously, the Member State holding the presidency tended to act as a spokesperson for the EU, but now the president of the European Council tends to do this (remember that after the Lisbon Treaty, the presidency of the European Council is held by a separate appointed official). The presidency rotates between all the Member States for six-month periods. As an institution, the presidency is only briefly referred to in the treaties, although the president of the Council is conferred with various tasks in specific treaty provisions[23] (usually informing another institution of a particular matter[24]).

4.2.5 THE EUROPEAN PARLIAMENT

4.2.5.1 INTRODUCTION

The European Parliament consists of representatives from all Member States who are directly elected. It was originally called the Common Assembly (in the European Coal and Steel Community Treaty). It has been directly elected since 1979. Prior to that, it consisted of national parliamentarians appointed to it. It does not have as much power as a parliament in a national system, in that it must cooperate with the Council (of Ministers) in the passing of laws. In fact, as noted above, it is probably best considered as a chamber in a bicameral parliament, along with the Council (of Ministers). As noted in Chapter 2, until 1992, it had very little power to participate in passing laws and was a largely consultative body.

EXPLAINING THE LAW

THE PARLIAMENT IN THE LEGISLATIVE PROCESS

Now, it is centrally involved under the legislative procedure. It makes sense to think of the EU as having a bicameral legislature consisting of the Council (of Ministers) and the European Parliament as the two chambers.

The Parliament currently has over 700 members and cannot have more than 750 members, plus its president, who acts as speaker.[25] Under the Lisbon Treaty, the European Council determines its composition, acting by unanimity, but on the initiative and consent of the European Parliament itself.[26] The term of the Parliament is five years.[27] Unlike in many national systems, there is no provision for early elections, because the executive of the EU is separate to parliament and does not need parliamentary support or approval to continue its functions (this is also the situation in the USA, for example).

....

23 See art 16(9) TEU and art 236 TFEU. Article 236 provides that the European Council acting by qualified majority may decide on the Presidency of Council configurations (other than the Foreign Affairs configuration, when the High Representative for Foreign Affairs and Security Policy is designated as chairperson or president).

24 See e.g. arts 121(5) TFEU (on multilateral surveillance) and 219 TFEU (on Euro exchange rates).

25 Article 14(2) TEU.

26 Ibid art 14(2) TEU and art 2 of the Protocol on Transitional Provisions.

27 Article 14(3) TEU.

KEY LEARNING POINT

THE OVERALL FUNCTIONS OF THE EUROPEAN PARLIAMENT

Under Article 14(1) TEU, the European Parliament, jointly with the Council (of Ministers), exercises (1) a legislative function, (2) a budgetary function, (3) political oversight and consultation as laid down in the treaties, and (4) has a role in appointing the president of the European Commission, as well as the Commission collectively, along with the president of the European Council.

The European Council nominates a president of the European Commission, which the Parliament must then approve.[28] A similar process applies to the president of the European Council.[29] The Parliament must also approve the choice of members of the Commission collectively (which involves the Member States nominating commissioners individually and collectively agreeing to the nominations in the Council, in cooperation with the Commission president).[30]

The European Parliament exercises oversight and a degree of accountability over the EU executive through parliamentary debates. The president of the European Commission delivers an annual 'State of the Union' address before the Parliament.[31]

4.2.5.2 PARLIAMENTARY SCRUTINY

As well as passing legislation, the European Parliament, like any parliament, debates important issues and seeks to hold the executive of the EU to account. The executive in the EU consists mainly of the Commission, but also it involves the Member States (as it is the Member States who implement EU law at national level). As noted above, the Commission must answer to written and oral questions posed by Parliament. The European Parliament has around 30 committees, most of which are 'standing' or permanent committees.[32] Committees are established under the Parliament's Rules of Procedure, which the Parliament is empowered to adopt under Article 232 TFEU.[33]

As in a national parliament, committees consist of a smaller number of members and specialise in scrutinising a particular topic. For example, the European Parliament has committees on Civil Liberty, Justice and Home Affairs and on Economic and Monetary Affairs. The committees participate in the legislative process by scrutinising and offering

....

28 Ibid art 17(7).
29 Ibid art 15.
30 Ibid art 17(7).
31 Rules of Procedure of the European Parliament, Annex XIII: Framework Agreement on relations between the European Parliament and the European Commission, Annex 4 para 5 OJ L 304 20.11.2010 p. 47.
32 Note that the term 'standing committee' has a different meaning in the UK Parliament, where it refers to a committee established temporarily to scrutinise a particular piece of legislation as it is passed through Parliament.
33 See especially rr 45–52 at 183–97.

opinions on draft legislation. Under Rules 184 and 185 of its Rules of Procedure, the European Parliament may also establish temporary committees for specific reports.

KEY LEARNING POINT

SPECIFIC FUNCTIONS OF THE EUROPEAN PARLIAMENT

As well as jointly with the European Council appointing the president of the European Commission and the Commission collectively, the European Parliament is given three specific important powers other than legislating and scrutinising the executive: (1) to censure the European Commission, (2) to approve the EU budget, and (3) to pose parliamentary questions to the EU executive, as the Commission is required, under Article 230 TFEU, to reply to oral and written questions from Parliament.

4.2.5.3 POWER OF CENSURE

Under Article 234 TFEU, the Parliament can censure the European Commission. The effect of a motion of censure being passed is that the European Commission must resign en masse. The censure must be passed by two-thirds of the Members of the European Parliament (MEPs) present, and these two-thirds must amount to a majority of all the MEPs. The European Parliament came close to passing one motion of censure to date, which resulted in the resignation of the Commission in 1999 and of its then president Jacques Santer, although it has discussed the possibility on several other occasions. The background to it was claims of corruption against a number of Commissioners and an ineffective response by the Commission to the problems.[34]

4.2.5.4 BUDGETARY POWERS

Under Article 310(1) TFEU, spending and revenue by the EU must be drawn up in estimates on an annual basis and approved by both the Council and the European Parliament using a procedure set out in Article 314 TFEU. The EU is not allowed to run a budget deficit, a rule also set out in Article 310(1) TFEU. Article 314 sets out a special legislative procedure. However, this procedure is quite similar to the ordinary legislative procedure in that in essence the Commission makes a proposal, the Council (of Ministers) ultimately acts by qualified majority, and the European Parliament approves by a majority (one of the main differences with the ordinary legislative procedure relates more to the detail of what happens where there is a failure of agreement).

As well as the annual budget, the EU has a 'multi-annual financial framework'. This sets out the broad outlines of the budget. This is agreed in cycles of seven years. It will set, for example, a ceiling of expenditure, which may not be spent subsequently in annual budgets.[35] This is what occurred with the most recent budget framework period ending in 2012.

....

34 See the useful research note prepared by the UK House of Commons Library in V. Miller, R Ware 'The resignation of the European Commission' Research Paper 99/32 (1999) www.parliament.uk/briefing-papers/RP99–32.pdf (last accessed 18 January 2015).
35 See art 312 TFEU.

ANALYSING THE LAW

HOW EFFECTIVE IS THE EUROPEAN PARLIAMENT?
THE NO-*DEMOS* THESIS

In an influential academic paper, the well known EU specialist Joseph Weiler proposed the question of the democratic effectiveness of the EU can be understood by referring to concept of the *demos*.[36] '*Demos*' is a Greek term, referring to 'the people'. In the EU, there is no single people in the sense of a population sharing a common identity and political consciousness for a single political space, as political consciousness is primarily directed still at the individual Member State level. This results in a lack of focus by the peoples of the Member States on political work at the European level. It is still the case, for example, that elections to the European Parliament are dominated by national issues.

4.2.6 THE EUROPEAN COMMISSION

The European Commission is, compared to national systems, one of the peculiarities of the EU system.

EXPLAINING THE LAW

COMPARING THE EUROPEAN COMMISSION

In general, the Commission can be said to be part of the executive of the EU. The closest comparison with a national system is with the central civil service, but the European Commission has important additional powers to initiate policy and legislation.

4.2.6.1 FUNCTIONS

One of its roles is to monitor the implementation of EU law in Member States, while it also (and it often does) bring legal action before the ECJ against Member States for inadequate implementation of EU law.[37]

Perhaps the most distinctive feature of the Commission is that it has a largely exclusive right to propose new legislation. This means that, ordinarily, only the Commission can propose new legislation;[38] neither the Member States nor members of the European Parliament may do so.

....

36 J H H Weiler 'The state *"über alles"*; *Demos, Telos*, and the German Maastricht decision' *NYU Jean Monnet Working Paper No 6/1995* (1995).

37 Article 258 TFEU.

38 See art 17(2) TEU and art 289 TFEU.

One of the vice presidents of the Commission is responsible for coordinating and implementing EU foreign policy[39] and is known as the High Representative for Foreign Affairs and Security Policy. The High Representative also chairs meetings of the Council (of Ministers) consisting of foreign ministers of the Member States.[40] Expanding this role was one of the major reforms of the Lisbon Treaty. It takes over from Presidencies of the Member States in chairing the Foreign Affairs configuration of the Council (of Ministers). The High Representative also has a right of initiative in the Common Foreign and Security Policy (CFSP).[41]

EXPLAINING THE LAW

THE RIGHT OF INITIATIVE OF THE EUROPEAN COMMISSION

The Commission's right of initiative is also not without any analogy in national systems; for example, the negative legislative role enjoyed by the US president, whereby the president may veto legislation passed by both Houses of Congress.[42] Whereas the president's power takes effect at the final stage of the legislative process, the Commission's occurs at the beginning, but given the Commission's more or less exclusive right of initiative, the effect is not dissimilar to a veto.

Moreover, Articles 242 and 255 TFEU provide respectively that Parliament and the Council (of Ministers) may *request* the Commission to initiate a piece of legislation.[43] While the Commission is under no formal obligation to do so, it might be difficult politically for it to reject such a request.[44] In addition, it is increasingly common for legislation to require the Commission to make proposals, making the Commission's initiative power increasingly less important in practice.[45] Moreover, the Parliament has a right to censure the Commission, which effectively entails dismissing the Commission (under Article 234 TFEU). Thus, if the Commission was to act in a manner disrespectful of the representative function of the Council or the Parliament by ignoring a request under Articles 241 or 255 TFEU, it could conceivably move to censure the Commission.[46]

39 Article 220(2) TFEU.
40 Ibid art 18(3).
41 See e.g. art 218(9) TFEU, art 238(2) TFEU.
42 See art I(7) of the US Constitution. A bill that is vetoed by the president may be passed by Congress through a two-thirds majority of each house.
43 In criminal matters, under art 76 TFEU, one-quarter of the Member States also have a right of initiative.
44 See e.g. K Lenaerts, P Van Nuffel *Constitutional Law of the European Union* (2nd edn Sweet & Maxwell 2005) 581–83.
45 J-P Jacqué 'The principle of institutional balance' (2004) 41 *Common Market Law Review* 383–91 at 390.
46 See ibid for a contrary view and generally. As Dashwood notes, the Commission itself lacks democratic legitimacy. See A Dashwood 'The institutional framework and the institutional balance' in M Dougan, S Currie (eds) *Fifty Years of the European Treaties: Looking Back and Thinking Forward* (Hart 2009) 7.

4.2.6.2 COMPOSITION

The president of the Commission is appointed jointly by the European Council, acting by qualified majority, and the European Parliament, acting by a majority.[47] The European Council makes a nomination that is then proposed to Parliament. The term of office of the Commission is five years and coincides with parliamentary terms. A curious feature of the provision (Article 17(7) TEU) is that the European Council in nominating someone is to 'take into account the elections to the European Parliament', but what 'taking into account' means is not specified.

EXPLAINING THE LAW

POLITICAL PARTIES AND THE PRESIDENT OF THE EUROPEAN COMMISSION

Article 17(7) TEU refers to taking into account elections to the European Parliament in appointing the president of the European Commission. However, what taking into account the elections means is not always obvious. When Commission President Barroso was appointed in 2004, he had the support of one of the major voting blocs in the Parliament, but not necessarily of a majority. He was prime minister of Portugal and so not a member of the European Parliament. As noted above, Commission President Juncker had the support of the largest party grouping in the European Parliament.

4.2.7 THE EUROPEAN COURT OF JUSTICE (ECJ) OR COURT OF JUSTICE OF THE EUROPEAN UNION (CJEU)

4.2.7.1 INTRODUCTION

The European Court of Justice (ECJ) has played a remarkable role in the development of EU law, much more so than a traditional understanding of the role of a court would suggest, which we will look at more in the next chapter. This is the Court of the EU and decides legal disputes concerning the laws of the EU. Member States must accept its decisions and put them into effect. This follows from the principle of supremacy: supremacy means that where there is a conflict between EU law and the law of a Member State (e.g. UK law), the Member State must apply the EU law over and above its law (see Chapter 6).

Under the procedural law relating to the ECJ, which is quite complex, there are a number of different types of actions that can be brought before it. The most common and perhaps important is the preliminary reference procedure under Article 267 TFEU, whereby national courts refer a question of EU law to the ECJ for clarification. The

---

47 Article 17(7) TEU.

ECJ then answers the question(s) posed and returns the case to the national court. The national court decides on the facts according to the interpretation by the ECJ of the requirements of EU law.

We will look at the European Court of Justice in more detail in Chapter 5.

4.2.7.2 THE GENERAL COURT

Prior to Lisbon, what is now the General Court was known as the Court of First Instance (CFI). It was established in 1988 initially to assist the ECJ, but it has since become more important and has jurisdiction over a wide variety of cases. Some of its decisions may be appealed on a point of law to the ECJ. We will look in more detail at its jurisdiction in Chapter 5.

4.2.8 THE COURT OF AUDITORS

This is not really a court as we normally understand, rather it is a regulatory body that makes sure the EU and its institutions spend money properly. The Court of Auditors acts as an auditor for the EU, just as accountants act as auditors for companies.[48]

4.2.9 THE EUROPEAN CENTRAL BANK (ECB)

Until recently an institution with a low profile, since the crisis in the Eurozone, the European Central Bank (ECB) has been at the centre of public attention. Debate has centred on what role it should have played to help avert the crisis and what additional powers it might be given to improve matters in the future. A key feature of the role of the ECB is that it only has powers relating to countries that are members of the Eurozone, i.e. that have the Euro currency. For these countries, it is responsible for monetary policy, which includes the single currency (Euro) and bank interest rates. Article 3(1) TFEU states that the EU has exclusive competence over monetary policy of the Member States with the Euro currency.

ANALYSING THE LAW

THE POWERS OF THE ECB?

The ECB is responsible for the monetary policy of those Member States who have adopted the Euro currency. Article 282(1) TFEU states that 'the European Central Bank, together with the national central banks, shall constitute the European System of Central Banks' (ESCB). The European Central Bank, together with the national central banks of the Member States whose currency is the Euro, which

---

....

48 Articles 285–87 TFEU.

constitute the Euro system, shall conduct the monetary policy of the Union.' More specifically, the ECB has these powers:

- The ECB has sole power to issue the Euro currency.[49]
- Currently, the ECB is prohibited from granting loans to the Member States or EU institutions and from purchasing debts from them, although this does not apply to 'publicly owned credit institutions' (i.e., public banks, but it does apply to other public bodies, including governments),[50] and as we shall see in Chapter 17, the way the ECB has exercised this power in the context of the Eurozone is very controversial.
- It is also given a kind of delegated legislative power to pass regulations necessary to fulfil its main tasks.[51]
- The Bank is independent of other Union institutions.[52]

The details of its powers are set out in the Statute of the ESCB (European System of Central Banks) and of the ECB.[53]

The adoption of the Euro currency and the creation of the ECB to support it is perhaps the most obvious example of flexible cooperation in the EU, whereby some Member States can push ahead with further integration, leaving other Member States to adopt a more independent course of action.

EXPLAINING THE LAW

THE EUROZONE AS AN EXAMPLE OF FLEXIBLE OR ENHANCED COOPERATION

Since the Treaty of Maastricht, the treaties now permit enhanced cooperation. In other words, they do not always insist on a one-size-fits-all policy: some Member States may move further ahead with integration if they wish. The Euro currency is the best example of this. Article 5(1) TFEU states that 'specific provisions shall

....

49 Ibid art 128.

50 Ibid art 123.

51 Ibid art 132(1). Interestingly, this power coexists alongside a power of the Council (of Ministers) and European Parliament, under the ordinary legislative procedure, to pass legislation necessary for the use of the Euro currency, but the power of the Union legislature is without prejudice to the special legislative power of the ECB. This seems to give a purely technocratic institution priority over a more democratic institution.

52 Article 130 TFEU.

53 OJ C 83 30.3.2010 p. 230.

apply to those Member States whose currency is the Euro'. 17 countries have joined. Although the treaty seems to create a legal aspiration for all Member States to join, it does not make it compulsory. Articles 136–138 TFEU set out the specific provisions (see further Chapter 17). Article 136(2) TFEU, for example, provides that 'only members of the Council representing Member States whose currency is the Euro shall take part in the vote'.

Article 133 TFEU establishes the ordinary legislative procedure as applicable to EU secondary legislation on measures necessary for the use of the Euro as the single currency, but it also requires that the ECB is consulted when these laws are adopted by the Council (of Ministers) and Parliament.

ANALYSING THE LAW
_____

WHAT DOES THE EUROZONE CRISIS TELL US ABOUT THE POWERS OF THE ECB?

We will examine the crisis in the Eurozone in Chapter 17, but it may be useful to highlight here some background to the role of the ECB in the affair, as the ECB is one of the least popularly understood institutions. The main problem underlying the crisis in the Euro is one of excess debt and difficulties Eurozone Member States have in paying back the debts, which has created a crisis of economic confidence. Although government debt is a matter of fiscal policy (how much money a government borrows or spends), debt can also result from a monetary policy problem. Monetary policy is concerned with the supply of money.

The problems experienced by Ireland illustrate how a monetary policy issue can have an overall impact on debt. The Irish Government acquired excess debt not due to its own spending, but through taking on bad debts by Irish banks. Irish banks had loaned too much money too easily during the Irish economic boom of the first years of this century, many of which were not being repaid. However, the debt came as a result of overly generous policies on the granting of loans. Many Irish banks borrowed money from other European banks (especially German banks) to provide the loans.

Although the granting of loans is an aspect of monetary policy, the supervision of banks' loan policies ('prudential supervision') is not in the competence of the ECB under the treaties. It is still a matter for national central banks. Article 136(6) TFEU states that the Council may unanimously, and after consulting the European Parliament and the ECB, confer specific tasks upon the ECB concerning policies relating to the prudential supervision of credit institutions and other financial institutions (with the exception of insurance undertakings). This has not yet been used.

Concerning the Irish problem, warnings from the ECB that too much loan money was being channelled in to Ireland from other Member States might have helped avoid over-lending by banks. Requiring the ECB to issue regular reports on the pattern of loans in Member States would not require the use of Article 136(6) TFEU to remove the right of national central banks to make a final decision on prudential supervision. However, proposals for a 'banking union' by the European Commission do propose prudential supervision should be an EU competence.[54]

We shall look at the ECB actions in the Eurozone crisis in more detail in Chapter 17.

The ECB is based in Frankfurt, Germany.

4.3 LEGISLATIVE PROCEDURES

4.3.1 SOME GENERAL POINTS

As we saw in Chapter 2, when the Communities were founded, the Council (of Ministers) had sole legislative power. Although the treaties did provide for majority voting, from the mid-1960s on it became the norm to allow individual Member States to block a legislative proposal if the Member State thought its vital national interests were under threat (under the Luxembourg Accord). From the Single European Act 1986 onward, qualified majority voting in the Council (of Ministers) increased, while the European Parliament was gradually given a greater role until it became in effect the co-legislature with the Council (of Ministers).

The Parliament was given more power in some areas more quickly than in others. This led to a series of different legislative procedures being used in Community law, with the main difference between them being the extent of the role of the European Parliament: it was merely to be consulted ('consultation procedure'); it could force the

....

54 http://ec.europa.eu/internal_market/finances/banking-union/index_en.htm (last accessed 18 January 2015).

Council (of Ministers) to act by unanimity instead of qualified majority voting, but could not otherwise block a legislative proposal ('the cooperation procedure'); or it was to decide jointly with the Council (of Ministers) (known as either the 'co-decision procedure', in which there was a conciliation procedure for reconciling disagreement between the Council (of Ministers) and the European Parliament; or the 'assent procedure', in which the European Parliament simply said yes or no). With the Treaty of Lisbon, co-decision was renamed the ordinary legislative procedure.

Article 294 TFEU sets out the ordinary legislative procedure, including the role of the conciliation committee, which, (some details omitted), goes as follows:

- *First reading*: The Commission submits a proposal to the Council and to the European Parliament. The Parliament has a first reading to consider and adopt a position, which it then sends to the Council. If the Council approves of the position at its first reading, the legislative proposal is adopted. If the Council proposes amendments, it is then transmitted to the European Parliament for it to consider.[55]
- *Second reading*: The Parliament may, within three months, decide to adopt or reject the proposal as amended by the Council, but if the Parliament proposes amendments after a second reading, the text is sent back to the Council. If the Council then agrees to the amendments following the second reading by Parliament, the text is adopted but if the Council does not agree, a conciliation committee is established,[56] consisting of an equal number of representatives of the Parliament and of the Council, along with representatives of the Commission. Only representatives of the Council and Parliament vote (a qualified majority of the members of Council representatives and by a majority of European Parliament members). Once an agreed text is decided upon, it is then sent to the Council and Parliament for a third reading.[57]
- *Third reading*: Within six weeks, if either the Council or Parliament vote it down, it is deemed not adopted; if both approve (the Council by qualified majority and the Parliament by majority), it is adopted.[58]

The Parliament's role takes effect after the Council has first voted. In effect, it has a veto on what the Council has decided, but usually does not exercise its power in the form of a veto, as the conciliation procedure is generally successful.

....

55 Article 294(3)–(6) TFEU.
56 Ibid art 294(10)–(12).
57 Ibid art 297(7)–(10).
58 Ibid art 294(13)–(14).

KEY LEARNING POINT

THE ORDINARY LEGISLATIVE PROCEDURE UNDER ARTICLE 294 TFEU

Under the ordinary legislative procedure, set out in Article 294 TFEU, the following applies:

– Only the Commission may normally make a legislative proposal;

$$\nabla$$

– The Parliament must then consider and vote, usually by absolute majority (*First reading*);

$$\nabla$$

– The Council adopts by QMV or proposes amendments (*First reading*);

$$\nabla$$

– If amendments proposed by Council, Parliament has *second reading*: A special *conciliation procedure* is used to achieve agreement between the Council (of Ministers) and the European Parliament, where there is a disagreement between them.

$$\nabla$$

Third reading: rejection or adoption by both Council and Parliament.

4.3.2 THE LISBON TREATY

The following are among the main changes to law-making made by the Treaty of Lisbon:

– the *separate second and third pillar instruments were abolished* in favour of unified instruments for the Union as a whole, which are the standard instruments since the founding of the Communities: Regulations, directives, and decisions
– the *Commission retains rights of initiative except* when the treaties state otherwise.[59] This provision for exceptions is an innovation; the main example is regarding police and judicial cooperation in criminal matters, when one-quarter of the Member States may initiate[60]
– a new *right of popular initiative* is established, whereby if 1 million citizens sign a petition, a new law may be proposed (Article 11(4) TEU)

....

59 Article 17(2) TEU and art 289 TFEU.
60 Article 76 TFEU. See also art 289(4) TFEU.

– the *co-decision procedure is renamed* the ordinary legislative procedure (Article 294 TFEU), and its application is extended to, e.g. agricultural policy,[61] the common commercial policy;[62] and across all of Area of Freedom, Security and Justice[63]
– methods of passing legislation other than the ordinary legislative method are renamed *special legislative procedures*. Generally, these procedures require unanimity in the Council (of Ministers), instead of qualified majority voting, and either just consultation or straightforward assent by the European Parliament (like the pre-existing consultation and assent procedures for passing legislation). Provision is made for some of these special procedures to transition to the ordinary legislative method, under what are called '*passarelle* clauses' (there is a general *passarelle* clause in Article 48(7) TEU). The general *passarelle* clause requires unanimity in the Council (of Ministers), the consent of the European Parliament, and a provision is also made for a veto by national parliaments. In some provisions, 'emergency breaks' are established, whereby Member States can exercise a veto where fundamental national interests are affected (e.g. Article 48 TFEU regarding the social security system).

4.3.3 SPECIAL LEGISLATIVE PROCEDURES

The special legislative procedures reduce the role of the European Parliament, consequently leaving greater power to the Council (of Ministers), as used to be the case more generally. Individual Member States may be given a veto through unanimity applying in the Council (of Ministers) instead of qualified majority voting, e.g., Article 153 TFEU on social security and protection in employment. Or the European Parliament may be just consulted, e.g., Article 22 TFEU on electoral rights of Union citizens. Some provisions exceptionally require unanimity in the Council *and* the consent of Parliament, e.g. Article 19(1) TFEU on anti–discrimination measures.

ANALYSING THE LAW
_____

THE REASONS FOR SPECIAL LEGISLATIVE PROCEDURES
Special legislative procedures apply because the Member States are more concerned to preserve their individual sovereignty. This is generally in more politically important areas, for example, criminal justice, where 'emergency breaks' are more common. In politically sensitive matters, the Member States are seen as having greater political legitimacy. This can be related to the debate about whether there exists a *demos* so as to make the European Parliament a satisfactorily democratic body, genuinely representing the peoples of the Member States.

....

61 Article 43 TFEU, previously subject to cooperation procedure; see art 37 ECT.
62 Article 207 TFEU; previously the European Parliament was not involved under Article 133 ECT.
63 Title V Part Three TFEU.

4.4 TYPES OF LEGISLATION: ARTICLE 288 TFEU

4.4.1 INTRODUCTION

> **KEY LEARNING POINT**
> ....
>
> **TYPES OF SECONDARY LEGISLATION**
> A somewhat curious feature of EU law is the way in which legislation is
> distinguished depending on: (i) how detailed it is; (ii) how it takes effect in
> national law; and (iii) to whom it is directed.

Although variations in legislation in these ways are also found in national systems,
different terminology is not generally used as a consequence: the single term
'legislation' or 'Act' is generally used (different terminology is usually only used for
delegated legislation). Prior to the Lisbon Treaty, the situation was further complicated
by the use of different legislative instruments again under the Second and Third pillars,
such as 'Common Positions', 'Joint Actions', and 'Framework Decisions', although
these are now abolished.

Article 288 TFEU now uses the same distinctions as had been used since the beginning
of the Communities and applies them throughout EU law. They can be summarised as
follows:

- Regulations:
    - of general application
    - are 'directly applicable' in national law according to the treaty
      wording
    - detailed and specific
- Directives:
    - of general application
    - require national implementation, usually through national
      legislation
    - set out objectives or purposes, although sometimes quite detailed
- Decisions:
    - directed at individuals, not of general application
    - not stated to be directly applicable, but they tend to be because
      they are quite detailed and direct effect doctrine supplies the rest

4.4.2 LEGISLATIVE AND NON-LEGISLATIVE ACTS

The Lisbon Treaty makes what is in some respects a somewhat confusing distinction
between *legislative* and *non-legislative acts*.[64]

....

64 Ibid art 290.

(1) REGULATIONS, DIRECTIVES, AND DECISIONS AS NON-LEGISLATIVE ACTS AND (2) NON-LEGISLATIVE ACTS AS (I) DELEGATED ACTS AND AS (II) IMPLEMENTING ACTS

The standard legal instruments – regulations, directives and decisions – can be adopted in a non-legislative form by the institutions, under Article 297(2) TFEU. Individual treaty articles state which institution can adopt non-legislative acts adopted in the form of regulations, directives or decisions. Further, in the case of the European Commission as the adopting institution, the category of non-legislative acts is divided into two additional, and also somewhat unclear, categories of non-legislative acts adopted as delegated acts (governed by Article 290 TFEU) and non-legislative acts adopted as implementing acts (governed by Article 291 TFEU).

Article 290(1) TFEU states that: 'A legislative act may delegate to the Commission the power to adopt non-legislative acts of general application to supplement or amend certain non-essential elements of the legislative act.' In the UK, this would simply be considered delegated legislation, and Article 290(2) does use the term 'delegation', stating that legislative acts shall explicitly lay down the conditions to which the delegation is subject, but this is not called delegated *legislation*.

LEGISLATIVE VERSUS NON-LEGISLATIVE ACTS

The standard legal instruments can be issued in legislative or non-legislative form. The usefulness of the distinction is open to doubt, as it tends to muddy the waters between legislative and executive action. In any legal system, legislation can be implemented either by delegated legislation or implementing measures. Adopting legislative instruments in a non-legislative form creates a rather vague layer of decision-making.

There are some practical implications of the distinction:[65]

- national parliaments' right to object to union measures on the grounds of alleged incompatibility with the principle of subsidiarity (Article 5(3)

---

65 Dougan (n 4) 638–39.

TEU and Protocol on the Application of the Principles of Subsidiarity and
Proportionality) only applies to legislative acts
- the Council (of Ministers)' obligation to deliberate and vote in public only
  applies to draft legislative acts (Article 16(8) TEU and Article 15(2) TFEU)
- the distinction may also be relevant to standing to bring annulment actions,
  which may not be available for 'merely' implementing measures.

EXPLAINING THE LAW

NON-LEGISLATIVE ACTS AS (1) DELEGATED ACTS (ARTICLE 290 TFEU) OR (2) IMPLEMENTING ACTS (ARTICLE 291 TFEU)

This distinction between non-legislative acts *as delegated acts* under Article 290
TFEU and non-legislative acts *as implementing acts* under Article 291 TFEU is not
clear conceptually: both involve measures implementing legislation, and it is not
clear what is different between 'delegation' and 'implementation'. In a national
system, they could both simply be described as 'delegated legislation'. Two clear
procedural differences exist between the measures in Articles 290 and 291 TFEU:

(i) measures under Article 290 TFEU can only be adopted by the European
     Commission
(ii) measures under Article 291 TFEU must involve uniform implementation across
     the Member States.

Further, it was unclear to what extent the comitology system (see next) applied
to Article 290 TFEU, whereas it had traditionally applied to implementing powers
of the Commission (now these are exercised under Article 291 TFEU). However,
Article 290(2) TFEU provides a separate legal basis to comitology for the control
of delegated powers.

The distinction between the two types of act or instrument has been the subject of
recent case law.

KEY CASE *COMMISSION V PARLIAMENT AND COUNCIL*

In a recent judgment, the European Court of Justice has attempted an
explanation of the distinction. *Commission v Parliament and Council*[66] concerned
Regulation No 528/2012[67] establishing harmonised rules concerning the

66 Case C–247/12 *Commission v Parliament and Council* judgment of 30 June 2014.
67 Regulation No 528/2012/EU of the European Parliament and of the Council of 22 May 2012 concerning the
   making available on the market and use of biocidal products OJ L 167 27.6.2012 p. 1.

making available on the market and the use of biocidal products. Article 80(1) of Regulation No 528/2012 conferred on the Commission powers to adopt an implementing regulation specifying the fees payable to the European Chemicals Agency for the tasks carried out in implementing the regulation as well as the conditions governing payment of those fees. The Commission sought annulment of Article 80(1) on the grounds that it should have given the Commission a power to adopt delegated acts, which the Commission described as completing the normative framework, and not being just about detail.[68] The relevant paragraphs from the Court's judgment are paragraphs 38 and 39:

> 38 When the EU legislature confers, in a legislative act, a delegated power on the Commission pursuant to Article 290(1) TFEU, the Commission is called on to adopt rules which supplement or amend certain non-essential elements of that act. In accordance with the second subparagraph of Article 290(1) TFEU, the objectives, content, scope and duration of the delegation of power must be explicitly defined in the legislative act granting such a delegation. That requirement implies that the purpose of granting a delegated power is to achieve the adoption of rules coming within the regulatory framework as defined by the basic legislative act.

> 39 By contrast, when the EU legislature confers an implementing power on the Commission on the basis of Article 291(2) TFEU, the Commission is called on to provide further detail in relation to the content of a legislative act, in order to ensure that it is implemented under uniform conditions in all Member States.

Thus, one clear difference is that delegated acts may amend legislation in non-essential matters. However, it seems that both delegated acts ('rules which supplement certain non-essential elements') and implementing acts may supplement legislation in matters of detail, so the case still seems to leave potential overlap between the concepts, since on an ordinary understanding of the word 'detail', it could include adding non-essential elements. The Council and Parliament seemed to consider the difference was the *degree of* detail: Article 80(1) was sufficiently detailed, meaning the Commission's role was confined to purely implementing it,[69] but again degree of detail does not seem a very clear ground of distinction either. The Court went on to note that the EU legislature had discretion whether to confer a power to adopt delegated or implementing measures on the Commission.[70]

....

68 Case C–247/12 paras 23–24.
69 Ibid para 31.
70 Ibid para 40.

KEY LEARNING POINT

UNDER THE TREATY OF LISBON, THE COMMISSION DOES NOT GENERALLY ADOPT DELEGATED *LEGISLATION*, BUT THERE ARE TWO CASES WHERE IT HAS A SPECIAL LEGISLATIVE POWER

Under the Treaty of Lisbon, the European Commission is not given power to pass delegated legislation. It is given powers to adopt non-legislative acts as delegated acts under Article 290 TFEU and non-legislative acts as implementing acts under Article 291 TFEU, as discussed above (in substance, these two powers are more or less the equivalent to delegated legislative power). However, there are two places in the treaty where a formal, *special legislative power* is given to the Commission:

1. Under Article 106(3) TFEU, the Commission may address appropriate directives or decisions to Member States to ensure public undertakings and undertakings to which Member States grant special or exclusive rights;
2. Under Article 45(3)(d) TFEU, in the area of free movement of workers, the Commission may adopt regulations governing the conditions under which a worker may remain in the territory of a Member State after having been employed in that State.

Another situation also arises: a legislative instrument might give the European Commission power to amend it in some limited way. When this is the case, a special comitology procedure applies (see below).

4.4.3 COMITOLOGY

Article 291(3) TFEU provides that the European Parliament and the Council, acting by means of regulations in accordance with the ordinary legislative procedure, shall lay down in advance the rules and general principles concerning 'mechanisms for control by Member States of the Commission's exercise of implementing powers', and the term 'comitology' is used to describe these mechanisms. They have been established since the 1960s. If comitology committees think the Commission is not exercising implementing powers properly, the Comitology Committee may, for example, refer the matter to the Council (of Ministers), who can of course revoke the Commission's implementing powers. The exact powers of comitology committees are set out in Directive 1999/468/EC.[71] There are four types of comitology procedure, although there is a basic distinction between the advisory procedure and the other three 'examination' procedures:

1. Advisory procedure: this involves the least influence for the Comitology Committees, which simply advise the Commission.
2. Management procedure: this has the power, acting by qualified majority voting, to refer the implementation back to the Council (of Ministers).

----

71 OJ L 184 17.7.1999 p. 2, as amended by Council Decision 2006/512 OJ L 200 22.7.2006 p. 11.

3. Regulatory procedure: this automatically refers implementation back to the Council unless a qualified majority of the Comitology Committee positively supports the Commission's implementation.

4. Regulatory procedure with scrutiny: this involves referral to both the Council and the European Parliament. It only applies where the implementing measure of the Commission in some way amends the parent instrument, which the parent instrument itself must permit, and where the parent instrument is passed by the ordinary legislative procedure. It was introduced in 2006.[72]

KEY LEARNING POINT
....

COMITOLOGY

'Comitology' refers to the system of committees of experts established by the Member States, i.e. sitting in the Council (of Ministers) to supervise the exercise by the European Commission of powers delegated to it to implement EU legislation. There are two basic categories of Comitology Committee and four specific types. The two categories are 'advisory' and 'management'. In the management category, there are three types: the standard management procedure, the regulatory procedure, and the regulatory procedure with scrutiny. The regulatory procedure with scrutiny applies where the parent legislation has been passed under the ordinary legislative procedure.

4.5 INSTITUTIONAL BALANCE AND THE SEPARATION OF POWERS IN THE EU

In political theory, the idea of a tripartite separation of powers has been widely accepted since Montesquieu's famous articulation of it in the eighteenth century.[73] Montesquieu distinguished between elements of government based on the nature of the function: he proposed that there were three conceptually distinct exercises of government power: making law (legislating), executing or implementing the law (the executive), and adjudicating disputes about the law (the judiciary). Montesquieu proposed that these should be exercised by different people and separated in their functioning. Later separation of powers theorists emphasised the idea of checks and balances, that is, the idea that one branch could exercise part of the power of another branch to prevent any branch having absolute power in its own sphere (a 'check' between branches), or that power could be divided within a branch (a 'balance' within a branch).[74]

....

72 Council Decision 2006/512/EC, ibid.

73 H de Charles Montesquieu *L'Esprit des Lois* (1748); in English *The Spirit of Laws* (T Nugent trans) (Nourse & Vaillant 1752).

74 A S Diamond 'The zenith of separation of powers theory: the Federal Convention of 1787' (1978) 8(3) *Publius* 45–70.

Separation of Powers in the EU

- Montesquieu, *Esprit des Lois* (1734)
- Separate personnel for each branch
- Founding fathers of US developed more on idea of checks and balances (Madison)
- 'Check' = partial exercise of power of one branch by another branch
- 'Balance' = division within a branch
- Rationale: to de-concentrate power so as to prevent (or minimise) its abuse
- **'Institutional balance'** as EU alternative?

Check

Check

Legislature

→

'Bicameral' ordinary legislative under Article 294

TFEU procedure (balance): Council + European Parliament vote on Commission proposal*

(*though Council and EP can ask Commission to propose)

+

Special legislative procedures
(EP has lesser role)

+

'Yellow-card system' involving national Parliaments (Protocol to the Treaty of Lisbon)

Executive

→

(1) Commission:
  i. monitoring
  ii. Enforcement actions

+ (balance)

(2) Member States:
  i. individually in domestic legal systems
  ii. collectively in Council of Ministers and European Council

Judiciary

→

General Court

+

Court of Justice

–

Judges appointed by Member States

–

ECJ as law-maker through meta-teleological interpretation? + Problem of 'unusually permissive environment' in role which the ECJ operates: reversal of its approach to Treaty interpretation requires unanimity from Member States

> KEY LEARNING POINT
>
> ## 'INSTITUTIONAL BALANCE' INSTEAD OF SEPARATION OF POWERS
>
> The ECJ has not referred to a Montesquieuean-style separation of powers, but has instead developed the concept of institutional balance.[75] As we will see, one of the difficulties with this concept is that it has not been very fully defined by the ECJ in its case law.

Jacqué links the principle of institutional balance with an *ultra vires* doctrine,[76] and thus implicitly links it with the rule of law. *Ultra vires* means acting outside of allocated powers. 'Institutional balance' can thus be linked to the principle of conferral, whereby the Union institutions may only exercise the competences attributed to them in the treaties (the EU law expression of an *ultra vires* principle).[77] Thus, the concept seems to refer to the balance of powers as established for each institution by the treaties. Presumably, this must generally depend on the text of the treaty.

However, the ECJ has not always followed the treaty text in its approach to interpreting the powers of the institutions. The concept of institutional balance has been of greatest significance in case law on the standing of the European Parliament to bring an annulment action before the ECJ. Article 173 of the EC Treaty initially provided for no standing for the European Parliament to bring annulment actions against acts of the Council or Commission.[78]

The ECJ followed this lack of textual support, in Case 302/87 *European Parliament v Council*,[79] by rejecting a claim by the European Parliament that it should have the same unlimited standing as other privileged applicants. The Court appeared to base its decision primarily on a literal reading of Article 173(1) EEC Treaty. The Court also examined to what extent the overall role of the Parliament required a right to bring an annulment action, noting, amongst other matters, that the European Parliament had political controls available to it, including the power to censure the Commission and its ability to conduct debates in order to ensure oversight over the Commission.

....

75 Jacqué (n 45) 384.
76 Ibid. Jacqué also links it to the idea of protection of the individual, although he suggests this concern has been superseded by human rights protection.
77 Article 7(1) TEU. See Jacqué (n 45) 386.
78 Now art 230(2) ECT and now art 263(2) TFEU. The Nice Treaty formally added the Parliament to the list in the text of art 230(2) of applicants with privileged standing.
79 Case 302/87 *European Parliament v Council* [1988] ECR 5615.

The Court reached the opposite conclusion to *European Parliament v Council* on the same issue of the standing of Parliament shortly after in *European Parliament v Council of the European Communities*,[80] observing:

> . . . However, the circumstances and arguments adduced in the present case show [compared to Case 302/87 *European Parliament v Council*] that the various legal remedies provided for both in the EURATOM Treaty and in the EEC Treaty, however effective and diverse they may be, may prove to be ineffective or uncertain.[81]

Thus, here the ECJ emphasised its view of effective powers, not the treaty text. The Court went on to base its decision on three specific considerations:[82] first, that an action for failure to act cannot be used to challenge the legal basis of a measure already adopted; second, that the possibility of an objection similar to that of Parliament could be raised subsequently in a national court and might then result in a preliminary reference was, as an alternative legal remedy, a mere contingency; and third, that the Commission's duty to ensure the Parliament's prerogative are respected could not oblige the Commission to bring an action when it did not share the Parliament's objection to it.

The Court invoked the concept of institutional balance, saying the treaties had 'assigned to each institution its own role in the institutional structure of the Community'[83] and that the absence of textual support 'cannot prevail over the fundamental interest in the maintenance and observance laid down in the treaties establishing the European Communities'.[84] In criticism of this approach, it might be said that the concept of institutional balance does not seem to have much meaning unless it is stable and identifiable, and it is difficult to see how that can be without reference to the treaty text.

The principle has also been addressed in more recent case law. In *Parliament v Council*,[85] the ECJ annulled a directive that created an alternative legislative procedure to that envisaged in (then) Article 67 EC Treaty in the area of asylum, visa and immigration, in that it provided for a cooperation procedure combined with the use of QMV in the Council[86] instead of either of the two procedures envisaged in Article 67. That article provides for either the cooperation procedure using unanimity in the Council or co-decision.[87] The Court's reasoning seemed essentially to be based on the principle that the specific provisions of the treaty could not be circumvented through secondary

....

80 Case C–70/88 *European Parliament v Council of the European Communities* [1990] ECR I–2041 (the case concerned the equivalently worded provisions of the EURATOM Treaty).

81 Ibid para 16.

82 Ibid paras 17–19.

83 Ibid para 21.

84 Ibid para 26.

85 Case C–133/06 *European Parliament v. Council* [2008] ECR I-3189.

86 See art 36(3) of Council Directive 2005/85 OJ 2005 L 326 1.12.2005 p. 13.

87 The latter is to be used where the Council has previously adopted, using the cooperation procedure and unanimity in the Council legislation defining the common rules and basic principles.

legislation, the Court noting that the Council's position effectively accorded provisions of secondary legislation priority over primary legislation.[88]

Here, the ECJ treated the treaty as *lex specialis*, which could not be supplemented through secondary legislation, and adopted an implicitly textual approach to interpretation. This seems contrary to the decision in Case C–70/88 *European Parliament v Council of the European Communities*, in which the ECJ was prepared to supplement the treaty beyond the text. However, the Court did not make this reasoning at all explicit. It only briefly referred to institutional balance, noting the principle 'requires that each of the institutions must exercise its powers with due regard for the powers of the other institutions' and actually citing Case C–70/88 *European Parliament v Council of the European Communities* in support of this.[89] The Court did not seek to link institutional balance with the principle of conferral, which it had earlier noted in its judgment.[90]

ANALYSING THE LAW

WOULD IT BE BETTER TO APPLY A SEPARATION OF POWERS ANALYSIS TO THE EU?

A difficulty with this concept appears to be the lack of clear criteria for determining its correct application. This is a problem that relates to the issue of balancing in general: balancing involves weighing incommensurable interests against each other, and it therefore entails the risk of subjectivity.[91] This problem does not arise in a similar way with a tripartite separation of powers, because that depends on a conceptual definition of function (legislative, executive, judicial); it is thus a matter of defining the type of power involved, rather than weighing the exercise of power by one institution with its exercise by another.

The incommensurability problem with balancing may be thought to arise more with the concept of checks and balances in separation of powers theory, but it does to a much lesser extent, because the idea of checks and balances in separation of powers theory is more clearly definable as the *partial* exercise of the power of one branch by another, and is thus still primarily a matter of defining a function. Therefore, it may be preferable for the ECJ to adopt a standard separation of powers approach in its case law, perhaps using the idea of institutional balance to support the idea of the principle of conferral based on the text of the treaties.

The most problematic aspect of the EU from the point of view of separation of powers theory is the role of the European Commission. This has both an executive and legislative role. However, its legislative role – its right of initiative – is limited

---

88 Case C–133/06 (n 85) para 58.

89 Ibid para 57.

90 Ibid para 44.

91 See generally, e.g. T A Aleinikoff 'Constitutional law in the age of balancing' (1987) 96(5) *Yale Law Journal* 943–1005 at 958, 972.

and can be considered a 'check' in traditional separation of powers theory. The law-making role of the ECJ is also problematic as regards a separation of powers, but it is not inevitable that the ECJ would play such a role (see further next chapter).

4.6 CONCLUSION

We have covered a large amount of issues in this chapter, but it covered four main themes: the institutions of the EU, the procedures for passing laws in the EU, types of laws in the EU, and the institutional balance or separation of powers at EU level. The institutions of the EU are in many respects like those at national level. The most distinct institution is the European Commission, which acts as a civil service, but also has a special role in developing new policies and proposing new laws. The Member States are represented in the EU by ministers in the Council (of Ministers), by heads of government in the European Council, and by directly elected representatives in the European Parliament.

The ECJ has played a very important role in the development of EU law, and we will look further at this in the next chapter. In recent years, the ECB has become much more prominent, and there has been debate about whether it should be given more powers. Law-making in the EU is somewhat more complicated than at national level, in that there are several different types of procedure for passing laws and several different types of legislation. However, the ordinary legislative procedure can be compared with the working of a bicameral parliament, with the Council (of Ministers) and the European Parliament acting as individual chambers.

The Treaty of Lisbon has somewhat unfortunately introduced some additional complexity concerning quasi-legislative powers of the European Commission (non-legislative delegated acts and non-legislative implementing acts). We completed the chapter by looking at the concept of 'institutional balance' in the case law of the ECJ, and considered whether it would be preferable for the ECJ to adopt a separation of powers analysis to the workings of the EU institutions.

POINTS TO REVIEW

- The main institutions of the EU are the European Council (meeting of heads of government of the Member States), the Council (of Ministers) (ministers from the Member States meeting), the European Commission (a centralised civil service), the European Parliament (consisting of directly elected representatives from the Member States), the Court of Justice, the Court of Auditors and the European Central Bank.

– The European Commission may seem the institution least comparable to an institution at national level. Broadly speaking, it can be compared to a civil service, in that its main function is to ensure EU law is enforced. It does this through monitoring implementation at national level and through taking proceedings against the Member States before the ECJ. It has a central role in the legislative process by having a more or less exclusive right of legislative initiative, but in practice the Council (of Ministers) and European Parliament can ask the Commission to propose new laws.

– Although it is somewhat complicated, law-making in the EU basically works along the lines of a bicameral Parliament: under the ordinary legislative procedure, the Council (of Ministers) and European Parliament pass laws proposed by the European Commission.

– In addition to the ordinary legislative procedure, there are a number of special legislative procedures. They differ mainly in giving the European Parliament a reduced role.

– The ECJ does not apply a separation of powers analysis in interpreting the powers of the EU institutions in its case. Instead, it has adopted the concept of institutional balance. This concept may be open to criticism for being poorly defined.

CHAPTER GLOSSARY

Bicameral parliament is a parliament with two legislative chambers. The ordinary legislative procedure in the EU, in which the Council (of Ministers) and the European Parliament jointly pass legislation, could be compared to a bicameral parliament. A parliament with a single legislative chamber is called a 'unicameral' parliament.

Co-decision is the old term (pre-Lisbon Treaty) for what is now called the ordinary legislative procedure.

Comitology refers to the system of committees established by the Member States to scrutinise the exercise of delegated legislative power by the European Commission.

Configuration refers to the different composition of the Council (of Ministers) when it is meeting, depending on which area of EU competence is being dealt with. Article 16(6) TEU provides that the Council shall meet in different configurations, the list of which is to be adopted in accordance with Article 236 TFEU. Apart from Foreign Affairs and General Affairs, there are eight other configurations currently in use.

Cooperation procedure refers to one of legislative methods used by the European Parliament prior to the Treaty of Lisbon 2009. Under the cooperation procedure, the European parliament could force the Council (of Ministers) to act by unanimity instead of qualified majority voting.

Emergency break refers to the use, under the Treaty of Lisbon, of a veto in the legislative process by a Member State to protect its essential interests.

Institutional balance is a concept used by the European Court of Justice as a substitute for a separation of powers in determining the proper scope of the power of the EU institutions. The concept of institutional balance can be criticised as poorly defined.

Ioannina compromise is a modification of the ordinary legislative procedure whereby the legislative process can be delayed to consider more fully the objections of some Member States.

Luxembourg Accord refers to an agreement reached among the Member States in the late 1960s whereby Member States were allowed to veto a proposed piece of legislation where it perceived its vital national interests were affected, even where the treaties provided for majority voting.

Non-legislative acts is a concept introduced by the Treaty of Lisbon, it refers to the standard EU legal instruments being introduced in a non-legislative form, as a type of administrative measure. The concept is poorly defined in the treaties, and confusion is added by a further unclear distinction being introduced between non-legislative acts adopted as delegated acts (in Article 290 TFEU) and non-legislative acts adopted as implementing acts (in Article 291 TFEU).

Ordinary legislative procedure refers to main procedure for passing EU (secondary) legislation since the coming into effect of the Lisbon Treaty in 2009. It involves the European Commission making a proposal for a new piece of legislation and then the Council (of Ministers) and the European Parliament jointly deciding whether to adopt it. If there is disagreement between the Council and the Parliament, a conciliation procedure is applied.

Passarelle refers to a type of clause in the EU treaties allowing for a change in the voting procedure in the Council (of Ministers) from unanimity to (qualified) majority voting. Article 48(7) TEU contains a general *passarelle* clause (there are also some specific *passarelle* clauses) stating that the European Council acting unanimously and with consent of the European Parliament may replace a special legislative procedure with ordinary legislative procedure. Unusually for EU law, under this provision, national parliaments have right of veto within six-month period.

Population initiative is a new procedure introduced by the Treaty of Lisbon as Article 11(4) TEU whereby a legislative initiative can be put before the EU legislature where it is supported by a petition with 1 million signatures from EU citizens.

Primary legislation as a term in EU law refers to the founding treaties of the EU and to amending treaties.

Qualified majority voting refers to the system of majority voting in the EU Council (of Ministers), under which the vote of a Member State is weighted according to its population size.

Right of initiative refers to the power the European Commission has to propose new laws at EU level. Only the Commission may generally propose a new law (an exception is in Article 76 TFEU), although the Council (of Ministers) and the European Parliament can ask the Commission to do so or can require it to do so by putting a clause to that effect in some other piece of legislation.

Secondary legislation is the term used in EU law to describe laws other than the treaties. The types of secondary legislation are regulations, directives and decisions.

Special legislative procedure refers to any procedure for passing secondary legislation in the EU that differs from the ordinary legislative procedure.

TAKING THINGS FURTHER

H Xanthaki 'The problem of quality in EU legislation: what on earth is really wrong?' (2001) 38 *Common Market Law Review* 651–76 This article looks at criticisms of the difficult drafting style of EU legislation. Among the conclusions reached are that the problem is not so much with the guidelines for drafting adopted by EU institutions, but that not enough care and attention is made to simplifying legislative language.

J-P Jacqué 'The principle of institutional balance' (2004) 41 *Common Market Law Review* 383 This article provides an overview of the concept of institutional balance, which, in the case law of the ECJ, seems to replace the concept of a separation of powers. The article is favourable toward the approach of the ECJ, adopting the orthodox view of the issue amongst EU lawyers.

F Häge 'Who decides in the Council of the European Union?' (2008) 46(3) *Journal of Common Market Studies* 533–58 This political science article analyses the influence of ministers and officials (mainly COREPER) in the process of passing legislation, arguing that ministers do exercise greater influence than officials.

G Conway 'Recovering a separation of powers in the European Union' (2011) 17(3) *European Law Journal* 304–322 This article offers a critique of the standard view of institutional balance adopted in the case law of the ECJ. It argues that the concept of a separation of powers, found at the state level, can and should be applied to horizontal relations between the institutions at EU level.

5

CHAPTER 5
THE SPECIAL ROLE OF THE EUROPEAN COURT OF JUSTICE

This chapter examines the remarkable role of the European Court of Justice (ECJ) in the EU legal system. It is widely agreed that the Court of Justice has made a fundamental contribution to enhancing integration, with a corresponding reduction in Member State sovereignty. Many of the key constitutional features of the EU were not explicitly established in the treaties, but by the case law of the Court of Justice, including: direct and indirect effect, supremacy, parallelism in external relations, human rights, a prohibition on non-discriminatory obstacles to free movement, and the basis of merger control, to identify some of the Court's more notable contributions. The Court of Justice has an expansive jurisdiction, which has facilitated this development of case law. It hears preliminary references from national courts, enforcement actions brought by the Commission or another Member State, reviews of the legality of acts of the EU institutions, and actions for damages against the Union institutions. However, what really facilitated the central role the Court has played in enhancing integration has been its methods of interpretation. The dominant method of interpretation of the Court of Justice is 'meta-teleological': purposive interpretation, with purpose geared toward a high level of generality of enhancing integration overall in the EU legal system. Controversy exists over the legitimacy of some of the Court's case law in this respect. In this chapter, we will look first at the procedures before the Court of Justice and the appointment of its judges. This is followed by an overview of its methods of interpretation and some of its most important cases to illustrate its role. Finally, we will examine the debate as to the legitimacy of the Court's approach to its role.

AS YOU READ . . .

The key questions that will be answered in this chapter are as follows:

– What kind of jurisdiction does the ECJ have?

– What is the role of the General Court?

– How are judges appointed?

— What are the methods of interpretation employed by the Court and what is its preferred or dominant style?

— How important has the role of the ECJ been in the process of integration?

— What normative criticisms can be made of the Court's approach to its role?

5.1 INTRODUCTION

In this chapter, we will examine the central role played by the Court of Justice of the EU (the ECJ or, as it is now more commonly called, the CJEU) in the development of the EU and how the Court of Justice functions today. We will look in particular at its methods of interpretation, which are distinctive and merit study in their own right. These methods are central to the role the ECJ has carved out for itself in the integration process. First, we will examine the jurisdiction and procedure of the Court, including the appointment of its judges, as well as how it relates to the separate European Court of Human Rights (ECtHR). The Court's role is set out in Article 19 TEU. As with any court, it is there to ensure that 'the law is observed'.

ARTICLE 19 TFEU

1. The Court of Justice of the European Union shall include the Court of Justice, the General Court and specialised courts. It shall ensure that in the interpretation and application of the Treaties the law is observed.

   Member States shall provide remedies sufficient to ensure effective legal protection in the fields covered by Union law.

2. The Court of Justice shall consist of one judge from each Member State. It shall be assisted by Advocates-General.

   The General Court shall include at least one judge per Member State.

   The judges and the Advocates-General of the Court of Justice and the judges of the General Court shall be chosen from persons whose independence is beyond doubt and who satisfy the conditions set out in Articles 253 and 254 of the Treaty on the Functioning of the European Union. They shall be appointed by common accord of the governments of the Member States for six years. Retiring judges and Advocates-General may be reappointed.

3. The Court of Justice of the European Union shall, in accordance with the Treaties:

   (a) rule on actions brought by a Member State, an institution or a natural or legal person;

> (b) give preliminary rulings, at the request of courts or tribunals of the Member States, on the interpretation of Union law or the validity of acts adopted by the institutions;
>
> (c) rule in other cases provided for in the Treaties.

The Court has contributed a great deal to the development of the constitutional structure of the EU, albeit that this is controversial.

5.2 JURISDICTION AND PROCEDURE OF THE COURT

Articles 251–281 TFEU and the Statute of the Court of Justice of the European Union (which is like a protocol to the treaties[1]) set out rules on the functioning of the Court.

5.2.1 SOME PRELIMINARY POINTS

5.2.1.1 COMPOSITION OF THE COURT

Under Article 19(2) TFEU, there is one judge for each Member State, so at present there are 28 judges.[2] Judges are appointed by the governments of the Member States acting collectively.[3] In the past, there has been little scrutiny of this process. Since the Treaty of Lisbon, the Member States are to be advised by a panel comprising seven persons chosen from among former members of the Court of Justice and the General Court, members of national supreme courts, and lawyers of recognised competence, one of whom shall be proposed by the European Parliament.[4] The process will thus be dominated by legal élites.

The term of the judges is for six years, and they may be reappointed.[5] The judges normally sit in chambers. The rules governing chambers are set out in the Statute of the Court. Chambers consist of three or five judges, and each chamber elects a president. Occasionally, the Court sits in a Grand Chamber (13 judges, but a quorum is 9 judges), over which the president of the Court presides, and rarely as a full court (literally, this would be 28 judges, but a quorum is 15 judges). The Court sits as a Grand Chamber

---

1 Article 281 TFEU provides that the Statute shall be laid down in a separate protocol.
2 Article 254 TFEU states that the Statute of the Court of Justice shall determine the number of judges, and art 48 of the Statute states that there shall be 27 judges (the Statute is in the form of a protocol to the treaties, Protocol No 3 of the Statute of the Court of Justice of the European Union).
3 Ibid art 254.
4 Ibid art 255.
5 Ibid art 253.

when requested to do so by a Member State or an EU institution. The Court sits as a Full Court when dealing with disputes under Article 228(2), Article 245(2), Article 247 or Article 286(6) TFEU.[6]

> ## KEY LEARNING POINT
>
> ### THE ROLE OF THE ADVOCATE GENERAL
> The role of the Advocate General is a distinct feature of the Court of Justice: the Advocate General provides a detailed and public advisory opinion to the Court prior to the Court's own judgment. The Opinions of Advocates General tend to go into more depth than the judgments of the Court. However, the Court is not bound by the Opinion of the Advocate General, although it quite often reaches the same conclusion. Even where the Court does reach the same conclusion, it may be for different reasons. The Advocate General is independent of the Court, although a part of the institution.

Under Article 252 TFEU, there are eight Advocates General. A declaration annexed to the Final Act of the Inter-governmental Conference which adopted the Treaty of Lisbon states:

> . . . if, in accordance with Article 252, first paragraph, of the Treaty on the Functioning of the European Union, the Court of Justice requests that the number of Advocates General be increased by three (eleven instead of eight), the Council will, acting unanimously, agree on such an increase. In that case, the Conference agrees that Poland will, as is already the case for Germany, France, Italy, Spain and the United Kingdom, have a permanent Advocate General and no longer take part in the rotation system, while the existing rotation system will involve the rotation of five Advocates General instead of three.[7]

In October 2013, the Court of Justice requested that the number be increased, citing the effects of enlargement, the effects of the Treaty of Lisbon, and the greater volume of case law facing the Court. In status, Advocates General are equal to judges of the Court. Germany, France, Italy, Spain, the United Kingdom and now Poland have a permanent Advocate General because of the size of their populations. The function of the Advocate General is to provide a preliminary advisory opinion in each case, as set out in the second paragraph of Article 252 TFEU:

> It shall be the duty of the Advocate-General, acting with complete impartiality and independence, to make, in open court, reasoned submissions on cases which, in accordance with the Statute of the Court of Justice of the European Union, require his involvement.

....

6   Articles 16–17 of the Statute of the European Court of Justice.
7   Court of Justice of the European Union, Press release No 139/13, Luxembourg (23 October 2013).

The Court of Justice is not bound by the Advocate General's Opinion, but tends to decide the same way.[8] It is sometimes observed that the Advocates General provide a more thorough discussion of the legal issues, and this is frequently the case. The judgments of the ECJ can be notoriously brief (although this is not always so; see especially in its competition law judgments). To some extent, the role of the Opinions of Advocates General 'take the heat' from this criticism of the Court of Justice. This is positive in one sense, as the Advocates General do generally discuss the issues in more depth, but negative in the sense that their role can act as a disincentive to the Court of Justice to offer more substantial reasoning.

Finally, Article 253 TFEU sets out the qualifications of the judges and Advocates General:

> The judges and Advocates-General of the Court of Justice shall be chosen from persons whose independence is beyond doubt and who possess the qualifications required for appointment to the highest judicial offices in their respective countries or who are jurisconsults of recognised competence.[9]

5.2.1.2 LUXEMBOURG, NOT STRASBOURG

A very common source of confusion about the ECJ, which sits in Luxembourg, is its relationship with the European Court of Human Rights, which sits in Strasbourg. It is not altogether uncommon for the two courts to be confused. All the EU Member States have signed the European Convention on Human Rights (ECHR)[10] and permit cases to be taken against them before the European Court of Human Rights. However, apart from this, the two courts are entirely separate and originate in separate legal systems as discussed in Chapter 2. The Court of Justice has no jurisdiction over the ECHR, although it does look to the ECHR as a source of inspiration for human rights, which are general principles of EU law.[11]

KEY LEARNING POINT

DISTINGUISHING THE LUXEMBOURG AND STRASBOURG COURTS
Remember that the European Court of Human Rights, which sits in Strasbourg, is separate to the EU system. The European Court of Human Rights has jurisdiction only over one law, the European Convention on Human Rights.

---

8 C J Carrubba, M Gabel and C Hankla 'Judicial behavior under political constraints: evidence from the European Court of Justice' (2008) 102(4) *American Political Science Review* 435–52 at 449 suggesting that, statistically, opinions of the AG '[have] a systematic positive influence on ECJ decisions'.

9 'Jurisconsult' refers to legal academics.

10 ETS No 5.

11 Case 46/87 *Hoechst* [1989] ECR I–283 paras 18–19; Case 26/75 *Rutili v Minister for the Interior* [1975] ECR 1219; Case 149/77 *Defrenne v Sabena III* [1978] ECR 1365.

Another key difference between the two is their scope of application in national law. In particular, three differences can be highlighted in this regard:

1. EU law only applies where the EU has competence (see Chapter 7), which does not extend to the whole of national law, whereas a claim before the Strasbourg court on compatibility with the ECHR can relate to any part of national law.
2. EU law produces effects between individuals through horizontal direct effect, whereas the ECHR is generally only available as a remedy against the state.
3. No supremacy or direct effect doctrines automatically apply to the ECHR; it is up to each national system to decide what effects the ECHR produces in national law.

This situation is rendered slightly more complex by Article 6 TEU (as amended by the Treaty of Lisbon), which provides that the EU shall accede to the ECHR. When it does so, an implication is that, in human rights matters, the European Court of Human Rights will function as a kind of court of appeal from the Court of Justice.

Chart: Going from National Courts to European Courts

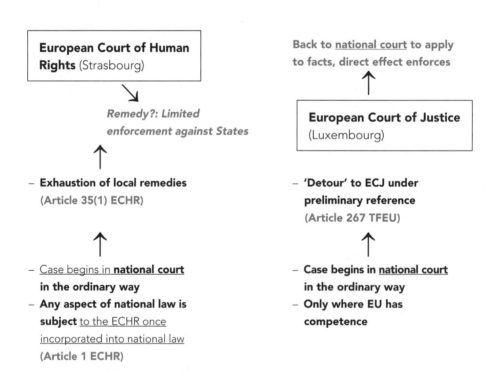

5.2.1.3 PRECEDENT IN THE ECJ

There is no doctrine of binding precedent in EU law. This reflects the approach of the civil law tradition of continental Europe. However, 'the Court does not often depart from its previous decisions'.[12] In other words, there is a de facto system of precedent, related to the universally accepted principle of formal justice that like cases be treated alike.[13] Any court, whether it is in the common law tradition of the UK in which precedent is a distinct source of law or not, will need an informal system of precedent of treating like cases alike.[14]

In this context, Stone Sweet and McCowan have argued that precedent has been central to the effectiveness of the ECJ in carving out its role in the integration process.[15] They point to data indicating extensive citation by the ECJ of its own cases.[16] More generally on precedent, they note its connection with the concept of analogy, which is the thought process by which similarity and dissimilarity are evaluated.[17]

5.2.1.4 PROCEDURE AND JURISDICTION OF THE ECJ

Procedure before the Court of Justice differs with UK procedures in three main respects: (i) procedure is more written than oral; (ii) the Advocate General delivers a preliminary opinion (there is no equivalent to this in UK courts); and (iii) there are no dissenting judgments.

EXPLAINING THE LAW

SINGLE JUDGMENTS IN THE COURT OF JUSTICE OF THE EU

The last point, that there is only one majority judgment and no dissenting judgments at the ECJ, is important in practice, because it contributes to the brevity and sometimes the superficiality of the Court's judgments. In the UK, where there is more than one judge hearing case in the High Court or above, each judge delivers an opinion. This is also the case in the European Court of Human Rights for dissenting judges. The advantage of this is that it results in more open and explicit debate between judges when they disagree. This helps illustrate more fully the legal reasoning in judgments, thereby improving the quality of their justification.

---

12 A Arnull *The European Court and its Court of Justice* (Oxford University Press 1999) 533. Cases where the ECJ has departed from previous decisions include criminal proceedings in Case C–267/91 *Keck and Mithouard* [1993] ECR I–6097 (selling arrangements) and Case 127/08 *Metock v Minister for Justice, Equality & Law Reform* [2008] ECR I–6241 (prior lawful entry or residence in the EU).

13 N MacCormick *Legal Reasoning and Legal Theory* (Clarendon Press 1978) 6, 99.

14 M Cappelletti 'The law-making power of the judge and its limits: a comparative analysis' (1981–1982) 15 *Monash University Law Review* 63, noting that the authority of precedents has always been recognised even in the civil law tradition.

15 A Stone Sweet, M McCowan 'Discretion and precedent' in A Stone Sweet *The Judicial Construction of Europe* (Oxford University Press 2004) 109–115. See also L Conant *Justice Contained: Law and Politics in the European Union* (Cornell University Press 2002) 63–68.

16 Stone Sweet and McCowan (n 15) refer to data from the years 1961–1998 in which a total of 2674 rulings cite 2057 different cases. They note, however, that they conflate citation with precedent, but do take citation as a highly reliable indicator of precedent, subject to future research.

17 Ibid, citing S Vosniadou, A Ortony (eds) *Similarity and Analogical Reasoning* (Cambridge University Press 1989).

In the context of an alleged breach of EU law and of proceedings before the ECJ arising from the breach, different entities may be the victim/aggrieved party: an individual may be a victim of a breach of EU law by (i) a Member State or (ii) a Union institution. Where there is a violation by a Member State of EU law, another Member State or the Union itself may be the aggrieved party. Although it may seem an obvious observation to make, it is always useful when dealing with any cases to consider 'who is suing who over what and in what court', i.e. always bear these four elements in mind, as this will help make clearer the differences between different types of Court of Justice proceedings: (i) who is suing (individual, Member State or institution); (ii) who is being sued (individual, Member State or institution); (iii) on what basis is the claim being brought (national law or administrative action is being challenged or EU law and administrative action?); and (iv) in which court is the claim being brought?

Different remedies are available to deal with this range of situations. There are three main categories of proceedings before the ECJ/CJEU.

5.2.2 THE PRELIMINARY REFERENCE[18] FROM A NATIONAL COURT TO THE COURT OF JUSTICE

Where a point of EU law has arisen in a national court in a dispute between an individual and the Member State in question, the national court refers the point of law to the Court of Justice asking it to make a decision (or answer the question) on a point of EU law so that the national court correctly applies EU law in finally giving judgment in the case (Article 267 TFEU).

KEY LEARNING POINT

PRELIMINARY REFERENCES AND WHO IS SUING WHO, OVER WHAT, AND IN WHAT COURT?

In a preliminary reference under Article 267 TFEU, an individual is suing either his or her own government or another individual *in a national court* on the basis that EU law is not being properly applied in national law (usually, because of the government, but it can be because of an individual if there is horizontal direct effect). The national court will refer an issue of EU law to the ECJ, which will answer it, and refer it back to the national court to apply to the facts of the case.

EXPLAINING THE LAW

THE IMPORTANCE OF THE PRELIMINARY REFERENCE SYSTEM

The preliminary reference system plays a key role in EU law. It ensures a connection between national courts and the ECJ, allowing the ECJ to influence

---

18 The exact wording of art 267 TFEU refers to a 'preliminary ruling'. In this book, the common UK shorthand of 'preliminary reference' is used.

and usually determine the interpretation of EU law in national courts. Due to national courts being under a duty in cases of doubt to refer a preliminary reference to the ECJ, the ECJ can ensure the consistency of EU law throughout the Member States. In this way, the preliminary reference system complements through procedure the EU law doctrines of direct effect and supremacy. As we will see in Chapter 6, one of the reasons given by the Court of Justice for developing the doctrine of direct effect was that it was necessary for the preliminary reference system to function.

From a political science perspective, the impact of the preliminary reference system can be understood in terms of rivalry between judicial institutions. Alter locates the largely successful relationship between the ECJ and national courts within the context of inter-court rivalry and the self-interested motivation of courts as institutions; they are primarily concerned with enhancing their own status and jurisdiction.[19]

Lower level national courts were motivated to circumvent the national judicial hierarchy through using the preliminary reference system to determine authoritatively legal issues independently of national supreme or constitutional courts. In systems without constitutional review, courts in general were motivated by the increasing power vis-à-vis national legislatures and executives that the supremacy doctrine implied:[20] national courts were now able to assert a de facto power of constitutional review based on the supremacy of EC law to disapply national legislation.

The success of the preliminary reference system, therefore, is largely attributable to self-empowerment by national courts lower than supreme or constitutional courts; this thesis is consistent with the much greater resistance to supremacy manifested in national constitutional and supreme courts.

Three key issues arise with the preliminary reference system concerning the division of labour between national courts and the ECJ:

....

19 K Alter *Establishing the Supremacy of European Law: The Making of an International Rule of Law* (Oxford University Press 2001) 28. See also A-M Burley, W. Mattli 'Europe before the court: a political theory of integration' (1993) 47(1) *International Organization* 41–76 at 43–44; J H H Weiler 'Journey to an unknown destination: a Retrospective and prospective of the European Court of Justice in the arena of political integration' (1993) 31(4) *Journal of Common Market Studies* 417–46 at 42.

20 Alter (n 19). Motivation might vary depending also on whether the specific legislation in question accorded with the substantive policy preferences of the judge. See W Mattli, A-M Slaughter 'Revisiting the European Court of Justice' (1998) 52(1) *International Organization* 177–209 at 190 ff.

5.2.2.1 WHEN SHOULD A NATIONAL COURT MAKE A PRELIMINARY REFERENCE TO THE ECJ?

By the *acte clair* doctrine in the *Da Costa* case, where the Court has clearly ruled on a point of law, national courts are not under a duty pursuant to Article 267 TFEU to make a preliminary reference to the ECJ for clarification of the requirements of Union law.[21] However, this has been further determined especially by the *CILFIT* case, where the ECJ held that a preliminary reference should not be made only where the issue of interpretation of Community law was so obvious as to leave no room for any reasonable doubt.[22] Thus, the position of the ECJ on this point has evolved, from leaving the issue largely to the national court to now requiring that in any cases of any doubt of the interpretation of EU law, a preliminary reference must be made from the national court to the ECJ, which retains the right to refuse the reference.[23]

> KEY LEARNING POINT
> ....
>
> **WHEN ARE PRELIMINARY REFERENCES MANDATORY?**
> The text of Article 267 TFEU envisages two types of preliminary reference:
> (1) optional and (2) mandatory. If a national court or tribunal considers that it
> is necessary to decide a question of EU law in giving judgment, it *may* make
> a preliminary reference. If it is a national court against whose decisions there
> is no appeal, it must make a preliminary reference. The effect of the *acte clair*
> as clarified in *CILFIT*, however, is that unless the question of EU law is clear,
> a national court against whose decision there is an appeal is still under an
> obligation to make a preliminary reference.

In a number of cases, the ECJ has set requirements about the formulation of question by the national court, which if not met will lead to the Court refusing to hear the reference. First, in *Telemarsicabruzzo SpA*,[24] for example, the ECJ said the questions of law and the relevant facts must be clearly stated in the reference from the national court.[25] Secondly, the facts must not be hypothetical,[26] (although courts in other jurisdictions

....

21 Joined Cases 28–30/62 *Da Costa* [1963] ECR 31.

22 Case 283/81 *CILFIT v Ministry of Health* [1982] ECR 3415 para 21.

23 The judgment in Case 244/80 *Pasquale Foglia v Mariella Novello (No 2)* [1981] ECR 3045 can be interpreted as important in the development of the approach of the ECJ to determine itself how the preliminary reference system was to work. The ECJ stated that it was for it to examine the conditions under which a preliminary reference is sent to it in order to confirm its own jurisdiction (see para 21).

24 Case C–320/90 *Telemarsicabruzzo SpA v Circostel, Ministero delle Poste e Telecommunicazioni and Ministerio della Difesa* [1993] ECR I–393.

25 Similarly see Case C–83/91 *Meilicke v ADV/ORGA* [1992] ECR I–4871. Case 93/78 *Mattheus v Doego Fruchimport und Tiefkuhlkost eG* [1978] ECR 2203 is somewhat different. Here, the ECJ rejected jurisdiction on the grounds that the question was non-justiciable before it, rather than that the question was unclear, because the measures in issue were not yet a part of Community law in that they concerned countries that were soon to join, but had not yet joined, the Communities.

26 See e.g. Case 244/80 *Pasquale Foglia v Mariella Novello* [1980] ECR 3045 para 18; Case C–467/04 *Criminal proceedings against Gasparini and Others* [2006] ECR I–9199.

sometimes do answer hypothetical legal questions) on the rationale that this would be a waste of the Court's resources. Thirdly, the question asked must be relevant to the resolution of the facts before the national court.[27] This differs from the previous situation, in that the question is not purely hypothetical to the facts of the case, but it is not necessary to answer the question to deal with the case.

5.2.2.2 HOW FAR CAN THE ECJ GO IN DETERMINING THE APPLICATION OF THE LAW TO THE FACTS?

In theory, it is for the ECJ to answer an abstract question of law. Once the ECJ gives the answer, it then sends it back to the national court to apply to the facts. This suggests the ECJ has no role in application to the facts. However, this is not really the case in reality. As we have seen above, the ECJ insists that the factual background must be clear in the preliminary reference, it will not accept a purely abstract legal question without the facts on which it is based being explained. Quite often, the way the ECJ answers the question will leave the national court with a minimal role in deciding how to apply the ECJ's answer to the facts.[28]

5.2.2.3 WHAT IS THE POSITION OF NATIONAL FINAL COURTS OF APPEAL?

Article 267 TEU distinguishes between final courts of appeal, from which there is no further appeal in national law, and other courts, from which there is an appeal. In the case of the former, it states:

> Where any such question is raised in a case pending before a court or tribunal of a Member State against whose decisions there is no judicial remedy under national law, that court or tribunal shall bring the matter before the Court.

Bearing in mind the rule in *CILFIT*, which means that in any case of doubt a national court or tribunal will need to refer questions of EU law to the ECJ, the specific obligation on the final court of appeal may not seem so significant. However, the provision means that the *acte clair* doctrine does not really apply to final courts: even if the final court of appeal believes the EU law in issue seems clear, it generally should still refer the question to the ECJ.

5.2.2.4 WHAT IS A 'COURT OR TRIBUNAL' FOR THE PURPOSES OF ARTICLE 267 TFEU?

The definition of what is a court or tribunal under Article 267 TFEU is an autonomous concept of EU law, i.e. the Court of Justice defines it, rather than individual Member States. What this means is that if a national system designates a body as court or tribunal, i.e. uses that expression, it will not necessarily fall under Article 267, it must satisfy the criteria established in the Court of Justice's case law. Conversely, bodies that are not

....

27 See e.g. Case 18/93 *Corsica Ferries Italia Srl v Corpo dei Piloti del Porto di Genova* [1994] ECR I–1783.

28 For an example see Case C–144/04 *Werner Mangold v Rüdiger Helm* [2005] ECR I–9981 (concerning age discrimination in employment).

described in their titles as courts or tribunals under national law may satisfy the criteria of the Court's case law.[29]

A leading authority is *Broekmeulen*, where the Court of Justice held that a body established under the auspices of the Royal Medical Society for the Promotion of Medicine was a 'court or tribunal' within the meaning of the treaty, even though that society was a private association. In order to practise as a doctor in the Netherlands it was necessary to be registered with the Royal Medical Society. The Court stated:

> If, under the legal stem of a Member State, the task of implementing such provisions [relating to freedom of movement of services and of establishment] is assigned to a professional body acting under a degree of governmental supervision, and if that body, in conjunction with the public authorities concerned, creates appeal procedures which may affect the exercise of rights granted by Community law, it is imperative, in order to ensure the proper functioning of Community law, that the Court should have an opportunity of ruling on issues of interpretation and validity arising out of such proceedings.
>
> In the absence in practice of any right of appeal to the ordinary courts, the appeals committee, which operates with the consent of the public authorities and with their cooperation, and which, after an adversarial procedure, delivers decisions which are in fact recognised as final, must, in a matter involving the application of Community law, be considered as a court or tribunal of a Member State within the meaning of Article 177 of the Treaty. Therefore, the Court has jurisdiction to reply to the question asked.[30]

As Broberg and Fenger note, although there is no abstract definition of court or tribunal under Article 267 TFEU, it is possible to deduce considerations relevant to the court and to assess the relative importance of these considerations.[31] In *Dorsch Consult*, the Court of Justice listed the following criteria:

1. it is established by law
2. it is permanent
3. its jurisdiction is compulsory
4. it has an *inter partes* procedure
5. it applies rules of law and
6. it is independent.[32]

....

29 M Broberg, N Fenger *Preliminary References to the European Court of Justice* (Oxford University Press 2014) 61.

30 Case 246/80 *Broekmeulen v Huisarts Registratie Commissie* [1980] ECR 2311 paras 16–17.

31 Broberg and Fenger (n 29) 61.

32 Case C–54/96 *Dorsch Consult Ingenieurgesellschaft mbH v Bundesbaugesellschaft Berlin mbH* [1997] ECR I–4961 para 23, citing Case 61/65 *Vaassen (née Göbbels)* [1966] ECR 261; Case 14/86 *Pretore di Salò v Persons Unknown* [1987] ECR 2545 para 7; Case 109/88 *Danfoss* [1989] ECR 3199 paras 7–8; Case C–393/92 *Almelo and Others* [1994] ECR I–1477; and Case C–111/94 *Job Centre* [1995] ECR I–3361 para 9. See also Joined Cases C–110–147/98 *Gabalfrisa and Others* [2000] ECR1–1577, where a tax tribunal was found to satisfy the criteria.

Established by law: In *Dorsch Consult*, a body established by a framework budgetary law was allowed to refer a dispute to the Court of Justice concerning public service contracts. It did not matter that the law had not conferred power concerning the subject matter of the dispute.[33] In contrast, bodies that are set up purely by administrative decisions will not generally be considered 'established by law'.[34] This can be described as a formal, rather than functional criterion, i.e. it depends on the formal legal basis of a body, rather than its function. However, the Court treats it in a minimalist way, it is not difficult to satisfy. *Broekmeulen* illustrates this. It is enough that there is some involvement of public authorities in the ongoing work of the body, rather than that it has been originally established by law.

Similarly to *Broekmeulen*, in *Gebhard*, the National Council of the Bar of Italy was found to be a court or tribunal,[35] and in *Abrahamsson and Anderson*, a special appeals committee to examine appeals against certain decisions taken in relation to higher education was found to be a court or tribunal.[36] In *Abrahamsson and Anderson*, of the eight members of the body in question, the chair and vice chair had to be former judges, three members had to be lawyers, all of whom were appointed by the government.[37]

A borderline category in this regard is arbitrators or arbitral tribunals. These will normally be established by law. Most jurisdictions have a legal framework governing arbitration. In particular cases, arbitrators will be established normally in a contract. However, this will typically be a contract between private parties. The Court of Justice has held that arbitrators established under a contract are not courts or tribunals under Article 267 TFEU.[38] It was not sufficient that an arbitrator gave legally binding conclusions, arbitration was chosen as an alternative to the normal courts, and public authorities were not involved in the decision to choose arbitration.[39]

All this meant that the link between the arbitration procedure in this instance and the organization of legal remedies through the courts in the Member State in question was not sufficiently close for the arbitration procedure to fall under 'court or tribunal'[40] (so it is not impossible that if elements of these circumstances were different, in a particular case, an arbitration procedure might come within Article 267 TFEU).

In *Criminal proceedings against X*, the Court of Justice held that a reference may be made under Article 267 TFEU only by a body required to give a ruling in complete

....

33 Case C–54/96 *Dorsch Consult* (n 32) paras 22–38.
34 Broberg and Fenger (n 29) 61–62.
35 Case C–55/94 *Gebhard v Consiglio dell'Ordine degli Avvocati e Procuratori di Milano* [1996] ECR I–4165.
36 Case C–407/98 *Abrahamsson and Anderson v Fogelqvist* [2000] ECR I–5539.
37 Some of the members of the appeals committee of the Royal Medical Society were appointed in *Broekmeulen*.
38 Case 102/81 *Nordsee* [1982] ECR 1095. See also Case C–125/04 *Denuit and Cordenier* [2005] ECR I–923. See further G Beber 'Arbitration tribunals and art 177 of the EEC Treaty' (1985) 22 *Common Market Law Review* 489–504.
39 Case 102/81 *Nordsee* (n 38) paras 10–12.
40 Ibid para 13.

independence in proceedings intended to result in a judicial decision; as a result, prosecutors were not included.[41]

It is permanent: Broberg and Fenger note that this has never appeared to be decisive of itself as a requirement, but that it is unlikely a body established regarding a particular dispute would satisfy the requirement.[42] This is consistent with the Court's case law on arbitrators.

Its jurisdiction is compulsory: This means that the body in question gives a binding ruling and whose jurisdiction cannot be avoided. It does not need to be the case, however, that it is the only such body to have jurisdiction.[43] In *Gabalfrisa*, decisions of the Spanish tax authority could be challenged before the administrative courts only after complaint proceedings have been brought before the Tribunales Económico-Administrativos and, thus, the jurisdiction of those tribunals was found to be compulsory.[44]

It has an inter partes *procedure:* This is not a very strict requirement, it can be related to the idea of the existence of a legal dispute, rather than that there are two parties to a dispute in an adversarial type process. Thus, in *Cartesio*, the Court of Justice found that an appellate body hearing an appeal from a decision by a lower court relating to a register fell within, even though the lower court's decision was not *inter partes*:

> 56. With regard to the *inter partes* nature of the proceedings before the national court, Article 234 EC does not make reference to the Court subject to those proceedings being *inter partes*. None the less, it follows from that article that a national court may make a reference to the Court only if there is a case pending before it and if it is called upon to give judgment in proceedings intended to lead to a decision of a judicial nature (see to that effect, inter alia, Case C–182/00 *Lutz and Others* [2002] ECR I–547, paragraph 13 and the case law cited).

> 57. Thus, where a court responsible for maintaining a register makes an administrative decision without being required to resolve a legal dispute, it cannot be regarded as exercising a judicial function. Such is the case, for example, where it decides an application for registration of a company in proceedings which do not have as their object the annulment of a measure which allegedly adversely affects the applicant (see to that effect, inter alia, *Lutz and Others*, paragraph 14 and the case law cited).

> 58. In contrast, a court hearing an appeal which has been brought against a decision of a lower court responsible for maintaining a register, rejecting such an application, and which seeks the setting-aside of that decision, which allegedly adversely affects

---

41 Joined Cases C–74/95 & 129/95 *Criminal proceedings against X* [1996] ECR I–6609.
42 Broberg and Fenger (n 29) 62–63.
43 Case C–259/04 *Emanuel* [2006] ECR I–3089.
44 Joined Cases C–110–147/98 *Gabalfrisa and Others* [2000] ECR I–1577 para 35.

the rights of the applicant, is called upon to give judgment in a dispute and is exercising a judicial function.

59. Accordingly, in such a case, the appellate court must, in principle, be regarded as a court or tribunal within the meaning of Article 234 EC, with jurisdiction to refer a question to the Court for a preliminary ruling (see for similar situations, inter alia, Case C–300/01 *Salzmann* [2003] ECR I–4899; *SEVIC Systems*; and Case C–117/06 *Möllendorf and Others* [2007] ECR I–8361).

60. It is apparent from the court file that, in the main proceedings, the referring court is sitting in an appellate capacity in an action for the setting-aside of a decision by which a lower court, responsible for maintaining the commercial register, rejected an application by a company for registration of the transfer of its seat, requiring the amendment of an entry in that register.

61. Accordingly, in the main proceedings, the referring court is hearing a dispute and is exercising a judicial function, regardless of the fact that the proceedings before that court are not *inter partes*.

62. Consequently, in the light of the case law cited in paragraphs 55 and 56 above, the referring court must be regarded as a court or tribunal for the purposes of Article 234 EC.[45]

It applies rules of law: This means that the national body is deciding on the basis of legal rules, rather than making a decision on a discretionary basis, e.g. on a sense of the equity of the case.[46]

It is independent: This criterion will generally be satisfied by any body that is a part of the ordinary courts system of a Member State. The focus of the court is to look to a legal basis for independence, rather than to examine factual independence in a particular case.[47] In *Syfait*, the Court of Justice considered whether the Greek Competition Commission was a court or tribunal.[48] The Court decided that it lacked independence in that it carried out both the investigation of breaches of competition law and adjudication of them.

In *Wilson*,[49] the Court elaborated on the idea of independence in the context of interpreting 'independent court or tribunal' in Directive 98/5/EC.[50] It said a basic

....

45 Case C–210/06 *Cartesio Oktató és Szolgáltató bt* [2008] ECR I–9641 paras 56–62.
46 Case 61/65 *Vaassen-Göbbels v Beambtenfonds voor het Mijnbedrijf* [1966] ECR 261, where the body in question applied a regulation under Dutch law relating to social insurance.
47 Ibid 63.
48 Case C–53/03 *Syfait* [2005] ECR I–4609.
49 Case C–506/04 *Wilson* [2006] ECR I–8613.
50 OJ L 77 14.03.1998 p. 36.

feature is acting in the role of a third party relative to a dispute.[51] Further, it involved immunity from external pressure,[52] such as guarantees against removal from office.[53] Finally, the Court emphasised impartiality and objectivity regarding the dispute in the sense that there was a level playing field between the parties.[54]

5.2.3 AN ENFORCEMENT ACTION BROUGHT AGAINST A MEMBER STATE IN THE ECJ

5.2.3.1 INTRODUCTION

An enforcement action is brought by either the European Commission or a Member State, for a breach of EU law by the accused State: Article 258 TFEU governs enforcement actions brought by the Commission, and Article 259 TFEU governs actions brought by Member States. However, the Member States hardly ever sue each other under Article 259 TFEU. Case law has supplemented the enforcement procedure by creating the doctrine of State liability: Member States must provide a remedy to individuals aggrieved for their breaches of EU law, including damages:[55] see the following chapter.

KEY LEARNING POINT
....

ENFORCEMENT ACTIONS: WHO IS SUING WHO OVER WHAT, AND IN WHAT COURT?

In an enforcement action, an individual is not involved in the litigation. The European Commission or a Member State may sue another Member State for failing to properly implement or comply with EU law in national law. Although Member States rarely sue each other in enforcement actions (because doing so would be very politically sensitive), a recent example is *Hungary v Slovakia*,[56] concerning a refusal by Slovakia to permit the president of Hungary to enter Slovakia (to attend a commemorative event) and whether this was a violation of free movement. The ECJ held that the derogations to free movement, interpreted in light of public international law, allowed Slovakia to refuse entry.[57]

The European Commission often brings enforcement actions, it is part of its normal work.

....

51 Case C–506/04 *Wilson* (n 49) para 49, citing Case C–24/92 *Corbiau v Administration des Contributions* [1993] ECR I–1277 para 15 and Case C–516/99 *Schmid* [2002] ECR I–4573 para 36.

52 Case C–506/04 *Wilson* (n 49) para 51, citing Case C–103/97 *Köllensperger and Atzwanger* [1999] ECR I–551 para 21; Case C–407/98 *Abrahamsson & Anderson* above (n 36) para 36; and the European Court of Human Rights in *Campbell and Fell v United Kingdom*, judgment of 28 June 1984 Series A No 80 § 78.

53 Case C–506/04 *Wilson* (n 49) para 51, citing Joined Cases C–9/97 and C–118/97 *Jokela and Pitkäranta* [1998] ECR I–6267 para 20.

54 Case C–506/04 *Wilson* (n 49) para 52.

55 Joined Cases C–6 & C–9/90 *Francovich & Ors* [1991] ECR I–5357.

56 Case C–364/10, judgment of 16 October 2012.

57 Ibid paras 49–51.

5.2.3.2 ENFORCEMENT ACTIONS BY THE COMMISSION AGAINST MEMBER STATES UNDER ARTICLE 258 TFEU

ARTICLE 258 TFEU

If the Commission considers that a Member State has failed to fulfil an obligation under the Treaties, it shall deliver a reasoned opinion on the matter after giving the State concerned the opportunity to submit its observations. If the State concerned does not comply with the opinion within the period laid down by the Commission, the latter may bring the matter before the Court of Justice of the European Union.

Article 258 allows for the enforcement of EU law directly before the Court of Justice either at the initiation of the Commission (usually) or the Member States (under Article 259, which is rarely used). The enforcement procedure under Article 258 has two stages.

Administrative stage Although the Commission has a discretion to sue a Member State, Article 258 TFEU makes it clear that this is not the first option: there is first an administrative exchange of opinions between the Commission and Member State. A number of alternatives to the enforcement procedure (which only the Commission under Article 258 TFEU and Member States under Article 259 TFEU can use) are relevant to the Commission's decision:

1. The use of direct effect, indirect effect, and State liability may address a problem of compliance at national level.
2. Petitions to the European Parliament under Articles 20(2)(d), 24 and 227 TFEU, which may bring about a solution through a political route.
3. A complaint to the Ombudsman under Article 228 TFEU about a failure of the Commission to enforce EU law, which will only result, however, in a non-binding report to the European Parliament.

In practice, the Commission cannot be expected to monitor every aspect of implementing EU law, and it responds to complaints brought to its attention by individuals. It then decides itself how to pursue the matter. A register is kept of individual complaints (and the European Ombudsman exercises a degree of oversight about how effectively the Commission responds to individual complaints).

The administrative stage consists of up to two elements. The first entails negotiations between the Commission and the Member States, which will attempt to resolve the matter informally (sometimes called the 'pre-contentious stage'). If the matter is not then resolved, the Commission will send a letter of formal notice to the Member State, requesting a response usually within a two-month period, and this may be followed by a reasoned opinion ('contentious stage'). The purpose of the letter of formal notice is, first, to delimit the subject-matter of the dispute and to indicate to the Member State, which is invited to submit its observations, the factors enabling it to prepare its defence and, secondly, to enable the Member State to comply before proceedings are brought to the Court.[58]

If the informal stage is unsuccessful in resolving the matter, and the Member State does not respond as the Commission wishes to the formal letter of notice, the Commission may deliver a reasoned opinion. This reasoned opinion sets out exactly the grounds of complaint, and it must be sufficiently detailed and specific to explain the Commission's reasons for initiating the enforcement procedure; the Court of Justice has held the reasoned opinion must be 'detailed and cogent'.[59]

The delivery of the opinion sets the time running within which the Member State must comply with the Commission recommendations in order to avoid the Commission bringing a case. The Commission determines the time limit for compliance, but it must be reasonable in allowing the Member State enough time to achieve compliance.[60]

EXPLAINING THE LAW

THE COMMISSION'S DISCRETION UNDER ARTICLE 258 TFEU

The Commission enjoys wide discretion in whether and when to bring an enforcement action, and a decision to not bring an enforcement action is not subject to judicial review.[61] However, the Commission can only take into account matters occurring before it commences the enforcement action, e.g. it cannot take account of changes to national legislation during the course of proceedings that might create or aggravate a Member State's liability under EU law, as this could impair the capacity of the defence to submit its case.[62] Conversely, the Court of Justice cannot take into account factors that might reduce a Member State's liability when those factors have occurred after the expiry of the period for compliance set out in the Commission's reasoned opinion and it may persist in bringing the action, in that it will establish liability on the part of the Member State with regard to the rights of an affected party.[63]

58 Case C–1/00 *Commission v France* [2001] ECR I–9989.
59 Case 74/82 *Commission v Ireland* [1984] ECR 2793.
60 Case C–207/96 *Commission v Italy* [1997] ECR I–6869 para 18; Case C–439/99 *Commission v Italy* [2002] ECR I–305 para 12.
61 Case 247/87 *Star Fruit Company v Commission* [1989] ECR 291; Case C–200/88 *Commission v Greece* [1990] ECR I–4299.
62 Case 7/69 *Commission v Italy* [1970] ECR 111.
63 Case 240/86 *Greece v Commission* [1988] ECR 1835; Case C–230/99 *Commission v France* [2001] ECR I–1169 para 31.

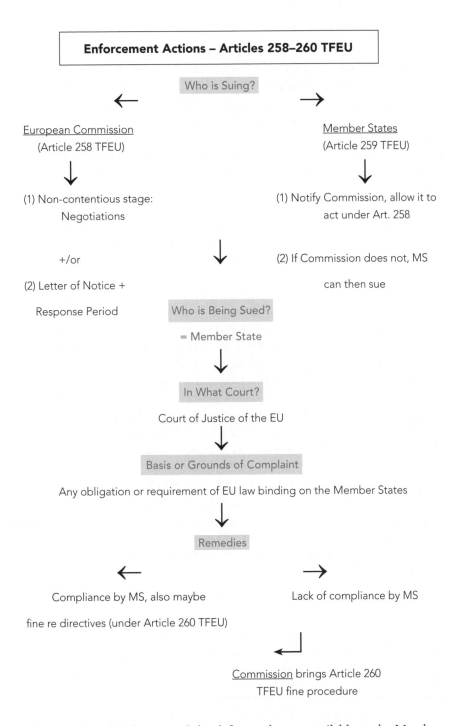

Enforcement Actions – Articles 258–260 TFEU

Who is Suing?

European Commission
(Article 258 TFEU)

Member States
(Article 259 TFEU)

(1) Non-contentious stage:
Negotiations

(1) Notify Commission, allow it to
act under Art. 258

+/or

(2) If Commission does not, MS

(2) Letter of Notice +

can then sue

Response Period

Who is Being Sued?

= Member State

In What Court?

Court of Justice of the EU

Basis or Grounds of Complaint

Any obligation or requirement of EU law binding on the Member States

Remedies

Compliance by MS, also maybe

Lack of compliance by MS

fine re directives (under Article 260 TFEU)

Commission brings Article 260
TFEU fine procedure

Next, there is the judicial stage and the defences that are available to the Member
State.

This is the final stage, and it arises where the Member State has failed to comply with
the recommendations in the letter of formal notice as supported by the reasoned opinion
and within the time limit stated in the latter.

KEY LEARNING POINT

CONCEPT OF THE STATE UNDER ARTICLE 258 TFEU
A Member State's failure to fulfil obligations may, in principle, be established
under Article 258 TFEU whatever the agency of that State whose action or
inaction is the cause of the failure to fulfil its obligations, even in the case of a
constitutionally independent institution.[64] For example, in *Commission v Italy*,
the complaint of the Commission related to Italian judicial procedure and
practice in the exercise of the right to claim back tax levied but not actually
owed.

Case law has established quite a strict approach towards enforcement, with relatively little scope for defences excusing a failure by the Member States to comply with EU law.

Force majeure *or necessity*: This is a defence under international law for failing to comply with a legal obligation,[65] and while the Court of Justice has indicated that it can apply in EU law, it is rarely pleaded successfully. In *Commission v Belgium (Belgian Wood)*, Belgium pleaded the dissolution of a government as a justification for a delay in complying with (then) Community law. The ECJ did not accept this, although it did try explain the scope of *force majeure* as a possible defence. *Commission v Italy* concerned a Community law obligation in a directive to compile statistical data on the carriage of goods by road. Italy claimed that a bomb attack at the Ministry of Transport damaged its capacity to gather statistics. The ECJ accepted a bomb attack could amount to *force majeure*, but not for as long as the Italians claimed it did in this case, for a period of several years.[66]

In a previous case, also involving Italy, the Court had held that where the treaty provides for exceptional circumstances (e.g. as now in Article 78(3) TFEU or Article 122 TFEU[67]), it is exhaustive of the relevance of those circumstances for complying with EU law; Member States must use the treaty procedure, and they may not take unilateral action.[68] In *Commission v Italy*, Italy had suspended imports of meat products in order to address an artificially low market price in the pig-meat sector.

64 Case 77/69 *Commission v Belgium (Belgian Wood)* [1970] ECR 237 paras 15–16; Case C–129/00 *Commission v Italy* [2003] ECR I–14637 para 29, citing Case 77/69 *Commission v Belgium (Belgian Wood)* [1970] ECR 237 para 15.
65 See, e.g., Article 62 of the Vienna Convention on the Law of Treaties, 23 May 1969 1155 UNTS 331, 8 ILM 679 (1969).
66 Case 101/84 *Commission v Italy* [1985] ECR 2629 para 16.
67 The provision in question was art 226 EEC Treaty, which only applied during the transitional phase of the Communities and which allowed the Commission to take measures independently of the Council. The current treaties contain more general exception clauses. Article 122(1) TFEU provides that, without prejudice to any other procedures provided for in the treaties, the Council, on a proposal from the Commission, may decide, in a spirit of solidarity between Member States, upon the measures appropriate to the economic situation. See also Article 78(3) TFEU.
68 Case 7/61 *Commission v Italy* [1961] ECR 317 at 329.

Thus, the Court of Justice is reluctant to accept *force majeure*, while not ruling it out in principle.

Political or economic difficulties: Member States may not plead general economic or political difficulties as a defence. For example, in *Commission v UK (Tachographs)*, the UK pleaded political difficulties of resistance from trade unions for not fulfilling a Community obligation to install recording equipment in road transport. The ECJ rejected this as a defence, stating that Member States could not obtain economic benefits from Community membership and then refuse to apply Community law for economic gain.[69]

Reciprocity: One of the fundamental features of EU law is that, in general, reciprocity is not a condition of the application of EU law: Member States may not decide to disapply EU law in retaliation for a failure of another Member State or of an EU institution to fulfil its obligations under EU law, i.e. there is no form of legal self-help in EU law. This is one of the key differences between EU law and general public international law (legal self-help exists in the form of counter-measures, as discussed in Chapter 2).

In *Commission v Belgium and Luxembourg (Re import of Powdered Milk Products)*, the facts related to a decision by Belgium and Luxembourg to introduce levies for import licences for certain milk products, which both countries justified by what they said was a failure of the Council to comply with time limits in one of the Council's own resolutions. The Court of Justice rejected this argument:

> In [the defendants'] view, . . . international law allows a party, injured by the failure of another party to perform its obligations, to withhold performance of its own . . .
>
> However, this relationship between the obligations of parties cannot be recognized under Community law. In fact, the treaty is not limited to creating reciprocal obligations between the different natural and legal persons to whom it is applicable, but establishes a new legal order that governs the powers, rights and obligations of the said persons, as well as the necessary procedures for taking cognizance of and penalizing any breach of it. Therefore, . . . the basic concept of the treaty requires that the Member States not take the law into their own hands. Therefore the fact that the [other party] failed to carry out its obligations cannot relieve the defendants from carrying out theirs.[70]

Commission v France concerned restriction by France on the import of lamb and mutton from the UK, which France partly defended on the basis that the UK also had restrictions. The ECJ stated:

> A Member State cannot under any circumstances unilaterally adopt, on its own authority, corrective measures or measures to protect trade designed to prevent any

---

69 Case 128/78 *Commission v UK (Tachographs)* [1979] ECR 41 para 12.
70 Joined Cases 90–91/63 *Commission v Belgium and Luxembourg (Re import of Powdered Milk Products)* [1964] ECR 625, 632.

failure on the part of another Member State to comply with the rules laid down by the Treaty.[71]

It is debatable whether this is sound doctrine in all circumstances (as discussed in Chapter 2), but remains valid in all but extreme cases.

Threat to public order: It would take something quite overwhelming for a threat to public order to justify non-compliance with EU law by a Member State. In *Commission v France (Spanish Strawberries)*,[72] protests by French farmers were interfering with the free movement of fruit goods. The Court rejected an argument that 'apprehension of internal difficulties' by a Member State cannot justify a refusal to enforce Union law:[73]

> . . . it is for the Member State concerned, unless it can show that action on its part would have consequences for public order with which it could not cope by using the means at its disposal, to adopt all appropriate measures to guarantee the full scope of EU law so as to ensure its proper implantation in the interests of all economic operators.[74]

Uncertainty of law: As generally in legal systems, uncertainty of law is not a defence.[75]

Acquiescence: The Commission is free to bring an enforcement action whenever it wishes, it cannot be prevented from doing so on the grounds of delay or a claim of acquiescence by the Commission.[76]

Lack of prejudice to another Member State: The Commission does not need to demonstrate prejudice to another Member State to bring an enforcement procedure.[77]

Compliance within time limit: It follows from the logic of the administrative stage and the wording of Article 258 TFEU that if a Member State complies within the time limit set out in the Commission's reasoned opinion, this will operate as a defence if the Commission seeks to bring a subsequent enforcement action. In *Commission v Italy*,[78] the facts related to Italian rules governing trade fairs, exhibitions, and markets, which the Commission claimed was contrary to the freedom to provide services. Italy had repealed some of the relevant laws prior to expiry of the time limit in the Commission's reasoned opinion, so any Commission legal action relating to those laws was inadmissible:

> It is clear from the very terms of the second paragraph of Article 226 EC [now Article 258 TFEU] that the Commission may not bring proceedings before the Court for

....

71 Case 232/78 *Commission v France* [1979] ECR 2729 para 9.
72 Case C–265/95 *Commission v France (Spanish Strawberries)* [1997] ECR I–6959.
73 Ibid para 55.
74 Ibid para 56.
75 Case 7/71 *Commission v France* [1971] ECR 453 para 47.
76 Ibid paras 5–6.
77 Ibid para 50.
78 Case C–439/99 *Commission v Italy* [2002] ECR I–305.

Treaty infringement unless a Member State has failed to comply with the reasoned opinion within the time-limit notified to it for that purpose.[79]

5.2.3.3 ENFORCEMENT ACTIONS BY A MEMBER STATE AGAINST ANOTHER MEMBER STATE UNDER ARTICLE 259 TFEU

ARTICLE 259 TFEU

A Member State which considers that another Member State has failed to fulfil an obligation under the Treaties may bring the matter before the Court of Justice of the European Union

Before a Member State brings an action against another Member State for an alleged infringement of an obligation under the Treaties, it shall bring the matter before the Commission.

The Commission shall deliver a reasoned opinion after each of the States concerned has been given the opportunity to submit its own case and its observations on that of the other party's case both orally and in writing.

If the Commission has not delivered an opinion within the three months of the date on which the matter was brought before it, the absence of such an opinion shall not prevent the matter from being brought before the Court of Justice.

Under this procedure, if a Member State believes another Member State is violating EU law, it must first notify, not the Member State in question, but the European Commission, which then has the option (not the obligation) to apply a similar procedure as under Article 258 TFEU. If the Commission does not take any action after three months have passed since the Commission was notified, the complainant Member State may bring an action under Article 259 TFEU. The procedure is rarely used, as it would signal the failure of diplomacy.

Examples are *France v UK*,[80] where France, supported by the Commission, successfully sued the UK over a fishing dispute, and *Belgium v Spain*,[81] where Belgium unsuccessfully sued Spain over Spanish rules that required wine from certain regions to be produced in a certain way or bottled in their region of origin before they could be exported (the Spanish rules on bottling in the region of origin were found to be justified under free movement rules). A more recent example is *Spain v UK*, where Spain lost in a case against the UK over voting in Gibraltar (the Court of Justice found that the EU could extend to residents of Gibraltar the right to vote in European elections).[82]

....

79 Ibid para 16, citing Case C–362/90 *Commission v Italy* [1992] ECR I–2353 para 9.
80 Case 141/78 *France v UK* [1979] ECR 2923.
81 Case C–388/95 *Belgium v Spain* [2000] ECR I–0312.
82 Case C–145/04 *Spain v UK* [2006] ECR I–7917.

5.2.3.4 LACK OF COMPLIANCE UNDER ARTICLE 260 TFEU

ARTICLE 260 TFEU

1. If the Court of Justice of the European Union finds that a Member State has failed to fulfil an obligation under the Treaties, the State shall be required to take the necessary measures to comply with the judgment of the Court.

2. If the Commission considers that the Member State concerned has not taken the necessary measures to comply with the judgment of the Court, it may bring the case before the Court after giving that State the opportunity to submit its observations. It shall specify the amount of the lump sum or penalty payment to be paid by the Member State concerned which it considers appropriate in the circumstances.

If the Court finds that the Member State concerned has not complied with its judgment it may impose a lump sum or penalty payment on it.

This procedure shall be without prejudice to Article 259.

3. When the Commission brings a case before the Court pursuant to Article 258 on the grounds that the Member State concerned has failed to fulfil its obligation to notify measures transposing a directive adopted under a legislative procedure, it may, when it deems appropriate, specify the amount of the lump sum or penalty payment to be paid by the Member State concerned which it considers appropriate in the circumstances.

If the Court finds that there is an infringement it may impose a lump sum or penalty payment on the Member State concerned not exceeding the amount specified by the Commission. The payment obligation shall take effect on the date set by the Court in its judgment.

Article 260 TFEU provides for a second enforcement procedure where a Member State has failed to comply with a judgment under Articles 258 or 259.[83] The ECJ is not bound in imposing a payment under Article 260(1) TFEU to follow the amount set by the European Commission. The Commission itself has published communications or guidelines on how it calculates the amount of payment, taking into account the following considerations: seriousness of the infringement, consequences of the infringement, duration of the infringement, and capacity to pay of the Member State.[84]

---

83 For a recent evaluation see B Jack 'Article 260(2) TFEU: an effective judicial procedure for the enforcement of judgments?' (2012) 19(3) *European Law Journal* 404–421.

84 European Commission MEMO/05/482 http://europa.eu/rapid/press-release_MEMO-05-482_en.htm (last accessed 18 January 2015).

Case law has addressed the scope of the Commission's role relative to the Court and the nature of the fines that can be imposed. In *Commission v Spain*,[85] the Court of Justice pointed out that it was not bound by the Commission suggestion as to the payment to be made and went on to discuss the scope of penalty payment.[86] In *Commission v France*, the Court of Justice decided that it would impose both a lump sum and a penalty payment, and this was related to both the duration of the breach and the likelihood of persistence.[87] The combination of lump sum and penalty payment is meant to address both (a penalty payment applies cumulatively until the breach is ceased, e.g. a daily payment).

ARTICLE 7 TEU WHEN ARTICLE 260 FAILS . . .

1. On a reasoned proposal by one third of the Member States, by the European Parliament or by the European Commission, the Council, acting by a majority of four fifths of its members after obtaining the consent of the European Parliament, may determine that there is a clear risk of a serious breach by a Member State of the values referred to in Article 2. Before making such a determination, the Council shall hear the Member State in question and may address recommendations to it, acting in accordance with the same procedure. The Council shall regularly verify that the grounds on which such a determination was made continue to apply.

2. The European Council, acting by unanimity on a proposal by one third of the Member States or by the Commission and after obtaining the consent of the European Parliament, may determine the existence of a serious and persistent breach by a Member State of the values referred to in Article 2, after inviting the Member State in question to submit its observations.

3. Where a determination under paragraph 2 has been made, the Council, acting by a qualified majority, may decide to suspend certain of the rights deriving from the application of the Treaties to the Member State in question, including the voting rights of the representative of the government of that Member State in the Council. In doing so, the Council shall take into account the possible consequences of such a suspension on the rights and obligations of natural and legal persons. The obligations of the Member State in question under this Treaty shall in any case continue to be binding on that state.

To date, the procedure in Article 7 TEU has never been used. Article 7 is the closest EU law comes to a kind of self-help (discussed above under the heading of reciprocity).

---

85 Case C–278/01 *Commission v Spain* [2003] ECR I–14141.
86 Ibid paras 41–42.
87 C–304/02 *Commission v France* [2005] ECR I–6263 paras 42 ff.

5.2.4 REVIEW OF LEGALITY[88]

5.2.4.1 INTRODUCTION

A review of legality is a direct action brought in the ECJ by an individual or another EU institution against one of the EU institutions alleging an act of the institution is contrary to EU law. It is worth looking at the wording of Article 263 TFEU in some detail, as it sets out the essential criteria for the use of this procedure. The procedure is available if:

> . . . *an act* adopted jointly by the European Parliament and the Council, or an act of the Council, or of the Commission and of the ECB (other than recommendations and opinions), or an act of the European Parliament intended to produce legal effects vis-à-vis third parties *is unlawful* because of a lack of competence, infringement of an essential procedural requirement, infringement of the Treaty (i.e. TEU or TFEU) or of any rule of law relating to its application, or misuse of powers between the Treaties and an EC law (as for contracts**) *and the action can be brought by either* a Member State, an institution of the EU (Commission, Council, EP) or a private party/individual (to whom the law is directed or for whom the law is of direct and individual concern) (Article 263 TFEU).

> *Note*: A review of legality lies against acts of the institutions that have legal effects, so for example general administrative decisions as to policy implementation may not be reviewable under Article 263 TFEU if they do not involve legal effects.

Similarly, under Article 265 TFEU, a direct action brought for *failure to act*, in infringement of the treaty, of the European Parliament, Council (of Ministers) or Commission can be brought by the same parties/categories of litigant as under Article 265 TFEU.

KEY LEARNING POINT

REVIEWS OF LEGALITY: WHO IS SUING WHO OVER WHAT, AND IN WHAT COURT?

In a review of legality a person, including a legal person, affected by an act of an EU institution having legal effects may sue that institution alleging illegality in the act, either illegality of commission (doing something illegal) (Article 263 TFEU) or omission (failing to carry out a legal duty) (Article 265 TFEU). It is an EU act, not a national law, that is being challenged before the ECJ (or General Court). An individual may only sue under these provisions if the act being challenged is (i) directed at the individual *or* (ii) is of direct and individual concern to the individual. *This means that if the act being challenged is not specifically directed at the individual, he or she must as an alternative show the act is of 'direct and*

---

88 Various terms tend to be used to describe this procedure. The TFEU uses the expression 'review of legality'. Using the terminology of UK public law, it is a judicial review (although this expression is not used in the treaties).

individual concern' to him or her. The 'direct and individual concern' requirement
(the alternative to the act being directed at the individual) has been narrowly
interpreted, and the ECJ had been criticised for this (see next).

5.2.4.2 STANDING OR CAPACITY TO BRING A REVIEW OF LEGALITY: THE DIRECT AND INDIVIDUAL CONCERN REQUIREMENT

EXPLAINING THE LAW

PRIVILEGED AND NON-PRIVILEGED APPLICANTS UNDER ARTICLES 263 AND 265 TFEU

Article 263 distinguishes between two categories as regards standing, i.e. the
right or capacity to bring a review of legality against an EU institution in the Court
of Justice. The first category relates to EU institutions or the Member States who
automatically have the right to sue. They do not need to show they have been
affected in a particular way, and this category is called 'privileged applicants'. The
second category do have to show that they have been affected in a particular
way. The standing requirement Article 263 establishes for this category is that a
measure they complain of is of direct and individual concern to them. Because
they have to satisfy this standing requirement (which, as we shall see below, the
Court of Justice interprets restrictively), this category is called 'non-privileged
applicants'.

Privileged applicants: Privileged applicants are those specifically listed in Article 263
TFEU, i.e. those EU institutions and the Member States listed as being entitled to
sue. The institutions are the European Parliament, the Council and the Commission.
Article 173 EEC Treaty (now Article 263 TFEU) initially provided no standing for
the European Parliament. At first, the ECJ followed in this text in *European Parliament
v Council (Comitology)*,[89] where it refused to accept that the Parliament could being
a review of legality. In *Comitology*, the European Parliament attempted to challenge
the Council's Decision formalising the structures of comitology (comitology refers to
committees established and appointed by the Member States to oversee the exercise by
the Commission of delegated legislative powers).

The Court of Justice reversed itself shortly afterwards in *European Parliament v Council
(Chernobyl)*,[90] based on arguments related to the effectiveness of the remedies or
procedures available to the Parliament. Contrary to its reasoning in *Comitology*, the
Court in *Chernobyl* observed that the absence of textual support 'cannot prevail over
the fundamental interest in the maintenance and observance laid down in the treaties

....

89 Case 302/87 *European Parliament v Council (Comitology)* [1988] ECR 5615.
90 Case C–70/88 *European Parliament v Council (Chernobyl)* [1990] ECR I–2041.

establishing the European Communities'.[91] The facts concerned a regulation relating to radioactivity in foods, and the Parliament objected to the legal basis and the form of the legislation. The ECJ held that Parliament should be allowed to protect its prerogatives. In effect here, the Court decided on the basis of what it thought the law should be, not on what the then text of the treaty stated. Since the judgment, the treaty text has been amended to provide for standing for Parliament.

Non-privileged applicants and the 'direct and individual concern' standing requirement: Non-privileged applicants are parties other than the EU institutions (which are individually listed), i.e. individuals or legal persons who are directly and individually concerned by an act of an EU institution and wish to challenge it. This standing requirement has two elements: (i) direct concern; and (ii) individual concern. Untypically, the Court of Justice has taken a narrow approach to the standing of non-privileged applicants. In particular, it interprets the 'individual concern' element narrowly (albeit with some variations in the emphasis in the case law): to have standing to bring a review of legality of an act of an EU institution, a person must be able to show that he or she has been affected virtually in a unique way.

The Lisbon Treaty removed the individual concern requirement (but not the direct concern requirement) for 'regulatory acts . . . not entail implementing measures'. It remains to be seen how the Court of Justice will interpret 'regulatory acts'. However, the General Court has stated that a literal, historical and purposive analysis of the term 'regulatory act' indicated that it should be defined as 'an act of general application which is not a legislative act'.[92] An example of a successful action to review a regulatory act is *Microban International and Microban (Europe) v Commission*,[93] which involved a Commission decision on additives adopted under a comitology procedure. It is not clear that 'not entailing impending measures' adds much to direct concern, since the definition of direct concern excludes any discretion in implementation. One view is that this element can be equated with direct applicability of regulations and decisions.

Direct concern: The main issue of definition to arise with the 'direct concern' element is the presence of an intermediary party in the relationship between the individual suing and the EU institution being sued. The general approach of the Court of Justice has been that the presence of an intermediary party does not prevent direct concern existing, it depends on the decision-making discretion exercised by the intermediary relating to the subject matter of the dispute.

In *Piraiki-Patraiki v Commission*,[94] cotton producers in Greece brought an action against a Commission decision authorising France to impose quotas on cotton imports from Greece during November and December 1981 and January 1982. The Commission

....

91 Ibid para 26.
92 Case T–18/10 *Inuit Tapiriit Kanatami v European Parliament* [2011] ECR II–5599 para 50.
93 Case T–262/10 *Microban International and Microban (Europe) v Commission* [2011] ECR II–7697.
94 Case 11/82 *Piraiki-Patraiki v Commission* [1985] ECR 207.

decision, which was not addressed to the applicants, was adopted under a provision
of the Accession Treaty of Greece to the then EEC. The ECJ noted as regards
direct concern that it was merely theoretical that France would not make use of the
authorisation, and that the decision was thus of direct concern to the applicants, even if
implementing measures were needed at national level.

Dreyfus v Commission[95] set out the standard test on 'direct concern'. It concerned a loan
from the EC/EU to the Soviet Union and its former republics to enable agricultural
and food products and medical supplies to be imported. The contested decision was
a Commission decision refusing to approve part of the contract between an agent of
the borrower (the borrower being the USSR and its Republics) and an undertaking
that had been awarded a supply contract. The contract provided that it was subject to
Commission approval.

The applicant here was the undertaking that had been awarded the supply contract.
The ECJ noted that in previous case law it had held that an individual can be directly
concerned, even if (s)he has not entered into legal relations with the Commission, but
whose legal and factual situation is directly affected.[96]

KEY LEARNING POINT

THE STANDARD TEST FOR 'DIRECT CONCERN'
In *Dreyfus*, the test for 'direct concern' was whether the measure directly
affected the person's legal position and left no discretion to the addressees of
that measure who were entrusted with its implementation, that being a purely
automatic matter flowing solely from the Community/Union legislation without
the application of other intermediate rules.[97]

Compared to *Piraiki-Patraiki*, for example, *Dreyfus* makes clear that national
implementation must not involve discretion and seems to minimise the existence of any
kind of implementing national rules (compare direct applicability of regulations). The
applicant was found to be directly concerned by the contested measure, including on the
ground that the addressees of that measure did not have a margin of discretion as regards
its implementation.

The ECJ stated (paragraphs 52 and 53) that the option available to the addressee of the
contested decision to forgo Community/EU financing at issue was 'purely theoretical',
so that that decision, refusing such financing, deprived the applicant 'of any real

---

95 Case C–386/96 P *Dreyfus v Commission* [1998] ECR I–2309.
96 Ibid para 24, citing e.g. Joined Cases 41–44/70 *International Fruit Co and Ors v Commission* [1971] ECR 411;
   Case C–135/92 *Fiskano v Commission* [1994] ECR 1–2885; and Case T–83/92 *Zunis Holding and Others v Com-*
   mission [1993] ECR 11–1169.
97 Ibid para 43.

possibility of performing the contract awarded to it, or of obtaining payment for supplies made thereunder'. For that reason, the Court held that the applicant was directly concerned by that decision.

Instituoto N. Avgerinopoulou and Others v Commission[98] involved an application for the annulment of a Commission decision not to bring to an end alleged discrimination between public and private vocational training bodies in Greece regarding their access to financing from EU Structural Funds. The applicants were providers of or associations of providers of private vocational training.

Confirming earlier case law, the (then) CFI stated that only measures having binding legal effects of such a nature as to affect the interests of the applicant by having a significant effect on his legal position constitute acts or decisions against which proceedings for annulment may be brought under (then) Article 230 ECT (now Article 263 TFEU) and that the refusal by a Community institution to withdraw or amend an act could itself be reviewable under Article 230 EC only if the act that the Community institution refused to withdraw or amend could itself have been reviewed.

On the facts, the CFI found that the Commission decision was of general scope in being addressed to the Hellenic Republic, but also noted that an act of general scope could in certain circumstances still be of direct and individual concern if it satisfied the test in *Dreyfus*. The CFI found that on the facts this test was not satisfied, as structural funds were mainly with the competence of the Member States.[99]

Regione Siciliana v Commission[100] also concerned structural funds. The CFI found that the contested Commission decision had simply requested Italy to refund money that should not have been spent, Italy could have made up any shortfall itself, and the reimbursement of the funds paid to the applicant would be the direct consequence, not of the contested decision, but of the action taken by the Italian Republic on the basis of national legislation in order to fulfil obligations under the Community rules on the subject. The applicant was found to be not directly concerned by the contested Commission decision since it produced effects only between the Commission and the Italian Republic.

In *CISAC & EBU v Commission*,[101] a professional association representing parties affected by a Commission decision on competition law was held to be directly concerned with the Commission decision as it was in a clearly defined position as a negotiator intimately linked to the subject matter of the Commission decision.[102] The CFI also noted it was 'settled case law' that the test for direct concern was whether an applicant's legal

---

98 Case T–139/02 *Instituoto N. Avgerinopoulou and Others v Commission* [2004] ECR–II 875.
99 Ibid paras 63–65.
100 Case T–341/02 *Regione Siciliana v Commission* [2004] ECR II–2877.
101 Case T–442/08 *CISAC & EBU v Commission*, judgment of 12 April 2013.
102 Ibid para 77.

situation was directly affected by the contested decision and that the contested decision left no discretion in implementation to the addressees.[103]

Individual concern: Among the most criticised of all the decisions of the ECJ is its early judgment in *Plaumann & Co v Commission*, concerning the standing of individuals to challenge acts of the Community institutions.[104] Somewhat untypically for the ECJ, this decision has been attacked for being overly narrow and leaving individuals without a legal remedy (although in its judgment the ECJ started by stating it was taking a broad approach to the interpretation of individual entitlements).[105] The decision turned on the meaning of 'other person' and 'individual concern' in Article 173 EEC Treaty. The Court of Justice declared, with little discussion, that:

> Persons other than those to whom a decision is addressed may only claim to be individually concerned if that decision affects them by reason of certain attributes which are peculiar to them or by reason of circumstances in which they are differentiated from all other persons and by virtue of these factors distinguishes them individually just as in the case of the person addressed.[106]

The applicant in *Plaumann* failed on this test, because it carried out a commercial activity that anyone else could at any time. It is very difficult to show that an act not specifically directed at someone is nonetheless of direct and individual concern, since in practice, if anybody else is also concerned, the claim fails. It made it very difficult to claim that any legislative act could be of direct and individual concern.

Shortly afterwards, however, in *Töpfer v Commission*[107] an applicant, the importer of cereals, was found to be individually concerned in circumstance where there were others in a similar position. The applicant was found to be individually concerned because the disputed decision involved only those importers who applied for an import licence (and were rejected by the decision) on a particular day. The case illustrates how the *Plaumann* test can restrict standing to a defined, fixed category.

EXPLAINING THE LAW

THE 'PROBLEM' WITH *PLAUMANN*

Plaumann is the leading authority interpreting the criteria in Article 263 TFEU allowing an individual to bring a case in the ECJ claiming illegality in an act of one of the EU institutions. On the phrasing in Article 263 (and Article 265 TFEU

---

103 Ibid para 66.

104 Case 25/62 *Plaumann & Co v Commission* [1963] ECR 95.

105 Ibid at 106–107. For criticism see e.g. P Craig, G de Búrca *EU Law: Text, Cases, and Materials* (4th edn Oxford University Press 2008) 511–14; A Kaczorowska *European Union Law* (2nd edn Routledge 2011) 445–47.

106 Case 25/62 *Plaumann & Co v Commission* (n 104) 107.

107 Cases 106–107/63 *Töpfer v Commission* [1965] ECR 177.

on omissions), an individual can only bring such an action (with one exception, see below) if the act is 'of direct and individual concern' to him or her. This makes it very difficult for individuals to challenge legislation adopted under Article 288 TFEU (apart from decisions), because of the narrow interpretation of the ECJ to the issue. The Court of Justice interprets 'direct and individual concern' almost to mean that the person bringing the action must be exclusively affected: if other people are affected, this makes it very difficult to bring an action. This very much limits the ability of individuals to sue the EU institutions.

Calpak,[108] for example, suggested that in any situation where the people affected by legislation were not a closed category, they could not claim that the legislation was of direct and individual concern: the ECJ stated that the possibility of being able to identify the number or identity of persons (producers of wine on the facts) affected (by a regulation) did not make the act in question a matter of direct and individual concern.[109]

The ECJ adopted a somewhat less strict approach in practice in *Codorníu* (although it stated that it was applying *Plaumann*),[110] in which it held that a regulation could be of direct and individual concern, though the ECJ said it was still applying *Plaumann*. *Codorníu* concerned legislation that reserved the term *crémant* for certain sparkling wines from France and Luxembourg. The applicant was Spanish and would be required to stop using the same term for his wine. Even though there were other Spanish wine producers in the same position, the ECJ said the *Plaumann* test had been satisfied.

Despite saying it was following *Plaumann*, the ECJ was really relaxing it to some extent (although the extent of that relaxation was not made clear). This ambiguity essentially remains in the case law and has not been fully clarified. In *Buralux*,[111] for example, shortly after *Codorníu* the Court of Justice seemed to revert to its stricter approach in *Calpak*, even though the facts seemed similar to those in *Codorníu* in that there were a small number of individuals affected.

Piraiki-Patraiki v Commission,[112] discussed above under 'direct concern', suggests that the presence of pre-existing legal contracts affected by the contested decision of an EU institution was a significant consideration in favour of a finding of individual concern. To recall the facts, cotton producers in Greece brought an action against a Commission decision authorising France to impose quotas on cotton imports from Greece.

....

108 Joined Cases 789–790/79 *Calpak SpA and Società Emiliana Lavorazione Frutta SpA v Commission* [1980] ECR 1949.

109 Ibid para 9.

110 Case C–309/89 *Codorníu SA v Council* [1994] ECR I–1853.

111 Case C–209/94 P *Buralux SA v Council* [1996] ECR I–615.

112 Case 11/82 *Piraiki-Patraiki v Commission* (n 94).

The Court of Justice found that the Commission decision affected the applicants only as regards exporting to France, and not more generally in their business, and that it applied to any Greek exporters of cotton. However, having cited *Plaumann*, the ECJ held that traders who had already entered into contracts with French undertakings prior to the adoption of the Commission decision were individually concerned. They related this finding of standing to the substance of the case, noting that the contracts could have been and should have been ascertained by the Commission in evaluating the impact of its decision, as it was required to do under the Accession Treaty. However, pre-existing contracts are not decisive, as is apparent from *Buralux*.

Buralux concerned a regulation on the supervision and control of waste shipments and an action brought by undertakings specialising in waste shipment. The regulation provided for the authorisation into and out of and within the EC/EU of shipments. The undertakings were found not to be individually concerned as they were involved only in their objective capacity as economic operators in the area of waste shipment in the same way as any operator in that sector and were not in a limited class of identified or identifiable individuals who were particularly concerned because of their special situation.

The ECJ also noted that it was settled caselaw that being able to determine the number or identity of persons affected does not make them individually concerned and reasserted the *Plaumann* test.[113] The regulation here was concerned with legal effects on categories of person envisaged generally and in the abstract.[114] *Piraiki-Patraiki* was distinguished on the basis that it involved an obligation on the part of the Commission to assess the impact of decisions on a particular Member State, and so the fact that there were pre-existing contracts also in this case did not mean the same result followed as in *Piraiki-Patraiki*.[115]

KEY CASE *THE BASIS OF THE DECISION IN* PLAUMANN

In *Plaumann*, the Advocate General had proposed a slightly differently formulated test to that adopted by the ECJ later in the case, suggesting that direct concern must stem from the individuality of particular persons, rather than from membership of an abstractly defined group, and that the mere fact a measure applied to a small number of identifiable people did not render it of individual concern to them.[116] The text did suggest that the test for individual

---

113 Case C–209/94 P, *Buralux SA v Council* [1996] ECR I–615 paras 24–25, citing the judgment in Case C–264/91 *Abertal and Others v Council* [1993] ECR I–3265 para 16, and the order in Case C–131/92 *Arnaud and Others v Council* [1993] ECR I–2573 para 13.

114 Ibid para 26.

115 Ibid paras 31–34, noting the context in *Paraiki-Patraki* (n 94) of the provisions of the Act concerning the Conditions of Accession of the Hellenic Republic and the Adjustments to the Treaties OJ L 291 19.11.1979 p. 17.

116 Case 25/62 *Plaumann & Co v Commission* opinion of 28 May 1960 of Advocate General Römer at 116.

concern must entail more than just that the measure was not of a general legislative character, because the text already made this distinction between regulations and decisions,[117] and to repeat it would have rendered the individual concern requirement superfluous. However, the ECJ here could have engaged in a degree of consequentialist or results-based reasoning so as to avoid as narrow an approach as it took so as to facilitate access to justice, while still respecting the textual significance of the distinct individual concern requirement. This is eventually what it did to some extent in modifying the strictness in practice of the *Plaumann* test.[118] *Töpfer v Commission* is an early example (*Codorníu* is a later example), one of a number of cases where the Court has not applied *Plaumann* in a literal way as meaning a person must be in a unique position, i.e. no others must be in the same position regarding the subject-matter of the complaint.

Both Advocates General and the General Court have asked the Court of Justice to reconsider its approach in *Plaumann*, but the Court declined to do so.

In *Jégo Quéré v Commission*, the Court of Justice considered an appeal from the CFI, where the CFI found admissible an action brought by the company Jégo-Quéré & Cie SA for the annulment of part of a Commission regulation on the recovery of the stock of hake (a type of fish), and associated conditions for the control of activities of fishing vessels.[119]

Jégo-Quéré was a fishing company established in France and operated on a regular basis in the waters south of Ireland, in an area covered by the regulation. The CFI had held that the fact that a provision is of general application does not prevent it from being of direct and individual concern to some of the economic operators whom it affects and that it was necessary to consider whether, where an individual applicant is contesting the lawfulness of provisions of general application directly affecting its legal situation, the inadmissibility of the action for annulment would deprive the applicant of the right to an effective remedy, of the kind guaranteed by EU law and Articles 6 and 13 of the ECHR.

The CFI held that as there were no national implementing measures, the only way to raise the issue in a national court would be to breach the regulation and have its legality addressed in the subsequent legal proceedings, which was not a satisfactory remedy (it would require an individual to break the law to achieve access to justice), and similarly an action for damages on the basis of non-contractual ability (a special procedure under the treaties) would not fully address all issues of the legality of the regulation.

---

117 Ibid.
118 See e.g. the discussion of case law in Kaczorowska *European Union Law* (n 105) 447–52.
119 Case C–263/02 P *Jégo Quéré v Commission* [2004] ECR I–3443 (appeal from Case T–177/01 *Jégo Quéré v Commission* [2002] ECR II–2365).

The CFI considered it should follow the argument of Advocate General Jacobs in *Unión de Pequeños Agricultores v Council*[120] that there is no compelling reason to read into the notion of individual concern a requirement that an individual applicant seeking to challenge a general measure must be differentiated from all others affected by it in the same way as an addressee, i.e. affected in a unique way.

The CFI proposed a new test for individual concern, in the circumstances of this case where there was no remedy at national level for the breach of EU law:

> . . . a natural or legal person is to be regarded as individually concerned by a Community measure of general application that concerns him directly if the measure in question affects his legal position, in a manner which is both definite and immediate, by restricting his rights or by imposing obligations on him. The number and position of other persons who are likewise affected by the measure, or who may be so, are of no relevance in that regard.[121]

On the facts, the CFI went on to conclude that the contested Commission regulation imposed obligations on *Jégo Quéré* that rendered it of individual concern, while the CFI had noted that under the previous test (i.e. *Plaumann*), the applicant would not have been individually concerned. On appeal, the ECJ stated that it should be noted, first, that individuals are entitled to effective judicial protection of the rights they derive from the Union legal order, and the right to such protection is one of the general principles of law stemming from the constitutional traditions common to the Member States, but it rejected the CFI approach there should be a change to the meaning of individual concern where no remedies were available at national level.

The ECJ held the CFI approach would involve an inquiry into national procedural law that was beyond the Court of Justice's jurisdiction[122] (however, the ECJ itself did go on to note the possibility could exist of the issue being addressed in a national court, even if there was no national implementing legislation).

As noted above, the Lisbon Treaty has created an exception to the *Plaumann* test: individual *and* direct concern does not need to be shown for 'a regulatory act that does not entail implementing measures' (see the fourth paragraph of Article 263 TFEU); instead, it is enough to show 'direct concern'. More generally, the distinction drawn by the Lisbon Treaty (see the previous chapter) between the standard legal instruments adopted in a legislative and non-legislative form makes the *Plaumann* test more complicated to apply. In general, anything that is in a legislative form is harder to fit within *Plaumann*, but the standard instruments adopted in non-legislative form are more open to being included in *Plaumann*. How this will play out in the case law remains to be seen.

....

120 Case C–50/00 P *Unión de Pequeños Agricultores v Council* [2002] ECR I–6677.
121 Case T–177/01 *Jégo Quéré v Commission* para 51.
122 Case C–263/02 P *Jégo Quéré v Commission* para 33.

```
┌─────────────────────────────────────────────────┐
│   Reviews of Legality – Articles 263–265 TFEU    │
│                                                   │
│          (Judicial Review in EU Law)             │
└─────────────────────────────────────────────────┘
```

Who is Suing?

←   →

Privileged Applicants   Non-Privileged
                                                 Applicants

- Member State(s)   Individuals *'directly and*
- Council (of Ministers)   *individually concerned'*
- European Commission
- European Parliament

                              Complex test: i. no discretion for MS in
                              implementation ('direct concern')

                              ii. individual affected in unique or almost
                              unique way ('individual concern')

Who is Being Sued?

Any EU institution, agency or official body

In What Court?

Court of Justice of the EU (or General Court)

Basis or Grounds of Complaint

Any obligation or requirement of EU law binding on

the EU institution/body

Remedies

Compliance by EU institution/body as directed by Court of Justice

5.2.4.3 SUBSTANTIVE GROUNDS FOR REVIEW

Article 263 TFEU identifies several substantive grounds of judicial review, i.e. legal bases for suing an EU institution or body: lack of competence, infringement of an essential procedural requirement, infringement of the treaties or of any rule of law relating to their application, or misuse of powers. The categories are not mutually exclusive. In a general sense, any error of law could be considered to reflect a 'lack of competence'. Similarly, this overlaps with 'infringement of the Treaties'.

Lack of competence: Competence is a fundamental aspect of the legal regulation of governmental bodies: such bodies can only act within the powers specifically attributed to them under the law. In the EU, this is reflected in the principle of conferral in Article 5 TEU. An example from EU case law is *France v Commission*,[123] where France sued the Commission seeking annulment of the conclusion by the Commission of an international agreement. The Court of Justice held that the Commission action was intended to produce legal effects and was reviewable and that the Commission was not competent to conclude on behalf of the EEC an international agreement with a non-Member State in the area of competition rules, as this power was vested in the Council (of Ministers).

The Commission could not base its powers internally in the (then) EC in the area of competition to conclude an international agreement, i.e. to give itself external powers that the treaty vested in the Council. The treaty article, Article 228 EEC Treaty (now the equivalent provision in the TFEU is Article 218 TFEU), provided for a balance of powers whereby the Commission would negotiate, but the Council would adopt/conclude the agreement.

Breach of procedural requirement: Eugénio Branco v Commission[124] concerned withdrawal/reduction of a European Social Fund (ESF), and an application for the annulment of this decision by the recipient of the funding. The CFI cited a series of cases in which it had been held that recipients of ESF financing are directly and individually concerned by the funding decision (a point of contrast with cases involving structural funds).[125] No reasons were given by the Commission in its decision on withdrawal and the Commission simply followed what the Member State authorities decided should have been done. The CFI held this violated a consistent requirement in its case law that EU institutions must give reasons for their decisions in order to enable judicial review.

....

123 Case C–327/91 *France v Commission* [1994] ECR I–1409.
124 Case T–85/94 *Eugénio Branco v Commission* [1995] ECR II–45.
125 Ibid para 26, citing Case C–291/89 *Interhotel v Commission* [1991] ECR I–2257 para 13; Case C–304/89 *Oliveira v Commission* [1991] ECR I–2283 para 13; Case C–157/90 *Infortec v Commission* [1992] ECR I–3525 para 17; Case C–181/90 *Consorgan v Commission* [1992] ECR I–3557 para 12; and Case C–189/90 *Cipeke v Commission* [1992] ECR I–3573 para 12.

Transocean Marine Paint Association v Commission concerned the application by the
Commission of Article 85 EEC Treaty (now Article 101 TFEU) on competition law.[126]
The Commission, acting under Article 85(3) EEC Treaty, granted an exemption to
undertakings in the marine paint sector from the application of the competition law
rules in Article 85(1) EEC Treaty, subject to a requirement that the firms/undertakings
concerned notify the Commission of links they have with other undertakings in the
paints sector. The undertakings sought an annulment of this notification condition.

The Court of Justice found that the secondary legislation governing competition law
procedure reflected a general rule that a person whose interests are perceptibly affected
by a decision of a public authority must be in a position to make his or her view on
the decision known. The Court found that this procedural requirement had not been
fulfilled, that the condition in the Commission decision should be annulled and that
the Commission should take the opportunity to retake the decision after hearing and
considering the objections of the parties concerned.

Infringement of the treaties or any rule relating to their application:

KEY CASE *A PARTICULARLY SERIOUS OR MANIFEST ERROR LEADS
TO A NULLITY*

Commission v BASF AG and Others[127] where acts of a Community/ EU institution
are marked by an irregularity that is so obvious that it cannot be accepted (i.e.
the error is particularly serious and manifest), the act can be considered a nullity
(like the distinction between void and voidable acts in UK law), even though
ordinarily an irregularity will not normally invalidate an act until the irregularity is
adjudicated by a court (i.e. ordinarily, an act remains valid until a court decision
to the contrary). In the area of competition law, the Commission must act as
a college and so an individual Commissioner or another party cannot amend,
beyond matters of management and administration of the original decision,
a decision taken by the Commission collegiately. Note that this judgment
could conceivably be considered to involve a lack of competence on the part
of the individual Commissioner or a breach of procedure in the absence of
endorsement by the Commission as a body of the decision.

Misuse of powers: Misuse of powers does not arise as often as the other categories.
An example is the *Giuffrida v Council* case,[128] which involved an application for the
annulment of a Council (of Ministers) decision to appoint someone to the post of
principal administrator of the Commission directorate-general on regional policy.

126 Case 17/74 *Transocean Marine Paint Association v Commission* [1974] ECR 1063.
127 Case C-137/92P [1994] ECR I 2555.
128 Case 105/75 *Giuffrida v Council* [1976] ECR 1395.

The Commission acknowledged that, in organising the recruitment procedure, it had intended to appoint the successful candidate from the beginning (as the candidate was assigned a grade lower than that at which he was actually working for several years, which was equivalent to principal administrator, prior to the appointment). The Court of Justice found this pursuit of such a specific objective was contrary to the aims of the recruitment procedure and was a misuse of powers.

5.2.5 AN ACTION FOR DAMAGES

In an action for damages brought before the ECJ under Articles 268 or 340 TFEU, the Union may be held non-contractually liable to make good any damage caused by its institutions or by its servants in the performance of their duties. It is an independent cause of action, so it does not depend on a declaration of annulment pursuant to Article 263 or 265 (i.e. the treaty basis for action for damages is Articles 268 and 340 TFEU).

EXPLAINING THE LAW

DISTINGUISHING THE TREATY-BASED ACTION FOR DAMAGES FROM STATE LIABILITY

Articles 268 and 340 TFEU are concerned with damages awarded against an EU institution for a breach of EU law. In other words, it is a remedy in EU law at EU level. State liability is a remedy of damages in national law (although required by EU law) available against a national public authority for failing properly to implement EU law (see next chapter). Another key difference is the legal basis: the treaty in one case, the case law of the ECJ in the case of Member State liability.

The ECJ has drawn an analogy, however, between the two causes of action and in *Brasserie du Pêcheur* between the elements of liability: the factors indicating liability are the same in both cases (see further the next chapter).[129] For example, the greater the degree of discretion granted to an EU institution, the less likely it is that there will be a breach, although fundamental principles of EU law must always be respected.[130] The Court of Justice has also developed the concept of liability of the Member States for judicial error, i.e. national courts can be liable for improperly applying EU law. We will look at this in the next chapter.

---

129 Joined Cases C–24/93 & 48/93 *Brasserie du Pêcheur v Germany* [1996] ECR I–1029.
130 On the latter see e.g. Joined Cases T–481/93 and 484/93 *Vereniging van Exporteurs in Levende Varkens v Commission* [1995] ECR II–2941.

The ECJ set out the criteria for the existence of non-contractual liability of an EU institution in *Bergaderm*:[131]

- the conduct of the institution must infringe a rule of law intended to confer rights on individuals
- the breach of EU law must be sufficiently serious
- there must be a direct causal link between the breach by the EU institution and the damage sustained by the applicant.

Finally, it seems open to interpretation that Article 340(3) TFEU imposes contractual as well as non-contractual liability on the European Central Bank. The provision states:

> Notwithstanding the second paragraph, the European Central Bank shall, in accordance with the general principles common to the laws of the Member States, make good any damage caused by it or by its servants in the performance of their duties.

5.3 THE GENERAL COURT

Prior to the Lisbon Treaty, the General Court was known as the Court of First Instance (reflecting its function). Article 19(1) states:

> The Court of Justice of the European Union shall include the Court of Justice, the General Court and specialised courts. It shall ensure that in the interpretation and application of the Treaties the law is observed.

It is a subordinate court to the Court of Justice and was established by the Single European Act 1986 (SEA). It came into operation in 1989 and hears a more limited class of cases, as set out in Article 256 TFEU, e.g. competition and trade mark cases (see below). The same rules govern the appointment of judges to the General Court as to the Court of Justice. Appeals go from here to the Court of Justice on points of law only.[132] It works like a lower court or court of first instance, from which an appeal may be made to the ECJ itself on a point of law. Its jurisdiction has been added to by the treaties since the Single European Act 1986.

....

131 Case C–352/98 P *Laboratoires Pharmaceutiques Bergaderm v Commission* [2000] ECR I–5291.
132 Article 256 TFEU.

Summary Chart of Proceedings before the EU Court of Justice

	Who is suing?	Who is being sued?	Court?	Legal basis?	Remedy?
Preliminary References (Article 267 TFEU)	Individual	1) Member State or 2) other individual	National court ECJ → National court	Any directly effective EU law	ECJ answers legal question
Enforcement Action (Articles 258–260 TFEU)	Commission (usually) or Member State	Member State	Court of Justice	Any obligation of EU law on Member States	Compliance by Member State or fine
Judicial Review (Articles 263, 265 TFEU)	Member State, Commission, EP, or Council or individual with standing	EU institution/body	Court of Justice	Any obligation of EU law on an EU institution/ body	Compliance by EU institution/ body
Also:					
Action for Damages (Articles 263 and 340 TFEU)	EU institution or agency/ body	Any legal person with standing	Court of Justice	Any damage caused by EU in course of its duties	Compensation

> KEY LEARNING POINT
> ....
>
> **THE JURISDICTION OF THE GENERAL COURT**
> Article 256 TFEU states that the General Court shall have jurisdiction under:
>
> - Article 263 TFEU, review of legality of acts of the institutions
> - Article 265, review of failure to act by the institutions
> - Article 268 TFEU, disputes regarding compensation from the contractual liability of the EU
> - Article 270 TFEU, disputes relating to employment by the EU and
> - Article 272 TFEU, disputes arising from an arbitration agreement with the exception of those under Article 257 (cases before the specialised courts) and those reserved to the Court of Justice/ECJ.
>
> It currently does not have jurisdiction over:
>
> - preliminary references in most cases (Article 256(3) TFEU)
> - actions by or against Member States.

In the absence of Court of Justice precedent on a point of law, General Court precedents are commonly cited instead where they exist on the point.

5.4 THE APPROACH OF THE ECJ TO INTERPRETATION

5.4.1 INTRODUCTION

Methods of interpretation are an aspect of the practice and application of law that is often insufficiently studied. Lawyers 'do' interpretation often without reflecting explicitly on the underlying interpretative method. Sometimes interpretation is seen as the preserve of those with an academic interest. However, this view is misconceived. Since different methods of interpretation can yield very different results, justifying the choice of interpretative method should be understood as a normal and central aspect of the interpretation of legal texts.

5.4.2 METHODS OF INTERPRETATION IN GENERAL

All law students will be familiar with different methods of interpretation. Interpretation features in every legal system: at its most basic, it is the simple act of attributing meaning to a text. In English law, for example, the dominant method of interpretation has traditionally been the literal or plain meaning rule, followed by the golden rule whereby a literal interpretation that is absurd will be discarded in favour of an interpretation that achieves the purpose of the law. Thirdly, the mischief rule looks at the problem the law was trying to address (to some extent, the mischief rule and golden rule overlap in pushing toward purposive interpretation). In modern terminology, the mischief rule would be called purposive interpretation.

KEY LEARNING POINT

THE BASIC FEATURES OF INTERPRETATION
In every legal system, there is more than one method of interpretation, but normally the ordinary meaning or literal method is the first one used.

A related distinction is that between first and second order justification. First-order justification relates to clear legal rules where meaning is straightforward in that a readily applicable legal rule can be identified: typically, this involves a straightforward literal interpretation that does not result in any ambiguity or absurdity. Second-order justification relates to the choice between different methods of interpretation, e.g. when a textual approach on its own results in ambiguity.[133] As Maduro has noted in criticism of the ECJ, the Court is generally quite poor at second-order justification, leaving its choices largely unjustified.[134]

KEY LEARNING POINT

FOUR ASPECTS OF INTERPRETATION
Four main aspects or types of interpretation can be identified:

1. Ordinary meaning or literal interpretation.
2. Purposive or teleological interpretation, including meta-teleological interpretation.
3. Consequentialist legal reasoning.
4. Historical or originalist interpretation.

Ordinary meaning or literal interpretation: The reasons for ordinary meaning being the first rule of interpretation, i.e. its underlying values, were well summarised by Summers and Taruffo:

First, these types of arguments require for their construction the least by way of materials. . . . The second . . . is that, when competing with other arguments, the

---

133 MacCormick (n 13) 100 ff.

134 Maduro comments that '[second-order justification] has rarely been the case in the ECJ case law' and that this is a 'remarkable' feature of the Court's adjudication. See M P Maduro *We the Court: The European Court of Justice and the European Economic Constitution* (Hart Publishing 1997) 20. However, more recently, Maduro tempers his criticism on this point, merely noting that: 'It may be true that the Court does not always fully articulate why it identifies a particular goal as the predominant one in a certain area of the law'. See M P Maduro 'Interpreting European law: judicial adjudication in a context of constitutional pluralism' (2007) 2(1) *European Journal of Legal Studies* 1–27 at 13.

linguistic arguments are relatively more difficult to cancel, or relatively less often subordinated pursuant to a mandatory rule or maxim of priority, or relatively more difficult to outweigh, than other arguments. Their superior comparative force is presumably attributable mainly to the great weight of the substantive rationales behind them, including democratic legitimacy of the legislature.[135]

Teleological or purposive: This approach is broader than the literal one in identifying the purpose or aim underlying a provision as a primary interpretative consideration and thus goes beyond the self-evident meaning at first reading. Although it is often now associated with EU law, it is equivalent to the mischief rule of interpretation at common law, whereby the problem that a statute was trying to address could be examined as a way of supplementing the meaning derived on the basis of the ordinary meaning approach.[136]

Teleological interpretation can be related to the term 'systematic' interpretation: systematic interpretation looks beyond the immediate provision to be interpreted, putting it in a broader context of surrounding law in the legal system.

EXPLAINING THE LAW

WHAT IS DISTINCTIVE ABOUT ECJ INTERPRETATION: META-TELEOLOGICAL INTERPRETATION

What is different about EU law then compared to the traditional common law approach is not in having a concept of purposive interpretation, but in the degree to which it influences interpretation. Lasser has aptly described a distinct characteristic of the use of purposive interpretation by the ECJ as 'meta-teleological'.[137] This means that purposes are stated at a broad level of generality. This points to a more general aspect of legal reasoning, which is the extent to which purposes (amongst other legal concepts) can be stated at varying levels of generality. The broader the level of generality, the broader the scope and impact of the provision being interpreted. Very often, the level of generality is an issue that is left unarticulated,[138] which raises questions concerning choice, discretion and objectivity in judging and legal reasoning.

---

135 R Summers, M Taruffo 'Interpretation and comparative analysis' in D N MacCormick, R Summers (eds) *Interpreting Statutes: A Comparative Study* (Dartmouth Publishing Aldershot 1991) 481–82.

136 (1844) 8 ER 1034; 11 Cl & Fin 85 at 143.

137 See M. Lasser *Judicial Deliberations in Comparative Perspective* (Oxford University Press 2004) 288; 'Comparing constitutional review by the European Court of Justice and the U.S. Supreme Court' 4(4) *International Journal of Constitutional Law* 618–51 (2006) 648.

138 J. Stone 'The *Ratio* of the *Ratio Decidendi*' 22(6) *Modern Law Review* 597–620 (1959); G. Conway 'Levels of Generality in the Legal Reasoning of the European Court of Justice' 14(6) *European Law Journal* 787–805 (2008).

Consequentialist: This approach allows consideration of the consequences of a particular interpretation to be decisive or important in legal reasoning. This relates to an aspect of interpretation that arises anytime there exists interpretative choice, it is thus a consideration that attaches to other interpretative considerations, rather than being a free-standing one by itself, unless on the basis of consequentialism, a judge entirely ignores an otherwise applicable legal text. The term 'results-oriented' is also used.

Historical or originalist interpretation: This privileges the understanding of a legal text prevalent at the time of its adoption (in US literature, the term 'originalist'[139] is more commonly used and is the term used in the present work). Two types of originalist interpretation can be identified. One looks to the intention of the authors or signatories of those who ratified legal texts, e.g. as evidenced by preparatory or drafting materials. A more objective type of originalist interpretation looks to the understanding that the legal terms had generally in the legal system or body politic at the time of its adoption, as evidenced by legal tradition. A text itself is objective evidence of historical intention, but it may result in ambiguity, calling for reference to other legal materials to fill in the gap in meaning.

5.4.3 STATEMENTS BY THE ECJ ON INTERPRETATION

The early opinions of Advocate General Lagrange[140] and of Advocate General Römer were somewhat more explicit than the ECJ itself often is on matters of interpretation. These opinions could be said to have set the scene for the Court's emphasis on teleological interpretation. In *France v High Authority* Advocate General Lagrange stated that the approach of reading one treaty provision in light of the treaty overall 'is always legitimate'[141] and in *Fédération Charbonnière Belgique v High Authority* it was suggested that the ECJ may refer to *travaux préparatoires*, but had no obligation to do so;[142] in contrast, an originalist or historical approach to interpretation would give stronger weight to such material.

KEY LEARNING POINT

COURT OF JUSTICE STATEMENTS ON INTERPRETATION
Where the Court of Justice is explicit about questions of interpretation, it tends to avoid any statement of hierarchy between the different techniques; in particular, it tends to avoid attributing any priority to ordinary textual meaning.

139 See e.g. K Whittington *Constitutional Interpretation: Textual Meaning, Original Intent, & Judicial Review* (Kansas University Press 1999).
140 See generally R Greaves 'Selected opinions delivered by Advocate General Lagrange' (2003–2004) 6 *Cambridge Yearbook of European Legal Studies* 83–103.
141 Case 1/54 *France v High Authority of the European Coal and Steel Community* [1954–1955] ECR 1 at 26. Advocate General Lagrange referred to the 'ultimate aim of beginning to unite Europe', but on the specific situation of the case identified the treaty aim as 'ensuring the establishment, maintenance and observance of normal competitive conditions': ibid.
142 Opinion of Advocate General Lagrange in Case 8/55 *Fédération Charbonnière Belgique v High Authority* [1954–1956] ECR 260 at 271. See also Opinion of Advocate General Römer in Case 6/54 *Netherlands v High Authority* [1954–1956] ECR 118 at 125–26.

Where the Court of Justice is explicit about questions of interpretation, it tends to avoid any statement of hierarchy between the different techniques; in particular, it tends to avoid attributing any priority to ordinary textual meaning. For example, in *CILFIT*, it stated:

> Every provision of Community law must be placed in its context and interpreted in the light of the provisions of Community law as a whole, regard being had to the objectives thereof and to its state of evolution at the date on which the provision in question is to be applied.[143]

In this passage, the emphasis is on context and object and purpose, with the additional implication that interpretation may be evolutionary, i.e. it may change over time.

In its very first reported decision, the statements of the Court on interpretation suggested a more conserving approach:

> It is not for the Court to express a view as to the desirability of the methods laid down by the Treaty, or to suggest a revision of the Treaty, but it is bound in accordance with Article 31, to ensure that [in] the interpretation and application of the Treaty as it stands the law is observed.[144]

Here, interpretation is implicitly contrasted with treaty revision. The review of case law below suggests that this implicitly more conserving approach has often been superseded by more expansive teleological interpretation, although sometimes originalist interpretation does still feature in the Court's reasoning. In the more recent case of *Kaur*, for example, the Court indicated it would attribute a meaning to a Treaty provision in accordance with the intention of the Member States at the time of its adoption as indicated by a declaration attached to the treaty by the UK, which is contrary to the suggestion of an evolutionary interpretation in *CILFIT* above.

5.5 AN OVERVIEW OF THE IMPORTANCE OF THE COURT OF JUSTICE IN THE INTEGRATION PROCESS

This section briefly overviews some of the leading cases of the ECJ that have helped to create a constitutional structure for the EU and shows its key role in the integration process. The cases are only briefly referred to here, as we will look at them in more detail in the chapters on each of the topics.

....

143 Case 283/81 *CILFIT v Ministry of Health* [1982] ECR 3415 para 20.
144 Case 1/54 *France v High Authority* (n 141) at 13.

5.5.1 DIRECT EFFECT

The first of the creative judgments of the ECJ that contributed to the Constitution of the EU was *Van Gend en Loos*,[145] where the ECJ held that Community law had direct effect in the legal systems of the Member States. This was not obviously supported by the wording of the treaty, which appeared only to attribute such effect to regulations.[146] On the wording of the relevant treaty provisions, the ECJ observed:

> The wording of Article 12 contains a clear and unconditional prohibition which is not a positive but a negative obligation. This obligation, moreover, is not qualified by any reservation on the part of States which would make its implementation conditional upon positive legislative measure enacted under national law.[147]

So to infer the existence of a doctrine of direct effect, it was not necessary that the text contained an explicit statement, rather it was enough that the text did not explicitly exclude it. In *Van Gend en Loos*, the ECJ seemed to suggest direct effect applied to negative obligations[148] but later, in *Lütticke*,[149] the Court held that (ex) Article 95 EEC Treaty (now Article 110 TFEU) had direct effect, even though it imposed a positive obligation to remove discriminatory internal taxes on imports.

The direct effect doctrine was later further extended in *Walrave & Koch* by rendering it applicable to cases between private individuals, i.e. where the violation of Community law was by an individual ('horizontal direct effect'),[150] with the ECJ doing so again in relation to a treaty provision that was explicitly addressed to the Member States.[151] Here, the ECJ did not make reference at all to the text, but to consequences and effectiveness, arguing that Community law would be less effective and unequal in application in the absence of such direct effect being applied to a body, a sporting association, which did not have standing in public law.

What Stein described as the most radical extension of direct effect came in *Franz Grad*,[152] where the ECJ broadened it to cover secondary legislation, and not just treaty provisions. The ECJ made two major arguments: first, the effectiveness of

....

145 Case 26/62 *Van Gend en Loos* [1963] ECR 1, which concerned the requirement in (ex) art 12 EEC Treaty that Member States refrain from increasing customs duties on imports from other Member States.
146 See E Stein 'Lawyers, judges, and the making of a transnational constitution' (1981) 75(1) *American Journal of International Law* 1–27 at 7.
147 Case 26/62 *Van Gend en Loos* (n 145) at 13.
148 As noted in Stein (n 146) 10.
149 Case 57/65 *Lütticke GmbH v Hauptzollamt Saarlouis* [1966] ECR 205.
150 See Case 36/74 *Walrave & Koch v Association Union Cycliste Internationale* [1974] ECR 1405, taken against a private bicycle association. See also Case C–415/93 *Bosman* [1995] ECR I–4921, taken against a sporting association.
151 In Case 43/75 *Defrenne v SABENA (Defrenne II)* [1976] ECR 455, the ECJ held (ex) art 119 of the EEC Treaty on equal pay for equal work to have direct effect.
152 Case 9/70 *Franz Grad v Finanzamt Traunstein* [1970] ECR 825.

binding measures would be impaired in the absence of direct effect; and, secondly, the preliminary reference procedure implied individuals could exercise their rights in national courts.

5.5.2 SUPREMACY

What really gave the direct effect doctrine its significance was its combination with a new principle of the supremacy of Community law over that of all the Member States. *Costa v ENEL*[153] similarly resulted in a doctrine of fundamental significance, without explicit treaty support. The ECJ could have simply left the matter up to each Member State according to traditional principles of monism or dualism (see Chapter 2). In a later judgment, the Court confirmed that Community law takes precedence over all national including constitutional law, relying on an argument as to effectiveness and on the need for uniformity of approach among the Member States. As one commentator noted:

> In 1957, neither the doctrine of direct effect nor the doctrine of supremacy had emerged. If they were nascent, as the Court later claimed, they were certainly very well hidden, and the introduction of these concepts involved a series of daring acts of judicial activism.[154]

The Court later strengthened the supremacy principle at a procedural level, holding in *Simmenthal* that a national court was required to disapply any national legislation that conflicted with Community law and should not wait before making a preliminary reference to the ECJ.[155]

5.5.3 HUMAN RIGHTS

There was no treaty basis for the Court's original human rights jurisprudence,[156] and the Court itself even held later that the Community did not have the power to ratify the European Convention on Human Rights (ECHR),[157] but it is widely accepted that the ECJ was motivated primarily by a desire to support the supremacy doctrine against human rights challenges. More recently, the decision of the Court in *Mangold*[158] that a ban on age discrimination could be considered a general principle of EU law has been sharply attacked by Roman Herzog,[159] a former president of Germany and also former

....

153 Case 6/64 *Costa v ENEL*.

154 J H H Weiler 'Eurocracy and distrust' (1986) 61(3) *Washington Law Review* 1103–42 at 1112–13.

155 Case 106/77 *Amminstrazione delle Finanze dello Stato v Simmenthal* [1978] ECR 629 para 20 and see also para 18.

156 Case 29/69 *Stauder v City of Ulm* [1969] ECR 419; Case 4/73 *Nold v Commission* [1974] ECR 491.

157 In *Opinion 2/94 (Accession of the Community to the European Convention on Human Rights)* [1996] ECR 1–1759.

158 Case C–144/04 *Mangold v Helm* [2005] ECR 1–9981. The judgment in *Mangold* was later upheld in Case C–555/07 *Kücükdeveci* [2010] ECR I–365 and Case C–282/10 *Dominguez*, judgment of 24 January 2012.

159 Co-authoring with Lüder Gerken: '[Comment] Stop the European Court of Justice' *EU Observer.com* (10 September 2008) http://euobserver.com/9/26714 (last accessed 18 January 2015).

president of the German Federal Constitutional Court, as an example of unacceptable methods of interpretation. In its judgment, the ECJ stated that various international instruments and the constitutional traditions common to the Member States supported its conclusion.[160] Herzog and Gerken, however, observed that:

> . . . this 'general principle of community law' was a fabrication. In only two of the then 25 member states namely Finland and Portugal is there any reference to a ban on age discrimination, and in not one international treaty is there any mention at all of there being such a ban.[161]

A prohibition on discrimination on grounds of age had been included in Article II–81 of the Treaty establishing a Constitution for Europe.[162] This treaty was not ratified, a fact that tends to confirm the creativeness of the Court's conclusion in *Mangold*.

5.5.4 STATE LIABILITY

The ECJ also developed the doctrine of state liability in the absence of an explicit basis in the treaties. In *Francovich*,[163] the ECJ invoked primarily the effectiveness of Community law and the principle of loyal cooperation in support of its decision.[164] Although these principles are certainly not inconsistent with the doctrine of state liability, equally they do not necessarily entail it.[165] In *Brasserie*,[166] the ECJ supplemented its reasoning by suggesting that in many national legal systems the essentials of the legal rules governing state liability have been developed by the courts;[167] however, in the EU, doctrines of state liability were more often established by statute. More recently, the ECJ has extended the state liability principle to encompass liability for the decision of the highest courts of the Member States.[168] The Court went on to refer to the principle of the effectiveness of the remedies.[169]

5.5.5 FREE MOVEMENT CASE LAW

The development of the free movement principle in *Dassonville*[170] to cover non-discriminatory obstacles to free movement greatly expanded the scope of free

....

160 Case C–144/04 *Mangold* (n 158) paras 74–75.

161 Herzog and Gerken 'Stop the Court' (n 159).

162 Treaty Establishing a Constitution for Europe Brussels (29 October 2004) CIG 87/2/04 Rev 2. Article 21 of the EU Charter on Fundamental Rights also contained a prohibition on discrimination on grounds of age.

163 Cases C–6/90 & 9/90 *Francovich* [1991] ECR I–5375.

164 Ibid paras 33 and 36 respectively.

165 Distinguishing between loose and tight coherence see L. Alexander & K. Kress 'Against legal principles' in A Marmor (ed) *Law and Interpretation: Essays in Legal Philosophy* (Clarendon Press 1995) 313–14.

166 Cases C–46 & C–48/93 *Brasserie du Pêcheur* [1996] ECR I–1029 para 57.

167 Ibid paras 29–30.

168 Case C–224/01 *Köbler* [2003] ECR I–10239. We will look further at this topic in the next chapter.

169 Ibid paras 33–34.

170 Case 8/74 *Procureur du Roi v Benoît and Gustave Dassonville* [1974] ECR 837.

movement. The ECJ seems to have gone beyond original intention in its interpretation, although there was at least some textual ambiguity in Article 30 EEC Treaty read on its own. Another clear example of extra-textual, consequentialist reasoning by the ECJ was the creation of exceptions to the prohibition on non-discriminatory or indistinctly applicable measures, the latter itself being a development of the Court rather than of the treaty.

The treaties themselves provide for exceptions to the free movement principles, which the ECJ supplemented with its case law. In *Bachmann*, for example, the ECJ held that national rules allowing the deductibility from income tax of various insurance and pension contributions only if the contributions were paid in Belgium could be justified to ensure the cohesion of the tax system, since the Belgian authorities could not be sure of the tax regulations of other countries and compliance with them.[171]

MAKING CONNECTIONS
+ + + + + + + + + + + + + + + + +

THE INFLUENCE OF THE ECJ ACROSS SUBSTANTIVE AREAS OF LAW

The above section has provided a brief survey of some of the more important judgments of the ECJ. These judgments are important because they have established key new doctrines, which impact across all subsequent development of EU law because they work as precedents. We have looked at cases briefly in the following areas: direct effect, supremacy, state liability, human rights and free movement.

Numerous other areas of EU law can be analysed to show the importance of the ECJ also, and we will look at some of these in other chapters: the doctrine of parallelism in external relations, the interpretation of competences generally, criminal sanctions, and merger control in competition law.

5.6 ASSESSING THE ECJ: A NORMATIVE ASSESSMENT OF INTERPRETATION

Not surprisingly, a court that has been in existence for over 60 years has attracted considerable commentary. However, two things stand out about commentary and criticism on the Court: first, for the initial 30 years of its existence, it attracted relatively little attention, yet it was during this period that many of its most important precedents were delivered (this was at a time when the Community was much less significant

---

171 Case C–204/90 *Bachmann v Belgium* [1992] ECR I–249.

than the EU is today, but these precedents still apply throughout EU law) and when it established its approach to interpretation. Secondly, there has been a reluctance to criticise the ECJ in much academic literature. Many EU law academics favour the integration project and resist criticism of an institution that has played such an important role in it, even though there is considerable scope for questioning why a court should play such a political role.

Two aspects of the legal reasoning of the ECJ seem open to criticism: the political and empirical nature of 'effectiveness' (or *effet utile*, frequently invoked by the Court) as a criterion of interpretation,[172] and thus the difficulty in conceptualising its limits; and secondly, the wide scope the ECJ gives to meta-teleological interpretation. Identifying purposes in the law goes beyond the text, and when the way in which purposes are stated is open to variation and even manipulation, predictability in the law is undermined.

In many cases the ECJ has clearly gone beyond what can reasonably be attributed to the Member States as authors of the treaties. Rasmussen was the first to launch a sustained criticism of the reasoning of the Court.[173] Although he did not propose in detail an alternative methodology, he implicitly favoured textual interpretation.[174] Rasmussen, in particular, focused on the role of non-legal policy, often expressed in the case law of the ECJ by an argument about effectiveness. Hartley and Neill made similar criticisms.[175]

ANALYSING THE LAW

WHAT SHOULD WE UNDERSTAND THE LIMITS OF LEGAL REASONING TO BE?[176]

Legal reasoning is generally understood to be distinct from 'ordinary practical reasoning', i.e. ordinary decision-making about what should be the case. In legal reasoning, we naturally consider that the law requires something that is not a matter of individual judgment or discretion, i.e. the law entails objective requirements. These requirements should bind judges also. Thus, it is helpful to think of the idea of a shared (and thus objective) framework or system of interpretation in a legal system, that every reasonable participant in a legal system can 'access'. In this way, there are conventions or standard practices

....

172 F Snyder 'The effectiveness of European community law: institutions, processes, tools, and techniques' (1993) 56(1) *Modern Law Review* 19–54 at 24, 56.

173 H Rasmussen *On Law and Policy of the European Court of Justice* (Martinus Nijhoff 1986).

174 H Rasmussen 'Between activism and self-restraint: a judicial policy for the European Court' (1988) 13 *European Law Review* 28–39; H Rasmussen 'Towards a normative theory of interpretation of Community law' (1992) *University of Chicago Legal Forum* 135–78.

175 Sir Patrick Neill's *The European Court of Justice: A Case Study in Judicial Activism* (European Policy Forum 1995); T Hartley 'The European Court, judicial objectivity and the constitution of the European Union' (1996) 112 *Law Quarterly Review* 95–109.

176 See further G Conway *The Limits of Legal Reasoning and the European Court of Justice* (Cambridge University Press 2012).

that are usually followed and should be followed for the law to work effectively throughout the community.

This idea of shared or objectively valid interpretation is central to the rule of law. This understanding of interpretation supports giving priority to certain elements in legal reasoning: the priority of the explicit text, downplaying implication, focusing on the most specifically relevant laws (i.e. following *lex specialis* and not more general laws), considering what the law-maker intended. All these elements are often understated in the case law of the ECJ, and the Court is very much open to the criticism of being too creative in its approach, downplaying express texts, emphasising overall purposes in the law instead of the purpose of specific provisions, and ignoring the intentions of the Member States as authors of the EU treaties. The ECJ has undoubtedly played a key role in increasing European integration, but whether this law-making and constitution-building is appropriate for a court is very much open to debate.

5.7 CONCLUSION

The ECJ has undoubtedly played a key role in the development of EU law. In this respect, it is not typical of courts. It could even be said that the Court has been almost as important in building the constitution of the EU as have the Member States. The role the Court has played has been facilitated by the variety of procedures available before it, in particular by the preliminary reference procedure, which has allowed it to influence the application of EU law in all the Member States.

The Court's methods of interpretation have been controversial, though they have not always been as fully debated as might be expected, given the extent of the influence of the Court. The characteristic method of the ECJ is meta-teleological: it downplays the centrality of specific textual provisions, preferring broad purposive interpretation aimed at enhancing the overall goal of integration. As the competence of the EU grows, it remains to be seen if the Court will continue to play the same role to the same extent.

POINTS TO REVIEW

– The ECJ has functioned as a general court and constitutional court for the EU since the European Communities were founded.

– The ECJ has a wide range of jurisdiction encompassing preliminary references, enforcement actions, reviews of legality and actions in damages for non–contractual liability.

- Following the Lisbon Treaty, the Court of First Instance has been renamed the General Court. Its jurisdiction has expanded since it was founded by the Single European Act 1986, and it acts as a tribunal of first instance in many cases.

- The ECJ is distinctive as a court in the creativity of its methods of interpretation. Its distinctive approach can be described as meta-teleological: it often engages in purposive interpretation, downplaying specific textual provisions, in favour of advancing an overall purpose of the EU legal system of enhancing integration.

- The ECJ has developed some of the central constitutional features of the EU legal system, including: direct effect, supremacy, state liability, broad readings of competence, a human rights jurisdiction, and parallelism in external relations.

- The ECJ had often caused controversy with its rulings, but there has been surprisingly little discussion of an alternative normative approach to interpretation. One alternative to its method is to envisage the ECJ (and any court) having a shared hermeneutic or interpretative perspective with the law-maker and all reasonable participants in the legal system.

CHAPTER GLOSSARY

Court of First Instance refers to the lowest rung in the general court system of the EU as it was described from 1986 to 2009. It is now known as the General Court.

Effet utile refers to the idea of effectiveness of EU law as a guide to legal reasoning by the ECJ.

Enforcement action refers to a procedure before the ECJ initiated by either the European Commission or another Member State claiming a failure by another Member State to comply with EU law.

General Court refers to the general court of first instance of the EU judicial system. Appeals from this court to the ECJ can be heard on points of law. The two courts together make up the CJEU.

Hermeneutic is another term for 'interpretative'.

Judicial activism refers to judicial creativity in interpretation.

Levels of generality refers to the degree of abstraction used to describe a legal provision or the purpose of a legal provision.

Meta-teleological interpretation refers to purposive interpretation guided by purpose stated at a very high or systemic level of generality.

Pre-contentious stage refers to the use of the enforcement procedure up until the delivery of a letter of notice by the Commission to a Member State.

Preliminary reference refers to a procedure before the ECJ in which a national court refers a question of EU law, to which the answer is not very clear, for a judgment on the correct legal answer, after which the national court is responsible for applying the ECJ judgment to the facts of the case.

Review of legality refers to a procedure before the ECJ or CJEU in which privileged applicants (a Member State, the European Commission, the Council of the European Parliament) or non-privileged applicants can challenge the legality of an act of an institution.

Teleological is another term for 'purposive', usually applied to legal interpretation in EU law.

TAKING THINGS FURTHER

H Rasmussen *On Law and Policy of the European Court of Justice* (Kluwer 1986) This is a landmark study of the European Court of Justice. Whereas generally speaking scholarship on the Court had praised and celebrated its role, with little fundamental critique, this work identified a fundamental objection to the Court's preference for policy-oriented reasoning, instead of the legal analysis more typically expected of courts.

J Shaw 'European Union legal studies in crisis? Towards a new dynamic' (1996) 16(2) *Oxford Journal of Legal Studies* 231–53 This is a seminal article in EU studies that accurately captures the culture of the discipline as favouring an automatic pro-integration perspective, which, it argues is too narrow for a satisfactory understanding of what EU studies as a discipline should be concerned with, especially when it comes to the role of the ECJ.

G Conway *The Limits of Legal Reasoning and the European Court of Justice* (Cambridge University Press 2002) This work by the present author offers a normative critique of the dominant meta-teleological approach to interpretation of the ECJ. It argues that the ECJ should be seen as sharing a hermeneutic perspective with the law-maker, and that this would result in much greater emphasis on *lex specialis*, legal traditions and the intention of the Member States in the legal reasoning of the Court.

J Komárek 'Judicial law-making and precedent in supreme courts: the European Court of Justice compared to the US Supreme Court and the French Cour de Cassation' in C Barnard, O Odudu (eds) *Cambridge Yearbook of European Legal Studies* (Hart Publishing 2009) 399–434 This offers a comparative assessment of the use of legal reasoning by the Court of Justice, relative to both a constitutional court (the US Supreme Court) and an 'ordinary' court of appeal.

G Beck *The Legal Reasoning of the European Court of Justice* (Hart Publishing 2013) This book offers a detailed account of how the Court of Justice has approached legal reasoning, including cases relating to economic governance.

B de Witte, E Muir and M Dawson (eds) *Judicial Activism at the European Court of Justice* (Edward Elgar 2013) This offers an inter-disciplinary, and largely sympathetic, discussion of different aspects of the criticisms of judicial activism of the European Court of Justice. It does not offer a normative account of interpretation, but rather an analysis of the existing legal and political context.

W Phelan *In Place of Inter-state Retaliation: The European Union's Rejection of WTO-style Trade Sanctions and Trade Remedies* (Oxford University Press 2014) This work is the first full-scale treatment of the elimination of international law countermeasures as an aspect of dispute settlement in the EU system in its broader 'constitutional' context. The author argues that this feature of the EU should be seen as being as important as the doctrines of supremacy and direct effect to the particular character of the EU in international law.

6

CHAPTER 6
THE EU AND NATIONAL LAW

This chapter examines how EU law takes effect in and influences national law. The way in which EU law impacts on national law is one of the key differences between EU law and other international law. Three key doctrines of EU law combine to achieve this effect: the doctrines of direct effect, supremacy and state liability. These doctrines are best understood as working together to give EU law real 'teeth' in national legal systems. They ensure that individual citizens can invoke EU law in a national court and have that EU law applied over and above any contrary or different national law, failing which there is a remedy in damages. The three doctrines were the creation of the Court of Justice, and they illustrate very well the key role that the Court has played in the EU legal system. National courts have always accepted the doctrines of direct effect (and indirect effect) and state liability, but there have been important differences of principle in how national courts have reacted to the supremacy doctrine of the Court of Justice. Some national courts have resisted the supremacy doctrine in its strongest form, although they all accept the doctrine on a day-to-day basis. As well as looking at case law from the Court of Justice, we will look at examples of the reception of the supremacy doctrine in national constitutional law. It is appropriate to say 'national constitutional law' here because the doctrines of direct effect, indirect effect and supremacy are central to the constitutional nature and importance of the EU: the EU, through these doctrines, has a very big impact on the constitutional law of the Member States.

AS YOU READ . . .

The key questions that will be answered in this chapter are as follows:

— How does law made at a central level in the EU take effect in national law?

— What do direct effect and indirect effect mean?

— What does the more recent doctrine of 'incidental direct effect' mean?

- Do, and in what way, direct effect, indirect effect and incidental direct effect empower the individual in national courts?

- How and why did a supremacy doctrine become a part of EU law?

- How do the doctrine of direct effect, indirect effect and supremacy combine to make a practical difference in national courts?

- What differences can be seen in the way national courts have reacted to the supremacy doctrine?

- What is the extent of the doctrine of the liability of Member States for breaches of EU law?

6.1 INTRODUCTION

The relationship between EU law and national law is governed by the doctrines of *supremacy*, *direct effect* and *indirect effect*. This is a very important area as it determines the practical significance of EU law in the legal systems of the Member States. The combination of supremacy and direct effect of EU law is most significant: it means (1) that nationals of the EU Member States can invoke EU law in their own courts (direct effect) and (2) have conflicting national law set aside and disapplied in favour of the application of EU law (supremacy).

In addition, national courts are under an obligation to interpret national law, in so far as possible, in a way that maximises its compatibility with EU law (indirect effect, sometimes called conforming interpretation). The operation of supremacy and direct effect combined with the preliminary reference system (see Chapter 5) has been described as a 'magic triangle', in that the three combined powerfully to greatly expand the impact of EU law in national legal systems.[1]

It is first useful to understand the background in public international law of these doctrines. EU law is a product of public international law, but it has important distinct characteristics that greatly extend the impact of EU law in national legal systems compared to the impact of public international law in national systems. We have already looked at this generally in Chapter 2. We will briefly recap on this and also look at (i) the novelty of direct effect as a way of incorporating transnational or international law (EU law here) into national law (ii) the novelty of direct effect for the individual.

----

1   A Vauchez 'Embedded law – political sociology of the European Community of law: elements of a renewed research agenda' *European University Institute Working Paper 2007/23* (2007) 8.

After outlining the principle of direct effect and the related interpretative principle of indirect effect, we will look at how national constitutional courts have reacted to the supremacy doctrine stated by the Court of Justice. In addition, we will briefly examine the doctrine of incidental direct effect (which arises less often).

As we will see, the Court of Justice has played a very important role in this area of EU law. The treaties did not (and still do not) set out the supremacy doctrine explicitly. Instead, the Treaty of Lisbon incorporated supremacy indirectly by reference to case law of the Court of Justice and the Council Legal Service's opinion on supremacy of *Community* law in Declaration No 17 annexed to the Final Act. It is a product of the Court's case law, and this is also the case with the doctrines of direct effect and indirect effect.

6.2 INTERNATIONAL LAW BACKGROUND TO DIRECT EFFECT

The doctrines of *supremacy* and *direct effect* distinguish EU law from other kinds of international law in its impact on national systems. By the doctrine of supremacy, when there is a conflict between EU law and national law, national law must be disapplied.

KEY LEARNING POINT

DIRECT EFFECT
By the doctrine of direct effect, an individual can invoke an EU law in a national court. Traditionally, individuals have not been allowed to invoke international law in a national court: only states could do this. Individuals were said not to be 'subjects of international law'.

As noted here, a first key change brought by direct effect concerns the international law doctrine that the individual could not be a subject of international law. In traditional international law, the individual could not be a subject of the law. This meant that an individual who had suffered as a result of a breach of international law could only achieve a remedy if his or her government sued on his or her behalf. In the second half of the twentieth century, this traditional position of the individual began to change with the development of international human rights law, but it otherwise remains the case. EU law now works very differently, in that most EU laws can be directly invoked in a national court by an individual. Further, when there is a conflict with national law, EU law must be applied over and above national law.

The direct effect doctrine of EU law changes how international law normally impacts on national law in another way also: the way EU is incorporated into national law. Primarily, in the context of international treaties a basic distinction exists as to how national legal systems accept international law as part of national law (remember that international law and national law are separate legal systems). We have looked at this in Chapter 2, and it is worth recalling now briefly that:

1. once a treaty has been signed/ratified by the government (i.e. the executive, e.g. foreign minister), the treaty is automatically a part of national law (monism)
2. two steps are necessary to make a treaty part of national law, i.e. signature ratification by the government/executive and incorporation by parliament, usually by legislation (dualism).[2] The two types of monism are: (i) strong monism (once the international treaty is part of domestic/national law *and* has the same standing or a higher standing than constitutional law) and (ii) weak monism (the international treaty is part of domestic/national law, but has the same status as an ordinary statute).

EXPLAINING THE LAW

EU LAW PUSHES NATIONAL SYSTEMS TOWARDS MONISM
The direct effect doctrine of EU law means that once the Member States ratify the founding and amending treaties (which, remember, are like a Constitution), they are monist towards ordinary EU laws, i.e. EU secondary legislation: once secondary legislation is adopted in Brussels, it can be invoked (assuming certain conditions are met) in a national court without national implementing legislation, once the conditions for direct effect are satisfied, irrespective of whether a Member State is monist or dualist towards 'ordinary' international law (i.e. non-EU law). If a Member State is dualist, it remains dualist as regards the founding and amending treaties, but it becomes monist as regards secondary legislation.

6.3 OUTLINE OF THE SUPREMACY DOCTRINE

To understand the supremacy doctrine, it is again useful to bear in mind the international law background. The two main EU treaties – the Treaty on European Union (TEU) and Treaty on the Functioning of the European Union (TFEU) – are international treaties and, as such, they bind any state that has signed them in international law, just like any international law treaty. Article 4(3) TEU states that Member States have an obligation to ensure the fulfilment of the obligations arising under the treaties.

....

2 Note, however, that many systems that are dualist are more receptive to other sources of international law than treaties, such as custom and general principles (e.g. the latter are part of common law).

Did the original Treaty of Rome and its equivalent provisions mean supremacy over national law (in national law as well as international law)? In the absence of express treaty provisions on it, traditional dualism would suggest not: but direct effect *now applied to the supremacy doctrine* gives it effect in national law, not just in EU law. This is how supremacy and direct effect combine. It does so to produce 'strong monism': EU law, at least according to the Court of Justice, prevails over all national constitutional law (not simply ordinary statute law or common law).

The issue of supremacy was first directly considered by the Court of Justice in *Costa v ENEL*, where the Court stated:[3]

> The integration into the laws of each Member State of provisions which derive from the Community, and more generally the terms and the spirit of the Treaty, make it impossible for the States, as a corollary, to accord precedence to a unilateral and subsequent measure over a legal system, accepted by them on a basis of reciprocity . . . The executive force of Community law cannot vary from one State to another . . . Wherever the Treaty grants the States the right to act unilaterally, it does this by clear and precise provisions (for example Articles 15, 93(3), 223, 224 and 225). Applications, by Member States for authority to derogate from the Treaty are subject to a special authorisation procedure . . . which would lose their purpose if the Member States could renounce their obligations by means of an ordinary law. The precedence of Community law is confirmed by Article 189, whereby a Regulation shall be binding and 'directly applicable in all Member States'.[4]

The Court of Justice described the transfer of sovereignty to the Communities as 'permanent'.[5]

ANALYSING THE LAW

THE TREATY BASIS FOR THE SUPREMACY DOCTRINE

The Court had sought some textual support by suggesting that the express provisions on derogation from the treaty carried the implication that they alone were the means by which Member States could deviate from Community law and that a supremacy doctrine could be thus inferred.[6] This is a somewhat doubtful argument: many international treaties have derogation provisions (e.g. Article 13 of the European Convention on Human Rights), without claiming that as a matter of national law (and not just as a matter of international law) the treaty is supreme over national law. Nonetheless, the supremacy doctrine stated by the ECJ in *Costa v ENEL* has become accepted as part of EU law.

---

3   Case 6/64 *Costa v ENEL* [1964] ECR 585.
4   Ibid 593.
5   Ibid 594.
6   Ibid.

Two other cases from the ECJ later identified other important elements of the supremacy doctrine. In *Internationale Handelsgesellschaft*,[7] the ECJ clarified its view that supremacy extended to cover national constitutional law, relying on an argument as to effectiveness and a principle of uniformity of Community law across the Member States.[8] This means that even if the national law that is contrary to EU law is the most important national constitutional law, EU law still prevails. In the UK, this might seem less significant because Acts of Parliament are the highest source of law, but the significance is more obvious where national constitutions are harder to amend than an ordinary Act of Parliament. The case showed the full implications of *Costa v ENEL*.

In *Simmenthal*,[9] the ECJ had to consider the related issue of how a national court could give effect to a prevailing provision of EU law when it clearly conflicted with domestic law. The ECJ made it clear that national courts should be willing to disapply national law themselves and should not wait to make a preliminary reference, justifying this on the basis of effectiveness for EU law:

> The effectiveness of [the preliminary reference procedure] would be impaired
> if the national court were prevented from forthwith applying Community law in
> accordance with the decision or the case law of the Court.[10]

In addition, the ECJ has held that national procedural law must not prevent national courts of their own motion, when no party to the proceedings has raised the issue, from considering whether domestic law is compatible with EU law.[11]

As an aside, it is worth noting that the absolute claims of the ECJ regarding supremacy have been strongly contested, most notably by the German Federal Constitutional Court. We will return to this at the end of the chapter. First, we will look in more detail at the doctrine of direct effect. This is more multifaceted and somewhat more complicated in its detail.

KEY LEARNING POINT

THE SCOPE OF THE SUPREMACY DOCTRINE

The supremacy doctrine applies to all national law, including national constitutional law (*Internationale Handelsgesellschaft*). The effect of the doctrine is that when there is a conflict of norms between EU law and national law, national law must be set aside and EU law applied instead (*Simmenthal*).

---

7 Case 11/70 *Internationale Handelsgesellschaft mbH v Einfuhr- und Vorratsstelle für Getreide und Futtermittel* [1970] ECR 1125.
8 Ibid para 3.
9 Case 106/77 *Simmenthal* [1978] ECR 629.
10 Ibid para 18.
11 Case C–312/93 *Peterbroeck, Van Campenhout & Cie SCS v Belgium* [1995] ECR I–04599.

6.4 OUTLINE OF THE DIRECT EFFECT OF TREATY ARTICLES: *VAN GEND EN LOOS*

The principle of direct effect treaty articles was first declared by the ECJ in the leading case of *Van Gend en Loos*.[12] There was no explicit treaty basis for the ECJ decision in *Van Gend en Loos* (as with its decision on supremacy in *Costa v ENEL*), and the two judgments are often taken as prime examples of judicial activism or interpretative licence by the ECJ. As in *Costa v ENEL*, the ECJ in *Van Gend en Loos* focused on an argument about effectiveness of Community law, suggesting that in the absence of direct effect, Community nationals could be deprived of an effective remedy. Two types of direct effect exist, namely *vertical*, which refers to the entitlement of a citizen to invoke EU law in suing his or her own government in a national court and *horizontal*, which refers to the entitlement of a citizen to invoke EU law in suing another citizen.

> KEY LEARNING POINT
> ....
>
> **CONDITIONS FOR DIRECT EFFECT OF TREATY ARTICLES**
> For any provision of EU law to be directly effective it must satisfy certain conditions. The EU law must be:
>
> a. sufficiently clear and precise
> b. unconditional
> c. capable of involving an individual right.

Following the *Van Gend en Loos* case, the ECJ has held that a substantial number of treaty provisions are directly effective, and it does not require a great deal of clarity. They include:

- Article 21 TFEU: Citizens' rights of free movement and residence (*Baumbast and R v Home Department*[13])
- Article 45 TFEU: the free movement of workers (*Walrave and Koch v Association Union Cycliste Internationale* and *Van Duyn v Home Office*[14])
- Articles 30, 34, 35 and 110 TFEU: the free movement of goods (*Van Gend en Loos*)
- Articles 49 and 56 TFEU: freedom of establishment and services (*Reyners v Belgium* and *Van Binsbergen*[15])
- Article 157 TFEU: equal pay for men and women (*Defrenne v SABENA*[16]).

------

12 Case 26/62 *Van Gend en Loos* [1963] ECR 1.
13 Case C–413/99 *Baumbast and R v Home Department* [2002] ECR I–7091.
14 Case C–36/74 *Walrave and Koch v Association Union Cycliste Internationale* [1974] ECR 1405 and Case 41/74 *Van Duyn v Home Office* [1974] ECR 1337.
15 Case 2/74 *Reyners v Belgium* [1974] ECR 631; Case 33/74 *Van Binsbergen v Bestuur van de Bedrijfsverening voor de Metaalnijverheit* [1974] ECR 1299.
16 Case 43/75 *Defrenne v SABENA* [1976] ECR 455.

6.5 HORIZONTAL DIRECT EFFECT OF TREATY ARTICLES: *DEFRENNE V SABENA*

The ECJ developed the horizontal direct effect doctrine in *Defrenne v SABENA*.[17] The case involved an equal pay claim brought by an airline stewardess (Gabrielle Defrenne) using what is now Article 157 TFEU against her ex-employer (the Belgian airline company, SABENA). Other examples of horizontal direct effect include *Angonese*,[18] in which an Italian national successfully relied on Article 45 TFEU in a claim against an Italian bank, and *Courage Ltd v Crehan*,[19] in which Article 101 TFEU was invoked in a dispute between the Courage brewery and a publican.

> **KEY LEARNING POINT**
>
> **SUMMARISING HORIZONTAL VERSUS VERTICAL DIRECT EFFECT**
> With vertical direct effect, an individual may invoke EU law in a national court only against the national government. With horizontal direct effect an individual may invoke EU law in a national court against the national government as well as against individuals. To summarise the position in EU law, all the main EU laws (Treaty articles, regulations and decisions) have both vertical and horizontal direct effect (assuming the conditions for direct effect are met), except directives, which can only have vertical direct effect. Regarding directives not having direct effect, on the 'plus side' from the point of view of an individual, in the absence of full transposition by a Member State within the time allowed in a directive, a public authority of a Member State may not rely on an untransposed provision of a directive against an individual.[20]

6.6 DIRECT EFFECT OF SECONDARY LEGISLATION

6.6.1 INTRODUCTION

In the very significant judgment in *Franz Grad v Finanzamt Traunstein*,[21] the ECJ broadened direct effect to cover secondary legislation, and not just treaty provisions. Remember from the types of secondary legislation in the EU: *regulations,*

17 Ibid.
18 Case C–281/98 *Angonese* [2000] ECR I–4139.
19 Case C–453/99 *Courage Ltd v Crehan* [2001] ECR I–6297.
20 Case C–168/95 *Criminal proceedings against Arcaro* [1996] ECR I–4705.
21 Case 9/70 *Franz Grad v Finanzamt Traunstein* [1970] ECR 825.

directives and *decisions* (Article 288 TFEU). In *Franz Grad*, the ECJ made two major arguments: (1) the effectiveness of binding measures would be impaired in the absence of direct effect; and (2) the preliminary reference procedure implied individuals could exercise their rights in national courts.[22] This follows the type of reasoning in *Van Gend en Loos*.

The judgment in *Franz Grad* involved a decision, whereas only regulations appeared to be attributed with such effect under the treaty in that regulations were at least described as 'directly applicable'.[23] The ECJ addressed this point, noting that the express attribution of direct applicability to regulations did not mean that other measures did not have such effect (this in the broad interpretative approach of the ECJ, it was enough that the text did not exclude something, rather than it being required by the text[24]).

6.6.2 DIRECT EFFECT OF REGULATIONS

Regulations may also be directly effective, both vertically and horizontally, if they satisfy the tests laid down in *Van Gend en Loos*. Regarding regulations, the text of the treaty offers more support for the idea of direct effect, because the treaty refers to them as 'directly applicable', although direct effect still goes beyond the idea of direct applicability. The idea of direct applicability is now interpreted to mean that a provision needs no implementing measure (this, it will usually satisfy the conditions for direct effect).

KEY LEARNING POINT

THE DIFFERENCE BETWEEN DIRECT EFFECT AND DIRECT APPLICABILITY

In the early days of Community law, there was some confusion about the relationship between the concepts of direct effect and direct applicability. The treaties did not (and still do not) use the term 'direct effect', but they did describe regulations as directly applicable. What 'directly applicable' means is that no national implementing legislation is needed for an EU law, as there is no discretion in national implementation of it and it is sufficiently detailed. Regulations and Decisions under Article 288 FEU are directly applicable. Direct effect means that an individual can invoke an EU law in a national court proceeding. Directly applicable laws will usually satisfy two of the conditions of direct effect, namely, they must be clear and precise and they must also be unconditional. However, they may not satisfy the final condition of affording an individual right.

22 Ibid paras 5–6.

23 Owing to the use of the expression 'directly applicable' in the treaties, rather than directly effective, there was an early debate in Community law about the relationship between direct effect and direct applicability. It is now clear that direct effect relates to the capacity of an individual to invoke EU law in a national court, whereas direct applicability relates to the lack of a need for national implementing legislation for an EU legislative measure. Generally, what is directly applicable will satisfy the conditions for direct effect, but not necessarily so.

24 Case 9/70 *Franz Grad* (n 21) para 5.

Commission v Italy[25] concerned a regulation that concerned the slaughtering of cows. The ECJ criticised the Italian Government for implementing the regulation in an ineffective way, applying horizontal direct effect. *Muñoz & Superior Fruiticola v Frumar Ltd & Redbridge Ltd*[26] referred to the 'very nature' and 'place in the system of sources' of EU law of regulations as justifying their direct effect. This relates to the fact that regulations need no implementing legislation, meaning they will normally fulfil the criteria for direct effect. The same applies to decisions, although more so, since decisions are by their nature directed to individuals, they are thus more likely to create individual rights.

6.6.3 DIRECT EFFECT OF DIRECTIVES: *VAN DUYN*

Directives were once considered incapable of being directly effective in that they are conditional and require implementation by the Member States. However, in *Van Duyn v Home Office*,[27] the ECJ held that directives are capable of direct effect and that the existence of discretion as to their implementation did not preclude direct effect, so long as the result to be achieved was clear.[28]

However, the ECJ further held in *Pubblico Minister v Tullio Ratti*[29] that a directive cannot have direct effect until its deadline for implementation has expired. If a Member State fails to implement a directive on time[30] (either at all or properly), then an individual can invoke the directive if it meets the conditions of direct effect otherwise, i.e. once the period for implementation has expired. Although a Member State cannot be sued by an individual before the time period for implementation of a directive has expired, the Member States are during this time supposed to refrain from taking any measures liable gravely to jeopardise the attainment of the result prescribed by the directive.[31]

If a Member State does jeopardise the attainment of an objective in this way, it is likely that its position regarding state liability could be aggravated (see further below on the doctrine of state liability), but national courts must not apply pre-existing national rules contrary to directives only after the period prescribed for its transposition has expired.[32]

---

25 Case 39/72 *Commission v Italy* [1973] ECR 101.

26 Case C–253/00 *Muñoz & Superior Fruiticola v Frumar Ltd & Redbridge Ltd* [2002] ECR I–7289.

27 Case 41/74 *Van Duyn v Home Office* [1974] ECR 1337.

28 See also the earlier case of Case 33/70, *SpA SACE v Finance Minister of the Italian Republic* [1970] ECR 1213.

29 Case 148/78 *Pubblico Minister v Tullio Ratti* [1979] ECR 1629.

30 The Member States are not allowed to vary the time period to a subsequent date from the date specified in the directive: Case C–140/97 *Walter Rechberger and Others v Austrian Republic* [1999] ECR I–3499.

31 Case 157/02 *Rieser International Transporte GmbH v Autobahnen-und-Schnellstrasse Finanzierurgs AG (Asfing)* [2004] ECR I–7477.

32 Case C–156/91 *Hansa Fleisch Ernst Mundt* [1992] ECR I–5567 para 20.

6.7 NO HORIZONTAL DIRECT EFFECT OF DIRECTIVES: *MARSHALL*

Although it was established in *Van Duyn v Home Office* that directives are capable of direct effect, the ECJ has differentiated between the enforcement of a directive against the state (i.e. vertical effect) and against an individual (i.e. horizontal direct effect) in *Marshall v Southampton Area Health Authority*.[33] The facts concerned a woman working at a hospital who was obliged to retire at 60, even though male workers could retire at 65. She sought to rely on EC Directive 76/207[34] on equal treatment; she was successful as the defendant was held to be a public body, but the principle of no horizontal direct effect for directives was established.

> KEY LEARNING POINT
> ....
>
> ### DIRECTIVES DO NOT HAVE HORIZONTAL DIRECT EFFECT
> An unimplemented directive may be invoked in court by employees of a public authority against that authority (as part of the state), but not by a private sector employee in court against his/her employer.

In *Faccini Dori v Recreb Srl*,[35] Advocate General Van Gerven suggested that the ECJ reconsider the *Marshall* decision, but the ECJ confirmed *Marshall*.[36] The plaintiff sought to rely on a directive permitting her to withdraw from a contract for an English language course she had signed away from business premises. She could not rely on the directive against a private company, but she could sue the Italian State in state liability for failing to implement a directive on time.

In this way, the ECJ has indirectly reduced the significance of directives not having horizontal direct effect. On the absence of horizontal direct effect for directives, this ECJ decision has been criticised for reducing the effectiveness of EU law,[37] but it is a textually justified decision as the treaty provision on directives addresses it to the Member States and an effectiveness criterion of adjudication is open to criticism as being too political. The Court continues to follow *Marshall/Faccini Dori*.[38]

---

33 Case 152/84 *Marshall v Southampton Area Health Authority* [1986] ECR 723.

34 Directive 76/207/EC OJ L 039 14.02.1976 p. 40.

35 Case C–91/92 *Faccini Dori v Recreb Srl* [1994] ECR I–3325, on Council Directive 85/577/EEC, concerning protection of the consumer in respect of contracts negotiated away from business premises (OJ L 372 31.12.1985 p. 31).

36 Ibid paras 19–25.

37 See e.g. F Becker, A Campbell 'The direct effect of European directives: towards the final act?' (2007) 13(2) *Columbia Journal of European Law* 401–26.

38 Case C–192/94 *El Corte Inglés v Blázquez Rivero* [1996] ECR I–1281; Case C–443/98 *Unilever Italia v Central Food SpA* [2000] ECR I–7535; Case C–235/03 *QDQ Media v Omedas Lecha* [2005] ECR I–1937; Case C–80/06 *Carp v Ecorad* [2007] ECR I–4473.

6.8 DEFINITION OF THE STATE AND EMANATION OF THE STATE IN THE CONTEXT OF HORIZONTAL DIRECT EFFECT (*FOSTER V BRITISH GAS*) AND STATE LIABILITY

MAKING CONNECTIONS
+ + + + + + + + + + + + + + + + + +

THE DEFINITION OF THE 'STATE'

The question of defining what is the state arises in two contexts when considering the application of EU law in national law: (1) for the purpose of applying the rule that directives only have vertical direct effect and (2) for the purpose of the state being liable in damages under the doctrine of state liability (see section 6.14 below).[39] This is similar to the issue that raises in UK public law defining a public body or a body exercising function for the purpose of bringing a judicial review.

6.8.1 DEFINITION OF THE STATE IN THE CONTEXT OF HORIZONTAL DIRECT EFFECT

In *Marshall*, concerning the direct effect of a directive, the ECJ held that the Southampton Area Health Authority was part of the state even in its capacity as employer.[40] However, the ECJ held that it is generally for the national courts to determine whether a particular body is part of or 'an emanation of' the state on the facts of a case. Nonetheless, the ECJ has developed a quite broad interpretation of the state (this is a good example of how the preliminary reference system is meant to present an abstract legal question to the Court, which then answers it in the abstract and leaves the application to the national court). The leading case is *Foster v British Gas*,[41] where the ECJ held that for an organisation to be an emanation of the state, it should be responsible for providing a public service under state control and have special powers to do so.[42]

---

39 Technically in UK public law the 'crown' is a more correct term than the 'state'.
40 Case 152/84 *Marshall* (n 33) paras 49–50.
41 Case C–188/89 *Foster v British Gas* [1990] ECR I–3133.
42 Ibid paras 18–20.

KEY CASE *'EMANATION OF THE STATE'*

The leading authority on defining the state is *Foster v British Gas*:

18 On the basis of those considerations, the Court has held in a series of cases that unconditional and sufficiently precise provisions of a directive could be relied on against organizations or bodies which were subject to the authority or control of the state or had special powers beyond those which result from the normal rules applicable to relations between individuals.

19 The Court has accordingly held that provisions of a directive could be relied on against tax authorities (the judgments in Case 8/81 *Becker*, cited above, and in Case C–221/88 *ECSC v Acciaierie e Ferriere Busseni (in liquidation)* [1990] ECR I–495), local or regional authorities (judgment in Case 103/88 *Fratelli Costanzo v Comune di Milano* [1989] ECR 1839), constitutionally independent authorities responsible for the maintenance of public order and safety (judgment in Case 222/84 *Johnston v Chief Constable of the Royal Ulster Constabulary* [1986] ECR 1651), and public authorities providing public health services (judgment in Case 152/84 *Marshall*, cited above).

20 It follows from the foregoing that a body, whatever its legal form, which has been made responsible, pursuant to a measure adopted by the state, for providing a public service under the control of the state and has for that purpose special powers beyond those which result from the normal rules applicable in relations between individuals is included in any event among the bodies against which the provisions of a directive capable of having direct effect may be relied upon.

Satisfying just one of the conditions in *Foster v British Gas* is not enough. However, the relative importance of the different conditions is not as clear from the case law, so the courts may require 'more' or 'less' of one of the conditions. In *Doughty v Rolls Royce*, the UK Court of Appeal found that Rolls Royce was not an emanation of the state, even though it was 100 per cent owned by the UK Government, as the other criteria in *Foster* were not satisfied.[43]

In *Kampelmann v Westfallen*, for example, the ECJ stated the tests in similar terms to *Foster*, stating that individuals may rely on a directive directly before the national courts as against the state and any organisations or bodies which are subject to the authority or control of the state or have special powers beyond those which result from the normal rules applicable to relations between individuals, either where the state has failed to transpose the directive into national law within the prescribed period or where it has not done so correctly.[44]

---

43 [1992] 1 CMLR 1045.
44 Joined Cases C–253–256/96 *Kampelmann v Westfallen* [1998] ECR I–6907 para 47.

Foster v British Gas has been applied in a range of subsequent cases: public administration generally, including local government (e.g. *Jiménez Melgar v Ayuntamiento de Los Barrios*),[45] health authorities and hospitals (*Marshall*[46] and *Medipac-Kazantzidis v Venizelio-Pananio*[47]), the police (*Johnston v Chief Constable of the RUC*[48]), state-owned industry (*Foster* itself). The Court of Justice has decided that all three branches of government – the legislature, the executive or administration, and the judiciary – can be liable in state liability.

6.8.2 DEFINITION OF THE STATE IN THE CONTEXT OF STATE LIABILITY

In the context of state liability (discussed below in section 6.14), many cases have involved the legislature as the cause of liability,[49] followed by the executive.[50] Recognition in EU law that judicial decisions can give rise to state liability is more recent. This was first held in *Köbler v Austria*, but the ECJ held also that liability only arose for judicial error where it was committed by a national court from which there is no right of appeal. The ECJ clarified the exact scope of *Köbler* in *Traghetti del Mediterraneo SpA v Italy*,[51] a case involving a claim against the Italian Supreme Court.

In another case from Italy, *Commission v Italy*, the Court of Justice held that, first, by excluding all liability of the Italian State for damage caused to individuals through an infringement of EU law on the part of a court adjudicating at last instance when that infringement resulted from an interpretation of the rules of law or an assessment of the facts and evidence carried out by that court and, second, by limiting that liability by legislation to cases of intentional fault or serious misconduct, Italy had failed to fulfil its obligations under the general principle that Member States are liable for the infringement of EU law by one of their courts adjudicating at last instance.[52] In this case, the fault was with the legislature, but related to the subject of liability for judicial error.

> KEY LEARNING POINT
> ....
>
> **THE CONDITIONS OF STATE LIABILITY FOR JUDICIAL ERROR**
> The ECJ stated that state liability for judicial error could be incurred only exceptionally where there was a manifest infringement of EU law by a national court from which there is no right of appeal (*Köbler*, as clarified by *Traghetti*).

....

45 Case C–438/99 *Jiménez Melgar v Ayuntamiento de Los Barrios* [2001] ECR I–6915.
46 Case 271/91 *Marshall* (n 33) paras 49–50.
47 Case C–6/05 *Medipac-Kazantzidis v Venizelio-Pananio* [2007] ECR I–4557.
48 Case 222/84 *Johnston v Chief Constable of the RUC* [1986] ECR 1561.
49 See e.g. Joined Cases C–46 and C–48/93 *Brasserie du Pêcheur*; Case C–140/97 *Rechberger* (n 30); Case C–5/94 *The Queen v Ministry of Agriculture, Fisheries and Food, ex parte Hedley Lomas (Ireland) Ltd* [1996] ECR 1–2553 (concerning a refusal by the UK to grant an export licence for the export of sheep on the basis of a suspicion that exported animals would be treated in conditions contrary to EU law).
50 Case C–302/97 *Konle v Austria* [1999] ECR I–3099; C–424/97 *Haim* [2000] ECR I–5123.
51 Case C–173/03 *Traghetti del Mediterraneo SpA v Italy* [2006] ECR I–5177.
52 Case 379/10 *Commission v Italy* [2011] ECR I–180.

6.9 'INCIDENTAL' DIRECT EFFECT OF DIRECTIVES

Although directives cannot be directly effective against other individuals, the ECJ has further circumvented this (in addition to state liability and a broad definition of 'emanation of the state') to some extent by holding that a directive could be relied on in a national court to prevent other individuals from enforcing national law that is clearly contrary to a directive. This is called 'incidental direct effect'.

KEY LEARNING POINT

....

'BYPASSING' HORIZONTAL DIRECT EFFECT THROUGH INCIDENTAL EFFECT

The doctrine or concept of incidental effect is one of three ways the ECJ has reduced or bypassed the significance (at least to some extent) of the decision in *Marshall* that directives do not have horizontal direct effect (i.e. an individual cannot sue another individual on the basis of a directive). Incidental effect prevents a national law contrary to an unimplemented directive from being applied in a national court.

In *CIA Security International*,[53] CIA Security, a manufacturer of alarms, sued the private defendant companies, arguing the defendants had libeled it by claiming that the alarm system that CIA marketed had not been approved as required under Belgian legislation. CIA did not have approval, but argued that the Belgian legislation had not been notified to the Commission as required by Article 8 of Directive 83/189[54] on technical standards (and, therefore, that the Belgian legislation was not valid). The ECJ held that Directive 83/189 laid down a precise obligation on Member States to notify draft technical regulations to the Commission before they were adopted, and that therefore those provisions could be relied on by individuals before national courts. In what is a good example of the tendency of the ECJ to consequentialist or results-based reasoning (rather than looking at legal texts), the ECJ declared at paragraph 48:

> . . . effectiveness of Community control will be that much greater if the directive is interpreted as meaning that breach of the obligation to notify constitutes a substantial procedural defect such as to render the technical regulations in question inapplicable to individuals.

....

53 Case C–194/94 *CIA Security International* [1996] ECR I–2201, in particular paras 41–48.
54 OJ L 109 26.4.1983 p. 8.

The private claimant, CIA Security, was allowed to rely on Belgium's failure to comply with the directive in its legal action against the private defendants, thereby depriving the defendants of a defence (i.e. a provision of national law) that they would otherwise have had. In effect, this is a manifestation of supremacy: national law contrary to EU law could not be applied.

EXPLAINING THE LAW

THE APPLICATION OF INCIDENTAL EFFECT
Two things are apparent from *CIA Security* about incidental effect:

1. It is notable that here, incidental effect was used as a sword and not just as a shield: i.e. it provided a basis for an action, and not just a defence to an action brought by somebody else. In *CIA Security*, the result of incidental direct effect was to deprive a defendant of a defence based on national law. It could also happen that a claim based on national law could fail because the national law in question was contrary to an unimplemented directive.
2. However, there still had to be a separate cause of action in national law other than the EU directive: here, the separate cause of action was libel under national law.

Another example is *Unilever Italia v Central Food SpA*.[55] The company Unilever supplied Central Food with a consignment of olive oil. Central Food refused to pay for the consignment of oil because it claimed it was not labelled as required under national (Italian) law. Unilever argued that Italian law was not compliant with Community law. Unilever sued Central Food for non-payment, relying on *CIA Security*.

The ECJ found that a national technical regulation should not be applied as a legal consequence of its non-compliance with the obligation of notification under Article 8 of Directive 83/189 (laying down a procedure for the provision of information in the field of technical standards)[56] and that its non-applicability could be relied on in proceedings between individuals, so Unilever could rely on the directive to prevent the application of the Italian law. Further, the Court held that national rules not compliant with the obligation to observe the periods of postponement of adoption of a draft technical regulation pursuant to Article 9 of that directive should not be applied either.

....

55 Case 443/98 *Unilever Italia v Central Food SpA* [2000] ECR 1–753.
56 Council Directive 83/189/EEC laying down a procedure for the provision of information in the field of technical standards and regulations OJL 109 26.4.1983 p. 8 (as amended).

It is, moreover, possible to rely on a directive vertically where the result incidentally imposes obligations on another individual. In *R (on the application of Wells) v Secretary of State for Transport, Local Government & the Regions*, a British woman was able to require the British Government to implement an environmental impact assessment under Directive 85/337[57] of proposed mining operations, even though the assessment would impact adversely on the quarry owners.[58]

6.10 INDIRECT EFFECT AS AN OBLIGATION OF INTERPRETATION: *VON COLSON*

A final technique the ECJ has adopted that reduces the impact of the *Marshall* rule is the doctrine of indirect effect.

KEY LEARNING POINT

THE DOCTRINE OF INDIRECT EFFECT
Where national legislation has been enacted to implement a directive, national courts are under a duty to interpret the implementing legislation *and national legislation generally* (see further below on this point) to achieve the results required by the directive. However, a national court is only required to do this insofar as it is possible to do so and after the implementation date has expired.

This duty can be related to the obligation on Member States under Article 288 TFEU to achieve the results of a directive and their general duty under Article 4(3) TFEU to take all appropriate measures to ensure fulfilment of their obligations. The doctrine was first fully set out in *Von Colson and Kamann v Land Nordrhein Westfalen*.[59] This case concerned incorrect implementation of a directive on equal treatment (the facts involved the refusal of the German prison service to employ a female in a male prison; the EU directive in question was on the equal treatment of men and women[60]). The ECJ held that national courts have a duty to interpret national implementing legislation

---

57 OJ L 175 5.7.1985 p. 40.
58 Case C–201/02 *R (on the application of Wells) v Secretary of State for Transport, Local Government & the Regions* [2004] ECR I–723; see in particular paras 56–57.
59 Case 14/83 *Von Colson and Kamann v Land Nordrhein Westfalen* [1984] ECR 1891.
60 Directive 76/207/EEC OJ L 039 14.2.1976 p. 40, on the implementation of the principle of equal treatment for men and women as regards access to employment, vocational training and promotion, and working conditions.

in a way that gives effect to the directive 'in so far as it is given discretion to do so under national law'.[61] The directive in question did not have direct effect on the facts.

KEY LEARNING POINT

WHEN INDIRECT EFFECT ARISES

A national court is only required to comply with the duty of interpretation under the doctrine of indirect effect only after the implementation date for a directive has expired, unless the directive relates to a general principle of EU law. Indirect effect can in principle arise in the context of any national law implementing EU law, but it usually arises with directives, because these generally require national implementing legislation.

In *Adeneler & Others*,[62] the ECJ decided when the interpretative obligation in *Von Colson* arises. The ECJ stated that the general obligation owed by national courts to interpret domestic law in conformity with a directive exists *only once the period for its transposition or implementation has expired*. However, the ECJ has extended the interpretative obligation to the period before the implementation of a directive when the obligation relates to a general principle of Union law.

Mangold v Helm[63] concerned Directive 2000/78[64] (which required Member States to introduce legislation to tackle age discrimination), the implementation date of which was still in the future at the time of the dispute. The ECJ held that the observance of the general principle of equal treatment, in particular in respect of age, could not be conditional upon the expiry of the period allowed the Member States for the transposition of the directive. As the category of general principles of EU law is quite broad (see Chapter 2), this decision has the potential to be often relevant in future cases.[65]

KEY CASES *CONFORMING INTERPRETATION UNDER THE DOCTRINE OF DIRECT EFFECT IN UK LAW IN* LISTER *AND* DUKE

The case of *Lister v Forth Dry Dock & Engineering Co Ltd* is a leading authority on acceptance of indirect effect in UK law.[66] It concerned the interpretation of a UK statutory instrument, the Transfer of Undertakings (Protection of Employment) Regulations 1981, adopted specifically to implement Directive 77/187.[67] The facts concerned whether workers dismissed very soon before

---

61 Case 14/83 *Von Colson* (n 59) para 28.
62 Case C–212/04 *Adeneler & Others* [2006] ECR I–6057 paras 108–115.
63 Case C–144/04 *Mangold v Helm* [2005] ECR I–9981 paras 66–68, 74–77.
64 OJ L 303 16 2.12.2000.
65 The *Mangold* case is examined in more detail in ch 8.
66 [1990] 1 AC 546, [1990] ILLR 250.
67 OJ L 061 5.3.1977 p. 26.

the transfer of ownership of a company had a claim against the new owner on the basis of unfair dismissal. The House of Lords concluded that there should be implied into regulation 5(3) of the Transfer Regulations these words: 'or would have been so employed if he had not been unfairly dismissed in the circumstances described by regulation 8(1)'. Lord Templeman observed in his judgment that: '. . . the courts of the United Kingdom are under a duty to follow the practice of the European Court of Justice by giving a purposive construction to directives and regulations issued for the purpose of complying with directive . . .'.[68]

Another significant judgment is *Duke v GEC Reliance*,[69] which illustrates some of the tension between the traditional methods of UK statutory interpretation and the new purposive orientation of (now) EU law. The issue was whether the exclusion of issues relating to retirement from the Sex Discrimination Act 1975 could be interpreted to confirm with the Equal Treatment Directive. Lord Templeman stated:

> Of course a British court will always be willing and anxious to conclude that United Kingdom law is consistent with Community law. Where an act is passed for the purpose of giving effect to an obligation imposed by a directive or other instrument, a British court will seldom encounter difficulty in concluding that the language of the Act is effective for the intended purpose. But the construction of a British Act of Parliament is a matter of judgment to be determined by the British courts and to be derived from the language of the legislation considered in the light of the circumstances prevailing at the date of enactment . . . Section 2(4) of the European Communities Act 1972 does not . . . enable or constrain a British court to distort the meaning of a British statute in order to enforce against an individual a Community directive which has no direct effect between individuals.[70]

In emphasising both the wording and purpose, Lord Templeman was showing a willingness to accept the teleological method of the Court of Justice. Nonetheless, the influence of the more restrained UK tradition is apparent in the reference to the circumstances prevailing at the date of enactment, which is somewhat different, to the more prospective orientation of the Court of Justice (see Chapter 5 discussion on the *CILFIT* case, and see below on *Marleasing*).

This is a somewhat different emphasis than is traditional in UK law, where ordinary meaning is the primary principle of statutory interpretation, albeit that the UK 'mischief rule' of statutory interpretation is quite similar to purposive interpretation. Indirect effect then had the impact in the UK of making purposive interpretation more prominent in the context of UK legislation applying EU law.

68 *Lister v Forth Dry Dock Co Ltd* (n 66) 254.
69 [1988] IRLR 118.
70 Ibid 122–23.

6.11 DEVELOPMENT OF THE INTERPRETATIVE OBLIGATION AND ITS LIMITS: *MARLEASING, PFEIFFER* AND *IMPACT*

The obligation of interpretation (the *Von Colson* approach) was extended to cover all national legislation and not just the implementing legislation in *Marleasing*.[71] The facts concerned conformity of Spanish company legislation with an as yet unimplemented Directive. The ECJ stated:

> . . . in applying national law, whether the provisions in question were adopted before or after the directive, the national court called upon to interpret it is required to do so, as far as possible, in the light of the wording and the purpose of the directive in order to achieve the result pursued by the latter . . .[72]

The obligation of interpretation identified in *Marleasing* was confirmed in *Pfeiffer v Deutsches Rotes Kreuz*.[73] This case involved Directive 93/104 (the working time directive)[74]. The ECJ stated that the principle of interpretation in conformity with [Union] law requires the referring court to do whatever lies within its jurisdiction, having regard to the whole body of rules of national law, to ensure that the directive in question is fully effective.[75] The UK courts accepted this approach in *Webb v EMO (Air Cargo) Limited*.[76]

| KEY LEARNING POINT

THE DUTY OF INTERPRETATION EXTENDS TO ALL RELEVANT NATIONAL LAW

In its judgments in *Marleasing* and *Pfeiffer*, the ECJ decided that duty to interpret in conformity with a directive if possible extended to all national law. The rationale for this approach was that it would make directives more effective. Consistently with this approach, in *Wagner Miret*, the Court held that the principle of interpretation in conformity with directives must be followed, in particular, where a national court considers that the pre-existing provisions of its national law satisfy the requirements of the directive concerned.[77]

---

71 Case C–106/89 *Marleasing v La Comercial Internacional de Alimentacion* [1990] ECR I–4135.
72 Ibid para 8.
73 Case C–397/01 *Pfeiffer v Deutsches Rotes Kreuz* [2004] ECR I–8835.
74 OJ L 307 13.12.1993 p. 18.
75 Ibid paras 113–18.
76 [1993] 1 WLR 49.
77 Case C 334/92 *Wagner Miret v Fondo de Garantía Salarial* [1993] ECR I–06911.

In *Pupino*, the Court went some way towards *identifying the limits of indirect effect*.[78] The ECJ stated that the principle *of conforming interpretation* 'cannot serve as the basis for an interpretation of national law *contra legem*'.[79] *Contra legem* is Latin for 'counter to the law', i.e. interpretation should not change the law. Given that the ECJ on the facts of this case was dealing with the compatibility of Italian criminal procedure with EU legislation, it is not surprising that the issue of the limits of interpretation became relevant. In criminal law, it is widely recognised that courts should not be creative in interpretation of criminal laws so as to extend liability in an unpredictable way (strict construction of criminal law). A similar issue arose in other cases, where the obligation of interpretation has been limited by the general principles of legal certainty and non-retroactivity, so that national courts should not use unimplemented directives to interpret national legislation in such a way as to create, or exacerbate, criminal liability against individuals.[80]

In *IMPACT v Minister for Agriculture and Food*,[81] the ECJ applied this also to non-criminal law. It stated indirect effect requires national courts to do whatever lies within their jurisdiction, taking the whole body of domestic law into consideration and applying the interpretative methods recognised by domestic law, with a view to ensuring that the directive in question is fully effective and achieving an outcome consistent with the objective pursued by it, but interpretation could not be *contra legem*.[82] Related to this is the ruling in *Arcaro* that there is no method of procedure in EU law allowing the national court to eliminate national provisions contrary to a provision of a directive which has not been transposed where that provision may not be relied upon before the national court.[83]

KEY LEARNING POINT

INDIRECT EFFECT DOES NOT REQUIRE INTERPRETATION *CONTRA LEGEM*

National courts, in applying the doctrine of direct effect, are not required to change national law by means of interpretation. This was established in cases such as *Pupino* and *IMPACT*.

---

78 Case C–105/03 *Criminal proceedings against Maria Pupino* [2005] ECR I–5285. The case concerned Council Framework Decision 2001/220/JHA OJ L 82 1 22.03.2001 p. 1, on the standing of victims in criminal proceedings. For useful discussion see C Lebeck 'Sliding towards supranationalisation? The constitutional status of EU framework decisions after Pupino' (2007) 8(5) *German Law Journal* 501.

79 Case C–105/03 *Maria Pupino* (n 78) para 47.

80 Case 80/86 *Officier van Justitie v Kolpinghuis Nijmegen* [1987] ECR 3969 and Case C–168/95 *Criminal proceedings against Arcaro* [1996] ECR I–4705. The ECJ has adopted at least one decision that goes against this line of reasoning, although not in the context of indirect effect. In Case 238/84 *Criminal proceedings of Hans Röser* [1986] ECR 795, the ECJ had to decide the meaning of a piece of Community legislation in the context that the language versions varied. The ECJ decided that, although a German citizen being prosecuted for breach of a Community law acted within the meaning of the German text of the legislation, the German text was incorrect and had to be altered to conform to the Community-wide meaning, although with the unfair consequence on the facts of the subsequent prosecution of the Community national concerned: for criticism see H Rasmussen 'Towards a normative theory of interpretation of Community law' (1992) *University of Chicago Legal Forum* 135–78 at 169–71.

81 Case C–268/06 *IMPACT v Minister for Agriculture and Food* [2008] ECR I–2483.

82 Ibid paras 100–101.

83 Case C–168/95 *Arcaro* (n 80) paras 39–40.

In other words, the ECJ has acknowledged that some national legislation is entirely unambiguous and, therefore, incapable of being interpreted by national courts to be compatible with Union law.[84]

ANALYSING THE LAW

UNDERSTANDING THE IDEA OF INTERPRETATION
CONTRA LEGEM

The conclusion of the ECJ in cases such as *Pupino* and *IMPACT* that a duty of interpretation in conformity with EU law, i.e. the doctrine of indirect effect, does not extend to interpretation *contra legem* implies that there is a conceptual distinction between interpretation and law-making or law-changing. In other words, the ECJ is recognising that at some point, interpretation has a limit, and that beyond that point or limit the law is being changed by judicial act, not interpreted. Although this is an obviously correct view, it is surprising how little the idea has been identified and explored in the overall body of ECJ case law. What are the limits on interpretation? We have looked at this briefly in Chapter 5, but one clear way of determining the limits of interpretation is to identify shared conventions of understanding between the law-maker and the judiciary. If the judiciary goes beyond what could reasonably be inferred to be the intention of the law-maker, the judiciary is over-stepping its role and engaging in law-making.

6.12 THE LEGAL EFFECT OF EU LAW IN UK LAW

6.12.1 LEGISLATION

In accordance with the doctrine of dualism, membership of the UK in the then European Communities was given effect in UK law through an Act of Parliament, the European Communities Act 1972. Section 2(1) is the central provision and states:

> All such rights, powers, liabilities, obligations and restrictions from time to time created or arising under the Treaties, and all such remedies and procedures from time to time provided for by or under the Treaties, as in accordance with the Treaties

---

84 See e.g. Case C–111/97 *EvoBus Austria* [1998] ECR I–541; Cases C–240–244/98 *Océano Grupo Editorial & Others v Murciano Quintero & Others* [2000] ECR I–4941.

are without further enactment to be given legal effect or used in the U.K. shall be recognised and available in law, and be enforced, allowed and followed accordingly; and the expression 'enforceable Community right' and similar expressions shall be read as referring to one to which this subsection applies.

Debate has arisen over the effect of this provision on the UK Constitution. One view is that even though the result was the acceptance in UK law of the EU doctrine of supremacy, this was only so because of the 1972 Act and that Parliament can at any time repeal the 1972 Act so as to remove the effect of EU law in UK law. Another view is that it is not politically possible to do this, and so the effect of EU law is a kind of revolution in the UK legal system.[85]

Parliament generally gives effect to the founding EU treaties through an amending Act to the 1972 Act. The most recent such Act was the European Union Act 2008, giving effect in UK law to the Lisbon Treaty.

However, in 2011, Parliament passed an Act relating to the status of EU law in UK law that did not arise from treaty amendment at EU level, but rather from a desire of the Coalition Government to clarify the relationship between EU and UK law. This is a very important piece of legislation constitutionally. It confirms the constitutional entitlement of the UK to withdraw from the European Union, which also reflects new Article 50 TEU as inserted by the Treaty of Lisbon, which provides that Member States may withdraw from the EU.

KEY LEARNING POINT

THE EUROPEAN UNION ACT 2011

The European Union Act 2011 is unusual for an Act of Parliament relating to the EU, in that it did not result from treaty amendment at EU level, but from a desire by the Coalition Government to clarify the relationship between UK law and EU law. The European Union Act 2011 has two main components:

1. It sets out a requirement for a referendum for any transfer of further powers from the UK to the EU.
2. Section 18 confirms that *EU law only has effect in UK law because of being recognised by UK law*, i.e. it does not have a status in UK law independent of recognition by the UK Parliament. Case law from the ECJ suggests differently: *Costa v ENEL* and *Handelsgesellschaft*, which together suggests a transfer of power to the EU is permanent and overrides all national constitutional law.

....

85 For references, see the further reading at the end of the chapter.

6.12.2 CASE LAW

Although the UK joined in 1973, it was several years before the higher courts ruled on issues relating to UK membership:

KEY CASE MCCARTHYS LTD V SMITH

McCarthys Ltd v Smith[86] concerned interpretation of the Equal Pay Act 1970. Lord Denning MR said the courts must look to relevant European Economic Community Treaty (EEC Treaty) (now TFEU) provision (then Article 119) that the Act was intended to give effect to. This was *implicitly* to accept the supremacy of Community law, but Lord Denning formulated his response in an interesting way by considering the issue in monist terms to the effect that Community law *was now in effect UK law*:

> . . . the provisions of Art. 119 of the EEC Treaty take priority over anything in our English statute on equal pay which is inconsistent with Art. 119. That priority is given by the European Communities Act 1972 itself. Community law is now a part of our law: and whenever there is any inconsistency, community law has priority. It is not supplanting English law. It is part of our law which overrides any other part which is inconsistent with it.[87]

KEY CASE FACTORTAME *AND SUPREMACY*

R v Secretary of State for Transport, ex parte Factortame Ltd[88] was the first UK case to explicitly turn on the question of supremacy of EC law. The facts concerned the Merchant Shipping Act 1988, which contained certain requirements for registering a fishing vessel as a British fishing vessel, the effect of which was to make it more difficult for nationals from other Member States to have their fishing boats registered as such in Britain. The Divisional Court (a three-judge chamber of the High Court, with one Court of Appeal judge) wished to refer the question to the ECJ on the questions of *Community law*, but in the meantime, pending the decision of the ECJ, the question of interim relief under English law arose, i.e. should the Court suspend the operation of the Merchant Shipping Act 1988 and how could it do so in light of the doctrine of parliamentary sovereignty?

---

86 [1981] QB 199.

87 Ibid 200. See also *Garland v British Rail Engineering* [1982] 2 All ER, where Lord Diplock LJ stated that anything short of an express positive statement in an Act of Parliament passed after 1 January 1973 that a particular provision is intended to be made in breach of an obligation of Community would not justify a court in construing that provision in a manner inconsistent with a Community treaty obligation.

88 [1989] 2 All ER 692, [1989] 2 WLR 997.

The Divisional Court ordered suspension of Part II of the 1988 Act. However, the Court of Appeal held the Divisional Court could not suspend an Act of Parliament in this way. The House of Lords agreed with the Court of Appeal that, *as a matter of English law*, the 1988 Act had to be applied by the courts. The House of Lords then referred a second preliminary reference to the ECJ as to what was the requirement of *Community law* as to remedies, as opposed to the substantive issues (the ECJ had already ruled on those[89]). Unsurprisingly, and consistently with its case law on supremacy, the ECJ said EC law must take priority and interim relief should have been granted suspending the application of the Merchant Shipping Act 1988.[90]

After receiving the judgment of the ECJ following the preliminary ruling procedure, the House of Lords then agreed to suspend application of the relevant provisions of the 1988 Act.[91]

EXPLAINING THE LAW

FACTORTAME AND THE VALIDITY OF UK ACTS OF PARLIAMENT

Factortame may seem to suggest that it results in Acts of Parliament being invalid if they are contrary to EU law. Strictly speaking, this is not correct: it is not that the Act is invalid, it is that the application of the Act is suspended. In practice, it may not make much difference. But underlying the difference in phrasing is the important constitutional issue referred to above: suspending the Act is consistent with the idea that Parliament retains sovereignty since the reason for the suspension is another Act, i.e. the European Communities Act 1972. It is as if Parliament is saying 'for the time being, apply this Act, and not that one (because they are in conflict)'. In contrast, saying that Acts of Parliament were invalid would question parliamentary sovereignty by suggesting Parliament did not have the power to pass them.

6.13 NATIONAL RECEPTION OF THE SUPREMACY DOCTRINE

6.13.1 INTRODUCTION

Not all of the highest courts in the Member States have accepted the expression of supremacy by the ECJ in *Costa v ENEL* and *Internationale Handelsgesellschaft*, the most well known of such judgments being those of the German Federal Constitutional Court based in Karlsruhe,

---

89 [1989] 2 CMLR 353 (Court of Appeal).
90 Case C–213/89 *Factortame I* [1990] I–2433 (ECJ).
91 [1990] 2 AC 85, [1991] 1 AC 603 (both House of Lords judgments).

Germany. The potential for conflict arises especially in the context of the problem of *kompetenz-kompetenz*,[92] i.e. on the question of who has authority to decide ultimately the competence of the EU vis-à-vis the Member States.

> KEY LEARNING POINT
> ....
>
> **THE PROBLEM OF *KOMPETENZ-KOMPETENZ***
> One of the basic constitutional issues of the EU is who has ultimate competence or jurisdiction to decide the respective competences of the EU and the Member States: is it the ECJ or the highest courts in the Member States? The ECJ has said it is for itself to decide this. However, the treaties are silent on the issue, and the highest courts have not simply accepted this because the ECJ has said it. From the point of view of national supreme or constitutional courts, it is their highest duty to guard their own Constitution. For example, if the ECJ itself is acting outside of its authority by being overly creative in interpreting EU competences, there is no legal reason why a national constitutional court should give up its responsibility to guard national constitutional competences. This issue is known as *kompetenz-kompetenz* in German: i.e. who has the competence to decide competence issues. Underlying it are key issues of constitutional theory. In a number of Member States, the highest courts have reached a conclusion that ultimately they, and not the ECJ, should decide the issue.

6.13.2 GERMANY

The German Federal Constitutional Court in Karlsruhe has indicated in a series of cases that the validity of Community or Union law in the German constitutional order depended upon satisfactory compliance with human rights as protected by German constitutional law and that the Federal Constitutional Court has competence to determine the compatibility of the degree of transfer of competence to the EU with the German constitutional order.[93]

On the *kompetenz-kompetenz* question, it required in its *Lisbon Treaty* judgment that increases in the competence of the Union institutions through the use of *passarelle* clauses and the use of the enhanced flexibility procedure in the Lisbon Treaty both require the prior approval of the two houses of the German Parliament in order for

....

92 See e.g. G Beck 'The problem of *Kompetenz-Kompetenz*: a conflict between right and right in which there is no *Praetor*' (2005) 30(1) *ELR* 42–67.

93 *Internationale Handelsgesellschaft* BVerfGE 37, 271 [1974] 2 CMLR 540 *(Solange I)*; *Wüensche Handelsgesellschaft* BVerfGE 73, 339, [1987] 3 CMLR 225 *(Solange II)*; *Brunner v European Treaty* BVerfGE 89, 155 [1994] 1 CMLR 57; *Lisbon Treaty Case* BVerfG 2 BvE 2/08, judgment of 30 June 2009 http://www.bundesverfassungsgericht. de/entscheidungen/es20090630_2bve000208en.html (in English, last accessed 18 January 2015). For academic commentary on the Lisbon Treaty judgment see e.g. A Steinbach 'The Lisbon judgment of the German Federal Constitutional Court: – new guidance on the limits of European integration?' (2010) 11(4) *German Law Journal* 367–90.

Germany to agree to them, and the Karlsruhe court asserted its own jurisdiction to determine the matter of *kompetenz-kompetenz*.[94]

The constitutional courts of a number of other Member States, including both old and new members of the Union, have expressed similar reservations to an absolute, unqualified statement of the supremacy of Union law – for reasons of space, only a few can be surveyed here.

6.13.3 FRANCE

In France, the situation is somewhat complicated by the various judicial organs that have relevant jurisdiction, which are the *Conseil Constitutionnel*, the *Conseil d'État* and the *Cour de Cassation*.[95] The *Conseil d'État* initially resisted accepting the supremacy of Community law,[96] but then accepted it in practice.[97] However, the basis of the *Conseil d'État's* reasoning was that such supremacy as Community law had was based on Article 55 of the French Constitution,[98] which concerns the incorporation of international agreements into national law and not on the nature of the Community legal order as identified by the ECJ in *Costa v ENEL*. The *Conseil d'État* thus apparently does not accept the supremacy of Community or EU law over the French Constitution, although it has not stated this explicitly, but it has ruled that international agreements under Article 55 do not have supremacy over the Constitution.[99]

The *Conseil Constitutionnel* or Constitutional Council has tended to base its acceptance of supremacy on Article 88–I of the French Constitution, which provides for the participation of the Republic in the EU, but the *Conseil Constitutionel* has ruled that an EU directive that is in conflict with an express provision of the Constitution cannot be transposed and enter into force.[100] The Constitutional Council adopted the same

....

94 Ibid.

95 The *Conseil d'État* provides the executive branch with legal advice, but without having the power to declare proposed legislative acts impermissible or invalid as unconstitutional (so it exercises advisory review only). It also acts as the administrative court of last resort. The *Conseil Constitutionnel* also exercises an advisory jurisdiction before legislation is finally approved, but does so after a legislative measure has been voted on by Parliament and before signature by the president, plus it has the power to prevent enactment by a declaration of unconstitutionality. The *Cour de Cassation* is the highest court in general civil matters.

96 Decision of 1 March 1968 in *Syndicat Général de Fabricants de Semoules de France* [1970] CMLR 395, on the ground that as it had no jurisdiction to rule on the invalidity of legislation, it could not accord primacy to Community law.

97 *Raoul Georges Nicolo* [1990] 1 CMLR 173.

98 See further the decision of the *Cour de Cassation* in Decision of 24 May 1975 in *Administration des Douanes v Sociétés 'Café Jacques Vabre' et Sàrl Weigel et Cie* [1975] 2 CMLR 336, which based its acceptance of supremacy on art 55 of the Constitution also.

99 Decision of 30 October 1998, *Sarran and Levacher* (RFDA 1998 at 1091). International law does not *have supremacy over national constitutional law in France.*

100 See generally C Richards 'The supremacy of Community law before the French Constitutional Court' (2006) 31 *ELR* 499–517.

general reasoning in its approach to the Treaty of Lisbon, basing its constitutionality on
Article 88–I,[101] and stating:

> When however undertakings entered into for this purpose contain a clause running
> counter to the constitution, call into question constitutionally guaranteed rights
> and freedoms or adversely affect the fundamental conditions of the exercising of
> national sovereignty, authorisation of such measures requires prior revision of the
> Constitution.[102]

This has been interpreted by some as similar to the German constitutional position.[103]

6.13.4 ITALY

In Italy, the Constitutional Court in *Frontini* stated that it would subject Community
law to judicial review as to its compatibility with fundamental rights and with the basic
principles of the Italian constitutional order.[104] In *Granital*, the Constitutional Court
further asserted jurisdiction to determine the *kompetenz-kompetenz* question.[105] In *Fragd*,
it confirmed its willingness to subject specific rules of Community law to review on
human rights grounds.[106]

6.13.5 SPAIN

Also from Southern Europe, the Spanish Constitutional Court has denied absolute
supremacy of EU law in the Spanish legal order and asserted *kompetenz-kompetenz*,
although it was keen to state that the eventuality in which it would have to exercise its
powers in this regard were 'scarcely conceivable':[107]

> In the scarcely-conceivable event that in the ultimate functioning of European Union
> Law this Law were [as a] result [be] irreconcilable with the Spanish Constitution, and
> without the hypothetical excesses of European Law with regard to the European
> Constitution itself being remedied by the ordinary channels provided for in the
> latter, ultimately the preservation of the sovereignty of the Spanish people and of
> the supremacy of the Constitution as it provides for itself could lead this Court to
> tackle the problems that would arise in such a case, and which from the current

....

101 Décision n° 2009-595 DC (3 décembre 2009) cons 14 et 22 *Journal officiel* du 11 décembre 2009 at 21381,
       texte n°2 para 7, as quoted in J Ziller 'The law and politics of the ratification of the Lisbon Treaty' in S Griller,
       J Ziller (eds) *The Lisbon Treaty: EU Constitutionalism Without a Treaty* (Springer 2008) 324.
102 Décision n° 2009-595 DC (n 101) para 9.
103 Griller and Ziller (n 101) 284.
104 *Frontini v Ministero delle Finanze* [1974] 2 CMLR 372.
105 *Spa Granital v Amministrazione delle Finanze* Decision 170 of 8 June 1984, unofficial translation at (1984) 21
       CMLRev 756.
106 *Spa Fragd v Amministrazione delle Finanze* Decision 232 of 21 April 1989 (1989) 72 RDI.
107 Constitutional Court of Spain, Declaration on the consistency of the European Constitutional Treaty with the
       Spanish Constitution, DTC 1/2004 (13 December 2004).

point of view are considered to be non-existent, by way of the relevant constitutional procedures. . . . This is aside from the fact that the safeguarding of the said sovereignty is always ultimately assured by Article I–60 of the Treaty [Establishing a Constitution for Europe] . . . which may not override the exercise of a withdrawal, which remains reserved for the sovereign, supreme, will of the Member States.[108]

The Constitutional Court went on to distinguish between supremacy and primacy, indicating that EU law can take effect in priority to national law (i.e. EU law can have primacy), but cannot invalidate or nullify national law (i.e. EU law does not have supremacy).[109]

ANALYSING THE LAW

PRIMACY VERSUS SUPREMACY

The distinction drawn by the Spanish Constitutional Court between primacy and supremacy of EU law or Spanish law is a useful one. It can be related to the debate in UK constitutional law: Parliament has granted primacy to EU law over its own Acts on a day-to-day basis, but retains supremacy in that it can repeal the European Communities Act 1972 (it is only the 1972 Act that gives EU law primacy).

6.13.6 POLAND AND THE CZECH REPUBLIC

Amongst the newer Member States, the Polish Constitutional Court has been amongst the most inclined to assert a sovereignty reservation concerning EU membership. It did so in its decision on the Polish Accession Treaty[110] to the EU, in 'a clear refusal of supremacy of this Treaty over [the] national Constitution'.[111] The Court stated that in the event of a conflict between the Constitution and Community law, the conflict would not lead to the invalidity of the applicable constitutional norms or to their automatic change: such a conflict 'cannot be solved by recognition of supremacy of Community norm towards the national constitutional norm'.[112]

....

108 As cited in R Alonso García 'The Spanish Constitution and the European Constitution: the script for a virtual collision and other observations on the principle of primacy' (2005) 6(6) *German Law Journal* 1001 at 1001–1002.

109 See http://www.tribunalconstitucional.es/es/jurisprudencia/restrad/Paginas/DTC122004en.aspx (last accessed 18 January 2015).

110 Judgment of 11 May 2005 in the case K 18/04 [Wyrok z dnia 11 maja 2005 r. Sygn. akt K 18/04] OTK Z.U. 2005/5A, item 49, as cited and discussed in K Kowalik-Bańczyk 'Should we polish it up? The Polish Constitutional Tribunal and the idea of supremacy of EU law' (2005) 6(10) *German Law Journal* 1355–66 and A Lazowski 'Case note: Polish Constitutional Tribunal conformity of the Accession Treaty with the Polish Constitution. Decision of 11 May' (2007) 3(1) *European Constitutional Law Review* 148–62.

111 Kowalik-Bańczyk (n 110) 1358.

112 Ibid 1364.

Also from the newer Member States, in its first judgment on the Lisbon Treaty,[113] the Czech Constitutional Court has asserted *kompetenz-kompetenz*, i.e. the power to determine if the Union institutions are acting within conferred powers,[114] though it has been suggested that in its second judgment on the Lisbon Treaty,[115] it was notably more positive towards the EU than the German Federal Constitutional Court in the latter's *Lisbon* judgment.[116]

ANALYSING THE LAW

WHY HAS THE UK HOUSE OF LORDS OR SUPREME COURT NOT ADDRESSED THE SUPREMACY DEBATE AS FULLY AS OTHER NATIONAL HIGHEST COURTS?

It might be asked why the compatibility of EU law with UK law has not been more fully addressed by the UK House of Lords or Supreme Court. In *Factortame*, the House of Lords simply accepted the decision of the ECJ that Acts of Parliament should be suspended where they appeared to be incompatible with EU law. This may in large part be explained by the role of parliamentary sovereignty in UK law: Parliament is the highest source of law, and as it has authorised EU membership, the courts can say that suspending an Act of Parliament incompatible with EU law can be implicitly justified by the European Communities Act 1972. In the UK, Parliament is the ultimate constitutional guardian. However, perhaps it might have been desirable for the House of Lords and now the Supreme Court to be somewhat more explicit about these issues.

6.14 STATE LIABILITY

A final important aspect of the relationship between national and EU law that we will now examine is the EU doctrine of state liability. This refers to the doctrine that when the Member States breach EU law, they are liable to pay damages to the person affected. As with so many of the important constitutional doctrines of EU law, this doctrine was created by the ECJ.

....

113 Decision of 26 November 2008 Case No Pl ÚS 19/08 (published as No 446/2008 Coll).

114 Ibid para 120, as quoted in Editors & J Komárek 'The Czech Constitutional Court's second decision on the Lisbon Treaty of 3 November 2009' (2009) 5(3) *ECLR* 345–52 at 351.

115 Judgment of 3 November 2009 Case No Pl ÚS 29/09.

116 The editors of the *ECLR* interpret the judgment as conceiving of a pooling of sovereignty in positive terms as a reinforcement of sovereignty: Editors and Komárek (n 114) 351.

6.14.1 ESTABLISHING THE PRINCIPLE: *FRANCOVICH*

Most legal systems face a practical question in their public law: should the state/government be liable in damages where an organ of the state fails to apply the law correctly and the individual suffers damages? This is dealt with in various ways in legal systems, and not all accept the principle that the state should be liable in damages in this way.

KEY LEARNING POINT

ESTABLISHING STATE LIABILITY

Francovich v Italy[117] first established the principle of Member State liability in damages for breach of Community law.

In *Francovich*, an action was taken against Italy for failure properly to implement Directive 80/987/EEC,[118] and the ECJ held that Member State liability in damages is available in cases of non-implementation, or misimplementation, of a directive or of any other provision of EC law by a Member State. The ECJ first observed that the EEC Treaty had created its own legal system, that both the nationals and the Member States were subjects of the legal system and that individuals have rights. Further, it stated that those rights are expressly granted and such rights arise by virtue of obligations that the treaty imposes in a clearly defined manner both on individuals and on the Member States and Community institutions.

The Court went on to state that the full effectiveness of Community rules would be impaired and the protection of rights granted to individuals would be weakened if individuals were unable to obtain redress, especially where action by the Member State was necessary to give effect to Community rules and the Member State fails to take this action. It also referred to the duty of cooperation and loyalty of the Member States towards the Community. The Court thereby concluded that:

> It follows that the principle whereby a Member State must be liable for loss and damage caused to individuals as a result of breaches of Community law for which the Member State can be held responsible is inherent in the system of the treaty.[119]

---

117 Joined Cases C–6/90 & 9/90 *Francovich v Italy* [1991] ECR I–5357. The case concerned a failure by Italy to implement a directive requiring employers to pay minimum insurance to cover non-payment of wages to employees.

118 OJ L 283 20.10.1980 p. 23.

119 Ibid paras 31–35.

ANALYSING THE LAW

FRANCOVICH AS AN EXAMPLE OF TELEOLOGICAL INTERPRETATION

Francovich is a good example of teleological reasoning by the ECJ: there was no express textual basis for the doctrine of state liability. Regarding the fact that the Community was a legal system, it is not obvious that this *necessarily* entails state liability in damages. State liability is not a feature, for example, of US law,[120] where individual states are subject to a doctrine of sovereign immunity, meaning that for most purposes they are not liable in damages for misimplementation of federal law. Moreover, state liability had not always been a feature of the law of national legal systems, for example, those of Ireland,[121] Sweden[122] and the United Kingdom;[123] on the other hand, these three Member States developed doctrines of state liability in damages for legal torts in the last 60 years of the twentieth century (albeit through legislation) and, moreover, the tendency in civil law states in general has been to provide for some form of state liability for damages in tort.[124]

EXPLAINING THE LAW

STATE LIABILITY IN CONTEXT REGARDING DIRECTIVES

The doctrine of state liability reinforces direct effect, supremacy and the preliminary reference procedure in national law. State liability gives a remedy in damages enforceable by a national court for failure of a Member State to comply fully with EU law. It is another way (added to indirect effect and incidental direct effect) for the ECJ to overcome the lack of horizontal direct effect of directives: an individual who is affected by the failure of another individual to comply with a directive because the directive has not been implemented in national law, now has a remedy against the state in damages.[125]

6.14.2 THE CONDITIONS OF STATE LIABILITY

However, the *Francovich* case left a number of unanswered questions. The *Francovich* case had been concerned specifically with the failure of the Italian State to implement a

....

120 See e.g. D Meltzer 'Member state liability in Europe and the United States' (2006) 4(1) *International Journal of Constitutional Law* 39–83 at 49.
121 Established judicially in *Byrne v Ireland* [1972] IR 241.
122 Act on Torts 1972.
123 Crown Proceedings Act 1947.
124 See generally J F Pfander 'Government accountability in Europe: a comparative assessment' (2003) 35(3) *George Washington International Law Review* 611–52; A Olowofoyeku 'State liability for the exercise of judicial power' (1998) *Public Law* 444–62 at 450.
125 Case C–111/97 *Evobus Austria v Niederosterreichischer Verkehrsorganisations* [1998] ECR I–5411.

directive. The obligation imposed on states to implement directives is clear (see Articles 4(3) TEU and 288 TFEU). However, two issues remained unclear from the case: (i) what the position might be in relation to other types of breaches; and (ii) what is the level of fault required to establish liability?

The ECJ addressed the issues further in the joined cases *Brasserie du Pêcheur SA v Germany; Factortame III*.[126] The Court stated that there are three conditions:[127]

KEY LEARNING POINT

THE CONDITIONS FOR STATE LIABILITY
1. The rule of law infringed must be intended to confer rights on individuals.
2. The breach must be sufficiently serious.
3. There must be a direct causal link between the breach of the obligation resting on the state and the damage sustained by injured parties.[128]

6.14.2.1 AN INTENTION TO CONFER RIGHTS ON INDIVIDUALS

There is a clear equivalence to direct effect in this condition (the first condition for *Francovich* liability is the same as the third condition for direct effect). This first *Brasserie/Factortame III* condition has been held to have been satisfied in the case of the following directly effective treaty articles, for example: Article 34 TFEU on free movement of goods;[129] Article 35 TFEU on free movement of goods;[130] Article 45 TFEU on free movement of workers;[131] and Article 49 TFEU on freedom of establishment.[132]

6.14.2.2 A SUFFICIENTLY SERIOUS BREACH

The test for determining whether an infringement is sufficiently serious 'is whether the Member State concerned – manifestly and gravely disregarded the limits on its discretion'.[133] Although this is generally a question of fact to be decided by national courts, the ECJ did identify in *Brasserie/Factortame III* criteria national courts may use

---

126 Joined Cases C–46 and C–48/93 *Brasserie du Pêcheur SA v Germany; Factortame III* [1996] ECR I–1029 (the facts concerned liability of Germany for refusing imports of beer from France).

127 See in particular ibid paras 37–39, 51 and 54–57 (emphasis added).

128 These are very similar to the conditions for contractual liability of the EU in damages: see Case C–6/49 *Alfons Lütticke v Commission* [1971] ECR 325. However, a major difference between Member State liability and contractual liability of the EU institutions is that the latter has a treaty basis: see art 340 TFEU.

129 Joined Cases C–46 and C–48/93 *Brasserie du Pêcheur v Germany/Factortame III*; Case C–112/00 *Schmidberger v Austria* [2003] ECR I–5659; Case C–445/06 *Danske Slagterier v Germany* [2009] ECR I–2119.

130 Case C–5/94 *Hedley Lomas Ltd* [1996] ECR I–2553.

131 Case C–224/01 *Köbler v Austria* [2003] ECR I–10239 (the facts concerned a professor at an Austrian University who claimed indirect discrimination existed where previous employment in a university in another Member State was not taken into account in length-of-service pay increases).

132 Joined Cases C–46 and C–48/93 *Brasserie du Pêcheur v Germany/Factortame III*; Case C–524/04 *Thin Cap Group v Commissioners of Inland Revenue* [2007] ECR I–2107.

133 Joined Cases C–46 and C–48/93 *Brasserie du Pêcheur/Factortame III* at para 55.

in order to determine whether the state should be liable. These can be summarised as follows:

- the clarity and precision of the rule breached
- the measure of discretion left by that rule (this was identified as important in Synthon[134])
- whether the infringement and the damage caused was intentional or involuntary
- if there was an error of law, whether the error was excusable or not
- any position taken by the Union's institutions
- the adoption or retention of national measures contrary to that rule.

The exact balance between these factors cannot be stated in the abstract, although the larger the degree of discretion, the less likely there is to be a breach.[135] Where the Member State or national institution has only considerably reduced, or even no, discretion, the mere infringement of EU law may be sufficient to establish the existence of a sufficiently serious breach.[136] The doctrine of state liability applies to both breaches of the Treaty[137] and breaches of secondary legislation.[138]

KEY CASES *FAILURE TO IMPLEMENT A DIRECTIVE AND STATE LIABILITY IN* DILLENKOFER *AND* EMMOTT

The ECJ has held, in *Dillenkofer*, that failure to implement a directive will generally be sufficiently serious to attract state liability:

26 So where, as in *Francovich*, a Member State fails . . . to take any of the measures necessary to achieve the result prescribed by a directive within the period it lays down, that Member State manifestly and gravely disregards the limits on its discretion.

27 Consequently, such a breach gives rise to a right to reparation on the part of individuals if the result prescribed by the directive entails the grant of rights

---

134 Case C–452/06 *Synthon* [2008] ECR I–7681 para 38.
135 For an example where an error was not sufficiently serious see Case C–392/93 *R v HM Treasury, ex parte British Telecom plc* [1996] ECR 1–1631.
136 Case C–5/94 *Hedley Lomas* [1996] ECR I–2553 para 28; Case 352/98P *Laboratoires Pharmaceutiques Bergaderm SA, in Liquidation and Jean-Jacques Groupil v Commission of the European Communities* [2000] ECR 5291 para 44.
137 For example the breach of art 34 TFEU in *Brasserie du Pêcheur/Factortame III* was held to be not serious in that it was an excusable error in law. A breach of art 35 TFEU was serious enough in Case C–5/94 *Hedley Lomas Ltd* [1996] ECR 1 2553.
138 Case C–140/97 *Rechberger & Others v Austria* [1999] ECR I–3499 (incomplete implementation by Austria of a directive on package holidays). Complete failure to implement a directive will obviously be sufficiently serious to engage state liability: see e.g. Joined Cases C–178, 179, 188, 189 & 190/94 *Dillenkofer & Others v Germany* [1996] ECR I–4845 (Germany failed to implement a directive on package holidays).

to them, the content of those rights is identifiable on the basis of the provisions of the directive and a causal link exists between the breach of the State's obligation and the loss and damage suffered by the injured parties: no other conditions need be taken into consideration.[139]

Moreover, the ECJ has also held, in *Emmott*, that until a directive has been fully implemented in national law, which may be after a judgment from the Court of Justice relating to national implementation, the rights a person may gain under a directive still suffer from legal uncertainty and that, as a consequence, national time limits for initiating actions related to the protection of rights under a directive should only run from when the directive has been transposed into national law:

> 22 Only the proper transposition of the directive will bring that state of uncertainty to an end and it is only upon that transposition that the legal certainty which must exist if individuals are to be required to assert their rights is created.

> 23 It follows that, until such time as a directive has been properly transposed, a defaulting Member State may not rely on an individual's delay in initiating proceedings against it in order to protect rights conferred upon him by the provisions of the directive and that a period laid down by national law within which proceedings must be initiated cannot begin to run before that time.[140]

Emmott dealt with a procedural aspect of state liability, when time limits can run. Another procedural aspect of state liability addressed in the case law is the issue of effectiveness and equivalence of the national remedy.

KEY LEARNING POINT

THE PRINCIPLES OF EQUIVALENCE AND EFFECTIVENESS IN THE CONTEXT OF STATE LIABILITY AND NATIONAL PROCEDURAL AUTONOMY

The principle of equivalence in the context of remedies in EU law is a requirement in the case law of the Court of Justice that the protection of rights in national law should be the equivalent to the protection of national law rights in national law. This means that national procedural law, which under the principle of national

---

139 Joined Cases C–178, 179, 188, 189 & 190/94 *Dillenkofer & Others v Germany* (n 138) paras 26–27. On the facts in *Dillenkofer*, Germany had adopted implementing legislation, but it did not come into effect within the period required under the directive in question.

140 C–208/90 *Emmott v Minister for Social Welfare and Attorney General* [1991] ECR I–04269 paras 22–23. See also Case C–445/06 *Danske Slagterier v Germany*.

procedural autonomy is still a Member State competence,[141] must ensure that it is as easy procedurally to protect rights under EU law as it is to protect rights under national law.[142] The related principle of effectiveness means that procedures and sanctions imposed in national law for violating EU law must be adequate to ensure the effective implementation of EU law.[143]

In *Transportes Urbanos y Servicios Generales*, the ECJ addressed whether it is compatible with the EU law principles of equivalence and effectiveness that an action to establish state liability should be subject to differing procedural rules according to whether the legislation at issue contravenes a constitutional provision or a rule of EU law.[144] The Court found that if the EU law principle of equivalence is to be observed, it is not justified that an action to establish state liability because of the breach by national legislation of EU law is subject to the condition that all remedies *not only administrative but also judicial* against the administrative measure based on that legislation must have first been exhausted, while such a condition is not imposed in the case of an action to establish liability because of the infringement by national legislation of the Constitution.[145]

6.14.2.3 DIRECT CAUSAL LINK BETWEEN BREACH AND DAMAGE

This is normally for the national courts to decide according to national rules on causation (this reflects the principle of national procedural autonomy).[146]

6.14.3 DEFINING THE 'STATE' IN STATE LIABILITY

It is also possible to consider the definition of the 'state' for the purpose of state liability to be a kind of fourth condition or a prior condition. The expression used in this context is 'emanation of the state'. The ECJ has been quite flexible here (as it has been with the definition of emanation of the state for the purposes of vertical direct effect). As noted above at section 6.7, the Court of Justice has decided that all three branches of government – the legislature, the executive or administration, and the judiciary – can be liable in the EU in state liability.

6.14.4 LIMITATION ON THE RECOVERY OF DAMAGES

The Member States can impose certain restrictions on the amount of damages that a claimant can recover, but the amount of damages recoverable must be equivalent to

....

141 On national procedural autonomy see generally e.g. N Zingales 'Member state liability versus national procedural autonomy' (2010) 11(4) *German Law Journal* 419–38.

142 This is found in a wide range of case law see e.g. Case 33/76 *Rewe v Landwirtschaftskammer für das Saarland* [1976] ECR 1989 para 5; Case 45/76 *Comet v Produktschap voor Siergewassen* [1976] ECR 2043 paras 12 to 16; Case 199/82 *Amministrazione delle Finanze dello Stato v San Giorgio* [1983] ECR 3595 para 14; Joined Cases 331/85, 376/85 and 378/85 *Bianco and Girard v Directeur Général des Douanes des Droits Indirects* [1988] ECR 1099 para 12; Case 104/86 *Commission v Italy* [1988] ECR 1799 para 7; Joined Cases C–6/90 and C–9/90 *Francovich* (n 117) para 43.

143 Case 79/83 *Harz* [1984] ECR 1921 para 28.

144 Case C–118/08 *Transportes Urbanos y Servicios Generales* [2010] ECR I–635.

145 Ibid paras 38–40.

146 See e.g. Case C–140/97 *Rechberger* (n 30).

the damages available in its domestic legal system, i.e. a principle of equivalence with national remedies applies, e.g. in *Brasserie du Pêcheur*, the ECJ stated:

> The conditions laid down by the applicable national laws must not be less favourable than those relating to similar domestic claims or framed in such a way as in practice to make it impossible or excessively difficult to obtain reparation.[147]

A similar principle of equivalence applies to limitation periods.[148]

APPLYING THE LAW

PROBLEM-SOLVING WITH DIRECT EFFECT AND STATE LIABILITY
Question

The German Parliament has recently enacted new legislation regulating the sale of meat in Germany (the Meat Laws). According to the Meat Laws, bacon rashers may be sold individually or by weight. However, pork rashers (which tend to be larger) must be sold individually wrapped and with distinct markings. The German Trade Ministry has explained that this will help busy customers to distinguish between different types of meat, especially because of recent health scares concerning meat and, in particular, pork. The German Government is confident that its restriction on free movement of goods is compatible with EU law, owing to relevant ECJ case law on public health derogation from the free movement principles. The German legislation also states that the German administrative authorities may implement the law over a period of 18 months, to be exercised at their discretion.

The Big Pig Meat Company of London produces pork rashers and has sold them to supermarkets throughout the United Kingdom and the EU, including Germany, for many years. The Big Pig Meat Company of London has a subsidiary in Germany. However, the company is very concerned about the effect that the Meat Laws may have upon its ability to export meat to the lucrative German meat market. It believes that Germany has failed properly to implement the (fictitious) EU Council Directive on the Trade in Meat between Member States 2012. This EU directive, inter alia, requires advance notice to existing suppliers of goods before changes in conditions of sale on health grounds, but which establishes a six-month period after which it must be implemented in full by the Member States. The directive is meant to help suppliers of meat goods avoid having to comply abruptly with new health and safety rules. The German Government believes it can comply with the directive as a matter of administrative practice, and so it does not need to amend its Meat Laws.

---

147 Joined Cases C–46 and C–48/93 *Brasserie du Pêcheur* para 74.
148 Case C–445/06 *Danske Slagterier v Germany* [2009] ECR I–2119.

The Big Pig Meat Company is also dissatisfied that some German supermarket retailers have decided to go ahead and apply the German Meat Laws immediately, even before the German authorities decide to apply it within the 18-month period. The German retailers believe this will be good for consumer confidence.

Advise the Big Pig Meat Company of London and its German subsidiary of any remedies it may have under EU law. Your answer should concentrate on issues related to direct effect and state liability, rather than free movement.

Outline answer
There are two aspects to this problem: direct effect and state liability. First, with regard to direct effect:

- The situation in the question relates to a new German law and its compatibility with new EU secondary legislation, in the form of a directive. On the facts, a particular issue arises about the timing of the implementation of both the German law and the new EU law.
- A directive has vertical direct effect but not horizontal direct effect (*Marshall*). Thus, if the German law is incompatible with the EU directive, the Big Pig Meat Company may be able to sue the German Government on the basis of vertical direct effect.
- It is best to say 'may be able to sue the German Government' because this depends on the time period issue. The German Government has six months under EU legislation. It says it can satisfy the EU requirements through administrative practice. This suggests that it is willing to allow the German courts to apply indirect effect by interpretation to avoid any incompatibility between its law and the EU directive after the time period for applying the directive has elapsed (an obligation of indirect effect only arises after the time period for implementation of a directive has expired: *Adeneler*; there does not seem to be any general principle of EU law at stake to impose a duty prior to the implementation deadline, unlike in *Mangold*). However, if interpretation could not achieve this, then the Big Pig Company will have a basis for an action for failure to implement EU law after the time period for implementation of the EU directive has expired.
- Although a directive has no horizontal direct effect, it may have incidental direct effect. The question is whether this might arise in this situation. Could the Big Pig Company sue German retailers for failing to comply with the directive? Not if this was the sole cause of action; they would need some other cause of action based on national law and would then be able to prevent the German retailers relying on national law to avoid the obligation in the directive (*CIA Security*). For example, the Big Pig Meat Company might be able to sue the German retailers for failing to carry out a previous contractual obligation to sell the Big Pig Meat Company's products.

The German retailers would not be able to rely on German law to get out of the contract if German law was incompatible with the directive (assuming the time period for implementing the directive had passed).

Second, with regard to state liability:
– You should first explain how state liability generally works. It is available in *national* courts as a remedy of damages for an individual who has suffered loss as a result of the incorrect implantation of EU law. It works in combination with direct effect and supremacy to give EU law practical effect in a national system. Explain how it interacts with direct effect and supremacy to do this.
– You then need to explain the scope of and conditions for the doctrine to apply, which means going through *Francovich* and *Brasserie du Pêcheur*, especially *Brasserie*, as this sets out the conditions (to give a full answer you could also address the possibility of state liability for judicial error, first set out in *Köbler v Austria* and then clarified in *Traghetti*, but this is not required on the facts of the situation).
– A good answer will assess whether the conditions for state liability have been satisfied. The most obvious issue in this regard is the degree of discretion (e.g. *Synthon*): did the EU directive prevent more stringent standards being adopted by Germany (not clear on the facts)? Generally, directives leave the means of implementation to the Member States themselves. However, if the result required by the directive is not achieved, then state liability will arise. Germany has chosen to allow the courts to achieve compatibility through indirect effect. This is permissible, so long as the result is ultimately achieved.

6.15 CONCLUSION

EU law takes effect in national law in a way that gives it a much bigger impact in national than is the case for other international laws. Whereas under public international law, each state decides how – whether by monism or dualism (see further Chapter 2) – to incorporate international law into its national law, membership of the EU entails acceptance of a doctrine of direct effect. Direct effect involves monism being applied to EU law, apart from the treaties, which still need to be incorporated individually according to each country's national constitutional requirements. Direct effect allows EU citizens to involve EU law in a national court without the need for implementing legislation at national level.

The direct effect of EU law has been supplemented by a number of other doctrines that apply when the conditions for direct effect are not satisfied, especially in the case of directives, which do not have horizontal direct effect (i.e. they cannot be invoked in a national court against individuals). These are the doctrine of indirect effect (a duty of interpretation), incidental direct effect (which can prevent the application of national law contrary to an EU law that is not itself directly effective), and a broad interpretation of 'the state' for the purposes of vertical direct effect.

What really gives EU law its effect in national law is its combination with the doctrine of supremacy. Under the doctrine of supremacy, when there is a conflict in a national court between an EU law and national law, EU law must be applied. Although some of the highest courts of the Member States have said that national constitutional law ultimately has supremacy over EU law, on a day-to-day basis supremacy is accepted in national courts throughout the Member States. The effectiveness of EU law in national law has been further strengthened by the development of the doctrine of state liability, under which Member States must compensate citizens who have suffered loss as a result of failure of the Member State to comply with EU law.

All these doctrines together – direct effect, supremacy and Member State liability – result in EU law having a very substantial impact in the legal systems of the Member States. All three doctrines were also developed by the ECJ and were not set out in the treaties, so they also illustrate well the remarkable role played by the ECJ in increasing integration.

POINTS TO REVIEW

- EU law impacts in a very substantial way on national law: this is chiefly achieved through the doctrines of direct effect and supremacy. These doctrines are supported by the doctrine of state liability. All three were developed in the case law of the ECJ, without an explicit treaty basis.

- Direct effect applied across both primary and secondary EU legislation and was first established in *Van Gend en Loos*. Although the founding and amending treaties have to be agreed according to the constitutional requirements of each Member State, once these have been satisfied, they have direct effect in national law even if not specifically incorporated. For example, the European Communities Act 1972 refers to the founding Community treaties from the 1950s, but without incorporating them in any detail. The doctrine of direct effect makes more comprehensive incorporation unnecessary. Secondary legislation is also directly effective.

- The conditions for direct effect must be satisfied for it to be applied: clarity, unconditionality and conferment of an individual right.

- Once these conditions are satisfied, direct effect allows an individual to invoke EU law in a national court. This is its second element, apart from making national implementing legislation unnecessary. The ability of individuals to rely on EU law contrasts with traditional international law, which could only be invoked by a state in a national court suing another state.

– Two varieties of direct effect exist: vertical and horizontal. Vertical direct effect refers to reliance by an individual on EU law in a national court against his or her government. Horizontal direct effect refers to reliance by an individual on EU law in a national court against his or her government. The treaties have both vertical and horizontal direct effect, as do regulations and decisions. Directives only have vertical direct effect.

– Although directives only have vertical direct effect, the ECJ has developed a number of doctrines that can compensate for their lack of horizontal direct effect: a broad interpretation of 'the state' for the purposes of vertical direct effect, indirect effect and incidental direct effect.

– The doctrines of direct effect and supremacy work together. When EU law is being invoked in a national court by an individual (direct effect), when a conflict arises with national law, the supremacy doctrine, first developed in *Costa v ENEL*, means EU law is to be applied. In the UK, this means that any Act of Parliament contrary to EU law must not be applied by the courts; EU law should be applied instead. This was accepted by the House of Lords in *Factortame*. Note that this does not mean Acts of Parliament are invalid as a result, merely that they are not being applied in this situation.

– Although there is debate amongst UK constitutional lawyers about the impact of the EU supremacy doctrine on parliamentary sovereignty in the UK, section 18 of the European Union Act 2011 makes clear that EU law only has effect in UK law because of the European Communities Act 1972. The 1972 Act can be repealed by the UK Parliament at any time.

– The effect of EU law in national law was further strengthened by the doctrine of state liability. This was first developed by the ECJ in *Francovich*, and the conditions for its application were developed in *Brasserie du Pêcheur*. The doctrine means national governments are obliged to compensate their citizens who have suffered loss as a result of failure by the government to comply with EU law. The doctrine was later extended to liability for judicial error in *Köbler* and *Traghetti*, although in limited circumstances.

CHAPTER GLOSSARY

***Contra legem* interpretation** refers to interpretation that contradicts or tries to change the meaning of a law. Under the doctrine of indirect effect, national courts are not under a duty to engage in *contra legem* interpretation of national law.

Direct applicability is a term used in the EU treaties, in Article 288 TFEU, to describe the way in which regulations impact on national law. It means regulations do not need any additional legislation to be fully applied in a national legal system. It should not be confused with direct effect.

Direct effect is the doctrine of EU law governing its incorporation into national law so as to affect individual citizens. Once certain conditions are met, EU law (both primary legislation in the treaties and second legislation) can be invoked by an individual in a national court. The conditions for direct effect are: clarity, unconditionality, and conferment of an individual right.

Factortame is the leading UK case on the reception of the supremacy doctrine in UK law. In this case, the House of Lords agreed with the ECJ to suspend Acts of Parliament that were contrary to EU law.

Horizontal direct effect refers to the direct effect of EU law in an action between two individuals, i.e. an EU citizen is allowed to invoke EU law in a national court in an action against another private citizen.

Incidental direct effect is a doctrine related to direct effect. It applies where direct effect itself cannot apply, mainly in the situation where there is no horizontal direct effect. It prevents a national law contrary to an EU law from being applied in a national court, even though the EU law in question cannot be applied because it does not have direct effect.

Indirect effect refers a duty imposed by EU law on a national court to try to interpret national law in a manner compatible with EU law is so far as it is possible to do so. It is one way in which an absence of direct effect of an EU law can be compensated for. The duty only arises in the case of directive after the period for implementation has expired.

Kompetenz-kompetenz is a German term meaning literally 'competence-competence'. It refers to the issue of who has competence to determine the competences of the EU: is it the ECJ or the highest courts of the Member States?

Sölange is the name commonly given to a series of cases from the German Federal Constitutional Court in which the German Court held it would only accept the supremacy of EU law so long as EU law was compatible with the guarantees of fundamental rights and competences attributed to the German State in the German Basic Law (the German Constitution) (*sölange* means 'so long as' in German).

State liability is a doctrine of EU law under which Member State governments are required to compensate their own citizens if their citizens have suffered loss or damage as a result of a failure by the Member State government to comply with EU law.

Supremacy refers to a doctrine of EU law under which EU law prevails over national law in the case of a conflict between the two in national courts.

Vertical direct effect is the direct effect of EU law in an action between an individual and his or her government, i.e. an EU citizen is allowed to invoke EU law in a national court in an action against his or her government.

TAKING THINGS FURTHER

P Pescatore 'The doctrine of direct effect: an infant disease of Community law' (1983) 8 *European Law Review* 155–57 This article discusses the earlier doubt and confusion created by the way in which the terms direct applicability and direct effect were used in the case law of the ECJ.

T R S Allan 'Parliamentary sovereignty: law, politics and revolution' (1997) 113 *Law Quarterly Review* 443–52 This article was a response to the article by Wade below and argued that UK membership of the European Communities did not compromise parliamentary sovereignty and that EC law took effect in UK law because of the European Communities Act 1972.

W Wade 'Sovereignty: revolution or evolution?' (1996) 112 *Law Quarterly Review* 568–75 In contrast to Allan's article above, this article argues that the supremacy doctrine of EC law represented a revolution in the UK Constitution in that Parliament can no longer be considered supreme.

M Kumm 'The jurisprudence of constitutional conflict: constitutional supremacy in Europe before and after the constitutional treaty' (2005) 11(3) *European Law Journal* 262–307 This article argues that national constitutional courts should be willing to accept the supremacy doctrine if the EU respects national constitutional values. In this way, it seeks to offer an account of 'constitutionalism beyond the state'.

H Schepel 'The enforcement of EC law in contractual relations: case studies in how not to "constitutionalise" private law' (2004) 12(5) *European Review of Private Law* 661–75 Offers a critical discussion of the approach of the ECJ to incidental direct effect, arguing that EC law values should only be imposed upon national private law where they can be translated into subjective rights and, on the other, that the application of EC law provisions on private parties should be limited to cases where these can reasonably be said to carry responsibility for the implementation of those provisions.

7

CHAPTER 7
DETERMINING COMPETENCES IN THE EU

This chapter examines the issue of competences of the EU relative to the competences of the Member States. This is a key issue in studying the nature and effect of the EU as an organisation and legal system and in understanding the scope of its role. There are several aspects to the subject of EU competences. The chapter first provides an overview of how the competence question arises in EU law: what is the general scope of extent of the activities of the EU and its institutions. This involves looking at the focus of the original treaties and then recapping on the expansion of competences dealt with in more detail in Chapter 3. This part introduces an important distinction between general and specific competences, a distinction that has not always been fully appreciated in EU law. It is partly for this reason that the Member States have sometimes found it difficult to 'control' the competences of the EU, although they have attempted to do so through the principle of conferral. The chapter goes on to look at the different categories of competence defined by the Treaty of Lisbon – exclusive, shared, concurrent – and the role of the EU in external relations (both the general law of external relations and the Common Foreign and Security Policy). In addition, it looks at the principles of conferral and subsidiarity. The chapter concludes by identifying competence as an important constitutional issue that is central to debates on the role and legitimacy of the EU.

AS YOU READ . . .

The key questions that will be answered in this chapter are as follows:

— What does the concept of competence mean?

— What was the original core competence of the European Communities?

— What is the significance of the distinction between general and specific competences and how can this be applied to the competences of the EU? In particular, how does the 'common market' competence interact with other competences of the EU?

— What are the categories of EU competence recognised by the Lisbon Treaty?

— What is the relationship between the internal competences of the EU and its external competences under the doctrine of parallelism developed by the European Court of Justice (ECJ)?

— What is the general approach of the ECJ to issues of competence?

7.1 INTRODUCTION

> There is a school of thought that no opportunity should be missed of moving the Community caravan forward, if necessary by night marches . . . there was a time when it would have been considered impolite in Community circles to talk about drawing lines at all. That has changed; and I believe the change is healthy, and evidence of the growing maturity of the order.[1]

This comment from a leading EU law academic expresses two important points about the competences of the EU: (1) there has always been ambiguity about defining the limits of EU competence and (2) defining these limits has become more of a concern of Member States in more recent years. The main reason it has been difficult to define the limits of EU competence is because the term 'common market' (now called the 'internal market') and its associated principles of freedom of movement and undistorted competition (or freedom of competition) – this is what made up the European Communities from the beginning – can be interpreted in a very broad way.

This is because almost any difference in laws amongst the Member States on any subject can in the abstract be understood as an obstacle to full free freedom of movement or of freedom of competition, and the European Court of Justice (ECJ) has interpreted the treaties as prohibiting *any such* obstacles (and not just *discriminatory* obstacles). The role of the ECJ in interpreting and expanding the competences of the EU through its case law is one of the strongest examples of the central role the Court has played as a 'motor of integration', but the Member States have also played a role through treaty amendment.

KEY LEARNING POINT

THE CONSEQUENCE OF THE EU ACTING OUTSIDE OF COMPETENCE

Competence is a fundamental legal concept. When a body acts outside its legal competence, its action is invalid. In the language of UK public law, it is *ultra vires*.

A different interpretative approach could have been adopted. On the issue of limiting competence, a key distinction in legal reasoning is very relevant: the difference between

---

1   A Dashwood 'The limits of European Community powers' (1996) 21 *European Law Review* 113 at 133, 128.

general laws (*lex generalis*) and specific laws (*lex specialis*). The ECJ, however, usually avoids (probably deliberately) drawing this distinction in its reasoning. However, the ECJ implicitly drew the distinction in one high-profile case, *Tobacco Advertising*,[2] and the difference between its approach in this case compared with other cases will help illustrate how the reasoning of the ECJ is central to the issue of defining EU competences.

The Member States have become increasingly alert to the issue of defining EU competences over time, especially from the Treaty of Maastricht in 1992 onwards. In particular, the inclusion of the principles of subsidiarity and conferral in the treaties since the Treaty of Maastricht was intended to clarify the question of the competences of the EU. It is debatable how much difference these have made in practice, as we shall discuss below.

7.2 UNDERSTANDING COMPETENCE – ASPECTS OF THE COMPETENCE QUESTION IN THE EU

There are several different aspects to understanding legal competences, and this can make the topic seem complicated and difficult at first. When a number of significant distinctions are understood first, it becomes easier to understand and analyse the issue.

7.2.1 WHAT DOES LEGAL COMPETENCE MEAN?

We may all have a general understanding of what the word competence means, as involving an ability to do something, but it can be useful to define more precisely what a legal competence means. Essentially, it does involve the idea of an ability or capacity of a natural or legal person or institution to do something that is legally binding or has some legally valid effect.

> KEY LEARNING POINT
>
> **THE CONCEPT OF COMPETENCE**
> Competence can be explained more fully as the capacity *to change legal relations or make binding legal decisions* (this was how it was understood by a famous legal theorist named Wesley Hohfeld[3]).

Thus, a person or body of institution may have a capacity or freedom to express an opinion, but we would not really think of this as a legal competence in a specific sense

---

2   Case C–376/98, *Germany v Parliament and Council* [2000] ECR I–8419.

3   W Hohfeld 'Some fundamental legal conceptions as applied in judicial reasoning' (1913–1914) 23 *Yale Law Journal* 16–59 at 55.

of the term. The idea of competence is related to the idea of legal validity. If a person or body does not have the competence to do something, then that person or body cannot make a legally valid decision on the matter in question.[4] We have come across this idea already when we looked at the procedures of the ECJ, e.g. reviews of legality of the acts of the EU institutions by the ECJ involve an assessment by the ECJ of whether an institution acts within its powers (*intra vires*) or outside is powers (*ultra vires*).

7.2.2 VERTICAL VERSUS HORIZONTAL COMPETENCES IN THE EU

When it comes to defining competences in the EU, one significant distinction is the difference between competence looked at vertically and horizontally.

KEY LEARNING POINT

VERTICAL VERSUS HORIZONTAL COMPETENCES IN THE EU
Vertical competences in the EU involve the relationship and differences between competences of the Member State and the EU. Horizontal competences relates to the different competences of the EU institutions. The focus of this chapter is on vertical competence. Chapter 4 examines the issue of horizontal competences in the context of the separation of powers in the EU.

7.3 THE ORIGINAL COMPETENCES OF THE EU AND THEIR GROWTH

At its origins, the Communities of what is now the EU – the European Coal and Steel Community (ECSC), the European Atomic Energy Community (EURATOM) and the European Economic Community (EEC) – sought to create a common market.

KEY LEARNING POINT

THE TWIN PRINCIPLES OF THE COMMON MARKET
The common market entails two principles: first, freedom of movement of goods, workers, services and capital; and, second, freedom of competition or, more accurately, undistorted competition between enterprises across the Member States.

Although these two competences are essentially economic in nature, it can be difficult to separate the idea of a common market from non-economic competences. It will be

---

4   T Spaak 'Norms that confer competence' (2003) 16(1) *Ratio Juris* 89–104 at 91–92.

easier to see this by examining the concepts of freedom of movement and freedom of competition in a little more detail.

Freedom of movement refers to the capacity of economic actors or economic commodities – goods, workers, service providers, capital and goods – to move or be moved from one Member State to another. The most obvious way in which this can happen is if no taxes are imposed when moving these from one Member State to another. Take goods as an example. Freedom of movement here means that a Member State into which the goods are being imported does not impose (a) taxes, (b) quotas ('quantitative restrictions') or (c) restrictions comparable to quotas such as product requirements, for example, requirements that certain goods are packaged and labelled in a certain way. This last type of restriction is a less obvious restriction than (a) or (b). This is because (a) and (b) are directly discriminatory: they clearly only apply to imported goods; (c) is an example of indirect discrimination, in that it applies equally to both imported and domestic goods, so there is no direct discrimination, but it is likely that it is harder for imported goods to satisfy as domestic goods will probably already comply with it.

However, in its case law, the ECJ has decided that any obstacle to free movement, whether directly or indirectly discriminatory or not, is contrary to the treaties.[5] It is because of the very broad scope of the concept of an 'obstacle to free movement' that it is difficult to define the limits of EU competence in the area of free movement. Almost any differences in national legal systems can be understood as a possible obstacle to free movement of goods and economic actors.

For example, the investigation and prosecution of customs fraud by different police forces could be understood as more time-consuming and difficult to implement if there are separate police forces. Does such investigation and prosecution fall within the free movement principles? Similarly, any differences in national laws on any aspect of the law that might be encountered by enterprises engaging in competition could be understood as being within the common market.

EXPLAINING THE LAW

THE BROAD SCOPE OF THE IDEA OF A COMMON MARKET (NOW INTERNAL MARKET)

This general point, about the potential of the concept of common market to drag in all kinds of competences that might not at first sight seem to be part of it, was well expressed by Davies:

> Alas, as every Community lawyer knows, there could hardly be more open-ended and ambiguous competences than those assigned to the Community. As if the individual policies, notably the legislative competence for the internal

---

5   Case 8/74 *Procureur du Roi v Dassonville* [1974] ECR 837.

> market, were not open enough, there is a mop-up clause allowing legislation that may be necessary 'in the course of the operation of the common market' to achieve 'one of the objectives of the Community'?
>
> These objectives include 'the raising of the standard of living and quality of life' in the Community. What kind of rules might be necessary in operating an international common market? Shared criminal law, at least concerning fraud? Common tax rules? A common contract code? Harmonized education systems to ease migration of persons? A single language? All are arguable.[6]

As noted, the problem is that almost any national rules in the abstract could be understood as an obstacle to free movement or as a distortion on competition (in the sense that cross-border movement could be said to be freer the fewer the differences are between the national laws of the Member States, even if the actual effect on free movement was only potential or slight). Davies identifies in the quote above a 'mop-up clause'. This is the general competence clause provided for in Article 352 TFEU, which we will look at next. This same risk was identified by the ECJ itself in *Tobacco Advertising* in the context of competition law:

> 106. In examining the lawfulness of a directive adopted on the basis of Article 100a of the Treaty, the Court is required to verify whether the distortion of competition which the measure purports to eliminate is appreciable (*Titanium Dioxide*, cited above, paragraph 23).
>
> 107. In the absence of such a requirement, the powers of the Community legislature would be practically unlimited. National laws often differ regarding the conditions under which the activities they regulate may be carried on and this impacts directly or indirectly on the conditions of competition for the undertakings concerned. It follows that to interpret Articles 100a, 57(2) and 66 of the Treaty as meaning that the Community legislature may rely on those articles with a view to eliminating the smallest distortions of competition would be incompatible with the principle, already referred to in paragraph 83 of this judgment, that the powers of the Community are those specifically conferred on it.[7]

Here, the ECJ states that, in order to impact on the comment market from a competition point of view, there must be an appreciable impact demonstrated, otherwise there would be no way to limit Community competences. However, the ECJ has not followed up on this in its case law. Nor has it recognised the same issue arising with free movement and it has rejected the idea that free movement under the Union only becomes relevant when a certain threshold of impact is reached.[8]

....

6   G Davies 'Subsidiarity: the wrong idea, in the wrong place, at the wrong time' (2006) 43 *CMLRev* 63–84 at 63, 65.

7   Case C–376/98, *Germany v Parliament* paras 106–107.

8   Joined Cases 177 & 178/82 *Van de Haar and Kaveka de Meern* [1984] ECR 1797 para 13.

7.4 THE DEVELOPMENT OF COMPETENCES UNDER THE TREATIES

At its origins, the EU was understood as being about a free trade area or common market. However, as noted, it is hard to limit the scope of this idea.

> KEY LEARNING POINT
>
> **THE DEVELOPMENT OF EU COMPETENCES AT TREATY LEVEL**
> The Member States clearly understood the common market to be a concept with limitations, because they subsequently gave the EU additional competences in specific matters. This process began with the Single European Act 1986 and has continued with subsequent treaty amendments.

The Single European Act 1986 added the following elements.

– new provisions on monetary capacity (while the idea of monetary convergence was already part of the treaties)
– improvements, especially in the working environment, as regards the health and safety of workers, and the development of dialogue between management and labour at European level
– a policy of economic and social cohesion to counterbalance the effects of the completion of the internal market on the less developed Member States and to reduce development differences between the regions
– research and technical development, to strengthen the scientific and technological basis of European industry and to encourage it to become more competitive at international level
– environmental protection as a more explicit concern. It specified that the Community can only intervene in environmental matters when this action can be attained better at Community level than at the level of the individual Member States (subsidiarity)
– principle of cooperation in foreign policy.

Interestingly, in adopting more explicit provisions on the environment, the SEA provided the first treaty reference to the principle of subsidiarity.[9] Later, in the Treaty of Maastricht, the principle of subsidiarity was inserted as a general treaty provision to deal with a perceived problem that Community/Union competences were too vaguely defined in practice and that the Community/Union institutions tended to act outside their competence without a check being exercised by the ECJ.

The Treaty of Maastricht was the next treaty amendment after the SEA and it added further new competences. As we have seen in more detail in Chapter 3, the most sensitive of these competences – the Common Foreign and Security Policy and Justice

---

9   The SEA inserted art 130r(4) European Economic Community Treaty (EEC Treaty).

and Home Affairs (JHA) – were adopted within a pillar structure that provided inter-governmental competences only for the EU in these two areas. JHA encompassed two elements, namely asylum, visa and immigration policy and criminal justice issues.

Among the main changes introduced by the Treaty of Amsterdam was the transfer of visa, asylum and immigration policy to the first or Community pillar, i.e. it was made largely supranational.

The Lisbon Treaty has continued a trend of transferring intergovernmental elements to a supranational framework. Most of criminal justice has now been supranationalised (but note that the EU only has a limited competence in criminal justice[10]). For the most part, the Treaty of Lisbon reorganised existing competences (including by defining categories of competence, see further below), rather than by adding new competences. However, the Lisbon Treaty did add some new elements:

- shared competence on general economic interest[11]
- shared competence on energy policy[12]
- complementary competence on space[13]
- complementary competence on tourism[14]
- complementary competence on sport[15]
- complementary competence on civil protection[16]
- complementary competence on administrative cooperation for the effective implementation of Union law.[17]

KEY LEARNING POINT

THE AREA OF FREEDOM, SECURITY AND JUSTICE (AFSJ) AS SUCCESSOR TO JUSTICE AND HOME AFFAIRS (JHA)

At the Treaty of Maastricht, JHA encompassed asylum, visa and immigration policy as well as criminal justice cooperation in the intergovernmental third pillar. At the Treaty of Amsterdam, visa, asylum and immigration were transferred to the supranational first pillar, splitting JHA. Later the term Area of Freedom, Security and Justice came to supersede JHA. The AFSJ also has a connotation of including free movement. In that respect, it becomes a somewhat inexact term by being overly broad, since freedom of movement makes up a large part of the internal market.

---

10 See arts 67, 82–89 TFEU.
11 Ibid art 14.
12 Ibid art 21.
13 Ibid art 189.
14 Ibid art 22.
15 Ibid art 12.
16 Ibid art 23.
17 Ibid art 24.

7.5 CATEGORIES OF COMPETENCE UNDER THE LISBON TREATY

As noted above, concern and criticism about the inexact nature of Community and Union competences has been a recurrent theme at least since the run-up to the Treaty of Maastricht in 1992. As a concept, exclusive competences were introduced by the ECJ, rather than by the Member States, in its judgments in the *ERTA* line of cases on external relations.[18] In relatively limited areas, the EU has exclusive competences, but more commonly has shared competence, or 'supporting', 'coordinating' or 'complementary' competences with the Member States, as these concepts were defined by the Lisbon Treaty.

7.5.1 EXCLUSIVE COMPETENCES (ARTICLE 3 TFEU)

Under Article 3 TFEU, the areas of exclusive competence are the customs union, competition law, economic and monetary policy, conservation of marine biological resources and the common commercial policy. Under Article 3(2) TFEU, the EU has also exclusive competence for the conclusion of an international agreement when its conclusion is provided for in a legislative act of the Union or is necessary to enable the Union to exercise its internal competence, or in so far as its conclusion may affect common rules or alter their scope. In the area of exclusive competences, the Member States no longer exercise any competence independently of the EU.

7.5.2 SHARED COMPETENCES (ARTICLE 4 TFEU)

The term 'shared competences' is used to describe competences that are not fully exercised by either the Member States or the EU.

EXPLAINING THE LAW

SHARED COMPETENCES

The term 'shared competences' is perhaps somewhat misleading. It suggests that the Member States and the EU equally exercise competences. However, in the area of shared competences, once the EU acts on the competence, the Member States lose their competence to the extent that the EU has acted. So the Member States retaining competence is temporary or conditional upon the EU not exercising competence.[19]

---

18 Case 22/70 *Commission v Council (Re European Road Transport Agreement) (ERTA))* [1971] ECR 263; Joined Cases 3, 4 & 6/76 *Kramer* [1976] ECR 1279.

19 R Schütze 'Lisbon and the federal order of competences: a prospective analysis' (2008) 33(5) *European Law Review* 709–22 at 715.

The Lisbon Treaty lists the following as shared competences, now in Article 4 TFEU:

(a) internal market
(b) social policy, for the aspects defined in this treaty
(c) economic, social and territorial cohesion
(d) agriculture and fisheries, excluding the conservation of marine biological resources
(e) environment
(f) consumer protection
(g) transport
(h) trans-European networks
(i) energy.

7.5.3 'SUPPORTING', 'COORDINATING' OR 'COMPLEMENTARY' COMPETENCES (ARTICLE 6 TFEU)

Article 6 states that the Union shall have competence to carry out actions to support, coordinate or supplement the actions of the Member States in these areas:

(a) protection and improvement of human health
(b) industry
(c) culture
(d) tourism
(e) education, vocational training, youth and sport
(f) civil protection
(g) administrative cooperation.

KEY LEARNING POINT

'SUPPORTING', 'COORDINATING', OR 'COMPLEMENTARY' COMPETENCES

'Supporting', 'coordinating', or 'complementary' competences give the most power to the Member States. The EU is to assist the Member States with their exercise of the competences.

ANALYSING THE LAW

THE IMPACT OF THE LISBON TREATY ON EU COMPETENCES

On the categories of competences, one of the reasons the Lisbon Treaty introduced them was to enhance clarity and thus safeguard competences remaining with the Member States, in particular, by defining competences that were not exclusive. Lisbon set out two non-exclusive categories, shared and complementary. However, as noted, the term 'shared competences' may be misleading and better considered as 'conditional competence'. Overall on Lisbon, Schütze comments that:

> In many ways, by way of conclusion, the chance to enhance the constitutional clarity of the European Union's federal order of competences will be missed. Worse, the Lisbon Treaty – if it ever enters into force – may represent a serious step backwards. Instead of three clear-cut competence categories, the Reform Treaty would give us three official and a number of 'unofficial' competence types, none of which impresses by defined contours. Nor will there be any clearer distinction between different types of competences.[20]

On 'unofficial competences', Schütze suggests the competences in Article 4(3) TFEU (Article 4 is the provision on shared competences, Article 4(3) relates to research, technological development and space) should not really be there, since Article 4(3) effectively provides for something different to shared competences by stating that the Member States do not lose their competence when the Union exercise its competence. Thus, Schütze suggests, the term 'parallel competence' might be better. Article 4(3) raises the possibility of conflict between Member State and EU action in this area, which will presumably be resolved by applying the supremacy principle. The second 'unofficial' category Schütze identifies[21] is 'coordinating competences', referred to in Article 2(3) TFEU, which states 'The Member States shall coordinate their economic and employment policies within arrangements as determined by this Treaty, which the Union shall have competence to provide' (see also Article 5). Given that the same term 'coordinate' is also used in Article 6 on supporting competences, it seems unclear why they were not simply included in that provision.[22]

....

20 Ibid 721. Dougan observes that 'the underlying legal framework governing the existence and exercise of Union competences has not changed; the Treaty of Lisbon's amendments affect only the detailed application'. See M Dougan 'The Treaty of Lisbon 2007: winning minds, not hearts' (2008) 45 *Common Market Law Review* 617–703 at 654.

21 Schütze (n 19) 717–18.

22 Ibid. Joerges uses the term 'diagonal' to describe situations where the Union does not have exclusive competence and may need to rely on the Member States' competence for the effective exercise of its own competence. See C Joerges (with comments by D Chalmers, R Nickel, F Rödl and R Wai) 'Rethinking European law's supremacy' *EUI Working Paper Law 2005/12* (2005) 16; C Joerges 'The impact of European integration on private law: reductionist perceptions, true conflicts and a new constitutional perspective' (1997) 3(4) *European Law Journal* 378–406 at 398–99.

KEY LEARNING POINT

'SOFT LAW' AND THE OPEN METHOD OF COOPERATION
The term soft law refers to the use of non-binding instruments that take a legal
form. The main example in the treaties is recommendations and opinions
under Article 288 TFEU. A more recent kind of soft law is the 'Open Method of
Cooperation (OMC)'. It was created as part of EU employment policy in the 1990s
leading up to the Treaty of Amsterdam (it is sometimes called the Luxembourg
process because it was stimulated by the European Council Session of 20–21
November 1997). It involves a process of peer evaluation amongst the Member
States of policies they adopt implementing EU law. The Commission monitors
the process while the Court of Justice and European Parliament are not involved.
It can thus be described as intergovernmental. The OMC process involves
the Council deciding on an objective, means of implementation and then a
benchmarking and peer review process amongst the Member States of how
and if implementation is achieved in each Member State. The process is binding
informally in the sense that there is an expectation the Member States will follow
through on what has been decided, but it is not legally enforceable. An example
is Article 148 TFEU on employment policy.

7.6 THE PRINCIPLE OF CONFERRAL AND THE DISTINCTION BETWEEN GENERAL AND SPECIFIC COMPETENCES

To understand competence in EU law further, it is important to understand the
distinction between general and specific competences. This can be more important in
practice than the categories of competence recognised in the Lisbon Treaty for the issue
of limiting EU competences. As was noted at the start of the chapter in the quote from
Dashwood, from the beginnings of the Community there has been a reluctance to state
clearly the limits of Community/Union competences.

The notion of a common market suggested a purely economic concern, but the
principles of free movement and freedom of competition can drag in within their scope
non-economic matters. The idea of a common market is a general competence, specific
competences (such as, e.g. regarding the environment) are more narrowly defined and
are not wholly within the scope of a common market, although they may be related to
it, e.g. the environment.

Perhaps the problem with defining the limits of competence is because of insufficient
attention to this distinction. The general competence of the Union has sometimes been
allowed to drag in other competences in a poorly defined way that makes it hard to
respect the principle of conferral.

THE PRINCIPLE OF CONFERRAL

Vagueness as to the scope of Union competences is in conflict with the principle of conferred powers in Article 5 TEU, namely, that the Union can only act on the basis of the limited powers accorded in the treaty:

1. The limits of Union competences are governed by the principle of conferral. The use of Union competences is governed by the principles of subsidiarity and proportionality.
2. Under the principle of conferral, the Union shall act only within the limits of the competences conferred upon it by the Member States in the treaties to attain the objectives set out therein. Competences not conferred upon the Union in the treaties remain with the Member States.

In Article 5, with the principle of subsidiarity, the TEU recognises both that Union competence is limited in not applying to areas that remain the exclusive preserve of the Member States (the principle of conferral) and that in areas of shared competence, the exercise of Union competence depends on the achievement of better results, by reason of scale or effects, than if the Member States acted individually (the principle of subsidiarity, see below). Both the principles of conferral and subsidiarity thus sit uneasily with and can be opposed to the 'conceptual pull' of the common, now internal, market principles of the abolition of obstacles to free movement and undistorted competition. The right to strike provides a good example of this.

ANALYSING THE LAW

CONTRASTING *TOBACCO ADVERTISING* WITH *VIKING* AND *LAVAL*

The ECJ judgment in *Tobacco Advertising* was quoted above concerning the need to set some threshold for an impact on competition to be sufficient to give the EU competence. Moreover, the ECJ in *Tobacco Advertising* stated that limitations on competence in one treaty provision could not be circumvented by reliance on another treaty provision.[23] This is an important issue in limiting competences: if a specific provision limits or excludes competence, it can be gotten around by relying on a more general competence to deal with the same matter. In the EU context, the general competences are freedom of movement and freedom of competition.

On the facts of *Tobacco Advertising*, the ECJ held that the specificity of (then) Community competence in public health of (then) Article 129/152 ECT (now Article 168 TFEU) could not be circumvented by the Community legislature by relying on the *more general* internal market power in then Article 100a/95

23 Case C–376/98 *Germany v Parliament and Council (Tobacco Advertising)* [2000] ECR I–8419 paras 77–79.

ECT (now Article 114 TFEU) (in order to harmonise legislation on public health concerning tobacco). This reflects the distinction between *lex generalis* (general law) and *lex specialis* (specific law) applied to competence. The reason for this is clear: to hold otherwise would render the existence of a more specific competence, in which the EU has a more limited role, irrelevant in practice, since the same matter could simply be included under a more general competence in which the EU has a bigger role. This could not be the intention of the legislature, since specific laws are a stronger expression of legislative intention.

The ECJ took the opposite approach to *Tobacco Advertising* in *Viking* and *Laval*.[24] Despite the specific exclusion of the rights to strike from the social competence of the Union by then Article 137(5) ECT (now Article 153(5) TFEU)), the ECJ held that national rules permitting strikes where such strikes has the effect of being an inhibition to the posting of workers from one Member State to another were contrary to Community law on free movement (now in Article 45 TFEU).[25] The ECJ did not try to explain the inconsistency between its approach in *Tobacco Advertising* and its approach in *Laval* and *Viking*.

In *Tobacco Advertising*, the more general internal market power attempted to be relied on is now Article 114 TFEU.

EXPLAINING THE LAW

GENERAL COMPETENCES IN ARTICLES 114 AND 352 TFEU

Article 114 TFEU is one of two general competence clauses in the treaties, the other being Article 352 TFEU. Article 114 TFEU provides for the approximation (harmonisation) of laws relating to the establishing or functioning of the internal market. It uses the ordinary legislative procedure. Article 352 TFEU is a residual powers clause allowing the Union to adopt measures necessary for attaining treaty objectives when no more specific legal basis is available. It relies on unanimity in the Council (of Ministers).

One academic has described the potential scope of (then) Article 308 European Community Treaty (ECT) (now Article 352 TFEU) in the following words: '. . . it became virtually impossible to find any activity which could not be brought within

---

24 Case C–438/05 *The International Transport Workers' Federation and the Finnish Seamen's Union v Viking Line ABP and OÜ Viking Line Eesti* [2007] ECR I–10779; Case C–341/05 *Laval un Partneri Ltd v Svenska Byggnadsarbetareföbundet* [2007] ECR I–11767.
25 Case C–438/05 *Viking* (n 24) paras 39–40; Case C–341/05 *Laval* (n 24) paras 87–88.

the "objectives of the Treaty'".[26] This is because of the generality with which the treaty objectives can be described: anything that enhances integration is consistent with the preamble's exhortation to 'an ever-closer Union'.[27] The more the EU institutions rely on Articles 114 and 352 TFEU, the less significant are any limitations set out in the treaties on EU competences. In *Opinion 2/92*, the ECJ qualified the scope of Article 352 as follows:

> That provision, being an integral part of an institutional system based on the principle of conferred powers, cannot serve as a basis for widening the scope of community powers beyond the general framework created by the provisions of the Treaty as a whole and, in particular, by those that define the tasks and activities of the Community. On any view, [Article 308] cannot be used as a basis for the adoption of provisions whose effect would, in substance, be to amend the Treaty without following the procedure which it provides for that purpose.[28]

This passage suggests that Article 352 TFEU should not be used to extend Union powers, but given that the 'general framework' of the treaties is so broad, it is hard to see that this judgment places practical limits on EU competence.

EXPLAINING THE LAW

THE CHOICE OF LEGAL BASIS FOR LEGISLATION AND THE CENTRE-OF-GRAVITY TEST

It is often possible that a given legislative proposal or instrument could be based on more than one specific legal basis, because it overlaps two policy areas. In this situation, the approach of the ECJ is to determine the legal basis through a centre-of-gravity test, i.e. whichever legal basis captures or reflects most fully the core or essence of the legislative proposal is the correct or more correct legal basis:

> If examination of a measure reveals that it pursues two aims or that it has two components and if one of those aims or components is identifiable as the main one, whereas the other is merely incidental, the measure must be founded on a single legal basis, namely, that required by the main or predominant aim or component.[29]

....

26 J H H Weiler 'The transformation of Europe' (1991) 100(8) *Yale Law Journal* 2403–83 at 2445–46 (in contrast with (ex) art 308 ECT/now art 352 TFEU, (ex) art 95 ECT/now art 114 TFEU does not require unanimity).

27 T Schilling 'Subsidiarity as a rule and a principle, or: taking subsidiarity seriously' *New York University Jean Monnet Working Paper No 10/1995* (1995) 13, 17, noting that there were no limits to Community competences because they are expressed in terms of ends (and of course the ECJ relies on teleological interpretation).

28 *Opinion 2/94 Re Accession of the Community to the European Convention on Human Rights* [1996] ECR 1–17 para 30.

29 Case C–155/07 *Parliament v Council* [2008] ECR I–8103 para 35, citing Case C–155/91 *Commission v Council* [1993] ECR I–939 paras 19, 21; Case C–36/98 *Spain v Council* [2001] ECR I–779 para 59; Case C–338/01 *Commission v Council (Recovery of Indirect Taxes)* [2004] ECR I–4829 para 55; and Case C–91/05 *Commission v Council (ECOWAS)* [2008] ECR I–3651 para 73.

This quite often arises for example concerning development cooperation. A recent example is *Commission v Council*,[30] concerning the Council's decision to pursue a Partnership and Cooperation Framework Agreement between the EU and the Philippines. The Council identified several legal bases for this: firstly, the Council identified the two most obvious legal bases, which were Article 207 TFEU on the common commercial policy (the external aspect of the internal market) and Article 209 on development cooperation policy. In conjunction with Article 218(5) TFEU, the treaty provision on the power of the EU to enter into agreements with third countries. In addition, it identified the following:

– Article 79(3) TFEU on the power of the EU to conclude international agreements on the readmission of third country nationals
– Article 91 TFEU on international transport
– Article 100 TFEU on transport by rail, road and inland waterway
– Article 191(4) TFEU cooperation with third countries and international organisations concerning the environment.

At issue in the judgment was the unanimous decision of the Council on 12 May 2012 to authorise the Framework Agreement with the Philippines and the choice of legal basis for the decision. The Framework Agreement involved cooperation over a wide range of EU activities, including migration, development cooperation, the environment and natural resources, and transport. The Commission argued that the latter four treaty bases were unnecessary and unlawful in that the provisions of the Framework Agreement which accounted for the addition of Articles 79(3) TFEU, 91 TFEU, 100 TFEU and 191(4) TFEU were entirely covered by Article 209 TFEU.[31] The Council argued that the Framework Agreement was intended to establish comprehensive cooperation and that a particular aspect of cooperation was not predominant and that particular policy areas were not just aspects of development cooperation in this case.[32] The ECJ in its judgment summarised the standard test for determining the legislative basis:

> According to settled case law, the choice of the legal basis for a European Union measure, including the measure adopted for the purpose of concluding an international agreement, must rest on objective factors amenable to judicial review, which include the aim and content of that measure. If examination of a European Union measure reveals that it pursues a twofold purpose or that it has a twofold component and if one of those is identifiable as the main or predominant purpose or component, whereas the other is merely incidental,

30 Case C–377/12, *Commission v Council*, judgment of 11 June 2014.
31 Ibid paras 16–17.
32 Ibid paras 27–32.

the measure must be founded on a single legal basis, namely, that required by the main or predominant purpose or component. By way of exception, if it is established that the measure pursues several objectives which are inseparably linked without one being secondary and indirect in relation to the other, the measure must be founded on the various corresponding legal bases. However, no dual legal basis is possible where the procedures required by each legal basis are incompatible with each other (see, inter alia, Case C130/10 *Parliament v Council* EU: C:2012:472, paragraphs 42 to 45 and the case law cited).[33]

Having analysed the relative importance of the different elements of the Framework Agreement between the EU and the Philippines, the ECJ concluded, in favour of the Commission, that the provisions of the Framework Agreement relating to readmission of nationals of the contracting parties, to transport and to the environment did not contain obligations so extensive that they could be considered to constitute objectives distinct from those of development cooperation that are neither secondary nor indirect in relation to the latter objectives.[34] The 'centre of gravity' (the ECJ itself does not use this term) of the contested decision and resulting Framework Agreement was, therefore, development cooperation.

7.7 THE PRINCIPLE OF SUBSIDIARITY

The ECJ has made limited use of the principle of subsidiarity, which was intended to be a means of restricting, or clarifying limits on, EU competence.

EXPLAINING THE LAW

THE PRINCIPLE OF SUBSIDIARITY
Introduced by the Treaty of Maastricht in 1992 as a general constitutional principle, the principle requires, in essence, that it must be demonstrated that action can be better achieved at Union level to justify the exercise of competence by the EU, instead of leaving matters to the Member States. Subsidiarity only applies to areas of shared EU competence. In matters of exclusive EU competence, the Member States no longer have any competence and so subsidiarity is not relevant. Where the EU has only

---

33 Ibid para 34.
34 Ibid paras 47–59.

complementary competence, the Member States may exercise competence individually as they see fit, the role of the EU is simply to support the Member States. Subsidiarity matters in the context of shared competence because once the EU has acted in an area of shared competence, the Member States lose their competence, under Article 2(2) TFEU. Article 5(3) TEU states:

> Under the principle of subsidiarity, in areas which do not fall within its exclusive competence, the Union shall act only if and in so far as the objectives of the proposed action cannot be sufficiently achieved by the Member States, either at central level or at regional and local level, but can rather, by reason of the scale or effects of the proposed action, be better achieved at Union level.

> The institutions of the Union shall apply the principle of subsidiarity as laid down in the Protocol on the application of the principles of subsidiarity and proportionality. National Parliaments ensure compliance with the principle of subsidiarity in accordance with the procedure set out in that Protocol.

Subsidiarity is thus intended as a kind of protection for the Member States against the unjustified exercise of competence by the EU and a resulting loss of Member State competence. Areas of shared competence are listed in Article 4(2) TFEU and the list, noted above, is quite extensive, including such matters as the internal market; social policy, for the aspects defined in this treaty; agriculture and fisheries; the environment; consumer protection; transport; energy; and the area of freedom, security and justice.

The concept behind subsidiarity is that power should be exercised as close to those affected as it can be without impairing its effectiveness. It is a principle of social organisation and entails a kind of presumption against the centralisation of power and has its origins in Catholic social teaching (or at least that any centralisation or de-localisation of power must be clearly justified).[35]

Subsidiarity is primarily thought of as applying to shared competences,[36] although the Treaty wording applies it to 'areas which do not fall within the Union's exclusive competence' (Article 5(3) TEU). It is most relevant in the context of shared competences, because the exercise of shared competence by the EU has the effect of the Member States losing their competences, whereas with supporting, coordinating or supplementary competence, the Member States can always still act. Nonetheless, in principle subsidiarity could also be applicable to the latter: the EU should only exercise supporting, coordinating or supplementary competence when it can usefully add to what the Member States can individually achieve.

....

35 See the papal encyclicals *Rerum Novarum* 1892 of Pope Leo XIII and *Quadregisimo Anno* 1932 of Pope Pius XI.
36 See, e.g. European Parliament Factsheet on the EU, 'The Principle of Subsidiarity' (2015), sec. C 1.

Article 5(3) TEU also refers to the Protocol on the Application of the Principles of Subsidiarity and Proportionality.

Subsidiarity is concerned with the *exercise*, rather than the existence of competence, and only applies to non-exclusive EU powers. In *Germany v European Parliament and Council*,[37] the Court held that it was not necessary for Community measures to refer to the subsidiarity principle. In a later decision, the Court set a threshold of review that would render the subsidiarity principle of very limited legal significance as a limit on Community action, by suggesting that a diversity of national rules could of itself create barriers to the common market and that harmonisation thus satisfied subsidiarity in that situation:

> With regard to the principle of subsidiarity, since the national provisions in question differ significantly from one Member State to another, they may constitute, as is noted in the fifth recital in the preamble to the PPE Directive, a barrier to trade with direct consequences for the creation and operation of the common market. The harmonisation of such divergent provisions may, by reason of its scope and effects, be undertaken only by the Community legislature.[38]

However, as noted already, given that almost any diversity of national rules could be understood as a potential obstacle to a common market, on this approach, harmonisation is almost necessarily rendered consistent with subsidiarity at a conceptual level. As Estella has noted:

> Even in those areas in which there seem to be clear reasons in favour of national, or even regional or local regulation . . . it will always be possible to argue that due to the close relationship between these areas and the development of the single market, some Community intervention will always be necessary.[39]

ANALYSING THE LAW

THE PRINCIPLE OF SUBSIDIARITY AND THE ECJ
Subsidiarity is not a straightforward or simple concept. However, the ECJ could adopt some standard of scrutiny, such as a requirement for reasons or justification for the exercise of Union competence going beyond an assertion that national

....

37 Case C–233/94 *Germany v European Parliament and Council* [1997] ECR I–2405 paras 26–28.
38 Case C–103/01 *Commission v Germany* [2003] ECR I–5369 paras 46–47. Similarly see Case C–491/01 *R v Secretary of State for Health, ex parte British American Tobacco (Investments) Ltd* [2002] ECR 1–11453 paras 181–83; Cases C–154 & 155/04 *The Queen, on the application of Alliance for Natural Health and Nutri-Link Ltd v Secretary of State for Health* [2005] ECR I–6451 paras 106–108.
39 A Estella *The EU Principle of Subsidiarity and its Critique* (Oxford University Press 2002) 113–14.

divergences of laws are enough to justify EU intervention.[40] With the current approach of the ECJ, the treaty provisions on subsidiarity make little difference to the reasoning of the Court.

The Lisbon Treaty has introduced a new procedure, called the yellow card system, involving national parliaments in the legislative process as a way of implementing the subsidiarity principle.

KEY LEARNING POINT

YELLOW CARD SYSTEM AND SUBSIDIARITY
Under Article 7 of Protocol No 2 to the treaties on the application of the principles of subsidiarity and proportionality, a draft European legislative act must be reviewed within an eight-week time limit if one-third, or one-quarter in the AFSJ, of the national parliaments object to its subsidiarity arguments.

So far, this procedure has not been used a great deal, perhaps because it requires quite a high degree of coordination between national parliaments. Whoever has initiated the legislative proposal (usually the Commission, but it may be a group of Member States or another European institution from which the draft originates), may decide to maintain, amend or withdraw the draft and reasons must be given for each decision. So national parliaments are not given a veto.

The first use of the yellow card system came in 2012, concerning a proposed regulation on the exercise of the right to take collective action within the context of the freedom of establishment and the freedom to provide services. Subsequently, the Commission decided to withdraw the proposal,[41] although it seems that this was not because or at least solely because of the use of the yellow card system by national parliaments.[42]

The second use of it occurred with the Commission's proposal to establish a European Prosecutor under Article 86 TFEU.[43] However, the Commission decided to proceed with

....

40 See generally M Kumm 'The jurisprudence of constitutional conflict: constitutional supremacy in Europe before and after the constitutional treaty' (2005) 11(3) *European Law Journal* 262–307.

41 Commission decision to withdraw the Proposal for a Council Regulation on the exercise of the right to take collective action within the context of the freedom of establishment and the freedom to provide services Brussels 21.3.2012 COM(2012) 130 final 2012/0064 (APP).

42 G Vara Arribas, D Bourdin 'What does the Lisbon Treaty change regarding subsidiarity within the EU institutional framework' (European Institute of Public Administration 2012) 15.

43 Proposal for a Council Regulation on the establishment of the European Public Prosecutor's Office COM/2013/0534 final 2013/0255 (APP).

the proposal.[44] One consequence of the greater use of the yellow card procedure may be the development of a set of principles relevant to the use of subsidiarity, which could facilitate greater respect for subsidiarity in the approach of the ECJ to judicial review.

7.8 EXTERNAL RELATIONS

The role of the ECJ has been especially central in the development of the Union's external relations law. The ECJ has been instrumental here chiefly through the development of the doctrine of parallelism, whereby it held that the exercise of an internal Community/Union competence gave rise to external Community/Union competence that pre-empted Member States exercising an equivalent or overlapping competence, i.e. that Union competence could be exclusive.[45] The founding decision on the parallelism doctrine is *ERTA*. It went considerably beyond the text of the treaties,[46] which did not specify either parallelism or pre-emption.

EXPLAINING THE LAW

THE ROLE OF THE ECJ IN DEVELOPING THE DOCTRINES OF PARALLELISM AND PRE-EMPTION IN EXTERNAL RELATIONS

In *ERTA*, the ECJ held that when the Community/Union exercises its internal powers, this creates a parallel external power for the Community/Union in international relations. The effect is to allow the EU to engage in external relations, e.g. conclude treaties, in that area. In addition and, very importantly, the ECJ held that that this implied power was exclusive and pre-empted that of the Member States where common rules were adopted (instead of concluding, for example, that its general treaty-making power was concurrent, as suggested by the Commission[47]). This means that when the EU adopts common internal policies, the EU automatically gets exclusive competence to develop external relations and policies on that matter, and the Member States may no longer engage in an independent foreign policy on that matter.

Differences emerged in the case law on the question of the extent of exercise of internal powers as a prerequisite for the existence of parallel external powers: *Kramer* suggested there must

....

44 European Commission, Communication from the Commission to the European Parliament, the Council and the National Parliaments on the review of the proposal for a Council Regulation on the establishment of the European Public Prosecutor's Office with regard to the principle of subsidiarity, in accordance with Protocol No 2, Brussels 27.11.2013 COM(2013) 851 final.

45 Case 22/70 *Commission v Council (ERTA)* [1971] ECR 263 paras 17–19, 28–31.

46 Ibid paras 12–17.

47 Ibid para 11.

first be internal exercise of competence,[48] *Inland Waterways* suggested the opposite.[49] Later, in *Opinion 1/94*, the ECJ clarified that *Inland Waterways* applied only where external competence could not realistically be exercised without the initial exercise of external competence.[50]

Later cases further clarified that this competence only became exclusive when the area of competence in question is 'already covered to a large extent by Community rules progressively adopted . . . with a view to achieving an ever greater degree of harmonization';[51] when internal measures become sufficiently harmonised to have the effect of pre-emption is not fully clear.[52] Exclusive competence arises where international action by the Member States, individually or collectively, would affect internal rules or distort their scope.[53]

ANALYSING THE LAW

THE ECJ JUDGMENT IN *OPINION 1/91*:[54]

Perhaps the high point of the creativity of the Court on competence involved the issue of the proposed creation of a new court for wide economic integration under the European Economic Agreement (EEA).[55] In *Opinion 1/91*, the ECJ held that the creation of such a court was contrary to Community law if its jurisdiction overlapped with that of the ECJ itself, as it would threaten the foundations of the Community itself.[56] Shaw observed that here '[the ECJ] intervened directly in the exercise of sovereign will by the Member States'.[57] Constantinesco suggests that what the ECJ did was to give priority to some constitutionally expressed principles over others and that this is a kind of super-constitutionality.[58] The legitimacy of the Court limiting the Member States in this way is open to debate.

48 Cases 3, 4 & 6/76, *Kramer* (n 18).
49 *Opinion 1/76 Re Draft Agreement Establishing a Laying-up Fund for Inland Waterway Vessels* [1977] ECR 741.
50 *Opinion 1/94 Re WTO Agreement* [1994] ECR I–5267 paras 85–86.
51 *Opinion 2/91 Re Convention No 170 International Labour Organisation on Safety in the Use of Chemicals at Work* [1993] ECR I–1061 para 25.
52 See e.g. P Craig *EU Administrative Law* (Oxford University Press 2006) 412.
53 Case C–467/98 *Commission v Germany* [2002] ECR I–9855 para 74. See Craig (n 52) 414–15.
54 *Opinion 1/91 Re European Economic Area Agreement I* [1991] ECR 6079.
55 The European Economic Area (EEA) is an international organisation set up in Europe in 1994 to facilitate economic relations between EU and non-Member State countries Iceland, Liechtenstein and Norway. It allows these countries to participate in the internal market without being members of the EU. The European Free Trade Association (EFTA) was founded in Europe in 1960 as an alternative free-trade association for countries that did not wish to join the EU. Current members are Iceland, Liechtenstein, Norway and Switzerland.
56 Ibid 6081–82.
57 J Shaw 'European Union legal studies in crisis? Towards a new dynamic' (1996) 16(2) *Oxford Journal of Legal Studies* 231–53 at 239.
58 V Constantinesco 'The ECJ as law-maker: *Praeter aut Contra Legem?*' in D O'Keeffe, A Bavasso (eds) *Judicial Review in European Law: Essays in Honour of Lord Slynn* (Kluwer 2001) 79.

The ECJ in the more recent case of *MOX Plant* has held that it has exclusive jurisdiction over mixed agreements, thereby precluding a Member State from bringing proceedings in an international tribunal.[59] Mixed agreements are international treaties in which both the EU and Member States are parties, because the EU does not have competence over the entirety of the agreement. The case represents an interesting example of the interaction of *lex generalis* and *lex specialis*, because the treaties contain a provision that quite specifically addresses the question of the exclusivity of ECJ jurisdiction.

Article 292 ECT (retained as Article 344 TFEU following Lisbon) provided that the Member States undertake 'not to submit a dispute concerning the interpretation or application of the treaty to any method of settlement other than those provided therein'. Based on a teleological argument about the effectiveness of the Community/Union legal order, the ECJ ruled out any overlap of jurisdiction between it and another court or tribunal. This was not inevitable on the wording, since Article 344 TFEU could be interpreted as applying to the EU treaties only, for example. However, characteristically, the ECJ did not focus on the text, but on the effectiveness of integration.

7.9 CASE STUDY – CRIMINAL LAW COMPETENCE OF THE EU

Criminal law is one of the more recently acquired competences of the EU. It was first a part of the inter-governmental third pillar, along with visa, asylum and immigration, following the Treaty of Maastricht. At the Treaty of Amsterdam, visa, asylum and immigration were transferred to the first pillar, leaving criminal law matters in the third pillar. At Lisbon, the criminal law competence of the EU was partly supranationalised, in the process of the dropping of the pillar structure.

Criminal law is a part of the Area of Freedom, Security and Justice (AFSJ) (discussed earlier in this chapter). Under Article 4(2)(j) TFEU, the AFSJ is a shared competence, meaning that the Member States lose their competence to the extent that the EU has exercised its own. However, an important difference concerning the AFSJ is that the doctrine of parallelism appears not to apply to it, i.e. the Member States seem to retain their external competences in this area, even when the EU adopts legal instruments that may amount to a common policy.[60]

59 Case C–459/03 *European Commission v Ireland* (*MOX Plant*) [2006] ECR I–4635. For discussion see e.g. C P R Romano (Case Note) 'Case C–459/03 *Commission of the European Communities v Ireland*' (2007) 101(1) *American Journal of International Law* 171–79.
60 Article 7(3) TFEU, which states that it shall be open to Member States to organise between themselves and under their responsibility such forms of cooperation and coordination as they deem appropriate between the competent departments of their administrations responsible for safeguarding national security. It seems logical that the Member States would retain the same faculties to cooperate with third states.

The main provisions of the treaties on criminal law now are:

- Judicial cooperation in criminal matters in the Union shall be based on the principle of mutual recognition of judgments and judicial decisions and shall include the approximation of the laws and regulations of the Member States in the areas referred to in Article 83(2) (Article 82), and measures: (a) to lay down rules and procedures for ensuring recognition throughout the Union of all forms of judgments and judicial decisions; (b) to prevent and settle conflicts of jurisdiction between Member States; (c) to support the training of the judiciary and judicial staff; and (d) to facilitate cooperation between judicial or equivalent authorities of the Member States in relation to proceedings in criminal matters and the enforcement of decision (Article 82(1)), as well as minimum rules on: (a) the mutual admissibility of evidence between Member States; (b) the rights of individuals in criminal procedure; (c) the rights of victims of crime; and (d) any other specific aspects of criminal procedure which the Council has identified in advance by a decision (upon which the Council shall act unanimously after obtaining the consent of the European Parliament) (Article 82(2)).
- Article 83(2) provides for the minimum rules concerning the definition of criminal offences and sanctions in the areas of particularly serious crime with a cross-border dimension resulting from the nature or impact of such offences or from a special need to combat them on a common basis, namely terrorism, trafficking in human beings and sexual exploitation of women and children, illicit drug trafficking, illicit arms trafficking, money laundering, corruption, counterfeiting of means of payment, computer crime and organised crime.
- In addition, Article 83(2) provides that on the basis of developments in crime, the Council may adopt a decision identifying other areas of crime that meet the criteria specified in this paragraph, acting unanimously after obtaining the consent of the European Parliament.
- Article 84 provides for measures concerning crime prevention.
- Article 85 provides for Eurojust, which is to facilitate practical cooperation between the prosecution agencies of the Member States.
- Article 86 provides a legal basis for a European public prosecutor (EPP) (Article 86 TFEU).
- Articles 87–89 deal with police cooperation.

More or less parallel with the development of treaty competence, the ECJ developed the concept of effectiveness of remedies at national level so that Member States are required to adopt criminal sanctions where this is necessary to ensure effective and dissuasive enforcement of EU law at national level.[61] The latter point was clarified to some extent in the later case of *Commission v Council*,[62] where the Court more cautiously held, without really any argument specifically on the point, that '[b]y contrast, and

....

61 Case C–176/03 *Commission v Council (Environmental Crimes)* [2005] ECR I–7879.
62 Case C–440/05 *Commission v Council (Sea Pollution)* [2007] ECR I–9097.

contrary to the submission of the Commission, the determination of the type and level of the criminal penalties to be applied does not fall within the Community's sphere of competence'.[63]

Presumably, however, by the logic of the case law, the Court could review the effectiveness, proportionality and dissuasiveness of whatever criminal sanctions are chosen at national level. This line of authority can be related to the *lex specialis–lex generalis* distinction; the ECJ allowed the *lex generalis* of the internal market to spill over into the more specific competence or *lex specialis* of criminal law.

ANALYSING THE LAW

THE LIMITS OF THE CRIMINAL LAW COMPETENCE OF THE EU

An important practical question concerns the limits of EU criminal law competence. An obvious answer might be that the limits are set out in the treaties and on the basis of the principle of conferral: whatever the treaty does not attribute as a power in this sphere to the EU remains with the Member States. However, the issue also needs to be addressed in terms of ambiguity in the provisions that do attribute competence to the EU in criminal matters. Two points of ambiguity seem to arise:

(1) Article 82(2)(d) seems to open any aspect of criminal procedure to EU action
(2) Article 83(2) seems to extend jurisdiction to define substantive crimes over any crime with a 'serious cross-border dimension', a criterion that seems open to differing interpretations.

A more practical limitation on EU powers in this sphere is procedure: the so-called emergency break provisions mean a Member State can opt out of a measure, whilst Article 83(2) TFEU requires unanimity in the Council and only consultation for the European Parliament. Some matters are clearly outside the competence of the EU:

- minor crimes
- police powers
- the structure of courts and legal officials in the Member States
- prisons and means of criminal punishment generally.

A final point concerns the interaction of the Council of Europe and the EU in criminal matters. The Council of Europe has traditionally been the focus of efforts between European countries to cooperate in criminal law. Legal instruments adopted under its auspices have concerned the typical issues affecting inter-state enforcement of national criminal law: extradition[64] and mutual legal assistance (e.g. transmission of evidence from

....

63 Ibid para 70.
64 European Convention on Extradition ETS No 24.

one jurisdiction to another[65]). The EU has adopted its own instruments in this area, expanding cooperation and facilitation of requests from one Member State to another.[66]

In this case, the new EU instruments apply as between the EU Member States; the previous Council of Europe conventions or agreements will apply as between the EU Member States and non-EU Member States individually. This is because, as noted above, the doctrine of parallelism does not appear to apply to the AFSJ.

7.10 CONCLUSION

Competence is an important topic in EU law because it is central to the constitutional identity of the EU and is about one of the most basic questions as to the function of the EU: what can it do and how does this impact on the powers of the Member States?

This is a surprisingly difficult question to address, not least because the ECJ tends to creatively interpret treaty provisions to enhance EU competence. This remains the case despite the attempt by the Treaty of Lisbon to categorise EU competences. In particular, a distinction between general and special competences has often not been followed closely in the EU. It is difficult to limit the scope of the idea of common market with its twin principles of freedom of movement and freedom of competition. As a result, the twin constitutional principles of conferral and subsidiarity have not had a big impact on the practice of EU law since their introduction by the Treaty of Maastricht in 1992.

POINTS TO REVIEW

- Competence (another word for which is power) refers to the basic capacity to do something that has a legal effect and/or is legally valid. Competence is a basic issue prior to the deciding legal validity of an act.

- The original competences of the European Communities involved the idea of a common market. This suggests an essentially economic idea of free trade. However, it is difficult to state clearly what matters lie outside the core ideas of the common market, namely, freedom of trade and freedom of competition.

65 European Convention on Mutual Legal Assistance in Criminal Matters ETS No 30.
66 Replacing extradition arrangements between the Member States, the EU has adopted the Council Framework 2002/584/JHA on the European arrest warrant and the surrender procedures between Member States OJ L 190 18.7.2002 p. 1; in the area of mutual legal assistance, the EU has recently adopted Directive 2014/41/EU regarding the European Investigation Order in criminal matters OJ L 130 1.5.2014 p. 1.

- One way of limiting EU competence is to distinguish between specific and general powers. The ECJ took this approach in *Tobacco Advertising*, in which it held that a public health matter could not be regulated under a general competence clause, but had to be regulated under the specific clause in the treaty on public health. However, the ECJ did not make this explicit and has not generally followed it in other case law, e.g. in *Laval* and *Viking* on the right to strike.

- The Lisbon Treaty distinguished between exclusive, shared and complementary/supporting/coordinating EU competences. The term shared competence is perhaps misleading, because in those areas that do fall within shared competences, the Member States lose their competences to the extent that the EU exercises its own competence.

- The ECJ has exercised a very significant role in developing the external relations of the EU through creating the doctrines of parallelism and pre-emption. This means the EU possesses matching external powers to its internal powers and the Member States correspondingly losing their powers externally when the EU gains parallel powers.

- The approach of the ECJ to competence is marked by a pro-integration teleological method of interpretation that emphasises the effectiveness of EU law and which can result in a reduction in Member State competences.

CHAPTER GLOSSARY

Area of Freedom, Security and Justice refers to the competence of the EU to achieve security goals and cooperate in security matters as an extension of the principles of free movement. It encompasses what used to be referred to as Justice and Home Affairs, which included visa, asylum and immigration matters and criminal justice cooperation.

Common Foreign and Security Policy refers to the foreign relations of the EU other than the external aspects of the common market.

Common market is the term that was originally used to describe the project of European integration. For example, this term was used when Britain first joined to describe the European Communities. It focuses on the idea of market integration, which is the original core of the EU.

Conferral is a principle of EU law introduced by the Treaty of Maastricht, to the effect that the EU only possesses those powers actually conferred by the EU treaties.

European Economic Area (EEA) refers to an international organisation in Europe, and it regulates economic relations between the EU and Iceland, Liechtenstein and Norway.

European Free Trade Area (EFTA) refers to an international organisation in Europe that is an alternative free-trade association to the EU. Current members are Iceland, Liechtenstein, Norway and Switzerland.

Exclusive competence refers to those powers of the EU where the EU possesses sole power and the Member States individually have no remaining power. Although first established as result of doctrine of the ECJ, exclusive competences are now defined in Article 2(1) TFEU ('only the Union may legislate and adopt legally binding acts the Member States being able to do so themselves only if so empowered by the Union or for the implementation of Union acts'). Article 3(1) TFEU identifies the following exclusive competences: (a) customs union; (b) the establishing of the competition rules necessary for the functioning of the internal market; (c) monetary policy for the Member States whose currency is the Euro; (d) the conservation of marine biological resources under the common fisheries policy; (e) common commercial policy. Article 3(2) TFEU provides that the EU also has exclusive competence in international agreements if provided for in a legislative act of the Union or if necessary to enable the Union to exercise its internal competence or where the agreements relate to common EU policies.

External relations refers to the competence of the EU to deal with non–EU states and international organisations regarding EU laws and policies.

Internal market refers to market integration in the EU, but implies just internal aspects of market integration, and not external aspects (whereas as the term 'common market' can be taken to also include external aspects of integration).

Mixed agreements are international agreements where both the Member States and the EU are signatories. They arise where the EU does not have exclusive competence, i.e. where mixed competence exists.

Open method of coordination (OMC) is a kind of soft law instrument by which the Council of the EU sets objectives for the Member States to achieve, it involves a process of evaluation by the Council and the Commission of Member State implementation.

Parallelism is a doctrine developed in the case law of the ECJ whereby the EU has the same powers in external relations, in relations with states and organisations outside the EU, as it has in internal competence.

Power is another term for 'competence'.

Pre-emption is a doctrine related to parallelism and it entails that the Member States may not exercise competence in external relations when internal competence has been exercised to the extent of involving common policies.

Shared competence refers to areas of EU law and policy where both the Member States and the EU have competence, but where the Member States may only exercise their competence to the extent that the EU has not done so. It is defined in Article 2(2) TFEU.

Soft law is a term used to describe policy instruments that are expected to be followed and respected, but which are not legally enforceable.

Subsidiarity is a principle introduced generally in EU law by the Treaty of Maastricht. In essence, the principle states that competence or decision-making should be exercised at Member State level unless it can more effectively be exercised at EU level. It is set out in Article 5(3) TEU.

Supporting competence refers to areas of EU law and policy where both the Member States and the EU have some competence and the EU may only support and not replace Member State competence. It is defined in Article 2 TFEU.

'Yellow card' system is the procedure introduced under the Lisbon Treaty whereby national parliaments may formally express concern that proposed EU legislation may not comply with the principle of subsidiarity.[67]

TAKING THINGS FURTHER

W A Dashwood 'The limits of European community powers' 21 (1996) *European Law Review* 113 This is one of the first considered discussions of the limits of competence of the Community/Union.

R Schütze 'Lisbon and the federal order of competences: a prospective analysis' (2008) 33(5) *European Law Review* 709–22 This article provides a clear and helpful analysis of the impact of the Lisbon Treaty on the competences of the EU.

G Conway 'Conflicts of competence norms in EU law and the legal reasoning of the European Court of Justice' (2010) 11(9) *German Law Journal* This article discusses the nature of competence norms and different ways in which legal reasoning by the ECJ can deal with competence norms. It argues that the distinction between specific and general competences is very important for determining the limits of competence.

H Haukeland Fredriksen 'Bridging the widening gap between the EU treaties and the agreement on the European Economic Area' (2012) 18(6) *European Law Journal* 868–86 This article explores the relationship between the EEA and the EU, a little studied topic but a significant one, especially in light of possible UK withdrawal from the EU.

....

67 See art 12 TEU and arts 5 and 6 of the Protocol on the Application of Subsidiarity and Proportionality.

8

CHAPTER 8
FUNDAMENTAL RIGHTS AND CITIZENSHIP

This chapter examines the protection of fundamental human rights in the EU. Initially, the EU was not seen as being concerned with human rights and, instead, the focus was on what was then seen as an essentially economic idea of a common market. In response to concerns raised by national constitutional courts in some Member States, especially Germany, that human rights protection at then Community level needed to satisfy national constitutional guarantees of human rights, the European Court of Justice (ECJ) began to develop a human rights jurisprudence in its case law. The European Convention on Human Rights existed as a backdrop to these developments, and the ECJ in its case law drew inspiration from the ECHR, as well as from national constitutional traditions. In 2000, the EU adopted the EU Charter of Fundamental Rights, which was initially given soft-law status. The perhaps more obvious option of the EU acceding to the ECHR was only decided by the Lisbon Treaty, while the treaty also gave formal legal standing to the EU Charter. For the future, a major question in a human rights context in the EU will be how the relationship between the EU Charter and the ECHR will be worked out, including the relationship between the ECJ and the European Court of Human Rights.

AS YOU READ . . .

The key questions that will be answered in this chapter are as follows:

— To what extent does the EU have competence and jurisdiction in human rights matters?

— What are the obligations of the EU to uphold human rights?

— What are the main conceptual and philosophical issues that arise in the adjudication of rights, including the defining in judicial interpretation the concrete implications of abstractly stated rights and the problems of the legitimate limitations or restrictions on rights and of the conflict of rights?

- How did the human rights law of the EU develop over time? Relatedly, what is the relationship between the protection of human rights at national level and the protection of human rights in the EU?

- What is different about the protection of human rights in the EU compared to the protection of human rights in the Council of Europe legal system (the Council of Europe governs the European Convention on Human Rights)?

- What is the relationship between the fundamental freedom of movement principles and more traditional or typical understandings of human rights?

- How will the current relationship between the European Convention on Human Rights and human protection in EU law be affected by EU accession to the European Convention on Human Rights (ECHR)?

- What are the main features of the approach of the European Court of Justice (ECJ) to the protection of human rights?

- What does the concept of citizenship add to the rights of EU citizens?

8.1 INTRODUCTION

Although the EU was initially concerned with an essentially economic idea of a common market, this concept of a common market has a broad scope. EU competence, as a result, always had the potential to spill over in to matters that are not purely economic, meaning that human rights protection was always likely to become of concern for the EU institutions.

It was the European Court of Justice (ECJ) that first developed human rights principles in the then European Economic Community (EEC), the original treaties contained no references to human rights. Partly, the reason for this may have been that human rights were separately protected in Europe by the European Convention on Human Rights (ECHR)[1] of the Council of Europe (and indeed the relationship between EU law and the ECHR is becoming an increasingly important issue, as we will see below).

It is widely thought that the motivation of the ECJ for doing so was to protect the EEC from challenges in national systems on the ground that the protection of rights

---

1   ETS No 5.

in Community law at the time was not adequate. Perhaps the easiest way for the EU to address the issue of human rights would be for it simply to adopt the ECHR as part of EU law.

Indeed, the Lisbon Treaty provides for the EU to accede to the ECHR, in the same way a country accedes (although the EU is of course not a country and may never achieve the characteristics of a state). However, perhaps unsurprisingly for the EU, the least complicated route was not chosen to deal with the human rights issue. As well as acceding to the ECHR, the EU has adopted its own bill of rights called the EU Charter of Fundamental Rights.[2]

KEY LEARNING POINT

PARALLEL SYSTEMS OF HUMAN RIGHTS PROTECTION IN EUROPE: (I) THE ECHR; AND (II) THE EU CHARTER OF FUNDAMENTAL RIGHTS

For Member States of the EU, there are two systems of rights protection at European level. The EU has its own system, which is now based on the EU Charter of Fundamental Rights (adopted in 2000 and given formal legal standing in EU law by the Treaty of Lisbon in 2009). The ECHR has been in existence since the early 1950s and all EU Member States have also acceded to the ECHR.[3]

EXPLAINING THE LAW

THE STATUS IN UK LAW OF: (I) THE ECHR AND (II) THE EU CHARTER OF FUNDAMENTAL RIGHTS

The ECHR became a part of UK law with the coming into effect of the Human Rights Act 1998. Unlike EU law, the ECHR is not supported by any doctrine of supremacy. The two main elements of the HRA in this context are sections 3 and 4. Section 3 established a principle of conforming interpretation between the ECHR and UK statutory law (quite like the principle of indirect effect in EU law). Section 4 establishes that if UK primary legislation cannot be interpreted compatibly with the ECHR, the UK courts (High Court and above) may issue declaration of incompatibility. This declaration of incompatibility has no formal legal effect: it is up to Parliament to change the UK primary legislation or not.

Although the Treaty of Lisbon in Article 6 TEU fully incorporated the EU Charter of Fundamental Rights into EU law, a special Protocol on the application of the Charter of Fundamental Rights to Poland and the United Kingdom was attached

---

2 OJ C364/01 18.12.2000 at 1.
3 Ratification of the ECHR is now a condition of EU membership for any country planning to join the EU under the 'Copenhagen criteria' agreed by the European Council on 21–22 June 1993.

to the treaty at the insistence of the UK and Poland. This Protocol is intended to clarify the limits of the application of the EU Charter in the UK and Poland. In particular, the UK was concerned that the economic and social rights contained in Title IV of the EU Charter would provide the basis for the Court of Justice to undermine aspects of UK employment law, such as restrictions on the right to strike or rules on termination of employment.

Article 1(1) of the Protocol provides that the Charter does not extend the ability of the Court of Justice, or any court or tribunal of Poland or the UK, to find that the laws, practices or action of Poland or the UK are inconsistent with the fundamental rights, freedoms and principles that it reaffirms. Article 1(2) then states that, in particular, and for the avoidance of doubt, nothing in Title IV of the Charter creates justiciable rights applicable to Poland or the UK except in so far as Poland or the UK has provided for such rights in its national law. Finally, according to Article 2, to the extent that a provision of the Charter refers to national laws and practices, it shall only apply to Poland or the UK to the extent that the rights or principles it contains are recognised in the law or practices of Poland or the UK.

It has not happened to date that the UK courts have decided to avoid any Court of Justice judgment relating to the EU Charter on the basis of the Protocol. Nonetheless, the Protocol may have the effect of highlighting judicial activism by the Court in this sphere; to date, the Court of Justice has been quite cautious in its interpretation of the Charter. However, the potential for a conflict may be increased by the judgments of the Court treating the EU Charter as having horizontal application (discussed below in this chapter).

8.2 SUMMARISING THE CURRENT FRAMEWORK OF HUMAN RIGHTS PROTECTION IN THE EU

It is perhaps easiest to divide up the story of human rights protection in the EU into four stages. Initially, the ECJ refused to review Community law for its compliance with fundamental human rights contained in national constitutions for the reason that this approach would challenge the supremacy of Community law.[4] In the second stage, the ECJ reversed this approach: it started to review the compliance of then EEC law with human rights standards in order to protect the supremacy of Community law from

....

4   Case 1/58 *Stork v High Authority* [1959] ECR 17 at 26.

challenges in national courts that rights were not properly protected at Community (now Union) level. In doing so, the ECJ stated it would base its human rights protection both on the constitutional traditions of the Member States and on the ECHR, but the standard of protection developed was not simply based on either, it was an 'autonomous' Community standard.[5]

In this way, national constitutional law became a source of an independent standard that was part of Community law. More usually, the ECJ referred to the ECHR standards. A third stage was the adoption by the EU of the EU Charter on Fundamental Rights in 2000. However, the Charter was initially only given 'soft law status': it was not binding in EU law, though it could be referred to by the EU institutions in their decision-making as a standard to be followed. In effect, it became a source that the EU could use in human rights adjudication.

A fourth stage is the accession of the EU to the ECHR, which at the time of writing is due imminently (see section 8.5 below). Accession to the ECHR will raise the potentially complicated issue of the relationship between the EU Charter and the ECHR in EU law and the possibility for conflict between them. This is discussed further below.

KEY CASE *THE FIRST ECJ CASE ON HUMAN RIGHTS,* STAUDER v ULM

The first case in which the ECJ declared that human rights protection was a part of Community law was *Stauder v Ulm*.[6] The facts were somewhat unusual: it concerned a claim that a requirement that a person had to reveal their names in order to obtain a coupon from the government to buy subsidised butter had their right to privacy infringed. The scheme for subsidised butter was regulated under EEC law. The ECJ in its judgment said that there was no violation as the scheme could be implemented in such a way so as not to require the identification of the beneficiaries. Interpreted in that way, the ECJ said, the scheme 'contains nothing capable of prejudicing the fundamental human rights in the general principles of Community law and protected by the Court'.[7] The human rights that have been infringed were not really identified in the very brief judgment (only the Commission submitted observations and it referred to discrimination and a general principle of proportionality, but rejected the argument that either was infringed).

---

5   See Case 4/73 *Nold v Commission* [1974] ECR 491 at 503, where the ECJ stated that, in the context of property rights, account should be taken of the highest standard of protection amongst the Member States, which was Germany, although this may have been related to the facts, which arose in Germany.

6   Case 6/69 *Stauder v Ulm* [1969] ECR 419.

7   Ibid para 7.

The next major decisions were *Internationale Handelsgesellschaft* and *Nold*. In *Handelsgesellschaft*, the facts concerned the validity of a system of licensing exports which required sale of the goods for which the licence was granted within a specified period. If the goods were not exported in this period, a deposit was forfeited by the exporter. This scheme operated on the basis of EEC legislation. The German court considered this contrary to the German Basic Law (Constitution) provisions on economic liberty and proportionality of government measures. The ECJ was somewhat more specific on the place of human rights in Community law than it was in *Nold*:

> In fact, respect for fundamental rights forms an integral part of the general principles of law protected by the Court of Justice. The protection of such rights, whilst inspired by the constitutional traditions common to the Member States, must be ensured within the framework of the structure and objectives of the Community.[8]

Here the ECJ makes clear that while it will use the constitutional traditions of the Member States as an inspiration in its decisions on human rights, human rights protection must exist independently within the structure of Community law. This paragraph might be considered somewhat ambiguous on this point: does the structure of Community law ultimately have priority over human rights? We will return to this issue later.

The ECJ was criticised as regards its motivation for developing human rights protection as a part of Community law.

EXPLAINING THE LAW
───────

THE MOTIVATION OF THE ECJ IN THE EARLY HUMAN RIGHTS CASES

It is generally considered that, in developing human rights case law, the ECJ was concerned that Community acts would start to be reviewed by national courts for their compatibility with national law on human rights grounds. One former judge stated the ECJ was forced to do so to defend the independence of Community law from challenges at national level.[9] The most influential national system in this regard was Germany. The German Federal Constitutional Court declared that it would only accept the validity of EEC law in the German legal system *so long as* EEC law provided satisfactory protection of the human rights standards set out in the German Basic Law. As a result, this case law is sometimes described as the *sölange* cases (*sölange* is German for 'so long as'). As we saw in Chapter 6, similar case law exists in other Member States.

....

8   Case 11/70 *Nold v Commission* [1970] ECR 1161 para 4. On the facts, the ECJ found that there was no violation of human rights.

9   F Mancini 'The making of a constitution for Europe' (1989) 26 *Common Market Law Review* 595–614 at 609–11.

ANALYSING THE LAW

THE STATUS OF HUMAN RIGHTS AS 'GENERAL PRINCIPLES OF EU LAW'

Note that in *Nold* and subsequently, the ECJ identified human rights as 'general principles of Community law'. This is significant because general principles of law in any legal system are considered to be inherent in the legal system and thus independent of the legislature. By describing human rights as general principles of Community (now Union) law, the ECJ was allowing itself the freedom to develop case law on them independently of the legislature.

Recently, in *Åklagaren v Åkerberg Fransson*, the Court found that the application of the Charter where national legislation falls within the scope of EU law is the same as the previous scope human rights had when developed by the ECJ as general principles of EU law.[10] This implies its judgment in *ERT* (discussed below in this chapter in section 8.6) applies in the context of the Charter, i.e. that EU human rights apply to national law when applying a derogation from EU law. Article 6(1) TEU is unusual in that it contains a directive about how the Charter is to be interpreted:

> The rights, freedoms and principles in the Charter shall be interpreted in accordance with the general provisions in Title VII of the Charter governing its interpretation and application and with due regard to the explanations referred to in the Charter, that set out the sources of these provisions.

This suggest that the Court of Justice should interpret the rights carefully, according to the intentions of the Member States. In contrast, treating the Charter rights as general principles of law could indicate a more autonomous approach to interpretation. However, the text of Article 6(1) is probably too specific to allow the Court to be creative or activist without a political backlash from the Member States.

EXPLAINING THE LAW

STAGES OF HUMAN RIGHTS PROTECTION IN THE EU

First stage	Approach to human rights
1950s–late 1960s	ECJ refuses to review the compliance of Community acts with human rights standards in national law
Late 1960s–2000	ECJ decides to develop a human rights jurisprudence in its own case law

---

10 Case C–617/10 *Åklagaren v Åkerberg Fransson*, judgment of 26 February 2013 para 18.

| 2000–2009 | The ECJ continues its previous approach, but with the addition of the EU Charter of Fundamental Rights as one of the sources it draws on |
| 2009– | Under the Lisbon Treaty, the EU Charter of Fundamental Rights becomes formally a part of EU law *and* the EU is to accede to the ECHR |

The EU Charter goes beyond the basic standards of the ECHR in a number of respects and potentially on some points at least may conflict with it, although for the most part it incorporates ECHR standards wholesale. Two sources of human rights conflict could arise here: (a) between fundamental rights protection at EU level compared to the Member States and (b) between the ECHR and the EU Charter. The role of judicial interpretation in elaborating on the EU Charter will be decisive in addressing this potential of conflict.

KEY CASE *THE* MANGOLD *CASE AND THE HORIZONTAL APPLICATION OF THE EU CHARTER*

Mangold v Helm is a very significant judgment, as it illustrates the willingness of the Court of Justice to be creative in its approach to the interpretation of human rights in the EU legal order, but also illustrates that fundamental rights have a horizontal direct effect. The dispute was between a private employer and his employee. As seen in Chapter 5, the judgment was controversial because the EU declared a right against discrimination on grounds of age to be a general principle of EU law.

Mangold was confirmed by *Kücükdeveci* to the effect that the general principle of EU law of non-discrimination on grounds of age applied in relationships between private parties, i.e. had horizontal direct effect.[11] In *Kücükdeveci*, having worked for 10 years in Germany since the age of 18 for the company Swedex, Ms Kücükdeveci was dismissed with one month's notice in circumstances where the employer calculated the period of notice as if the employee had only three years' length of service. The employer's calculation was in accordance with the German legislation in force, providing that periods of employment completed before the age of 25 were not to be taken into account in this calculation. In *Kücükdeveci*, the Court concluded that under EU law, on the basis of non-discrimination on grounds of age, national legislation could not provide that periods of employment completed by an employee before reaching the age of 25 are not taken into account in calculating the notice period for dismissal.

In *Mangold* and in *Kücükdeveci*, the Court seemed to implicitly assume that general principles of law are capable of conferring substantive rights and

---

11 Case C–555/07 *Kücükdeveci* [2010] ECR I–365.

imposing substantive obligations in legal relations between individuals, but did not develop any clear doctrine. Around the same time, however, as Advocate General Kokott noted in *Roca Álvarez v Sesa Start España ETTSA*: 'prior to any further development . . . it would be necessary to discuss the dogmatic foundations of that contested horizontal direct effect and its limits'.[12]

8.3 CONCEPTUAL ISSUES IN THE LEGAL PROTECTION OF HUMAN RIGHTS

In this section we will look briefly at two related issues: (a) problems of interpretation that arise in the adjudication of human rights cases by the courts generally and in the EU, and, relatedly, (b) the problems of determining the legitimate limitations on rights and of resolving conflicts of rights. Human rights clauses present a particular problem for legal reasoning because of their relative *interpretative indeterminacy*. This means that their meaning is not self-evident and can be open to different interpretations. Another way of putting this is that bills of rights are often under-specified.

ANALYSING THE LAW

ABSTRACTION IN THE DEFINITION OF RIGHTS, RIGHTS ARE OFTEN UNDER-SPECIFIED

Rights are usually abstractly defined, as are the limitations on them. There can be reasonable disagreement about the scope of rights and of their limitations. For example, how far is freedom of expression to be limited in order to protect privacy?

The abstract text of a right to freedom of expression or a right to privacy will not answer this question. Interpretation, therefore, becomes of central importance.

Secondly, rights often conflict. Traditional rules of legal reasoning for resolving conflicts such as *lex posterior* (apply the most recently enacted law) and *lex specialis* (apply the most specific law) may not be that helpful when dealing with conflicts between rights.[13]

---

12 Case C–104/09 *Roca Álvarez v Sesa Start España ETTSA* [2010] ECRI–8661 para 55. Unlike in *Mangold*, in *Kücükdeveci*, the Court of Justice made a reference to the Charter: 'It should also be noted that art 6(1) TEU provides that the Charter of Fundamental Rights of the European Union is to have the same legal value as the treaties. Under art 21(1) of the Charter, "[a]ny discrimination based on . . . age . . . shall be prohibited"' (para 22).

13 E-U Petersmann 'Time for a United Nations "global compact" for integrating human rights into the law of worldwide organizations: lessons from European integration' (2002) 13(3) *European Journal of International Law* 621–50 at 635; L Zucca *Constitutional Dilemmas: Conflicts of Fundamental Legal Rights in Europe and the USA* (Oxford University Press 2007) 54–55.

Rights provisions are usually all enacted simultaneously, meaning *lex posterior* does not provide a solution: it is not possible to apply the most recently enacted right in this situation, because both rights in conflict will have been enacted at the same time. Even if rights were enacted at different times, their normative status as inherent 'goods' makes questionable any *lex posterior* rule, i.e. it is not obvious that being more recently enacted makes one right more important than another.

Lex specialis is unlikely to be helpful in many cases of rights conflicts because these rights clauses, the way they currently tend to be drafted, generally tend to have a relatively high degree of generality, and indeed some degree of generality is necessary.[14] When two abstract rights conflict, it is not possible to decide between them on the basis of specificity: they may well be both equally unspecific.

Since such rights apply across all public law, it is very difficult to enumerate them in considerable detail relative to the circumstances of their application (detention and trial rights may be something of an exception under current practice[15]), i.e. competing rights claims in abstract Bill of Rights may not be resolvable on grounds of specificity, since they may be expressed in equally general terms. However, the articulation of rights claims at a very high level of generality is not inevitable either, as the trial rights (Article 6 of the ECHR) example demonstrates, and it is certainly true that more could be done to specify rights so as to reduce indeterminacy and differences of interpretation.

ANALYSING THE LAW

CONFLICTS OF RIGHTS AND INTERESTS AND THE IDEA OF BALANCING

A metaphor that is often used to describe what judges should do when faced with a conflict of rights or a conflict between a claimed right and a legitimate limitation on rights is 'balancing'. The judges must weigh up competing claims and decide which deserves to be treated as more important. Some scholars and others, however, criticise the idea of balancing as a statement of what judges need to do, but not a solution as to how to do it.[16]

The same criticism can be made of the idea of proportionality, which also involves balancing. Sometimes proportionality can be applied in a straightforward, factual way, i.e. when it can be shown that 'a sledgehammer is being used to crack a nut'. But often, proportionality, especially in a human rights context, involves weighing up two abstract values (e.g. freedom of expression versus privacy), in which case it is hard to say that there is a single correct answer to what is a disproportionate interference with privacy in the interests of freedom of expression.

14 F Schauer 'The generality of rights' (2000) 6(3) *Legal Theory* 323–36 at 329–30.
15 See arts 5 and 6 of the ECHR.
16 T A Aleinikoff 'Constitutional law in the age of balancing' (1987) 96(5) *Yale Law Journal* 943–1005.

This criticism suggests that balancing really involves judges making a moral decision and that this might vary from court to court or judge to judge. One concept that can help decide how to balance conflicting rights is the idea of a hierarchy of rights. This idea has not been invoked much by the European courts. However, the European Court of Human Rights has recognised the principle of hierarchy in describing the right to life as 'the supreme value in the hierarchy of human rights'.[17]

In the background to this issue of interpreting rights is a more basic issue of what is distinct about rights compared to other legal interests, e.g. the community interest. Why is it important to define individual human rights in advance relative to other interests?

ANALYSING THE LAW

RIGHTS VERSUS UTILITY IN THE EU

The idea of rights has often been contrasted with the philosophy of utilitarianism. Traditional utilitarianism proposes that the state or government should protect by law whatever achieves 'the greatest happiness for the greatest number'. Although different versions of utilitarianism have been developed, a consistent criticism of it as a political philosophy is that it fails to take into account minority rights: under (traditional) utilitarianism, what is best for the majority always prevails. We can see significant echoes of this debate in the way the EU Charter of Fundamental Rights is drafted, as will be discussed below: what are the limitations that can be placed on rights in the general interest of the EU? Sometimes, the ECJ is a bit ambiguous about this in its case law, although it is a difficult issue.

8.4 THE EU CHARTER OF FUNDAMENTAL RIGHTS

The EU Charter of Fundamental Rights offers a mixture of quite detailed statements of rights in parts and some quite vaguely stated rights in other parts. However, it is greatly elaborated on through accompanying Explanations formally adopted by the Member States.[18] In several places,[19] it is surprisingly brief, while some new rights or

---

17 See e.g. *Streletz, Kessler and Krenz v Germany* (2001) EHRR 31 paras 72–94. See also *Tysiqc v Poland* (2007) 45 EHRR 42 para 102.

18 Bureau of the Convention on a Charter of Fundamental Rights of the European Union *Explanations by the Convention relating to the Charter of Fundamental Rights* document Convent 49 of 11.10.2000 Charte 4473/00 Convent 50, OJ C 326 26.10.2012 p. 391. The Explanations have since been updated as regards some details, see: OJ C 303 14.12.2007 p. 17.

19 It is much briefer than the ECHR on the limitations on rights, which are set out in a general clause in art 52.1, rather than being set out for each individual right, as under the ECHR: as noted in R Alonso García 'The general provisions of the Charter of Fundamental Rights of the European Union' (2002) 8(4) *European Law Journal* 492–514 at 497.

novel clauses are addressed specifically that are not found in other Bills of Rights. For example, Article 3.2 contains a prohibition on eugenics and reproductive cloning[20] and Article 29 a right of access to a placement service. Some provisions are very brief and do not even mention the issue of the limits on a right or the grounds on which it may be permissibly restricted.

However, Article 6(1) of the TEU works toward specifying the content of the Charter in stating that 'rights, freedoms and principles in the Charter shall be interpreted in accordance with the general provisions in Title VII of the Charter governing its interpretation and application and with due regard to the Explanations referred to in the Charter, that set out the sources of those provisions'. The reference to the Explanations or Notes from the Praesidium[21] accompanying the text of the Charter appears to endorse originalist interpretation, i.e. the Charter should be interpreted as the Member States intended (although this kind of interpretation of interpretation is not very common in EU law generally). Moreover, Article 52(3) provides:

> Insofar as this Charter contains rights which correspond to rights guaranteed by the Convention for the Protection of Human Rights and Fundamental Freedoms, the meaning and scope of those rights shall be the same as those laid down by the said Convention. This provision shall not prevent Union law providing more extensive protection.

EXPLAINING THE LAW

ADOPTING ECHR STANDARDS AS PART OF THE EU CHARTER OF FUNDAMENTAL RIGHTS

The Explanations that accompany the Charter refer in a wholesale way to ECHR standards to flesh out the bare essentials contained in the Charter itself, and this reflects what is said in Article 52(3) of the EU Charter just noted. In many instances, the Explanations start by stating that the content of the rights is the same as the equivalent provisions of the ECHR. At the end of the Explanations, 12 provisions are listed as corresponding with the ECHR,[22] while the clear implication from this list (and from Article 52(3) of the Charter stating there is correspondence between them) is that case law from Strasbourg also applies to EU law.[23]

---

20 A Torres Pérez *Conflicts of Rights in the European Union* (Oxford University Press 2009) 11 notes EU Charter rights mostly reflect existing rights, and that examples of novelty are art 3.2 prohibiting eugenic practices and reproductive cloning and article 5.3 banning the trafficking of human beings, along with Title IV on social rights.

21 Text of the Explanations relating to the complete text of the Charter (n 18).

22 Ibid 49–50.

23 Alonso García (n 19) 498. This could be further inferred from the statement in the preamble of the EU Charter that the Charter reaffirms, inter alia, the ECHR, and is further confirmed in the details of the Explanations themselves.

The fact over 50 years of ECHR case law has now built up a recognisable body of standards[24] goes a long way to achieving some predictability in interpretation, albeit that many of the standards will have been judge-made because the text of the ECHR is under-specified.

MAKING CONNECTIONS
+++++++++++++++++++

THE EU CHARTER ON FUNDAMENTAL RIGHTS AND THE ECHR
There is a large degree of overlap, and the EU Charter itself expressly states in Article 52(3) where it adopts corresponding rights to the ECHR, the content of the EU Charter is the same:

> 3. In so far as this Charter contains rights which correspond to rights guaranteed by the Convention for the Protection of Human Rights and Fundamental Freedoms, the meaning and scope of those rights shall be the same as those laid down by the said Convention. This provision shall not prevent Union law providing more extensive protection.

In effect, this gives the jurisprudence of the European Court of Human Rights indirect status in EU law. The EU Charter is more specific and enumerates more rights (although the ECHR itself has been elaborated on or added to in a number of Protocols).

The following table sets out the EU Charter rights compared to the equivalent provisions under the ECHR and Protocols to the ECHR.

	EU Charter of Fundamental Rights	ECHR equivalent
Article 1	Human dignity	
Article 2	Right to life	Article 2
Article 3	Right to integrity of the person	
Article 4	Prohibition of torture of inhuman and degrading treatment or punishment	Article 3

---

24 There is a possible 'get-out clause' in the Explanations to art 52.3 of the EU Charter regarding the autonomy of EU Law, which state: 'This means in particular that the legislator, in laying down limitations to those rights, must comply with the same standards as are fixed by the detailed limitation arrangements laid down by the ECHR without thereby adversely affecting the autonomy of Community law and of that of the Court of Justice of the European Communities' (48 (33)). However, now that the Lisbon Treaty requires accession to the ECHR (art 6(2) TEU), the balance seems to have tilted more strongly in favour of the Strasbourg standard rather than any Union claim to autonomous standards in conflict with the ECHR. The firm commitment by the Member States to the ECHR may reflect what Torres Pérez (n 20) 14 describes as 'increasing uneasiness' with ECJ rights discourse.

Article 5	Prohibition of slavery and forced labour	Article 4
Article 6	Right to liberty and security	Article 5
Article 7	Respect for private and family life	Article 8
Article 8	Protection of personal data	Article 8
Article 9	Right to marry and found a family	Article 12
Article 10	Freedom of thought, conscience and religion	Article 9, Article 16
Article 11	Freedom of expression and information	Article 10
Article 12	Freedom of assembly and association	Article 11
Article 13	Freedom of the arts and sciences	
Article 14	Right to education	Article 2, Protocol 1[25]
Article 15	Freedom to choose an occupation and right to engage in work	
Article 16	Freedom to conduct a business	
Article 17	Right to property	Article 1, Protocol 1
Article 18	Right to asylum	
Article 19	Protection in the event of removal, expulsion or extradition	Article 4, Protocol 4;[26] Article 1, Protocol 7 (ECHR provisions relate to aliens)
Article 20	Equality before the law	
Article 21	Non-discrimination	Article 14; Article 1, Protocol 12[27]
Article 22	Cultural, religious and linguistic diversity	
Article 23	Equality between men and women	Article 14; Article 5, Protocol 7[28]
Article 24	Right of the child	
Article 25	Rights of the elderly	
Article 26	Integration of persons with disabilities	

25 ETS No 9.
26 ETS No 46.
27 ETS No 177.
28 ETS No 117.

Article 51	Scope – specifies Charter applies to the EU institutions with regard to subsidiarity and to the Member State implementing EU law + that the Charter does not create any new EU competence	
Article 52	Scope of guaranteed rights – specifies general grounds of limitation of rights, conditions and limits in treaties apply, and correspondence with ECHR	Article 18
Article 53	Level of protection – states Charter without prejudice to protection of rights in other international legal instruments	Not applicable
Article 54	Prohibition of abuse of rights	Article 17

EXPLAINING THE LAW

EU ACCESSION TO THE ECHR AND ITS PROTOCOLS

Under the accession agreement of the EU to the ECHR (see section 8.5 below), the EU will accede to the ECHR itself, the first protocol, and the Protocol No 6. The reason for this is that not all Member States have acceded to all the other protocols to the ECHR, and the idea is to ensure a consistent, minimum approach across the Member States.[29]

ANALYSING THE LAW

THE CONTINUING POSSIBILITY OF CONFLICTS BETWEEN THE ECHR AND THE EU CHARTER OF FUNDAMENTAL RIGHTS

Although Article 6(1) TEU and accompanying explanations to the EU Charter considerably reduce the possibility for conflict with the ECHR by stating that the EU Charter is to be interpreted consistently with the ECHR, the possibility for conflict between the two is not fully removed. More generally, Article 53 of the EU Charter states in effect that it is without prejudice to human rights protection under international law and national law. The actual wording states 'Nothing in this Charter shall be interpreted as restricting or adversely affecting . . .'. At first glance this would seem to subordinate the EU Charter

---

29 P Gragl 'A giant leap for European human rights: the final agreement on the European Union's accession to the European Convention on Human Rights' (2014) 51(1) *Common Market Law Review* 13–58 at 17–18.

to all other existing human rights instruments to which the Member States are bound, but the Explanations state that it is just intended that the Charter is to maintain the level of protection already existing.[30] If the ECHR is interpreted as requiring a higher standard, which could happen because the ECHR is interpreted in an evolutionary way, i.e. its interpretation is updated by the European Court of Human Rights, then a conflict could occur with the lower standard protected in EU law. Article 52(3) of the EU Charter refers to the possibility of the EU providing more protection for a particular right, but does not address the possibility of EU law providing less protection or different protection.[31]

As an example of under-specification in the EU Charter itself, no hierarchy is established between more traditional rights and the free movement principles. The free movement principles are converted into the language of rights, in the form of a freedom to choose an occupation and right to engage in work (applicable to any EU citizen in any Member State) (Article 15) and the freedom to conduct a business (in accordance with Community law) (Article 16). We will examine this further in section 8.6 below.

8.5 THE LISBON TREATY AND EU ACCESSION TO THE ECHR

The Lisbon Treaty in Article 6(2) provides for the EU to accede to the ECHR, just as a country would.[32] Article 6(2) states:

The Union shall accede to the European Convention for the Protection of Human Rights and Fundamental Freedoms. Such accession shall not affect the Union's competences as defined in the Treaties.

Currently, both the EU and Council of Europe are preparing for EU accession. The ECHR is already an important source drawn on by the ECJ in its case law on human

---

30 Text of the Explanations relating to the complete text of the Charter 50 (and 35, which states more briefly and more clearly that: 'This provision is intended to maintain the level of protection currently afforded . . .').

31 See the Opinion of Advocate General Maduro in Case C–465/07 *Meki Elgafaji and Noor Elgafaji v Staatssecretaris van Justitie* [2009] ECR I–921 (9 September 2008), where he stated 'Community provisions, irrespective of which provisions are concerned, are given an independent interpretation which cannot therefore vary according to and/or be dependent on developments in the case-law of the European Court of Human Rights' (para 18).

32 Within the Council of Europe system, art 59(2) of Protocol No 14 provides the legal basis for EU accession to the ECHR.

rights. There are several implications or issues that will arise with the accession by the EU to the ECHR:

(1) it will make more systematic the reliance of the EU on ECHR standards in its activities and in ECJ case law (somewhat similarly to the way the Human Rights Act 1998 did in UK public law);
(2) whether the ECHR will have a higher status in EU law than EU law itself, i.e. whether the ECHR will have supremacy;
(3) related to the second point, the relationship between the ECJ and the European Court of Human Rights will need to be worked out;
(4) the extent of divergences between EU Charter and the ECHR, already discussed, is not great, but some divergence may occur, and it is in this situation, in particular, that the supremacy issue would arise.

The issue of conflict between EU law and the ECHR predates the adoption of the EU Charter and the European Court of Human Rights has arrived at a solution in the *Bosphorus* case. In this judgment, the Strasbourg Court stated that it would presume compliance by the EU with the ECHR.[33] An example is *Matthews v United Kingdom*.[34] Here, the European Court of Human Rights was willing to review on human rights grounds an EU law, although the EU law in question did not come within the jurisdiction of the ECJ.[35] The facts concerned the right of residents of Gibraltar who were EU citizens to vote in elections of the European Parliament.

> **KEY CASE** *THE EQUIVALENT PROTECTION DOCTRINE IN THE BOSPHORUS CASE*
>
> The *Bosphorus* case confirmed earlier case law from the Strasbourg Court[36] that the role of the ECJ in reviewing EU law for human rights protection provided 'equivalent protection' as available under the ECHR and so the Strasbourg Court did not need to exercise a second review. However, this is a presumption, and it may be that the European Court of Human Rights would be persuaded in particular case to take a different approach and to test the compatibility of EU law with the ECHR, as occurred in the *Matthews* case.

---

33 *Bosphorus Hava Yollari Turizm v Ireland* (2006) 42 EHRR 1.

34 1999-I 251, (1999) 28 EHRR 361.

35 Act Concerning the Election of the Representatives of the European Parliament by Direct European Suffrage, which was based on the EC Treaty and has been ratified by the Member States. It was found to be contrary to art 3 Protocol No 1 to the ECHR.

36 See the decision on the European Commission on Human Rights (this was previously an organ under the European Court of Human Rights but has since been abolished) in *M & Co v Federal Republic of Germany* (1990) 64 DR 138. For background discussion see C Costello 'The *Bosphorus* ruling of the European Court of Human Rights' (2006) 6(1) *European Human Rights Law Review* 87–130.

In December 2014, the ECJ delivered its judgment in *Opinion 2/13* on the accession agreement of the EU to the ECHR drafted by the Commission.[37] The ECJ found the draft accession agreement to be incompatible with EU law on numerous grounds, primarily: that it failed to coordinate higher protection than the ECHR that Member States could apply under Article 53 ECHR with Article 53 of the EU Charter; that it allowed Member States to be a party against each other before the European Court of Human Rights; that a problem could arise in the future under Protocol 16 to the ECHR whereby Member States could request an advisory opinion to the Strasbourg Court in a way incompatible with the preliminary references procedure under Article 267 TFEU; that it did not preserve the exclusive jurisdiction of the ECJ under Article 344 TFEU; that it provided the possibility for the Strasbourg court to rule on the division of powers between the EU and the Member States and on EU secondary law independently of an ECJ interpretation of them; that it did not provide for the Strasbourg court to be bound by a judgment of the ECJ on the same issue of law; and that it could provide for Strasbourg to have jurisdiction over an aspect of the Common Foreign Security Policy over which the ECJ did not have jurisdiction. Overall, a key concern of the Court of Justice is that the draft accession agreement did not preserve its own institutional powers as the Court of the EU to give a definitive interpretation of EU law, including on the division of powers between the EU and the Member States. National supreme and constitutional courts do not object to the role of the European Court of Human Rights in national systems on comparable grounds. It is likely that the Strasbourg court would be sensitive of its own initiative to many of these concerns, but the Court of Justice clearly wishes them to be addressed in advance.

8.6 THE RELATIONSHIP BETWEEN THE FUNDAMENTAL FREEDOMS OF MOVEMENT, FUNDAMENTAL HUMAN RIGHTS AND OTHER LEGAL CONSIDERATIONS

In the 1990s, a well known debate took place in which the academics Coppel and O'Neill claimed the ECJ manipulated fundamental rights in its legal reasoning to enhance its own role and power and encourage further integration, which prompted a detailed response from the academics Weiler and Lockhart defending the ECJ.[38] Coppel

---

37 *Opinion 2/13 on Accession of the EU to the ECHR* judgment of 18th December 2014.
38 J Coppel, A O'Neill 'The European Court of Justice: taking rights seriously?' (1992) 29 *Common Market Law Review* 669–92; J H Weiler, N J S Lockhart 'Taking rights seriously: The European Court of Justice and its fundamental rights jurisprudence: Part I' (1995) 32 *Common Market Law Review* 51–94; J H Weiler, N J S Lockhart 'Taking rights seriously: the European Court of Justice and its fundamental rights jurisprudence: Part II' (1995) 32 *Common Market Law Review* 579–627.

and O'Neill began by noting their purpose was to question the easy assumption that
the use of the language of fundamental rights by the ECJ translated into the actual
protection of rights within the then EC. The motivation of the ECJ in its early rights
case law was, they noted, beyond question about securing its own supremacy claims
rather than rights *per se*,[39] while a reading of its more recent case law suggested an
'offensive' use of rights to extend the influence of the EC/EU over the Member States
(as opposed to a defensive use to maintain supremacy). In other words, rights were being
used to enhance integration at the expense of Member State autonomy.[40]

First, Coppel and O'Neill noted that the ECJ had begun to apply Community rights
norms directly to national legal acts, instead of confining them to Community law.
Rutili[41] signalled this trend in referring to the ECHR as a limit on the derogation by
Member States from the free movement of workers principles. The ECJ noted that
the exceptions in the treaties to free movement were to be determined by Community
law and reflected the limitations permitted in the ECHR under Articles 8 (right to
respect for private and family life), 9 (freedom of thought, conscience, and religion),
10 (freedom of expression) and 11 (freedom of assembly and association).[42] The facts
of *Rutili* concerned an Italian national living in France, who was restricted from living
in certain areas of France (amongst the Court's conclusions were that this was only
permissible if similar restrictions would also be imposed on French nationals in this
situation).

The first case where the ECJ openly assessed the validity of an act of a Member
State on the basis of fundamental rights considerations was *Wachauf v Federal Republic
of Germany*.[43] On the facts, German law required the consent of a landowner for
a farmer to be able to surrender to and claim compensation from the state for his
milk production quota, which quota was provided for under Community secondary
law.[44] The ECJ held that this violated a fundamental right of the farmer concerned,
in depriving the lessee, without compensation, of the fruits of his labour and of his
investments in the tenanted holding. The Court held and that the Member States must,
so far as possible, implement Community law in accordance with the protection of
fundamental rights in the Community legal order.[45] The ECJ went on to note that
the Community law in question could have been implemented so as to comply with
fundamental rights; in effect, therefore, the problem lay with implementation.[46]

----

39 Coppel and O'Neill (n 38) 669, 672, citing e.g. Weiler's comment that the 'deep structure' of the early rights case
     law was 'all about supremacy'. See J H H Weiler, A Cassese and A Clapham (eds) *Human Rights and the European
     Community Vol II* (Nomos 1990) 580–81.
40 Coppel and O'Neill (n 38) 669–70.
41 Case 36/75 [1975] ECR 1219.
42 Ibid para 32.
43 Case 5/88 [1989] ECR 2609.
44 Ibid, paras 1, 5.
45 Case 5/88 paras 16, 19.
46 Ibid para 22.

ANALYSING THE LAW

THE ECJ IN *WACHAUF*: NO RIGHT IS ABSOLUTE?

Interestingly, the ECJ also stated in *Wachauf* that no fundamental right was absolute and that account had to be taken of its social function.[47] Restrictions were to be allowed where they 'correspond to objectives of general interest pursued by the Community and do not constitute, with regard to the aim pursued, a disproportionate and intolerable interference, impairing the very substance of those rights'.[48] This might be taken to reflect a certain ambiguity in ECJ case law as to the fundamental status of human rights relative to the structure and goal of integration. On the other hand, the ECJ recognises that the very substance of the rights cannot be interfered with.

Generally in human rights law, not many rights are considered absolute in the sense that they can never be subject to restriction. A right that can never be subject to restriction is, in the language of contemporary human rights law, 'non-derogable'. Under the ECHR, the following are described in non-derogable terms: the right to life excepting death resulting from lawful action in war (Article 2); the ban on torture or inhuman or degrading treatment (Article 3); the prohibition on slavery or servitude (Article 4(1)); and the prohibition on retroactive criminal penalties (Article 7).

The EU Charter of Fundamental Rights does not identify any particular rights as non-derogable. In international law, certain principles are considered to be non-derogable and these are referred to as 'peremptory norms' or *jus cogens*.[49] However, beyond the prohibitions on genocide and slavery, there is not much agreement on what can be considered *jus cogens*.

The ECJ judgment in *ERT* is worth quoting at some length because it provides a good summary of the approach of the ECJ to human rights and to an issue that has provoked debate and criticism:

41 With regard to Article 10 of the European Convention on Human Rights, referred to in the ninth and tenth questions, it must first be pointed out that, as the Court has consistently held, fundamental rights form an integral part of the general principles of law, the observance of which it ensures. For that purpose the Court draws inspiration from the constitutional traditions common to the Member States and from the guidelines supplied by international treaties for the protection of human rights on which the Member States have collaborated or of which they are signatories

---

47 Case 5/88 para 18.

48 Ibid para 18.

49 Article 53 of the Vienna Convention on the Law of Treaties 1155 UNTS 331, 8 ILM 679 (1969), which states that a treaty provision shall be void if it conflicts with *jus cogens*.

(see, in particular, the judgment in Case C–4/73 *Nold v Commission* [1974] ECR 491, paragraph 13). The European Convention on Human Rights has special significance in that respect (see in particular Case C–222/84 *Johnston v Chief Constable of the Royal Ulster Constabulary* [1986] ECR 1651, paragraph 18). It follows that, as the Court held in its judgment in Case C–5/88 *Wachauf Federal Republic of Germany* [1989] ECR 2609, paragraph 19, the Community cannot accept measures which are incompatible with observance of the human rights thus recognized and guaranteed.

42 As the Court has held (see the judgment in Joined Cases C–60 & C–61/84 *Cinéthèque v Fédération Nationale des Cinémas Français* [1985] ECR 2605, paragraph 25, and the judgment in Case C–12/86 *Demirel v Stadt Schwaebisch Gmund* [1987] ECR 3719, paragraph 28), it has no power to examine the compatibility with the European Convention on Human Rights of national rules which do not fall within the scope of Community law. On the other hand, where such rules do fall within the scope of Community law, and reference is made to the Court for a preliminary ruling, it must provide all the criteria of interpretation needed by the national court to determine whether those rules are compatible with the fundamental rights the observance of which the Court ensures and which derive in particular from the European Convention on Human Rights.

43 In particular, where a Member State relies on the combined provisions of Articles 56 and 66 in order to justify rules which are likely to obstruct the exercise of the freedom to provide services, such justification, provided for by Community law, must be interpreted in the light of the general principles of law and in particular of fundamental rights. Thus the national rules in question can fall under the exceptions provided for by *the combined provisions of Articles 56 and 66 only if they are compatible with the fundamental rights the observance of which is ensured by the Court.*

The facts of *ERT* concerned the granting of a television monopoly for considerations of a non-economic nature relating to the public interest. The decision in *ERT* allowed the Court of Justice to scrutinise national implementing measures in cases such as *Carpenter*, *Zhu* and *Chen* (discussed below under citizenship).

KEY LEARNING POINT
....

NATIONAL IMPLEMENTATION OF EU LAW MUST COMPLY WITH FUNDAMENTAL RIGHTS PROTECTED BY EU LAW AND THIS ALSO APPLIES TO NATIONAL DEROGATIONS FROM EU LAW

The view that national implementing measures had to comply with Community/ EU fundamental rights was confirmed in *ERT*.[50] Coppel and O'Neill identified this and other case law[51] as a trend of assessing Member States' public policy

---

50 Case C–260/89 *ERT* [1991] I–2925 para 41.
51 Case 353/89 *Commission v Netherlands* [1991] ECR I–4069.

derogations from EU law from the standpoint of Community/EU law protection of fundamental rights.[52] In other words, even when involving derogations from EU law, e.g. under freedom of movement, the Member States must comply with EU protection of human rights. For Coppel and O'Neill, this seemed like the ECJ was using human rights to encroach upon the competences of the Member States. One aspect of national implementation that the ECJ tends to be very willing to review is their proportionality.[53]

In *SPUC v Grogan*, the ECJ classified abortion as a service and held that Ireland could prohibit the provision of information in circumstances where such provision was not part of an economic activity. Coppel and O'Neill criticised this as an avoidance of the human rights issue involved, which was instead dealt with as a matter of technical classification.[54] Instead of relating to the issue of abortion in terms of 'a profound moral dilemma', that 'abortions are carried out for money . . . is the only relevant factor for the Court'.[55]

In defence of the ECJ, Weiler and Lockhart note that the preliminary reference was itself framed in technical terms, asking the question: 'Does the organized activity or process of carrying out an abortion . . . come within the definition of "services" . . . [in] Article 60 of the Treaty . . .'[56] and that the broader rights issue was moot on the facts and did not need to be addressed.[57]

Coppel and O'Neill then went on to argue that fundamental human rights should be seen as having more importance than the fundamental freedoms of movement. They cite ECJ case law equating the free movement provisions of EU law with fundamental rights. In *Heylens*, for example, the ECJ stated:

> Since free access to employment is a fundamental right which the Treaty confers individually on each worker of the Community, the existence of a remedy of a judicial nature against any decision of a national authority refusing the benefit of that right is essential in order to secure for the individual effective protection for this right.[58]

This seems to consider that there is no hierarchical distinction between the free movement market principles and human rights and this undermines the idea that the

---

52 Coppel and O'Neill (n 38) 677.

53 See e.g. Case 227/82 *Van Bennekom* [1983] ECR 3883 para 40; Case C–42/02 *Lindman* [2003] ECR I–13519 para 25.

54 They also noted its inconsistency with a statement by Advocate General Werner in Case 7/76 *IRCA* [1976] ECR 1213 at 1237, that a fundamental right 'recognized and protected by the Constitution of any Member State must be recognized and protected by Community law'. See Coppel and O'Neill (n 38) 685–86.

55 Coppel and O'Neill (n 38) 687.

56 Weiler and Lockhart (n 38) 599.

57 Ibid 601.

58 Case 222/86 *UNECTEF v Heylens* [1987] ECR 4098 para 14. Petersmann suggests that in the EU the judicial protection of market freedoms and the non-discrimination principle are fundamental individual rights, although he suggests that the ECJ avoids human rights language for the common market freedoms, for the right to property, and the freedom to pursue a trade or business. See E-U Petersmann (n 13) 626–28.

ECJ can be trusted to protect fundamental rights.[59] In response, Weiler and Lockhart contend the fact the ECJ uses the term 'fundamental' to describe two things, human rights and free movement, does not have to mean both are equally important.[60] In reply to this latter point, it remains the case, however, that the ECJ did not attempt, and to date has not, to explain whether it considered the freedom of movement principles to have the same status as fundamental rights.

Since this academic debate took place in the 1990s, the adoption of the EU Charter of Fundamental Rights was an opportunity for the Member States to decide the relationship between the fundamental freedoms of movement and human rights. In the Charter, Article 45 states that: 'Every citizen of the Union has the right to move and reside freely within the territory of the Member States'. However, the explanations accompanying the EU Charter do not discuss how 'freedom of movement and residence' (the heading of Article 45) relate to other rights. The case law of the ECJ tends to still describe the freedom of movement principles as 'fundamental'.

Similarly, the EU Charter could be considered quite ambiguous on the status of human rights relative to other interests. Article 52.1 on the scope of guaranteed rights states:

> Any limitation on the exercise of rights and freedoms recognised by this Charter must be provided for by law and respect the essence of those rights and freedoms. Subject to the principle of proportionality, limitations may be made only if they are necessary and genuinely meet objectives of general interest recognised by the Union or the need to protect the rights and freedoms of others.

This paragraph recognises the possibility of conflict (i) between rights and (ii) between rights and the general interest and for rights to be limited in order to resolve the conflict. Two conflicting tendencies can be discerned from the wording. On the one hand, the wording, echoing the formula in *Wachauf*, that rights have an essence that may not be impaired at all suggests a strong conception of rights. However, this essence is not identified. Moreover, there is a vague reference to a 'general interest' as a ground for limiting rights.[61] The Explanations to the Charter elaborate on the meaning of 'general interest' and state:

> The reference to general interests recognised by the Union covers both the objectives mentioned in Article 2 [of the European Community Treaty] and other interests protected by specific Treaty provisions such as Articles 30 or 39(3) of the EC Treaty.[62]

---

59 Coppel and O'Neill (n 38) 692. See also Case 240/83 *Procureur de la République v ADBHU* [1995] ECR 531.
60 Weiler and Lockhart (n 38) 594–95.
61 The expression in the Charter reflects its use in ECJ case law: see e.g. Case 44/79 *Hauer v Land Rheinland Pfalz* [1979] ECR 3727 at 3746.
62 Explanations relating to the Charter of Fundamental Rights (n 18), explanation to art 52.

ANALYSING THE LAW
_____

**THE EU CHARTER IS DOUBTFUL ON THE STATUS OF
TRADE-RELATED RIGHTS?**

The Explanations seem to reflect a doubtful status of trade-based rights by
stating that Article 16 may be subject to the limitations in Article 52.1 of the
Charter and that Article 16 is 'Of course . . . to be exercised with respect for
Community law and national legislation'.[63] Article 52.2 provides that: 'Rights
recognised by this shall be exercised under the conditions and within the limits
defined by those Charters which are based on the Community Treaties or the
Treaty on European Union Treaties'.

Overall, the EU Charter on Fundamental Rights mostly confirms ECHR standards. It
does contain some additional rights as noted above, e.g. the right to a placement service.
The possibility for conflict between the ECHR and the EU Charter is not removed
despite Article 52(3) stating that where the EU Charter and the ECHR contains the
same rights the EU Charter is to be interpreted in the same way as the ECHR., as it is
possible that the ECHR or the EU Charter could set a higher standard protection of a
particular right than each other.

8.7 MORE RECENT CASE LAW ON
HUMAN RIGHTS

Case law since the adoption of the Charter also sheds light on how human rights relate
to other interests or considerations in EU law.

In *Schmidberger*,[64] the facts concerned a protest mounted on an Alpine road route over
which Austrian authorities had control. The aim of the protest was to demand from
national and Community/Union authorities a strengthening of the various measures
designed to limit and reduce heavy goods traffic on the Brenner motorway and the
pollution thereby caused.[65]

The effect of the protest was to prevent the passage of trucks operated by the plaintiff,
Schmidberger, which was a German transport operator. The firm's vehicles did not
breach environmental guidelines. The Austrian authorities considered that they had
to allow the demonstration to go ahead because the demonstrators were exercising

....

63 Ibid 18–19 (23).
64 C–112/00 *Schmidberger v Austria* [2003] ECR I–5659.
65 Opinion of Advocate General Jacobs (12 July 2002) para 8.

their fundamental rights of freedom of expression and freedom of assembly under the Austrian constitution.[66] Schmidberger complained of a breach of free movement.

SCHMIDBERGER AND LIMITS ON FREE MOVEMENT TO PROTECT HUMAN RIGHTS

The Advocate General noted that this appeared to be the first case in which a Member State had invoked the necessity to protect fundamental rights to justify a restriction of one of the fundamental freedoms of movement of the treaty.[67]

The Advocate General proposed that in such a case the Court should follow the same two-step approach as it did in analysis of the traditional grounds of justification such as public policy or public security, which are also based on the specific situation in the Member State concerned: it was therefore to be established: (a) whether Austria was, as a matter of Community law, pursuing a legitimate objective in the public interest capable of justifying a restriction on a fundamental treaty freedom; and (b) if so, whether the restriction in issue is proportionate.[68] The ECJ contrasted the rights in issue here to non-derogable rights:

> . . . unlike other fundamental rights enshrined in that Convention, such as the right to life or the prohibition of torture and inhuman or degrading treatment or punishment, which admit of no restriction, neither the freedom of expression nor the freedom of assembly guaranteed by the ECHR appears to be absolute but must be viewed in relation to its social purpose. . . . In those circumstances, the interests involved must be weighed having regard to all the circumstances of the case in order to determine whether a fair balance was struck between those interests. The competent authorities enjoy a wide margin of discretion in that regard. Nevertheless, it is necessary to determine whether the restrictions placed upon intra-Community trade are proportionate in the light of the legitimate objective pursued, namely, in the present case, the protection of fundamental rights.[69]

ANALYSING THE LAW

SCHMIDBERGER RIGHTS AND FREEDOMS

In *Schmidberger*, the ECJ invoked a classic balancing metaphor to solving rights conflicts. It avoided making any claim that either human rights or free movement prevailed or was more important. On the facts, it in effect created an exception

---

66 Ibid para 88.
67 Ibid para 89.
68 Ibid para 95.
69 C–112/00 *Schmidberger v Austria* paras 80–83.

out of free movement on the basis of human rights. Klabbers suggests that if the ECJ had stated in *Schmidberger* that human rights were more important in principle, it would be hard in future cases for the ECJ to weight rights against free movement and decide that free movement was more important on the facts.[70]

In *Omega*,[71] the German police had made an order forbidding Omega from operating a 'playing at killing' game in a laserdrome on the ground that the act of simulated homicide and the trivialisation of violence engendered was a violation of human dignity. In Germany, the protection of human dignity is a constitutional principle.[72] As the equipment was lawfully made in the UK, Omega argued that the order breached its rights under the EU principle of freedom to provide services.

The Advocate General expressly addressed the issue of the ranking of human rights relative to the fundamental freedoms, but she noted that the ECJ does not rank them more highly than the treaties or fundamental freedoms.[73] The Advocate General went on to suggest that the fundamental freedoms could be equated with fundamental rights.[74] In a much briefer judgment, the ECJ noted the balancing exercise between Community and national competence:

> The fact remains, however, that the specific circumstances which may justify recourse to the concept of public policy may vary from one country to another and from one era to another. The competent national authorities must therefore be allowed a margin of discretion within the limits imposed by the Treaty.[75]

In concluding on the facts, the ECJ accepted the restriction and stated:

> . . . according to the referring court, the prohibition on the commercial exploitation of games involving the simulation of acts of violence against persons, in particular the representation of acts of homicide, corresponds to the level of protection of human dignity which the national constitution seeks to guarantee in the territory of the Federal Republic of Germany.[76]

---

70 J Klabbers *Treaty Conflict and the European Union* (Cambridge University Press 2009) 165–66.
71 Case C–36/02 *Omega* [2004] ECR I–9609. For discussion see J Morijn 'Balancing Fundamental rights and Common Market Freedoms in Union law: *Schmidberger* and *Omega* in light of the European Constitution' (2006) 12(1) *European Law Journal* 15–40.
72 See art 1 of the German Basic Law or *Grundgesetz*.
73 Opinion of Advocate General Stix-Hackl (18 March 2004) paras 48–49.
74 Ibid para 50 (reference omitted).
75 Case C–36/02 *Omega* para 31.
76 Ibid para 39.

The ECJ further stated that the German measure was not disproportionate. On the facts, the ECJ was quite sensitive to German law and its protection of human dignity as constitutional principle.

EXPLAINING THE LAW
———————————————

INTER-RELATED LEGAL SYSTEMS: NATIONAL LAW, EU LAW AND INTERNATIONAL LAW

Whereas *Schmidberger* and *Omega* involved the relationship between national law and EU law, the *Kadi* case involved a different relationship above: namely the relationship between the Community and Union legal order and international law. Thus, in an EU context, human rights involves three different, but inter-related legal systems:

<u>**Human Rights and Three Inter-related Legal Systems**</u>

    1.   2.   3.

National Law $\longrightarrow\longrightarrow$ **EU Law** $\longrightarrow\longrightarrow$ **International Law (including ECHR)**

                  $\downarrow$ $\downarrow$

       Schmidberger,   *Kadi,*

         Omega   *Bosphorus*

Here, the ECHR can be considered part of international law, because it does not have the distinct supranational characteristics we discussed in Chapter 2. However, with EU accession to the ECHR, the ECHR will become a part of EU law, which complicates the picture slightly. When this happens, it is not clear whether the ECJ will view the European Court of Human Rights in Strasbourg as a kind of higher court or supreme court when it comes to human rights.

The facts of *Kadi* related to the adoption by secondary legislation in EU law of measures against individuals resulting from requirements posed by UN Security Council resolutions. The Advocate General held that the EU could accept the direct application of UN Security Council resolutions in the EU legal order, so long as equivalent human rights protection as reflected in EU law was to be found in the UN system.[77]

Whereas the Advocate General was prepared to subject the EU implementing measures to judicial review, the Court of First Instance accorded an automatic priority to UN Security Council resolutions, excluding judicial review save for violations of *jus cogens*. In contrast, the ECJ reached a similar conclusion to the Advocate General in subjecting EU implementing measures to fuller judicial review on human rights grounds (and not

....

77 Opinion of Advocate General Maduro (16 January 2008) paras 34–40, 54 (the Advocate General did not draw any parallel with national reception of Community/Union law).

just on *jus cogens* grounds), but the EU was more concerned to assert the autonomy of the EU from international law.[78]

The Court stated that the Community was an autonomous legal system with respect to international law[79] and that: 'the obligations imposed by an international agreement cannot have the effect of prejudicing the constitutional principles of the EC Treaty'.[80] The Court declared that UN rules could not have priority over:

> . . . the principles that form part of the very foundations of the Community legal order, one of which is the protection of fundamental rights, including the review by the Community judicature of the lawfulness of Community measures as regards their consistency with those fundamental rights.[81]

The ECJ further held that the guarantee of fundamental rights in the Community, inspired by the constitutional traditions of the Member States and the European Convention on Human Rights,[82] formed part of the very foundations of the Community.[83] The ECJ held that it thus did have jurisdiction to determine the validity of international legal norms within the Community legal system, which did not entail any challenge to the primacy of (in this case) the Security Council resolution in international law.[84] On the facts, the ECJ held that the appellant's rights of defence[85] and his right to property were breached.[86]

ANALYSING THE LAW

THE SIGNIFICANCE OF THE ECJ JUDGMENT IN *KADI*

The approach of the ECJ in *Kadi* might be thought a victory for human rights, and the judgment was welcomed for affording greater human rights protection than had the CFI.[87] However, the exact status of human rights remains under-discussed. In particular, it is not clear that human rights have the highest importance, since they were included into a broader category of constitutional

---

78 See G de Búrca 'The European Court of Justice and the international legal order after *Kadi*' *Jean Monnet Working Paper 01/09* (2009) 4.

79 Joined Cases C–402/05 P & 415/05 P para 282 (ECJ). See also ibid para 316.

80 Ibid para 285.

81 Ibid para 304.

82 Ibid para 283.

83 Ibid para 290. See also ibid paras 303–304.

84 Ibid para 288.

85 Joined Cases C–402/05 P & 415/05 P *Kadi* para 348. Similarly see ibid para 353, noting these procedures violated the right to be heard and the principle of effective judicial protection.

86 Ibid para 369, the Court having noted that some restriction of property rights could in principle be justified: ibid para 366. See also e.g. the decision of the CFI (now the General Court) in Case T–47/03 *Sison v Council* [2005] ECR II–1429, which adopted an approach more consistent with the ECJ rather than the CFI in *Kadi*.

87 As noted in de Búrca (n 78) 2.

principles making up the character of the EU as a legal system. Klabbers accurately concludes that the ECJ 'remained silent about the possible conflict of norms created' by concluding international agreements, such as with the ECHR.[88]

One of the main reasons the ECJ was called on to decide how compatible with human rights were UN Security Council resolutions on blacklisting individuals (i.e. subjecting individuals to sanctions because of terrorist links) is because there is a lack of human rights protection at UN level when it comes to the Security Council. There is no way of legally enforcing the UN bills of rights, the Universal Declaration of Human Rights and the ICCPR, at international level it is largely a matter of political decision-making.

The ECJ gave indirect legal status to the EU Charter on Fundamental Rights, prior to its incorporation into EU by the Treaty of Lisbon, in several cases. For example, in Case *EP v Council*,[89] the Court noted that the Charter recognised in Article 7, the right to respect for private or family life and observed that this provision must be read in conjunction with the obligation to have regard to the child's best interests, in Article 24(2) of the Charter, and taking account of the need, expressed in Article 24(3), for a child to maintain on a regular basis a personal relationship with both his or her parents.

This supported the Court's conclusion as to what the Member States had to take into account in applying the Directive 2003/86 on the right to family reunification[90] to determine the conditions for the exercise of the right to family reunification by third country nationals residing lawfully in the territory of the Member States. In *Advocaten voor de Wereld*, which related to a European Arrest Warrant under the framework of the pre-Lisbon third pillar, the Court referred to the Charter in support of the status of legality of criminal offences and penalties as a general principle of EU law.[91]

The Court for the first time referred to the EU Charter after the Lisbon Treaty entered into force in *Detiček v Maurizio Sgueglia* when it referred to Article 24(3) of the Charter on the right of children to maintain on a regular basis a personal relationship and direct contact with both parents.[92] *Kücükdeveci*, noted above, was the second post-Lisbon reference.[93]

----

88 Klabbers (n 70) 5.
89 C–540/03 *EP v Council* [2006] ECR I–5769.
90 Directive 2003/86/EC on the right to family reunification, OJ L 251 3.10.2003 p. 12.
91 Case C–303/05 *Advocaten voor de Wereld* [2007] ECR I–3633 paras 45–46.
92 Case C–403/09PPU *Detiček v Maurizio Sgueglia* [2009] I–2193 paras 53–54, 58.
93 N Lazzerini '(Some of) the fundamental rights granted by the Charter may be a source of obligations for private parties: Case C–176/12 *Association de médiation sociale v Union locale des syndicats CGT and Others*, judgment of the Court of Justice (Grand Chamber) of 15 January 2014, nyr' (2014) 51 *Common Market Law Review* 907–34 at 912.

In *Dominguez*, the proceedings were between an employee and her private law employer, and concerned the compatibility with the Working Time Directive[94] of a provision of the *Code du Travail* (the French Labour Code) whereby the entitlement to paid annual leave was conditional on the employee having actually worked for a minimum number of days during the reference period.[95] The referring court only asked whether the national provision conflicted with the directive, and whether it should thus disapply it.

The Court of Justice itself asked the parties to address the relevance of Article 31(2) of the Charter (on workers' right to an annual period of paid leave). Analogously to arguments about the (lack of) horizontal effect of directives, Advocate General Trstenjak relied on the wording of Article 51(1) of the Charter, arguing that the addressees of fundamental rights therein are only those explicitly mentioned by the first sentence of Article 51(1), which are the institutions and bodies of the EU and member states (Opinion of 8th September 2011 paragraphs 80–83).[96]

The Court did not address the issue explicitly, it returned the case to the referring court to consider whether the employer could be considered a public employer and whether as an emanation of the state, state liability might apply to it, thus leaving open the scope of horizontal application of the Charter rights.

In *Association de médiation sociale v Union Locale des Syndicats CGT and Others (AMS)*,[97] the ECJ was in a preliminary reference requested to clarify whether a provision of the Charter, Article 27 on the 'Workers' right to information and consultation within the undertaking' could be invoked in order to disapply an arguably conflicting national provision in a dispute between private parties. The provision of national law concerned how to calculate employees in a company. One of the main Charter provisions in issue was Article 52(5):

> . . . [t]he provisions of [the] Charter which contain principles [. . .] They shall be judicially cognisable only in the interpretation of such acts and in the ruling on their legality.

Article 52(5) relates to the distinction between rights and principles in the last recital to the Charter's preamble and in the second sentence of Article 51(1). Article 52(5) suggests principles, from the point of view of the courts, are just aids to interpretation. Notwithstanding the text, Advocate General Cruz Villalón considered that principles could sometimes apply between individuals, when the provisions giving specific

---

94 Directive 2003/88/EC of the European Parliament and of the Council of 4 November 2003 concerning certain aspects of the organisation of working time, OJ L 299 18.11.2003 p. 9.

95 Case C–282/10 *Dominguez*, judgment of 24 January 2012.

96 Ibid. paras 80–83.

97 Case C–176/12 *Association de médiation sociale v Union Locale des Syndicats CGT and Others (AMS)*, judgment of 15 January 2014.

content to a 'principle' are contained in a directive, individuals may rely on them also in horizontal disputes, in order to review national acts.[98]

In its judgment, the Court of Justice distinguished *Association de médiation sociale* from *Kücükdeveci*. In *Kücükdeveci*, '. . . the principle of non-discrimination on grounds of age . . ., laid down in Article 21(1) of the Charter, is sufficient in itself to confer on individuals an individual right which they may invoke as such'. Article 27 of the Charter '. . . to be fully effective . . . must be given more specific expression in European Union or national law' before it could be invoked in the context of a horizontal dispute i.e. Article 27 was not specific enough to deal with the facts of the case.

This statement seems to leave open the possibility that secondary legislation could further specify it, but the Court did not consider that Directive 2002/14 could, which presumably relates to the status of directives themselves as addressed to the Member States only: '. . . since [Article 27] does not suffice to confer on individuals a right which they may invoke as such, it could not be otherwise if it is considered in conjunction with [Directive 2002/14]'.[99]

MAKING CONNECTIONS
+ + + + + + + + + + + + + + + + +

HORIZONTAL SCOPE OF THE CHARTER

In *AMS*, the Court appeared to accept in principle that the Charter could have horizontal direct effect, assuming the content of a particular provision was sufficiently specific, i.e. satisfied the normal conditions of direct effect. It did not state that provisions identified as containing principles automatically could not have direct effect, but this was the situation in *AMS* concerning Article 27 of the Charter because it was not specific enough.

8.8 CITIZENSHIP OF THE EU

8.8.1 OVERVIEW

The Treaty of Maastricht introduced the concept of EU citizenship, now contained in Article 9 TEU and Articles 18–25 TFEU. Apart from its rhetorical or symbolic significance, the chief practical effect of the concept of EU citizenship has been to extend the rights consequent on free movement. A second possible general impact has been to minimise the requirement of a cross-border element for EU law to apply: some cases seem to suggest that the mere fact of a person being an EU citizen is enough to

---

98 Opinion of 18 July 2013 paras 71–80.
99 Case C–176/12 paras 45–49.

engage EU law and cross-border movement is not needed (we will look at this briefly further below at the end of this chapter). However, there are also some more specific rights that the treaty gives to EU citizens.

> ### KEY LEARNING POINT
>
> ....
>
> #### SUMMARY OF TREATY RIGHTS GIVEN TO EU CITIZENS
> The following rights are given to EU citizens and not just the free movement categories of workers and service providers by the citizenship provisions in the TFEU:
>
> - The right to move and reside within the EU (Article 21 TFEU).
> - The right to vote and stand as a candidate in European and municipal elections in the Member State of residence (Article 22 TFEU).
> - The right to diplomatic and consular protection in third countries from other Member States where the home Member State is not diplomatically represented (Article 23 TFEU).
> - The right to petition the European Parliament and to apply to the ombudsman (Article 24 TFEU).

In a series of directives in 1990, the then EEC/EC began to extend the right of free movement to categories other than workers and the self-employed and their family members, but subject to the condition that nationals exercising the new free movement right have adequate resources so as not to become a burden on the social assistance schemes of the Member States and that they would be covered by sickness insurance – the rights granted were to enter other Member States and reside there: see Directive 90/366 (concerning students and vocational training);[100] Directive 90/365 (concerning the self-employed who had ceased to work);[101] and Directive 90/364 (concerning all other nationals).[102]

> ### KEY LEARNING POINT
>
> ....
>
> #### FINANCIAL SELF-SUFFICIENCY AND FREE MOVEMENT
> The right to free movement is not a fundamental human right in EU law (although, as we saw above, the ECJ does sometimes equate free movement with fundamental rights). This is clear from the fact that EU citizens can only exercise free movement if they have enough financial resources not to become an unreasonable burden on the state where they move to: the host Member State is not obliged to finance EU citizens e.g. through social welfare provision.

....

100 OJ L 180 13.07.1990 p. 30.
101 Ibid 28.
102 Ibid 26.

Cases extending rights based on citizenship have concerned EU citizens claiming a (non–contributory[103]) *subsidiary* type of social benefit and who are turned down by the host state because they do not have the right nationality, or have not got sufficiently long residence in the Member State in question, or for some other reason that seems to put them at a disadvantage compared to citizens of the host state, or because they exercised their free movement rights.

ANALYSING THE LAW

CITIZENSHIP IN THE CONTEXT OF EQUALITY AND NON-DISCRIMINATION

Whereas the treaty wording in Article 21 TFEU suggests citizenship rights are only as specifically granted (applying a *lex specialis* principle), the ECJ in some cases seems to suggest equal treatment applies unless specifically excluded (applying *lex generalis* over *lex specialis*). Note that this approach has a remarkably broad potential: equality and non-discrimination could be taken to mean that all legal entitlements must be harmonised for all EU citizens. The ECJ has not stated the point in such broad terms, but the possibility exists conceptually because of the breadth of the idea of equality and non-discrimination.

Future developments in citizenship may seek to expand the rights of EU citizens on the grounds of equality. In some of its case law, the ECJ has rather dramatically stated that EU citizenship is 'destined to become the fundamental status of nationals of the Member States, enabling those who find themselves in the same situation to enjoy the same treatment in law irrespective of their nationality, subject to the exceptions as are expressly provided for'.[104] This is consistent with the role the ECJ has played in the process of integration: it suggests the ECJ sees the EU as supplanting the Member States in the long term.

Another way in which the equality principle can be given a broad scope is through extending it to include associated persons regarding the grounds of non-discrimination. In *Coleman*, the ECJ decided that a person related to a disabled person could benefit from protection against discrimination applicable to her disabled son.[105]

First inserted into the ECT at the Treaty of Maastricht in 1992, Articles 17–22 ECT (prior to the TFEU) (and ex Articles 8–8e ECT), now in Articles 18–25 TFEU, were the first formal reference to a concept of citizenship of the Community/Union, although

---

103 A non-contributory benefit is one that does not require the person benefiting to have paid in to a fund in advance to support the benefit.

104 See e.g. Case C–184/99 *Grzelczyk v Centre Public d'Aide Sociale d'Ottignies-Louvain-La-Neuve* [2001] ECR I–6193 para 28; Case C–333/13 *Dano v Jobcenter Leipzig* judgment of 11th November 2014 para 58.

105 Case C–303/06 *Coleman v Attridge Law* [2008] ECR I–5603, interpreting the scope of Directive 2000/78/EC establishing a general framework for equal treatment in employment and occupation OJ L 303 2.12.2000 p. 16.

a general conception of citizenship of the Community/Union had been part of the thinking behind European integration for some time before.

Article 20(1) TFEU states:

> Citizenship of the Union is hereby established. Every person holding the nationality of a Member State shall be a citizen of the Union. Citizenship of the Union shall complement and not replace national citizenship.

EXPLAINING THE LAW

EU CITIZENSHIP IS DERIVATIVE FROM NATIONAL CITIZENSHIP

To become a citizen of the EU, a person must first be a national of one of the Member States, i.e. it is not possible for someone to acquire EU citizenship independently of the Member States. As the ECJ has confirmed, it is for each Member State to decide how a person acquires citizenship.[106] Similarly, the loss of citizenship is a matter primarily for national law. However, the ECJ has held that national rules on loss of nationality must respect proportionality.[107] In addition, a person can have dual nationality and still retain EU citizenship (i.e. a person can be a national of a third country, as well as a national of an EU Member State for the purpose of acquiring EU citizenship.[108]

Article 21(1) TFEU states:

> Every citizen of the Union shall have the right to move and reside freely within the territory of the Member States, subject to the limitations and conditions laid down in this Treaty and by the measures adopted to give it effect.

The wording in Article 21 is important. It states that the concept of citizenship is *in accordance with* the conditions and limits defined by the treaties and by measures adopted to give it effect (i.e. the latter refers to secondary legislation) – i.e. it is subject to the existing law. This suggests that these provisions do not add any new specific rights, rather they simply confirm a more general concept of citizenship already implicit in the scheme of the treaty (i.e. the *lex specialis* as mentioned above).

---

106 Case C–369/90 *Micheletti v Delegacion del Gobierno en Cantabria* [1992] ECR I–4239; Case C–192/99 *The Queen v Home Secretary, ex parte Kaur* [2001] ECR I–1237.
107 Case C–135/08 *Rottmann v Freistaat Bayern* [2010] ECR I–1449.
108 Case C–148/02 *Garcia Avello* [2003] ECR I–11613.

> KEY LEARNING POINT
> ....
>
> **CITIZENSHIP AND EXCEPTIONS TO FINANCIAL SELF-SUFFICIENCY**
> Despite the treaty wording that the concept of citizenship is in accordance with
> the conditions and limits defined by the treaties and by measures adopted
> to give it effect, the ECJ has used citizenship to make some inroads on the
> principle that nationals of the Member States exercising their right of free
> movement must be economically self-sufficient and must not become an
> unreasonable burden on the social assistance system of the host state: the
> approach of the Court has been that some social assistance may be reasonably
> expected.

> KEY LEARNING POINT
> ....
>
> **THE DIRECT EFFECT OF THE CITIZENSHIP PROVISIONS**
> The ECJ has held that the citizenship provisions of the treaty, Articles 20[109] and
> 21,[110] have direct effect. In *Baumbast*, the ECJ declared the right of residence
> set out in Article 21(1) TFEU was directly effective so as to allow a German
> national who was no longer a migrant worker a right to reside in the UK. Thus,
> even though Article 21(1) TFEU refers to conditions and limitations laid down
> in the treaties, the basic right of residence was justiciable in the absence of any
> exclusionary rule applicable to Mr Baumbast.

8.8.2 NON-WORKERS (I.E. CITIZENS OTHER THAN WORKERS) AND 'SOCIAL ADVANTAGES'

MAKING CONNECTIONS
+ + + + + + + + + + + + + + + + +

WHAT CITIZENSHIP ADDS TO WORKERS' RIGHTS
We will see in Chapter 10 how citizens of the Member States originally acquired
rights under the treaties as economic actors, either workers or self-employed.
One of the most important aspects of citizenship is that it gives, albeit still
relatively limited rights, to citizens of Member States who exercise free movement
other than in the capacity of a worker or service provider. Workers derive the
most benefit under EU law. One of the main benefits is the right to 'equal social
and tax advantages' when in employment. We will examine this in more detail
in Chapter 10. Here, it is important to make the link with citizenship, in order to
evaluate to what extent citizenship gives equivalent benefits to EU citizens who
are not workers.

....

109 Case C–184/99 *Grzelczyk* (n 103).
110 Case C–413/99 *Baumbast v Home Secretary* [2002] ECR I–7091.

In 1989 the ECJ had held in *Lebon* that a job-seeker fell outside Regulation 1612/68, Article 7(2), i.e. only those actually in employment could benefit i.e. from 'equal social and tax advantages'.[111] As a result, a job-seeker's claim for the Belgian *minimex* (non-contributory minimum subsistence allowance, which Belgian law gave only to Belgian nationals and to EU workers) failed. The ECJ said that Member States were under no obligation to give social advantages to job-seekers. The same general principle was thought to apply to all 'economically inactive' EU citizens: they only qualified for residence so long as they did not 'become a burden on the social security system of the host Member States' (which is still the rule, see Directive 2004/38,[112] Article 7(1)(b), (c)). As a corollary to that, the 'economically inactive' cannot claim the sort of state benefits that workers can claim. In other words, 'social advantages' are not within the scope of the treaty as far as these groups are concerned. However, the following are cases where the ECJ has granted some social assistance to citizens who were not workers.

Martínez Sala was the first case in which the ECJ began to explore to what extent non-workers/families might be able to claim social advantages in a host state.[113] Maria Martínez Sala was a Spanish national living in Germany for 25 years (apparently with the acquiescence of the German authorities). On the facts, she had a right to reside in Germany under German law (i.e. independently of her right of free movement under EU law). She was not a worker or family member of a worker. She claimed German non-contributory child-rearing allowance, which the German authorities refused to give her. The ECJ held that, in her particular circumstances, she fell within the scope of the treaty equal treatment provisions and *was* entitled to this particular social advantage. However, the scope of this for future cases was not made clear.

The next major case was *Grzelczyk*,[114] in which the ECJ made the statement quoted above that EU citizenship was destined to become the status of the nationals of the Member States. Grzelczyk was a Belgian national who had received his secondary schooling and diploma in France as a student and had returned to Belgium for university studies. When he ran out of money in his final year, he claimed a transitional study-to-work grant that was available to Belgian students coming to the end of their studies and entering the world of work. He was refused because the Belgian legislation required recipients to complete their secondary education in Belgium. The ECJ held that Grzelczyk was in a situation that was within the scope of the treaty equal treatment provisions because he was exercising a right of residence (and now would come under Directive 2004/38).

....

111 Case 316/85 *Centre public d'aide sociale de Courcelles v Lebon* [1987] ECR 2811.
112 OJ L 158 30.04.2004 p. 77.
113 Case C–85/96 *Martínez Sala v Freistaat Bayern* [1998] ECR I–2691.
114 Case C–184/99 *Grzelczyk* (n 104).

> ## KEY LEARNING POINT
>
> ### *GRZELCZYK*
>
> In *Grzelczyk*, the ECJ adopted a protective approach to citizenship that placed conditions on how Member States treated EU citizens: limitations or conditions can only be legally enforced by a host state in a proportionate, non-discriminatory way.[115]

On the facts, Belgium should have considered whether Grzelczyk had become an *unreasonable* burden on state finances, particularly as his difficulties were temporary. The fact of his having achieved a degree of social integration appears to have been significant.

In *Carpenter*, the ECJ held that Article 49 EC (now Article 56 TFEU), read in the light of the fundamental right to respect for family life, is to be interpreted as precluding a refusal, by the Member State of origin of a provider of services established in that Member State who provides services to recipients established in other Member States, of the right to reside in its territory to that provider's spouse, who is a national of a third country. The facts were that Mrs Carpenter, who was a Filipino national, entered the UK on the basis of a six-month visa, overstayed the visa without applying for an extension, but then married a UK national. The rationale for the judgment was partly related to the fact the Court held that Mr Carpenter would not be able to exercise free movement as effectively if he could not be with his wife.[116]

In *Zhu and Chen*,[117] the ECJ held that (then) Article 18 ECT (now Article 21 TFEU) and Council Directive 90/364/EEC[118] on the right of residence confer on a young minor who is a national of a Member State, is covered by appropriate sickness insurance and is in the care of a parent who is a third-country national having sufficient resources for that minor not to become a burden on the public finances of the host Member State, a right to reside for an indefinite period in that state. In such circumstances, the same provisions allow a parent who is that minor's primary carer to reside with the child in the host Member State.

In *Collins*, the ECJ signalled that the *Lebon* case was no longer incorrect in deciding that non-worker EU citizens were never entitled to equal treatment in social advantages.[119]

---

115 Ibid para 36. On proportionality see also Case C–413/99 *Baumbast* (n 110); Case C–138/02 *Collins v Secretary of State for Work and Pensions* [2004] ECR 1–6193; Case C–406/04 *De Cuyper* [2006] ECR I–6947. In *Baumbast*, the ECJ held that Court indicated that it would be disproportionate not to renew Mr Baumbast's residence permit given that, even though he did not have cover for emergency treatment, he had lived in the United Kingdom for several years; his family resided in the UK; neither he nor his family relied on British social welfare assistance; and both he and his family had comprehensive medical insurance in another Member State.

116 Case C–60/00 [2002] ECR I–6279 para 30.

117 Case C–200/02 *Zhu and Chen* [2004] ECR I–9925.

118 Council Directive 90/364/EEC, OJ L 180 13.07.1990 26, now replaced by Directive 2004/38.

119 Case C–138/02, *Collins*, (n 115).

Collins was an Irish national, who entered the UK on 31 May 1998 to seek work. On 8 June, he claimed jobseeker's allowance, but was not eligible under UK law because he was not 'habitually resident' in the UK. The UK argued that he was not entitled to it under EU law because of *Lebon*.

The ECJ said that *Lebon* in deciding that jobseekers were never entitled to equal treatment in relation to 'social advantages' was no longer an accurate statement of the law. The correct starting point was to ask whether he was an EU citizen with the right of residence (which he was) and, if so, was it discriminatory and disproportionate in his particular circumstances to deny him the allowance. The Court concluded that that the 'habitual residence' requirement attached was indirectly discriminatory against migrant jobseekers.[120] The UK therefore had to justify it on objective grounds proportionate to a legitimate aim, and could not simply refuse it point blank. Whether this was so was a matter for the national court/authorities to decide on the facts of the case. The ECJ stated:

> In view of the establishment of citizenship of the Union and the interpretation in the case law of the right to equal treatment enjoyed by citizens of the Union, it is no longer possible to exclude from the scope of Article 48(2) of the Treaty – which expresses the fundamental principle of equal treatment, guaranteed by Article 6 of the Treaty – a benefit of a financial nature intended to facilitate access to employment in the labour market of a Member State.[121]

Trojani[122] also concerned a *minimex* or transitional grant in Belgium. Trojani was a French national who had been in Belgium for two years, living first at a campsite, then at a youth hostel and finally at a Salvation Army hostel. In return for board, lodging and pocket money, he did miscellaneous jobs for about 30 hours a week as part of a 'personalised socio-occupational reintegration programme'. Belgium had granted him temporary leave to reside in Belgium, but he was now refused (i) the right of residence and (ii) *minimex*.

The ECJ held that it was up to the national court to decide on the facts whether he was a 'worker'. If it was decided that he was not a worker, he was not entitled to residence merely by virtue of Article 18 ECT (now Article 20 TFEU) because the 'sufficient resources' condition in Directive 90/364 (and now in Directive 2004/38) had to be satisfied, *but* that condition had to be applied in accordance with the principle of proportionality.

Further, the ECJ seemed to hint that there would be nothing disproportionate in using the conditions in Directive 90/364 (now in Directive 2004/38) against this particular individual (i.e. to deny free movement), except that because Belgium had chosen to give

120 Ibid para 65.
121 Ibid para 63.
122 Case C–456/02, *Trojani v Centre Public d'aide sociale de Bruxelles (CPAS)* [2004] ECR I–7573.

Trojani temporary leave to reside, in his case it would then be discriminatory under (ex) Article 12 ECT (now Article 18 TFEU) to deny him the *minimex*.

In *Bidar*,[123] the facts concerned maintenance grants for students. The ECJ held that national legislation that grants students the right to assistance covering their maintenance costs only if they are settled in the host Member State may not preclude a national of another Member State from obtaining the status of settled person as a student where that national was lawfully resident and had received a substantial part of his secondary education in the host Member State and had consequently established a genuine link with the society of that state. In *Ioannidis*,[124] the ECJ confirmed its approach in *Collins* and held it is contrary to Article 39 ECT (now Article 45 TFEU) for a Member State to refuse to grant a tideover allowance, i.e. a transitional grant from work to university, to a national of another Member State seeking his first employment who is not the dependent child of a migrant worker residing in the Member State granting the allowance, on the sole ground that he completed his secondary education in another Member State.

In *Vatsouras and Koupatantze*, the ECJ addressed whether Article 24(2) of Directive 2004/38 is compatible with (then) Article 12 EC (now Article 18 TFEU), read in conjunction with (then) Article 39 ECT (now Article 45 TFEU).[125] The ECJ did not deal explicitly with the compatibility issue, rather it clarified the scope of Article 45 TFEU and followed *Collins* and *Ioannidis* that it is no longer possible to exclude from the scope of (then) Article 39(2) ECT a benefit of a financial nature intended to facilitate access to employment in the labour market of a Member State, but it continued that it is, however, legitimate for a Member State to grant such an allowance only after it has been possible to establish a real link between the jobseeker and the labour market of the host Member State.[126]

KEY LEARNING POINT

THE PATTERN IN THE CASELAW

In the above cases, the ECJ has in effect used citizenship caselaw to create exceptions to the previous approach that only workers or service providers could benefit from any social or tax advantages as a requirement of EU law. Citizenship has been used as a basis for some social assistance claims by economically non-active EU citizens exercising free movement, i.e. the host Member State may now be required to provide some limited financial assistance to EU citizens other than workers or the self-employed/service providers. There is no clear dividing

---

123 Case C–209/03 *R (on the application of Bidar) v London Borough of Ealing* [2005] ECR I–2119.
124 Case C–258/04 *Office National de l'Emploi v Ioannidis* [2005] ECR I–8275.
125 Joined Cases C–22/08 & C–23/08 *Vatsouras and Koupatantze* [2009] ECR I–4585.
126 Case C–224/98 *D'Hoop v Office National d'Emploi* [2002] 3 CMLR 12 para 38, and Case C–258/04 *Ioannidis* para 30.

line between what is and what is not required of the Member States in this regard: however, it must not be an unreasonable burden on the host Member State, and the degree of social integration of the EU citizen concerned is an important factor. The Member States must consider these factors on a case-by-case basis. In its recent *Dano* judgment, the ECJ did not offer much clarification of where the boundary lies as to what financial assistance Member States are required to give.[127] The facts related to a Romanian national living in Germany who was mother to a son born in Germany. She had a limited command of the German language and had never worked in Germany, although she had been there for several years. The Court concluded that Germany was not required to provide special non-contributory cash benefits where a citizen from another Member State who was not working did not qualify for residence due to having insufficient resources.[128]

ANALYSING THE LAW

CITIZENSHIP MEANS A CROSS-BORDER ELEMENT NO LONGER NEEDED TO PROTECT THE 'SUBSTANCE OF RIGHTS'?

Some case law on the citizenship provisions suggests that it is enough for a person to be an EU citizen, that movement across a border can protect rights in the *home* member state. For example, in *Tas-Hagen and Tas*,[129] the ECJ held that a residence condition should not be imposed on an entitlement to a pension for civilian war victims (the condition meant that moving to another Member State disentitled a person to the pension): 'As Netherlands nationals, Mrs Tas-Hagen and Mr Tas enjoy the status of citizens of the Union under Article 17(1) EC and may therefore benefit from the rights conferred on those having that status, such as, inter alia the right to move and to reside freely within the territory of the Member States conferred by Article 18(1) EC' (paragraph 19). However, the ECJ has tended not to be explicit about this: it has not directly said it is now abandoning the cross-border element in free movement of citizens,[130] perhaps because this would open up a difference between free movement of citizens (workers and service providers) and the other free movement principles. Under pre-citizenship case law, this kind of pension would more easily have been considered outside the scope of the treaty: see, e.g. *Ministère Public v Even*, although a difference between *Tas-Hagen and Tas* and *Even* was that *Even* related to a refusal to give a pension to a non-national (not because a national changed residence).

Whereas *Tas-Hagen and Tas* suggests the possibility of citizenship on its own grounding a right with a minimal cross-border element, the more recent case of

---

127 Case C-333/13 *Dano v. Jobcenter Leipzig* judgment of 11th November 2014.
128 Ibid paras. 80–83.
129 Case C–192/05 *Tas-Hagen and Tas* [2006] ECR I–10451.
130 Case C–148/02 *Garcia Avello* above para 26, stating the treaties do not apply to purely internal situations.

Zambrano comes very close to eliminating it. In this case,[131] Colombian nationals living in Belgium were able to rely on EU citizenship in a derivative way due to their children being EU citizens, having been born in Belgium. The Belgian authorities sought to deport Zambrano, who had applied for temporary unemployment benefit during a period of suspension of his employment. His application for a benefit resulted in an inspection being conducted at his place of work, and the inspection revealed he had no work permit. The ECJ stated that to protect the 'substance of the rights' of his children to reside in the EU as EU citizens, it was necessary to grant Zambrano a right to reside and work in Belgium.[132]

However, the ECJ refused to extend this approach to an EU national living in the UK who wished to assert for her third-country spouse an entitlement to enter the UK to be with her where she had not crossed the UK border (she had dual Irish and UK nationality).[133] It also later clarified that its 'substance of rights' approach only applied where an EU citizen would be forced to leave the EU altogether in order to be able to enjoy a right the substance of which was guaranteed by EU law.[134]

In *O and S*, the situation arose that both parents were third country nationals, but children from a previous relationship were EU citizens and the mothers were lawful residents. The ECJ held that the new partner of the mother who was not otherwise lawfully resident could be refused a right to remain on grounds of insufficient resources so long as this did not impair the substance of the rights of the EU citizens involved (the children).[135] The right at risk here was the right of the children to family life.

Somewhat similar facts to *Zambrano* arose in the *Iida* case.[136] The ECJ distinguished the two cases by noting that 'the present case displays a peculiarity in that the third-country national is not applying for a right of residence in the Member State in which his daughter, the Union citizen, is living' (this distinguished it from *Zambrano*).[137] The facts involved Mr Iida claiming a right to stay in Germany as a family member of an EU national, but where his EU family members were living separately to him in Austria.[138]

The Court seems more cautious in stating that 'It must be recalled that the purely hypothetical prospect of exercising the right of freedom of movement does not establish a sufficient connection with EU law to justify the application of that law's provisions.[139]

131 Case C–34/09 *Gerardo Ruiz Zambrano v Office National de l'Emploi* [2011] ECR I–1449.
132 Ibid para 42.
133 Case C–434/09 *McCarthy v Home Secretary* [2011] ECR I–3375.
134 Case C–256/11 *Dereci v Bundesminesterium für Inneres* [2011] ECR I–11315 para 66.
135 Joined Cases C–356 & 357/2011 *O and S*, judgment of 6th December 2012 paras 46–51, 82.
136 Case C–40/11 *Yoshikazu Iida*, judgment 8th November 2012.
137 Ibid Opinion of Advocate General Trstenjak of 15 May 2012 at para. 1.
138 Case C–40/11 para 77.
139 See Case C–299/95 *Kremzow* [1997] ECR I–2629 para 16.

The same applies to purely hypothetical prospects of that right being obstructed'. The approach in the area of free movement of goods, whereby actual or potential obstacles to free movement are prohibited, is thus not applied here: the substance of rights test requires an actual breach on the facts.

The ECJ noted the limits of the scope of the Charter of Fundamental Rights when it ruled that: 'Under Article 51(2) of the Charter, it does not extend the field of application of European Union law beyond the powers of the Union, and it does not establish any new power or task for the Union, or modify powers and tasks as defined in the Treaties'[140] and that the German authorities' refusal to grant Mr Iida a residence card of a family member of a Union citizen 'does not fall within the implementation of European Union law within the meaning of Article 51 of the Charter'.[141]

Amongst the most recent judgments is *Alokpa and Moudoulou*.[142]

EXPLAINING THE LAW

NATIONAL COURTS TO DECIDE ON THE FACTS OF SUBSTANCE OF RIGHTS INFRINGED

Alokpa and Moudoulou confirms the 'substance of rights' approach under Article 20 TFEU (removing the requirement for prior exercise of freedom of movement), though without clarifying its scope other than deciding that it was for national courts to decide on the facts if the substance of rights has been infringed.

However, the Court of Justice has so far avoided being explicit about two key conceptual issues its substance of rights raises: (1) what is the connecting factor with EU competence if there is no proper exercise of free movement (is it a potential exercise?) and (2) what is the core of rights, which the term suggest, that must be respected by the Member States under EU law?

Mrs Alokpa, a third country national, had twins prematurely in Luxembourg. The twins were EU citizens as they were French nationals on account of their father being a French national. The mother was the sole carer of the twins as the father had absconded, and Mrs Alokpa applied for an extension of temporary discretionary residence in Luxembourg. This was granted to her on account of her twins requiring care due to their prematurity.[143] However, she was denied permission to stay longer on the grounds that she did not fall within the permitted categories of an EU citizen's family member as this 'is restricted to dependent relatives in the direct ascending line', and secondly, the twins had not exercised their right of free movement.[144]

---

140 Case C–40/11 *Yoshikazu Iida* para 78. This then raises the problem that the ECJ is not always clear in its general case law on the limits of EU powers.
141 Case C–40/11 *Yoshikazu Iida* para 81.
142 Case C–86/12 *Adzo Domenyo Alokpa, Jarel Moudoulou, Eja Moudoulou v Ministre du Travail, de l'Emploi et de l'Immigration*, judgment of 10 October 2013.
143 Ibid paras 13–16.
144 Ibid para 18.

The Court of Justice defined the question referred to it as: whether, in a situation such as that at issue in the main proceedings, Articles 20 TFEU (on the general rights of EU citizens) and 21 TFEU (on the exercise of rights of free movement and residence) must be interpreted as meaning that they preclude a Member State from refusing to allow a third-country national to reside in its territory, where that third-country national has sole responsibility for her minor children who are EU citizens, and who have resided with her in that Member State since their birth, without possessing the nationality of that Member State and having made use of their right to freedom of movement?

The ECJ found that it was for the national court to decide whether, pursuant to Article 7(1)(b) of Directive 2004/38[145] the children, as EU citizens, had sufficient resources and comprehensive sickness insurance cover either 'on their own or through their mother'.[146] If such conditions were not met, the national court was able to refuse residence under Article 21 and the Article 7(1)(b) of the Directive,[147] although the origin of resources of the child did not matter.[148]

Notwithstanding Article 21, the Court found a stronger right could be based on Article 20 TFEU. The Court noted previous case law where it had held that there are very specific situations in which, despite the fact that the secondary law on the right of residence of third-country nationals does not apply and the Union citizen concerned has not made use of his freedom of movement, a right of residence cannot, exceptionally, without undermining the effectiveness of the Union citizenship that citizen enjoys, be refused to a third-country national who is a family member of him or her. This is so if, as a consequence of refusal, that citizen would be obliged in practice to leave the territory of the EU altogether, thus denying him the genuine enjoyment of the substance of the rights conferred by virtue of the status of EU citizen (referring to *Iida*[149] and *Ymeraga and Ymeraga-Tafarshiku*[150]).

8.9 CONCLUSION

Although Europe has now over six decades of experience in the protection of rights at European level, many questions remain about the protection of rights in the EU. In particular, it is not fully clear what the relationship will be in all contexts and

---

145 Article 7 (1)(b) (on the right of residence for more than three months) states: 'All Union citizens shall have the right of residence on the territory of another Member State for a period of longer than three months if they: (a) are workers or self-employed persons in the host Member State; or (b) have sufficient resources for themselves and their family members not to become a burden on the social assistance system of the host Member State during their period of residence and have comprehensive sickness insurance cover in the host Member State . . .'.

146 Case C–86/12 ibid para 30.

147 Ibid para 31.

148 Ibid paras 27–28.

149 Case C–40/11 para 71.

150 Case C–87/12, judgment of 8 May 2013 para 36.

circumstances between the EU Charter of Fundamental Rights and the ECHR. In the case of many provisions, the EU Charter of Fundamental Rights is mostly the same as the ECHR in the scope of protection it gives to rights and this is expressly set out in it. However, the potential for difference remains in the case of rights that are included in the EU Charter, but that are not in the ECHR, or where one or the other offers more protection to a particular right. In addition, a continuing ambiguity in EU law is the status of the fundamental freedoms of movement relative to more traditional rights. Finally, imminent EU accession to the ECHR will also raise important practical questions of the relationship between the ECJ and the European Court of Human Rights and whether the ECJ will accept the Strasbourg court as having the final say in human rights questions.

EU citizenship, introduced at the Treaty of Maastricht, can be seen as an umbrella concept that supersedes the more functional idea of free movement of economic actors, workers and service providers, and one that is more consistent with a constitutional understanding of the EU. To date, citizenship has been of practical effect in the granting of certain specific rights for citizens in other Member States (in the form of limited social benefits), although the Court of Justice is seeking to strengthen it, gradually, through the concept of the substance of rights, which it has introduced independently of free movement. The extent of its development will be tied up with the future development of the EU overall and whether it results in greater political union amongst the Member States.

POINTS TO REVIEW

- The European Communities were not initially conceived as having a human rights dimension, but as the scope of the common market expanded, it became necessary to address human rights issues.

- Today, the EU is bound both by the ECHR and its own EU Charter of Fundamental Rights, it also draws on national constitutional traditions, but is not bound to any particular constitutional tradition.

- Rights present particular problems of interpretation, because they are expressed in general terms and need to be applied to a wide range of specific factual situations, while they also can conflict with each other.

- The EU Charter of Fundamental Rights only has formal legal standing since the Treaty of Lisbon came into effect in 2009. It has many similarities with the ECHR, but also contains some differences, including some newly protected human rights.

- It is as yet unclear what relationship will exist between the EU Charter and the ECHR when the EU accedes to the ECHR, which the EU is required to do under Article 6 TEU.

- EU citizenship has so far developed as an umbrella concept for the rights of those exercising free movement; in practical terms, it facilitates the rights of citizens when moving to other Member States. Its future development, albeit with the assistance of the Court of Justice, will ultimately depend on how much the Member States are willing to strengthen political integration and especially regarding financial support for non-nationals, i.e. EU citizens from other Member States.

CHAPTER GLOSSARY

Bill of rights is the term used to describe the concept of a catalogue or list of fundamental human rights.

Conflicts of rights refers to a clash between two different rights that cannot be resolved in a way that fully satisfies both rights.

Derogations from rights refers to exceptions permitted to countries in exceptional circumstances to not comply with human rights obligations.

EU Charter of Fundamental Rights refers to the EU bill of rights adopted in 2000.

European Convention on Human Rights refers to a bill of rights agreed by Western European countries in the early 1950s as part of the Council of Europe system.

Jus cogens refers to peremptory norms of international law, which are considered fundamental moral principles that cannot be violated.

Limitations on rights refers to the concept that rights can rarely be protected in an absolute way and have to compete with other interests that may justify restricting rights in certain circumstances.

Margin of appreciation is a doctrine developed in the case law of the European Court of Human Rights that allows some differences of interpretation between the countries that have ratified the ECHR on how to protect human rights.

Originalism is an approach to judicial interpretation that seeks to give effect to the original intention of the law-maker.

'Sölange' refers to a line of case law from the German Federal Constitutional Court stating that EU law would only be accepted in the German legal system so long as it satisfied the guarantees of fundamental rights in the German Constitution.

TAKING THINGS FURTHER

J Coppel, A O'Neill 'The European Court of Justice: taking rights seriously?' (1992) 29 *Common Market Law Review* 669–92 A relatively old article, but one that is well known as being amongst relatively few academic critiques of the approach of the ECJ to fundamental rights until that point. It generated a response from Weiler and Lockhart.

C Costello 'The *Bosphorus* Ruling of the European Court of Human Rights' (2006) 6(1) *European Human Rights Law Review* 87–130 This article provides a detailed discussion in context of the important decision of the European Court of Human Rights on the *Bosphorus* judgment, in which it discussed its attitude to EU law.

S Douglas-Scott 'EU admission to the ECHR' (2012) 19 *Maastricht Journal of European and Comparative Law* This article provides one of the most recent discussions of EU accession to the ECHR and its consequences.

E Spaventa 'Seeing the wood despite the trees? On the scope of Union citizenship and its constitutional effects' (2008) 6(1) *Common Market Law Review* 13–45 This article offers an overall assessment of the introduction of citizenship in the EU since the Treaty of Maastricht 1992. It distinguishes between the material scope of citizenship laws and its personal scope and suggests that the case law indicates a loosening of the requirement for a cross-border effect of EU rights to arise, which has materialised to some extent in recent case law.

A Torres Perez *Conflicts of Rights in the European Union* (Oxford University Press 2009) This book offers a detailed discussion of the important issue of conflicts of rights, advocating an approach based on judicial dialogue between different courts to resolve differences in human rights protection.

S de Vries, U Bernitz and S Weatherill (eds) *The Protection of Fundamental Rights in the EU After Lisbon* (Hart Publishing 2013) This book is divided into three parts: the first looks at the tension between fundamental rights and fundamental freedoms of movement; the second looks at the horizontal effect of EU fundamental rights; and the third looks at the interaction among national, supranational and international courts and rights from a systemic perspective.

K Lenaerts 'Exploring the limits of the EU Charter of Fundamental Rights' (2013) 8(3) *European Constitutional Law Review* 375–403 This article examines Title VII of the EU Charter of Fundamental Rights (Articles 51 to 54) specifying the situations under which the Charter may be invoked and how the provisions of the Charter are to be interpreted, as well as looking at the meaning of the term 'principle' in Article 52(5) of the Charter and its overlap with the concept of 'general principles of EU law'.

D Kostokopoulou 'When EU citizens become foreigners' (2014) 20(4) *European Law Journal* 447–63 This article examines the limits of current EU law on the rights of citizens, taking a perspective that sees tension between national citizenship and EU citizenship.

Part 2

SUBSTANTIVE LAW

CHAPTERS IN THIS PART:

9

CHAPTER 9
FREE MOVEMENT OF GOODS I: CUSTOMS DUTIES, TAXES AND CHARGES OF EQUIVALENT EFFECT

This chapter looks at one of the two main aspects of free movement of goods in the EU: the prohibition on customs taxes on imports and exports and the prohibition on discriminatory or protective internal taxes targeted at imports or exports. A prohibition on taxes and customs duties is usually understood as a basic feature of a free trade area. In EU law, this prohibition is quite absolute; it admits of few exceptions. It is accompanied by a Common Customs Union, which means a common set of customs duties is applied by all EU Member States to goods coming from third countries into the EU. This prohibition on customs duties, and charges of equivalent effect, on goods being exported and imported between the Member States is accompanied by a prohibition on discrimination in internal taxation. This is a necessary complement to the prohibition on customs duties: if goods from other Member States could be made subject to higher taxes, e.g. at the point of sale, this could negate the prohibition on customs duties.

AS YOU READ . . .

The key questions that will be answered in this chapter are as follows:

– What do the different terms in the treaty provisions Article 30 on customs duties and charges of equivalent effect and Article 110 TFEU on internal taxation mean?

– What is the scope of Article 30 and Article 110? In what sense are they mutually exclusive?

– What are typical examples of kinds of national measures or rules that are prohibited?

– What exceptions or derogations exist both under the TFEU and as a result of the case law?

— What are the main points of difference between the two areas, chiefly regarding the relatively strict approach to the prohibition on customs and charges of equivalent effect?

— What way should problem situations in this area be approached?

9.1 INTRODUCTION

The treaty provisions on customs duties are one of the foundational principles of the common market (later the single market and now the 'internal market'). This prohibition is a key feature of a fully free trade area. Internationally, the World Trade Organization (WTO) tends to focus on what we will examine in the next chapter, which is a second important dimension of free trade: a prohibition on quotas or quantitative restrictions and equivalent measures.

The EU, the most advanced free trade area in the world, addresses fully the two aspects of free trade. The prohibition on customs duties and equivalent charges is quite absolute in EU law, with limited exceptions (as we will see in the next chapters, there are more exceptions to the prohibition on quotas or quantative restrictions and equivalent measures). This prohibition on customs duties, and charges of equivalent effect, on goods being exported and imported between the Member States is accompanied by a prohibition on discrimination or protection in internal taxation.

The two sets of rules are contained in Article 30, on customs duties, and Article 110 TFEU, on internal taxation.

> **KEY LEARNING POINT**
> ....
>
> **THE IMPORTANCE OF THE DIVIDE BETWEEN ARTICLE 30 TFEU ON CUSTOMS DUTIES AND ARTICLE 110 TFEU ON INTERNAL TAXATION**
> A particular charge or levy on goods is either: (i) a customs duty or CEE or (ii) an internal tax: it cannot be both, as *they are mutually exclusive categories*.[1] The distinction is vital:
>
> (1) A customs duty/CEE caught is automatically *unlawful* and can only escape the consequences of Article 30 TFEU by coming within one of the three 'exceptions'.
> (2) Charges that are part of internal taxation are caught by Article 110 TFEU and are judged under entirely different rules, i.e. direct discrimination and indirect discrimination is prohibited on similar goods (Article 110(1)),

---

....

1 See e.g. Case C–347/95 *UCAL* [1997] ECR I–4911 para 17 and Case C–213/96 *Outokumpu* [1998] ECR I–1777 para 19.

whilst indirect discrimination is prohibited on related goods if it has a protective effect under Article 110(2).

(3) Whilst the exceptions to Article 30 TFEU are quite narrow and specific, under Article 110 TFEU an open-ended category of exception exists in relation to indirect discrimination.

9.2 CUSTOMS DUTIES AND CHARGES OF EQUIVALENT EFFECT UNDER ARTICLE 30

KEY LEARNING POINT

THE MEANING OF 'GOODS'

As with Articles 34 and 35 TFEU, Article 30 does not define the term 'good'. The ECJ has interpreted it to mean any product capable of having a monetary value and being the object of commercial transactions.[2] One practical issue here is to distinguish goods from services. Anything that can be valued in money and that is capable of forming the subject of commercial transactions does not necessarily fall within the category of goods. In *Jägersköld*, the Court concluded that fishing rights were not goods. The Court stated that the activity consisting of making fishing waters available to third parties, for consideration and upon certain conditions, constitutes a provision of services[3] (whereas the fish themselves, once caught, would constitute goods). A lottery would also amount to a service, rather than goods (even though tickets are used).[4]

When what seems a service is connected with a good and the good is the predominant element of the transaction or process, all will be considered as 'goods', e.g. the process of depositing waste.[5]

EXPLAINING THE LAW

THE COMPETENCE OF THE EU CONCERNING TAXATION[6]

In general, taxation is a competence of the Member States, and not for the EU. However, the EU has some competence concerning tax matters, including under Articles 28–30 TFEU concerning goods. The tax competences of the EU can be

---

2   See, e.g. Case 7/68 *Commission v Italy* [1968] ECR 423 para 1.

3   Case C–97/98 *Jägersköld* [1999] ECR I–7319 paras 32–36.

4   Case C–275/92 *Schindler* [1994] ECR I–1039.

5   Case C–221/06 *Stadtgemeinde Frohnleiten Gemeindebetriebe Frohnleiten GmbH v Bundesminister für Lund- und Forstwirthschaft, Umwelt und Wasserwirtschaft* [2007] ECR I–9643.

6   J Thygesen 'National tax law: under influence of EU rules for the free movement of goods' (2013) 41(6/7) *Intertax* 351–59 at 351.

summarised by noting the ways in which the Member States may violate EU law by the way in which they organise their tax affairs:

- Violating the prohibition on customs duties and charges of equivalent effect the rules on the Common Customs Union under Articles 28–30 TFEU
- Violating the prohibition on discrimination or protection in favour of domestic goods in internal taxes under Article 110 TFEU
- Violating the general prohibition on state aid (subsidies to domestic industry) under Article 107(1) TFEU
- Violating limited EU rules on Value Added Tax (VAT) and excise duties, under Article 113 TFEU, which provides that:

   The Council shall, acting unanimously in accordance with a special legislative procedure and after consulting the European Parliament and the Economic and Social Committee, adopt provisions for the harmonisation of legislation concerning turnover taxes, excise duties and other forms of indirect taxation to the extent that such harmonisation is necessary to ensure the establishment and the functioning of the internal market and to avoid distortion of competition.[7]

9.2.1 COMMON CUSTOMS UNION (CCU)

KEY LEARNING POINT

THE COMMON CUSTOMS UNION

Articles 28–29 TFEU both envisage the abolition of tax barriers on trade in goods between Member States (whether the goods originated from within the EU or originally from a third country, i.e. a country outside the EU, having entered into circulation in to the EU), as well as providing for the formation of a common systems of customs, i.e. a Common Customs Union (CCU), for goods entering in to the EU for the first time from third countries. Under Article 3(1)(a) TFEU, the customs union is an exclusive competence of the EU. The CCU means that goods entering into the EU from a third country are charged the same level of customs duty, regardless of which Member State they first enter. After a good has entered the EU and any customs duty due has been paid, it can then circulate freely from one Member State to another without any further customs duties being payable, in the same way as goods produced in the Member States. The abolition of customs duties and CEEs came fully into effect on 1 July 1968. It was enhanced

---

7   Excise duties are indirect taxes on the consumption or the use of certain products. They are usually taxes expressed as a monetary amount per quantity of the product, rather than in percentages. Council Directive 2008/118/EC, OJ L 9 14.01.2009 p. 12, concerning the general arrangements for excise duty. Amongst the products regulated are energy products, alcoholic drinks and manufactured tobacco products.

with the completion of the internal market on 31 December 1992, which resulted
in the elimination of most administrative formalities involved in goods crossing
borders within the EU.

ARTICLE 28 TFEU

1. The Union shall comprise a customs union which shall cover all trade in goods
and which shall involve the prohibition between Member States of customs
duties on imports and exports and of all charges having equivalent effect, and
the adoption of a common customs tariff in their relations with third countries.

2. The provisions of Article 30 and of Chapter 2 of this Title shall apply to
products originating in Member States and to products coming from third
countries which are in free circulation in Member States.

ARTICLE 29 TFEU

Products coming from a third country shall be considered to be in free circulation
in a Member State if the import formalities have been complied with and any
customs duties or charges having equivalent effect which are payable have been
levied in that Member State, and if they have not benefited from a total or partial
drawback of such duties or charges.

The customs tax collected by the authorities of the Member States from the CCU go
directly to the 'own resources' of the EU.[8]

9.2.2 CUSTOMS DUTIES

ARTICLE 30 TFEU

Customs duties on imports and exports and charges having equivalent effect
shall be prohibited between Member States. This prohibition shall also apply to
customs duties of a fiscal nature.

---

8   See Article 2(1) of Council Decision 2007/436/EC and EURATOM, OJ L 163 23.6.2007 p. 17, on the system of
    the European Communities' own resources, adopted under Article 311 TFEU (ex Article 267 ECT). Article 311
    TFEU provides for the Union's own resources, to be determined by decision of the Council acting unanimously
    and after consulting with the European Parliament.

A customs duty is a tax on imports or exports imposed because the good is an import or export, i.e. because the good crosses a border, and so it is not imposed on domestic products, which have not crossed the national border.[9] Usually, a customs duty is imposed at the physical stage of crossing a border (although it could be imposed at a later stage in the case of imports or an earlier stage in the case of exports, but this is not usual).

Around the world, customs duties are commonly placed on imported goods. They represent a kind of protection of domestic goods: the competing domestic good does not have to pay the customs duty, and so can compete more easily. It is much less common for a country to impose a custom duty on a domestically produced good being exported (since this would make a country's own goods less competitive by increasing their price). In practice, therefore, customs duties generally relate to imports. EU law prohibits customs duties on goods circulated from one Member State to another, in order to facilitate trade between the Member States as much as possible.

MAKING CONNECTIONS
++++++++++++++++++

THE PROHIBITION ON CUSTOMS DUTIES AND CEES IS DIRECTLY EFFECTIVE BOTH VERTICALLY AND POSSIBLY, IN EFFECT, HORIZONTALLY

The ban on customs duties is directly effective. However, it was what is now Article 30 that was in issue in e.g. *Van Gend en Loos*,[10] the case that first established the doctrine of direct effect. Given the centrality of free movement of goods to the idea of a common market (most free trade areas focus primarily on some aspect of free movement of goods), perhaps it is not surprising in retrospect that the Court of Justice chose this case to announce the new doctrine.

Although it is usually the case that customs duties of CEEs will be imposed by Member States, a CEE can be created by a private entity, in which case the CEE is still prohibited, i.e. Article 30 can, unusually, have horizontal direct effect. An example is *Dubois et Fils SA and General Cargo Services v Garoner Exploitation SA*,[11] where Garoner Exploitation was the owner of an international road station near Paris where the customs authorities had offices. Garoner Exploitation imposed a charge on vehicles being cleared through customs to offset the costs of the customs authorities operating on its premises. The ECJ held that this was prohibited.

---

9 See e.g. Case 90/79 *Commission v France* [1981] ECR 283 para 13; Case C–109/98 *CRT France International v Directeur Régional des Impôts de Bourgogne* [1999] ECR I–2237 para 11.

10 Case 26/62 *Van Gend en Loos* [1963] ECR 1.

11 Case 16/94 *Dubois et Fils SA and General Cargo Services v Garoner (GA) Exploitation SA* [1995] ECR I–2421.

In *Dubois v Garoner Exploitation*, the ECJ did not explicitly state that Article 30 has horizontal direct effect, but it indirectly achieved the same result by finding that the CEE arises from a failure of the Member State:

> 20 The nature of the measure requiring economic agents to bear part of the operating costs of customs services is immaterial. Whether the pecuniary charge is borne by the economic agent by virtue of a unilateral measure adopted by the authorities or, as in the present case, as a result of a series of private contracts, it arises in all cases, directly or indirectly, from the failure of the Member State concerned to fulfil its financial obligations under Articles 9 and 12 of the Treaty.

> 21 It follows that the answer to be given to the national court is that Articles 9 and 12 of the EC Treaty apply to a transit charge designed to compensate a private undertaking for bearing costs arising from the performance by the customs and veterinary services of their tasks as providers of services in the public interest even if it has not been imposed by the State but arises from an agreement concluded by that undertaking with its customers.[12]

9.2.3 CHARGES HAVING EQUIVALENT EFFECT (CEES)

A charge having an equivalent effect (CEE) relates to charges imposed on goods being imported or exported because of the fact of crossing the Member State's border, which are not called or labelled as customs duties, but which nonetheless are equivalent to a customs charge. The ECJ has defined a CEE as:

> . . . any pecuniary charge, however small and whatever its designation and mode of application, which is imposed unilaterally on domestic or foreign goods by reason of the fact that they cross a frontier . . . constitutes a CEE . . .[13]

> *or*

> . . . [It can be a CEE] even if it is not imposed for the benefit of the State, is not discriminatory or protective in effect and if the product on which the charge is imposed is not in competition with any domestic product.[14]

So it is not the fact that a tax is imposed physically at a border that counts or makes it contrary to Article 30 TFEU: it is any tax imposed solely by virtue of a good being an import from another Member State.[15] The ECJ has applied this logic to deal with

---

12 Ibid paras 20–21.

13 See e.g. Case 158/82 *Commission v Denmark* para 18; Case C–90/94 *Haahr Petroleum* [1997] ECR I–4085 para 20; Case C–347/95 *UCAL* [1997] ECR I–4911 para 18; and Case C–213/96 *Outokumpu* para 20; Case C–293/02 *Jersey Produce Marketing Organisation* [2005] ECR I–9543 para 55; Case C–72/03 *Carbonati Apuani* [2004] ECR I–8027 para 20.

14 See e.g. Case C–24/68 *Commission v Italy* [1969] ECR 193 para 9.

15 Case 78/76 *Firma Steinike und Weinlig v Bundesamt für Ernährung und Forstwirtschaft* [1977] ECR 595.

cases where goods cross an internal frontier, but which is analogous to crossing a border, in the case of charges imposed on goods entering French overseas territories from France.[16] The fact that there need not be any discrimination in favour or protection of comparable or related domestic goods indicates the absolute nature of the prohibition compared with Article 110 TFEU below.

> KEY LEARNING POINT
>
> ### WHEN A CHARGE OR TAX IMPOSED AT THE BORDER WILL BE REGARDED AS INTERNAL TAXATION FALLING UNDER ARTICLE 110 TFEU
>
> Although in general, taxes imposed at the border will be considered to be a customs tax, a charge levied at the border will be regarded as an internal tax, rather than as a CEE, where the comparable charge levied on national products is applied at the same rate, at the same marketing stage and on the basis of an identical charging event.[17]

The ECJ has consistently followed this definition. In *Commission v Italy (Statistical Levy)*, the facts concerned a small Italian levy or charge on goods being exported or imported.[18] The ostensible purpose was to collect statistical material for use in tracking patterns of trade and to assist traders by providing such information. The Court of Justice found it to be contrary to the treaties:

> As it is imposed universally on goods crossing the frontier, the charge in question hampers the interpenetration at which the Treaty aims and thus has an effect on the free circulation of goods equivalent to a customs duty.

> The very low rate of the charge cannot change its character with regard to the principles of the Treaty which for the purpose of determining the legality of those charges, do not admit of the substitution of quantitative criteria for those based on the nature of the charge.[19]

In another case from Italy, *Commission v Italy (Art Treasures)*, Italy imposed a tax on the export of art-historical items, the rationale being to protect Italy's national heritage.[20] This too was found to be contrary to the treaties:

> A tax levied on the exportation of articles possessing artistic or historic value falls within the prohibition contained in [now Article 30 TFEU] by reason of the fact that

16 See Case C–163/90 *Legros* [1992] ECR I–4625; Joined Cases C–363 & C–407–411/93 *Lancry and Ors v Direction Générale des Douanes and Others* [1994] ECR I–3957.

17 Joined Cases C–441 & 442/98 *Kapniki Michaïlidis & Idrima Kinonikon Asphalise* [2000] ECR I–7145 para 24.

18 Case 24/68 *Commission v Italy (Statistical Levy)* [1969] ECR 193.

19 Ibid para 14.

20 Case 7/68 *Commission v Italy (Art Treasures)* [1969] ECR 42.

export trade in the goods in question is hindered by the pecuniary burden which it imposes on the price of the exported articles.[21]

EXPLAINING THE LAW

THE STRICT CHARACTER OF THE PROHIBITION UNDER ARTICLE 30 TFEU

This example illustrates the strict character of Article 30 TFEU; under the other free movement rules, including under Article 36 TFEU (relating to exceptions or derogations to the prohibition on quantitative restrictions and measures of equivalent effect), the protection of national heritage is recognised as a ground of derogation. The rationale for the claimed derogation is irrelevant, however socially useful it may be, under Article 30 TFEU.

This is also apparent from *Sociaal Fonds voor de Diamantarbeiters v Brachfeld*, where a Dutch levy of 0.43 per cent was charged on imported diamonds, with the proceeds being paid to a social fund for workers in the industry.[22] This was also contrary to Article 30 TFEU.

EXPLAINING THE LAW

THE 'EXOTIC IMPORT'

The term 'exotic import' is sometimes used to describe an import with no domestic equivalent, i.e. the importing country does not manufacture a similar or equivalent good. Of course, such goods are not very rare or unusual. A common example is cars. Not every country has a car manufacturer. In this situation, any tax will generally be a customs duty, since there is no comparison for the purposes of discrimination under Article 110 TFEU.[23] A tax on an imported 'exotic' good can still be an internal tax if it is part of a general system of internal taxes.

9.2.4 'DISGUISED' CUSTOMS DUTIES

EXPLAINING THE LAW

THE STRICT CHARACTER OF THE PROHIBITION UNDER ARTICLE 30 TFEU

If a charge is imposed on both imported and domestic products, but the proceeds are used *exclusively* to help the domestic products, this is considered CEE on

---

21 Ibid para 3.

22 Joined Cases 2 & 3/69 *Sociaal Fonds voor de Diamantarbeiters v Brachfeld* [1969] CMLR 335.

23 Case C–47/88 *Commission v Denmark* [1990] ECR I–4509. See also e.g. Case 193/79 *Cooperativa Cofruta v Amministrazione delle Finanzo dello Stato* [1987] ECR 2085.

imports because all the money paid by the importers is used to assist their domestic competitors. The domestic competitors are being fully compensated, albeit indirectly, for the tax burden they bear. This is a kind of 'disguised' customs duty. An example is *Capolongo v Azienda Agricola Maya*, concerning an Italian charge on cardboard applied to all products, imported or domestic, but the proceeds of the tax were used entirely to promote the industry in Italy.[24]

Nygård[25] is one of a number of cases[26] in which the ECJ departed from its previous approach of considering charges imposed solely on exported goods[27] so as not to contravene (now) Article 30 TFEU. In *Nygård*, Danish law provided that a production levy was to be charged for every pig – including sows, boars, store pigs and piglets – bred and slaughtered in Denmark and declared fit for human consumption following inspections carried out by the public authorities. The levy was also payable in respect of pigs slaughtered for private consumption.

Germany provided for a similar levy. Nygård refused to pay the Danish levy, having paid the German levy when he exported pigs to Germany, and was sued before the Danish courts for refusing to pay the Danish levy. Nygård argued that the Danish levy was a CEE or, alternatively, if it was not a CEE it constituted discriminatory internal taxation prohibited by (now) Article 110 of the TFEU in so far as the levy resources are allocated to activities benefiting exclusively, or to a proportionately greater degree, the breeding of pigs for slaughter on the domestic market.

Proceeds of the Danish levy were used for a variety of purposes connected with the pigmeat industry in Denmark. The details of the Danish rule were that the levy was payable by the producer when pigmeat was destined for the domestic market at the point of delivery for slaughter, whereas in the case of export it was payable by the exporter, irrespective of whether or not he was also the producer. The Commission had authorised the Danish levy under state aid, so the issue in this case concerned the interaction of state aid and Articles 30 and 110 TFEU. On the question of characterising the Danish levy, the ECJ observed:

21. It also follows from the Court's case law that, for the purposes of the legal characterisation of a charge levied on national products processed or marketed on the national market and on national products exported in an unprocessed state in accordance with identical criteria, it may be necessary to take into account the purpose for which the revenue from the charge is applied (see, by way of analogy, *UCAL*, cited above, paragraph 20).

24 Case 77/72 *Capolongo v Azienda Agricola Maya* [1973] ECR 611.
25 Case C–234/99 *Nygård* [2002] ECR I–3657.
26 See e.g. Case 222/82 *Apple and Pear Development Council v K.J. Lewis* [1983] ECR 4083.
27 See also, e.g. Joined Cases C–441 & 442/98 *Michaïlidis* [2000] ECR I–7145.

22. Thus, if the revenue from such a charge is intended to finance activities for the special advantage of the taxed national products processed or marketed on the national market, it may follow that the charge imposed on the basis of the same criteria nevertheless constitutes discriminatory taxation in so far as the fiscal burden on products processed or marketed on the national market is neutralised by the advantages which the charge is used to finance whilst the charge on the products exported in an unprocessed state constitutes a net burden (see, by way of analogy, Case 73/79 *Commission v Italy* [1980] ECR 1533, paragraph 15, Joined Cases C–78/90 to C–83/90 *Compagnie Commerciale de l'Ouest and Others* [1992] ECR I–1847, paragraph 26, and *UCAL*, paragraph 21).[28]

The discrimination here is similar to the position in *Capolongo*, except the discrimination is between goods for the domestic market and goods for the export market: goods for the domestic market had their tax burden reduced or neutralised by the benefits from the way in which the levy was spent.

The Court went on to note its standard approach: if the tax burden on the domestic goods is fully neutralised or offset, the levy amounts to CEE; if the tax burden on the goods for domestic consumption is only partly offset, the situation falls under Article 110 as discriminatory internal taxation.[29] The Court rejected the argument that the charging event in this case was different, noting its previous case law on the marketing of animal meat that the relevant marketing stage was withdrawal from the national herd, which can be applied to both the pigs intended for domestic and export markets in this case.[30]

Further, the ECJ held in *Nygård* that it did not matter for the purpose of classifying the levy as not being a CEE and thus falling under internal taxation subject to Article 110 TFEU that the levy was payable by the producer or exporter; this did not differentiate the charging event.[31] This factor might have been considered relevant in that different marketing stages could be identified in the sense of production and distribution, but the Court did note that any difference in prices would be passed on to the producer by the exporter.[32] On the facts, it was found that the levy fell to be considered under

....

28 Case C–234/99 *Nygård* [2002] ECR I–3657 paras 20–21.

29 Ibid para 23, citing *Compagnie Commerciale de l'Ouest and Others* para 27; Case C–17/91 *Lornoy and Others* [1992] ECR I–6523 para 21; and Case C–72/92 *Scharbatke* [1993] ECR I–5509 para 10.

30 Case C–234/99 *Nygård* [2002] ECR I–3657 paras 28–30, citing Joined Cases 36/80 & 71/80, *Irish Creamery Milk Suppliers Association and Others* [1981] ECR 735 para 23.

31 This aspect of the judgment in *Nygård* might be contrasted with the earlier judgment in Case 29/72 *Mirimex SpA v Minister for Finance of Italy* [1972] ECR 1309, where inspections of imported meat were found not to fall under Article 110 TFEU (i.e. were not a part of a general system of internal taxation) because the inspections of imported meat were conducted by a body different from that inspecting domestic meat and each body applied criteria different from those applied by the other. It seems the analogous character of the taxes is open to different interpretations, depending on how specifically and strictly the test of comparison is applied.

32 Case C–234/99 *Nygård* [2002] ECR I–3657 paras 31–32.

(now) Article 110 TFEU, since revenue was not solely allocated to financing activities exclusively benefiting the production of pigs for slaughter on the national market.[33]

> **KEY CASE** *VARIATIONS ON THE* CAPOLONGO *SITUATION*
>
> Apart from the specific situation in *Capolongo*, where the burden of taxation on the domestic good (or the good intended for the domestic market) is entirely cancelled out by the reinvestment of the proceeds of the levy to help domestic industry (in which case the tax is a CEE), two other, related situations can possibly arise:
>
> (1) If the proceeds are not used exclusively (rather, they are used only *partially*) to help domestic products, this is considered a discriminatory internal tax and to fall under Article 110 TFEU, since the domestic goods too bear a tax burden that is not fully offset, as in *Nygård*.
> (2) If the proceeds from the imported products go back into the national exchequer and are not used specifically to help competing domestic products, the use of them to help domestic industry more generally is considered as a subsidy or 'state aid' and is dealt with under competition law (we will look at state aids briefly in Chapter 14).

9.2.5 EXCEPTIONS

The ECJ has formulated what are treated as three 'exceptions', although the first one is really a prior issue of categorisation as to whether Article 30 or Article 110 TFEU applies.

9.2.5.1 CHARGES FALLING INTO 'INTERNAL TAXATION'

This is sometimes treated as an exception, but it is really a question of whether Article 30 applies in the first place, i.e. it is a prior issue of correct categorisation, rather than an exception. If a charge or levy is properly labelled 'internal taxation' it must be judged according to Article 110, *not* Article 30 TFEU. The ECJ set out the standard test in *Nygård*, reflecting previous case law:

> 21. . . . a charge may not be . . . characterised [as a customs duty or CEE] if it forms part of a general system of internal dues applying systematically to categories of products according to objective criteria applied without regard to the origin of the products, in which case it falls within the scope of [now Article 110] of the Treaty.
>
> 20. . . . This latter case, however, presupposes that the charge is imposed on national products processed or marketed on the national market and on national

---

33 Ibid para 39.

products exported in an unprocessed state at the same marketing stage, and that the chargeable event is identical for both classes of products (see, by way of analogy, in regard to charges levied on national products and imported products, Joined Cases C–149/91 & C–150/91 *Sanders Adour and Guyomarc'h Orthez Nutrition Animale* [1992] ECR I–3899, paragraph 17, and *Outokumpu*, paragraph 24).[34]

9.2.5.2 CHARGES FOR SERVICES RENDERED

If a charge is imposed to meet the cost of a service actually rendered to the importer, it is not a CEE. However, the conditions are strict:

- the charge to the importer/exporter must not exceed the cost of the service (i.e. the fee must be proportionate, a charge will be deemed to be a CEE if it is a flat-rate charge based on the value of the goods and not on the costs of the service[35]) and
- the service must confer a tangible, *individual* benefit on the trader concerned.

EXPLAINING THE LAW

CHARGING FOR SERVICES RENDERED

The effect of the case law is almost that, although the ECJ has not said this quite explicitly, the importer or exporter must voluntarily agree to or ask for the service before it is legitimate for the Member State to charge for it. However, if a service is imposed but it is necessary and clearly for the benefit of the specific goods, i.e. it is an *individualised* benefit[36] on which it is imposed, this could be justified.

In *Cadsky v Istituto Nazionale per il Commercio Estero*, fees were imposed for quality control inspections on vegetables exported from Italy to improve the reputation of Italian produce abroad, and the ECJ held that any benefit from this:

> . . . relates to the general interest of all exporters, so that the individual interest of each of them is so ill-defined that a charge imposed in payment for this inspection cannot be regarded as consideration for a specific benefit actually and individually conferred.[37]

The checks were in the general public interest, but it was not fair or reasonable to impose the costs on importers who did not benefit from them specifically. In *Bresciani*,

---

34 Case C–234/99 *Nygård* [2002] ECR I–3657 paras 19–20. The question of double taxation (the fact that Nygård had to pay both Danish and German levies) was not at the time regulated by EC law.

35 See e.g. Case 170/88 *Ford España v Spain* [1989] ECR 2305.

36 A Kaczorowska *EU Law* (3rd edn Routledge 2013) 505.

37 Case 63/74 *Cadsky v Istituto Nazionale per il Commercio Estero* [1975] 2 CMLR 246.

the ECJ similarly held that charges for general health or quality checks at frontiers (in this case imported raw cowhides) did not satisfy the requirement for specific benefit on the importer.[38]

9.2.5.3 CHARGES FOR INSPECTIONS CARRIED OUT UNDER EU LAW REQUIREMENTS

Fees can be charged for mandatory inspections under EU law (as opposed to the law of a Member State), again provided the fee does not exceed the actual cost. An example is *Commission v Germany*, where veterinary inspections on imported animals mandated by Community law were exempted from (now) Article 30 TFEU.[39]

9.3 INTERNAL TAXATION UNDER ARTICLE 110 TFEU

Article 110 TFEU is concerned with internal taxation, in other words, tax that is imposed internally within a Member State and that is not related to the fact that a good has crossed the Member State's border for the purpose of export or import. The most common form of internal taxation on goods is valued added tax, which is usually imposed at the retail stage. However, internal taxation could be imposed at any stage in the production, distribution or sale of a good within a given Member State. A preliminary point is that Article 110 applies equally to exports and to imports, although in practice,[40] the question arises much more often in the context of imports. In *Nygård*, discussed above, there was a breach where an internal tax applied to goods intended for the domestic market and goods intended for the export was used in such a way as partially to offset the burden of the levy on the domestic goods, but not on the exported goods. The levy was prohibited to the extent that it was used to offset the tax burden on goods for the domestic market.[41]

9.3.1 ARTICLE 110, FIRST PARAGRAPH: DIRECT OR INDIRECT DISCRIMINATION

ARTICLE 110(1) TFEU

No Member State shall impose, directly or indirectly, on the products of other Member States any internal taxation of any kind in excess of that imposed directly or indirectly on similar domestic products.

---

38 Case 87/75 *Bresciani* [1976] ECR 129. See also Case 24/68 *Commission v Italy* [1969] ECR 193 and Case C–389/00 *Commission v Germany* [2003] ECR I–2001.

39 Case 18/87 *Commission v Germany* [1988] ECR 5427.

40 Case 142/77 *Larsen and Kjerulff* [1978] ECR 1543 para 27; Case C–234/99 *Nygård* [2002] ECR I–3657 para 41.

41 Case C–234/99 *Nygård* [2002] ECR I–3657 para 42, citing Case 94/74 *IGAV* [1975] ECR 699 para 13; Case C–72/92 *Scharbatke* [1993] ECR I–5509 para 10 and Case C–347/95 *UCAL* [1997] ECR I–4911 para 23.

What Article 110(1) targets is discrimination in internal taxation of goods between goods based on their country of origin.[42] It reflects the non-discrimination on grounds of nationality principle that is fundamental to all the free movement principles. Unlawful discrimination can only occur between things that are similar, and thus a key issue under Article 110(1) is the test for the similarity of goods.

KEY LEARNING POINT

SIMILARITY OF GOODS UNDER ARTICLE 110(1) TFEU
The ECJ interprets 'similarity' widely and takes into account: the 'objective characteristics' of the product. The relevant characteristics may, depending on the product, concern aspects such as:

– composition; method of manufacture
– taste, alcohol content etc
– whether two products are capable of meeting the same needs from the point of view of the consumer (though the court is not particularly taken by evidence of national habits or customs if that is used as a justification for lower taxes on domestic products).

As we will see, a similar issue arises under Article 102 TFEU in the definition of a product market (where the idea of interchangeability is also central).

In *Commission v France*, France taxed grain-based spirits at FF 2110 per hectolitre, while it taxed wine-based spirits at FF 710.[43] On the facts, it was found that there was no significant production of spirits obtained from cereals in France. The Court avoided ruling whether these were similar products, as it held they were in any case caught under (now) Article 110(2) TFEU.[44]

EXPLAINING THE LAW

GOODS CAN FALL UNDER ARTICLE 110(2) TFEU IF THEY ARE NOT SIMILAR
If goods are not similar, but still can be competing with each other, they are subject to Article 110(2) TFEU. In borderline cases, where it can be difficult to assess the similarity of goods, the easiest approach to take is simply to apply Article 101(2) without getting into possible awkward and technical analysis of how similar goods are.

---

42 The level of taxation, e.g. that it is very high, cannot be challenged: see Case C–47/88 *Commission v Denmark* [1990] ECR I–4509 paras 9–10.

43 Case 168/78 *Commission v France* [1980] ECR 347.

44 Ibid paras 39–40. The Court said it was unnecessary to address similarity since clearly the products fell under paragraph 2.

Another example is *Commission v Italy*, where an Italian tax on bananas was not levied on other table fruit, in the circumstances that Italy produced very few bananas and more of other table fruit.[45] These were found to be not similar, but the ECJ found a breach of Article 110(2). The ECJ here did engage in an analysis of similarity:

> 9. It must therefore be considered, as the Court pointed out in its judgment of 17 February 1976 in Case 45/75, *Rewe-Zentrale Des Lebensmittel-Grosshandels GmbH v Hauptzollamt Landau Pfalz* [1976] ECR 181, whether bananas and other table fruit typically produced in Italy have similar characteristics and meet the same consumer needs. Consequently, in order to assess similarity, account must be taken, on the one hand, of a set of objective characteristics and their water content, and, on the other hand, of set of objective characteristics of the two categories of the product in question, such as their organoleptic[46] characteristics and their water content, and, on the other hand, whether or not the two categories of fruit can satisfy the same consumer needs.

> 10. It must be observed in this case that the two categories of fruit in question, that is to say, on the one hand, bananas, and, on the other, table fruit typically produced in Italy mentioned above have different characteristics, as the Commission has conceded, the organoleptic characteristics and the water content of the two categories differ. By way of example, the higher water content of pears and other fruit typically grown in Italy give them thirst-quenching properties which bananas do not possess. Moreover, the observation of the Italian government, which has not been challenged by the Commission, that the banana is regarded, at least on the Italian market, as a foodstuff which is particularly nutritious, of a high energy content and well-suited for infants must be accepted. It must therefore be held that those two categories of fruit are not similar within the meaning of the first paragraph of [now Article 110 TFEU].[47]

In *Commission v Denmark*, wine made from grapes (all imported) was taxed at between DKK 11 and DKK 20 per litre, while wine made from other fruit (a typical Danish product) was taxed at between DKK 7 and DKK 11 per litre.[48] These were found to be similar products, an easier assessment to make given the common designation of them as wine. The differential treatment by Danish tax law was thus contrary to (now) Article 110(1) TFEU.

In *Nygård*, an issue arose as to the similarity of animals as products depending on whether they were dead or alive. Relying on previous authority, as noted above, the Court did not consider it decisive whether animals were taxed when alive or after slaughter; the charging event could be defined as a withdrawal from the national herd.[49]

---

45 Case 184/85 *Commission v Italy* [1987] ECR 2013.
46 This refers to the sensory qualities of food such as taste, colour, smell and moisture.
47 Case 184/85 *Commission v Italy* [1987] ECR 2013 paras 9–10.
48 Case 106/84 *Commission v Denmark* [1986] ECR 833.
49 Case C–234/99 *Nygård* [2002] ECR I–3657 para 28.

9.3.2 ARTICLE 110 TFEU, SECOND PARAGRAPH: INDIRECT PROTECTION

ARTICLE 110(2) TFEU

Furthermore, no Member State shall impose on the products of other Member States any internal taxation of such a nature as to afford indirect protection to other products.

There is a protective effect in taxation if the tax rules in question are not discriminatory because the goods in question are not similar to each other, but, nevertheless, imported goods from another Member State are put in a disadvantageous position vis-à-vis domestic goods. Protective effect overlaps with the idea of indirect discrimination, but the difference is that, with protective effect, the goods in question are not direct competitors, which are not immediate substitutes for each other or interchangeable, but nonetheless there is some kind of market relationship between them.

It could be said that indirect discrimination and protective effect for related goods shade into each other as categories. Quite often, the ECJ will not look at the issue of similarity in any depth and will simply apply paragraph 2 of Article 110, where it is enough to show goods are in competition without a close analysis of the exact degree of similarity. Where there is such a relationship, it has to be shown that the tax system actually has a protective effect on the competing domestic product, putting the imported product at a disadvantage.

In *Commission v UK*, the UK applied excise duty rates on wine that was five times that on beer.[50] The ECJ applied (now) Article 110(2) TFEU and found that the UK's tax system had the effect of subjecting wine imported from other Member States to an additional tax burden so as to afford protection to domestic beer and that this protection was most marked in the case of the most popular wines. The effect of the UK tax system was to stamp wine with the hallmark of a luxury product, which meant that it was not seen in the eyes of the consumer as a genuine alternative to the typical domestically produced beverage.

In *Humblot v Directeur des Services Fiscaux*, France had an annual car tax calculated by reference to engine size, with a significantly higher tax on larger cars, of which France did not produce many.[51] The French rating meant that buying a larger car meant accepting a much higher tax rate, which reduced the competition French car industries faced from large imported cars. The ECJ applied Article 110 here, concluding that

50 Case 170/78 *Commission v UK* [1983] ECR 2265.
51 Case 112/84 *Humblot v Directeur des Services Fiscaux* [1986] ECR 1367.

the special tax reduced competition, although the Court did not say expressly which paragraph it was basing its judgment on.[52]

Commission v Italy concerned bananas and whether a tax on them violated now Article 110(2) TFEU relative to the treatment of competing Italian fruit. The ECJ noted that the function of Article 110(2) was to cover all forms of indirect tax protection in the case of products which, without being similar within the meaning of Article 110(1), are nevertheless in competition, even partial, indirect or potential competition, with each other.[53] The tax here was unlawful because it did not apply to competing Italian goods, giving them an advantage by reducing competition, especially as the tax amounted to almost half the price of the imported goods.[54]

In *Commission v Belgium*, it was not incompatible with Article 110(2) TFEU for Belgium to introduce a higher tax on wine than on beer, even though a higher tax on wine could lead consumers to choose beer as an alternative to wine.[55] Reflecting previous case law the ECJ found that only commonly consumed wines, which are in general cheap wines, have enough characteristics in common with beer to constitute an alternative choice for consumers and may therefore be regarded as being in competition with beer for the purposes of Article 110(2) TFEU.[56]

EXPLAINING THE LAW

DIFFERENT TESTS UNDER ARTICLE 110 TFEU

In *Commission v Belgium*, the ECJ went on to note that, while discrimination under Article 110(1) related to a comparison of tax burdens relative to rates of tax, the mode of assessment or the detailed rules of application, Article 110(2) involved a more general criterion of protection, given the difficulty of making sufficiently precise comparison between the products in question.[57] It followed that an assessment under paragraph 2 had to take into account the impact of the tax on the competitive relationship of the products concerned.[58]

However, the Court went on to focus on price, which perhaps inevitably is a key consideration under both paragraphs of Article 110 TFEU since it is a key factor for consumers. On the facts of this case, the ECJ found that the Commission had not established that the difference in prices between beer and wine was so

---

52 Ibid paras 14–16.
53 Case 184/85 *Commission v Italy* [1987] ECR 2013 para 11.
54 Ibid para 13.
55 Case 356/85 *Commission v Belgium* [1987] ECR 3299.
56 Ibid para 11.
57 Ibid para 14.
58 Ibid para 15.

small that a 6 per cent difference in tax would influence consumer behaviour.[59] What emerges from the case is that it may be more difficult to prove a violation of paragraph 2, even though it is easier for products to fall within the scope of paragraph 2 than is the case under paragraph 1. Under paragraph 1, the mere fact of differences in treatment of themselves are enough.

9.3.3 PERMITTED PREFERENCES UNDER ARTICLE 110 TFEU

The ECJ may permit a Member State to give a preference to certain products in certain situations, *but only indirect discrimination* or protective effect; direct discrimination could never be justified in this way. There must be shown to be a legitimate social justification for the measure in question, and it must be based on objective factors.

KEY LEARNING POINT
....

OBJECTIVE JUSTIFICATION UNDER ARTICLE 110 TFEU
As with the other areas of free movement, the ECJ has developed case law in which it accepts a reason for not applying Article 110 TFEU. However, as with all the other free movement principles, case law developed exceptions can only justify indirect discrimination or a protective effect (protective effect could here be seen as equivalent to non-discriminatory obstacles overriding other free movement principles, except the concept of protective effect is explicit in the treaty).

The concept of objective justification, as with the other free movement principles, where there is an equivalent concept, is an open-ended category of sound policy reasons as to why indirect discrimination or protective effect may be permitted to the Member States. For example, in *Chemical Farmaceutici v DAF SpA*, synthetic ethyl alcohol was taxed more highly than the same product obtained from natural fermentation, in order to encourage the distillation of agricultural products as against the manufacture of alcohol from petroleum derivatives.[60] The ECJ noted that the system of taxation pursued an objective of industrial policy and that it was not discriminatory in its application.[61]

In *Commission v France*, French taxation of sweet wines produced in the traditional manner was lower than that on liqueur wines.[62] The ECJ found that this was justified, since it was intended to encourage production in agriculturally poor soil, which could

....

59 Ibid paras 18–20.
60 Case 140/79 *Chemical Farmaceutici v DAF SpA* [1981] ECR 1.
61 Ibid paras 15–16.
62 Case 196/85 *Commission v France* [1987] ECR 1597.

more easily sustain grapes for sweet wines, i.e. it was justified to stimulate production in agriculturally underdeveloped areas, and it was not discriminatory in its application.[63]

```
┌─────────────────────────────────┐
│   Article 30 or Article 110     │
│   (TFEU): one or the other      │
└─────────────────────────────────┘
```
↙   ↘

Customs duty or CEE (Article 30 TFEU)

Internal taxation (Article 110 TFEU)

(i) Direct or indirect discrimination (Article 110(1)) (similar goods)
(ii) Protective effect (Article 110(2) (goods not similar, but related, i.e. in competition)

↓   ↓

Only justifiable:
(i) Service rendered
(ii) Requirement of EU Law

Justifiable under open-ended caselaw category of objective justification

APPLYING THE LAW

ANSWERING A PROBLEM QUESTION ON ARTICLES 30 AND 110 TFEU

A problem question should be approached in a series of logical steps:

(1) Classifying the tax charge as either (i) a customs tax or CEE under Article 30 TFEU or (ii) an internal tax under Article 110 TFEU:
   (i) *if it is imposed solely on the imported good and not on any competing domestic good*, then it is a customs duty or CEE
   (ii) *if it is imposed on goods destined for the export market to other EU Member States*, but is not imposed or is smaller or is compensated for, for the same goods intended for the domestic market, the additional charge is a custom duty or CEE
   (iii) *if it is imposed on both imported goods and competing domestic goods*, then it will be internal taxation, but it must (a) satisfy the test of being part of a general system of internal dues applying systematically to categories of products according to objective criteria applied without regard to the origin of the products and at the same marketing stage, and that the chargeable event is identical for both classes of products and (b) it must

---

63 Ibid paras 9–10.

not be a disguised customs duty whereby the burden on domestic goods is fully offset (see *Capolongo*)

(2) *If it is a customs duty or CEE, determining if an exception applies:* (i) charges for services rendered or (ii) charges to cover costs of checks/inspections required by EU law

or

(2) *If it is internal taxation, which paragraph of Article 110 TFEU applies?* Paragraph 1 if the goods are similar and there is discrimination (direct or indirect) and paragraph 2 if the goods are not similar, but are competing and there is protective effect involving a competitive disadvantage.

(3) *If it is internal taxation, can it be objectively justified?*

SAMPLE PROBLEM QUESTION AND ANSWER ON ARTICLES 30 AND 110 TFEU

Sample problem

(a) A 15 per cent tax is imposed on all pasta sold in Denmark. No pasta is produced in Denmark. Potatoes are subject to a low 10 per cent tax because the Danish Government says that potatoes are a healthy food and wishes to encourage their consumption. It claims that in some regions of Denmark where soil is shallow and poor, only potatoes will grow among commonly eaten vegetables and it wishes to encourage the agriculture in these areas. The pasta importers XYZ Ltd and the European Commission consider that there must be something they can do about this discrepancy.

(b) TLC Ltd manufactures high-quality cheddar cheese in the UK and has been building up an export market in the Netherlands. The Dutch Government has just reduced the sales tax on all cheeses with low cholesterol levels, on the grounds of health. This means that cheeses such as Edam and Brie now get the benefit of a lower tax rate; cheeses such as Cheddar are higher in saturated fats, must pay the higher rate of tax and are correspondingly more expensive. All Edam cheese is manufactured in the Netherlands.

(c) ABC Ltd is a UK company specialising in production of fruit-flavoured, low-alcohol drinks directed at young drinkers. Sales of its product in Scandinavian countries are low. There is considerable competition in these countries from traditional fruit-based soft drinks and flavoured beers, manufactured by domestic companies. In Sweden, a 10 per cent sales tax is payable on the soft drinks; ABC's product falls into a different tax category and pays 17.5 per cent. ABC objects to this tax differential and also complains of a health check on all fermented products, imposed at the time of import and involving a fee of 2.5 per cent of the value of the imported product. The proceeds of this charge are used to help fund the development by Swedish researchers of healthy alcoholic drinks.

Advise XYZ Ltd, TLC Ltd and ABC Ltd as to the applicable rules of EU law regarding free movement of goods.

Suggested answer

(a) (i) First step: Article 20 or Article 110 TFEU?

- If pasta and potatoes are not in competition, then the pasta is an exotic import and the charge will be a customs duty or CEE unless it is part of a general system of internal taxes.
- If they are in competition, Article 110 likely applies, but must satisfy test above (part of general system of internal taxation etc.).

(ii) Second step:

- If a customs duty or CEE under Article 30, does an exception apply? Does not seem to, no service rendered, no information on EU law requirements.
- If Article 110 applies, which paragraph? If goods are similar, paragraph 1 applies and need to identify direct or indirect discrimination. Indirect discrimination here, as Denmark produces no such goods and not affected by higher rate. If paragraph 2 applies, identify protective effect. NB: *The end result is not affected whether paragraph 1 or paragraph 2 is the applicable paragraph (although it can be more difficult to demonstrate protective effect).*

(b) and (c) Same sequence of steps, but note some additional issues:

(b) Seems to fall under Article 110 TFEU, as both domestic and imported cheese pay taxes. Not direct discrimination, but could fall under paragraph 1 (if different cheeses deemed similar products) or paragraph 2 (if not similar, but are in competition). The question raises the issue of objective justification.

(c) Could be either Article 30 or Article 110 TFEU here:

- If no Swedish substitutes for the imported fruit-flavoured, low-alcoholic drinks, Article 30 applies, so 17.5 per cent tax would be an unlawful customs duty or CEE + next step is apply the rules on exceptions to Article 30 ((i) services rendered or (ii) requirements of EU law).
- If goods deemed similar or in competition, Article 110 applies; determine if objective justification applies.

9.4 CONCLUSION

The prohibition on taxes and customs duties (including charges of equivalent effect or CEEs) and on discrimination or protection in the Member States tax systems is a key element of the establishment of the common market, now the internal market. The prohibition on customs duties is almost absolute, with just two narrow exceptions relating to services rendered and requirements of EU law. Customs duties and CEEs are within the exclusive competence of the EU.

In contrast, internal taxation is still mostly within the competence of the Member States. The Member States are free to determine their own levels of internal taxation, but they are prohibited from discriminating on grounds of the origin of the goods relative to other Member States and their own domestic goods, as well as being prohibited from providing indirect protection. This is a reasonably stable area of EU law. Although technical aspects of the Common Customs Union (CCU) are continually adjusted (beyond the coverage of this book), Articles 30 and 110 TFEU represent one of the most well established and stable areas of EU law.

POINTS TO REVIEW

- Articles 30 TFEU on customs duties and charges of equivalent effect (CEEs) relates to the imposition of charges on a good as a tax due to the good having crossed a border from one Member State to another. The concept of CEEs covers taxes imposed not literally at the border, but which are imposed because of a cross-border transfer.

- Article 110 TFEU relates to discriminatory treatment of goods from other Member States in internal taxation, such as VAT. In addition to discriminatory treatment in favour of the equivalent of a domestic good compared to a similar imported good from another Member State, more indirect protective treatment for domestic goods is also prohibited.

- Articles 30 and 110 TFEU are mutually exclusive. This does not mean that either one or the other applies to a particular good; what it means is that a tax can either be a customs duty (or a CEE) or internal taxation, but not both.

- The significance of the distinction in practice is that the prohibition on discrimination or protection in internal taxation is not as absolute as the prohibition on customs duties and CEEs, in that the exceptions to the prohibition on the latter are very narrow, and they are not as narrow for internal taxation under Article 110 TFEU.

- For customs duties and CEEs under Article 30 TFEU, there are two limited exceptions or derogations: (1) for charges imposed as a result of requirements of EU law and (2) charges of services rendered.

- For internal taxation under Article 110 TFEU, discrimination and protection in favour of domestic goods relative to goods from other EU Member States are prohibited. The prohibition under Article 110 is not as absolute, in that objective justification has been developed as an open-ended category in the case law of the ECJ to justify indirect discrimination or protection.

CHAPTER GLOSSARY

Charges of equivalent effect (CEE) refers to a charge imposed on a good due to it having crossed a border, even though the charge is not labelled as a customs duty.

Common Customs Union (CCU) refers to the establishment of a common system of customs applied by all EU Member States to goods from third countries being imported into the EU.

Customs duty refers to a charge imposed on a good as a tax due to it having crossed a border. It is usually imposed at the physical point of crossing a border, but this is not always so.

Direct discrimination in the context of goods in the EU refers to explicit discrimination or differential treatment of goods based on their country of origin/ manufacture.

Disguised customs duty refers to a tax imposed on domestic and similar imported goods, but which discriminates in its application in favour of domestic good so that the effect of the tax on the domestic good is fully compensated for. In effect, a tax is only imposed on the imported good.

Excise duties are indirect taxes on the consumption or the use of certain products. They are usually taxes expressed as a monetary amount per quantity of the product, rather than in percentages.

Indirect discrimination in the context of goods in the EU refers to a tax arrangement that puts an imported good from another Member State in a disadvantageous position relative to a competing domestic good.

Internal taxation in the context of goods refers to taxes imposed on goods in the domestic market, e.g. taxes imposed at the point of sale, such as value added tax (VAT).

Protective effect refers to an advantage conferred on domestic goods relative to imported goods with which the domestic good has some kind of market relationship, even if the goods are not substitutes.

Services rendered refers to a service provided by a Member State to importers or exporters of goods. In effect, case law establishes that such services may be charged for so long as they are voluntarily requested by the importer or exporter and confer an individualised benefit.

Value added taxation (VAT) is a common type of internal taxation on goods, and it is usually imposed by the retailer at the point of sale according to VAT rates determined in a country's annual budget.

TAKING THINGS FURTHER

C Barnard *The Substantive EU* (4th edn Oxford University Press 2013) The fourth edition of this book provides authoritative and comprehensive coverage of Articles 30 and 110 TFEU in Chapter 3.

J Snell 'Non-discriminatory tax obstacles in Community law' (2007) 18(2) *International and Comparative Law Quarterly* 339–70 This article looks at the relevance of taxation issues to the jurisprudence of the ECJ across free movement, as well as looking at the issue of double taxation.

J Thygesen 'National tax law: under influence of EU rules for the free movement of goods' (2013) 41(6/7) *Intertax* 351–59 This article provides a very clear discussion of how EU rules on free movement of goods and rules on competition law (specifically state aid) interact with tax law.

CHAPTER 10
FREE MOVEMENT OF GOODS II: QUANTITATIVE RESTRICTIONS AND MEASURES OF EQUIVALENT EFFECT

In the previous chapter, we looked at one of the two main aspects to free movement of goods in the EU: the prohibition on customs taxes on imports and exports and the prohibition on discriminatory or protective internal taxes targeted at imports or exports. In this chapter, we will look at the second major aspect of free movement of goods: the prohibition on quantitative restrictions (such as quotas on the number of goods allowed into a country) and measures of equivalent effect. The two areas of free movement complement each other. One is directed at taxation (in its various forms), and the other addresses other product-related restrictions. The ECJ and the European Commission have worked in tandem in this area to achieve a very broad scope for the relevant treaty provisions on quantitative restrictions and measures of equivalent effect. This broad scope has meant that this area of EU law should not be viewed in its technical, 'market' dimension only, but also as having an important constitutional dimension in illustrating the overall character of the EU and in expanding the competences of the EU relative to the Member States. The structure of the free movement rules can be compared across the free movement areas. Thus, in this area also, there are the basic treaty rules prohibiting restrictions on free movement, there are treaty-based derogations or exceptions to the prohibition, there is important case law from the ECJ giving a broad reading to the free movement rules, and correspondingly ECJ case law that has expanded the derogations or exceptions (other than in cases of direct discrimination).

AS YOU READ . . .

The key questions that will be answered in this chapter are as follows:

– What do the different terms in the treaty provisions, Articles 34 and 35 TFEU, mean (especially 'measures' and 'measures having equivalent effect (MEQRs)')?

- How has the ECJ interpreted these rules over time to give them a broad effect or scope?

- What are typical examples of kinds of national measures or rules that are prohibited?

- What exceptions or derogations exist, both under the treaty and as a result of the case law?

- What does this area of the law tell us about this area of European integration and the role of different institutional actors in it?

- What way should problem situations in this area be approached?

10.1 INTRODUCTION

The treaty provisions on free movement of goods are amongst the most fundamental in the treaties. They are foundational principles of the common market (now described as the internal market). Free movement of workers developed more slowly, whereas free movement of goods took effect more quickly and obviously because the Member States already traded with each other to a substantial extent. When the term 'free trade' is used, it generally refers to goods: the EU is a free trade area *par excellence*.

Two separate aspects of free movement of goods exist: the treaty provisions on (1) prohibiting customs duties and charges of equivalent effect (CEEs) and (2) prohibiting quantitative restrictions (QRs) and measures of equivalent effect (or measures equivalent to a quantitative restriction (MEQRs)). We have looked at customs duties and internal taxation in the previous chapter. On QRs and MEQRs, the relevant treaty provisions are now in Articles 34 and 35 TFEU,[1] which read:

> ### ARTICLE 34 TFEU
>
> Quantitative restrictions on *imports*, and all measures having equivalent effect shall be prohibited between Member States.
>
> ### ARTICLE 35 TFEU
>
> Quantitative restrictions on *exports*, and all measures having equivalent effect, shall be prohibited between Member States.

---

1   Note that the frequent changes in the numbering of the same provision owing to treaty revision can make this area seem difficult to keep up with. Previously, for example, art 34 TFEU used to be art 30 EEC Treaty and later art 28 EC Treaty.

The first step to understanding these terms is to look at the ECJ's interpretation of them. The ECJ has adopted a very wide approach to their interpretation, which has had the effect of significantly expanding the scope of the common or internal market.

10.2 DEFINITIONS UNDER ARTICLES 34 AND 35 TFEU

10.2.1 DEFINING 'GOODS'

No definition of 'goods' is given in the treaty. In *Commission v Italy*, the ECJ defined 'goods' in a common-sense way as 'products which can be valued in money and which are capable, as such, of forming the subject of commercial transactions'.[2] They are thus any product capable of being bought and sold.

10.2.2 DOES A QUANTITATIVE RESTRICTION ENCOMPASS A BAN?

As a matter of common sense, it might seem obvious that a prohibition on quantitative restrictions also includes a complete ban on the export or import of a certain good. A quantitative restriction is a quota on the number of goods that can be imported or exported; if quotas are prohibited, all the more so should outright bans be prohibited. The ECJ confirmed that this was so in a number of cases. In addition, a study of the preparatory materials of the relevant treaty provisions shows that the authors of the treaty intended this to be so.[3] In *Geddo v Ente Nazionale Risi*, the ECJ stated that a prohibition on quantitative restrictions covers measures that amount to a total or partial restraint, although the Court stated this without discussing it in detail.[4]

The issue was again dealt with in *R v Henn and Darby*.[5] This was the first preliminary reference from the UK to the ECJ (the preliminary reference was made from the House of Lords), and concerned a UK ban on obscene products from Germany. The ECJ stated that it was clear that Article 30 EEC Treaty (now Article 34 TFEU) included outright bans, though it did not elaborate on this.

The Opinion of Advocate General Warner did, however, address the issue in more depth. The Advocate General stated that the UK Court of Appeal was plainly wrong in thinking that 'quantitative restrictions' did not include a total prohibition. He observed in support of this that the point had not been argued, that there was ample ECJ authority on it, that the text of Article 36 EEC Treaty supported this approach by equating a prohibition

....

2   Case 7/68 *Commission v Italy (Export of Art Treasures)* [1968] ECR 423 at 428.
3   G Conway *The Limits of Legal Reasoning and the European Court of Justice* (Cambridge University Press 2012) 266–272.
4   Case 2/73 *Geddo v Ente Nazionale Risi* [1973] ECR 865 para 7.
5   Case 34/79 *R v Henn and Darby* [1979] ECR 3795.

with a restriction and that such an interpretation was consistent with the purpose of free movement of goods as one of the foundations of the Community.[6]

> KEY LEARNING POINT
> ....
>
> **OUTRIGHT BANS**
> The term 'quantitative restrictions', as well as quotas, includes outright bans on or prohibitions of goods.

10.2.3 DEFINING 'MEASURES HAVING EQUIVALENT EFFECT TO QUANTITATIVE RESTRICTIONS' OR 'MEQRS'

Undoubtedly, the most significant interpretative issue under Articles 34 and 35 was defining 'measures having equivalent effect to quantitative restrictions' or 'MEQRs'. The ECJ has adopted a very wide approach indeed, suggesting that any national rules that make it more difficult to import or export goods are MEQRs and thus contrary to the treaty. This had the potential to make any national trading rules contrary to the treaty, since in theory the mere fact of having to satisfy national rules at all makes the import or export of goods more difficult. This resulted in a problem of overreach, and the development of EU law in this area has related to this issue.

10.2.3.1 DEFINING A 'MEASURE'
A preliminary issue to defining MEQRs, however, is first to define a 'measure'.

> KEY LEARNING POINT
> ....
>
> **WHAT IS A MEASURE?**
> The position in the case law essentially is that the measure need not be in the form of legislation and, secondly, it should originate from the state. Another way of putting this second point is that Articles 34 and 35 TFEU do not have horizontal direct effect[7] (we will return to this briefly at the end of this chapter). Here, the approach of the ECJ to defining what can be a measure is again quite broad.

In *Apple & Pear Development Council v Lewis*,[8] the ECJ held that a promotional campaign sponsored by a government could be a measure. In other words, a national rule or policy does not have to be in legislative form to be a measure. This flexible approach to what can be a 'measure' is also apparent from a case such as *Commission v France (Franking Machines)*.[9] This concerned an administrative decision by the French Post Office. The ECJ held that for an administrative practice to constitute a 'measure', the practice

....

6   Ibid 254.

7   See e.g. Case C–159/00 *Sapod Audic v Eco-Emballages SA* [2002] ECR I–5031 para 74.

8   Case 222/82 *Apple & Pear Development Council v Lewis* [1983] ECR 4083.

9   Case 21/84 *Commission v France (Franking Machines)* [1985] ECR 1355.

must show a certain degree of consistency and generality, which had to be assessed differently whether the market concerned had a small or large number of undertakings. Where there were only a few undertakings, treatment of a single undertaking could be a measure under Article 30 EEC Treaty (now Article 34 TFEU).[10] On the facts, it was held that an administrative practice of the French Post Office to permit franking machines made in France only violated Article 30 (in an action initiated by a UK manufacturer of franking machines).

EXPLAINING THE LAW

THE 'PURELY INTERNAL RULE' IN THIS AREA OF FREE MOVEMENT
We have seen how, in the area of free movement of workers and citizens, there is a 'purely internal' rule, meaning that an individual must have crossed a border for the treaty rules to apply. So, for example, a person moving from Wales to England cannot rely on free movement of workers or persons. The same principle applies to this area of free movement,[11] except that its application is narrowed by the very broad definition of MEQR in *Dassonville*, which we will examine next. *Dassonville* interpreted Article 34 TFEU as covering all trading rules enacted by Member States which are capable of hindering, directly or indirectly, actually or *potentially*, intra-Community trade. The word 'potentially' is emphasised because it has been interpreted by the ECJ to mean that Article 34 applies where it relates to a rule that *could* be a violation, even if on the facts of the case, the situation is purely internal.[12]

10.2.3.2 DEFINING AN 'MEQR'

On the question of what is an MEQR, the high point of the case law is *Procureur du Roi v Dassonville*, which is one of the most important decisions in the history of the ECJ.[13]

KEY CASE DASSONVILLE

....

The ECJ adopted almost the widest possible definition of 'MEQR'. The facts concerned a Belgian requirement for an official document issued by the government of an exporting country for the exported products to bear a designation of origin, so that when imported into Belgium the origin of the

....

10 Ibid para 13.

11 Case 286/81 *Oosthoek's Uitgeversmaatschappij* [1982] ECR 4575 para 9.

12 Case C–321–4/94 *Criminal proceedings against Pistre and Others* [1997] ECR I–2343, which concerned French legislation allowing the description 'mountain' to be used only in relation to products prepared on national territory from domestic raw materials. The facts involved proceedings brought against French nationals and concern French products marketed on French territory, but the ECJ held that free movement could still potentially be hindered by favouring the marketing of goods of domestic origin: ibid paras 44–45.

13 Case 8/74 *Procureur du Roi v Dassonville* [1974] ECR 837.

goods would be apparent to consumers. The particular circumstances were that Belgian traders imported Scotch whisky from France that had first been exported from the UK to France. The goods did not have any designation of origin, and traders based in Belgium were being prosecuted for violating the law on designations of origin.

The Belgian rule in *Dassonville* was held to be contrary to the treaty, with the ECJ making the following very important statement of what constituted an MEQR:

KEY LEARNING POINT

MEASURES HAVING EQUIVALENT EFFECT TO A QUANTITATIVE RESTRICTION (MEQRS)

All trading rules enacted by Member States which are capable of hindering, directly or indirectly, actually or potentially, intra-Community trade are to be considered as measures having an effect equivalent to trading restrictions.
Case 8/74 *Procureur du Roi v Dassonville* [1974] ECR 837 para 5

One of the effects of the above passage in *Dassonville* was that *all* indistinctly applicable national measures could be caught within its scope, which included the following:

1. *direct discrimination* (e.g. placing quotas on goods from certain countries, with no quotas on domestic goods)
2. *Indirect discrimination* (no explicit discrimination, but disproportionate impact on goods from other Member States compared to domestic goods)
3. *Any non-discriminatory obstacles to free movement or 'indistinctly applicable' measures* (which could impact equally in fact both domestic goods and goods from other Member States).

KEY LEARNING POINT

THE TERMINOLOGY OF 'DISTINCTLY APPLICABLE' AND 'INDISTINCTLY APPLICABLE'

One of the confusing aspects of the EU law on free movement is a tendency to use different terms to describe the same concept, depending on which area of free movement is in issue. In the area of quantitative restrictions, the term 'distinctly applicable' is used to mean 'non-discriminatory', but usually this means directly discriminatory (although logically it could be used to mean either directly or indirectly discriminatory). Similarly, 'indistinctly applicable' means 'non-discriminatory', but it is often used to encompass indirect discrimination and non-discriminatory obstacles.

Barnard has captured very clearly the broader significance of the judgment in *Dassonville*:

> The potential breadth of the so-called *Dassonville* formula is striking. In principle, measures having only an indirect, potential effect on trade fall within its scope and therefore breach Article 28 (now Article 30 TFEU). *Dassonville* therefore tends to support a reading of Article 28 as the basis for an economic constitution for the EU . . .[14]

> KEY LEARNING POINT
>
> ....
>
> *Dassonville* interpreted the treaty as prohibiting three types of national MEQRs:
>
> 1. direct discrimination
> 2. indirect discrimination
> 3. non-discriminatory obstacles.

An example of a distinctly applicable national measure is *Apple & Pear Development Council v Lewis*.[15] This case concerned an action taken by a government sponsored 'quango' (special agency), the Apple and Pear Development Council in the UK. The ECJ described the Development Council as being concerned 'essentially with publicity and promotion on the British market and improvement of the quality of the indigenous fruit marketed in the UK'.[16] As well as marketing pears in general, the Development Council organised campaigns relating specifically to English and Welsh apples and pears and, in particular, certain varieties typical of English and Welsh production.

The ECJ held that such a body could not seek to discourage the sale or purchase of goods from other Member States or recommend or promote consumption based solely on national origin, which would be an MEQR, but it was permitted to draw attention to the positive characteristics of domestically produced fruit and highlight the positive characteristics of certain varieties of fruit. Similarly, a designation of origin may be legitimate where it indicates a special value in the folklore or tradition of the region of origin.[17]

A case that might be thought to cause some difficulty of classification is *Decker v Caisse de Maladie des Employés Privés*.[18] The rule at issue in *Decker* might not be thought to fall within any of these categories, since it provided for a different regime according to

....

14 C Barnard *The Substantive Law of the EU: The Four Freedoms* (2nd edn Oxford University Press 2007) 92.

15 Case 222/82 *Apple & Pear Development Council v Lewis* [1983] ECR 4083.

16 Ibid para 15.

17 Case 113/80 *Commission v Ireland* [1981] ECR 1625.

18 Case C–120/95 *Decker v Caisse de Maladie des Employés Privés* [1998] ECR I–1831. See also Case 18/84 *Commission v France* [1985] ECR 1339.

the place where the good was to be purchased, and not according to where the good had been produced. It concerned a Luxembourg rule that subjected reimbursement of spectacles purchased abroad to prior authorisation, which was not required if the spectacles were purchased in Luxembourg.

The ECJ chose to describe it as an obstacle to free movement.[19] However, it seems also possible conceptually to consider that the rule involved indirect discrimination, since it was more likely not to accord the benefit of reimbursement to goods from other Member States.

APPLYING THE LAW

THE VARIETY OF QRS AND MEQRS

Member State X of the EU decides that, in order to protect its tractor construction industry, it will ban tractors from being imported that do not satisfy strict environmental emission standards. As it turns out, this means that only one of the five other Member States of the EU that produce tractors will be able to export to Member State X without major modifications to their tractor designs. Further, Member State X decides that in any case, no more than 500 such tractors may be imported in any year from any other Member State, justifying this restriction on the ground that it will need to assess all tractors imported to it claiming to satisfy its demanding standards and that it cannot administratively cope with more than 500 such inspections. Finally, Member State X decides to adopt an outright ban on six-wheeled tractors, whether produced domestically or in any other Member State, claiming that these are harder to drive and more prone to accidents.

There are at least three types of measures/MEQRs:

1. A distinctly applicable, outright ban on certain types of tractors (those with six wheels) (the ban is distinctly applicable in that it involves indirect discrimination, given that it only impacts in fact tractors from other Member States).
2. An indistinctly applicable product requirement, i.e. MEQR, on other types of tractors (relating to an environmental standard).
3. An indistinctly applicable quantitative restriction on the number of tractors satisfying its environmental standard that can be imported.

All three types of national 'measure' are prohibited under the treaty and ECJ interpretation of these articles, although there is a possibility of a derogation or exception being pleaded to justify the national rule.

---

19 Case C–120/95 ibid para 36.

ANALYSING THE LAW

THE SCOPE OF FREE MOVEMENT AND SPILL-OVER WITH OTHER LEGAL INTERESTS

In Chapter 1, we saw that neo-functionalists argue that integration in one area of integration has a 'spill-over' effect in that it draws in other elements of Member State regulation. This can be related to the distinction between specific and general competences outlined in Chapter 7. Free movement is one of the more general competences of the EU in the sense that it covers all aspects of trade in goods. This can be illustrated with reference to military products. The EU has no formal military competence, although under the Common Foreign and Security Policy, the Member States may cooperate if they wish. Military products can, however, fall under the free movement of goods principle, just like any other goods, and the treaty recognises this in Article 346(1)(b) TFEU, which provides that any Member State may take such measures as it considers necessary for the protection of the essential interests of its security which are connected with the production of or trade in arms, munitions and war *matériel*, but that such measures shall not adversely affect the conditions of competition in the internal market regarding products which are not intended for specifically military purposes.

In a recent article, Akkermans and Ramaekers suggest that free movement of goods encompasses aspects of property law. They argue that 'the refusal to recognise property rights validly created in another Member State violates the free movement of goods under Article 34 TFEU' and that the judgment in *Krantz*[20] should be decided differently today in light of the development of thinking about the internal market.[21]

Perhaps surprisingly, *Krantz* is the only case to deal indirectly with movable property as an instance of free movement of goods. The facts concerned a conditional transfer of title in a machine: this means that title is only transferred when the full payment is received. The owner of land on which the machine was located experienced difficulties in paying taxes and, as a result, the Dutch tax authorities seized the machine, which the owner of the land did not own because payment had not been made in full. The machine had been imported from Germany, and the German owner objected to the seizure as a violation of the free movement of goods (under the rules of private international law, the German

....

20 Case C–69/88 *H. Krantz GmbH & Co v Ontvanger der Directe Belastingen en de Staat der Nederlanden* [1990] ECR I–583.

21 B Akkermans, E Ramaekers 'Free movement of goods and property law' (2013) 19(2) *European Law Journal* 237–66. They also note the connection with free movement of capital: the free movement of capital and its application to immovable property law.

owner could assert a claim of ownership in Dutch law in recognition of his claim under German law[22]). The ECJ applied a remoteness argument to hold that free movement of goods did not apply, observing:

> . . . the possibility that nationals of other Member States would hesitate to sell goods on instalment terms to purchasers in the Member State concerned because such goods would be liable to seizure by the collector of taxes if the purchasers failed to discharge their Netherlands tax debts is too uncertain and indirect to warrant the conclusion that a national provision authorizing such seizure is liable to hinder trade between Member States.[23]

This is somewhat contrary to the Court's refusal to apply a *de minimis* test to the free movement of goods in *de Haar*.[24] The approach Akkermans and Ramaekers suggest is open to criticism in light of Article 345 TFEU, which states that the rules governing the system of property ownership shall not be prejudiced by the treaties. This is a competence exclusion clause; the argument put forward by Akkermans and Ramaekers applies the approach of the ECJ in *Viking* and *Laval* in the context of property and the free movement of goods (see Chapter 11): against this view, the *lex specialis* principle should apply to the effect that Article 345 overrides any spill-over of the internal market to property ownership.

10.3 THE RANGE OF CASE LAW ON MEASURES EQUIVALENT TO QUANTITATIVE RESTRICTIONS OR MEQRS UNDER ARTICLE 34 TFEU

As mentioned above, almost any national trading rules, in so far as they involve some extra effort in order to comply with them on the part of producers or manufacturers who want to export their goods, have the potential to be contrary to Articles 34 and 35 TFEU as interpreted by the ECJ in its judgment in *Dassonville*. The main examples of national measures that have come within the *Dassonville* definition of MEQRs are set out below.

....

22 The private international law rule of *lex rei sitae* applies and makes the substantive property law of the receiving Member State applicable: ibid 240.

23 Case C–69/88, *H. Krantz* (n 20) paras 10–11.

24 Joined Cases 177 & 178/82 *van de Haar and Kaveka de Meern* [1984] ECR 1797 para 13.

10.3.1 EXAMPLES OF TYPES OF MEQR

Import (or export) licences:
> e.g. *International Fruit Co v Produktschap voor Groenten en Fruit*[25]
> The ECJ held that (now) Articles 34 and 35 TFEU precluded a national measure, in this case legislation requiring, even as a pure formality, import or export licences or any other similar procedure for trade between the Member States.[26]

Health inspections for imported (or exported) goods:
> e.g. *Rewe-Zentralfinanz v Landwirtschaftskammer*[27]
> The facts concerned phytosanitary inspections on plant products (apples). The inspections were held to be an MEQR, but on the facts these were held to be capable of justification in so far as they could be required by Community secondary legislation.

Imposing obligations on importers of goods to buy a certain proportion of their supplies from the government at fixed prices:
> e.g. *Campus Oil Ltd v Minister for Industry and Energy*[28]
> This case concerned an Irish rule requiring importers of petrol to purchase a certain amount of petrol from Ireland's only refinery. However, although this rule was found to be contrary to what is now Article 34 TFEU, it was held to be justified under the treaty-based derogation for public policy (now in Article 36 TFEU, see further below), given the need to ensure a national supply of oil in an international market in which the supply of oil could be put at risk. The Irish measure was not of a purely economic nature.

*Prohibition on advertising of imported goods:**
> e.g. *Ortscheit*[29]
> The ECJ here held that a national prohibition of advertising for medicinal products that have not been authorised as required, but which could be imported from another Member State in response to an individual order if they have been lawfully put into circulation in that Member State, was to the extent that it affected only imported products an MEQR under now Article 34 TFEU. However, the ECJ also held the prohibition could be justified under the treaty derogation for the protection of the health and life of humans (now in Article 36 TFEU, see further below), because it was necessary for the effectiveness of the national authorisation scheme. Member States were entitled to maintain a national authorisation scheme in the absence of a procedure for Community authorisation or mutual recognition of national authorisations.

....

25 Cases 51–54/71 *International Fruit Co v Produktschap voor Groenten en Fruit* [1971] ECR 1107.
26 Ibid para 9.
27 Case 4/75, *Rewe Zentralfinanz v Landwirtschaftskammer* [1975] ECR 843.
28 Case 72/83 *Campus Oil Ltd v Minister for Industry and Energy* [1984] ECR 2727.
29 Case C–320/93 *Ortscheit GmbH v Eurim Pharm Arzneimittel GmbH* [1994] ECR I–5243.

e.g. *Gourmet International Products*[30]

This case concerned a Swedish law restricting alcohol advertising. The ECJ described the Swedish law as not only prohibiting a form of marketing a product, but in reality also prohibiting producers and importers from directing any advertising messages at consumers, with a few insignificant exceptions. On the facts, it was also found that it was easier for Swedish products to come within the limited exceptions. However, the ECJ held that the law could be justified on the public health treaty derogation to free movement under Article 36 TFEU, unless the same public health objective could be achieved by a lesser restriction of trade between Member States.

** *Note that following the important ECJ decision in* Keck and Mithouard *(which declared that* Dassonville *did not apply to 'selling arrangements', see further below), some special rules now apply to advertising.*

A minimum selling price:

e.g. *Fachverband der Buch- und Medienwirtschaft*[31]

The facts of this case are somewhat complicated. It involved Austrian legislation setting minimum prices for German-language books. Under the legislation, the publisher or importer was to fix and publish a retail price and the importer was not to fix a price below the retail price recommended by the publisher in the state of the publication (although value added tax on the price could be deducted from it). Libro, an Austrian importer of German goods, advertised books published in Germany for sale in Austria below the minimum price set for Austria on the basis of the German prices. This meant that books produced in Germany and sold in Austria were valued according to German market conditions, rather than Austrian ones, whereas books produced in Austria were sold in a way that reflected Austrian market conditions. We will look at this case further below as regards exceptions in ECJ case law to the strict rule in *Dassonville*.

KEY LEARNING POINT

RULES FIXING PRICES BY REFERENCE TO A MAXIMUM PERCENTAGE PROFIT

Price fixing is in general an MEQR, but not necessarily in every instance. In *Commission v Italy*,[32] the ECJ addressed price fixing in the form of a *maximum retail profit rule* in a situation where the Italian State had a monopoly on the production of tobacco. Italy further set uniform trading margins for the retail distribution of manufactured tobacco, i.e. sellers were only allowed to make a maximum level of profit relative to the cost of producing tobacco products.

---

30 Case C–405/98 *Gourmet International Products* [2001] ECR I–1795.
31 Case C–531/07 *Fachverband der Buch- und Medienwirtschaft v Libro Handelgesellschaft mbH* [2009] ECR I–3717.
32 Case 78/82 *Commission v Italy* [1983] ECR 1955.

Foreign suppliers of tobacco also had to follow this maximum profit level. The ECJ found that there was no discrimination, either directly or indirectly and no protective effect for Italian products. Price competition still existed, since foreign producers were free to seek to lower their production costs or to pass on production costs in their entirety. The Italian law set a maximum retail margin, but did not prevent a margin lower than that and so was not a prohibited MEQR. This means that in the area of price fixing, *Dassonville* targets straightforward rules specifying a particular price for a particular good, but not necessarily rules specifying a maximum range, within which competition can still take place.

Ingredients restrictions for all goods:
> e.g. *Cassis de Dijon*[33]

KEY LEARNING POINT

CASSIS DE DIJON

This is a very important case, which we will look at further below, because it developed the idea of mutual recognition as an alternative to harmonisation for furthering European cooperation and integration. It involved the fixing of a minimum alcohol content in liqueur drinks, and such a requirement was held to be an MEQR (the case is also for recognising the following grounds as mandatory requirements, or case law-based exceptions to the broad rule in *Dassonville*, on which see further below: the effectiveness of fiscal supervision, the protection of public health, the fairness of commercial transactions and the defence of the consumer).

Packaging requirements for all goods:
> e.g. *Walter Rau v De Smedt*[34]
>
> The ECJ held in this case that the application in one Member State to margarine (imported from another Member State and lawfully produced and marketed in the latter Member State) of legislation prohibiting the marketing of margarine or edible fats unless in a certain shape was an MEQR. It was not justified in a situation where consumer protection could be achieved by other means hindering trade to a lesser degree.

Origin-designation of all goods:
> e.g. *Commission v Ireland (Souvenir Jewellery)*[35]
>
> The ECJ here found that Ireland had adopted a distinctly applicable measure (which was directly discriminatory) by granting souvenirs imported from other Member

---

33 Case 120/78 *Rewe-Zentrale AG v Bundesmonopolverwaltung für Branntwein (Cassis de Dijon)* [1979] ECR 649.
34 Case 261/81 *Walter Rau v De Smedt* [1982] ECR 3961.
35 Case 113/80 *Commission v Ireland (Souvenir Jewellery)* [1981] ECR 1625.

States access to the Irish market solely on condition that they bear a statement of origin, when such a designation was not required of domestic products. The ECJ observed that the essential requirement of a souvenir was that it was a reminder of the place visited, which did not mean that it had to be manufactured in a particular country.

e.g. *Commission v UK (Origin Marking)*[36]

In this case, secondary legislation in the UK required that certain types of goods (clothing and textile goods, domestic electrical appliances, footwear, and cutlery) bear a designation of origin. The ECJ held that satisfying this requirement made the production of goods more difficult and could also have the effect of encouraging consumers to purchase domestic goods over imported ones from the Member States, even though the requirement was indistinctly applicable in that it applied to all goods, both domestic and imported.

Banning of the use of certain goods for a certain purpose:

e.g. *Commission v Portugal (Tinted Film)*[37]

Portuguese legislation prohibited affixing tinted film to the windows of passenger or goods vehicles. The Portuguese Government accepted that the law was capable of hindering trade (in tinted film) and thus that it was an MEQR, but argued that the legislation was justified on grounds of public safety and/or road safety. The ECJ agreed, in principle, but held that the legislation went beyond what was strictly necessary to achieve this intended outcome. We will discuss derogations/exceptions to freedom of movement further below.

Inspection and authorisation requirements for all goods:

e.g. *Dynamic Medien v Avides Media*[38]

This case concerned German legislation requiring all videos and DVDs to be inspected and classified by the German authorities, even if they had already been classified in the exporting state by the authorities there. The German law provided that 'image storage media' that have not been labelled or have been labelled 'Not suitable for young persons' under paragraph 14(2) by the highest authority of the *Land* or by a voluntary self-regulation body under the procedure, or which have not been labelled by the supplier, may not: (i) be offered, transferred or otherwise made accessible to a child or adolescent or (ii) be offered or transferred in retail trade outside of commercial premises, in kiosks or in other sales outlets which customers do not usually enter, or by mail order. The ECJ decided that the German legislation was an MEQR (but see further below as to its justification).

....

36 Case 207/83 *Commission v UK (Origin Marking)* [1985] ECR 1202.
37 Case C–265/06 *Commission v Portugal (Tinted Film)* [2008] ECR I–2245.
38 Case C–244/06 *Dynamic Medien v Avides Media* [2008] ECR I–505.

EXPLAINING THE LAW

THE PROBLEM OF OVERREACH IN *DASSONVILLE* AND THE ECJ RETREAT FROM IT

As noted above, one of the implications of the broad definition of MEQRs in *Dassonville* is that national rules that are obstacle to free movement are contrary to the Article 34 TFEU, even if they are not discriminatory. Potentially, this meant any national trading rules were contrary to the Treaty, since the mere fact of different national rules could in the abstract be considered an obstacle to free movement given the mere act of having to comply with a rule of a Member State to which a good was exported could be considered an additional burden for exporters. If *Dassonville* was taken to its logical conclusion, it would have meant the Member States should fully harmonise all trading rules. This they refused to do, and the ECJ was left with the problem of how to reconcile *Dassonville* with resistance to harmonisation on the part of the Member States. The ECJ, therefore, retreated from the full implications of *Dassonville*, and it did so in three ways:

1. In *Cassis de Dijon* (for the facts see above, see next for discussion), it developed what has come to be known as the principle of mutual recognition, which is an alternative concept of cooperation or integration to harmonisation. Mutual recognition means that each Member State should accept the regulatory standard of another, so that when goods are exported, the other Member State should assume they satisfy acceptable regulatory standards, e.g. as to health and safety, and the Member State to which they are imported should not impose another standard and should simply allow them to be sold.
2. It developed case law-based exceptions to the free movement principles. This category of exception is broader than the treaty-based exceptions now in Article 36 TFEU, which as we will see below, the ECJ has always interpreted narrowly.
3. In *Keck and Mithouard* (see further below), it decided that 'selling arrangements' were excluded from the scope of free movement and so could legitimately be the subject of differing national rules.

10.3.2 *CASSIS DE DIJON* AND THE PRINCIPLE OF MUTUAL RECOGNITION

The principle of mutual recognition, applied to free movement of goods, means that if a product is lawfully produced and/or manufactured in one Member State then it should be made available for sale in all other Member States:

– *Mutual recognition* implies that the Member States accept the validity of each other's regulation of products and do not impose a second system of regulation on imported goods from another Member State, e.g. regarding health and safety standards, or ingredient rules.

– Another way of expressing the effect of mutual recognition is to relate it to the idea of *avoiding a dual burden*. Exporters from one Member State to another Member State may have to satisfy two regulatory standards (e.g. concerning health and safety), one standard set by the Member State where the good was produced and one standard set by the Member State to which the good is exported. If the second Member State accepts the regulatory standard of the first Member State as being satisfactory, which is what the principle of mutual recognition requires, the good does not need to satisfy the second regulatory standard of the Member State to which the good is exported. This makes the good cheaper to produce and thus more competitive.

In effect, the principle creates a burden of proof on the other Member States to rebut a presumption that goods produced in one Member State satisfy all reasonable regulatory standards concerning the production of the good. One of the most effective ways to rebut the presumption is to identify national peculiarities that justify the adoption of special rules.

ANALYSING THE LAW

THE CONSTITUTIONAL SIGNIFICANCE OF *CASSIS DE DIJON* AND MUTUAL RECOGNITION

Although the facts of *Cassis de Dijon* may seem unremarkable, involving as they did alcohol content, the significance of the decision far transcended them. *Cassis de Dijon* is of great importance for developing an alternative method of integration to harmonisation, namely, mutual recognition. Several aspects of this are worth examining.

(i) *The distinction between negative and positive integration*: *Cassis de Dijon* can be related to a distinction that has been drawn in the academic literature between 'negative integration' and 'positive integration'. Negative integration involves the removal of national barriers to trade, whereas positive integration involved the adoption of uniform, harmonised rules across the EU. Mutual recognition enables negative integration, thereby providing an alternative method of integration to harmonisation. Harmonisation amounts to positive integration, and it is politically more sensitive and controversial because of the impact it has on Member State competences.[39] Harmonisation reduces the autonomy of the Member States compared to mutual recognition, much as a regulation leaves less implementing scope for the Member States than a directive does. Mutual recognition is thus more consistent with the principle of subsidiarity.

....

39 For rich discussion of this issue see M P Maduro *We the Court: The European Economic Constitution* (Hart Publishing 1999).

(ii) *The role of the ECJ: Cassis de Dijon* is one of the most important decisions of the ECJ, and it illustrates the central role the ECJ has played as 'a motor of integration'. The ECJ is considered to have acted as it did, with the support of the European Commission,[40] because of reluctance of the Member States to harmonise trading rules. Whatever one's views about whether the principle of mutual recognition is a beneficial one, a second, institutional issue arises: is it appropriate for a court to develop such an important principle of constitutional significance? When can and should the ECJ decide that the Union legislature is not doing what it should do and that it will step in to remedy the situation? Is the ECJ dealing with political matters, when it should stick to the more modest role of deciding what the current law actually is? This involves substantial constitutional questions of the proper role of a court. Many EU law academics praise the ECJ for this and other decisions furthering integration,[41] while a more critical tendency argues that the ECJ is overstepping the legitimate role of a court and trespassing on the role of the legislature.[42]

(iii) *The problem of a 'regulatory race to the bottom'*: One of the criticisms of mutual recognition is that it gives the Member State with the least demanding regulatory standard a competitive advantage, since its good will be cheaper to produce, and the other Member States must accept its regulatory standard and not impose a higher one. This makes goods from Member States with lower standards cheaper and thus more competitive. A possible consequence of this is that it will prompt Member States into a competitive race to lower regulatory standards, thereby reducing the quality and safety of goods in an effort to be more competitive. This has been described as a 'regulatory race to the bottom'.[43] As Barnard notes, one of the functions of the mandatory requirements or exceptions to the *Dassonville* formula, discussed further below, is to justify national restrictions that amount to MEQRs, but can be justified for good reasons, and thus to prevent such a decline in regulatory standards.[44]

---

40 In Directive 70/50/EEC OJ L 19.01.1970 p. 29 art 2(3) the Commission includes a list of MEQRs notably similar to what later emerged in ECJ case law, including packaging requirements, ingredient requirements, stipulations as to selling price, and advertising or publicity restrictions. The development of the law on MEQRs is thus a good example of the Commission and the ECJ working in tandem to increase integration. For discussion on this kind of interaction between the EU institutions, see L Conant *Justice Contained: Law and Politics in the European Union* (Cornell University Press 2002).

41 See the literature review in ch 2 of Conway *The Limits of Legal Reasoning and the European Court of Justice* (n 3).

42 H Rasmussen, *On Law and Policy of the European Court of Justice* (Martinus Nijhoff 1986); Conway *The Limits of Legal Reasoning and the European Court of Justice* (n 3).

43 M P Maduro *We the Court* (n 39) ch 4, discussing the phenomenon of 'competition between rules'.

44 Barnard *The Substantive Law of the EU* (n 14) 113.

10.4 MEQRS ON EXPORTS UNDER ARTICLE 35 TFEU

10.4.1 INTRODUCTION

> KEY LEARNING POINT
>
> ....
>
> **DISTINGUISHING ARTICLES 34 AND 35 TFEU**
> Case law on Article 35 TFEU *on exports* differs from Article 34 TFEU, not in the
> definition of an MEQR (this is the same under both Articles), but rather it differs in
> *distinguishing between the degree to which distinctly and indistinctly applicable
> national rules are prohibited.*

Under Article 35 TFEU, indistinctly applicable rules that are an obstacle to trade *must
be specifically targeted* at hindering trade before they are unlawful. Distinctly applicable
measures that clearly or explicitly discriminate against exports will generally be in breach
of Article 35 TFEU (as under Article 34), but non-discriminatory obstacles (indistinctly
applicable) will generally not be unless targeted at restricting exports. Export bans are
most obviously prohibited.

The application of Article 35 TFEU is illustrated by the case of *R v Thompson & Others*,[45]
which concerned a ban on the export of silver coins from the UK. The ECJ held that a ban
on the export from a Member State of silver alloy coins, which had once been but that were
no longer legal tender in that state and the destruction of which on national territory was
forbidden, was in principle contrary to (now) Article 35 TFEU. However, it held the UK
measure was justified as a derogation under the treaty on grounds of public policy because
it stemmed from the need to protect the right to mint coinage, as the right to mint coinage
traditionally has been regarded as involving the fundamental interests of the state.

The rationale for this approach is that the problem of a dual burden, i.e. having to satisfy
product rules in the home Member State as well as another Member State, does not
apply in the context of exports:[46] it will depend upon which Member State the state
goods are sent and what its regulations are. A dual burden can then be dealt with at that
stage under Article 34 TFEU.

10.4.2 DISTINCTLY APPLICABLE MEASURES ON IMPORTS UNDER ARTICLE 35 TFEU

Other examples of distinctly applicable measures that are prohibited under Article
35 TFEU are national rules that impose certain requirements on goods intended

....

45 Case 7/78 *R v Thompson, Johnson and Woodiwiss* [1978] ECR 2247.
46 P Craig, G de Búrca *EU Law: Texts, Cases, and Materials* (3rd edn Oxford University Press 2008) 681.

for export (but do not apply to goods intended for domestic sale), such as in, for example:

Bouhelier[47]

This concerned French rules requiring watchmakers to be licensed for export, apparently to ensure quality standards were maintained. The ECJ found that such licences were MEQRs even where no fee was charged.

Jongeneel Kaas[48]

At issue here was a Dutch law requiring cheese exporters to be in possession of an export licence. The ECJ held that in the absence of Community measures on the quality of cheese, Member States could adopt national measures so long as national measures did not discriminate between goods produced for the domestic market and those intended for export.

e.g. *Belgium v Spain (Rioja wine exports)*[49]

The facts involved Spanish rules that drew a distinction between Rioja wine intended for export, which had to be transported in bottles, and Rioja wine intended for distribution to consumers in Spain, which could be transported in bulk. The ECJ held that national rules applicable to wines bearing a designation of origin that make the use of the name of the production region conditional upon bottling in that region constitute an MEQR, since they had the effect of restricting patterns of exports of wine eligible to have the designation of origin and thereby created a difference of treatment between trade within a Member State and its export trade.

10.4.3 INDISTINCTLY APPLICABLE MEASURES

Indistinctly applicable measures will only be contrary to Article 35 where they have as their specific object or effect *the restriction of exports*:

Groenveld[50]

The ECJ held that in the state of Community law at that time (there were no Community rules regulating horsemeat), a national measure prohibiting all manufacturers of meat products from having in stock or from processing horsemeat was not contrary to the treaty if it did not discriminate between products intended for export and those marketed for the Member State (i.e. if it was applied objectively without distinction to goods produced domestically or imported from other Member States).

....

47 Case 53/76 *Procureur de la République v Bouhelier* [1977] ECR 197.
48 Case 237/82 *Jongeneel Kaas v Netherlands* [1984] ECR 483.
49 Case C–388/95 *Belgium v Spain (Rioja wine exports)* [2000] ECR I–3123.
50 Case 15/79 *Groenveld v Produktschap voor Vee en Vlees* [1979] ECR 3409.

> **KEY CASE** *INDISTINCTLY APPLICABLE MEASURES ON EXPORTS ARE LESS LIKELY TO BE IN BREACH OF ARTICLE 35 TFEU THAN ARE SUCH MEASURES ON IMPORTS UNDER ARTICLE 34 TFEU*
>
> An illustrative example is found in *Gysbrechts & Santurel Inter.*[51] The facts involved an online business that distinguished between how customers in Belgium could pay and how those in other Member States could pay. Belgian law prohibited the seller of a good from requesting any advance payment or payment during a seven-day 'withdrawal' period during which, under Belgian law, a consumer could withdraw from a distance contract. This was meant to protect the consumer. On the facts, the ECJ found that the effect of the Belgian law differed for customers buying from another Member State. This made it less attractive for Belgian firms to enter distance contracts in other Member States. The Court concluded that the treaty-based derogations did not apply (further, it held that although in principle the mandatory requirement of consumer protection could apply to this scenario, the Belgian prohibition on a seller even asking for card payment details without effecting payment before the period of withdrawal to be disproportionate to the objective of making effective a right of withdrawal.

10.5 SUNDAY TRADING AND SELLING ARRANGEMENTS AS EXCEPTIONS TO *DASSONVILLE*

10.5.1 INTRODUCTION

> **KEY CASE** KECK AND MITHOUARD *ON SELLING ARRANGEMENTS*
>
> In *Keck and Mithouard,*[52] the ECJ introduced a major exception to the scope of the *Dassonville* formula by holding that indistinctly applicable or non-discriminatory 'selling arrangements' regulated at national level were not unlawful even if they were an obstacle to market access. The ECJ has not defined in the abstract what a 'selling arrangement' is, but its case law has included the following national measures as selling arrangements:
> (i) Sunday trading rules
> (ii) rules on opening hours

51 Case C–205/07 *Gysbrechts & Santurel Inter* [2008] ECR I–9947.
52 Joined Cases C–267/91 & C–268/91 *Criminal proceedings against Keck and Mithouard* [1993] ECR I–6097.

(iii) restrictions on where goods are sold
(iv) restrictions on how goods are presented
(v) pricing requirements and
(vi) advertising restrictions.

The broader context of the judgment in *Keck and Mithouard* was increasing criticism of the activism of the ECJ. In particular, the Maastricht Treaty had excluded ECJ jurisdiction from Justice and Home Affairs and the Common Foreign and Security Policy. The scope of the internal market rules and their capacity to impact on national competences in light of ECJ case law was becoming more apparent. One of the very public points of criticism concerned the potential of *Dassonville* to outlaw national rules on Sunday trading.

KEY CASE *THE SUNDAY TRADING SAGA*

Prior to *Keck and Mithouard*, the ECJ had addressed this point in several cases, including *Torfaen Borough Council v B&Q* and *Stoke-on-Trent City Council v B&Q plc*,[53] where it created an *ad hoc* exception for Sunday trading rules (treating them in effect as a mandatory requirement, on which latter see below).

In *Torfaen Borough Council*, such rules were held not to be prohibited by the treaty. The ECJ adopted a somewhat awkward verbal formula to explain this, saying that where the restrictive effects on Community trade that might result from Sunday trading rules did not exceed the effects intrinsic to such rules and that the question of whether the effects of those rules actually remained within that limit was a question of fact to be determined by the national court, which appears to be simply a proportionality requirement.[54]

In *Stoke-on-Trent City Council*, the ECJ repeated its description in *Torfaen Borough Council* of Sunday trading rules as reflecting certain choices relating to particularly national or regional socio-cultural characteristics and that the Member States could make such choices, provided they complied with the principle of proportionality.[55]

In these cases on Sunday trading, it seemed the ECJ was making an *ad hoc* exception to *Dassonville*. In *Keck and Mithouard*, the ECJ generalised from this approach and declared

---

53 Case C–145/88 *Torfaen Borough Council v B&Q plc* [1989] ECR 3851; Case C–169/91 *Stoke-on-Trent City Council v B&Q plc* [1992] ECR I–6635.

54 Case C–145/88 *Torfaen Borough Council v B&Q plc* (n 52) para 15.

55 Ibid para 14, and Case C–169/91 *Stoke-on-Trent City Council v B&Q plc* (n 52) para 11.

that, contrary to what it had previously decided, Article 34 TFEU did not prohibit national legislation that only imposed restrictions on *the arrangements under which goods are sold*.[56]

The facts concerned a French law that made it an offence to resell goods at lower than the price for which they had been purchased. The law impacted on retailers; manufacturers were not prohibited from selling at a loss. Keck and Mithouard were retailers prosecuted for violating the law. The ECJ has not offered an abstract definition of 'selling arrangement'. However, it can be roughly defined as national laws concerning not the goods themselves, but issues such as the price at which they are sold (the issue in *Keck and Mithouard* itself); when and/or where they are sold; by whom or to whom they are sold; or how they are advertised.[57]

KEY LEARNING POINT
....

THE CONDITIONS FOR SELLING ARRANGEMENTS

16 By contrast, contrary to what has previously been decided, the application to products from other Member States of national provisions restricting or prohibiting certain selling arrangements is not such as to hinder directly or indirectly, actually or potentially, trade between Member States within the meaning of the *Dassonville* judgment . . . so long as those provisions apply to all relevant traders operating within the national territory and so long as they affect in the same manner, in law and in fact, the marketing of domestic products and of those from other Member States.

Joined Cases C–267/91 & C–268/91 *Keck and Mithouard* [1993] ECR I–6097, para 16

In other words, as regards the second condition, the ECJ is saying that selling arrangements are not to be considered non-discriminatory obstacles to market access contrary to the treaty, as *Dassonville* held they would be. However, discriminatory selling arrangements *will* still be unlawful under *Keck and Mithouard*. Further, restrictions on the *use of goods* tend to be treated by the ECJ as an obstacle to market access and so are not covered by *Keck and Mithouard*.[58]

....

56 Joined Cases C–267/91 & C–268/91 *Criminal proceedings against Keck and Mithouard* (n 52) para 16.

57 A number of cases decided prior to *Keck and Mithouard* would now be decided differently, including Joined Cases 60 & 611/84 *Cinéthèque* [1985] ECR 2605 (although it does still enjoy some precedent value as an example of the mandatory requirement of cultural protection), which concerned French rules restricting the availability of films on video to encourage cinema-going. An early precursor of the decision in *Keck and Mithouard* was Case 155/80 *Summary proceedings against Oebel* [1981] ECR 1993, where the ECJ held that national rules governing the hours of work, delivery and sale in the bread and confectionery industry constitute a legitimate part of economic and social policy, consistent with the objectives of public interest pursued by the treaty. In *Oebel*, the ECJ held that the treaty did not apply to national rules prohibiting the production of fine bakers' wares and also their transport and delivery to individual consumers and retail outlets during the night up to a certain hour.

58 For example Case C–110/05 *Commission v Italy* [2009] ECR I–519, which concerned an Italian rule prohibiting the towing of trailers by mopeds, motorcycles, tricycles and quadricycles, so that trailers could be towed only

TO *KECK* OR NOT TO *KECK*

Non-discriminatory obstacles that are not selling arrangements and that are thus not justified under *Keck and Mithouard* can be considered lawful by a different route; if they are not selling arrangements, then they fall within *Dassonville* if they restrict market access and are thus unlawful. But there is a possibility they can be justified either under the derogations in Article 36 TFEU or the exceptions in the case law called mandatory requirements; we will discuss both of these possibilities further below.

10.5.2 EXAMPLES OF SELLING ARRANGEMENTS

Sunday trading laws: Post-*Keck and Mithouard*, Sunday trading laws could be brought into the general category of selling arrangements and thus are no longer an exception on their own. Examples are *Punto Casa & PPV* and *Semararo Casa Uno and Others*, both concerning Italian legislation prohibiting Sunday trading.[59] Generally, retail hours are within the *Keck and Mithouard* exception for selling arrangements.[60]

Opening hours: In *Tankstation t'Heukske and JBE Boermans*, the ECJ held that Dutch legislation relating to the maximum opening hours and periods of compulsory closure of petrol stations comes within *Keck and Mithouard*.[61]

Restrictions on where goods are sold: Case law has dealt with a variety of factual situations under this heading. In *Commission v Greece (Processed Milk for Infants)*, the Court applied *Keck and Mithouard* to Greek legislation, which provided that powdered milk for infants was only to be sold in pharmacists' shops. Other cases have concerned, for example, Belgian legislation prohibiting the itinerant (meaning on the street) sale of subscriptions to periodicals[62] and Austrian legislation prohibiting the sale of jewellery by door-to-door salesmen to customers in their own homes.[63]

Restrictions on the prices at which goods can be sold: This was the issue in *Keck and Mithouard* itself. A similar case is *Belgapom v ITM Belgium SA and Vocarex*[64], concerning Belgian

---

by 'motor vehicles'. This was held to be justified, however, in the interests of road safety. See the discussion in E Spaventa 'Leaving *Keck* behind? The free movement of goods after the rulings in *Commission v Italy* and *Mickelsson and Roos*' (2009) 34(6) *European Law Review* 914–32.

59 Cases C–69/93 & C–258/93 *Punto Casa & PPV* [1994] ECR I–2355 and Case C–418/93 *Semararo Casa Uno & Others* [1996] ECR I–2975.

60 For a recent example see Case C–483/12 *Pelckmans Turnhout NV v Walter Van Gastel Balen NV and Others*, judgment of 8 May 2012.

61 Joined Cases C–401 & C–402/92 *Tankstation t'Heukske and JBE Boermans* [1994] ECR I–2199.

62 Case C–20/03 *Burmanjer and Others* [2005] ECR I–4133.

63 Case C–441/04 *A-Punkt Schmuckhandels v Schmidt* [2006] ECR I–2093.

64 Case C–63/94 [1995] ECR I–2467.

legislation that prohibited traders from offering a product for sale, or selling a product, at a loss. An example of a case where the ECJ found *Keck and Mithouard* inapplicable is *Fachverband der Buch- und Medienwirtschaft*.[65] This involved Austrian legislation setting minimum prices for certain imported books. The legislation was held not to be an (exempted) selling arrangement because it failed the second *Keck and Mithouard* criterion in that it discriminated between domestic and imported goods.

Restrictions on how goods are presented: In *Morellato*, the ECJ decided that a requirement under Italian legislation that bread that had been pre-baked and then frozen had to be wrapped before being handed to the customer constituted a selling arrangement.[66] Although this legislation appears indistinguishable from the packaging requirements cases, the ECJ decided that this requirement was a simple transformation process that did not affect the product itself and was, therefore, a selling arrangement.[67] This distinction is not altogether clear, since packaging does not really transform goods in any situation. It would make more sense to confine selling arrangements under this heading to marketing material external to the good.

Advertising restrictions: In principle, advertising restrictions fall within the scope of 'selling arrangements' and are thus not prohibited, but far-reaching prohibitions are likely to fail to satisfy the second criterion of *Keck and Mithouard* by having a disproportionate impact on the sale of goods from other Member States. In several cases, the ECJ has held that as long as advertising is only restricted, and not prohibited, *Keck and Mithouard* applied: *Hünermund and Others*,[68] *Leclerc-Siplec*,[69] *De Agostini v TV-Shop*.[70] *Gourmet International* dealt with a more far-reaching national measure, and the ECJ found it did not satisfy the *Keck and Mithouard* criteria.[71] This case involved Swedish legislation prohibiting all advertising of alcohol. The ECJ held that this legislation went beyond 'selling arrangements' because it had the effect, in fact, of discriminating between domestic (i.e. Swedish) alcohol and imported alcohol, in that Swedish consumers would already be familiar with Swedish brands. Thus, the second of the *Keck and Mithouard* criteria was not satisfied and the Swedish law was, therefore, an indistinctly applicable MEQR prima facie prohibited by Article 34 TFEU, unlawful unless it could be justified on health grounds under Article 36 TFEU.[72] The ECJ found that Article 36 could apply as a derogation for the Swedish measure.

....

65 Case C–531/07 *Fachverband der Buch- und Medienwirtschaft* [2009] ECR I–3717.
66 Case C–416/00 *Morellato v Commune di Padova* [2003] ECR I–9343.
67 Ibid paras 31–35.
68 Case C–292/92 *Hünermund and Others* [1993] ECR I–678, concerning a rule of professional conduct laid down by a pharmacists' professional body and prohibiting all pharmacists within the area over which it had jurisdiction from advertising outside the pharmacy quasi-pharmaceutical products which they are authorised to sell.
69 Case C–412/93 *Leclerc-Siplec* [1995] ECR I–179, concerning a prohibition on the broadcasting of advertisements for the distribution sector by television broadcasters.
70 Joined Cases C–34/95, C–35/95 & C–36/95 *De Agostini v TV-Shop* [1997] ECR I–3843, concerning national measures restricting the use of certain marketing practices in television advertising concerning a children's magazine.
71 Case C–405/98 *Gourmet International Products* [2001] ECR I–1795.
72 Ibid para 26.

DYNAMIC VERUS STATIC SELLING ARRANGEMENTS

Academic literature has distinguished between static and dynamic selling arrangements. Static selling arrangements are those that are location-specific, whereas dynamic selling arrangements can apply beyond specific locations.[73] For example, opening hours are static, advertising is dynamic. Dynamic selling arrangements, the argument goes, are more closely connected to the product and thus should not be distinguished from MEQRs. Whether this is so would require detailed market analysis by economic experts. The ECJ has not distinguished between these two types of selling arrangements, although it has not been very enthusiastic in recent years about applying *Keck and Mithouard*. However, the ECJ did not base its decision on economic expertise. The distinction between the market impacts of these different kinds of selling arrangements could be seen as a good illustration of Rasmussen's critique of the policy-making role of the ECJ: its failure to base its decision on adequate socio-economic data.[74] By seeing itself as legitimately basing innovative rulings on policy and effectiveness considerations, going beyond specific treaty rules, the ECJ is stepping outside judicial expertise. In this area, the blanket rule of the ECJ on selling arrangements lacks adequate economic evidence to justify it.

We have now considered how the ECJ has exempted non-discriminatory selling arrangements from the scope of Articles 34 and 35 TFEU as interpreted in *Dassonville*. Next we will consider how national measures that are caught within the scope of Articles 34 and 35 can be justified either (i) under the treaty derogations in Article 36 TFEU or (ii) under case law exceptions developed by the ECJ to limit the scope of its broad interpretation in *Dassonville*.

APPLYING THE LAW

PROBLEM-SOLVING AFTER *KECK*

Consider the following scenario, which will help you get used to applying the Dassonville *judgment in light of the qualification to it, as regards selling arrangements, set out in* Keck and Mithouard.

ABC Magazine Exporters Ltd is exporting magazines from the UK to Denmark. Some of these magazines are specialist trade magazines for wholesalers,

---

73 See K Mortelmans 'Article 30 of the EEC Treaty and legislation relating to market circumstances: time to consider a new direction?' (1991) 28(1) *Common Market Law Review* 115–36.

74 Rasmussen, *On Law and Policy* (n 42).

distributors and retailers in the electronics industry. These magazines are unlikely to be of interest to members of the public. ABC Magazine Exporters Ltd also supplies a number of special interest magazines to the Danish market, including magazines for aircraft, boat, firearms and fishing enthusiasts. These are in English, but are quite popular in Denmark, where many people can speak good English. ABC Magazine Exporters Ltd has just started this export to Denmark and is somewhat disappointed when it hears:

(i) that there is a legislative ban on advertising firearms magazines in Denmark. Selling firearms magazines is one of ABC's most profitable activities, as there are no Danish specialist firearms magazines, and the many firearms enthusiasts in Denmark buy English language material

(ii) further, under the same Danish legislation, ABC Magazine Exporters Ltd is not allowed to sell magazines advertising alcohol or cigarettes, which means it has to change the advertising content in several of its magazines specially to deal with this restriction, and this is quite costly

(iii) in addition, in order to encourage sales of print magazines, Denmark has adopted legislation requiring that online versions of magazines can only be made accessible online two months after the print version is available for sale and

(iv) finally, ABC Magazine Exporters Ltd is told by the Danish authorities that it must publish the magazines with a slightly larger than normal print type. It is told that this is to make it easier for people with poor eyesight to read magazines. Although there is no legislation on this requirement about print size, the Danish Government's Disability Rights Advisory Commission has recommended it. The Danish customs authorities take their advice and impose the requirement on importers of magazines into Denmark.

Tom is managing director of ABC Magazine Exporters Ltd. He is quite unhappy at having to comply with all these rules, as they reduce profits by almost 50 per cent. He asks your advice on whether the Danish rules are compatible with EU law.

Tip to get you started: You must first decide if the Danish rules in question are a 'measure' under Article 34 TFEU and then go on to consider if they are lawful.

Outline answer
The first step to answering this problem is to determine if there are national 'measures'. There clearly are, as the ECJ has interpreted government-sponsored initiatives, even though not in a legislative form, as 'measures' under Article 34 and 35 TFEU (*Apple & Pear Development Council* and *Franking Machines*). The rules here are in legislative form or are administrative decisions taken by public customs officials.

At this stage of your answer, you should also note that it is Article 34 that applies, as we are dealing with imports to Denmark from the UK and the rules at stake are Danish measures. Further, decide if the measures are distinctly or indistinctly applicable (this is relevant to which derogations apply).

It might be easiest to structure your answer by dealing with each of the four Danish measures in order:

(i)   The legislative ban on advertising firearms magazines in Denmark: A ban on advertising is an MEQR under *Dassonville*, but can be excepted as a selling arrangement under *Keck and Mithouard*. It applies to both Danish and imported products, so appears to be indistinctly applicable on the face of it. However, if the ban has a greater impact on imported products, it will not satisfy the criteria in *Keck and Mithouard* for a selling arrangement, and will still be contrary to Article 34: *Gourmet International*. The next step is to consider if the ban could be justified under the treaty or as under a mandatory requirement.

(ii) The legislative ban on selling magazines advertising alcohol or cigarettes: As for point (i), although it seems here that the rule applies equally to national and imported products, so it satisfies the criteria in *Keck and Mithouard* as a selling arrangement.

(iii) Legislative requirement that online versions of magazines can only be made accessible online two months after the print version is available for sale: This is quite similar to the facts of *Cinéthèque*. This is an indistinctly applicable measure and, under *Cinéthèque*, this would be contrary to *Dassonville*, but since *Keck and Mithouard* can be accepted as selling arrangement.

(iv) Requirement to publish the magazines with a slightly larger than normal print type: This appears to be an indistinctly applicable MEQR, not a selling arrangement, because it relates to the composition of the product. The question then is if it can be justified under Article 36 TFEU or under a mandatory requirement.

10.6 DEROGATIONS UNDER ARTICLE 36 TFEU

10.6.1 INTRODUCTION

As with the other areas of free movement,[75] the TFEU provides three standard exceptions to the prohibition on quantitative restrictions and of MEQRs: public security, public policy, and public health. In addition, there are grounds particular to goods, relating to the protection of health and life of humans, animals or plants; the

....

75 For example see art 45(3) TFEU regarding free movement of workers.

protection of national treasures possessing artistic, historic or archaeological value; or the protection of industrial and commercial property. In the discussion below, we will focus on the three standard exceptions and the protection of health and life of humans, animals or plants, as these are the most commonly invoked.[76] The text of Article 36 TFEU reads:

> The provisions of Articles 34 and 35 shall not preclude prohibitions or restrictions on imports, exports or goods in transit justified on grounds of public morality, public policy or public security; the protection of health and life of humans, animals or plants; the protection of national treasures possessing artistic, historic or archaeological value; or the protection of industrial and commercial property. Such prohibitions or restrictions shall not, however, constitute a means of arbitrary discrimination or a disguised restriction on trade between Member States.

The concepts referred to in Article 36 TFEU as justifying derogations/exceptions to free movement are quite-open-ended and abstract, especially the first two: 'public policy' and 'public security'. What they mean, therefore, very much depends on interpretation by the ECJ.

KEY LEARNING POINT

RESTRICTIVE INTERPRETATION OF TREATY DEROGATIONS

Consistently with its general approach to interpretation enhancing integration, the ECJ interprets derogations *restrictively*[77] and prefers to find in favour of whatever will enhance integration in the common market. When there is doubt, therefore, about the applicability of a derogation, the ECJ tends to hold that the claimed derogation is not permitted. This can be contrasted with the traditional approach to interpretation in international law, where the reverse applies: restrictions on state sovereignty are narrowly interpreted under the principle of *in dubio mitius*.[78] As such, this is a good example of the pro-integration, teleological approach to interpretation of the ECJ. Where a national rule is found to come within one of these exceptions, the ECJ adopts its standard approach that any restriction that is justified must satisfy two further criteria: (i) it must be *proportionate* and (ii) must *not be arbitrary discrimination or a disguised restriction* (or 'divert the derogation from its purpose').[79]

---

76 See also below in the discussion of the mandatory requirement of cultural diversity, discussing the recent case of *Fachverband der Buch* (n 30), which refers to the art 36 TFEU reference to the protection of national treasures possessing artistic, historic or archaeological value.

77 For a recent statement see e.g. in Case C–319/06 *Commission v Luxembourg* [2008] ECR I–4323 para 30.

78 H Lauterpacht 'Restrictive interpretation and effectiveness' (1949) 26 *British Yearbook of International Law* 26–85 at 58 ff; J Pauwelyn *Conflict of Norms in Public International Law* (Cambridge University Press 2003) 186. 'In dubio mitus' means more leniently in case of doubt.

79 For example Case C–405/98, *Gourmet International Products* (n 30) paras 28–33.

10.6.2 PUBLIC MORALITY

KEY LEARNING POINT

....

INTERPRETING 'PUBLIC MORALITY'
The approach of the ECJ in principle is that this is generally for Member States to decide according to their own values, but 'public morality' quite rarely succeeds as a claimed derogation.

The UK Government made a successful claim in *Henn and Darby*[80] concerning a restriction on the importation of obscene articles. The ECJ held that such a restriction could be justified on the grounds of the treaty-based category of public policy so long as it did not amount to disguised discrimination or indirect protection of domestic goods whereby domestic goods would not be subject to as strict a restriction as that for which the treaty-based derogation was to be invoked. A similar kind of UK rule was found to be not justified in *Conegate Ltd*,[81] because a UK ban on importing life-sized inflatable dolls was not matched by as similarly an absolute prohibition on such goods produced in the UK.

10.6.3 PUBLIC POLICY

KEY LEARNING POINT

....

INTERPRETING 'PUBLIC POLICY'
Although this appears at first glance to be a potentially broader category, it is not pleaded much, as it does not often succeed.

An attempt to invoke this derogation by France failed in *Cullet v Centre Leclerc*.[82] France sought to justify price fixing for fuels related to prices and costs in French oil refineries to avoid civil unrest. The ECJ rejected this, noting the French Government had the resources to deal otherwise with any civil unrest, although the wording of the ECJ decision suggested that if France could demonstrate civil unrest would occur to an extent that it could not deal with, the ECJ might have accepted the French argument.[83]

An example of where it was successful is *R v Thompson and Others*,[84] where UK legislation criminalising the export of old silver was found to be justifiable. An example of the narrow interpretation of 'public policy' is *Commission v Ireland (Souvenir Jewellery)*,[85] where the ECJ held that consumer protection could not be a factor under

....

80 Case 34/79 *R v Henn and Darby* [1979] ECR 3795.
81 Case 121/85 *Conegate Ltd v Commissioners of Customs and Excise* [1986] ECR 1007.
82 Case 231/83 *Cullet v Centre Leclerc* [1985] ECR 305.
83 Ibid para 33.
84 Case 7/78 *R v Thompson, Johnson and Woodiwiss* [1978] ECR 2247.
85 Case 113/80 *Commission v Ireland (Souvenir Jewellery)* [1981] ECR 1625.

this heading (consumer protection can be a 'mandatory requirement' under the case law of the ECJ, see further below).

A recent successful attempt by Finland to derogate on public policy grounds is *Ahokainen and Leppik*.[86] A Finnish law required import licences to be issued for the import of alcoholic products over 80 per cent proof. It was not in dispute that the Finnish measure could be justified under the treaty-based derogation public policy and public health. The ECJ stated the standard formula that it was necessary that the measure be proportionate to the objective to be achieved and not constitute a means of or a disguised restriction on trade between Member States. On the facts, the ECJ held that there was no evidence:

> . . . that the grounds of health and public policy relied on by the Finnish authorities have been diverted from their proper purpose and used in such a way as to create discrimination in respect of goods originating in other Member States, or indirectly to protect certain national products.[87]

The ECJ concluded that the question of proportionality was best left to the national court.[88]

10.6.4 PUBLIC SECURITY

> KEY LEARNING POINT
> ....
>
> **INTERPRETING 'PUBLIC SECURITY'**
> National attempts to plead 'public security' have rarely succeeded before the ECJ.

An example of a successful plea on this ground is *Campus Oil Ltd*.[89] This concerned an Irish rule requiring importers of petrol to purchase a certain amount from Ireland's only refinery. It was held to be justified under the treaty-based derogation for public security given the need to ensure a national supply of oil in an international market in which the supply of oil could be put at risk.

10.6.5 THE PROTECTION OF HEALTH AND LIFE OF HUMANS, ANIMALS OR PLANTS

The ECJ has limited the broad potential of the article by requiring scientific evidence to support its use. In *Sandoz*,[90] the facts concerned national rules prohibiting without prior authorisation the marketing of foodstuffs to which vitamins have been added, in circumstances where those goods had been lawfully marketed in another Member State. The ECJ classified this as an MEQR. Concerning public health, it was found that scientific uncertainty existed in the medical and health communities about the safety of vitamins. In this situation, the ECJ held that such an MEQR could be justified on

....

86 Case C–434/04 *Criminal proceedings against Ahokainen and Leppik* [2006] ECR I–9171.
87 Ibid para 30.
88 Ibid para 38.
89 Case 72/83 *Campus Oil Ltd v Minister for Industry and Energy* [1984] ECR 2727.
90 Case 174/82 *Officier van Justitie v Sandoz* [1983] ECR 2445.

grounds of public health, but that the Member State measures amounting to an MEQR for reasons of public health should be evidence-based.

10.6.6 INAPPLICABILITY OF DEROGATIONS IF NATIONAL MEASURE IS ARBITRARY OR AMOUNTS TO A DISGUISED RESTRICTION ON TRADE

> KEY LEARNING POINT
> ....
>
> **ARBITRARY RULES AND DISGUISED DISCRIMINATION**
> As noted by the ECJ, for example, in *Henn and Darby* and *Ahokainen and Leppik*,[91] even if a measure is covered by Article 36 TFEU, *it will still be unlawful if it is arbitrary or amounts to a disguised restriction on trade.*

An arbitrary measure appears to be essentially the same as disguised discrimination, since an arbitrary rule restrictively impacts on imports. *Conegate Ltd* is an example of arbitrary discrimination.[92] UK customs authorities had impounded a consignment of German articles on grounds of public policy, claiming that they were obscene. The ECJ held this was not justifiable as the UK did not prohibit domestic production or marketing of the goods.

A further example is *Commission v UK (French Turkeys)*.[93] This involved disguised discrimination by UK legislation restricting the import of turkeys from Member States apart from Ireland and Denmark, on health grounds. The ECJ applied a proportionality requirement to the treaty-based derogations and found that the UK measure was not justified. On the facts, the ECJ found that the possibility of infection by imported poultry products would be so much due to sheer hazard that it could not justify a complete prohibition of imports from Member States.[94]

10.7 EXCEPTIONS/DEROGATIONS UNDER CASE LAW: *CASSIS DE DIJON*, MUTUAL RECOGNITION AND MANDATORY REQUIREMENTS

10.7.1 OVERVIEW

The decision in *Cassis de Dijon*[95] applies to both Articles 34 and 35 TFEU and established two key principles:

....

91 Case 34/79 *R v Henn and Darby* [1979] ECR 3795; Case C–434/04 *Criminal proceedings against Ahokainen and Leppik* [2006] ECR I–9171.

92 Case 121/85 *Conegate Ltd v Commissioners of Customs and Excise* [1986] ECR 1007.

93 Case 40/82 *Commission v UK (French Turkeys)* [1983] ECR 2793.

94 Ibid para 47.

95 Case 120/78 *Rewe-Zentrale AG v Bundesmonopolverwaltung für Branntwein (Cassis de Dijon)* [1979] ECR.

1. *Mutual recognition* as a way of avoiding dual burdens, discussed above
2. *Mandatory requirements/rule of reason* or a case law-based category of exceptions for indistinctly applicable requirements. The concept had already been outlined in *Dassonville* in the following passage:

> 6. In the absence of a Community system guaranteeing for consumers the authenticity of a product's designation of origin, if a member State takes measures to prevent unfair practices in this connection, it is however subject to the condition that these measures should be reasonable and that the means of proof required should not act as a hindrance to trade between member States and should, in consequences, be accessible to all Community nationals.

On the basis of this 'rule of reason', the ECJ has developed justifications for national measures that are contrary to the broad interpretation of MEQRs in *Dassonville*. These justifications or exceptions are called 'mandatory requirements'. The development by the ECJ of these exceptions or derogations can be seen as essential given the problem of overreach in *Dassonville* (remember *Dassonville* could be interpreted as prohibiting all national trading rules applicable to imports or exports).

In other words, given that the ECJ had established a principle of strict interpretation of the treaty-based exceptions in Article 36 TFEU, its development of exceptions or derogations[96] in case law can be seen as an essential counterpoint to or retreat from this potential overreach of *Dassonville*. Mandatory requirements are an open–ended category of good reasons or genuine national policy concerns, which the ECJ gradually expands as various issues come before it concerning national measures contrary to *Dassonville* that are not covered by Article 36.

KEY LEARNING POINT

MANDATORY REQUIREMENTS DO NOT APPLY TO DIRECT DISCRIMINATION OR DISTINCTLY APPLICABLE MEASURES

Remember that mandatory requirements cannot justify direct discrimination i.e. distinctly applicable measures, they can only justify indistinctly applicable measures, i.e. indirect discrimination or non-discriminatory obstacles to free movement. Only the treaty-based derogations under Article 36 TFEU can justify direct discrimination, i.e. distinctly applicable measures,[97] although in one exceptional case on the environment the ECJ did seem to justify direct discrimination as a mandatory requirement, see further below on the judgment in *Aher-Waggon*.

Generally, it was initially thought that mandatory requirements could only justify indistinctly applicable measures, i.e. measures that did not discriminate *either*

---

96 In other area of free movement they are sometimes called 'overriding interests' or 'imperative requirements'.
97 Case 788/79 *Criminal proceedings against Gilli and Andres* [2004] ECR I–1333 para 6; Case 113/80 *Commission v Ireland (Souvenir Jewellery)* [1982] ECR 4575 para 11.

directly or indirectly. However, in practice and despite some indications to the contrary in earlier cases, mandatory requirements have been extended to justify indirect discrimination. This is partly due to the fact that there is a fine line between indirectly discriminatory measures and 'mere' obstacles to market access.[98]

Importantly, whether a rule is indirectly discriminatory is a question of fact, which the ECJ may not always be able to assess fully owing to a lack of evidence, so it may be hard to say whether a national measure is an example of indirect discrimination or a non-discriminatory obstacle. However, it is true that the ECJ has been more willing consistently to justify indirect discrimination under the other free movement principles than in relation to quantitative restrictions and MEQRs, and you should be careful to note this in an exam.[99]

The ECJ has refused to accept certain suggested mandatory requirements, principally those based on purely economic grounds. An example of the latter is *Duphar*, which concerned measures to reduce the costs of a sickness insurance scheme.[100]

EXPLAINING THE LAW

ECONOMIC REASONS FOR DEROGATIONS OR EXCEPTIONS
The approach of the ECJ rejecting purely economic reasons as mandatory requirements reflects its case law on the treaty-based derogations to free movement of persons, which is now codified in Article 27 of Directive 2004/38.[101]

The ECJ may also refuse to recognise a national objective as a mandatory requirement when it can be accommodated under the treaty-based derogations. In *Bluhme*,[102] the Court rejected a claimed mandatory requirement based on biological diversity, as it could be dealt with under Article 36 TFEU, which provides for derogating national measures related to the protection of the health and life of animals. The following discusses the main categories of mandatory requirement recognised to date in ECJ case law. They are first summarised in the text box.

....

98 Craig and de Búrca *EU Law* (n 46) 704, discussing Case C–320/03 *Commission v Austria* [2005] ECR I–9871, where the Advocate General thought that an Austrian rule banning lorries of a certain size from certain roads could involve indirect discrimination, but the ECJ without discussion treated a mandatory requirement as applicable.

99 See also the discussion in Barnard *The Substantive Law of the EU* (n 14) 126–27.

100 Case 238/82 *Duphar* [1987] ECR 1227. The ECJ also held here that restrictions on access to medicine under a national compulsory health insurance scheme did not concern access to the market and so were not contrary to free movement.

101 Directive 2004/38/EEC OJ L 158 30.04.2004 p. 77.

102 Case C–67/97 *Bluhme* [1986] ECR 1511.

A SUMMARY OF MANDATORY REQUIREMENTS
What are 'mandatory requirements'?

(i)   Mandatory requirements are reasons recognised as valid by the ECJ as to why Member States can make exceptions to the free movement principle.
(ii) They are exceptions created by the ECJ in its case law, and they supplement the treaty-based derogations or exceptions ('derogation' and 'exception' mean the same thing).
(iii) They can only be used to non-discriminatory obstacles to free movement and possibly indirect discrimination, they can never be used to justify direct discrimination.

What does the ECJ recognise as a good enough reason for a national restriction on free movement to be a mandatory requirement? This is an open-ended category, so it is a matter of looking to the case law. Here are the main mandatory requirements (i.e. justification for an exception to free movement) recognised to date:

(i)   consumer protection, e.g. *Walter Rau v De Smedt, Commission v UK (Origin Marking), Mars, Estée Lauder*
(ii)   environmental protection, e.g. *Commission v Denmark ('Danish Bottles'), Aher-Waggon, Aklagaren v Mickelsson and Roos*
(iii) cultural protection, e.g. *Cinéthèque, Fachverband der Buch- und Medienwirtschaft*
(iv)   protection of human rights, e.g. *Schmidberger v Austria*
(v)   diversity or pluralism in the media, e.g. *Familiapress*
(vi)   road safety, e.g. *Snellers Autos, Commission v Italy (Trailers), Commission v Finland (Transfer Licences)*
(vii) protection of the child, e.g. *Dynamic Medien*
(viii) crime prevention, e.g. *Commission v Portugal (Tinted Film)*.

10.7.2 EXAMPLES OF MANDATORY REQUIREMENTS

10.7.2.1 CONSUMER PROTECTION

This is the most commonly argued mandatory requirement. Examples include *Walter Rau v De Smedt*[103] and *Commission v UK (Origin Marking)*[104] discussed above. In *Mars*,[105] the ECJ refused to recognise an indistinctly applicable national rule on packaging as justified by this mandatory requirement. On the facts, it held that reasonably

103 Case 261/81 *Walter Rau Lebensmittelwerke v De Smedt PvbA* [1982] ECR 3961.
104 Case 207/83 *Commission v UK (Origin Marking)* [1985] ECR 1202.
105 Case C–470/93 *Köln v Mars GmbH* [1995] ECR I–1923.

circumspect consumers[106] may be deemed to know that there is not necessarily a link between the size of publicity markings relating to an increase in a product's quantity/ size and the size of that increase. Therefore, a national measure prohibiting the import and marketing of a product lawfully marketed in another Member State whose packaged units were increased in quantity/size during a short publicity campaign and had their wrapping marked '+ 10%' was unlawful.

Estée Lauder[107] concerned national legislation that prohibited the import and marketing of a particular cosmetic product whose name incorporated the term 'lifting'. The ECJ held this could be justified under Article 36, where the average consumer, reasonably well informed and reasonably observant and circumspect, is misled by that name, believing it to imply that the product possesses characteristics which it does not have. It was for the national court to decide, having regard to the presumed expectations of the average consumer, whether the name is misleading.

10.7.2.2 ENVIRONMENTAL PROTECTION

The protection of the environment was confirmed as a mandatory requirement by *Commission v Denmark (Danish Bottles)*,[108] involving Danish rules on the compulsory recycling of glass and plastic. The Court stated that 'protection of the environment is one of the Community's essential objectives, which may as such justify certain limitations of the principle of the free movement of goods'.[109] The case also contains a good general statement of the concept of mandatory requirements and the application of the principle of proportionality to them:

> 6. The first point which must be made in resolving this dispute is that, according to an established body of case-law of the Court (judgment of 20 February 1979 in Case 120/78 *Rewe-Zentral AG v Bundesmonopolverwaltung fuer Branntwein* (1979) ECR 649; judgment of 10 November 1982 in Case 261/81 *Walter Rau Lebensmittelwerke v De Smedt PvbA* (1982) ECR 3961), in the absence of common rules relating to the marketing of the products in question, obstacles to free movement within the Community resulting from disparities between the national laws must be accepted in so far as such rules, applicable to domestic and imported products without distinction, may be recognized as being necessary in order to satisfy mandatory requirements recognized by Community law. Such rules must also be proportionate to the aim in view. If a Member State has a choice between various measures for achieving the same aim, it should choose the means which least restricts the free movement of goods.[110]

....

106 Ibid para 24. See also Case C–210/96 *Gut Springenheide GmbH v Oberkreisdirektor des Kreises Steinfurt* [1998] ECR I–4657 para 31, which referred to the consumer being reasonably well informed also.

107 Case C–220/98 *Estée Lauder Cosmetics* [2000] ECR I–117.

108 Case 302/86 *Commission v Denmark (Danish Bottles)* [1988] 4607. See also the earlier case of Case 240/83 *Procureur de la République v ADBHU* [1985] ECR 352.

109 Ibid para 8.

110 Ibid para 6.

On the facts, it was held that a Danish rule establishing a deposit-and-return system for empty containers was necessary to achieve the protection of the environment. However, it was also held that the requirement that foreign manufacturers must either use only containers approved by the national authorities, or not market annually more than a certain volume of drinks in non-approved containers, was disproportionate.

ANALYSING THE LAW

A MANDATORY REQUIREMENT JUSTIFYING DIRECT DISCRIMINATION?

This area can be confusing because the ECJ in some case law seems to have suggested that the mandatory requirement of environmental protection could even justify direct discrimination. *Aher-Waggon*[111] involved German legislation on noise pollution from aircraft engines. German legislation made the first registration in Germany of aircraft previously registered in another Member State conditional upon compliance with stricter noise standards than those laid down in Community legislation. This is an example of direct discrimination, since planes registered in Germany were not subject to this stricter standard. In a short judgment, the ECJ held that this German rule was justifiable under public health or environmental protection and not disproportionate:

> 19. Such a barrier may, however, be justified by considerations of public health and environmental protection of the kind relied on by the German Government. The German Government states in particular that the Federal Republic of Germany, which is a very densely populated State attaches special importance to ensuring that its population is protected from excessive noise emissions.

The mandatory requirement recognised here was the prevention of noise pollution. Strangely, the ECJ did not remark on the fact that it was applying a mandatory requirement of environmental protection to direct discrimination. Normally, only the treaty derogations in Article 36 TFEU can justify direct discrimination. However, the ECJ also referred to public health (although not to the treaty provisions), and it is possible it was deciding that environmental protection came under the treaty derogation of public health. The ECJ did not clarify this and has not done so since.

Finally, a recent example of this mandatory requirement is *Aklagaren v Mickelsson and Roos*,[112] which concerned Swedish legislation prohibiting the use of 'personal watercraft' or jet-skis except on water designated as a 'general navigable waterway'. This was held to breach Article 34 TFEU. However, it was justifiable on environmental protection grounds.[113]

....

111 Case C–389/96 *Aher-Waggon v Germany* [1998] ECR 1–4473.
112 Case C–142/05 *Aklagaren v Mickelsson and Roos* [2009] ECR I–4273.
113 Ibid paras 34–36.

10.7.2.3 CULTURAL PROTECTION

The protection of national socio-cultural values was added by *Cinéthèque & Others*,[114] involving French rules restricting the availability of films on video to encourage cinema-going. Although it held the French rules were an MEQR, the ECJ held now Article 34 TFEU did not apply to national legislation regulating the distribution in this way because it was a justified objective to increase the production of cinematographic works (although it set out the usual condition that that any barriers to trade legitimated by a mandatory requirement were proportionate or did not exceed what was necessary to ensure that cinema availability had priority over other means of distribution).[115]

The ECJ noted that the purpose of the French rules, which were similar to those in a majority of Member States, was not to regulate trade, but to encourage cinematic production. The Court in *Cinéthèque* did not really set out any general criteria for determining what constituted similar cultural protection as a mandatory requirement (note by the way that following the decision in *Keck and Mithouard*, the French rules would now be considered to be a selling arrangement and so would not need to be justified by a mandatory requirement).

This ground has also arisen in the more recent case of *Fachverband der Buch- und Medienwirtschaft*, with a somewhat unusual set of facts discussed above.[116] The issue arose whether an Austrian rule setting prices on German language books could be justified under Article 36 on the basis of cultural protection. Characteristically, the ECJ did set out to narrow cultural protection, saying that the treaty derogation in now Article 36 relating to the 'protection of national treasures possessing artistic, historic or archaeological value' did not extend to protecting cultural diversity.[117]

However, the Court went on to hold that the protection of books as cultural objects could be legitimate as a mandatory requirement justifying a restriction on the free movement of goods.[118] It stated the usual requirement that the means had to be proportionate to this end and held on the facts of the case could have been better achieved by fixing a price taking into account Austrian market conditions.

10.7.2.4 PROTECTION OF HUMAN RIGHTS

Schmidberger v Austria added the protection of fundamental rights, such as the freedom of expression.[119] It concerned whether the Austrian Government's decision to sanction the closure of a motorway to facilitate a demonstration was a breach of EU law. The ECJ held that the road closure was capable of hindering trade, but then noted that the Austrian Government also had to respect the fundamental rights of the protestors: 'Since

---

114 Joined Cases 60 & 61/84 *Cinéthèque & Others SA and Others v Fédération Nationale des Cinémas Français* [1985] ECR 2605.

115 Ibid paras 22–23.

116 Case C–531/07 *Fachverband der Buch- und Medienwirtschaft* [2009] ECR I–3717.

117 Ibid para 32.

118 Ibid para 34.

119 Case C–112/00 *Schmidberger v Austria* [2003] ECR I–5659.

both the [European Union] and its Member States are required to respect fundamental rights, the protection of those rights is a legitimate interest which, in principle, justifies a restriction of . . . the free movement of goods'.[120]

10.7.2.5 DIVERSITY OR PLURALISM IN THE MEDIA

In *Familiapress*,[121] the ECJ has upheld a national rule prohibiting the offering of prizes for games in magazines when the objective of the national rule was to encourage smaller magazines that could not afford to compete by offering such games themselves.

10.7.2.6 ROAD SAFETY

In *Snellers Autos*,[122] the ECJ stated that road safety could be added to the list of mandatory requirements. More recent examples include *Commission v Italy (Trailers)*[123] and *Commission v Finland (Transfer Licences)*.[124] *Trailers* concerned Italian legislation prohibiting mopeds and motorcycles from towing trailers. The ECJ held that the legislation was capable of hindering trade in such trailers, but could be justified on safety grounds. In *Transfer Licences*, under Finnish legislation, a transfer licence was required before cars registered in other Member States could be imported into Finland, and the Commission alleged a breach of (now) Article 34 TFEU. The Finnish Government argued that it was justified on the grounds of protecting road safety in that licences could be refused to cars not deemed to be roadworthy.

The ECJ decided that the legislation was theoretically justifiable, though the Court held that the Finnish system did not actually promote road safety on the facts. The ECJ noted that the licence requirement did not apply to all vehicles registered in another Member State put into circulation in Finland. Further, pending the final registration of the vehicles in Finland, their technical characteristics could be identified because all Member States have a vehicle registration system. The case is a good example of the application of proportionality in a factual sense (in contrast to the use of proportionality as means to try to resolve a conflict or tension between two incommensurable values, see further Chapter 8 above).

10.7.2.7 PROTECTION OF THE CHILD

Dynamic Medien added the protection of the child as a mandatory requirement.[125] The case involved German legislation requiring all videos and DVDs to be inspected and classified by the German authorities, even if they had already been classified in the exporting state by the authorities there. The facts of this case have been set out above, and the ECJ decided that the German legislation did impose a trade barrier and that this requirement was not a selling arrangement, but was justifiable. The Court found

120 Ibid para 74.
121 Case C–368/95 *Vereinigte Familiapress Zeitungsverlags- und vertriebs Gmbh v Heinrich Bauer Verlag* [1997] ECR I–368.
122 Case C–314/98 *Snellers Auto's v Algemeen Directeur van de Dienst Wegverkeer* [2000] ECR I–8633.
123 Case C–110/05 *Commission v Italy (Trailers)* [2009] ECR I–519.
124 Case C–54/05 *Commission v Finland* [2007] ECR I–2473.
125 Case C–244/06 *Dynamic Medien* (fn 37).

that there was no doubt that the measure was suitable for protecting children from information harmful to them.

10.7.2.8 THE FIGHT AGAINST CRIME

Commission v Portugal (Tinted Film) added crime prevention as a mandatory requirement.[126] Portuguese legislation prohibited affixing tinted film to the windows of passenger or goods vehicles. The Portuguese Government accepted that the law was capable of hindering trade (in tinted film) but argued that the legislation was justified on grounds of public safety and/or road safety. It argued that the ban enabled the authorities to make a quick external inspection of the interior of vehicles in order (i) to ensure that the vehicle's occupants were wearing seat belts and (ii) to identify potential criminals. The ECJ agreed, in principle, but held that the legislation went beyond what was strictly necessary to achieve this intended outcome. The ECJ judgment in this case is another good example of how proportionality can be applied to a factual context.[127]

KEY CASE *THE* BEER PURITY *CASE AS AN EXAMPLE*

In *Commission v Germany (Beer Purity)*,[128] the drinking habits of the German population and the fact that it consumed beer in considerable quantities were raised in an attempt by the German Government to rebut the presumption of mutual recognition.[129] However, the ECJ found that the German rules still failed the requirements of proportionality in that the special dietary habits of the German population (i.e. they drank more beer per head of population than most other EU Member States) would justify certain special rules, but the complete abolition of all additives in beer went beyond what was strictly necessary to protect them. The ECJ held that there was a lack of scientific evidence to justify the complete banning of the additives and also that Germany was inconsistent in its approach in that not all drinks containing the same additives were banned.

APPLYING THE LAW

THE ROLE OF THE ECJ AS A 'MOTOR OF INTEGRATION'

Consider to what extent the ECJ has expanded its own jurisdiction through its decision in *Dassonville* and the discretion it has given itself to create new mandatory requirements. Does this give the ECJ a great deal of discretion over national policy in the area of trading rules? How has this impacted on the competences of the EU relative to the Member States? How is it a good idea for a court to have this kind of power?

---

126 Case C–265/06 *Commission v Portugal (Tinted Film)* [2008] ECR I–2245.
127 Ibid paras 41–47.
128 In Case 178/84 *Commission v Germany (Beer Purity)* [1987] ECR 1227.
129 Ibid paras 47–48.

MAKING CONNECTIONS
+++++++++++++++++++

THE SIMILAR STRUCTURE OF THE FREE MOVEMENT PRINCIPLES AND OF THEIR DEROGATIONS/EXCEPTIONS

A common pattern can be observed across the free movement principles and from which it is possible to adopt a framework for dealing with problem situations:

(i) What kind of national measure is in issue? Is it (a) direct discrimination, (b) indirect discrimination, or (c) a non-discriminatory obstacle to free movement?

(ii) Depending on your answer to (i), which of the following possibilities apply:

    a. If it involves direct discrimination, i.e. it is distinctly applicable, it can only be justified under the treaty (Article 36 TFEU)

    b. If indirect discrimination, it can be justified under Article 36 TFEU and might be justified under case law as a mandatory requirement

    c. If it is a non-discriminatory obstacle, it is not prohibited if it is a selling arrangement, and if it is prohibited, it might be justified by either Article 36 TFEU or the mandatory requirements case law.

NB: You should follow this sequence in any problem. This pattern of dealing with free movement can also be followed, with some modifications, for the other free movement principles.

An important point to bear in mind is that it is first necessary to classify a rule (direct or indirect discrimination or a non-discriminatory obstacle) in order to know which of the derogations/exceptions apply.

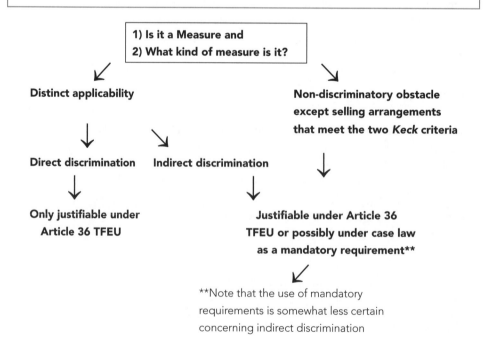

10.8 DIRECT EFFECT OF ARTICLES 34 AND 35 TFEU

MAKING CONNECTIONS
+ + + + + + + + + + + + + + + + +

FREE MOVEMENT DOES NOT HAVE HORIZONTAL DIRECT EFFECT

Since the doctrine of direct effect was declared by the EC in *Van Gend en Loos*, the treaty rules now contained in Articles 34 and 35 TFEU have had vertical direct effect, i.e. an individual can invoke the free movement provisions against his or her own government and national rules in a national court. However, the free movement principles generally do not have horizontal direct effect, i.e. an individual cannot sue another individual in a national court for violating free movement.

The ECJ has generally held that the free movement provisions of the treaty have vertical direct effect, while there are some conflicting indications in the case law on whether they have horizontal direct effect.[130] However, the general position appears to be that free movement of goods does not have horizontal direct effect. In *Sapod Audic*, the Court clearly stated that an obligation arising out of a private contract 'cannot be considered as a barrier to trade for the purpose of [Article 34 TFEU] since it was not imposed by a Member State but agreed between individuals'.[131]

Several considerations arise with the question of considering free movement of goods to have horizontal direct effect. Such horizontal direct effect could be quite intrusive in private economic relationships and could also be a considerable burden on private commerce, especially since the ECJ has extended the treaty to cover the idea of non-discriminatory obstacles (indistinctly applicable measures). Considerable legal uncertainty could result for private commercial enterprises if Articles 34 and 35 TFEU had horizontal direct effect.

Defining what is a state entity thus matters considerably in this area. The ECJ has been quite flexible in its approach to this, holding that a body that is funded by the government and whose membership is appointed by the government is a public entity[132] and that a statutory duty to pay levies to a body rendered it a public entity.[133]

....

130 See the excellent discussion in H Schepel 'Constitutionalising the market, marketising the Constitution, and to tell the difference: on the horizontal application of the free movement provisions in EU Law' (2012) 18(2) *European Law Journal* 177–200.

131 Case C–159/00 *Sapod Audic* [2002] ECR I–5031 para 74.

132 Case 249/81 *Commission v Ireland (Buy Irish)* [1982] ECR 4005.

133 Case 222/82 *Apple & Pear Development Council v Lewis* [1983] ECR 4083.

Further, the state can be liable for failing to prevent private bodies from restricting free movement in an enforcement action[134] and an individual can also sue the state for damages in a national court for failing to implement EU law, under the doctrine of state liability.

10.9 EFFECT OF HARMONISATION LEGISLATION

KEY LEARNING POINT

IMPACT OF HARMONISATION ON THE DEROGATIONS

Once the EU had adopted harmonising measures on an issue, the treaty-based derogations in Article 36 TFEU or the mandatory requirements can no longer be invoked by the Member States whenever harmonised rules apply.[135]

This could be seen as a logical approach, as the derogations could be used by a Member State to go back on something they had already agreed to and could undermine the legislative process. States have an opportunity during the adoption of legislation to seek to have their concerns inserted in legal instruments. Further, as the ECJ indicated in *Compassion in World Farming Ltd*,[136] harmonising measures may have as their purpose to protect the kind of concerns Article 36 addresses:

> . . . while Article 36 allows the maintenance of restrictions on the aforementioned grounds, which constitute fundamental requirements recognised by Community law, recourse to Article 36 is nevertheless no longer possible where Community directives provide for harmonisation of the measures necessary to achieve the specific objective which would be further by reliance on upon this provision [i.e. on Article 36][137]

The case concerned a conflict between international law norms[138] previously given effect by a Community decision[139] (and recommendation) and a later directive laying down minimum conditions for the protection of calves.[140]

---

134 Case C–265/95 *Commission v France* [1997] ECR I–6959.
135 Case C–320/93 *Ortscheit* [1994] ECR I–5243 para 18.
136 Case C–1/96 *The Queen v Minister of Agriculture, Fisheries and Food, ex parte Compassion in World Farming Ltd* [1998] ECR I–1251.
137 Ibid para 47.
138 The Council of Europe's European Convention on the Protection of Animals Kept for Farming Purposes, ETS No 78.
139 Council Decision 78/923/EEC OJ L 323 17.11.1978 p. 12.
140 Council Directive 91/629/EEC OJ L 340 11.12.1991 p. 28.

Against the approach taken by the ECJ in the above cases, it might be argued that since unanimity in the Council (of Ministers) is now the exception, rather than the norm, Member States have less opportunity for protecting their interests in the process of adopting legislation, as they may simply be outvoted. For this reason, perhaps in exceptional circumstances, the ECJ should be willing to consider Article 36 TFEU applying despite the existence of overlapping harmonising measures.

KEY LEARNING POINT

HARMONISATION IS TOTAL OR PARTIAL

Two distinct situations arise: where harmonisation is total, leaving no regulatory space for national measures to take effect, and where harmonisation is partial or involves setting minimum standards, in which case Member States will have scope for national rules that do not contradict the minimum rules set by EU harmonisation. Nonetheless, any national rules in this second situation would have to be generally consistent with the Treaty in the usual way. For example, in the second situation, any national rules in the 'space left over', i.e. not covered by EU harmonisation, that restricted free movement could be valid relying on the derogation in Article 36 TFEU, but they would need to be proportionate to the objective pursued under Article 36 TFEU.[141]

EXPLAINING THE LAW

ARTICLES 34 AND 35 TFEU IN THEIR INTERNATIONAL CONTEXT

It may be helpful to better understand the EU rules prohibiting quantitative restrictions and equivalent measures by looking at what rules would apply if the EU rules did not, e.g. if a Member State was to withdraw from the EU under Article 50 TEU. What rules would then apply? It may seem surprising, but largely similar rules apply under international law. All members of the EU are members of the World Trade Organization (WTO). As part of EU membership, each Member State has given up its right to decide trading rules with third countries itself, as the Member States have accepted the Common Custom Union. Now, the EU is represented as a bloc by the European Commission in the WTO, although the European Commission must follow directions by the Council (of Ministers).[142] Article XI of the General Agreement on Trade and Tariffs 1947 and WTO Agreement 1994[143] prohibits quantitative restrictions

---

141 Case C–323/93 *Société Agricole de la Crespelle* [1998] ECR I–1251 para 35; Case C–110/05, *Commission v Italy (Trailers)* [2009] ECR I–519 para 61.

142 Article 207 TFEU.

143 55 UNTS 224.

between WTO members subject to a number of exceptions. Although this GATT/WTO provision in Article XI has not been interpreted by the dispute settlement organs of the WTO quite as broadly as the ECJ has interpreted Articles 34 and 35 TFEU, the scope is quite similar: WTO members are required not to impose quantitative restrictions on trade with each other.

10.10 CONCLUSION

The prohibition on quantitative restrictions and on measures having an equivalent effect ('MEQRs') can seem a dauntingly technical topic at first. It is best understood if looked at in a chronological way and, in particular, if the 'problem' created by the broad interpretation of 'MEQR' in the *Dassonville* case is understood. *Dassonville* interpreted the TFEU, in what are now Articles 34 and 35 TFEU (following many confusing renumberings with each treaty revision), as prohibiting not only direct discrimination ('distinctly applicable' measures), but also as prohibiting indirect discrimination non-discriminatory obstacles to free movement in the abstract ('indistinctly applicable measures'). This meant that any national regulation of trade could be an MEQR and suggested that the Member States needed to harmonise trading rules fully.

What happened subsequently in this area was a response to the *Dassonville* case. The Member States refused to harmonise to this extent, leaving the ECJ with no option but to retreat from *Dassonville*. This the ECJ did through (1) the principle of mutual recognition in *Cassis de Dijon*, and (2) further through developing case law exceptions to *Dassonville* (which supplement the treaty derogations in Article 36) and (3) finally through exempting selling arrangements from the *Dassonville* rule on non-discriminatory obstacles/indistinctly applicable measures. A final general point to make is not to be confused by the terminology specific to this aspect of free movement of goods: in particular, 'distinctly applicable' simply means 'discriminatory' and similarly 'indistinctly applicable' simply means 'non-discriminatory'.

POINTS TO REVIEW

– The treaty prohibition on quantitative restrictions and equivalent measures (MEQRs) on exports and imports, in Articles 34 and 35 TFEU, make up the second element of the free movement of goods, the first element being the treaty rules on taxes. The treaty rules on quantitative measures and MEQRs prohibit bans, quotas, and equivalent restrictions on the export or import of goods. As well as the classic scenario of bans or quotas, therefore, restrictions on trade related to product composition, and equivalent measures to either of these, are prohibited.

- Articles 34 and 35 TFEU prohibit national 'measures', which as well as legislative rules, includes policy and administrative decisions by state organs.

- Bans and quotas are prohibited outright. It was initially thought that only MEQRs that discriminated, either directly or indirectly, between goods from other Member States and domestic goods were prohibited. However, in its leading case of *Dassonville*, the ECJ held that all potential obstacles to free movement were prohibited. This meant that national measures that amounted to non-discriminatory obstacles were contrary to the treaty.

- The *Dassonville* decision created a problem of the overreach of EU law, as almost any national rules on trading could be considered an obstacle to free movement since they had to be complied with by goods from other countries. The logical consequence of *Dassonville* would have been the full harmonisation of trading rules amongst the Member States. The Member States, however, refused to go this route, which meant the ECJ had to retreat from its decision in *Dassonville* to narrow the potential to invalidate virtually all national trading rules.

- The ECJ narrowed the impact of *Dassonville* in three ways: 1. In *Cassis de Dijon*, it declared that Member States did not have to harmonise their trading rules, they just had to accept a mutual recognition of the trading standards, e.g. of health and safety standards, thereby avoiding goods being imported or imported having to satisfy two health and safety standards (that of their domestic state and that of the state to which the goods are exported); 2. In *Keck and Mithouard*, it exempted non-discriminatory selling arrangements from the scope of prohibited obstacles to trade; 3. It developed a category of exceptions in the case law (instead of expanding its traditionally narrow approach to the treaty exceptions in Article 36 TFEU), usually called mandatory requirements, whereby the ECJ accepted trade restrictions for a sound policy reason (although the case law exceptions do not apply to distinctly applicable measures).

- The ECJ has not defined selling arrangements in the abstract, so it is a matter of looking to what has been identified in case law. Among the examples from case law are advertising methods (though very restrictive rules on advertising might not be considered a selling arrangement, but an MEQR instead), trading hours (e.g. rules on Sunday trading) and pricing-fixing requirements.

- Under Article 35 TFEU on exports (Article 34 TFEU, referred to above, deals with imports), a national rule must be distinctly applicable or discriminatory to be contrary to the treaty. Non-discriminatory obstacles to free movement or indistinctly applicable measures are not unlawful under Article 35 TFEU.

- Article 36 TFEU provides for the usual derogation related to public policy, public security and public health. These are strictly construed by the ECJ and cannot, for example, include economic motives. These derogations have been supplemented by case law exceptions developed by the ECJ, but note that direct discrimination (distinct applicability) can only be justified by the treaty derogations in Article 36 TFEU.

- Articles 34 and 35 TFEU do not have horizontal direct effect.

- Once EU harmonising measures have been adopted, the Member States may not invoke derogations under Article 36 relating to the same subject matter as the EU harmonising legislation.

CHAPTER GLOSSARY

A country of origin designation is an indication on a good of the country in which it was made. These are usually considered MEQRs and are usually thus contrary to Articles 34 and 35 TFEU.

A distinctly applicable measure is another term used to describe a non-discriminatory measure, i.e. a non-discriminatory national rule applicable to goods imported from other EU Member States and not applied to domestic goods. The term 'distinctly applicable' is used in EU law in the context of Articles 34 and 35, whereas 'discriminatory' tends to be used in other contexts. Note that the term 'distinctly applicable' is usually taken to mean directly discriminatory.

An indistinctly applicable measure is another term used to describe a non-discriminatory measure, i.e. a non-discriminatory national rule applicable to both domestic goods and goods imported from other EU Member States. The term indistinctly applicable is used in EU law in the context of Articles 34 and 35,

whereas 'non-discriminatory' tends to be used in other contexts.

A mandatory requirement refers to a national policy objective that the ECJ considers legitimate reason for restricting indistinctly applicable measures (note the concept is sometimes used to justify indirect discrimination).

Measures (under Articles 34 and 35 TFEU) are national practice or rules that impact on the free movement of goods. These national practices or rules do not have to be in the form of legislation, they can be contained in an administrative decision, practice or policy.

Measures having equivalent effect to quantitative restrictions (MEQRs) under Articles 34 and 35 TFEU are national measures that have a comparable effect to a quota on goods coming in to a Member State. The ECJ has interpreted 'MEQR' very broadly. It can be any national requirement on a good that makes it more difficult for an importer from a Member State to import their goods into another Member State. Among the things the ECJ has found to be an MEQR are ingredient requirements, packaging requirements and restrictions on advertising. Later in its case law, the ECJ decided that 'selling arrangements' did not come within the definition of 'MEQR'.

Minimum harmonisation refers to secondary EU legislation (i.e. regulations, directives or decisions but usually, in this context, directives) that harmonise basic or minimum rules in a particular area, leaving the Member States to regulate matters beyond the minimum rules.

Negative integration is a term used to describe the removal of national rules restricting the free movement of goods. It is contrasted with the term 'positive integration'.

A non-discriminatory obstacle to free movement is a national measure that does not discriminate between domestic goods and goods from other Member States, but that nonetheless makes it more difficult for goods to be moved freely between Member States.

Positive integration is a term used to describe the adoption of common rules across the EU, not just the removal of national rules (the latter is referred to as 'negative integration').

Quantitative restriction refers to a numeric limitation on the import or export of a good, i.e. a quota. It also includes absolute bans on the import or export of a particular type of good.

Rule of reason refers to the idea that the ECJ will accept certain limitations on distinctly applicable national measures that are indirectly discriminatory of the national measure is reasonably and proportionately connected to a legitimate objective. The development of the 'rule of reason' could be viewed as a consequence of the very broad interpretation of MEQR in *Dassonville*.

Selling arrangement is a term used by the ECJ to describe the way in which a good is sold, other than relating to packaging. It is contrasted with MEQR. This is a rough definition, as the ECJ has never defined it precisely. Instead it is a matter of looking to case law on what the term means. Among the examples from case law are advertising methods (though very restrictive rules on advertising might not be considered a selling arrangement, but an MEQR instead), trading hours (e.g. rules on Sunday trading) and pricing-fixing requirements.

TAKING THINGS FURTHER

M P Maduro *We The Court: The European Economic Constitution* (Hart Publishing 1999) This monograph offers an excellent overview of the case law of the ECJ and the differing policy reasons and choices that underlie Article 34 TFEU (on the prohibition on exports of quantitative restrictions and MEQRs) and ECJ case law interpreting it. The book demonstrates how several different visions of integration can be related to different approaches to Article 34 TFEU.

E Spaventa 'Leaving *Keck* behind? The free movement of goods after the rulings in *Commission v Italy and Mickelsson and Roos*' (2009) 34(6) *European Law Review* 914–32 This article provides a useful discussion of recent case law on national measures restricting the use of goods and explains how the reluctance of the ECJ to extend *Keck and Mithouard* can be compensated for by focusing on mandatory requirements as justifying obstacles to market access.

C Barnard *The Substantive Law of the EU* (3rd edn Oxford University Press 2010) The third edition of this very good book offers the most specialised and detailed treatment of the four freedoms, with clear and comprehensive analysis and discussion of case law.

H Schepel 'Constitutionalising the market, marketising the Constitution, and to tell the difference: on the horizontal application of the free movement provisions in EU law' (2012) 18(2) *European Law Journal* 177–200 This article offers an excellent analytical account of the reasons for and against applying horizontal direct effect to free movement provisions. It covers all of the free movement provisions, but is perhaps best read with the current chapter as it explains the different constitutional concerns underlying freedom of goods compared to freedom of persons very well.

M S Jansson, H Kalimo '*De Minimis* meets market access: transformation in the substance – and the syntax – EU free movement law' (2014) 51(2) *Common Market Law Review* 523–58 This article argues that the ECJ should develop a *de minimis* threshold for the application of free movement of goods, proposing how it could structure a *de minimis* test.

CHAPTER 11
FREE MOVEMENT OF PERSONS I: WORKERS

This chapter examines one of the most important aspects of the common market: the free movement of workers. Several aspects of free movement of workers arise: the right to go and seek work to access work opportunities, and to live in another Member State of the EU. We will look at all these aspects in this chapter. We will examine national measures or rules relating to workers and employment that are contrary to free movement of workers and citizens and when national measures can derogate or be excepted from EU law. It is worth keeping in mind that there is a similar structure or pattern to the different areas of free movement rules across EU law (relating to workers, services/establishment, goods and capital and payments), and that this is especially so for free movement of workers and services/establishment. The main practical legal effect that citizenship of the EU has had is to increase some of the rights of EU citizens who are neither working nor seeking work, but who nonetheless will not become an unreasonable burden on the financial resources of the 'host' Member State. Citizenship is examined in Chapter 8.

AS YOU READ . . .

The key questions that will be answered in this chapter are as follows:

- How has free movement of workers has been one of the key principles of the common market since the foundation of the European Communities in the 1950s?

- What are the different elements making up free movement of workers: right of entry/ travel to another Member State, right of residence, right of access to employment, right to seek work, rights to equal tax and social advantages once employed, the rights of family member of workers?

- What kinds of national measures are considered contrary to the free movement of workers?

- What are the derogations and exceptions to free movement of workers?

- What is the structure of free movement of workers, i.e. the sequence of issues that need to be addressed in answering any free movement of workers problem situations?

- How has the scope of free movement of workers been expanded through the case law of the European Court of Justice (ECJ)/Court of Justice of the EU (CJEU)?

- What is the scope of the equal rights to which workers are entitled? What equal rights are family members of workers entitled to? What equal rights are job seekers entitled to?

11.1 INTRODUCTION

Free movement of workers has been one of the central elements of the common market from the founding of the communities in the 1950s. This has remained the case, and the addition of citizenship of EU law by the Treaty of Maastricht in 1992 has provided some significant elements in this area of the law (as well as in in the law on free movement of services/establishment).

> KEY LEARNING POINT
>
> **WORKERS VERSUS SERVICES**
> It is useful here to distinguish clearly between workers and services/establishment: workers relates to employees, services/establishment to self-employed (we will look at free movement of services/establishment in the next chapter).

It might be wondered why citizenship is not considered here a more overarching idea that might be more obviously related to the topic of fundamental rights. The reason for this is that citizenship has not been a very dramatic development in EU law. It serves for the most part a rhetorical value, as a way of signifying a closer link between the nationals of the Member States and the EU as a political entity, although this feeling of belonging is probably still absent among ordinary Europeans. At a practical legal level, citizenship has been most significant in development of some aspects of free movement law and to date, fundamental rights protection in the EU has not drawn significantly on the concept of citizenship. Citizenship is examined in Chapter 8; it should be seen as an extension of free movement rights.

An important point to note here is that the structure of free movement of workers and free movement of services/establishment is very similar. In both cases, similar issues tend to arise. For example, common principles have been developed on the mutual recognition of educational qualifications.

> KEY LEARNING POINT
>
> **SOURCES OF LAW ON FREE MOVEMENT OF WORKERS**
> There are three sources of EU law on free movement of workers:
>
> – *Article 45 TFEU*: This is the primary treaty provision, it sets out the core elements or structure of free movement of workers.
> – *Directive 2004/38 and Regulation 492/2011*: These two pieces of legislation contain most the rules on free movement of workers. They have to some extent (especially Directive 2004/38) consolidated existing legislation and case law principles.
> – *Case law*: Much case law has been codified in the secondary legislation just mentioned, but the case law remains important in some respects, especially in the interpretation of Article 45 TFEU and Article 7 of Regulation 492/2011.

11.2 INTRODUCTION: THE HISTORY OF FREE MOVEMENT AND OF THE MAJOR LEGISLATION

A key element in the importance of free movement of workers has been the direct effect of free movement of worker provisions. This has meant that citizens in the Member States can involve free movement against contrary national rules or practices.

Under legislation, starting with the basic right in the treaty for workers to move freely, there was a gradual expansion to include family members of workers, students, retirees and all citizens, but the principle of economic self-sufficiency is central in all cases. Those benefiting from free movement cannot generally expect social assistance from the Member State they go to unless they are in employment or have been employed in the past for a substantial period (but the concept of citizenship has resulted in some limited exceptions to this, see Chapter 8).

1957[1]	The Treaty gives free movement rights to all workers; 'free movement' means the right to travel to, reside in and have equal treatment rights in, other Member States	(now) Article 45 TFEU
1964	Secondary legislation, a directive, sets out the situations in which Member States may legally deny free movement ('derogations')	Directive 64/221, now in Directive 2004/38

---

1   The idea for this chart came from a Lecture Workbook in EU Law developed by the teaching team at Leeds Metropolitan University led by Derek Martin, where I taught in 2006–2007.

1968	Secondary legislation, a directive, requires Member States to abolish administrative restrictions on free movement, and a Regulation sets out what equal treatment workers are entitled, and which includes rights for workers' families for the first time	Directive 68/360, now in Directive 2004/38 Regulation 1612/68 (now in Regulation 492/2011)
1970– 1993	Further residence rights are introduced: – right to reside after retiring from work in another Member State – right to reside given to non-economically-active persons **if** they have sufficient resources to support themselves – residence rights for students, **also if** they have sufficient resources	 Regulation 1251/70 Directive 90/364, Dir. 90/365 Directive 93/96 (now in Directive 2004/38)
1992	Citizenship of the EU introduced	Articles 17–18 TEU (now Article 9 TEU and Article 18–25 TFEU)
2004– 2006	Directive 2004/38 is adopted and implemented. It consolidates existing legislation and case law, while creating some new rights.	Directive 2004/38
2011	Regulation 1612/68 is updated and replaced. The amendments are minor.[2]	Regulation 492/2011

11.3 BASIC PRE-CONDITIONS FOR THE EXERCISE OF FREE MOVEMENT, INCLUDING DEFINITION OF A 'WORKER'

Some basic conditions must exist for free movement of workers rules to apply.

1. *EU nationals only can benefit:* only nationals of a Member State can benefit from the free movement rules. This is set out in Article 45(2) TFEU. So a third country national cannot benefit, unless they are or become a defined family member of a worker (see further below).

---

2   The main substantive differences are: art 4(2) is amended to update references to other secondary legislation; art 10 is amended to provide for equal access to educational provision for workers' resident children (it previously referred to a right of residence and access to housing and defined family member differently than the current provision in Directive 2004/38 art 2(2)); old arts 11 and 12 (also on family rights) are deleted.

2. *A linking factor with EU law must exist:* the free movement rules do not apply to activities which have no factor linking them with EU law and which are confined in all respects within a single Member State. This is sometimes called the purely internal rule. It creates a paradoxical situation that a Member State is free to restrict movement within their own territory but nationals restricted in this way have greater freedom to travel outside to another Member State.[3] Similarly, this can mean that a Member State is treating its own nationals less favourably than incoming migrant workers, sometimes called reverse discrimination. However, as discussed in Chapter 8, some more recent case law has seemed to dispense with any evident actual cross-border dimension when the 'substance of citizens' rights' are at stake.

KEY LEARNING POINT

REVERSE DISCRIMINATION AND THE REQUIREMENT OF A CROSS-BORDER ELEMENT

EU Member States are allowed to restrict movement within their territory of their own nationals, but they may not restrict the movement of other EU nationals. An example is *R v Saunders*, in which a UK national convicted of theft gave an undertaking not to return to England & Wales from Northern Ireland for three years.[4] Following a preliminary reference from Bristol Crown Court, the ECJ held that this situation was not covered by Community law. However, once there is a cross-border element, e.g. if its own national has worked in another Member State and returned home, (s)he has exercised the right of free movement and generally can rely on Article 45 TFEU as against his/her own Member State when (s)he returns. Notwithstanding this body of case law, it seems that the development of EU citizenship has had the effect of sidelining this requirement in the Court's case law (see further the final section of this chapter).

3. The claimant must come within a category entitled to free movement rights, although this has been extended over time to cover all EU citizens; nonetheless, the exact scope of the rights still depends on category (e.g. worker etc):
   – 'Workers' get the best 'deal' under EU law, along with their defined family members.
   – But other categories of individuals get rights as well, e.g. job seekers, students, retirees etc.
   – Recent ECJ case law (and the new Directive 2004/38) tends to emphasise rights being granted to some extent on the basis simply of being an EU citizen,

---

3 Case C–18/95 *Terhoeve v Inspecteur van de Belastingdienst* [2001] 1 CMLR 12 para 26. The issue in this case was whether a heavier social security contributions levied on a worker by his home Member State who transferred his/her residence from one Member State to another to take up work could be justified; the ECJ held they could not.
4 Case 175/78 *R v Saunders* [1979] 2 CMLR 216.

rather than depending on which category you fall into, but the categories remain significant.

- In particular, any citizen who is self-sufficient financially has the right to remain in another Member State but, in practice, only workers and retirees are financially self-sufficient.

A basic issue of definition that arises is the meaning of the term 'worker'. It is not defined in the TFEU and has been defined by the ECJ. The elements of the definition (which you can find repeated endlessly in the case law) are that a 'worker' is a person who:

> KEY LEARNING POINT
>
> **SUMMARISING THE DEFINITION OF A WORKER BY THE ECJ**
> A worker is defined autonomously by EU law, i.e. it is not for each Member State to define (*Hoekstra*):
>
> - 'performs services for and under the direction of another person', which excludes (*Bettray*) schemes of work that are for the purpose of medical rehabilitation
> - in return for which (s)he receives remuneration, but this does not have to be money or cash and can be payment in kind (e.g. food and accommodation) (*Steymann*)
> - part-time work is included, the activities must be 'economic' and 'real and genuine' and 'not on such a small scale as to be regarded as purely marginal and ancillary' (*Levin, Kempf*)
> - the work can be irregular (*Raulin*), and its duration does not matter (*Bernini, Ninni-Orasche*)
> - a trainee can be a worker if the elements above are present (*Lawrie-Blum*).
>
> It is the job of the national court to apply these principles to the facts of the individual case, which reflects the way the preliminary reference system works.

The following are the leading cases on the definition of a worker.

In *Hoekstra*,[5] the ECJ held that the establishment of as complete a freedom of movement as possible forms part of the foundations of the Community (now Union) and the definition of worker is a matter for Community/Union, not national, law. Another way of saying this is that the definition of a worker is autonomous of national laws, i.e. it does not depend on possibly varying definitions at national level.

In *Levin*,[6] the ECJ decided that part-time workers were included, even if this involves below-subsistence wages and supplementing income from other sources. The facts

---

5   Case 75/63 *Hoekstra v Bestuur der Bedrijfsvereniging* [1964] ECR 177.
6   Case 53/81 *Levin v Staatssecretaris van Justitie* [1982] ECR 1035.

concerned a British national in the Netherlands who was working part-time as a chamber maid; she supplemented her income from property she owned with her husband.

Kempf[7] confirmed and clarified the approach in *Levin*. It involved a German national living and working in the Netherlands as a music teacher and giving approximately 12 lessons a week and who was refused a residence permit. The ECJ held that it did not matter whether a person earning below the subsistence wage supplemented his or her income from public funds (i.e. social security) or private funds; that person could still be a worker.

Raulin[8] concerned infrequent and irregular work. Raulin was employed under a contract, which provided no guarantee as to the number of hours to be worked (on the facts, Raulin worked 60 hours over an eight-month period), with the result that she worked only a very limited number of days per week or hours per day and was not obliged to heed the employer's call for her to work. The ECJ held that, nonetheless, the person could still be a worker in so far as the activities pursued were 'effective and genuine activities to the exclusion of activities on such a small scale as to be regarded as marginal and ancillary'.[9] It was for the national court to decide on the facts whether this was so (the case was a preliminary reference, but clearly the ECJ did not rule out the possibility that on these facts a person could be a worker). Other case law has found that the duration of the work does not affect its character, i.e. a person can be a worker on just a short-term basis.[10]

Although the approach of the ECJ is to exclude work that is merely ancillary, it takes a broad view of how a person can be 'paid'. In *Steymann*, the facts concerned a person who worked in a religious community, and who was not paid as such but received benefits in kind.[11] The person, nonetheless, was found to be a worker. On the other hand, the fact payment in cash is given to a person for a certain activity does not necessarily mean the person is a worker.

In *Bettray*,[12] the facts concerned a rehabilitation scheme for drug addiction in which a person recovering from addiction was paid a certain amount in what was meant to be similar to a normal employment situation. The Court decided the person was not a worker. If the activity was merely for rehabilitation and reintegration, it did not

---

7 Case 139/85 *Kempf v Staatssecretaris van Justitie* [1987] 1 CMLR 764.
8 Case C–357/89 *Raulin v Minister van Onderwijs en Wetenschappen* [1994] 1 CMLR 227.
9 Ibid para 10.
10 Case C–3/90 *Bernini* [1992] ECR I–1071 para 16 and Case C–413/01 *Ninni-Orasche* [2003] ECR I–13187 para 25.
11 Case 196/87 *Steymann v Staatssecretaris van Justitie* [1989] 1 CMLR 449.
12 Case 344/87 *Bettray v Staatssecretaris van Justitie* [1991] 1 CMLR 459.

amount to work in the Court's view.[13] However, traineeships do amount to work in this context:

> The essential feature of an employment relationship, however, is that for a certain period of time a person performs services for and under the direction of another person in return for which he receives remuneration.[14]

In addition, employment among family members does not prevent a person being a worker.[15]

KEY LEARNING POINT

A JOB SEEKER IS A WORKER

Job seekers come within the definition of worker for the purpose of exercising the right to free movement, e.g. *Antonissen*.[16] However, job seekers only have limited rights to enter another Member State and look for work for a certain period of time which includes finding a residence or accommodation on the assumption that they have financial resources to support themselves. We will look further at what rights job seekers have compared to workers further below.

Deciding job seekers are workers for the purposes of free movement is very significant.

EXPLAINING THE LAW

A JOB SEEKER COMES WITHIN THE DEFINITION OF A WORKER

It has often been commented that the ECJ has played a central role in expanding the scope of the common market. A good example of this is its interpretation of the term 'worker'. The Treaty text did not define the term, so clearly the ECJ had a degree of choice, between narrow and broader interpretations. By deciding job seekers could be workers, the ECJ was substantially expanding the scope of the common market. If the ECJ had decided otherwise, the practical effect would be that a person would need to find a job in another Member State before being able to travel and reside in that Member State as worker. This would have restricted freedom of movement of workers and is unlikely to be what the Member States intended.

The difference between job seekers and workers helps to illustrate a key aspect of free movement: it involves a process or spectrum of rights or entitlements, rather than a single right or entitlement.

---

13 Ibid para 17.
14 Case 66/85 *Lawrie-Blum v Land Baden-Württemberg* [1987] 3 CMLR para 17.
15 Case C–337/97 *Meeusen* [1999] ECR I–3289 (spouse can employ the other spouse as a worker).
16 Case C–292/89 *R v Immigration Appeal Tribunal, ex parte Antonissen* [1991] 2 CMLR 373.

EXPLAINING THE LAW

FREE MOVEMENT OF WORKERS AS A SPECTRUM OR PROCESS OF ENTITLEMENTS

To give full effect to the idea that workers from one Member State of the EU can move to another Member State (the host state) and be treated in the same way for the purposes of employment as a worker of the host state involves several different stages of entitlement to equal treatment:

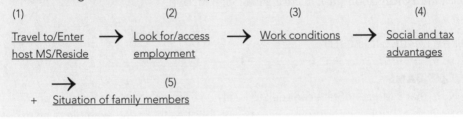

(1)   (2)   (3)   (4)

Travel to/Enter $\rightarrow$ Look for/access $\rightarrow$ Work conditions $\rightarrow$ Social and tax
host MS/Reside   employment   advantages

$\rightarrow$ (5)
+   Situation of family members

11.4 THE CONTENT OF FREE MOVEMENT RIGHTS: TRAVEL, RESIDENCE AND ACCESS TO EMPLOYMENT

RIGHTS	DEROGATIONS
1. Travel and residence rights, which contain the – A. right to leave home state, and B. right to enter the host state, and C. right to reside in the host state	1. Public policy[1] 2. Public security[2] 3. Public health[3]
2. Equal treatment rights: access to employment – A. no direct discrimination, and B. no indirect discrimination C. no non-discriminatory measures which might nevertheless have the effect of restricting the right of free movement	1–3. *All of the above, and -* 4. Public service posts[4] 5. Linguistic knowledge[5] 1–5. *All of the above, and -* 6. Measures justified by imperative requirements in the general interest[6]

[1] Treaty, Art 45(3) TFEU, Directive 2004/38, Article 27(1).

[2] Treaty, Art 45(3) TFEU, Directive 2004/38, Article 27(1).

[3] Treaty, Art 45(3) TEU, Directive 2004/58, Article 27(1).

[4] Treaty, Art 45(4) TFEU.

[5] Regulation 492/2011, Art 3(1).

[6] Case law.

The rights of free movement and residence are implicit in the treaty. The detailed application of these rights is spelled out in Directive 2004/38 (re-enacting Directive 68/360).

11.4.1 THE RIGHT TO LEAVE THE HOME MEMBER STATE

The home state can ask only for production of a valid identity card or passport when an EU citizen is leaving to go to another Member State. The right to leave is made explicit in secondary legislation (in Directive 2004/38, Article 4).[17]

> KEY LEARNING POINT
>
> **EXIT BANS**
> Note that a Member State can seek to justify an exit ban using derogations on grounds of public policy, public security or public health. For an example of an exit ban (on football hooligans), see, e.g. *Gough v Chief Constable of Derbyshire*.[18]

11.4.2 THE RIGHT TO ENTER THE HOST MEMBER STATE

The host state can ask only for production of a valid identity card or passport when an EU citizen exercises his or her right of entry under EU law. The right to enter the host state is in Directive 2004/38, Article 5.[19] No other document or formality can be demanded. In *Commission v Netherlands*, the issue in the case was whether the Dutch authorities could question entrants about the purpose and duration of their journey. The ECJ said no.

However, a Member State can seek to justify an entry ban using one of the applicable derogations/exceptions: public policy, public security, or public health. It is theoretically possible that the ECJ could apply its case law exception where a refusal of entry amounted to indirect discrimination or a non-discriminatory, but it has not generally done so. The public service and linguistic exceptions (in Regulation 492/2011) are not applicable.

11.4.3 THE RIGHT TO RESIDE IN THE HOST MEMBER STATE

There is no single, simple right of residence, a person can reside depending on the circumstances, *but economic self-sufficiency is still a central principle here.*

11.4.4 THE RIGHT OF RESIDENCE AND FORMALITIES

The host Member State may require an EU citizen to report his or her presence within a reasonable non-discriminatory period of time. Failure to comply with

---

17 Replacing Directive 68/360 art 2.
18 [2001] 4 All ER 289. See also Case 48/75 *Procureur du Roi v Royer* [1976] 2 CMLR 619.
19 Re-enacting Directive 68/360 art 3.

this requirement may make the person concerned liable to proportionate and non-discriminatory sanctions, as stated in Directive 2004/38, Article 5(5). Article 5(5) codifies pre-existing case law. In *Re Watson and Belmann*,[20] a British national in Italy failed to report her presence as a foreign national as required by Italian law. The ECJ held such a requirement is not incompatible with the treaty, but the penalties for its breach must be proportionate and must not negate the right of free movement itself. In this circumstance, deportation would be disproportionate, a fine or period of detention might not be.

> ### KEY LEARNING POINT
> ....
>
> ### REGISTRATION OF AN EU CITIZEN AFTER THREE MONTHS
> For periods of residence longer than three months, the host Member State may require the person concerned to register. This is provided for in Directive 2004/38, Article 8(1). This rule also must be administered in a non-discriminatory way. In *Commission v Belgium (Re Treatment of Migrant Workers)*,[21] Belgium issued to employed persons and seasonal workers, whose activity was not expected to last for more than three months, a document relating to their residence and which required payment of a charge for that document under (then) Article 48 EC Treaty (now Article 54 TFEU). This was found to be impermissible, as was a Belgian practice of issuing, during the first six months of residence, to workers from other Member States employment for at least one year two successive registration certificates, and charging for them, instead of issuing a residence permit.

11.4.5 THE RIGHT OF RESIDENCE AND RULES ON DURATION

The basic provisions on free movement are contained in the TFEU, while secondary legislation has elaborated on this as matters of detail. This secondary legislation has now been consolidated into Directive 2004/38.

11.4.5.1 THE THREE-MONTH RULE (DIRECTIVE 2004/38, ARTICLE 6)
All EU citizens have the right of residence in another Member State for three months. There are two preconditions:

1. The right is subject to holding a valid identity card or passport (Directive 2004/38, Article 6(1)).
2. The right lasts so long as the citizen does not become an unreasonable burden on the social assistance system of the host Member State (Directive 2004/38, Article 14(1)).

11.4.5.2 RIGHT OF RESIDENCE FOR MORE THAN THREE MONTHS (DIRECTIVE 2004/38, ARTICLE 7)
The right of residence beyond three months is given to the six categories of person below. The right of residence continues *so long as the person continues to have the relevant*

---

20 Case 118/75 *Criminal proceedings against Watson and Belmann* [1976] ECR 1185.
21 Case C–344/95 *Commission v Belgium (Re Treatment of Migrant Workers)* [1997] ECR I–1035.

status, and across all the categories, the principle of economic self-sufficiency applies (i.e. not being 'an unreasonable burden on the financial resources' of the host Member State) (Directive 2004/58, Article 14(2)). [22][23][24]

BEARER OF RIGHT OF RESIDENCE > 3 MONTHS	CONDITIONS APPLICABLE
(i) Workers/Employees (Directive 2004/58, Article 7(1)(a))	A worker keeps his Article 7 right of residence, i.e. 'worker' status when he is: – temporarily unable to work as a result of illness or accident (Article 7(3)(a)), or – involuntarily unemployed, so long as he has been employed for more than 1 year and registers as a job seeker (Article 7(3)(b) and (c)), or – undergoing 'vocational training', but generally on condition that <u>the training must be related to the previous employment</u> (Article 7(3)).[22] In *Lair v University of Hanover*, the ECJ interpreted 'vocational' narrowly, stating that it '. . . refers exclusively to institutions which provide only instruction either alternating with or closely linked to an occupational activity, particularly during apprenticeship' (para. 26).[23] However, a grant awarded for maintenance and training with a view to the pursuit of university studies leading to a professional qualification constitutes a social advantage within the meaning of Article 7 (2) of Regulation 1612/68 (now Regulation 492/2011), but it must have some link with the previous work.[24]
(ii) Self-employed persons (Directive 2004/38, Article 7(1)(a))	
(iii) Persons of independent means (Directive 2004/38, Article 7(1)(b))	Those who have: – sufficient resources for themselves and their family members not to become a burden on the social security system of the host Member State and – have comprehensive sickness insurance

22 Codifying previous case law interpreting art 7(3) of Regulation 1612/68.
23 Case 39/86 *Lair v Universitat Hannover* [1988] ECR 3161.
24 Case 235/87 *Matteucci v Communauté Français de Belgique* [1988] ECR 5589.

(iv) Students (Directive 2004/58, Article 7(1)(c), replacing Directive 93/96)	• A student has a right of residence so long as s/he satisfies the requirements of the directive
	• Thus, the student must
	  – be enrolled on a course of study at an establishment accredited or financed by the host Member State, and
	  – have sufficient resources for themselves and their family members not to become a burden on the social security system of the host Member State, and
	  – have comprehensive sickness insurance
	
	Family members of students
	The student's family have the same residence rights as the student, but 'family' in this context includes only spouse, registered partner and dependent children

(v) Job-seekers – see below	
(vi) Family members (Directive 2004/58, Articles 7(1)(d), 14(4))	Family members of any person falling into any of the above 5 categories; 'family member' is defined in Directive 2004/58, Article 2

11.4.5.3 THE FIVE-YEAR RULE (DIRECTIVE 2004/38, ARTICLE 16)

Any EU citizen who has resided legally in a host state for five years has the right of permanent residence there (Directive 2004/38, Article 16(1) – a new provision). Once the right of permanent residence has been acquired it is lost only:

– by absence for more than two consecutive years (Directive 2004/38, Article 16(4)) or
– by justified deportation, *but* the Member State's right to deport is restricted after five years, and further restricted after 10 years of residence.

11.4.5.4 OTHER PERMANENT RIGHTS OF RESIDENCE

In addition, there are permanent residence rights for the following, even if they do not satisfy the five-year rule:

For retired workers, a worker has the right to remain permanently in the Member State where he or she was employed, providing that (s)he is:

– retiring after certain minimum periods of employment and residence, or
– is an ill-health retiree (Directive 2004/58, Article 17(1))
– otherwise, i.e. retirees moving from home Member State to another Member State have the same rights as other citizens.

With regard to family members of a deceased worker, if a worker who has been in the host Member State for two years dies while still working, but before acquiring permanent residence rights, any family members residing with him acquire permanent residence rights (Directive 2004/58, Article 17(4)).

11.4.6 TRAVEL AND RESIDENCE RIGHTS OF JOB SEEKERS

The wording of Article 45 TFEU appeared to extend only to workers or those who already have offers of employment. However, as noted above, the ECJ took a broad interpretation of 'worker' and decided that it extended to job seekers. The Court then had to decide what residence rights should attach to this new status and said that the job seeker must be given a 'reasonable time' (probably six months) to find work; but even then deportation cannot be made automatic. The period must be extended if the individual shows that he or she still has a 'genuine chance' of getting a job.

KEY CASE *THE* ANTONISSEN *CASE ON JOB SEEKERS*

Antonissen is the leading case on job seekers.[25] It concerned a Belgian national looking for work in the UK, having arrived in October 1986, who was imprisoned for a drugs-related offence in March 1987. The UK authorities wanted to deport him on his release from prison in December 1987 (preliminary reference from the Queen's Bench Division to the ECJ). Characteristically, the ECJ emphasised the broad treaty purpose of ensuring free movement – this would be defeated if job seekers did not come within the definition of worker – but could deport after six months, unless the job seeker can show evidence that he or she is continuing to seek employment and that (s)he has a genuine chance of being engaged.

Directive 2004/38, Article 14(4) now states:

. . . an expulsion measure may in no case be adopted against . . .

(b) [a] Union citizen [. . . who] entered the territory of the host Member State in order to seek employment. In this case, the Union citizen . . . may not be expelled for as long as [he] can provide evidence that [he is] continuing to seek employment and that [he has] a genuine chance of being engaged.

KEY LEARNING POINT

JOB SEEKERS AND EQUAL TREATMENT
Note that job seekers do not enjoy the more general right to equal treatment guaranteed to workers under Regulation 492/2011 (the latter will be dealt with in

---

25 Case C–292/89 *R v Immigration Appeal Tribunal, ex parte Antonissen* [1991] 2 CMLR 373.

more detail below regarding actual workers).[26] In *Lebon*, the ECJ ruled that a job seeker fell outside Regulation 1612/68 (now Regulation 492/2011), Article 7(2).[27] However, the ECJ has modified this approach to some limited extent in light of the legal status given to EU citizenship since the Treaty of Maastricht. Case law on the treaty concept of citizenship is discussed in the final section of Chapter 8.

11.4.7 TRAVEL AND RESIDENCE RIGHTS – FAMILY MEMBERS

If an EU citizen is in one of the categories of persons entitled to travel and residence rights (see above), the citizen's 'family members' are given equal rights (Directive 2004/38, Article 3(1)).[28] To be a 'family member' it is necessary to fall within one of the four categories in the new Directive 2004/38, Article 2(2), i.e. spouse, registered partner, (grand)child or certain dependent relatives.

FAMILY MEMBER	DEFINITION
Spouse (Directive 2004/38, Article 2(2))	A separated spouse is still a spouse for this purpose. *Diatta v Land Berlin*[29] dealt with the now amended Article 10(1) of Regulation 1612/68 and held that separated but not-yet-divorced couples were still spouses for the purposes of Regulation 1612/68 (now Regulation 492/2011).
Unmarried partner (Directive 2004/38, Article 2(2)(b))	'. . . the partner with whom the Union citizen has contracted a registered partnership [. . .] if the legislation of the host Member State treats registered partnerships as equivalent to marriage and in accordance with the conditions laid down in [any such] legislation . . .' This puts some cohabitees in the same legal position as a spouse, but it depends on the host Member States having a 'registered partnership' law (not all have such a law). Article 2(2)(b) reflects *Netherlands v Reed*,[30] where the ECJ held that the now-amended Article 10(1) of Regulation 1612/68 did not require the Member States to treat unmarried partners as spouses, but that if the latter

---

26 OJ L 141 27.05.2011 p. 1.

27 Case 316/85 *Lebon* [1987] ECR 2811 para 26.

28 Replacing Regulation 1612/68 art 10(1).

29 Case 267/83 *Diatta v Land Berlin* [1986] 2 CMLR 164.

30 Case 59/85 *Netherlands v Reed* [1987] 2 CMLR 448.

	were recognised as spouses where the partners involved were both nationals, nationals from other Member States must be able to similarly benefit
Descendants (Directive 2004/38, Article 2(2)(c))	A direct descendant of the Union citizen, or of the citizen's spouse or partner, if aged under 21, or aged over 21, but still dependent.
Dependants (Directive 2004/38, Article 2(2)(d))	A dependent parent or grandparent of the Union citizen, or of the citizen's spouse or partner.

KEY LEARNING POINT

THIRD COUNTRY FAMILY MEMBERS

The general rule is that only nationals of a Member State can benefit from the free movement rules (Directive 2004/38, Article 39(2)). By way of exception, a third country national who is a family member of a person entitled to free movement rights is entitled to travel and residence rights (Directive 2004/38, Articles 4(1), 5(1), 6(2), 7(2), 16(2)).

As with most of Directive 2004/38, the above provisions largely reflect pre-existing ECJ case law. In *R v IAT and Surinder Singh, ex parte Secretary of State for the Home Department*,[31] the ECJ held that if a non-EU national married to a UK national who accompanies that UK spouse working in another Member State, then the non-EU national spouse has the same rights of re-entry as the spouse.

In *Secretary of State for the Home Department v Akrich*,[32] the ECJ held that if a non-EU national marries a UK national having unlawfully entered the UK, then that non-EU national cannot accompany the EU national spouse who goes to work in another Member State and then claim re-entry rights, i.e. the non-national must have been lawfully resident in one Member State before (s)he can benefit from EU law as a spouse of an EU national. Further, the ECJ held that EU law as to rights of non-national spouses of an EU citizen should be disapplied where the marriage is one of convenience and is not genuine.

However, in one of the few instances of the ECJ explicitly reversing itself, it overruled *Akrich* in *Metock v Minister for Justice, Equality and Law Reform*[33] on the ground of maintaining family life, although Member States could still deport if the marriage involved was a sham one.

---

31 Case C–370/90 *R v IAT and Surinder Singh, ex parte Secretary of State for the Home Department* [1992] 3 CMLR 358.
32 Case C–109/0 *Secretary of State for the Home Department v Akrich* [2003] ECR 19607.
33 Case C–127/08 *Metock v Minister for Justice, Equality and Law Reform* [2008] ECR I–6241.

11.5 EQUAL TREATMENT RIGHTS: THE SUBSTANTIVE RIGHTS OF WORKERS TO BE TREATED EQUALLY ONCE RESIDING IN ANOTHER MEMBER STATE

11.5.1 OVERVIEW

Once an EU citizen has acquired a right of residence in another Member State (s)he is entitled to equal treatment rights. There are two sources of equal treatment rights: (1) Regulation 492/2011 specifically on workers; and (2) general treaty/EU law applicable to all citizens of the EU. The rights are not unlimited, as mentioned previously; for example, citizens must in general be economically self-sufficient and so are not entitled to become an unreasonable burden on the social assistance/security system of another Member State.

KEY LEARNING POINTS

THE TREATY AND THE PRINCIPLE OF NON-DISCRIMINATION
Article 34(2) TFEU provides for 'the abolition of any discrimination based on nationality between workers of the Member States as regards employment, remuneration and other conditions of work and employment'.

Non-discrimination on grounds of nationality is the foundation of the common market idea of free movement of workers and Article 18 TFEU sets it out as a general principle applicable across the treaty: 'Within the scope of application of [the] Treaty, and without prejudice to any special provisions contained therein, any discrimination on grounds of nationality shall be prohibited'.

The general principle is also set out in Directive 2004/38, Article 24(1):

Subject to such specific provisions . . . expressly provided for in the Treaty and secondary law, all Union citizens residing on the basis of this Directive in the territory of the host Member State shall enjoy equal treatment with the nationals of that Member State within the scope of the Treaty.

KEY LEARNING POINT

LIMITATIONS ON THE PRINCIPLE OF NON-DISCRIMINATION
Two key limitations apply to the principle of non-discrimination/equal treatment:

1. Rights are given only 'within the scope of . . . the Treaty' – so it is not a blanket guarantee of equality across all areas of life, but only in those areas where the EU is competent (i.e. the common/internal market primarily).
2. Even if a matter *is* within the scope of the treaty, it may be subject to one of the exceptions or derogations, which we will look at further below.

The relationship between the general treaty principles and secondary legislation: as mentioned above, secondary legislation is *lex specialis*, in that it is more specific and so is looked to first in those matters which it governs (the treaty is looked to in default of a more specific rule in secondary legislation).

> KEY LEARNING POINT
>
> ### WHAT THE TREATY PROHIBITS: TYPES OF DISCRIMINATION AND NON-DISCRIMINATORY OBSTACLES
>
> The ECJ has recognised three types of national rules or practices that are contrary to free movement:
>
> 1. *Direct discrimination*, which involves express differentiation on grounds of nationality, e.g. a job is advertised stating that only UK nationals are eligible to apply;
> 2. *Indirect discrimination*, which does not involve express differentiation on grounds of nationality, but that does have a disproportionately negative impact on workers from other Member States (e.g. a job is advertised in the UK that requires applicants to have lived in the UK for three years, a requirement that is likely to be easier to satisfy for UK nationals);
> 3. *Non-discriminatory obstacles*, which do not involve discrimination either direct or indirect, but that make the free movement of workers between Member States harder to exercise, e.g. an employment contract that requires an employee to pay a fee to the employer before terminating employment to move to another job.

11.5.2 DIRECT DISCRIMINATION

Obvious examples of direct discrimination in the field of employment would be a prohibition on nationals from other or certain Member States applying or any quota system that limited the number of nationals from other Member States. Since direct discrimination is very obviously contrary to the treaties, it does not happen very often in practice.

An example is *Commission v France*,[34] which involved a French law stating that a certain proportion of the crews of French-registered ships had to be of French nationality and also certain posts had to be occupied by French nationals. Amongst the defences the French argued before the ECJ was that it did not apply it in practice, but the ECJ unsurprisingly held it incompatible with treaty.

---

34 Case 167/73 *Commission v France* [1974] 2 CMLR 216.

> **KEY LEARNING POINT**
> ....
>
> ## DEROGATING FROM DIRECT DISCRIMINATION
> Direct discrimination can be justified only by one of the derogations expressly
> provided for in the treaty (i.e. Article 45(3) on public policy, public health and
> public security grounds; or Article 45(4) on public service posts).

11.5.3 INDIRECT DISCRIMINATION

If a measure does not on the face of it make any distinction between a Member State's
own nationals and those of other Member States, but it is in practice more likely
to disadvantage the latter group, then it is indirectly discriminatory. A more typical
example of indirect discrimination is a residency requirement, e.g. a requirement to have
resided in a country/Member State for three years before applying for a job is obviously
easier for nationals than citizens of other Member States to satisfy, although on the
surface or explicitly it is not discriminatory.

An example is *Württembergische Milchverwertung-Südmilch-AG v Ugliola*,[35] which
concerned a rule of law that protected workers from the unfavourable consequences of
taking time off work to perform military service. The ECJ held it had to apply also to
nationals of other Member States who took time off work to perform military service in
their country of origin.

A further example is *Köbler v Austria* (a case of central importance in EU law on state
liability; see Chapter 6).[36] Köbler was a professor at a university in Austria and applied
for the special length-of-service increment for university professors. He claimed that,
although he had not completed 15 years' service as a professor at Austrian universities,
he had completed the requisite length of service if the duration of his service in
universities of other Member States of the EU were taken into consideration and that
the condition of completion of 15 years' service solely in Austrian universities, with no
account being taken of periods of service in universities in other Member States, was
indirect discrimination.

The ECJ held that special length-of-service increment did not solely have the effect
of rewarding the employee's loyalty to his employer (as Austria argued), but that it
also led to a partitioning of the market for the employment of university professors in
Austria and went against the very principle of freedom of movement for workers. The
case illustrates how it is the effect of a measure and not its purpose that determines the
assessment of the ECJ (this principle is also apparent in case law on free movement of
goods).[37]

....

35 Case 15/69 *Württembergische Milchverwertung-Südmilch-AG v Ugliola* [1969] CMLR 94.
36 Case C–224/01 *Köbler v Austria* [2003] ECR I–10239.
37 See generally paras 70–88 of the judgment in particular.

11.5.4 NON-DISCRIMINATORY MEASURES/OBSTACLES TO FREE MOVEMENT

Non-discriminatory obstacles are measures which apparently apply to nationals of the host state and to nationals of other Member States in the same way, but nevertheless restrict or create obstacles in the way of free movement. Remember that, in the *Dassonville* line of cases on free movement of goods (see Chapter 10), the ECJ started to declare such obstacles contrary to the treaties. In the following cases, Member State nationals successfully argued that they had been denied some benefit as a result of exercising a right of free movement:

Terhoeve v Inspecteur van de Belastingdienst concerned higher social security contributions for workers who resided in another Member State.[38] A Dutch rule required a worker to pay greater social security contributions compared to a worker who continued to reside in the Netherlands throughout the year, without any additional social benefits. The ECJ held it was prohibited by (now) Article 45 TFEU, even though there was no discriminatory effect as regards nationality.

ANALYSING THE LAW

BORDERLINE CASES

The rule in *Terhoeve* might be considered a borderline case between indirect discrimination and a non-discriminatory obstacle, since it might be argued that Dutch nationals were more likely to live continuously in the Netherlands. But the categorisation does not matter very much in practice, since the approach of the ECJ is to treat both kinds of national rules as prohibited.

Van Lent concerned criminal liability for using a vehicle registered in a Member State of employment different to a national's home Member State.[39] The ECJ held (now) Article 45 TFEU prohibited this national rule. The vehicle belonged to a leasing company established in the second Member State, and made available to the worker by his employer, who was also established in the second Member State.

D'Hoop v Office National d'Emploi involved Belgian legislation providing for the grant of unemployment benefits, known as tideover allowances, to young people who had just completed their studies and were seeking their first employment.[40] The ECJ held a Member State may not refuse to grant the tideover allowance to one of its nationals, a student seeking her first employment, on the sole ground that that student completed

---

38 Case C–18/95 *Terhoeve v Inspecteur van de Belastingdienst* [1999] ECR I–345.
39 Case C–232/01 *Van Lent* [2004] 3 CMLR 23.
40 Case C–224/98 *D'Hoop v Office National d'Emploi* [2002] 3 CMLR 12.

her secondary education in another Member State. The ECJ seemed to base this on citizenship provisions and not on Article 45 alone.

11.5.5 THE CONTENT OF EQUAL TREATMENT RIGHTS

As well as possessing the basic rights to leave their home Member States and entering another Member State to obtain employment in host/other Member States, workers (and their families) are entitled to equal treatment to the nationals of the Member States where they have moved to, i.e. to equal treatment more generally. Regulation 492/62011 spells out in detail the equal treatment rights for workers.

KEY LEARNING POINT

WORKERS' FAMILIES
Under Article 7(2) of Regulation 492/2011, members of the worker's family are entitled to the same rights as the worker. Remember that to be a 'family member', it is necessary to fall within one of the four categories as defined in Directive 2004/38, Article 3(1) (replacing Regulation 1612/68, Article 10(1)).

For example, a non–dependent child of over 21 is not within the definition and is thus not entitled to 'social advantages', as illustrated in *Centre Public d'Aide Sociale de Courcelles v Lebon*.[41] Here, the ECJ ruled that once a child of a worker reaches the age of 21, and is no longer dependent on the worker, benefits to the child cannot be construed as a benefit to the worker. This relates to the central provision of Article 7(2) of Regulation 492/2011 giving 'equal social and tax advantages' to workers, discussed further below.

KEY LEARNING POINT

WORKERS' RIGHTS UNDER REGULATION 492/2011
Note particularly the following, the main rights under Regulation 1612/68, now Regulation 492/2011:

a. equal treatment in employment-related matters
b. 'equal social and tax advantages' under Article 7(2) of Regulation 492/2011
c. housing
d. vocational training
e. maintenance grants/loans.

We will now look at each of these in more detail.

---

41 Case 316/85 *Centre Public d'Aide Sociale de Courcelles v Lebon* [1989] CMLR 337.

11.5.5.1 EQUAL TREATMENT IN EMPLOYMENT-RELATED MATTERS

PROVISION	EQUAL TREATMENT RIGHT IN EMPLOYMENT
Article 3 of Regulation 492/2011	Prohibits measures that directly or indirectly 'keep nationals of other Member States away from employment offered', e.g. measures that impose special recruitment procedures, or limit advertising of posts, impose special conditions, etc.
Article 4 of Regulation 492/2011	Prohibits measures limiting, by number or percentage, the employment of foreign workers, e.g. Case 167/73,*Commission v France* [1974] 2 CMLR 216
Article 6 of Regulation 492/2011	Vocational tests can be used, but not if they could have a discriminatory effect
Article 7(1) of Regulation 492/2011	The foreign worker must not be subjected to conditions of employment or work, in particular remuneration, dismissal or reinstatement, different from those applied to host state workers
Article 8 of Regulation 492/2011	Equal treatment in trade union rights

EXPLAINING THE LAW

MUTUAL RECOGNITION OF EDUCATIONAL QUALIFICATIONS OF WORKERS

Initially, legislation on the mutual recognition of educational qualifications of workers was only adopted regarding free movement of services and of establishment. The treaty only referred to the issue as regards services and establishment by providing a basis for secondary legislation (now Article 43 TFEU). This is because the issue more obviously arises in the services context: it is necessary to protect consumers and the public generally by regulating the way in which EU citizens exercising free movement can hold themselves out as having professional competence or expertise.

The issue first arose regarding freedom of movement of workers in *Heylens*.[42] This concerned a Belgian soccer player who played for a club in France but only had a

---

42 Case 222/86 *Heylens* [1987] ECR 4097.

licence or certificate to play in Belgium. The EC held that, although the Member States were entitled to adopt their own standards of recognition of professional qualifications since there were no Community standards, they had 'to reconcile the requirement as to the qualifications necessary in order to pursue a particular occupation with the requirements of the free movement of workers'.[43]

The ECJ later emphasised the unity of the principles applicable to mutual recognition in the areas of free movement of workers and of services[44] and also noted that national rules could constitute non-discriminatory obstacles.[45] Member States are essentially required to compare diplomas and qualifications in a way that fairly takes into account equivalence to qualifications in the Member State's own education system: 'assessment of the equivalence of the foreign diploma must be effected exclusively in the light of the level of knowledge and qualifications which its holder can be assumed to possess in the light of that diploma, having regard to the nature and duration of the studies and practical training to which the diploma relates'.[46]

Directive 2005/36/EC on the recognition of professional qualifications[47] consolidates previous secondary legislation and applies the same principles to both free movement of workers and free movement of services/establishment (the umbrella term 'free movement of professionals' for workers and service providers in this category tends now to be used). We will look at this in more detail in Chapter 12 on free movement of services and freedom of establishment.

11.5.5.2 'SOCIAL ADVANTAGES': THE CENTRAL PROVISION OF REGULATION 492/2011 IS ARTICLE 7(2) ON 'EQUAL SOCIAL AND TAX ADVANTAGES'

Migrant workers must enjoy the same 'social and tax advantages' as national workers: Article 7(2) of Regulation 492/2011. The ECJ initially defined 'social advantages' rather narrowly, confining it to benefits connected with employment. In *Michel S.*, the Court held that 'social advantages' concern only benefits connected with employment.[48] Thus, the disabled son of an Italian employee in Belgium who died could not obtain specific benefits available to similarly situated children of Belgian nationals to recover

---

43 Ibid paras 12–13.

44 Case 340/89 *Vlassopoulou* [1991] ECR I–2357 para 15; Case C–345/08 *Pesla* [2009] ECR I–11677 para 36.

45 Case C–340/89 *Vlassopoulou* ibid para 15; Case C–345/08 *Pesla* ibid para 36.

46 C–345/08 *Pesla* ibid para 39.

47 OJ L 255 30.9.2005 p. 22.

48 Case 76/72 *Michel S.* [1973] ECR 457.

their ability to work. However, the ECJ soon reversed this in favour of a broad interpretation:

> . . . the advantages which [the] regulation extends to workers who are nationals of other Member States are all those which, whether or not linked to a contract of employment, are generally granted to national workers primarily because of their objective status as workers or by virtue of the mere fact of their residence on the national territory and the extension of which to workers who are nationals of other Member States therefore seems suitable to facilitate their mobility within the community.[49]

This definition in *Reina* is repeated in many other cases. The facts involved an interest-free 'child-birth loan' given under German law to stimulate the birth rate of the population. The ECJ held that this was a social advantage under Article 7(2). The fact that the motivation behind the loan related to demographic policy or that it involved an assistance to German nationals, rather than an obstacle to the free movement of nationals of other Member States, did not rule out application of then EEC law or exclude it from Article 7(2) of Regulation 1612/68 (now Article 7(2) of Regulation 492/2011).

KEY LEARNING POINT

....

ARTICLE 7(2) APPLIES TO SOCIAL AND TAX ADVANTAGES EVEN IF NOT CONNECTED TO EMPLOYMENT

In *Cristini*,[50] an Italian widow of an Italian worker in France was refused a reduction card for rail fares for large families because of her nationality. The ECJ said that the term 'social and tax advantages' in Article 7(2) of Regulation 1612/68 was to be interpreted broadly so as to include all social and tax advantages *whether or not connected with employment.*

The approach in *Cristini* is reflected in cases such as *Inzirillo* and *Commission v Greece*. In *Inzirillo*, the ECJ ruled that an allowance for a dependent adult offspring could be considered an advantage to the worker who was the parent.[51] In *Commission v Greece*, a Greek law precluded by regulation or administrative practice employed or self-employed workers from other Member States and the members of their families from being attributed large-family status for the purpose of the award of special benefits for such families and from being awarded family allowances.[52] The ECJ found it to be contrary to (now) Article 45 TFEU.

....

49 Case 65/81 *Reina v Landeskreditbank* [1982] 1 CMLR 744 at para. 12.
50 Case 32/75 *Cristini v SNCF* [1976] 1 CMLR 573.
51 Case 63/76 *Inzirillo* [1976] ECR 2057.
52 Case C–185/96 *Commission v Greece* [1998] ECR I–6601.

> ## KEY LEARNING POINT
>
> ### EXCEPTIONS TO THE APPROACH IN *CRISTINI*
> There are some exceptional cases where a benefit is simply said by the Court
> not to be a social advantage. This occurs when a benefit has some peculiar
> association with the nationality of a Member State.

Ministère Public v Even is such an exceptional case.[53] It concerned early retirement
pensions in Belgium. Even was a French worker in Belgium, who received this pension
from the Belgian national pension office. A percentage reduction in the size of the
pension per year of early payment was made for all workers except Belgian nationals,
who were entitled to a pension for service in an allied army during the Second World
War. Even was entitled to this pension in France, but he received the reduced pension
in Belgium, and he claimed this was contrary to equality of treatment for workers from
other Member States.

The ECJ held that the aim of the benefit was to help those who rendered services in
wartime and thus '. . . [it] cannot therefore be considered as an advantage granted to a
national worker by reason primarily of his status of worker or resident on the national
territory' and was not a social advantage under Article 7(2) of Regulation 1612/68.

> ### ANALYSING THE LAW
>
> #### THE RIGHTS OF WORKERS' FAMILY MEMBERS
> The ECJ has used a broad interpretation of Article 7(2) of Regulation 1612/68 (now
> 492/2011) to conclude that rights granted to family members can be considered
> a benefit for the worker, and thus come under the scope of Regulation 1612/68;
> see, e.g. *Inzirillo* (above). However, the ECJ has not definitively stated that family
> members have *all* the same social and tax advantages as workers, so the exact
> scope of the rights of the family members to social and tax advantages is not fully
> clear. However, the development of the concept of citizenship has been used as
> a basis for additional rights to be given to EU citizens who are not workers, as we
> will discuss in the final section of this chapter.

11.5.5.3 HOUSING
Under Article 9 of Regulation 492/2011, there must be equal access to housing and
housing benefits for migrant workers, although this could be considered to be covered
already by the concept of 'social advantage' in Article 7(2) of the Regulation.

11.5.5.4 EQUAL TREATMENT AND VOCATIONAL TRAINING
Article 7(3) of Regulation 492/2011 states that workers shall, 'under the same conditions
as national workers have access to training in vocational schools and retraining centres'.

---

53 Case 207/78 *Ministère Public v Even* [1980] 2 CMLR 71.

Under Article 12 of Regulation 492/2011, children of migrant workers must be admitted to a Member State's 'general educational, apprenticeship and vocational training courses under the same conditions as the nationals of that state'.

The ECJ judgment in *Gravier* defined vocational training as:

> . . . any form of education which prepares for a qualification for a particular profession, trade or employment or which provides the necessary training and skills for such a profession, trade or employment is vocational training, whatever the age and the level of training of the pupils or students, and even if the training programme includes an element of general education.[54]

Gravier had no family members in Belgium and no right of residence there, apart from her claim as a student, i.e. she was not a worker (although she would now have a three-month right of residence as a citizen of the EU, under Directive 2004/38). She was charged an enrolment fee for a course in strip-cartoon art. The ECJ held imposition of the enrolment fee on non-national students as a condition of access to such training was contrary to the treaty. The ECJ did this by linking free movement law with the development of a common vocational policy by the Member States. Free movement and vocational policy combined to bring the situation within the scope of then Community law.

A 'general studies' part of a vocational course at university can itself be 'vocational', as in *Blaizot v University of Liège*.[55] The facts concerned conditions governing access to a preliminary diploma and a degree in veterinary medicine. The ECJ found that a supplementary enrolment fee for nationals of other Member States was contrary to the treaty.

Belgium v Humbel also helps to illustrate what sort of education is not 'vocational'. In *Humbel*, the ECJ held that a year of study that is part of a programme forming an indivisible body of instruction preparing for a qualification for a particular profession, trade or employment or providing the necessary training and skills for such a profession, trade or employment is vocational training for the purposes of the treaty.

However, it also held that the wording of Article 12 of Regulation 1612/68 places obligations only on those Member States in which the migrant worker resides. It did not prevent a Member State from imposing an enrolment fee as a condition for admission to ordinary schooling within its territory, on children of migrant workers *residing in another* Member State, even when the nationals of the other Member State in question are not required to pay such a fee.

---

54 Case 293/83 *Gravier v City of Liège* [1985] ECR 593 para 30.
55 Case 24/86 *Blaizot v University of Liège* [1989] 1 CMLR 57.

KEY LEARNING POINT

ARTICLE 7(3) OF REGULATION 492/2011 PROVIDES FOR EQUAL TREATMENT IN ACCESS TO VOCATIONAL TRAINING

Conditions [of] . . . access to vocational training are governed by Articles 7(3) and 12 of Regulation 492/2011. 'Access' includes all rules about eligibility, selection, as well as enrolment/registration fees (as illustrated in *Gravier* and *Blaizot*). Workers and workers' children are entitled to this equal access.

In addition, the ECJ takes the approach that vocational training is a general treaty right (under now Article 166 TFEU, which states, inter alia, that the Union shall implement a vocational training policy, which shall support and supplement the action of the Member States, while fully respecting the responsibility of the Member States for the content and organisation of vocational training available to all EU citizens who are legally resident in a host state). This is apparent, for example, in *Gravier* where the Court linked vocational training to free movement and described the common policy on vocational training as indispensable to the activities of the Community/Union.[56]

11.5.5.5 MAINTENANCE GRANT/LOANS

Articles 7(3) and 12 of Regulation 492/2011 apply to such things as enrolment and tuition fees (see *Gravier* and *Blaizot*). In respect of workers, maintenance grants are also covered by Article 7(2), i.e. such a grant is a 'social advantage' and thus the migrant worker has the same rights as nationals of the host Member State. *Lair v University of Hanover* is an example of a worker receiving a maintenance grant by virtue of Article 7(2) of Regulation 1612/68.[57] It concerned the interpretation of Article 7(3) of the Regulation.

The ECJ interpreted this narrowly, focusing on the term 'vocational' – '. . . refers exclusively to institutions which provide only instruction either alternating with or closely linked to an occupational activity, particularly during apprenticeship'.[58] However, the ECJ also held here that a grant awarded for maintenance and training with a view to the pursuit of university studies leading to a professional qualification is a social advantage within the meaning of Article 7(2) of Regulation 492/2011. In *Lair*, it is clear that there must be a link between the previous occupational activity and the studies in order to claim the status of 'worker'.

---

56 Case 293/83 *Gravier* (n 54) paras 23–24.
57 Case 39/86 *Lair v University of Hanover* [1989] 3 CMLR 545.
58 Ibid para 26.

11.6 EXCEPTIONS/DEROGATIONS TO FREE MOVEMENT OF WORKERS

11.6.1 OVERVIEW

There are 'three standard exceptions' within the free movement principles, which also apply to free movement of workers: public health, public policy and public security. These are contained in Article 45(3) TFEU, i.e. they are treaty-based, whilst the criteria for their application have been set out in Directive 2004/38, Articles 27–33 (having been mostly established before this in the case law of the ECJ). The derogations and exceptions to the free movement of workers (and similarly regarding the other free movement categories) are in practice very important: they indicate the scope of EU law by describing how Member States can validly depart from EC law principles in this context.

Regarding *workers*, there are six types of exception/derogation, four of which are in the TFEU itself, one of which is in secondary legislation, and one of which is a broad category established by the case law of the ECJ. In addition to the three standard exceptions just noted, the public service exception applies to free movement of workers (this means national governments do not have to apply free movement or equal treatment in recruiting for important civil service positions). One exception is set out in secondary legislation: the linguistic knowledge exception (this allows employers to require knowledge of a Member State's language, a requirement that would otherwise be an example of prohibited indirect discrimination.

The final category of derogation of exception is 'objective justification'. This is an open-ended category. It relates to some national policy that is in some way consistent with treaty objectives (also referred to as 'general or overriding requirements of the public interest') and that the ECJ thus considers can justify what would otherwise be a breach of free movement by a Member State.

> KEY LEARNING POINT
> ....
>
> **WHAT THE DIFFERENT DEROGATIONS CAN JUSTIFY**
> Only the four treaty-based exceptions (i.e. public policy, public security, public health and public service) can justify *direct discrimination* – all six categories can justify *indirect discrimination or non-discriminatory obstacles*. Note that a language requirement is, by definition, indirect discrimination.

The derogations of (a) public health, (b) public policy and (c) public security are generally taken together. Directive 1964/221 made rules designed to make Member States provide proof that they had an adequate reason in relation to the first three categories;[59] the ECJ was active in interpreting the directive strictly against Member

---

59 OJ 56 4.4.1964 p. 850.

States. Directive 2004/38 has now adopted and consolidated this case law and extended it somewhat (Articles 27–33).

11.6.2 RULES PARTICULAR TO THE PUBLIC HEALTH DEROGATION

This is a comparatively rare ground; it applies only to diseases with epidemic potential, which is now codified in Article 29 of Directive 2004/38. In order to rely on this exception, Member States must be able to provide credible scientific evidence. In other words, they may not simply assert that they believe a restriction on free movement is justified on health grounds. However, where scientific evidence is uncertain, the Member States are allowed to restrict free movement on a precautionary basis in order to protect the public from a public health risk.[60]

11.6.3 RULES PARTICULAR TO PUBLIC POLICY AND PUBLIC SECURITY

Note that the following particular situations apply to public policy and public security:

11.6.3.1 THE FIVE-YEAR RULE
If the person in question has acquired the right of permanent residence the Member States can only deport on 'serious grounds of public policy or public security' (Article 28(2), Directive 2004/38).

11.6.3.2 THE 10-YEAR RULE
Once a person has resided in the host state for 10 years, deportation can only be on 'imperative grounds of public security' (Article 28(3)(a), Directive 2004/38).

11.6.4 GENERAL RULES ON PUBLIC HEALTH, PUBLIC POLICY AND PUBLIC SECURITY

11.6.4.1 NO ECONOMIC MOTIVE
A Member State must not invoke a derogation 'to serve economic ends' (Article 27(1)).

11.6.4.2 PROPORTIONALITY
Measures taken by a Member State must comply with the principle of proportionality (Directive 2004/38, Article 27(2)).

11.6.4.3 PERSONAL CONDUCT
Measures must be based 'exclusively on the personal conduct of the individual concerned' (Directive 2004/38, Article 27(2), 1st paragraph).

11.6.4.4 WHEN IS A MEMBER STATE JUSTIFIED IN INVOKING 'PUBLIC POLICY'?
A Member State is only justified in invoking public policy where such conduct represents 'a genuine, present and sufficiently serious threat affecting one of the

---

60 Case 174/82 *Sandoz* [1983] ECR 2445 para 18.

fundamental interests of society'. Justifications that are isolated from the particulars of the case or that rely on considerations of general prevention 'shall not be accepted' (Directive 2004/38, Article 27(2)(2)). Article 27(2) of Directive 2004/38 is derived from existing case law, which we will discuss at the end of this section.

11.6.4.5 PREVIOUS CRIMINAL CONVICTIONS

Previous criminal convictions are not in themselves grounds for taking measures; the circumstances of the conviction and the evidence of a 'genuine, present and sufficiently serious threat . . .' must be taken into consideration (Directive 2004/38, Article 27(2)).

11.6.4.6 NO ARBITRARY DISTINCTION TO THE DETRIMENT OF NATIONALS OF OTHER MEMBER STATES

This principle is evident in the case law (e.g. *Adoui*), which we will now discuss.

11.6.5 CASE LAW ILLUSTRATING THE GENERAL RULES ON THE PUBLIC HEALTH, PUBLIC POLICY AND PUBLIC SECURITY EXCEPTIONS

Van Duyn v Home Office illustrates the public policy derogation.[61] It involved membership of the Church of Scientology, which was disapproved of by the UK Government. This was a specific pre-existing policy that had been defined by the UK Government (i.e. it was not merely manufactured for the purposes of the case), which considered the organisation to be anti-social and harmful. The case was referred to the ECJ, which concluded that the mere fact of membership itself did not amount to sufficient 'personal conduct' to justify public policy derogation, but that active participation and identification with the aims of the organisation would. In other words, membership of an organisation of itself will not usually satisfy the public policy derogation: the specific involvement of the individual concerned must be serious enough.

Adoui and Cornuaille v Belgium raised the question of whether Belgian law or practice make for 'arbitrary distinction' against French workers.[62] A and C worked in a bar 'suspect from the point of view of morals'. They were deported, and Belgium invoked the public policy exception in doing so. The ECJ held it could not do so if it did not take similarly repressive measures against its own nationals (although obviously these would not entail deportation).

In *R v Bouchereau*, a French national was twice convicted of unlawful possession of drugs, raising the question of whether he could be deported.[63] The ECJ said criminal convictions of themselves did not justify deportation; rather, it had to be determined whether there was a present threat to public policy or public security (in the event, Bouchereau was fined but not deported).[64]

....

61 Case 41/74 *Van Duyn v Home Office* [1975] 1 CMLR 1.
62 Joined Cases 115 & 116/81 *Adoui and Cornuaille v Belgium* [1982] 3 CMLR 631.
63 Case 30/77 *R v Bouchereau* [1977] 2 CMLR 800.
64 Ibid at 801.

Bonsignore v Oberstadtdirektor Köln concerned an Italian national who accidentally killed his younger brother in a firearms accident.[65] He had no arms permit/licence and was convicted of causing death by negligence, although no punishment was imposed. The case raised the question of whether a national could be deported for reasons of a general preventative nature, or whether the reasons had to be specific to the individual. The ECJ held that exceptions/derogations must be strictly construed and that in this case must relate to the individual specifically.

Calfa involved an Italian national expelled for life from Greece after conviction for being in possession of drugs whilst staying as a tourist in Crete.[66] The ECJ held an expulsion order justified by the public policy exception could be made only if, besides the national having committed an offence under drugs laws, his or her personal conduct created a genuine and sufficiently serious threat affecting one of the fundamental interests of society. This was not so where expulsion for life from the national territory had automatically followed a criminal conviction, and no account has been taken of the offender's personal conduct or of the danger which that person represents for the requirements of public policy. So EU law requires individualisation of the sanction.

In *Gough v Chief Constable of Derbyshire*,[67] the UK banned a football hooligan from travelling to another Member State, a ban that was upheld in the Court of Appeal as a legitimate derogation from free movement principles.[68]

Orfanopoulos and Oliveri v Land Baden-Württemberg is an example of a restriction on the freedom of movement of a foreign EU national with many years' residence in a host Member State.[69] The restriction was ordered on account of a criminal offence where there was a justified expectation that he would also commit future criminal offences. A complicating factor was whether his spouse and his children could reasonably be expected to live in his state of origin. The ECJ reiterated that derogations to be restrictively interpreted and also restated that the requirements for the public health, public policy and public security derogations to be invoked solely with regard to the personal conduct of an individual and not with reference to general preventative effect. The Court reiterated that he could not automatically be deported for a conviction, and left it for the national court to apply this to the case.

11.6.6 THE PUBLIC SERVICE EXCEPTION IN ARTICLE 45(4) TFEU

Article 45(4) TFEU states that the rest of Article 45 'shall not apply to employment in the public service'. Consistently with its broad interpretation of the term 'worker' and of

---

65 Case 67/74 *Bonsignore v Oberstadtdirektor* der Stadt Köln [1975] ECR 297.

66 Case C–348/96 *Calfa* [1999] 2 CMLR 1138.

67 *Gough v Chief Constable of Derbyshire* [2001] 4 All ER 289.

68 For comment on the case see e.g. G. Pearson 'Qualifying for Europe? The Legitimacy of Football Banning Orders "On Complaint" under the Principle of Proportionality' 3(1) *Entertainment & Sports Law Journal* 13 (2005).

69 Cases C–482/01 and C–493/01 *Orfanopoulos and Oliveri v Land Baden-Württemberg* [2005] 1 CMLR 18.

free movement rights in general, the ECJ tends to interpret the exceptions/derogations to free movement restrictively, and this is apparent in its approach to Article 45(4) on the public service exception.

▌ KEY LEARNING POINT
....

DEFINITION OF PUBLIC SERVICE
The ECJ defines 'public service' posts as: '. . . posts which involve direct or indirect participation in the exercise of powers conferred by public law and duties designed to safeguard the general interests of the state or of other public authorities. Such posts . . . presume on the part of those occupying them the existence of a special relationship of allegiance to the state and reciprocity of rights and duties which form the foundation of the bond of nationality' (*Commission v Belgium*[70]).

In *Commission v Belgium (No 2)*, Belgium tried to invoke the public service exception to discriminate against nationals from other Member States in the allocation of jobs in its local and national railway system.[71] The ECJ stated that employment within the meaning of the public service exception (now in Article 45(4) TFEU) must be connected with the specific activities of the public service in so far as it is entrusted with the exercise of powers conferred by public law and with responsibility for safeguarding the general interests of the state, and jobs within local authorities did not necessarily come under this category; rather, it was a question of looking at the characteristics or circumstances of each post.

On the facts, it held that jobs in the railway service were not within the public service exception, except for the jobs of head technical office supervisor, stock controller and night watchman with the municipality of Brussels and the job of architect with the municipalities of Brussels and Auderghem.

In *Lawrie-Blum v Land Baden-Württemberg*, the ECJ held that a post will benefit from the derogation in (now) Article 45(4) TFEU only if it involves *both* the exercise of power conferred by public law *and* safeguards the general interests of the state (i.e. these conditions are cumulative and not alternatives). On the facts, the ECJ held that preparatory service for the teaching profession could not be regarded as within the public service.

▌ KEY LEARNING POINT
....

COMMISSION NOTICE ON PUBLIC SERVICE JOBS
In order to clarify the meaning of the 'public service' and the type of posts it covered, the Commission published a document or Notice in 1988 in the

....
70 Case 149/79 *Commission v Belgium* [1980] ECR 3881 para 10.
71 Case 149/79 *Commission v Belgium (No 2)* [1982] 2 CMLR 413.

> *Official Journal* of the Communities giving guidelines as to what types of jobs were included or not. It stated that jobs in the armed forces, police, judiciary, tax authorities, and certain public bodies engaged in preparing or monitoring legal acts probably *would* be included and that jobs that probably *would not* be included were nursing, teaching and non-military research in public establishments.[72]

11.6.7 THE LANGUAGE/LINGUISTIC KNOWLEDGE EXCEPTION: REGULATION 492/2011, ARTICLE 3(1)

Employment conditions may relate 'to linguistic knowledge required by reason of the nature of the post to be filled' (Regulation 492/2011, Article 3(1)). This is an obvious, common sense requirement for most jobs, although it amounts to indirect discrimination. *Groener v Minister for Education* suggests the meaning of 'required by reason of the nature of the post' is not particularly difficult to satisfy.[73] The issue was whether Ireland could impose a requirement to know the Irish language for teaching posts, even though Irish was not needed actually to do the teaching.

The ECJ held that a permanent full-time post of lecturer in public vocational education institutions is a post that justifies the requirement of linguistic knowledge, within the meaning of Article 3(1) of Regulation 1612/68, provided that the language required is imposed as part of a policy for the promotion of the national language which is, at the same time, the first official language and provided that that requirement is applied in a proportionate and non-discriminatory manner.

A linguistic knowledge requirement in a job specification might be directly discriminatory, if it asked for a native speaker of the language – but is more likely to be indirectly discriminatory by asking simply for a high level of linguistic knowledge.

Thus, in addition to the five exceptions referred to in this section, Member States can plead that an indirectly discriminatory national rule *or* a non-discriminatory obstacle is justified by 'imperative requirements in the general interest' or 'objective justification'.

11.6.8 OBJECTIVE JUSTIFICATION UNDER CASE LAW

> KEY LEARNING POINT
> ....
>
> **CRITERIA FOR OBJECTIVE JUSTIFICATION**
> The Court may consider a national rule or practice as objectively justified if it is not directly discriminatory, is compatible with the objectives of the treaty, if the national rule is necessary to achieve the objective and is not disproportionate.

---

72 OJ C 72 18.03.1988 p. 2.
73 Case 379/87*Groener v Minister for Education* [1990] 1 CMLR 401.

This is an open-ended and rather vague category and is best illustrated by looking at actual cases where it has been adopted.

In *Commission v Bachmann*, the ECJ held that national rules allowing the deductibility from income tax of various insurance and pension contributions only if the contributions were paid in Belgium could be justified to ensure the cohesion of the tax system, since the Belgian authorities could be sure of the tax regulations of other countries and compliance with them.[74]

Finanzamt Köln-Altstadt v Roland Schumacker involved indirect discrimination based on the residence of the worker, whereby a national of another Member State employed, but not resident in a Member State, could not benefit from personal tax allowances.[75] The ECJ indicated this national rule could be justified in certain situations, because of the likely difference in position between workers from other Member States and workers resident in the Member State: the two workers were in a different position, since normally it is easier for the state of residence to offer an overall assessment of a person's tax situation.[76] The rationale seems to be based on the efficient working of national tax systems. However, the effect of the ECJ position was that that such indirect discrimination could not be justified where the non-resident worker could not benefit from personal allowances in the other Member States either.[77]

De Cuyper v Office National de l'Emploi concerned a Belgian rule containing a residence requirement imposed on an unemployed person over 50 years of age who was exempt from the requirement of proving that he was available for work, the residence requirement being a condition for the retention of entitlement to unemployment benefit.[78] The ECJ held that this was justified in light of the legitimate objective of monitoring the employment and family situation of unemployed persons and it was proportionate.

In *Tas-Hagen v Raadskamer WUBO van de Pensioen- en Uitkeringsraad*, the ECJ held that (now) Article 21(1) TFEU must be interpreted as precluding national legislation by which the Member State refused to grant to one of its nationals a benefit for civilian war victims solely on the ground that, at the time at which the application was submitted, the person concerned was resident, not in the territory of that Member State, but in the territory of another Member State.[79]

The ECJ rejected an argument that the Dutch rule was justified in order to limit the obligation of solidarity with civilian war victims to those who had links with the population of the Netherlands during and after the war. The Court held that the

---

74 Case C–204/90 *Commission v Bachmann* [1992] ECR I–249.
75 Case C–279/93 *Finanzamt Köln-Altstadt v Roland Schumacker* [1995] ECR I–225.
76 Ibid paras 33–35.
77 Ibid para 36.
78 *De Cuyper v Office National de l'Emploi* [2006] ECR I–6947.
79 Case C–192/05 *Tas-Hagen v Raadskamer WUBO van de Pensioen- en Uitkeringsraad* [2006] ECR I–10451.

objective was legitimate, but the residency requirement was not proportionate given that it applied to Dutch citizens who in all other respects were comparably integrated into Dutch society already.[80]

Förster v Hoofddirectie van de Informatie Beheer Groep concerned a Dutch rule that a student's entitlement to a maintenance grant depended on him or her being resident in the Netherlands for five years.[81] The ECJ held that this was justified and was not a violation of (now) Article 21 TFEU on citizenship. The Court held that it was justified in light of the legitimate objective of ensuring that students who are nationals of other Member States have, to a certain degree, integrated into its society.

11.7 CITIZENSHIP OF THE EU

For 'workers', the position on equal rights is now quite clear and well established. For *other EU citizens the position is slightly more fluid*, largely because of the ECJ case law in the last few years, which has sought to extend equal treatment rights – but only to a degree – to *all* EU citizens, whether they are 'workers' or not. This development reflects the introduction of the concept of citizenship of the EU in the Treaty of Maastricht 1992, now contained in Article 9 TEU and Articles 18–25 TFEU, and a move beyond what can be seen as more narrowly functional economic concepts of free movement of economic actors in the form of workers and service providers to a more constitutional understanding of the EU as not just an economic entity, but one that draws in a degree of political identity and connection with citizens.

Citizenship is discussed in more depth in Chapter 8. In practical terms, what EU citizenship adds to date is a number of treaty-based rights that those exercising free movement can exercise in other Member States, while case law has, first, enhanced to a limited extent the range of financial assistance citizens from one Member State may be entitled to in another Member State independently of being a worker or service-provider and, second, been a basis for EU citizens to assert rights independently of free movement under the substance of rights doctrine, although the scope of the latter has not been made clear to date.

APPLYING THE LAW

FRAMEWORK FOR ANSWERING FREE MOVEMENT PROBLEM QUESTIONS

(1) *Is the subject matter within the free movement principles?*
  - Is the person a worker? (Article 45 TFEU)
  - Is it a service (Articles 56–62 TFEU) or establishment (Articles 49–55)?

---

80 Ibid paras 30–33.
81 Case C–158/07 *Förster v Hoofddirectie van de Informatie Beheer Groep* [2008] ECR I–8507.

- Goods: (1) taxes and customs duties under Article 30 TFEU and internal taxation under Article 110 TFEU and (2) Quantitative restrictions and MEQRs under Articles 34–36 TFEU?

(2) *What kind of national rule/measure is in issue?* Is it direct discrimination, indirect discrimination or non-discriminatory obstacle (this matters because it determines which derogations apply)?[82]

(3) *Is a derogation applicable?* (only the Treaty can justify direct discrimination)
  (i)   the standard three: public policy, public security, public health
  (ii) public service/official authority
  (iii) linguistic exception (re workers only)
  (iv) case law (note different terminology across free movement principles).

(4) *Some further points:*
  - Mutual recognition of *educational* qualifications.
  - The ECJ sometimes somewhat confusingly says the case law exceptions must be non-discriminatory, whereas it would be clearer to state they must not involve direct discrimination.
  - Citizenship case law may further apply.

APPLYING THE LAW

SAMPLE PROBLEM QUESTION AND ANSWER

Problem

Nine months ago Sebastian, a 35-year-old from Vigo, Spain, travelled to the UK to look for work. He had applied for work as a hospital porter, but was told that UK nationals would be given priority for positions in the public sector, and has been doing some work as a part-time painter in a hotel.

Sebastian's partner, Helena, and Giuliano, Helena's son from a previous relationship, are due to travel to the UK to live with Sebastian next week. Helena was born in Canada and still holds Canadian nationality. Sebastian has been advised by the UK Ministry of Justice that, owing to a previous criminal conviction for smuggling wild animals, he may be deported and that, even if he is allowed to stay, it is unlikely that Helena and Giuliano would be allowed into the UK and that Helena would not be permitted to take up paid employment. Giuliano, who is deaf, would need special educational support.

Suppose that Sebastian, Helena and Giuliano had been allowed entry into the UK and had moved in to a flat together. However, last week, Helena announced that she wished to separate from Sebastian. She has already moved out of the flat and is presently living elsewhere with Giuliano in London.

---

82 Note different language in free movement of goods to describe direct discrimination: distinctly applicable.

Advise Sebastian and Helena as to his rights relevant to their situation under EU law.

Outline Answer

- What is Sebastian: is he a worker, job seeker or just an EU citizen? Job seekers have six–twelve months in practice (reasonable prospects of getting a job) (e.g. *Antonissen*), alternative rights as economically self-sufficient citizens under Directive 2004/38, and status as part-time workers (e.g. *Levin, Kempf, Steymann*) is sufficient in his case to give him full equal treatment rights (Article 7(2) of Regulation 492/2011).

- Has Sebastian been discriminated against or subject to a non-discriminatory obstacle? Direct discrimination regarding working as a hospital porter engages Article 45(4) TFEU and relevant case law (*Commission v Belgium (No 2)*, *Lawrie Blum* and Commission Notice 1988).

- What are the rights of Helena and Giuliano? It depends on their relationship with Sebastian, if married or subject to a recognised civil partnership (Articles 2–3 of Directive 2004/38) and if they are recognised as family members, they have equal treatment rights under Article 7(2) of Regulation 492/2011 (*Lebon* and *Cristini* on educational rights of dependents).

- Are citizenship rights in any way relevant (either in terms of financial assistance or the 'substance of rights doctrine'?). If Giuliano is by any chance an EU citizen, he may be able to assert a right to be with his father and mother once he is allowed to enter (*Carpenter*, *Alokpa*) and would not be an unreasonable financial burden on the UK.

APPLYING THE LAW

COMMON OMISSIONS IN ANSWERS TO FREE MOVEMENT PROBLEM QUESTIONS

Answers to free movement problem questions typically omit the following points:

(1) The applicability of derogations depending on the kind of national measure in issue (i.e. whether the national measure involves direct discrimination, indirect discrimination, non-discriminatory obstacles).

(2) The relevance of the citizenship provisions of the treaties and citizenship case law.

11.8 CONCLUSION

Free movement of workers has been central to the common market from the beginning of the Communities, and it remains so. Its scope has been supplemented by the development of EU citizenship, which has allowed non-worker EU citizens to gain subsidiary social benefits in certain circumstances, and has also been used to limit the importance of a cross-border dimension in some cases under the substance of rights doctrine. The basic rights of workers have been superseded by the more general rights of all citizens in Directive 2004/38, but equal treatment rights are still distinct to workers in important respects under Regulation 492/2011. Citizens' rights have gradually been expanded, but as yet it is clearly not the case that being citizens, as opposed to workers, is 'the fundamental status of nationals of the Member States',[83] as the ECJ has a habit of suggesting it would become.

―――――――――――――――

POINTS TO REVIEW

- Free movement of workers encompasses a spectrum of rights: right of entry/travel to another Member State, right of residence, right of access to employment, right to seek work, rights to equal tax and social advantages once employed, the rights of family member of workers.

- As with other areas of free movement, the ECJ has given a very broad interpretation of the scope of the treaty principle of free movement: national rules that are directly or indirectly discriminatory *and* non-discriminatory obstacles are contrary to the treaty.

- The standard derogations apply – public policy, public health, public security – along with the public service exception and the linguistic knowledge exception in secondary legislation. In addition, the ECJ has developed an open-ended category of case law exceptions or mandatory requirements that can justify indirect discrimination or non-discriminatory obstacles.

- Free movement of worker problem questions can be approached in a sequence or framework.

- Linking this chapter with Chapter 8, citizenship has to date supplemented the rights workers have enjoyed since the foundation of the Communities. It has been used as an umbrella category to encompass the extension of rights to EU nationals beyond workers or service-providers but the principle of economic self-sufficiency has only been partially qualified in citizenship case law. In addition, in some, to date limited, circumstances to protect the 'substance of rights', citizenship has been used in the case law to limit the traditional requirement for a cross-border element for EU rights to be engaged.

―――――――――――――――

83 See, e.g. Case C–50/06 *Commission v Netherlands* [2007] ECR I–4383 para 32 (the comment is made in numerous other cases).

CHAPTER GLOSSARY

Derogations refer to exceptions to the free movement of workers and citizens that EU law permits to the Member States. Here are three standard derogations across free movement law: public health, public policy, public security. In addition, there are three other derogations applicable to free movement of workers: the public service exception, the linguistic knowledge exception, and objective justification under case law.

Direct discrimination refers to explicit differentiation between nationals of the Member States in employment.

Indirect discrimination refers to a practice in a Member State that does not explicitly differentiate on grounds of nationality between nationals from that Member State and nationals in other Member States, but that put workers from other Member States at a disadvantage.

Mandatory requirements refers to reasons recognised in ECJ case law as justifying indirect discrimination or non-discriminatory obstacles.

Non-discriminatory obstacle refers to national rules or practices that do not involve discrimination either direct or indirect, but which amount to an obstacle or hindrance to free movement.

Objective justification refers to the development by the ECJ of an open-ended category of justification of national rules and practices restricting the free movement of workers. Objective justification can only justify indirectly discriminatory national rules or practices or obstacles to freedom of movement at national level.

Precautionary principle refers to the legality of Member State restrictions on free movement on grounds of public health where scientific uncertainty exists about a threat or risk to public health.

TAKING THINGS FURTHER

Publications Office of the EU, Volume 1, *Free Movement of Workers Online Journal* (2010) This online journal specialises in the free movement of workers. Its first issue addresses mutual recognition of educational qualifications of workers.

R White *Workers, Establishment and Services in the European Union* (Oxford University Press 2005) This provides a comprehensive overview of the categories of workers and service-providers under free movement.

C Barnard *The Substantive Law of the EU: The Four Freedoms* (4th edn Oxford University Press 2013) This provides an authoritative treatment of all the free movement principles, including workers in Chapters 11–14 and 16.

CHAPTER 12
FREE MOVEMENT OF PERSONS II: SERVICES AND ESTABLISHMENT

This chapter examines the second aspect of free movement of persons in the EU, namely, services and establishment. The essential difference between free movement of workers and of services and establishment is that between employees and the self-employed. Services and establishment relate to the self-employed. The difference between services and establishment is between short-term and long-term provision of services in another Member State. The structure of free movement of services and of establishment is similar to that of free movement of workers. Some issues are specific to, or more especially relevant to, free movement of services and establishment. For example, mutual recognition of educational qualifications is more of an issue in this area, although it also arises with workers.

AS YOU READ . . .

The key questions that will be answered in this chapter are as follows:

– What are the basic rights given to services providers moving to another Member State under EU law?

– What is the practical difference between services and establishment?

– What kinds of national measures are contrary to free movement of services and of establishment? What are the derogations to freedom of movement of services/establishment?

– What is the significance of the Services Directive?

– What rules govern mutual recognition of educational qualifications in free movement of services and of establishment?

12.1 INTRODUCTION

Remember that the EU treaties grant 'freedom of movement' to 'workers', but they also grant freedom of movement to self-employed persons who move to another Member State to 'establish' themselves in another Member State (Article 49 TFEU) and to those who, on a temporary basis, provide services in another Member State (Article 56 TFEU). The essential difference between workers and services/establishment is the difference between being employed by somebody else (workers) and providing services as a self-employed person or entity (services and establishment). Freedom of movement rights under Articles 49 and 56 TFEU are essentially the same rights as workers have under Article 45 TFEU. Note that a company is considered to be self-employed and so subject to free movement of services/establishment.

RIGHTS

1. Travel and residence rights, which include the:
   A. right to leave home Member State, and
   B. right to enter the host Member State, and
   C. right to reside in the host Member State

2. Equal treatment rights, which mean:
   A. no direct discrimination, and
   B. no indirect discrimination
   C no non-discriminatory measures that might nonetheless have the effect of restricting the right of free movement

---

MAKING CONNECTIONS
+ + + + + + + + + + + + + + + + +

SIMILAR STRUCTURE OF FREE MOVEMENT PRINCIPLES
In the leading decision in *Gebhard*,[1] the ECJ stated that the same principles underlie all the free movement categories.

There is much similarity between the structure of the law on free movement of services/establishment and that on free movement of workers. For example, they are both centrally concerned with eliminating discrimination on grounds of nationality and with equal treatment of persons from other Member States, and the derogations/ exceptions are similar (although there are some differences too). The rights under services/establishment are also subject to the three standard exceptions/derogations on the grounds of public health, public policy and public security and an exception for government posts (this exception is called 'official authority' in the case of services/

---

1   Case C–55/94 *Gebhard* [1995] ECR I–4165.

establishment, rather than 'public service' as with workers, but the concept is the same, i.e. an exception for government jobs).

Further, there is a general category of exception developed by the ECJ 'objective justification'. The language exception does not apply to services/establishment, simply because the question of the language ability of self-employed people tends to be self-regulating, i.e. someone who cannot speak a language is unlikely to offer themselves as a service provider in a Member State where he/she does not speak the language, as a consumer in that Member State is unlikely to hire such a service provider.

KEY LEARNING POINT

THE SIGNIFICANCE OF THE SERVICES–ESTABLISHMENT DISTINCTION

The main significance of the distinction between services (temporary provision of a service in another Member State) and establishment is that the general laws and regulatory system of the *home* Member State apply to service providers while in the host Member State, whereas those who are established in another Member State are subject to the general laws and regulatory system of the *host* Member State.

KEY LEARNING POINT

THE RIGHTS OF FAMILY MEMBERS OF SERVICE-PROVIDERS

The derivative rights granted to family members of service providers are the same as those granted to family member of workers. Directive 2004/38 applies equally to both categories (see Articles 2(2) and 3(1) of the directive as to the derivative rights of family members of workers or service providers).

EXPLAINING THE LAW

THE ENDURING SIGNIFICANCE OF DISTINGUISHING BETWEEN WORKERS AND SERVICE-PROVIDERS IN THE CONTEXT OF EU CITIZENSHIP

The derivative rights granted to family members of service providers are the same as those granted to family member of workers. Directive 2004/38 applies equally to both categories. Although there is thus a tendency to move away from distinct categories of persons and to develop an overall category of 'citizenship', for practical purposes, the distinction between workers on the one hand and services/establishment on the other is still important because:

(1) most obviously, the difference between services and establishment as to *the law of the home Member State versus that of the host Member State* as noted above.

But also:

(2) in the past, it appears that the approach of the ECJ to the category of case law exceptions may have been *more permissive of restrictions* on the free movement of services, than of restrictions on the right of establishment, but more recently the ECJ tends to adopt the same approach across both services and establishment;

(3) *mutual recognition of educational qualifications is more of an issue in the area of services/establishment*, because the latter are self-regulating to a greater degree than are workers/employees.

12.2 THE TFEU PROVISIONS ON SERVICES AND ESTABLISHMENT

KEY LEARNING POINT

THE PERSONAL SCOPE (SCOPE *RATIONAE MATERIAE*) OF SERVICES AND ESTABLISHMENT

Freedom of services and establishment applies to providers of services whether the service providers are:

– natural persons (Articles 49 and 56 TFEU)
– companies/firms/undertakings that are profit-making and formed in accordance with the law of a Member State and have their registered office, central administration or principal place of business in the EU (which means they can also be a subsidiary of a non-EU company) (Articles 54, 62 TFEU).

ARTICLE 49 TFEU

. . . restrictions on freedom of establishment of *nationals of a Member State in the territory of another Member State* shall be prohibited. Such prohibition shall also apply to restrictions on the setting up of agencies, branches or subsidiaries by nationals of any Member State established in the territory of any Member State. Freedom of establishment shall include the right to take up and pursue activities as self-employed persons and to set up and manage undertakings . . . *under the conditions laid down for its own nationals* by the law of the country where such establishment is effected . . .

ARTICLE 56 TFEU

. . . restrictions on freedom to provide services . . . shall be prohibited in respect of *nationals of Member States who are established in a State . . . other than that of the person for whom the services are intended . . .*

ARTICLE 57 TFEU

. . . the person providing the service may, in order to do so, temporarily pursue his activity in the state where the service is provided, *under the same conditions as are imposed by the State on its own nationals . . .*

KEY LEARNING POINT

DEFINING SERVICES

Services are within the TFEU if they come within the definition in Article 57 EC TFEU, i.e. services . . . *normally provided for remuneration*, insofar as they are *not* governed by the provisions relating to freedom of movement for . . . *persons*.

Thus, if a person is within the definition of 'worker', i.e. is employed, then Article 45 TFEU and case law on it should be applied. If a person is providing services in a self-employed capacity, then apply Article 49 (establishment) or Article 56 (services) TFEU.

KEY LEARNING POINT

THE REQUIREMENT FOR REMUNERATION

The requirement is for remuneration: i.e. voluntary or charitable services are not included. The ECJ has tended to interpret this quite broadly and has, for example, included state-funded essential (such as medical) services where payment is made for the latter directly by the service recipient.[2]

In *Bond van Adverteerders*,[3] the ECJ held that remuneration did not have to come from the recipient of the services, so long as there was remuneration from some party. The facts concerned provision of a cable TV service from one Member State to broadcasters

2 See e.g. Case C–158/96 *Raymond Kohll v Union des Caisses de Maladie* [1998] ECR I–931. The EU has now adopted secondary legislation in this area: Directive 2011/24/EU on the Application of Patients' Rights in Cross-border Healthcare, OJ L 88 04.04.2011 p. 45.

3 Case 352/85 *Bond van Adverteerders* [1988] ECR 2085.

in another Member State where the cable network operator received fees directly from subscribers, rather than from the broadcasters.

Deliège concerned high-ranking athletes involved in international competition.[4] The ECJ ruled that the mere fact that a sports association or federation unilaterally classified its members as amateur athletes did not necessarily mean that the athletes were not engaging in economic activities. The ECJ held that it can involve a number of separate, but closely-related services, and gave the example of advertising associated with sports events.[5]

In *Geraets-Smits*,[6] the ECJ held that a medical service provided in one Member State and paid for by the patient did not cease to fall within the scope of freedom to provide services merely because reimbursement of the costs of the treatment involved could be applied for under another Member State's sickness insurance legislation. Thus, the fact payment is made is itself decisive, whether or not there is any scheme of refunding.

EXPLAINING THE LAW

SPECIFYING THE DISTINCTION BETWEEN SERVICES AND ESTABLISHMENT

The distinction between 'establishment' and 'services' is 'one of degree rather than kind'. The ECJ has defined establishment as '. . . the actual pursuit of an economic activity through a *fixed* establishment in another Member State for an *indefinite period*'.[7] What this means is that the provisions on services should be applied where the service provider does not have any local, fixed base (in the host Member State), or is there for a limited period, i.e. only if establishment cannot first be applied.

Reyners v Belgium concerned a Dutch national, who had grown up and been educated in Belgium, where he applied to be called to the Belgian Bar.[8] He held the appropriate Belgian diploma necessary to practise as an *avocet*, but Belgian law provided that only Belgian nationals could practise at the Belgian Bar.

MAKING CONNECTIONS
+ + + + + + + + + + + + + + + + +

ARTICLE 49 TFEU ON ESTABLISHMENT HAS DIRECT EFFECT

The ECJ held that Reyners could rely on Article 49 TFEU ('. . . restrictions on freedom of establishment of nationals of a Member State in the territory of another Member State shall be prohibited'), i.e. that Article 49 TFEU was directly effective (as it met the conditions for direct effect).

---

4   Joined Cases C–51/96 & C–191/97 *Deliège* [2000] ECR I–2549.
5   Ibid para 56.
6   Case C–157/99 *Geraets-Smits* [2001] ECR I–5473.
7   Case C–221/89 *Factortame* [1991] 3 CMLR 589 para 20.
8   Case 2/74 *Reyners v Belgium* [1974] 2 CMLR 305.

Therefore, Reyners was entitled to rely on it in a national court.

KEY CASE GEBHARD

The leading case for some time on the distinction between services and establishment has been *Gebhard*. One of the key points established was that the temporary provisions of services is to be determined in the light of *duration, regularity, periodicity* and *continuity*. *Stable* and *continuous* provision of services amounts to establishment.

Gebhard concerned a German national who set up chambers as a lawyer in Milan and used the title *accovato* (lawyer, in Italian), although he had not been admitted to the Milan Bar and his training, qualifications and experience had not been formally recognised in Italy.[9] Disciplinary proceedings were brought against him by Milan Bar Council. Gebhard sought to rely on free movement principles to defend himself. The case is important for a number of reasons, including that it set out the test for distinguishing between services and establishment. The ECJ made a number of general statements concerning services and establishment and how to distinguish between them:

- The temporary nature of the provision of services, envisaged in the third paragraph of (then) Article 60 of the EC Treaty (now see Article 57 TFEU), is to be determined in the light of its *duration, regularity, periodicity* and *continuity*.[10]
- The provider of services, within the meaning of the TFEU, may equip himself or herself in the host Member State with the infrastructure necessary for the purposes of performing the services in question (so the mere fact that provision of a service entails some infrastructure does not make it establishment).[11]
- A national of a Member State who pursues a professional activity on a *stable* and *continuous* basis comes under the provisions of the chapter relating to the right of establishment and not those of the chapter relating to services.[12]

ANALYSING THE LAW

DOES *GEBHARD* PROVIDE CLEAR GUIDELINES?

The key point distinguishing services from establishment that the ECJ identified in *Gebhard* is the difference in continuity and stability. However, this still naturally leads on to the question: how stable and continuous must service provision be? The mere presence of infrastructure to support service provision is not enough, but the more stable and continuous the existence of the infrastructure, the more

---

9 Case C–55/94 *Gebhard* [1995] ECR I–4165.
10 Ibid para 39.
11 Ibid.
12 Ibid.

likely the service provision is to amount to establishment. It is a matter then
of looking to the case law for more precise indications. In *Gebhard* itself, the
facts concerned setting selling prices. In later case law, the ECJ has tended to
focus on the nature of the activity and the intent of the service provider, and has
downplayed the length of time or duration aspect of the test.

Schnitzer concerned a German national who was sued in Germany for having employed
a Portuguese construction company for three years, without completing registration of
skilled labourers as required by German law.[13] If the Portuguese company was deemed
to be established, Mr Schnitzer would have had to comply with German law, but if the
Portuguese company was deemed to be merely a service provider, then Portuguese law
(and not German law) would be applicable.

The ECJ said the fact that a service was provided even over several years did not
necessarily mean it came under establishment, pointing out that although in retrospect
a service may be provided for several years, it may not have been apparent at any given
time how long the service would be provided for:

> . . . the mere fact that a business established in one Member State supplies identical
> or similar services in a repeated or more or less regular manner in a second Member
> State, without having an infrastructure there enabling it to pursue a professional
> activity there on a stable and continuous basis and, from the infrastructure, to hold
> itself out to, amongst others, nationals of the second Member State, cannot be
> sufficient for it to be regarded as established in the second Member State.[14]

12.3 THREE FORMS OF CROSS-BORDER SERVICE AND THE CROSS-BORDER ELEMENT

12.3.1 FREE MOVEMENT OF THE SERVICE PROVIDER TO ANOTHER MEMBER STATE

The typical situation is where the provider of services goes temporarily to another
Member State to sell his or her services, as in *Van Binsbergen*.[15] In this case, a Dutch
lawyer, living in Belgium but practising in the Netherlands, was denied the right to

---

13 Case C–215/01 *Schnitzer* [2003] ECR I–14847.
14 Ibid para 40.
15 Case 33/74 *Van Binsbergen v Bestuur van de Bedrijfsvereniging voor de Metaalnijverheid* [1975] 1 CMLR 298.

appear as a legal representative because the Netherlands said only lawyers with Dutch residence were permitted to practise in the country.

> **KEY LEARNING POINT**
> ....
> **ARTICLE 56 TFEU ON ESTABLISHMENT HAS DIRECT EFFECT**
> In *Van Binsbergen*, the ECJ ruled that Van Binsbergen, a Dutch lawyer practising in the Netherlands but living in Belgium, could rely on Article 56 TFEU and that it was directly effective.

If Reyners or Van Binsbergen had been attempting to work in the Netherlands or Belgium as *employed* lawyers (i.e. as employees of another law firm, rather than setting up their own firms), the results would have been the same, although the decisions would have been made on the basis of the non-discrimination principles in Article 45 TFEU (i.e. under free movement of workers principles).

12.3.2 FREE MOVEMENT OF RECIPIENT OF SERVICES TO THE PROVIDER'S MEMBER STATE

The TFEU talks only of the free movement of those 'providing services'. The ECJ, by creative interpretation (emphasising, by a meta-teleological method, the effect and purpose of achieving overall integration, not focusing on actual wording of text) extended the rules to anyone who receives services in another Member State.

> **KEY LEARNING POINT**
> ....
> **FREE MOVEMENT ALSO APPLIES TO THOSE WHO RECEIVE SERVICES**
> Although the treaty texts only referred to those who provide services, the ECJ in its case law decided that anyone who received a service could also benefit from free movement.

A recipient does not even have to have travelled for the purpose of taking advantage of any particular service; thus he can receive services incidentally, e.g. as a tourist. Classic cases on these issues include the following.

Luisi and Carbone v Ministero del Tesoro concerned the export of currency to pay for medical services. Italian nationals were exporting more than the permitted amount of foreign currency under Italian law. The ECJ declared that this restricted Italians from buying services as tourists and was thus contrary to the treaty provisions on free movement of services/establishment.[16]

....

16 Case 26/83 *Luisi and Carbone v Ministero del Tesoro* [1985] 3 CMLR 52.

In *Cowan v Trésor Public*, the ECJ held that a UK tourist in France should be able to claim compensation for criminal injuries on the same basis as French nationals, by virtue of being a recipient of a service.[17] The ECJ did not appear to think it necessary in the case to specify what service was received; it was enough that tourists are in general recipients of services.[18]

On the other hand, somewhat more recently, the ECJ declared in *Oulane*[19] (discussed below under 'Cross-border element') that being a recipient of a service cannot be purely hypothetical.

12.3.3 FREE MOVEMENT WHERE THE SERVICE PROVIDER AND THE RECIPIENT EACH STAYS IN THEIR OWN MEMBER STATE

This situation falls squarely under Article 56 TFEU, as interpreted by the Court of Justice. It covers situations in which the service is provided at a distance, i.e. both the provider and the recipient remain in their own Member State. The following cases illustrate this situation.

Säger v Dennemeyer & Co concerned a firm operating from the UK (Dennemeyer & Co).[20] The firm provided a service renewing patents on behalf of clients, including those in Germany, and operated by post. German law only permitted such work to be done by individuals (i.e. not companies, such as Säger). The ECJ concluded that this was, prima facie, a restriction on the freedom of a firm in one Member State (in this case, the UK) to provide services in another Member State (in this case, Germany).

In the leading case of *Alpine Investments BV v Minister van Financien*,[21] which we will also discuss further below, the facts concerned cold calling by Alpine Investments, which sold financial products, from the Netherlands to another Member State. The Dutch Government decided to prohibit this practice, in order to preserve the reputation of the Dutch financial sector, which had been the subject of some complaints by investors from other Member States who lost out after purchasing financial products from the Netherlands in this sector/category. The ECJ held that this violated the treaty provisions as a (non-discriminatory) restriction on the freedom of services;[22] however, it could be justified to protect investor confidence in national financial markets.

....

17 Case 186/87 *Cowan v Trésor Public* [1990] 2 CMLR 613.
18 Notice here that a common market matter indirectly related to the criminal law, although the criminal law had not become part of Community law (and today the EU has rather limited competence in criminal law).
19 Case C–215/03 *Oulane* [2005] ECR I–1215.
20 Case C–76/90 *Säger v Dennemeyer* [1993] 3 CMLR 639.
21 Case C–384/93 *Alpine Investments BV v Minister van Financien* [1995] ECR I–1141.
22 Ibid para 35.

12.3.4 THE CROSS-BORDER ELEMENT

EXPLAINING THE LAW

THE CROSS-BORDER ELEMENT OF FREE MOVEMENT OF SERVICES

As with all the free movement principles, a basic requirement in the case law of the ECJ for the application of free movement rules is that there be a cross-border element, i.e. wholly internal situations were not included. However, particularly in more recent case law, the ECJ has interpreted this requirement very loosely, and it is enough that there is any cross-border element, even if it is quite tenuous.

Carpenter concerned the Filipino wife of a British national who had failed to renew her residence visa and was facing deportation.[23] The ECJ found that this was not a purely internal situation. The Court held that Mr Carpenter's profession entailed '. . . selling advertising space in medical and scientific journals and offering various administrative and publishing services to the editors of those journals' and came within (now) Article 56 TFEU as many of Mr Carpenter's clients were established in other Member States, even though Mr Carpenter did not cross a border.[24] The ECJ concluded that the expulsion of Mrs Carpenter would make her husband's everyday life, and hence professional activity, more difficult and thus constituted an obstacle prohibited by Article 56 TFEU.

However, at the same time, the ECJ has held that the cross-border element cannot be purely hypothetical for Article 56 TFEU to be engaged. In *Oulane*, a French national, Oulane, who had been based in the Netherlands without any form of identification, was detained and later deported to France.[25] He had been unable to give a fixed abode or show possession of any money or luggage. Oulane argued that he could be considered a tourist and, as such, a recipient of a service. The ECJ held the person invoking the status of service recipient must prove:

> Without prejudice to the questions pertaining to public policy, public security and public health, it is for the nationals of a Member State residing in another Member State in their capacity as recipients of services, to provide the evidence establishing that they are lawfully resident in that other Member State. If a national of a Member State is not able to prove that the conditions for a right of residence as a recipient of services within the meaning of Directive 73/148 are fulfilled, the host Member State may undertake deportation subject to the limits imposed by Community law.[26]

23 Case C–60/00 *Carpenter* [2002] ECR I–6279.
24 Ibid para 29.
25 Case C–215/03 *Oulane* [2005] ECR I–1215.
26 Ibid paras 53–56.

12.4 TREATY RIGHTS IN ESTABLISHMENT AND SERVICES

12.4.1 INDIVIDUALS' RIGHTS OF ENTRY AND RESIDENCE

> **KEY LEARNING POINT**
>
> ....
>
> **RIGHTS OF EXIT, ENTRY AND RESIDENCE**
> As with all the free movement principles, a basic requirement in the case law
> of the ECJ, for the application of free movement rules is that there be a cross-
> border element, secondary legislation further specified rights of entry and
> residence for an individual who intends to establish a business, or provide
> services, in another Member State, and they are equivalent to those given to
> a worker. They are now set out for EU citizens generally (not just workers and
> service providers) in Directive 2004/38,[27] discussed already in Chapter 11.

Thus, the rights are:

(a) the right to leave the home state (see Directive 73/148, Article 2; Directive 2004/38, Article 4)
(b) the right to enter the host state (see Directive 73/148, Article 3; Directive 2004/38, Article 5)
(c) the right to reside in the host state (see Directive 73/148, Article 4(1); Directive 2004/38, Articles 6–7).

12.4.2 RIGHTS NOT TO BE DISCRIMINATED AGAINST WHILST PROVIDING A SERVICE

> **KEY LEARNING POINT**
>
> ....
>
> **PROHIBITION ON DIRECT DISCRIMINATION, INDIRECT
> DISCRIMINATION AND NON-DISCRIMINATORY OBSTACLES**
> As in the area of workers, the fundamental rule that applies is that there must
> be no direct or indirect discrimination on the basis of nationality against those
> attempting to exercise their rights to establish or to provide services. This rule is
> contained in Articles 49 and 56 TFEU.

Concerning establishment, several cases can illustrate the application of the non-discrimination rule. *Reyners v Belgium*, which we looked at above, is one example.[28]

Steinhauser v City of Biarritz is another example.[29] It involved an artist of German nationality resident in France who was denied the right to rent premises for exhibition

....

27 OJ L 158 30.04.2004 p. 77.
28 Case 2/74 *Reyners v Belgium* [1974] 2 CMLR 305.
29 Case 197/84 *Steinhauser v City of Biarritz* [1986] 1 CMLR 53.

of his artwork, as such premises were reserved by local law for French nationals. The ECJ held that freedom of establishment includes the right not only to take up activities as a self-employed person but also to pursue them in the broad sense of the term, thus the renting of premises for business purposes furthers the pursuit of an occupation and therefore falls within the scope of (now) Article 49 of the TFEU.

It was not compatible with Article 49 for a tendering procedure for the allocation of public property belonging to a municipality to make the acceptance of applications conditional upon nationality. In *Commission v Italy*,[30] Italian law permitted only Italian nationals to apply for reduced-rate mortgages for residential premises and was held to be contrary to (now) Article 49 TFEU.

In the case of services, *Van Binsbergen*[31] and *Cowan v Trésor Public*,[32] both discussed above, provide examples.

We will look further below (at 12.4.4) at what substantive beyond exit, entry, residence and permission to provide services involve in the area of services and establishment, i.e. to what extent the 'equal social and tax advantages' principle in Regulation 492/2011 in relation to workers also applies to services and establishment.

12.4.3 BEYOND DISCRIMINATION: PROHIBITION ON NON-DISCRIMINATORY OBSTACLES

In the context of services and establishment, non-discriminatory obstacles arise where a (potential) host Member State has laws or regulations that affect the carrying on of a business or profession and which are more restrictive than the legal rules applicable to a business or profession in a home Member State (or even ban the activity completely), but such laws are apparently 'blind' to nationality either directly or indirectly. The ECJ has held that even *non-discriminatory obstacles to market access* are contrary to the TFEU.

Ordre de Avocats v Klopp[33] concerned a German lawyer, Klopp, who had been refused admission to the Paris Bar on the sole ground that he already maintained an office as a lawyer in another Member State. The Paris Bar required lawyers practising in Paris to have an office in Paris, but this applied equally to French lawyers with offices in other parts of France as it did to lawyers based in other Member States. On these facts, there was no indirect discrimination, because it was just as hard for French lawyers resident in France other than in Paris, as the Court noted, and the Paris Bar rule applied without distinction to lawyers from outside Paris, whether in France or other Member States.[34]

---

30 Case 63/86 *Commission v Italy* [1989] 2 CMLR 601.
31 Case 186/87 *Cowan v Trésor Public* [1990] 2 CMLR 613.
32 Case 33/74 *Van Binsbergen* [1975] 1 CMLR 298.
33 Case 107/83 *Ordre de Avocats v Klopp* [1984] ECR 2971.
34 Ibid para 12, although it might be said to be indirectly discriminatory in one respect, in that French lawyers were more likely to live in Paris than lawyers from other Member States.

Säger v Dennemeyer & Co Ltd concerned German legislation that reserved activities relating to the maintenance of industrial property rights to patent agents.[35] This was as likely to impact on service providers in the field of intellectual property rights from other Member States as those from Germany, a point the ECJ made very explicit in its judgment:

> It should first be pointed out that [then] Article 59 of the Treaty requires not only the elimination of all discrimination against a person providing services on the ground of his nationality but also the abolition of any restriction, even if it applies without distinction to national providers of services and to those of other Member States, when it is liable to prohibit or otherwise impede the activities of a provider of services established in another Member State where he lawfully provides similar services.[36]

A further example is *Alpine Investments*,[37] discussed above, concerning a Dutch prohibition on cold-calling (i.e. unsolicited sales calls) to sell financial products: calling from the Netherlands to other Member States had been prohibited by the Netherlands.

Gebhard confirmed the above case law holding that national rules that inhibited trade between the Member States, even if they affect own nationals in exactly the same way as nationals from other Member States (i.e. even where there is no discrimination, either direct or indirect) are contrary to the TFEU (unless justified by a derogation or caselaw).[38]

12.4.4 FREEDOM OF SERVICES/ESTABLISHMENT AND SUBSTANTIVE RIGHTS

There is no equivalent concerning services and establishment of Regulation 492/2011 (and in particular Article 7(2) of the latter), which gives workers from other Member States equal rights as national workers outside of the immediate context of employment.

KEY LEARNING POINT

EQUAL TREATMENT BEYOND EMPLOYMENT IN SERVICES AND ESTABLISHMENT

Although there is no equivalent in the area of services and establishment of Article 7(2) of Regulation 492/2011, the ECJ has developed a similar principle in relation to services/establishment, but the Court has tended to require some link between the social advantage and the ability to carry on the self-employed activity (whereas under Regulation 1612/68, Article 7(2), the ECJ has not insisted on this as a requirement in relation to social advantages and workers).

35 Case C–76/90 *Säger v Dennemeyer* [1993] 3 CMLR 639.
36 Ibid para 12.
37 Case C–384/93 *Alpine Investments* [1995] ECR I–1141.
38 Case C–55/94 *Gebhard* (n 9) para 37.

The *Meeusen* case concerned establishment,[39] where the ECJ ruled that the principle *of equal treatment of self-employed persons under now Article 49 TFEU precluded* national legislation that imposed a residence requirement on the children of self-employed EU migrants, but not on the children of nationals, before they could obtain finance for their studies.

The facts of the *Steinhauser* case on establishment related to renting premises for business purposes.[40]

Commission v Italy involved reduced-rate mortgage loans and social housing.[41] The ECJ said Member States had to provide to EU migrant workers on the same basis as nationals, and it noted how failing to do so would reduce equality of competition between EU migrant workers providing services and nationals providing services. In this way, the ECJ suggested the social advantage must have some connection with the ability to work/ provide the service. The ECJ further held that even if temporary providers of services would be unlikely to satisfy the eligibility criteria for social housing, they must still in principle be given the benefit of access to such on the same terms as nationals.[42]

12.5 THE SERVICES DIRECTIVE

For several years in the early 2000s, the European Commission promoted the adoption of a new framework directive on the cross-border provision of services in the Member States of the EU, a prospect that aroused opposition from some Member States who feared the impact of increased competition in certain areas of industry and the economy. The final text of Directive 2006/123, the Services Directive, was adopted on 12 December 2006, although it did not come into effect until 28 December 2009.[43]

ANALYSING THE LAW

EQUAL TREATMENT BEYOND EMPLOYMENT IN SERVICES AND ESTABLISHMENT

While the broad principles governing free movement of services have been established as set out above through the Treaty provisions, secondary legislation and case law from the ECJ, the 'Services Directive' is intended to place Member States under a duty to proactively remove obstacles to free movement of services – consistent with the trend of case law of the ECJ, the concern

---

39 Case C–337/97 *Meeusen* [1999] ECR I–3289.
40 Case 197/84 *Steinhauser* [1985] ECR 1819.
41 Case 63/86 *Commission v Italy* [1988] ECR 29.
42 Ibid paras 18–20.
43 Directive 2006/123 on services in the internal market OJ L 376 27.12.2006 p. 36.

is no longer with discriminatory national rules but more generally and more broadly with any obstacle to free movement. While it did not establish any new foundational principles governing free movement of services and establishment, it would establish a more systematic system of enforcement of EU law principles on free movement.

The main distinctive features of the directive are:

- It is comprehensive in applying to a wide range of services, although a significant range of services are excluded (Article 2(2)).
- It specifies a range of prohibited practices that may be non-discriminatory obstacles (e.g. an obligation to participate in a financial guarantee) (Article 14).
- It brings about administrative simplification for firms wanting to do cross-border business (Articles 5–8).
- It requires Member States to screen comprehensively for obstacles to free movement and to remove them (see Article 14 onward).
- It establishes greater consultation between the Commission, Member States and 'stakeholders' or business and other interests (see Articles 28, 29, 32, 33, 35).
- It establishes a broad framework for the exchange of information to facilitate cross-border services (Article 22) and a right to information for service providers (Article 21).
- It entails a general obligation of partnership and cooperation between the Member States.
- It sets out fully the rights of recipients of services (various provisions).

ANALYSING THE LAW

THE PROPOSED PRINCIPLE OF ORIGIN

In its initial proposal for the Services Directive, the European Commission proposed a principle of origin, under which services would be provided under the legal framework of the law of the home Member State of the service provider. This proposal eliminated rules applicable in the *host* Member State: it was the rules applicable in the *home* Member State of the service that were to now apply in the *host* Member State, including regarding establishment. This raised much opposition from trade unions, in particular, because of difficulties of enforcing it (it was the home Member State who was to enforce the service provision in the host Member State) and a fear that it would lead to a collapse in regulatory standards: Member States would be competing with each other to have lower standards in order to make their service providers more competitive. The Member States thus watered down this principle to a freedom to provide services principle, which really restated, albeit in a more systematic way, the pre-existing position that a presumption applied that the rules of the home Member State governed services, but that exceptions could be made in a non-discriminatory way in the interests of public policy, public security, public health or the protection of the environment.[44]

12.6 DEROGATIONS FROM THE FREE MOVEMENT OF SERVICES AND OF ESTABLISHMENT

There are five derogations to free movement of services/establishment:

- public health
- public policy
- public security
- official authority
- overriding/imperative reasons of the general interest.

12.6.1 THE THREE STANDARD EXCEPTIONS – PUBLIC POLICY, PUBLIC SECURITY AND PUBLIC HEALTH

Articles 52 and 65 TFEU allow Member States to deny or restrict the right of establishment or services rights on the grounds of:

- public policy
- public security or
- public health.

These exceptions are the standard exceptions, also applicable to workers under Article 45(3) TFEU. Similarly, the rules in Directive 2004/38 (ex-Directive 64/221), Articles 27–33, setting out detailed criteria for the use of the above exceptions/derogations apply, as they do in the case of workers, which we examined in Chapter 10.

12.6.2 THE EXERCISE OF OFFICIAL AUTHORITY

KEY LEARNING POINT

THE EXERCISE OF OFFICIAL AUTHORITY
The freedoms do not apply to positions of 'official authority'. This is the same concept as the public service exception under Article 45(4) TFEU in relation to workers, but it is simply labelled differently.

44 Article 16.

It is defined as: 'activities which in [a] State are connected, even occasionally, with the exercise of official authority' (Article 51 TFEU).

In *Reyners v Belgium*, Advocate General Mayras defined official authority as arising from '. . . the sovereignty and majesty of the State; for him who exercises it, it implies the power of enjoying the prerogatives outside the general law, privileges of official power and powers of coercion over citizens'.[45] In *Reyners*, it was also clarified that just because a particular profession may have some official authority functions, that does not mean that the whole profession is exempted from the free movement of services and establishment rules. The issue in the case was whether the entire legal profession came within the official authority exception. The ECJ pointed out that professional activities involving contacts, even regular and organic, with the courts, including even compulsory cooperation in their functioning did not necessarily amount to the exercise of official authority: many activities by lawyers did not involve official authority.[46]

In *Commission v Portugal*, technical inspection of vehicles resulting in certification of roadworthiness was not considered to amount to official authority.[47] Portugal imposed certain requirements on the private undertakings carrying out the certification, and it was these requirements (including limitations on share capital and company objects) that were found to be contrary to free movement.

12.6.3 LEGITIMATE REGULATION BY MEMBER STATES OF SERVICES/ESTABLISHMENT: THE CASE LAW EXCEPTIONS

As with workers, the ECJ has developed its own 'miscellaneous' category of exception or derogation whereby a national rule that restricts free movement of services/establishment may be justified, even though it does not come within one of the treaty exceptions above, *if* the ECJ believes the national rule in question pursues an objective that is in some way consistent with the treaty. The expression used in this context is 'overriding (or imperative) reasons of the general interest'. A reasonably full list is contained in paragraph 40 of the preamble of Directive 2006/123.

KEY LEARNING POINT

OVERRIDING OR IMPERATIVE REASONS OF THE GENERAL INTEREST
The case law exceptions to free movement of services and establishment are called overriding or imperative reasons of the general interest (objective justification is the term for free movement of workers and mandatory requirements is the equivalent term for free movement of goods). Only *indirectly*

---

45 Case 2/74 *Reyners v Belgium* [1974] 2 CMLR 305.
46 Ibid para 51.
47 Case 438/08 *Commission v Italy* [2009] ECR I–10219.

> *discriminatory measures* or *non-discriminatory obstacles* can be justified in this
> way – direct discrimination cannot be (direct discrimination can only be justified
> under one of the four treaty-based derogations).

The leading case is *Gebhard*, referred to above, where the ECJ set out the following
test – *if* a Member State's law *does* 'restrict', 'impede', 'hinder' or make 'less attractive'
cross-border activities and one of the four treaty-based exceptions/derogations is not
applicable, the ECJ will only consider the national rule to be justified if:

> [such] national measures . . . can be justified only if they fulfil four conditions:
>
> (1) they must be applied in a non-discriminatory manner [i.e. it must not involve
>   *direct* discrimination];
> (2) they must be justified by overriding reasons based on the general interest;
> (3) they must be suitable for securing the attainment of the objective which they
>   pursue; and
> (4) they must not go beyond what is necessary in order to attain that objective.
>
> (Gebhard, paragraph 36)

These conditions can now be looked at individually in more detail.

12.6.3.1 NON-DISCRIMINATORY MANNER

If a measure is *directly* discriminatory it is, of course, illegal, unless it can be justified
under one of the treaty derogations.

12.6.3.2 OVERRIDING REASON BASED ON THE GENERAL INTEREST

The 'overriding reasons based on the general interest' are an open-ended list the Court
is recognising reasons on a case-by-case basis. The overriding reasons include the
three treaty reasons of public policy, public security, public health (remember these are
interpreted restrictively for the purpose of the Treaty derogations), plus a range of other
public policy objectives.

12.6.3.3 SUITABILITY AND PROPORTIONALITY

Even if the national measure pursues a valid aim, the court (ultimately the national court) has
to judge whether this particular way of approaching the problem is suitable and proportionate.

The following case law can illustrate the courts doing such 'balancing acts'.

Säger v Dennemeyer, discussed already above, concerned a German law restricting who
could provide the service of renewing patents.[48] Dennemeyer & Co was a UK specialist
in patent renewal services, which consisted of monitoring patents by means of a
computerised system, advising the holders of those patents when the fees for renewing
the patents become due, and paying those fees on their behalf when they returned to
Dennemeyer the 'fees reminder' and asked Dennemeyer to pay the amounts indicated.

---

48 Case C–76/90 *Säger v Dennemeyer* [1993] 3 CMLR 639.

The ECJ held that, while it was legitimate to restrict the freedom to provide such a service in order to protect users of it against the harm which they could suffer as a result of legal advice given to them by persons who did not possess the necessary professional or personal qualifications, the service provided here was relatively straightforward and a national rule requiring a specific professional qualification in order to carry out this was disproportionate to the need to protect consumers from bad advice.

In *Alpine Investments BV*, also discussed above, Dutch legislation prohibited cold calling, whether the customers were in the Netherlands or in another Member State.[49] The ECJ held that this was a restriction on the cross-border offer of services, but that it could be justified to protect investor confidence in national financial markets.

MacQuen concerned a Belgian subsidiary of a UK company, which set up an optician's business in Belgium.[50] Belgian law stated that only qualified ophthalmologists could conduct eye tests. The company was charged with allowing non-qualified staff to do such tests (which would have been perfectly legal in the UK). The ECJ held that this national rule could be justified on the basis of a concern to maintain public health.

Mazzoleni involved a French security company that employed 13 workers as security officers at a shopping mall in Belgium.[51] The company paid them BFr 238 per hour (the equivalent of the French minimum wage), but the Belgian minimum legal hourly rate was BFr 357 per hour.

The question put to the ECJ on this point was: was there a breach of free movement principles where a Member State, for overriding reasons relating to the public interest, required any undertaking from another Member State employing persons, even temporarily, on the territory of the first state to comply with its legislation or national collective labour agreements relating to minimum wages, where that interest is already protected by the rules of the state in which the service provider was established/ originated and workers there were already in a comparable or similar position on the basis not solely of the legislation relating to minimum wages but of the overall position (impact of taxation, welfare protection in relation to illness, including under the obligatory supplementary insurance which applies in France, and to industrial accidents, widowhood, unemployment, retirement and death)?

The ECJ held that the host Member State could impose such a requirement, in order to protect workers, but that it might, however, prove to be disproportionate where the workers involved are employees of an undertaking established in a frontier region who are required to carry out, on a part-time basis and for brief periods, a part of their work in the territory of a Member State other than that in which the undertaking

---

49 In Case C–384/93 *Alpine Investments BV v Minister van Financien* [1995] ECR I–1141.
50 Case C–108/96 *MacQuen* [2001] ECR I–837.
51 Case C–165/98 *Mazzoleni* [2003] 2 CMLR 10.

is established/originates. In other words, the closer to services and the further from establishment, the harder it is to justify restrictions.

EXPLAINING THE LAW

THE *VIKING* AND *LAVAL* CASES AND THE RIGHT TO STRIKE

The decisions in *Viking* and *Laval*[52] provided the opportunity for the ECJ to clarify the status of human rights relative to the free movement principles. The judgments stand in contrast to the deferential approach to national human rights protection in free movement of goods cases such as *Omega* and *Schmidberger* (see Chapter 10). The cases concerned the relationship between free movement and the right to strike as protected in national laws. Despite the specific exclusion of the rights to strike from the social competence of the Union by then Article 137(5) ECT (now Article 153(5) TFEU), the ECJ held that national rules permitting strikes where such strikes has the effect of being an inhibition to the posting of workers from one Member State to another were contrary to Union law on free movement of services and establishment.[53] In *Viking*, the ECJ held that collective action initiated by a trade union or a group of trade unions against an undertaking in order to induce that undertaking to enter into a collective agreement, the terms of which were liable to deter it from exercising freedom of establishment, fell within (now) Article 49 TFEU.[54]

This could be considered as simply a limitation on the right to strike, and as such unremarkable given that few rights are absolute.[55] The ECJ held that the restriction on the freedom of establishment could be justified as an overriding interest to protect workers, but only if it was necessary and proportionate to this end (and the ECJ identified that this would not be the case where jobs or conditions of employment were not jeopardised or seriously under threat[56]). The ECJ went further in *Laval* and held that strikes to try to force a provider of services

---

52 Case C–438/05 *The International Transport Workers' Federation and The Finnish Seamen's Union v Viking Line ABP and OÜ Viking Line Eesti* [2007] ECR I–10779; Case C–341/05 *Laval un Partneri Ltd v Svenska Byggnadsarbetareföbundet* [2007] ECR I–11767.

53 Case C–438/05 *Viking* ibid paras 39–40; Case C–341/05 *Laval* ibid paras 87–88. There was no general discussion of human rights in either judgment, although various sources were referred to on the right to strike, which was described as a fundamental right (*Viking* ibid paras 43–44; *Laval* ibid paras 90–91). Article 11 ECHR provides for a right to join a trade union for the protection of a person's interests. Article 28 of the EU Charter of Fundamental Rights explicitly protects the right to strike. See also A Hinarejos 'Laval and *Viking*: the right to collective action versus EU fundamental freedoms' (2008) 8(4) *Human Rights Law Review* 714–29 at 728, noting that the judgments come close to establishing a hierarchy where the economic fundamental freedoms are placed higher than the right to collective action.

54 Case C–438/05 *Viking* [2007] ECR I–10779 paras 32–37.

55 See N Reich 'Free movement v social rights in an enlarged Union: the *Laval* and *Viking* cases before the ECJ' (2008) 9(2) *German Law Journal* 125–61 at 155.

56 Case C–438/05 *Viking* [2007] ECR I–10779 para 81.

into agreeing minimum pay or more favourable conditions than provided for in EU law were contrary to Article 49 TFEU.[57] The Court considered that this could amount to direct discrimination in that it did not take into account collective agreements already applicable in the home Member State and could not be justified under the Article 46 TFEU derogations.[58]

Whilst the ECJ has created exceptions in its case law, these exceptions were necessary given the huge scope of the doctrine of non-discriminatory obstacles (as was the case with the *Dassonville* formula in free movement of goods). *Viking* and *Laval* show the importance the ECJ can insist applies to free movement over other concerns.

12.6.4 IMMORAL OR ILLEGAL SERVICES OR CONTRARY TO PUBLIC POLICY

The question arises if a particular service is legal in the service provider's home Member State, but is immoral or illegal in the host state (i.e. if it comes within one of the exceptions, public policy, where individual Member States may have different policies), can a citizen (i.e. a provider of services from another Member State) say that his treaty freedom is being denied him if he is prevented from providing that service in the host country?[59] Or is the host country entitled to enforce its views of the particular activity and stop him?

On the whole, if the activity is not obviously universally illegal, the ECJ tends to say that it is a commercial service, and the service provider should be permitted to provide it. However, the host Member State has the chance to justify its laws on the grounds of public policy, security or health, or 'overriding reasons in the general interest', i.e. under one of the other exceptions/derogations.

In *Jany v Staatssecretarie van Justitie*, the Dutch authorities refused a residence permit to the applicant, who worked as a window prostitute in Amsterdam.[60] The ECJ held the applicability of the public-policy derogation is subject, in the case of citizens from other Member States wishing to pursue the activity of prostitution within the territory of the host Member State, to the condition that that state has adopted effective measures to monitor and repress activities of that kind when they are also pursued by its own nationals. That condition was not met in the present case, in which window prostitution

---

57 Case C–341/05 *Laval* [2007] ECR I–11767 para 111.

58 Ibid 113–19.

59 A different situation is where all Member States prohibit an activity, in which case the activity will fall outside art 56 TFEU. See Case C–137/09 *Josemans v Burgemeester van Maastricht* [2010] ECR I–3019, concerning a Dutch decision to close a coffee shop selling narcotic substances.

60 Case C–268/99 *Jany v Staatssecretarie van Justitie* [2001] ECR I–8615.

and street prostitution are permitted in the Netherlands and are regulated there at communal level.

Schindler concerned whether the UK could use a general prohibition on lotteries to prevent individuals established in Germany from selling in the UK (by post) tickets for a German lottery.[61] The ECJ noted that, although there was no discrimination, the UK law was an obstacle to free movement.[62] However, the ECJ held that the treaty provisions relating to freedom to provide services do not preclude legislation such as the UK lotteries legislation, in view of the concerns of social policy and of the prevention of fraud that justify it.

The decision is noteworthy also because the ECJ did not clearly state what exception/ derogation the UK law against lotteries fell into (was it justified on grounds of public policy or public security, or did it come within the case law category of exception?). The ECJ seemed to treat it as coming under the latter, but was not very specific about this.[63]

SPUC v Grogan concerned a ban by Ireland on publication of information on the provision of abortion.[64] The issue to be decided was could an Irish Students' Union be prevented from advertising, without commercial motive, the availability of such a service in the UK? The ECJ held first that provision of abortion could be considered a service and then held that provision of information in this way (without cooperation with the provider of the abortion service in other Member States) was not an economic activity, and thus the issue did not fall within freedom of movement of services (so there was no need to address the issue of exception/derogation from freedom of movement of services).

12.7 MUTUAL RECOGNITION OF EDUCATIONAL QUALIFICATIONS

12.7.1 INTRODUCTION

A similar issue arises with both workers and services/establishment, but especially with the latter: to what extent must Member States accept and recognise qualifications obtained in another Member State? The problem can vary depending on the profession. For example, medical qualifications are much more easily transferred from one country to another compared to legal qualifications; medicine is essentially the same everywhere,

---

61 Case 275/92 *Schindler* [1994] ECR I–1039.

62 Ibid paras 43–44.

63 Ibid paras 57–62.

64 Case C–159/90 *SPUC v Grogan* [1991] 3 CMLR 849.

whereas the law is not. The general approach to apply in the area of free movement of services was set out in *Gebhard*:

> Member States must take account of the equivalence of diplomas and, if necessary, proceed to a comparison of the knowledge and qualifications required by their national rules and those of the person concerned.[65]

However, the Member States perceived that because of wide differences in education and training systems across Europe, to ensure that service providers moving from their home Member State to another Member State would command confidence as to their qualifications and skills, it was necessary to regulate in more detail exactly what is required of Member States in terms of recognising qualifications or training or experience acquired in another Member State.

KEY LEARNING POINT

MUTUAL RECOGNITION OF SERVICES/ESTABLISHMENT

Mutual recognition of educational qualifications arises more in the context of services establishment, where a citizen from another Member State holds him- or herself out to be competent to provide a service to consumers who may not be able to evaluate adequately the qualifications, and the issue is how this might be regulated.

12.7.2 GENERAL POINTS

Some general points should be borne in mind when addressing mutual recognition of educational qualifications:

– *The rules apply only to nationals of Member States*: just as Article 45 TFEU applies only to workers from a Member State, so also do Articles 49 and 56 TFEU.
– Generally, EU law recognises only *qualifications obtained in a Member State*, although in some circumstances qualifications obtained outside the EU can be taken into account.
– *There must be a linking factor with EU law*, in that the rules do not apply to purely 'internal' situations, i.e. there must be a cross-border element.
– *When approaching a problem situation*, prior to Directive 2005/36 coming into effect, it was best to work from the specific to the general, as follows:
  1. if a specific or 'sectoral' directive covered the problem area, then there was no need to go further; if that is not the case, then
  2. consider whether a 'general' directive (Directives 1989/48 and 1992/51) provided the answer; if not, then
  3. apply the case law based on the treaty rules for establishment or services.

---

65 Case C–55/94 *Gebhard* [1995] ECR I–4165 para 39.

12.7.3 'UNREGULATED PROFESSION' AND 'REGULATED PROFESSION' UNDER DIRECTIVE 2005/36

KEY LEARNING POINT

UNREGULATED PROFESSION

If the host state does not 'regulate' the profession, then an EU citizen can practise subject to the same conditions as the host state's nationals (so long as those conditions do not contravene any treaty principles, such as non-discrimination).

In this case, the principles in *Vlassopoulou* apply,[66] such that a Member State must examine the knowledge and qualifications already recognised or acquired by the applicant in another Member State, provide reasons for a refusal to grant recognition and, further, provide access to a judicial remedy. In *Vlassopoulou*, a Greek lawyer was not permitted to establish in Germany because of a lack of German qualifications.

The ECJ confirmed previous case law that it must be possible for a national of a Member State to obtain judicial review of the decision of another Member State to refuse to recognise a diploma and, further, that if a qualification from another Member State is not deemed to be equivalent to qualifications required in the host Member State, the host Member State must assess whether any knowledge or practical training the person may have acquired in the host Member State is sufficient to make up for what was lacking in the qualification.[67]

KEY LEARNING POINT

REGULATED PROFESSION

If the profession in question is a 'regulated profession' in the host Member State then Directive 2005/36 applies.[68] A 'regulated profession' relates to professional activity where national rules state that pursuit of such activity in a Member State is subject to the possession of a diploma or other certificate of qualifications (Directive 2005/36, Article 3(1)(a)).

If the profession is regulated in both the EU citizen's state of origin and the host Member State, and the EU citizen is qualified to carry on the profession in the home Member State, then the host Member State must in principle recognise the qualification or 'diploma' from his state of origin that entitles him to carry on the profession there according to five levels of qualification specified in Article 11. The Member State must accept a qualification that is equivalent to or one level below its own level of requirement:

- Level 1: attestation of competence
- Level 2: certificate

---

66 Case C–340/89 *Vlassopoulou v Ministerium für Justiz* [1991] ECR I–2357.
67 See also Case C–31/00 *Conseil National de l'Ordre des Architectes v Dreessen* [2002] ECR I–663.
68 OJ L 255 30.9.2005 p. 22.

- Level 3: diploma of 1 year of full-time post-secondary study or equivalent
- Level 4: diploma of 3–4 years of full-time post-secondary study or equivalent at a university or equivalent establishment
- Level 5: diploma of at least 4 years of full-time post-secondary study or equivalent at a university or equivalent establishment.

Article 13 further provides that where the profession is regulated in the host Member State only, the host Member State must give access to the profession to applicants who provide evidence of having pursued the profession for a period of at least two years full-time over the preceding ten years.

In either case, under Article 14(1) and (2), Member States may require an aptitude test or adaptation period of up to three years where:

- *short training applies*: if the diploma from X's Member State shows a length of professional education and training at least one year shorter than that which is required in the host state
- *substantially different training*: if the education and training evidenced by X's diploma 'differ[s] substantially' from that which is required in the host state.

However, except in the case of the legal profession, the EU citizen may choose either the aptitude test or the adaptation period (Article 14(3)).

A particular situation arises where a profession is recognised in one Member State, but not in another, as in *Deutsche Paracelsus Schulen für Naturheilverfahren GmbH v Gräbner*.[69] Austria allowed only doctors to diagnose or treat physical disorders and, in particular, banned the profession of Heilpraktiker (lay health practitioner), which was recognised in Germany. The issue to be determined was whether Austria could ban the practice of the profession in Austria and/or the advertising in Austria of training for that profession in Austria or in any other Member State?

The ECJ held that (now) Articles 49 and 56 TFEU did not preclude a Member State from prohibiting the exercise of the activity of a Heilpraktiker by persons other than those with a doctor's qualification or from likewise prohibiting the organisation in its territory of training in that activity by unauthorised institutions, provided that that prohibition was applied in such a way that it covers only training of a kind liable to create confusion in the minds of the public as to whether the profession of Heilpraktiker could lawfully be exercised in the territory of the Member State in which the training is to take place.

However, Article 56 TFEU precluded a Member State that prohibits in its territory the exercise of the profession of Heilpraktiker and training in the activity of a Heilpraktiker

---

69 Case C–294/00 *Deutsche Paracelsus Schulen für Naturheilverfahren GmbH v Gräbner* [2002] ECR I–6515.

from likewise prohibiting the advertising of such training offered in a different Member State, if that advertising stated where the training is to take place and mentions the fact that the profession of Heilpraktiker may not be exercised in the first Member State.

12.7.4 THE SPECIFIC PROBLEM OF NON-EU QUALIFICATIONS

Neither the EU Treaty nor secondary legislation give any rights to non-EU citizens. In the case of EU citizens, can they insist on recognition of qualifications obtained in a third country? The position is not entirely clear, but the ECJ came very close to saying that they can in *Hocsman v Ministre de l'Emploi et de la Solidarité*.[70] Hocsman was a French national, who had an Argentinian basic medical qualification. This qualification was accepted and recognised in Spain. He went on to undertake specialist medical training there and then moved to France. In France, he was refused permission to practise on the basis that there was no obligation to recognise his Argentinian diploma. The ECJ stated:

> It is for the . . . competent national authorities to assess in the light of all the evidence in the case . . . whether Hocsman's diploma is to be accepted as equivalent to the corresponding French diploma. In particular, it will have to be considered whether recognition in Spain of Hocsman's diploma from Argentina as equivalent to the Spanish university degree . . . was given on the basis of criteria comparable to those intended . . . to ensure that Member States may rely on the quality of the diplomas in medicine awarded by the other Member States.

> Where . . . a Community national applies for authorisation to practise a profession . . ., the [host] State . . . must take into consideration all the diplomas . . . of the person concerned and his relevant experience, by comparing the specialised knowledge and abilities certified by those diplomas and experience with the knowledge and qualifications required by the national rules.[71]

APPLYING THE LAW

ANSWERING PROBLEM QUESTIONS ON FREE MOVEMENT OF SERVICES AND ESTABLISHMENT

The same general framework for answering free movement of workers questions discussed in Chapter 10 can be applied to free movement of services. Thus, any problem situation can be divided into a sequence of stages:

1. What kind of national rule is in issue? Direct discrimination, indirect discrimination, non-discriminatory obstacle?
2. What kind of equal treatments rights have been prohibited?

---

70 Case C–238/98 *Hocsman v Ministre de l'Emploi et de la Solidarité* [2000] 3 CMLR 102.

71 Ibid paras 39–40.

3. What derogation/exception is applicable (under the TFEU and the Services Directive)? Public policy, public health, public security, official authority (Treaty); environmental protection service directives; imperatives of the general interest (case law)?

12.7.5 CONTINUING SECTORAL DIRECTIVES FOR LAWYERS

Although the EU has moved towards general principles and away from sectoral directives, specific provisions still apply to lawyers. Two main directives have been adopted:

- Directive 77/249/EEC[72] provides that lawyers from another Member State do not have to satisfy residency requirements, but that they may practise, under conditions of the host Member State (Article 4), or be required to be accompanied by lawyers qualified in the host Member State for the pursuit of activities relating to the representation of a client in legal proceedings (Article 5).
- Directive 98/5/EC[73] provides that any lawyer may practise in any other Member State under the title used in his or her home Member State (Article 4) and may give legal advice (Article 2), after registering with the professional body of the host Member State, but must comply with the rules of procedure applicable in the courts of the host Member State. This does not allow a lawyer from one Member State to claim to be a lawyer qualified to practise in another Member State. Member States are entitled to determine the actual equivalence before allowing lawyers from one Member State to hold themselves out as qualified to practise in the host Member State;[74] this is subject to Article 10, which sets a three year period of practice in the host Member State after which a lawyer can register as qualified in that Member State, while leaving the merits of the decision to national professional bodies.

12.8 CITIZENSHIP

It is important to remember that the same citizenship principles governing workers apply equally to service providers. In practical terms, this means analysing the citizenship

---

72 Council Directive 77/249/EEC to facilitate the effective exercise by lawyers of freedom to provide services OJ L 78 26.03.1977 p. 7.
73 Directive 98/5/EC to facilitate practice of the profession of lawyer on a permanent basis in a Member State other than that in which the qualification was obtained OJ L 77 14.03.1998 p. 36.
74 See Case C–313/01 *Morgenbesser v. Consiglioni dell'Ordine degli Avvocati di Genova* [2003] ECR I–13467.

provisions to see how they supplement the rights of those who exercise free movement, as discussed in Chapter 8.

APPLYING THE LAW

SAMPLE PROBLEM QUESTION AND ANSWER ON FREE MOVEMENT OF SERVICES AND ESTABLISHMENT

Holiday Home Construction and Marketing Ltd is a firm based in England that specialises in the construction of holiday home complexes. A substantial part of its work is carried out in other EU Member States. It has recently been especially active in Spain and Portugal, where it has entered into contracts with local building firms to provide expertise and labour in the construction of leisure facilities and in the marketing of completed holiday home complexes. However, it is active in a range of European countries. It sometimes hires native or fluent speakers of the language of the other EU Member States where it operates, or if it intends to work short term, engages local translators. However, most of the time it can rely on English alone, even in other EU Member States. It has hired a number of Spanish- and Portuguese-speaking staff to work in the marketing of its business offerings in Spain and Portugal.

Holiday Home Construction and Marketing Ltd has several departments within its business, each department specialising in an aspect of it. It has a legal department as well as an auctioneering department. In Spain, its own legal department carries out legal advice work. Whilst its lawyers were trained in the UK, it has hired a number whose first university degree was a combination of English law and Spanish studies, which included studying both Spanish law and the Spanish language. However, one of its business rivals based in Spain has made a complaint to the Spanish authorities that Holiday Home Construction Ltd is illegally providing legal advice to Spanish consumers, as none of the lawyers working for it are registered as lawyers in Spain. The Spanish authorities then investigate the tax affairs of Holiday Home Construction and Marketing Ltd and decide that it should be paying Spanish corporate tax.

In Portugal, Holiday Home Construction Ltd has difficulty entering into business arrangements with local firms and it has been told that its auctioneering department is not qualified to organise auctions in Portugal. Holiday Home Construction Ltd has opened an office in Madrid, which it uses to cater to both its Spanish and Portuguese business. In addition, the Portuguese authorities tell Holiday Home Construction Ltd that Portuguese law prohibits its use of telesales marketing in the holiday home sector in order to protect more vulnerable consumers such as retirees from manipulative sales techniques that have been employed in this sector in the past.

Advise Holiday Home Construction Ltd on the relevance of EU law to its business in Spain and Portugal.

Outline answer

(1) Answers should note freedom of movement of services/establishment (Articles 49 and 56–57 TFEU) and the distinction between services and establishment and its significance concerning regulation by the home Member State or the host Member State:

   – The distinction is elaborated in case law: *Reyners*, *Gebhard* and *Schnitzer*; some detail on these is needed to apply it to the facts of the problem, e.g. concerning the existence of an office and an intention to provide services in the long term (*Schnitzer*).

   – A good answer should also note the issue of a cross-border element, but this is not a major issue on the facts (*Van Binsbergen*), apart from the issue of sales calls from Madrid to Portugal (e.g. *Alpine Investments*).

(2) Answers should note the general scope of the rights enjoyed by service providers not to be discriminated against or face non-discriminatory obstacles, and their limitation by derogations (Articles 51–52 and 62 TFEU and case law).

(3) Next, answers should address possible derogations: on the facts of the problem, the prohibition in Portugal on sales calling is similar to *Alpine Investments* as justified non-discriminatory obstacle on grounds of overriding reasons of the public interest (also should refer to *Gebhard*).

(4) The last part of the question relates to mutual recognition of educational qualifications. Answers should discuss Directive 2005/36, noting the difference between regulated and unregulated professions and apply the relevant rules to (a) lawyers and (b) auctioneers.

(5) A comprehensive answer will note the possible relevance of EU citizenship, although it is not obviously applicable on the facts given.

12.9 CONCLUSION

Free movement of services and establishment is structured very similarly to free movement of goods, but the difference between short-term and long-term exercise of service provision is one important distinction. The distinction is still important; it signifies the degree of regulation the host Member State may impose. National regulation is applicable across establishment despite a radical proposal completely to remove host Member State regulation of establishment.

The ECJ has adopted the same expansionary approach to the interpretation of the scope of the treaty provisions: as well as direct and indirect discrimination, non-discretionary obstacles are prohibited. As in the other areas of free movements, the ECJ has compensated for this broad reading by developing an open-ended category of case law exceptions that may justify national rules otherwise prohibited as indirectly discriminatory or acts constituting an obstacles to market access. Quite a wide range of grounds have been recognised.

This area of the law is subject to ongoing development: the exact rules governing mutual recognition of educational qualifications have recently been reformed and are currently under consideration for further reform. The exact balance between home Member State regulations and host Member State regulation is a recurring one and reflects the ongoing tension in the EU between the goals of cooperation and integration and the continuing desire for a degree of autonomy at national level.

POINTS TO REVIEW

- The basic rights given to services providers in EU law are to exit the home Member State, enter the host Member State, residence in the host Member State, and be subject to equal treatment for the purpose of the provision of services.

- The difference between services and establishment is between short-term and long-term provision of services. Free movement of services is generally presumed to be subject to the law of the home Member State (subject to justified exceptions e.g. national criminal law), while establishment, being more long term, is expected to comply generally with the laws of the host Member State.

- As in other areas of free movement, the ECJ has determined that, as well as direct and indirect discrimination, non-discriminatory obstacles are contrary to the treaty. Correspondingly, it has developed case law decisions to justify direct discrimination and non-discriminatory obstacles going beyond the treaty and legislative derogations of public policy, public health, public security and public authority.

- The Services Directive, as finally adopted, was less ambitious than its initial draft proposed by the European Commission, but it standardises rules designed to maximise the effect for some services and establishment, confirming a legal presumption in favour of free movement.

- Mutual recognition of educational qualification has become more systematic with the adoption of Directive 2005/36.

CHAPTER GLOSSARY

Country of origin principle refers to a proposal in an early draft of the Services Directive that free movement of services should be governed entirely by the law and organs of the home Member State.

Derogations refers to exceptions permitted to national law from the free movement of services and of establishment.

Direct discrimination refers to explicit differentiation by national laws or practices between EU citizens or legal persons based on nationality.

Establishment refers to long-term provision of services between Member States.

Indirect discrimination refers to national laws or practices that do not explicitly differentiate between EU citizens or legal persons based on nationality.

Non-discriminatory obstacle refers to national rules or practices that make free movement of services more difficult, even though they do not involve either direct or indirect discrimination.

Official authority refers to a derogation from free movement of services and establishment permitted to Member States in connection with governmental jobs.

Overriding/imperative reasons of the general interest refer to the case law category of exception that the ECJ has developed that can justify indirect discrimination or non-discriminatory obstacles in free movement of services or establishment.

Services refer to the short-term provision of services between Member States.

Services Directive refers to Directive 2006/123, which is the most comprehensive attempt to date to provide a legislative framework for free movement of services and establishment.

TAKING THINGS FURTHER

M Andenas, R Henning-Roth (eds) *Services and Free Movement in EU Law* (Oxford University Press 2003) Although now a decade old, this book provides one of the most comprehensive examinations of free movement of services and of establishment.

J Cremers 'Free movement of services and equal treatment of workers: the case of construction' (2006) 12(2) *European Review of Labour and Research* 167–81 This article looks at the issue of posting workers (which comes under services and establishment) in a broad context, examining the secondary legislation on the latter and relating it to the 'country of origin' principle.

S de la Rosa 'The directive on cross-border healthcare or the art of codifying complex case law' (2012) 49(1) *Common Market Law Review* 15–46 This article looks at the secondary legislation on healthcare as a type of service provision and/or establishment, exploring background case law.

C Joerges, F Rödl, 'Informal politics, formalised law and the "social deficit" of European integration: reflections after the judgments of the ECJ in *Viking* and *Laval*' (2009) 15(1) *European Law Journal* 1–19 This article examines the value choices the ECJ made in the judgments in the *Laval* and *Viking* cases concerning the right to strike. It argues that these judgments are not just technical decisions, but that they reveal important policy and political preferences.

13

CHAPTER 13
FREE MOVEMENT OF CAPITAL AND PAYMENTS

This chapter examines the final aspect of free movement in the EU, namely free movement of capital and of payments. This topic is generally less widely studied on university courses, but it is an important practical element of the free movement framework. Quite often, free movement of capital and payments operates in conjunction with the exercise of one of the other areas of free movement, in that capital or payments are made across a border because of the exercise of free movement of goods, workers or services/establishment, but of course it also arises independently as an aspect of commerce in the EU generally. For example, direct investment is significantly affected by free movement of capital. Free movement of capital and payments connects with broader issues of trade and economic governance. For example, banks within the EU may freely move credit to other Member States, and the easy availability of credit was one of the causes of the economic crisis in the Eurozone (we will look at this issue in Chapter 18 on Economic and Monetary Union). While the distinction between capital and payments was of significance in the past because only free movement of payments had direct effect, both now have direct effect.

AS YOU READ . . .

The key questions that will be answered in this chapter are as follows:

— What are the essential measures adopted to facilitate free movement of capital and payments?

— Why was free movement of capital and payments slower to develop in EU law compared to the other freedoms? What were the stages of this development?

— Why is it useful to distinguish between capital and payments, although it has become less significant over time?

- – What different kinds of national measures or rules are contrary to free movement of capital and payments? What are the derogations to free movement of capital and payments?

- – What particular rules apply to capital and payments compared to the other free movement principles?

- – How does freedom of movement of capital and payments interact with the other free movement principles?

13.1 INTRODUCTION

The basic premise of free movement of capital and payments is that money can be transferred without restriction from one Member State to another in the EU. The money so transferred may be used for several purposes: to pay for goods or services, or to invest in some commercial or other activity that requires finance to be sustained. Article 26(2) TFEU makes clear the link between all four free movement principles: 'The internal market shall comprise an area without internal frontiers in which the free movement of goods, persons, services and capital is ensured in accordance with the provisions of the Treaties'.

The connection between free movement of capital and free movement of services is also made clear in Article 58(2) TFEU, which states: 'The liberalisation of banking and insurance services connected with movements of capital shall be effected in step with the liberalisation of movement of capital'.

ANALYSING THE LAW

THE ECONOMIC CONTEXT OF FREE MOVEMENT OF CAPITAL AND PAYMENTS

The movement of capital and payments connects with broader issues of economic policy. For example, significant amounts of investment in a country can stimulate the growth of industry and entrepreneurship. It can also be important for the development of industrial expertise: foreign investors often bring superior technical expertise from which national industry can learn or be able to complement its own capacities. For this reason, foreign investment is often politicised. For example, in the recent political stand-off between some Western countries and Russia over the Russian annexation of Crimea, these Western countries have imposed sanctions on Russia, including foreign investment, with the aim of limiting Russian economic development.

Freedom of movement of capital and payments can also make credit more easily available (whether credit is actually more available will further depend on a country's rules on the availability of credit by banks[1]). The easy availability of credit can reduce interest rates, and low interest rates traditionally encourage investment in an economy (higher rates are needed less when credit is plentiful). Further, the easy availability of credit and finance can push up the demand for consumer goods, which can fuel imports and affect a country's balance of payments. In ways such as this, free movement of capital has a substantial impact on countries' overall economies.

The broad economic implications of free movement of capital explains why in the first period of integration with European Coal and Steel Community (ECSC), European Atomic Energy Community Treaty and the European Economic Community (EEC), free movement of capital was expressed as an aspiration, but was not legally enforced. Broader integration of the common market (now internal market) was needed before full liberalisation could be adopted. As noted by the ECJ in *Casati*, the original treaty provisions on capital were drafted in less 'imperative' terms than the other free movement principles.[2]

Reflecting the language of the treaty (which is not necessarily typical of the ECJ), the Court went on to hold that the requirements of the common market were primarily for the Council (of Ministers). On the facts, the ECJ held that the Council (of Ministers) had not incorrectly exercised its discretion in deciding that it was unnecessary to liberalise the exportation of banknotes at that stage of development of the common market.

Article 67(1) EEC Treaty stated that the Member States: 'shall progressively abolish between themselves all restrictions on the movement of capital . . . and any discrimination based on the nationality or on the place of residence of the parties or on the place where such capital is invested', but only 'to the extent necessary to ensure the proper functioning of the common market (now internal market)'.

The pace at which restrictions were progressively abolished was thus left to secondary legislation, based on Article (then) 69 EEC Treaty, although this did provide for qualified

....

1   Rules governing how banks may lend money are referred to as 'prudential supervision'. We will look at this further below in Chapter 18 on Economic and Monetary Union.
2   Case 203/80 *Casati* [1981] ECR 2595 para 19 and see C Barnard *The Substantive Law of the EU: The Four Freedoms* (4th edn Oxford University Press 2013) 580.

majority voting. This was achieved largely by secondary legislation in the late 1980s, which was in turn later reflected in a treaty amendment at the Treaty of Maastricht in 1992, expressing free movement of capital in more binding legal terms.[3] The following table summarises the development of legislation:

1960	Divided capital movements into four lists, with different degrees of liberalisation: List A – all foreign exchange transactions were to be authorised (direct investments in an undertaking in another MS and in real estate other than purely financial investments, certain personal capital movements, short and medium-term commercial credits, death duties, damages, transfers in performance of insurance contracts, authors' royalties, and transfers of moneys required for the provision of services) List B – general permissions had to be given (mainly concerned operations in securities[4]) List C – general permission had to be given, but MSs could introduce restrictions for economic objectives List D – did not have to be liberalised (funds on current or deposit accounts, and the physical import and export of financial assets and personal loans)	First Council Directive for the implementation of Article 67 of the EEC Treaty[5]
1963	Made some amendments to the First Directive, retained the same framework as it	Second Council Directive 63//21[6]
1986	– Merged Lists B into List A and added some new elements – List C became List B (could be subject to restrictions for economic objectives) – List C could still be subject to restrictions	Directive 86/566[7]

3 For a fuller discussion of the original treaty provisions on free movement of capital see J Usher 'The evolution of the free movement of capital' (2007) 31 *Fordham Journal of International Law* 1533–70 at 1533 ff.
4 A security is an interest or share in a publicly-traded corporation (i.e. stock), a credit owed by a governmental body or a corporation (i.e. a bond) or a right to ownership as in the form of an option.
5 OJ 43 12.7.1960 p. 921.
6 OJ 9 22.1.1963 p. 62.
7 OJ L 332 26.11.1986 p. 22

1990	Achieves more or less full liberalisation of movements of capital and payments, Article 1(1) providing that MSs shall abolish restrictions on movements of capital taking place between persons resident in MSs, while the previous List system was abolished in favour of general liberalisation	Council Directive 88/361, which came into force in 1990[8]
1992	The Treaty of Maastricht redrafts the free movement of capital and payments provisions to express them in legally binding terms (this is the only free movement principle for which the Treaty provisions have been amended)	Article 73a-h EC Treaty
1994	Following up on the Treaty amendment, the ECJ finds that free movement of capital and payments can be directly effective (in the context of vertical direct effect)	Case C-163, 165, and 250/94, *Criminal proceedings against Lucas Emilio Sanz de Lera, Raimundo Daz Jimnez and Figen Kapanoglu*[9]

RIGHTS – MORE LIMITED CONTEXT COMPARED TO OTHER FREE MOVEMENT PRINCIPLES

1. Travel and residence rights? Not applicable
2. Right to move capital from one MS to another
3. Right to make a payment for service or goods purchased in another MS

ARTICLE 63 TFEU

1. Within the framework of the provisions set out in this Chapter, all restrictions on the movement of capital between Member States and between Member States and third countries shall be prohibited.

2. Within the framework of the provisions set out in this Chapter, all restrictions on payments between Member States and between Member States and third countries shall be prohibited.

---

8 OJ L 178 08.07.1988 p. 5.
9 [1995] ECR I–4821.

THE AMENDED TREATY PROVISIONS ON FREE MOVEMENT OF CAPITAL AND THEIR DIRECT EFFECT

Article 63 TFEU was first adopted in the Treaty of Maastricht as Article 56 European Community Treaty (ECT), and it is clearly drafted in more binding terms than the original Treaty provisions. Originally, capital was dealt with in Article 67 EEC Treaty and subsequent articles, payments were dealt with in Article 106 EEC Treaty. Payments were now included by the Treaty of Maastricht within Article 56 ECT. Article 56 in its entirety (now Article 63 TFEU) was held to have direct effect in *Sanz de Lera*.[10] Previously, only the provisions on payments were found to be directly effective, in *Luisi and Carbone*; although the ECJ did not really discuss the point, it adjudicated on that assumption.[11]

In *Sanz de Lera*, the ECJ noted that, although Member States had discretion to decide how national law could be made compatible with these provisions, direct effect was still possible because national regulation was subject to judicial review. The ECJ did not specify that (then) Article 56 could be horizontally directly effective, but commentators have suggested that it could be, since individuals, such as financial institutions, could inhibit free movement of capital.[12]

To date, there has not been any case law establishing *horizontal direct effect* for free movement of capital and payments, but commentators suggest that this should be applicable because, for example, private financial institutions can restrict free movement of capital and payments.[13]

One of the striking features of Article 63 compared with the other areas of free movement is the inclusion of third countries. Article 63 TFEU provides for *the same* abolition of restriction that is to apply between Member States to the relationship between the Member States and third countries.

In contrast, the treaty provides for a Common Customs Union (CCU) applicable to goods, which means that all Member States impose the same level of customs duty to imported goods from third countries, instead of abolishing customs duties altogether. The motivation for the liberal approach in Article 263 TFEU towards third countries

---

10 Joined Cases C–163, C–165 & C–250/94 *Sanz de Lera* [1995] ECR I–4830.
11 The Belgian Government in its submissions did refer to the point, proposing that (then) art 106 EEC Treaty was directly effective.
12 See e.g. J Usher *The Law of Money and Financial Services in the European Community* (Oxford University Press 1994) 14–16.
13 Ibid 27; P Craig, G de Búrca *EU Law: Texts, Cases, and Materials* (5th edn Oxford University Press 2011) 694–95.

may have been to facilitate trade in the Euro currency, reassuring international money markets about ease of trading in the currency.[14]

However, Article 64 TFEU provides for significant exceptions to the abolition of restrictions on capital and payments with third countries.

EXPLAINING THE LAW

LEGISLATION ON FREE MOVEMENT OF CAPITAL AND PAYMENTS CONCERNING THIRD COUNTRIES

First, Article 64(1) TFEU exempts restrictions that existed prior to 1994 involving direct investment (including in real estate), establishment, the provision of financial services or the admission of securities to capital markets.[15] Article 64(2) TFEU provides for the ordinary legislative method to apply to measures achieving the greatest degree possible of free movement of capital between Member States and third countries. This is framed in aspirational terms, just as the original free movement of capital and payments provisions were. Furthermore, Article 64(3) TFEU provides that a special legislative procedure may apply to 'steps backwards' in the achievement of this goal of liberalisation of the movement of capital to or from third countries. Article 63(3) TFEU provides that the special legislative procedure is to involve unanimity in the Council (of Ministers) after consultation with the European Parliament. This is one of the few provisions of the treaties that provides for a retreat from 'ever-closer integration', should the Member States so decide.[16] This again reflects that movement of capital and payments is interlinked with a Member State's overall economy, and flexibility may be needed to deal with new economic conditions or problems.

The situation with sanctions against Russia taken in 2014 by EU Member States is an example of political events affecting free movement of capital and payments with third countries.[17]

....

14 Usher (n 3) 1543.

15 Article 64(1) further provides that in respect of restrictions existing under national law in Bulgaria, Estonia and Hungary, the relevant date shall be 31 December 1999. The original treaty provisions also provided for significant exceptions concerning third countries. This is rather similar to how free movement of goods was first developed under what are now arts 34 and 35 TFEU, when the initial concern was to prohibit new restrictions, rather than to prohibit all existing restrictions.

16 See also Protocol on Transitional Provisions provides for transitional period, art 10(4)–(5) of which gives the UK the possibility to opt-out of pre-existing third pillar (i.e. criminal justice) measures.

17 Statement of President of the European Council, EUCO 158/14 PRESSE 436 PR PCE 140 Brussels (29 July 2014). The legal basis for the sanctions, adopted within the framework of the Common Foreign and Security Policy, lies in the international law of countermeasures and self-help by Member States.

KEY CASE *THE DIFFERENCE BETWEEN CAPITAL AND PAYMENTS IN* LUISI AND CARBONE

The terms 'capital' and 'payment' are not defined in the treaties. The terms tend to be used to describe slightly different situations: capital refers to the movement of money across borders for the purposes of investment, whereas payment refers to consideration for a good or service. In the practice of the EU institutions, however, there is overlap between current payments under (ex) Article 106 ECT (concerning payments made by importers connected with the other free movement principles), and the definition of capital in the 1988 Directive. The significance of the overlap and distinction in the past was that Article 106 had been held to be directly effective,[18] whereas the provision on capital had not been.

This is illustrated by *Luisi and Carbone*, which concerned two Italian residents who had acquired more than the permitted amount of foreign currency, claiming it was to pay for various services in France and Germany. There was at that point no requirement to liberalise the physical transfer of banknotes as part of free movement of capital, but Article 106 did require payments for other services to be permitted. The ECJ explained the difference between capital and payments noted above: payments related to consideration for a good or service; capital related to investment.

On the facts in the case, this meant the transfer of banknotes did not amount to a movement of capital; rather, it was a payment subject to the directly effective Article 106. However, the secondary legislation examined above tended to include some items of consideration for goods or services as capital. This can matter even though the rules on both capital and payments are now directly effective, because of the narrow approach to payments of the ECJ: payments only applied to the purchaser of a good or service (i.e. the importer, see further below). A broad view of capital can compensate for this. Further, in some cases, other free movement principles can apply when free movement of payments does not.[19] The ECJ explained that, depending on the context, transfer of money could be either capital or payment:

> 21. The general scheme of the Treaty shows, and a comparison between [ex] Articles 67 and 106 confirms, that current payments are transfers of foreign exchange which constitute the consideration within the context of an underlying transaction, whilst movements of capital are financial operations essentially concerned with the investment of the funds in question rather than remuneration

---

18 Joined Cases 286/82 & 26/83 *Luisi and Carbone v Ministero del Tesoro* [1984] ECR 377.

19 Usher suggested a for-profit life assurance policy as an example of a transaction that is hard to classify as either payment or capital, as there are elements of both, in that some will be used for investment (capital) and some for expenses (payments): Usher (n 3) 1541.

for a service. For that reason movements of capital may themselves give rise to current payments, as is implied by [ex] Articles 67(2) and 106(1).

22. The physical transfer of bank notes may not therefore be classified as a movement of capital where the transfer in question corresponds to an obligation to pay arising from a transaction involving the movement of goods or services.

23. Consequently, payments in connection with tourism or travel for the purposes of business, education or medical treatment cannot be classified as movements of capital, even where they are effected by means of the physical transfer of bank notes.[20]

Usher listed the following as coming within the notion of capital in the 1988 Directive: direct investments, investments in real estate,[21] operations in securities, operations in units of collective investment undertakings, operations in current and deposit accounts with financial institutions, credits related to commercial transactions or to the provision of services in which a resident is participating,[22] financial loans and credits (including mortgages borrowed from a bank in another Member State[23]), sureties, other guarantees and rights of pledge, transfers in performance of insurance contracts, personal capital movements, physical import and export of financial assets and 'other capital movements'.[24] Overall, the approach of the ECJ is broad. The purpose of investment does not matter, for example, investment in real estate when the purpose is to establish a holiday home comes within free movement of capital.[25]

MAKING CONNECTIONS
+ + + + + + + + + + + + + + + + +

OVERLAP OF CAPITAL AND PAYMENTS WITH (1) SERVICES AND ESTABLISHMENT AND (2) GOODS

Although any difference of definition of capital and of payments no longer is of much practical significance because both treaty provisions are now directly effective, the definition of capital adopted in light of the nomenclature or

---

20 Joined Cases 286/82 & 26/83 *Luisi and Carbone v Ministero del Tesoro* [1984] ECR 377 para 21.
21 An example is Case C–386/04 *Centro di Musicologia Walter Stauffer v Finanzamt München für Körperschaften* [2006] ECR I–8203, which concerned investment in real estate where an Italian charitable foundation bought commercial premises in Munich. Note this example could also be considered an aspect of freedom of establishment if the premises were used for business purposes by the owner to provide services.
22 To clarify, investments other than those intended to confer management and control are included (those intended to confer management and control may fall under freedom of establishment): see G W Ringe 'Company law and the free movement of capital' (2010) 69(2) *Cambridge Law Journal* 378–409 (2010) 381.
23 Case C–484/93 *Svensson and Gustavsson v Ministre du Logement* [1995] ECR I–3955. See Usher (n 3) 1544.
24 Usher (n 3) 1538.
25 Case C–512/03 *Blanckaert v Inspecteur van de Belastingdienst/Particulieren/Ondernem- ingen buitenland te Heerlen* [2005] ECR I–7685 50. ·

terminology in the secondary legislation[26] can result in overlap between free movement of capital and free movement of services and of establishment. For example, 'direct investments' includes 'establishment and extension of branches or new undertakings belonging solely to the person providing the capital', which clearly falls under freedom of establishment. Similarly, the operation of current and deposit accounts, and loans, credits and sureties involve providing services.[27]

The close connection is illustrated in *Scheunemann*.[28] This concerned German law on inheritance tax, which granted a tax reduction on inheritance tax payable on assets in a company if the company was registered and based in the EU. Under now repealed EU secondary legislation, inheritance was defined as a capital movement. The principal issue in the case was whether this fell to be dealt with under free movement of capital or free movement of services. The Court of Justice held that it fell under services/establishment, since that holding enables the shareholder to exert a definite influence over the decisions of that company and to determine its activities, and thus free movement of capital was not applicable.

Restrictions on payment for goods can be seen as a restriction on the free movement of those goods. *Commission v Italy* is an example, where Italian rules designed to prevent currency speculation that provided that advance payments for exports had to be accompanied by an interest-free guarantee or security payment. The ECJ found that this was a measure equivalent to a quantitative restriction on goods.[29]

These overlaps are significant in that they allow free movement of services or free movement of goods principles to be applied where free movement of capital and payments is not applicable owing to the (uncharacteristically) narrow approach of the ECJ to interpreting the scope of payments.[30] In *Criminal proceedings against Lambert*, the ECJ held that free movement of capital and payments was not relevant to the way an exporter received payment; it was concerned only to

---

26 The ECJ did not change its approach to terminology following the treaty amendment at Maastricht: see Case C–222/97 *Trummer v Meyer* [1999] ECR I–1661 para 21.

27 Usher (n 3) 1539.

28 Case C–31/11 *Scheunemann v Bremerhaven* [2012] 3 CMLR 51 paras 31–35.

29 Case 95/81 *Commission v Italy* [1982] ECR 2187.

30 Sometimes, the ECJ has been willing to apply free movement principles simultaneously: see e.g. Case C–279/00 *Commission v Italy* [2002] ECR I–1425 concerning free movements of services and of capital (the facts concerned an Italian requirement that undertakings engaged in the provision of temporary labour established in other Member States had to lodge a guarantee with a credit institution having its registered office or a branch office in Italy). For further discussion and authority see Usher (n 3) 1544–49. However, if one freedom is clearly of secondary significance, the ECJ will apply the other freedom: see ibid 1551.

ensure that the importer was able to make the payment.[31] This meant restrictions on the exporter receiving a payment might not be covered. On the facts of *Lambert*, a farmer in Luxembourg was not allowed under Luxembourg law to receive payment for exports in the form of cash and, instead, he could only be paid by a bank transfer. This was not contrary to free movement of payments. Barnard notes that the case law overall is not very clear, with earlier cases preferring to apply goods or services and later cases trying to distinguish the primary purpose of a transaction.[32]

13.2 THE RANGE OF NATIONAL MEASURES PROHIBITED

ANALYSING THE LAW

NON-DISCRIMINATORY OBSTACLES ARE NOT PROHIBITED?

We have seen how in the areas of free movement of goods, workers and services/ establishment, the ECJ has held that not just national measures that are directly or indirectly discriminatory are prohibited: any national measure or practice that constitutes a restriction on free movement is also prohibited (with the exception of selling arrangements etc. in the context of goods). This is not the approach of the Court concerning free movement of capital and payments. In *Kerckhaert v Belgische Staat*,[33] for example, the ECJ found that a refusal by Belgium to grant a tax credit to a Belgian taxpayer for tax paid in France on a dividend on shares in a French company was not contrary to freedom of movement of capital if no tax credits would have been given for dividends paid by a Belgian company.

However, other cases have clearly extended the treaty principle to non-discriminatory obstacles, e.g. *Commission v Portugal*,[34] *Commission v Italy*,[35] and (especially) *Commission v UK*.[36] Peers noted the lack of clarity in ECJ case law on this point. The Court tends to use the expression 'liable to dissuade' instead of 'non-discriminatory obstacle' (language reminiscent of the 'market access'

---

31 Case 308/86 *Criminal proceedings against Lambert* [1988] ECR 4369.

32 Barnard (n 2) 580–85 and see further case law references therein. See also Ringe (n 22) 382.

33 Case C–513/04 *Kerckhaert v Belgische Staat* [2006] ECR I–10967 para 117.

34 Case 367/98 *Commission v Portugal* [2002] ECR I–4371 paras 44–45.

35 Case 174/04 *Commission v Italy* [2005] ECR I–4933 para 12.

36 Case C–98/01 *Commission v United Kingdom* [2003] ECR I–4641, one of the so-called golden shares cases. It concerned UK rules restricting ownership in the British Airport Authority. The Court of Justice stated, at para 43, that then art 56 ECT went beyond prohibiting discriminatory measures.

terminology that the Court now tends to use in the context of free movement of goods). However, the Court has not adopted as wide a formula as it did in *Dassonville* concerning goods: the more substantial the dissuasive effect of a national measure, the more likely it is to be recognised as contrary to Article 63, but how substantial remains unclear.[37]

EXPLAINING THE LAW

WHAT KINDS OF NATIONAL PRACTICES THE ECJ HAS FOUND TO BE PROHIBITED OR PERMITTED

Taking the terms capital and payment at face value, almost any commercial transaction involving the exchange or transfer of money is within their scope. This is reflected in the wide range of situations that the ECJ has found to fall within free movement of capital and payments:

- prohibition on the granting of a mortgage in a foreign currency (e.g. Case C–376/03, *D v Inspecteur van de Belastingdienst/Particulieren/ Ondernerningen/buitenland te Heerlen* [2005] ECR I–5821)
- limitations on the acquisition of property, such as administrative authorisation (as opposed to administrative formalities, which will nearly always be necessary concerning the purchase of land) (e.g. Case C–213/04 *Burtscher v Stauderer* [2005] ECR I–10309)
- restrictions on national citizens obtaining loans or investing in another Member State (e.g. Case C–513/03 *Heirs of van Hiltern-van der Heijden* [2006] ECR I–1957, para 44)
- discriminatory rules in direct taxation (e.g. Case C–346/04 *Conjin v Finanzamt Hamburg-Nord* [2006] ECR I–6137 paras 14–15), which would also be contrary to free movement of workers and Article 7(2) of Regulation 492/2011, but not double taxation, which is still a matter for national competence (e.g. Case C–446/03 *Marks & Spencer plc. v Halsey (Her Majesty's Inspector of Taxes)* [2005] ECR I–10837)
- non-discriminatory obstacles? Maybe, especially the more substantial the impact (Case C–98/01 *Commission v United Kingdom* [2003] ECR I–4641) (see previous textbox).

---

37 S Peers 'Free movement of capital: learning lessons or slipping on spilt milk?' in C Barnard, J Scott *The Law of the Single European Market: Unpacking the Premises* (Hart Publishing 2002) 340–46.

13.3 DEROGATIONS TO THE FREE MOVEMENT OF CAPITAL AND PAYMENTS

13.3.1 INTRODUCTION

KEY LEARNING POINT

SUMMARY OF DEROGATIONS FROM THE FREE MOVEMENT OF CAPITAL AND PAYMENTS IN ARTICLE 65 TFEU

Article 65 TFEU sets out the derogations to free movement of capital and payments. These can be summarised as follows, i.e. national rules governing the following are not incompatible with Article 63 TFEU:

1. national tax laws distinguishing between people on their basis of residence or where income is invested (remember that taxation generally is still within national competences)
2. prudential supervision (this is the regulation of banking, which as we will see in the chapter on EMU, is undergoing a process of transfer to Union competence for Member States of the Eurozone)
3. compilation of statistics
4. public policy
5. public security
6. objective justification or overriding interests under case law.

ARTICLE 65 TFEU

1. The provisions of Article 63 shall be without prejudice to the right of Member States:

(a) to apply the relevant provisions of their tax law which distinguish between taxpayers who are not in the same situation with regard to their place of residence or with regard to the place where their capital is invested;

(b) to take all requisite measures to prevent infringements of national law and regulations, in particular in the field of taxation and the prudential supervision of financial institutions, or to lay down procedures for the declaration of capital movements for purposes of administrative or statistical information, or to take measures which are justified on grounds of public policy or public security.

2. The provisions of this Chapter shall be without prejudice to the applicability of restrictions on the right of establishment which are compatible with the Treaties.

3. The measures and procedures referred to in paragraphs 1 and 2 shall not constitute a means of arbitrary discrimination or a disguised restriction on the free movement of capital and payments as defined in Article 63.

4. In the absence of measures pursuant to Article 64(3), the Commission or, in the absence of a Commission decision within three months from the request of the Member State concerned, the Council, may adopt a decision stating that restrictive tax measures adopted by a Member State concerning one or more third countries are to be considered compatible with the Treaties in so far as they are justified by one of the objectives of the Union and compatible with the proper functioning of the internal market. The Council shall act unanimously on application by a Member State.

We will look at each of the derogations now in turn, followed by discussion of additional exceptions created in the case law of the ECJ.

13.3.2 NATIONAL TAX LAWS

Direct taxation, i.e. taxation on income and value added tax, is still within the competence of the Member States.

MAKING CONNECTIONS
+ + + + + + + + + + + + + + + + + +

THE APPLICATION OF EU LAW TO NATIONAL TAXATION
However, as was noted in Chapter 7 on competences, the free movement principles are very broad conceptually and almost any aspect of Member States' competence could be brought within them. This is also the case with tax laws. Differing tax regimes could be considered to make a single or internal market less effective and united (or less 'single'). This is where the distinction between *lex generalis* and *lex specialis* becomes very important (see Chapter 7). Since the Member States have reserved taxation to themselves, these rules should be applied as *lex specialis* over the *lex generalis* of free movement. Taxation is a matter within the competence of the Member States unless it falls under Articles 30 or 110 TFEU on the free movement of goods. However, as we saw in earlier chapters, the treaty itself establishes that there should be no discrimination on grounds of nationality in national taxes applicable to workers, goods and services and establishment: so it is the existence and level of taxation that is within each Member State's competence (apart also from the Common Customs Union, which is a matter of exclusive EU competence).

Article 63(1)(a) allows the Member States to apply the relevant provisions of their tax laws which distinguish between taxpayers who are not in the same situation with regard to their place of residence or with regard to the place where their capital is invested.

Distinctions based on residence and on the location of capital investments are a type of indirect discrimination, and this is allowed to the Member States. However, the ECJ has taken a very narrow approach to this provision.

This is illustrated by *Petri Manninen*, which established that the prohibition of arbitrary discrimination in Article (now) 65(3) TFEU enables (now) Article 63(1)(a) TFEU to be interpreted in line with the case law on tax discrimination under the other treaty freedoms.[38] The facts concerned national rules designed to compensate for double taxation on dividend payments at the corporate and share-holder levels. Finnish tax law granted shareholders a tax credit related to the amount of the dividend payment, but the tax credit was limited to the dividend payments of Finnish corporations.

The ECJ held that this restricted the free movement of capital under (now) Article 63 and (now) Article 65 TFEU. The Court held that Article 65(1)(a) required, for differentiation of treatment, that the facts to be assessed were not comparable, impartially, or that common interest necessitated a differentiation between these facts. The ECJ found that shareholders who did not get the credit because their shares were not in Finnish companies were in a comparable situation, regardless of whether they received their dividend payment from a domestic or from a foreign Member State corporation.

In *Petri Manninen*, the ECJ did not accept the coherence of the national tax systems as a justification for a restriction of the freedom of capital movement. The Court accepted that the advantage of a tax credit directly related to the disadvantage that the dividend payment has already been subject to corporate income tax in that Member State, but the ECJ then stated that the double taxation of dividends could be avoided if the shareholders of corporations situated in other Member States were also granted such a tax credit. And so the Finnish rule was not essential to maintain the coherence of the national tax system.

ANALYSING THE LAW

THE JUDGMENT IN *PETRI MANNINEN* AND NATIONAL TAXATION
The judgment in *Petri Manninen* has been criticised, as it in effect seems to require Member States to grant a tax credit for shares in corporations in other Member States, even though the Member State granting the credit does not levy tax on that company. As well as granting a tax credit to the individual shareholder, a Member State is in effect granting a kind of benefit to the company. As Seer well expresses the point:

> Despite national sovereignty in respect of direct taxation being clearly defined in the EC Treaty, the ECJ ignored the fiscal competence of the Member States

---

38 Case C–319/02 *Petri Manninen* [2004] ECR I–7477. For critical discussion see R Seer 'The jurisprudence of the European Court of Justice: limitation of the legal consequences?' (2006) 46(10) *European Taxation* 470–77.

and expected the Member States to give a credit for a foreign Member State's tax without even explicitly stating this. It is the ECJ's silence on how a solution to a cross-border case could be decided so as to conform with Community law, whilst, at the same time, respecting the sovereignty of the Member States with regard to direct taxation, that gives rise to the destructive impact of the ECJ case law (footnotes omitted).[39]

Through a narrow interpretation, the ECJ is undermining Article 65(1)(a) TFEU. The criticism that can be made is that the ECJ does not explicitly confront this issue in its reasoning and attempt to justify its decision in light of it. What is 'comparable' is open to different interpretations, which the ECJ takes advantage of.

Bachmann v Belgium is an example of a judgment permitting (indirect) tax discrimination on the basis of the coherence of the tax system. The ECJ held that Belgium could limit tax deductions on life and sickness insurance premiums to insurers established in Belgium, on the basis that there was no other way of preserving the coherence of the tax system (which required tax to be paid on the ultimate benefits).[40]

The case was decided primarily on the grounds of freedom of services and establishment,[41] but it does illustrate the scope for a broader interpretation of (now) Article 65(1)(a) TFEU. In other words, if there is a genuine public policy reason, the ECJ has the scope to determine that the (indirect) discrimination will not be contrary to free movement of capital and payments. However, the ECJ is generally unwilling to do so in practice. In theory, direct discrimination on the grounds of the nationality of the taxpayer might also be thought to come within the scope of Article 65(1)(a), but it is unlikely ever to satisfy Article 65(3) in light of the narrow approach of the ECJ to the scope of the taxation exception.

13.3.3 PRUDENTIAL SUPERVISION

Prudential supervision involves the regulation of banking and credit institutions. For example, banks are only permitted to loan out a certain amount of their financial reserves, and there are also rules on the criteria for granting loans (e.g. concerning the percentage a loan amount

39 Seer ibid 471.

40 Case C–204/90 *Bachmann v Belgium* [1992] ECR 1–249. Contrast the decisions in Case C–80/94 *Wielockx v Inspecteur der Directe Belastingen* [1995] ECR 1–2493 and Case C–136/00 *Rolf Dieter Danner* [2002] ECR I–8147, and for discussion see Usher (n 3) 1552–53.

41 Concerning freedom of movement of capital and payments, the ECJ noted (*Bachmann* ibid para 34) that (then) art 67 ECT did not prohibit restrictions that do not relate to the movement of capital, but which result indirectly from restrictions on other fundamental freedoms and, secondly, that provisions such as those at issue before the national court preclude neither the payment of insurance contributions to insurers established in another Member State nor their payment in the currency of the Member State in which the insurer is established.

can be of a person's annual income). An absolute application of free movement of capital and payments would allow these rules to be circumvented by transaction taking place across borders within the EU. We will look at this in Chapter 17 on EMU.

One of the reasons for the crisis in the Eurozone was the excessive availability of credit between Member States. This arguably should have been addressed by national regulatory bodies (in the UK, the Financial Conduct Authority, in many countries, the Central Bank), and the crisis demonstrated weaknesses in national regulation. The Member States in the Eurozone have now decided to address this partly by creating a 'Banking Union', a process currently under way.

13.3.4 COMPILATION OF STATISTICS

The Member States are allowed to monitor the transfer of capital and payments for the purposes of data gathering.

13.3.5 PUBLIC SECURITY

This is one of the standard exceptions that applies across all free movement principles. One of the main instances of its use would be national laws regarding the proceeds of crime. Although the criteria for the use of the public security derogation are established in secondary legislation for free movement of persons only, similar principles apply to the free movement of capital and payments. The Member State must prove the existence of overriding grounds of public interest and the normal requirement for proportionality in use of derogations applies. *Scientology International* concerned a French rule requiring prior approval for capital investments on grounds of public security, but the French law did not specify the kind of threat to public security.[42]

The ECJ was willing to accept the possibility that such a rule could be justified, but the lack of criteria for determining the risk to public security meant that the French rule did not satisfy (now) Article 65(1)(b). However, public security was accepted in *Commission v Belgium* concerning a Belgian rule that allowed the government to possess a 'golden share' in privatised gas and electricity companies.[43] The justification was the need to ensure the supply of strategic sources of energy (this is comparable to the *Campus Oil* case in free movement of goods[44]).

13.3.6 PUBLIC POLICY

This is also one of the standard exceptions that applies across all free movement principles, and similar principles govern its use in the context of capital and payments,

....

42 Case C–54/99 *Association Eglise de Scientologie de Paris and Scientology International Reserves Trust v Prime Minister* [2000] ECR I–1355.
43 Case C–503/99 *Commission v Belgium* [2000] ECR I–4809.
44 Case 72/83 *Campus Oil and Others v Minister for Industry and Energy and Others* [1984] ECR 2727.

but as with the public security derogation, these are not set out in secondary legislation for the purposes of freedom of movement of capital and payments.[45]

13.3.7 CASE LAW EXCEPTIONS RECOGNISING OBJECTIVE JUSTIFICATION OR OVERRIDING INTERESTS

Although some case law suggests that non-discriminatory obstacles or national measures that dissuade free movement of capital are also contrary to the TFEU, this is less developed concerning free movement of capital compared to the other free movement principles, as noted above. As a result, the Court of Justice has not developed much in case law the idea of objective justification intended to counteract the extensive scope of including non-discriminatory obstacles within free movement.

Similarly, there is no equivalent to selling arrangement exceptions as there is with free movement of goods. However, in those cases where non-discriminatory obstacles have been found to be contrary to the treaty, the possibility of objective justification or overriding interests has been referred to.[46]

APPLYING THE LAW

ANSWERING PROBLEM QUESTIONS ON FREE MOVEMENT OF CAPITAL AND PAYMENTS

Freedom of movement of capital and payments are not typically examined in undergraduate courses, but the same general framework for addressing them can be used as for the other free movement principles:

(1) Determining the application of the most suitable freedom of movement principle:
  - This is more of an issue with free movement of capital and payments because capital and payments are generally necessarily a part of the free movement of goods and services. The approach of the ECJ is to concentrate on the primary free movement principle, as the *Scheunemann* case illustrates.
  - A second aspect is to distinguish between capital and payments. This is no longer of much practical significance, so it is not necessary to address it in any detail.
(2) Determining the nature of the national measure in issue (is it direct discrimination, indirect discrimination, or a non-discriminatory obstacle)
  - Remember that the case law is ambiguous as to whether non-discriminatory obstacles (or 'measures liable to dissuade') are contrary to the Treaty.

---

45 See e.g. Case C–367/98 *Commission v Portugal* [2002] ECR I–4731.
46 See e.g. Case C–98/01 *Commission v United Kingdom* [2003] ECR I–4641 para 49.

(3) Determining which derogation might apply:
  1. national tax laws
  2. prudential supervision
  3. compilation of statistics
  4. public policy
  5. public security
  6. objective justification or overriding interests in the case law.
  7. restrictions on the right of establishment that are compatible with the treaties

13.4 CONCLUSION

Freedom of movement of capital and payments began as the least mandatory of the freedom of movement principles, despite that it is connected to both freedom of movement of goods and of services. Since the Treaty of Maastricht it has all become directly effective. This has reduced the significance of the distinction between capital and payments (previously only payments were directly effective), the distinction relating essentially to the difference between payment for a good or service (payments) and investment (capital). Nonetheless, the free movement of payments still has the potential to be significant in a small number of cases, albeit that freedom of goods and freedom of services and establishment will probably be able to compensate for this, where a transaction is primarily about a payment rather than a good or service. As with the other free movement principles, derogations have been restrictively interpreted, including, perhaps surprisingly, in the sovereignty-sensitive area of taxation.

POINTS TO REVIEW

- The basic rights involved in freedom of movement of capital and payments are more straightforward than apply to the other free movement principles. Unlike with freedom of workers, there is no continuum or spectrum of rights from an initial entry into another Member State by an EU citizen through a process of residence by a family and through continuing employment.

- The distinction between capital and payments has never been fully elaborated in the treaties or in secondary legislation, instead the Court of Justice has relied on an interpretation of the terminology defined in secondary legislation.

- Payments have been narrowly interpreted to mean only the right of the recipient of a service or of goods to make payment: this is still of potential significance only when free movement of capital, goods or free movement of services are not applicable.

— The distinction between capital and payments is no longer of much practical relevance, but was of significance given that initially only free movement of payments was directly effective. The distinction relates now principally to the relevance of the other free movement principles: broadly speaking, payment means consideration or payment for the provision of goods or services, capital refers to investments. If payments are involved, then free movement of goods or free movement of services/establishment can be simultaneously applicable and perhaps more appropriate to apply.

— The Treaty of Maastricht redrafted the free movement of capital and payments provisions so that both are now dealt with in the same provision, namely Article 63 TFEU. Both are now directly effective.

— The ECJ has not made fully clear the extent to which non-discriminatory obstacles are contrary to free movement of payments and capital, but the more dissuasive a national measure of free movement is, the more open is it to being contrary to the TFEU.

— As with the other free movement principles, derogations may apply, and again these are narrowly interpreted.

CHAPTER GLOSSARY

Balance of payments refers to the difference between the amount of exports and imports of a country. It is considered favourable to have a surplus, which means a country's currency is in more demand and is worth more.

Capital refers to investment.

Direct discrimination refers to national laws or practices that explicitly differentiate between EU citizens or legal persons based on nationality.

Direct investment refers to investment that is not in return or consideration for a good or service.

Dissuasive effect is the expression commonly used in the case law of the European Court of Justice to convey the idea of an obstacle to free movement of capital and payment.

Indirect discrimination refers to national laws or practices that do not explicitly differentiate between EU citizens or legal persons based on nationality.

Non-discriminatory obstacle refers to national measures that dissuade or inhibit the free movement of capital or payments between Member States without involving any discrimination, direct or indirect, on grounds of nationality. The term 'dissuasive effect' is more commonly used in case law on freedom of capital and payments.

Payment is the consideration for a service or good.

Security is an interest or share in a publicly-traded corporation (i.e. stock), a credit owed by a governmental body or a corporation (i.e. a bond) or a right to ownership as in the form of an option.

TAKING THINGS FURTHER

C Barnard *The Substantive Law of the EU: The Four Freedoms* (4th edn Oxford University Press 2013) Chapter 15 of this established and specialist textbook has a comprehensive and updated overview of free movement of capital.

G W Ringe 'Company law and the free movement of capital' (2010) 69(2) *Cambridge Law Journal* 378–409 This article looks at the relationship between freedom of establishment and freedom of capital and comments on the potential for freedom of capital to provide a basis for increased involvement by the ECJ in national company law.

J Usher 'The evolution of the free movement of capital' (2007) 31 *Fordham Journal of International Law* 1533–70 After overviewing the evolution and scope of the free movement of capital rules, this article looks at the treatment of discriminatory taxation under the capital movement rules, and the approach of the European Court to the extension of the capital movement rules to third countries.

CHAPTER 14
COMPETITION LAW: CONTEXT AND ENFORCEMENT

This chapter first overviews the development of competition law as a type of legal regulation of a free market economy, its rationale and economic context, and the main different aspects or dimensions of competition law in the EU (cartels, dominant firms, state aid and mergers), as well as its scope (territorial and extra-territorial). It then examines the enforcement of competition law within the EU and how this has moved from a centralised model in which the European Commission played a dominant role to a decentralised model in which the Member States are primarily responsible for enforcing competition law. It is a broad topic, given that competition law is one of the two main pillars of the common market (now usually described as internal market) since the foundation of the Communities in the 1950s.

AS YOU READ . . .

The key questions that will be answered in this chapter are as follows:

– What is the aim of regulating free markets through competition or anti-trust law? For example, in what way do consumers benefit from competition law? In what way does it help business enterprises? Are there tensions between the aims of helping consumers and helping businesses?

– How did competition law develop as a response to the 'excesses' of free market economies?

– What are the different ways competition law intervenes in free markets, i.e. what types of intervention in what types of scenario does competition regulation involve?

– Are there any unique features of competition law in the EU compared with competition or anti-trust law in other systems?

– How is EU law enforced? How has its system of enforcement developed over time?

– Do the Member States have any remaining competence in the sphere of competition law?

14.1 INTRODUCTION

Competition law is a relatively new academic discipline, although regulation of competition has existed in various guises for several centuries. Modern competition law began in the United States with the Sherman Act 1890. Its concern is essentially with limiting the excesses of successful capitalism, which can result in a concentration of market power in a small number of powerful businesses or in a single business. Controlling or regulating market power is, therefore, a central concern for competition law.

More than 125 jurisdictions worldwide have adopted a regime of competition law, including China, the world's second largest economy since it transitioned from Communism (and which has been significantly influenced by EU competition law). The principle of undistorted competition has been central to the common market (later the single market and now the internal market)[1] since the founding treaties. Competition law, together with free movement, makes up the core of what is today termed the internal market.

It is difficult to generalise about free market economics in the context of competition. However, some basic points can be made. Generally, a monopoly, i.e. a situation where a product or service is provided by only one business in any given market, is considered undesirable. A given market is the supply and demand for a particular product or products. An example would be the car market in the UK, which could be further sub-divided into markets in a particular type of car (e.g. small cars versus large luxury cars). The supply in the small car market is the capacity of enterprises or businesses, referred to as 'undertakings' in EU competition law, to provide such cars to consumers in the UK. The demand is the extent of the capacity and desire of consumers to purchase cars. With modern transportation, car manufacturers in other countries can now respond to the demand.

> KEY LEARNING POINT
>
> **THE MEANING OF COMPETITION**
> By competition is meant the pressure on firms to provide better products or lower prices or better conditions of work due to the presence of other enterprises or undertakings offering the same products or services.

The key reason a monopoly is undesirable is that it allows the monopoly firm to act independently of competition from other firms, thus allowing the firm to charge higher prices or offer a low quality product without a fear that consumers will turn to another product. This concentration of market power (the ability of a firm or undertaking to act

---

1   J Snell 'The internal market and the philosophies of market integration' in C Barnard, S Peers (eds) *European Union Law* (Oxford University Press 2014) 302.

independently of consumers or competitors, or of producers regarding buying power[2])
is undesirable because it allows firms to escape the pressures of competition to reduce
prices or offer better products. This can be negative for consumers, competing businesses
and employees.

The less competition there is in the marketplace, the less incentive there is for businesses
to offer the best quality products at the lowest prices to consumers. The more dominant
an existing firm or small number of firms is in the marketplace, the more difficult for
new entrepreneurs to establish an enterprise and offer competitive products. Dominance
in the marketplace can also put workers at a disadvantage, because it limits the
possibilities for workers to find alternative employment in the same sector (this kind of
dominance and its impact on workers is central to the Marxist-socialist critique of law).

Competition law seeks to protect the natural development of supply and demand in
the marketplace. Attempts at limiting production or at maintaining prices at a higher
level than is justified under free market conditions is what competition law seeks to
prevent, as well as preventing the extreme capitalist outcome of a monopoly.

KEY LEARNING POINT

THE THEORY OF PERFECT COMPETITION

In a 'normal', 'ideal' or 'perfect' marketplace, operating under free and open
market conditions, prices for goods are subject to competitive pressures: a
producer will reduce prices for a particular good if the prices of competitor
goods are lower or if the quality of competitor goods is greater (but they are
being sold at the same price), because consumers will switch to the goods of
the competitor otherwise. There will be a large enough number of producers
of goods that an individual producer cannot unilaterally change supply and
demand. In a perfectly competitive market, no undertaking will have a very
large market share. Perfect competition rarely arises in practice; instead, the
typical market situation in reality is somewhere on a spectrum between a
monopoly and perfect competition.[3]

However, even when a firm does have a very large share of the market, the reality of
whether it can dominate a market depends also on other factors apart from price and
quality, especially on the type of good. If the good is a non-essential good, consumers
will still not likely buy an overly expensive or a poor quality product, even if there is
no competing product; consumers will just do without the good. In contrast, the classic
situation of a problematic monopoly arises when a firm is in a monopoly position for an
essential good, i.e. a good that consumers must buy.

---

2   R Whish *Competition Law* (6th edn Oxford University Press 2008) 8, citing UK Competition Commission
    Merger References: Competition Commission Guidelines (CC 2 June 2003) para 1.24.
3   Whish (n 2) 3–9.

NATURAL MONOPOLIES AND OLIGOPOLIES

Natural monopolies (as opposed to a state-imposed monopoly) do not often occur: they arise where it is most efficient, i.e. it costs less without unacceptably compromising the quality of the product, where a single firm can make the most of economies of scale. This can be the case, for example, when a unique and very difficult to produce product is made by a particular undertaking. Neither does the perfect competition outlined in the previous paragraph occur all that commonly. The most common market form in reality is an oligopoly, where a small number of firms dominate the market. A good example is the market in cars. Thus, competition law needs to be sensitive to the natural behaviours of oligopolies competing against each other.[4] They will often offer similar prices, not because they have collectively agreed to 'fix' prices at a higher level than they could be sold at without incurring a loss, but because they are tracking each other's behaviour and want to avoid being undercut in price or quality. We will look at this in the next chapter.

As noted above, competition law has been an important part of 'the European project' since its inception. Article 31(g) EEC Treaty provided that 'the activities of the Community shall include . . . the institution of a system ensuring that competition in the common market is not distorted'. Protocol 27 to the current treaties replaces this provision and refers to 'an open market economy with free competition'.

There are four main aspects to EU competition law and policy: the prohibition on agreement and concerted practices or cartel-like behaviour (Article 101 TFEU); the prohibition on the abuse of a dominant position in the marketplace (Article 102 TFEU); the limitation and regulation of state aids (Articles 107–109 TFEU); and the regulation of mergers (now under the Merger Regulation 139/2004[5]). This textbook concentrates on Articles 101 and 102 TFEU, but briefly examines state aids and merger control below in this chapter.

14.2 THE ORIGINS OF MODERN COMPETITION LAW

Modern competition law began in the United States with the passing of the Sherman Anti-Trust Act 1890.[6] However, the recognition of the existence of monopolies is not

---

4 Ibid 9–10.
5 Council Regulation 139/2004/EC on the control of concentrations between undertakings OJ L24 29.01.2004 p. 1–22.
6 15 U.S.C. §§ 1–7.

new, and various states regulated monopolies in one way or another, often actually to establish a monopoly. In the United Kingdom, for example, the monarch in the past granted monopolies to favoured subjects as a reward for their services to the crown and/or to secure their loyalty. The Statute of Monopolies 1623[7] in England was a way for the monarch to grant a patent, effectively creating a monopoly.

The context in which the Sherman Act was adopted was a growing practice in the US in the nineteenth century of corporations buying shares in other corporations, through the vehicle of a 'trust'. A trust is a legal relationship whereby the owner of a property interest holds it on trust for, i.e. for the benefit of, another party. These are common and generally legitimate kinds of legal relationship in the law of property, for example. However, in the US, trusts were used by firms to acquire influence and control in other corporations and to try to dominate or control the market in that way. The Act was particularly concerned with prohibiting anti-competitive practices across states, which had an inter-state effect or dimension in the US. The term 'restraint of trade' came to be employed to describe the kinds of behaviours prohibited (although this term has a different meaning in UK employment law).

The Sherman Act has three main sections. Section 1 provides that: 'Every contract, combination in the form of trust or otherwise, or conspiracy, in restraint of trade or commerce among the several States, or with foreign nations, is declared to be illegal' (thus agreements that unreasonably restrict inter-state trade are prohibited).

Section 2 provides that: 'Every person who shall monopolize, or attempt to monopolize, or combine or conspire with any other person or persons, to monopolize any part of the trade or commerce among the several States, or with foreign nations, shall be deemed guilty of a felony' (thus prohibiting monopolies or attempted monopolies that cannot be explained as resulting from growth or development as a consequence of a superior product, business acumen or historic accident).

Section 1 can be understood as targeting cartels. Section 2 does not prohibit monopolies; rather, it prohibits monopolies that do not result from free competition under normal market conditions. Later legislation further specified market activities that were to be prohibited. For example, the Clayton Anti-Trust Act of 1914[8] prohibited specific behaviours not encompassed by the Sherman Act: price discrimination between different purchasers, if such discrimination tends to create a monopoly; exclusive dealing agreements; tying arrangements; and mergers and acquisitions that substantially reduce market competition.

US law seeks to achieve a balance between prohibiting certain behaviour as automatically anti-competitive (an 'of itself' or 'per se' approach) and a more flexible approach of looking to actual market effects (a 'rule of reason'). These alternative

---

7 21 Jac 1 c 3.
8 15 U.S.C. §§ 12–27.

approaches, and an attempt to balance them, are also found in EU competition law, which also seeks to balance between them, as we shall see in the next chapter.

Gerber identifies intellectual developments in Austria in the late nineteenth century as decisive in the development of European competition law.[9] The political background to the development of competition law ideas in Austria was the political and social fragmentation of the Austro-Hungarian Empire and a rejection of classic free market liberalism in Austria, viewed as responsible for a prolonged period of economic depression in the 1870s and 1880s.

Cartels became major players in Austrian economic life as a way of achieving a degree of protection from completely free competition and as a way of achieving economies of scale, as a kind of 'organised capitalism':[10] 'They generally were viewed as the children of necessity (*Kinder der Not*) that served to establish order and to avoid the chaos of ruinous competition'.[11] However, by the 1890s cartels came to be seen as vehicles of economic exploitation by businesses previously advocating economic liberalism.

During this time, the legal regulation of cartels began to become more systematic, although an 1803 law had made it a criminal offence for members of a particular trade to increase the price of the good 'without work and to the detriment of the public'.[12] A more systematic approach was developed by a legal scholar Adolf Menzel, beginning at a conference held in 1894: 'The ideas were generated by a leading scholar in a superior academic forum and in response to political pressures'.[13] Menzel preferred an administrative approach to the issue of preventing the kind of cartel conduct that actually eliminated competition, i.e. which did not have an economic justification, through a system of state regulation.

In 1897 the Austrian Government presented draft legislation with an explanatory document. The Austrian approach could be considered sophisticated, in that it was attentive to distinguish carefully between negative and positive cartel behaviour and to the effects on competition, consumers and fiscal revenue of taxation. The behaviour primarily targeted was pricing without an economic justification. Although political circumstances meant the legislation was never actually adopted, it was influential in developments in other countries and is very significant as a first systematic approach to regulating competition in Europe.

---

9 D J Gerber 'The origins of European competition law in fin-de-siècle Austria' (1992) 36 *The American Journal of Legal History* 405–40.

10 Ibid 418.

11 Ibid 419, citing D Good *The Economic Rise of the Hapsburg Monarchy 1750–1914* (University of California Press 1984) 235–37.

12 Justizgesetzsammlung No 626.

13 Gerber (n 9) 423.

14.3 THE AIMS OF COMPETITION LAW

The aims of competition law[14] can be expressed simply as being to enhance competition between enterprises in a free market place. However, in terms of an underlying rationale, several different explanations can be given in an EU context. It is useful to bear in mind the question of who benefits from competition law. Consumers are the most obvious beneficiaries.

Competition encourages enterprises to provide better quality products or to lower the price of their products, or both. Better quality can relate to the characteristics of the goods, but can also include the supply of accessory products or after-sales service. Entrepreneurs also benefit from competition, because it facilitates access or entry to the market, thereby making it easier to start up a new business. However, the extent to which this is so varies with the business. In particular, the greater the degree of expertise or skill needed to enter a particular market, the more competition depends on additional factors such as the availability of training.

Competition law can benefit a particular country's economy, by making sure its national enterprises have well developed products and marketing techniques, thereby allowing them to compete more effectively internationally or in other countries. The market participant that benefits the least is the enterprise or undertaking that would, without the intervention of competition law, be able to dominate the market and to produce lower quality products at less cost and for greater profit.

Different views and approaches exist as to the *relative* protection competition law should give to competitors or to consumers. For example, in EU law, the notion of a common or single market (now the internal market) plays a role alongside consumer welfare and market efficiencies. The case law of the Court can be analysed for its integrative effect, rather than the concerns typical to national competition law of consumer welfare and opportunity for entrepreneurs. One of the strongest critiques of unregulated capitalism relates to what competition law seeks to prevent: the emergence of monopolies.

ANALYSING THE LAW

THE SOCIALIST-MARXIST CRITIQUE OF LAW

Karl Marx posited a materialist view of history, according to which societies develop according to historical laws of production. Marx supposed that the pursuit of capital and wealth eventually led to the emergence of monopolistic forms, which had out-competed all competitors. The capitalist class who owned the means of production would amount to a small number who had accumulated all the wealth of society through the acquisition of monopolistic market power

---

14 See generally e.g. D Zimmer (ed) *The Goals of Competition Law* (Edward Elgar 2012).

in a free market. This would lead to the exploitation of the working class or proletariat.

By preventing the emergence of monopolistic forms through managing or controlling individual undertakings or cartels in a dominant position, competition law prevents this monopolistic and exploitative outcome. Competition law is not conceived, however, in terms of class struggle and was not primarily directed at protecting workers. It has broader and primary aims of protecting consumers and enterprises, as well as workers.

The extent to which consumers or competing businesses have opposing interests is debatable. For example, it cannot be assumed that all large-scale firms in a strong market position will act in a way that harms consumers.

EXPLAINING THE LAW

THE IMPACT OF LARGE FIRMS ON CONSUMERS

Economies of scale can result from large firms, and these can be passed on to consumers. Breaking up a large firm like this or prohibiting monopolies can have the effect of eliminating these economies and thereby increasing prices. As we shall see in Chapter 16, EU law in Article 102 takes a more subtle approach. Dominance, even a monopoly, is not automatically prohibited; instead, dominant firms are restricted in the kinds of market behaviour they can engage in, compared with firms or undertakings not in a dominant position.

An additional, distinct aim of competition law is innovation and technical development,[15] sometimes called 'dynamic efficiency'.[16] This could be considered to fall under consumer benefit, which it does to an extent, but it also has a broader societal goal of the common good. Society in general, not only those engaged in consumption, can benefit from technological advances. For example, competition can stimulate technical advances in healthcare even though healthcare, at least basic healthcare, is often provided by society freely to all those in need, not merely to those who could afford to consume it in an economic sense.

15 I am grateful to Dr Jurgita Malinauskaite for drawing my attention to this point. Specifically on the EU see e.g. recently L Parret 'The multiple personalities of EU competition law: time for a comprehensive debate on its objectives' in Zimmer (n 14); D J Gerber 'The goals of European competition law: distortions in the literature – comment on Parret' in Zimmer (n 14).

16 M Bakhoum 'Reflection on the concepts of "economic freedom", "free competition" and "efficiency" from the perspective of developing countries' in Zimmer (n 14) 433.

Pharmaceutical companies engage in advanced research in order to earn greater profits, but a side effect is the development of more effective medical treatment.[17] This has a spin-off effect for all of society, since more effective drugs will eventually become more widely available to all, although in the shorter term this benefit may be limited by intellectual property rights.

In the UK, for example, such drugs can become freely available quickly through the state-funded National Health Service. The more developed an economy is, the more competition can stimulate innovation, since competition law creates the conditions within which innovation is incentivised by the appeal of more profit, while there are more firms with capacity or potential to lead innovation. In the context of a common or internal market, such as in the EU, a benefit of a single competition regime across the Member States is that it facilitates the diffusion of innovation by making market concentration easier.

EU competition law has an additional aim of ensuring the cohesiveness of the internal market and that competition occurs freely across border or inter-state amongst the EU Member States (this provides a basis for comparing EU competition law with US competition law, given that federal competence to regulate competition in the US is based on its impact on inter-state commerce). EU competition law is directed mainly at removing obstacles to trade in the private sector. A principle of liberalisation of trade is central to it.

This principle of liberalisation relates to a further rationale proposed for competition law, sometimes called ordoliberalism: this school of thought proposes that competition law exists to protect *individual* economic freedom by regulating and limiting the concentration of market power (not liberalism from the point of view of traders or undertakings), as part of a more general concern that government should exist to sustain social and political freedom.[18] Economic freedom is thus the ultimate goal, not market efficiency; market efficiency can be compromised in the interest of economic freedom.[19] Jones and Townley note that, while this approach has had some influence in EU competition law, it is not now a widely supported approach.[20]

---

17 See generally e.g. J Drexl, N Lee (eds) *Pharmaceutical Innovation, Competition and Patent Law: A Trilateral Perspective* (Edward Elgar 2013).

18 Associated in particular with Franz Böhm from the 1930s onwards. See F Maier-Rigaud 'On the normative foundation of competition law: efficiency, political freedom and freedom to compete' in Zimmer (n 14) 141–42 ff. Maier-Rigaud distinguishes ordoliberalism from neoliberalism, with neoliberalism focusing more on freedom to compete per se as a process of developing knowledge in society. A neoliberal position, for example, would be less restrictive of firms in a dominant position than ordoliberalism.

19 W Möschel 'The proper scope of government viewed from an ordoliberal perspective' (2001) 157(1) *Journal of Institutional and Theoretical Economics* 3–13.

20 A Jones, C Townley 'Competition law' in Barnard and Peers (n 1) 506.

Ordoliberalism has affinities with the 'Chicago School' of competition law; the broader context of both is the limitation of state power. The Chicago School is associated with, in particular, Robert Bork (who was both an academic and a federal appeals court judge), who argued that antitrust law in the US was originally intended to provide limited intervention in cases where business practice clearly had an anti-competitive effect, such as price fixing by cartels and predatory pricing by dominant firms, but that behaviours such as price discrimination could be justifiable economically (e.g. price discrimination could target the elasticity of demand more effectively for different consumers, vertical agreements could achieve greater efficiency).[21]

The thrust of the argument was that the protection of consumers was the key aim of competition law (not the protection of competitors and business undertakings in the market) and that a limited amount of state intervention could achieve this through targeting cartels especially.

The Court of Justice has not generally sought to outline a theory of the purpose of competition in its case law, but it has noted the twin concerns of consumer welfare and enabling market access for other undertakings:

> 25. In any case Articles 85 and 86 [now Articles 101 and 102 TFEU] cannot be interpreted in such a way that they contradict each other, because they serve to achieve the same aim.

> 26. [. . .] the condition imposed by Article 86 is to be interpreted whereby in order to come within the prohibition a dominant position must have been abused. The provision states a certain number of abusive practices which it prohibits. The list merely gives examples, not an exhaustive enumeration of the sort of abuses of a dominant position prohibited by the Treaty. As may further be seen from letters (c) and (d) of Article 86 (2), the provision is not only aimed at practices which may cause damage to consumers directly, but also at those which are detrimental to them through their impact on an effective competition structure, such as is mentioned in Article 3 (f) of the Treaty. Abuse may therefore occur if an undertaking in a dominant position strengthens such position in such a way that the degree of dominance reached substantially fetters competition, i.e. that only undertakings remain in the market whose behaviour depends on the dominant one.[22]

Recital 23 of the Merger Regulation 2004 also clearly identifies the single market goal:

> It is necessary to establish whether or not concentrations with a Community dimension are compatible with the common market in terms of the need to

---

21 R Bork *The Antitrust Paradox* (2nd edn New York Free Press 1993). See also R Posner 'The Chicago School of antitrust analysis' (1979) 127 *University of Pennsylvania Law Review* 925–48, identifying Aaron Director as the founder of the school.

22 Case 6/72 *Continental Can v Commission* [1973] ECR 215 paras 25–26.

maintain and develop effective competition in the common market. In so doing, the Commission must place its appraisal within the general framework of the achievement of the fundamental objectives referred to in Article 2 of the Treaty establishing the European Community and Article 2 of the Treaty on European Union.[23]

14.4 THE DIMENSIONS OF EU COMPETITION LAW: REGULATING CARTELS, DOMINANT FIRMS, STATE AIDS AND MERGERS

EU competition law has several aspects. The first two – cartels and abuse of a dominant position – are examined in detail in the following two chapters and are only briefly explained here. This section goes into somewhat more detail on the other two aspects of EU competition law: state aids and mergers.

14.4.1 CARTELS UNDER ARTICLE 101 TFEU

The term 'cartel' refers to collusion or collusive behaviour between different undertakings in order to limit competition in the marketplace. For example, competing supermarkets could all agree not to reduce the price of an essential good such as bread or milk below a certain level, even though some profit could still be made at a price lower than the agreed price. Collusion such as this artificially limits competition.

In an ideal competitive market, competitors are genuinely in competition, rather than cooperating to restrict it. Undertakings at the same level in the marketplace, e.g. distributors cooperating or retailers cooperating, hardly ever have a sound economic justification consistent with free competition. Cartels are thus, generally speaking, 'hard core' restraints on competition. This is dealt with in Article 101 TFEU, which we will look at in the next chapter.

14.4.2 ABUSE OF A DOMINANT POSITION UNDER ARTICLE 102 TFEU

The classic case of a dominant position in a marketplace is a monopoly, i.e. a situation where a single undertaking has a 100 per cent share of the market in a relevant good or service. In such a situation, there is no competition. However, monopolies are rare (they usually occur only where there is a statutory monopoly or a product is subject to a very high level of expertise and has been patented).

---

23 Council Regulation (EC) No 139/2004 on the control of concentrations between undertakings (the EC Merger Regulation), OJ L 24 29.1.2004 p. 1.

A more common situation is where a single undertaking has a very large share of the market in a good or service. This is not so unusual. This situation is dealt with in Article 102 TFEU, which places certain limits and obligations on the market behaviour of firms in a dominant position. In this situation, the freedom of a dominant firm can undermine the economic freedom of other firms, and competition law seeks a balancing of economic rights or freedoms.[24] We will look at this in Chapter 15.

14.4.3 STATE AIDS

'State aids' is the term used in EU law to describe subsidies by a government to domestic undertakings in order to help the undertaking compete. Since such subsidies are only given to domestic/national undertakings, they represent an interference in normal competitive conditions by giving the domestic undertaking an advantage not enjoyed by undertakings in the same market exporting into the domestic economy from other Member States. State aid can also distort competition in the domestic economy. Unsurprisingly, state aids are generally prohibited in EU law. Article 107(1) TFEU provides that:

> Save as otherwise provided in the Treaties, any aid granted by a Member State or through State resources in any form whatsoever which distorts or threatens to distort competition by favouring certain undertakings or the production of certain goods shall, in so far as it affects trade between Member States, be incompatible with the internal market.

Article 101(2)–(3) goes on to set out state aid that is considered compatible with the internal market:

– aid having a *social character*, granted to individual consumers, provided it does not discriminate based on the origin of the goods (an example from the UK is an aid scheme for air services for residents of specified areas within the Highlands and Islands of Scotland[25])
– aid to make good the damage caused by *natural disasters* or *exceptional occurrences*
– aid granted *following German unification* to the economy of certain areas of Germany
– aid to *promote the economic development of areas where the standard of living is abnormally low* or where there is serious underemployment, and of the regions referred to in Article 349 TFEU, in view of their structural, economic and social situation
– aid to promote the execution of an *important project of common European interest* or *to remedy a serious disturbance in the economy of a Member State*

---

24 See Bakhoum in Zimmer (n 14) 424.

25 European Commission *State Aid No N 27/2008 – United Kingdom Aid of a Social Character Air Services in the Highlands and Islands of Scotland (prolongation of N 169/2006)* Brussels 14.11.2008 C(2008) 685.

- aid *to facilitate the development of certain economic activities or of certain economic areas,* where such aid does not adversely affect trading conditions to an extent contrary to the common interest
- aid to promote *culture and heritage conservation* where such aid does not affect trading conditions and competition in the Union to an extent that is contrary to the common interest
- such other *categories as may be specified by decision of the Council* on a proposal from the Commission.

Article 108(2) TFEU provides for a special procedure for the Council acting by unanimity to approve in particular cases state aid that would otherwise be prohibited.

14.4.4 MERGERS

The treaties originally contained no provisions explicitly on mergers (a merger refers to two or more businesses combining to form one business). While the role of the Court of Justice has not generally been as instrumental in competition law as it has in other areas, the Court did provide the impetus for the development of EU merger control in the *Continental Can* case.[26] *Continental Can* involved a merger and its impact on the issue of the structure of the market in question. The Court of Justice referred to the spirit, general scheme and wording of Article 86 EEC Treaty (later Article 82 ECT, now Article 102 TFEU), and also to the system and objectives of the treaty (a good example of meta-teleological reasoning), and determined that the merger constituted abuse of a dominant position under Article 102 TFEU.

The Court held that clauses (a)–(d) in (now) Article 102 TFEU are not exhaustive and that the strengthening of a position of dominance through a merger may be abuse where it undermines the competitive structure of the market. Generally speaking, Article 102 is only engaged when there is abuse of a dominant position; a dominant position itself is not enough. By stretching the scope of (now) Article 102 TFEU to indicate that the mere fact of a merger could, of itself and without any specific market behaviours being identified, constitute abuse of a dominant position, the Court provided a basis for the regulation of mergers more generally in EU law. The possibility that mergers might result in over-dominance is a particular risk in an oligopolistic market, where there are already a small number of firms, or where a firm is already in a dominant position before merging with another undertaking.[27]

The EU legislature later took up the Court's implicit invitation to address mergers, by adopting Regulation 4064/1989,[28] which was amended several times and was replaced

---

26 Case 6/72 *Continental Can* [1973] ECR 215.

27 Merger Regulation 2004 recitals 25–26.

28 Regulation 4064/1989 on the control of concentrations between undertakings, OJ L 395 30.12.1989 p. 1, last amended by Regulation 1310/97/EC OJ L 180 09.07.1997 p. 1.

with Regulation 139/2004.[29] Recital 7 of Merger Regulation 139/2004 explained the legal basis for it:

> Articles 81 and 82 [now Articles 101 and 102 TFEU], while applicable, according to the case-law of the Court of Justice, to certain concentrations, are not sufficient to control all operations which may prove to be incompatible with the system of undistorted competition envisaged in the Treaty. This Regulation should therefore be based not only on Article 83 but, principally, on Article 308 of the Treaty, under which the Community may give itself the additional powers of action necessary for the attainment of its objectives, and also powers of action with regard to concentrations on the markets for agricultural products listed in Annex I to the Treaty.
>
> The provisions to be adopted in this Regulation should apply to significant structural changes, the impact of which on the market goes beyond the national borders of any one Member State. Such concentrations should, as a general rule, be reviewed exclusively at Community level, in application of a 'one-stop shop' system and in compliance with the principle of subsidiarity. Concentrations not covered by this Regulation come, in principle, within the jurisdiction of the Member States.

In adopting the 'one-stop shop' principle, therefore, the Merger Regulation gave the Commission sole control over all major cross-border mergers that had a European dimension. The 2004 Merger Regulation sought to ensure that the same merger does not have to be notified to several competition authorities in the Member States and EU and seeks to apply an approach more based on the principle of subsidiarity, whereby a merger is examined by the competition authority best placed to do so.

The Merger Regulation applies to all concentrations 'with an EU dimension', which is defined as follows as arising where:

- the combined aggregate worldwide turnover of all the undertakings concerned is more than €5 billion and
- the aggregate turnover in the EU of each of at least two of the undertakings concerned is more than €250 million, unless each of the undertakings concerned generates more than two-thirds of its aggregate EU-wide turnover within a single EU country[30]

or

- the combined aggregate worldwide turnover of all the undertakings concerned is more than €2.5 billion
- in each of at least three EU countries, the combined aggregate turnover of all the undertakings concerned is more than €100 million

---

29 Merger Regulation 2004.
30 Ibid art 2.

- in each of at least three EU countries, the aggregate turnover of each of at least two of the undertakings concerned is more than €25 million
- the aggregate EU-wide turnover of each of at least two of the undertakings concerned is more than €100 million, unless each of the undertakings concerned generates more than two-thirds of its aggregate EU-wide turnover in one and the same EU country.[31]

It is not required that the undertakings have their principal place of business within the EU; it is enough that they have substantial operations there.[32]

> ## KEY LEARNING POINT
>
> ### REGULATION 139/2004
> The new Merger Regulation 139/2004 sought to apply more subsidiarity to the system of merger control (compared to the original Merger Regulation 4064/1989), somewhat similarly to how Regulation 1/2003[33] did so for Articles 101 and 102 TFEU (see further below). It does so in two ways:
>
> - it provides for earlier notification to the Commission, which can then decide to refer to national competition authorities
> - it allows for the pre-notification procedure, whereby undertakings can inform the Commission of possible merger at an earlier stage again.
>
> The 2004 Regulation also simplified the procedure for notifications and investigations.

As a general rule, concentrations with an EU dimension must be notified to the Commission prior to their implementation and following either the conclusion of the agreement, the announcement of the public bid or the acquisition of a controlling interest.[34] The Merger Regulation allows notification before the conclusion of a binding agreement and abolishes the obligation to notify operations within a week of concluding an agreement. The Commission has the power to declare the concentration either compatible or incompatible with EU competition law.[35]

The Merger Regulation introduces a pre-notification procedure, which allows the undertakings to show the Commission that the proposed merger, while resulting in a concentration having a cross-border dimension, affects competition on the market of only one EU Member State.[36] Where pre-notification occurs, the agreement to merge

---

31 Ibid art 3.
32 Ibid recital 10.
33 OJ L1 4.1.2003 p. 1.
34 Ibid art 4(1)–(2).
35 Ibid art 4(3).
36 Ibid art 4(4).

should be suspended, unless the Commission agrees otherwise.[37] The Commission and national competition authorities can then decide if a referral to the Commission should be made. The Member State has 15 days within which to lodge an objection and the Commission has 25 days to refer the matter back to the national competition authority to apply national competition law.

The same pre-notification procedure applies to a '3+' rule under Article 4(5) independently of national competition authorities: an undertaking may refer to the Commission a merger that is capable of being reviewed by three or more national authorities and if none of the latter objects, the Commission then acquires exclusive competence.[38]

Further, an EU Member State may, within 15 working days of the date of receipt of the copy of the notification, acting on its own initiative or at the Commission's invitation, declare that a concentration significantly affects competition in the domestic market of that country. The result is that the competition authority of that Member State then deals with the case. The product or service market must present all the characteristics of a distinct market, but without constituting a substantial part of the common market.

Conversely, after the Commission has transmitted a notification to the Member States, an EU country can request the Commission to investigate whether a concentration, although without an EU dimension, significantly hampers competition between EU countries and is liable to have a significant effect on competition on the territory of the EU Member State or Member States making the request. The Commission must then inform the competent authorities of the relevant EU countries and companies concerned, fixing a time limit of 15 working days within which any other EU Member State can join the initial request. If, within 10 working days, the Commission has not adopted a decision to refer or not to refer to one of the other Member States, it is deemed to have adopted a decision in accordance with the request from the initiating Member State.[39]

Comparably to Article 101(3) TFEU in the context of cartels, the Merger Regulation 2004 recognises that mergers might result in efficiencies that outweigh anti-competitive effects. Therefore, it provides for the Commission to establish guidelines on the conditions under which it may take efficiencies into account in the assessment of a concentration.[40] The Commission has issued Guidelines. An important consideration it takes into account is the extent to which a merger will lead to foreclosure, which is any

....

37 Ibid art 7.
38 Ibid art 4(5).
39 Ibid art 9.
40 Ibid recital 29.

instance where actual or potential rivals' access to supplies or markets is hampered or eliminated as a result of the merger.[41]

The Commission is given generally similar powers to investigate mergers as it has to investigate other breaches of EU competition law.[42]

14.5 THE ORIGINAL SYSTEM OF ENFORCEMENT OF COMPETITION LAW

14.5.1 INDIVIDUAL AND BLOCK EXEMPTIONS

In the past, the Commission has had the power to grant both individual exemptions to agreements and block exemptions (which it still retains the power to grant).

An *individual exemption* was a formal, legally binding document from the Commission stating that, in its view, a particular type of agreement or concerted practice was not contrary to Article 101 TFEU (see further below regarding decentralisation of EU competition law enforcement).

A *block exemption* is a formal, legally binding statement from the Commission exempting a particular class or defined type of agreement from the effects of Article 101(1)–(2) TFEU. Block exemptions have been issued to cover specialisation agreements and research and development agreements. One of the most important concerns vertical restraints.[43]

An example of a block exemption specific to an industry is Commission Regulation 461/2010 on the application of Article 101(3) TFEU to categories of vertical agreements and concerted practices in the motor vehicle sector.[44] This is somewhat more restrictive than the block exemption on vertical restraints generally, because of high service and repair costs incurred by purchasers of new cars and less intra-brand competition at the retail level, as well as the tendency for car distribution agreements to operate sales along national lines, with significant price differences and restrictions on sales to buyers in other Member States.[45]

---

41 Guidelines on the assessment of non-horizontal mergers under the Council Regulation on the control of concentrations between undertakings OJ C 265 18.10.2008 p. 6.

42 Merger Regulation arts 11–13.

43 Commission Regulation 2790/1999/EC on the application of [now art 101(3)] of the Treaty to Categories of Vertical Agreements and Concerted Practices OJ L 336 29.12.1999 p. 21.

44 OJ L 129 28.5.2010 p. 5. See also Commission Regulation 330/2010/EU on the application of art 101(3) of the Treaty on the Functioning of the European Union to categories of vertical agreements and concerted practices OJ L 102 23.4.2010 p. 1.

45 A Stephan 'Editorial: reforming EU competition law' (2010) 6(2) *Competition Law Review* 139–43 at 142; 'Counting down Regulation 1400/2002: questioning the logic of sector-specific rules for the European car industry' (2010) 6(2) *Competition Law Review* 203–24.

Block exemptions were particularly important in the past when (now) Article 101(3) TFEU was not directly effective and when the Commission was largely responsible for the enforcement. A number of regulations[46] passed by the Council (of Ministers) empowered the Commission to apply (now) Article 101(3) TFEU of the Treaty to certain categories of agreements or decisions by associations of undertakings and concerted practices. Regulation 1/2003 makes it clear that the Commission may continue to issue such block exemptions.[47]

14.5.2 INDIVIDUAL EXEMPTIONS AND 'COMFORT LETTERS' IN THE ENFORCEMENT OF EU COMPETITION LAW

Comfort letters were informal statements of administrative decisions by the Commission not to pursue an action against a firm/undertaking for breach of EU competition law, in the context of the previous notification system, whereby undertakings engaging in an enterprise that was potentially contrary to Article 101 TFEU had to notify the Commission in advance.

After having investigated or examined a possible breach, the Commission, where it found there was no breach (or e.g. that the *de minimis* principle applied), could communicate this either through a formal individual exemption *or* an informal/non-binding 'comfort letter' to the firm/undertaking concerned. Comfort letters were more routine and had no legal standing as such; they simply amounted to an element of fact, which the national courts or third parties could take into account in deciding if there was a breach of EU competition law.[48]

14.6 REGULATION 1/2003 AND THE DECENTRALISATION OF ENFORCEMENT

14.6.1 DECENTRALISING ENFORCEMENT: REGULATION 1/2003

This notification system for cartel-like behaviour potentially contrary to Article 101 TFEU no longer exists and, as a result, comfort letters are now no longer issued. This has

---

46 Including Council Regulation 3976/87/EEC on the application of [now art 101(3) TFEU] to certain categories of agreements and concerted practices in the air transport sector OJ L 374 31.12.1987 p. 9 (later amended); Council Regulation 1534/91/EEC on the application of [now art 101(3) TFEU] of the Treaty to certain categories of agreements, decisions and concerted practices in the insurance sector OJ L 143 7.6.1991 p. 1; or Council Regulation 479/92/EEC on the application of [now art 101(3) TFEU] to certain categories of agreements, decisions and concerted practices between liner shipping companies (Consortia) OJ L 55 29.2.1992 p. 3 (later amended).

47 See recital 10.

48 Case 31/80 *L'Oreal* [1980] ECR 3775 especially paras 7–12.

arisen because of the decentralisation of the enforcement of competition law since 2004 with the passing of Regulation 1/2003, which came into effect on 1 May 2004.

The effect of Regulation 1/2003 is to make Article 101(3) TFEU directly effective (i.e. Article 81(3) can now be invoked before national courts and applied by national courts). Previously only Article 81(1) EC Treaty (now Article 101(1) TFEU) was directly effective (and so, before Regulation 1/2003, national courts could only deal with Article 81(1) if the issue came up in a case before it, but not Article 81(3)). Now, the Commission will make findings in important cases as to whether the criteria for exemption exist, rather than granting exemptions following a notification procedure as in the past.

The effect of (or one of the effects of) this change is that the Commission's role in enforcement has been reduced, and there will now be more competition cases dealt with at national level, rather than involving in all cases the Commission and often ending up before the ECJ in the case of disputes.

Firms/undertakings must now make their own decisions as to whether they comply with EU competition law (in the same way that a company would be responsible for ensuring its own compliance with, e.g. labour/employment law), on the basis of legal advice they obtain themselves from their own lawyers. They can no longer ask for individual exemptions or 'comfort letters' from the Commission (after having notified the Commission of a proposed/planned joint enterprise).

KEY LEARNING POINT

THE IMPORTANCE OF REGULATION 1/2003

Regulation 1/2003 enabled the enforcement of EU competition law to be decentralised. Previously, only the first two provisions of Article 101 were directly effective: the third paragraph, on exemptions/derogations, was not (because it did not satisfy all the conditions for direct effect). This meant that national courts could not themselves fully apply (now) Article 101 TFEU. At that stage in the development of (then) Community competition law, the Commission alone could fully apply its provisions in the first instance. Now national competition authorities can invoke the entirety of Article 101 in national courts, meaning that the Commission can concentrate on only major cases. One consequence of this is that the Commission can concentrate more resources on a smaller number of cases, and it has been suggested that the Commission as a result adopts a more adversarial and prosecutorial style,[49] which in turn strengthens due process rights in competition law procedures.

---

49 H Schweitzer 'The European competition law enforcement system and the evolution of judicial review' *EUI–RSCAS Competition 2009/Proceedings* (EUI 2009) 9, subsequently published in C-D Ehlermann, M Marquis (eds) *European Competition Law Annual 2009: Evaluation of Evidence and its Judicial review in Competition Cases* (Hart Publishing 2010).

The opening recitals to Regulation 1/2003 set out the context of its adoption:

(1) In order to establish a system which ensures that competition in the common market is not distorted, Articles 81 and 82 of the Treaty must be applied effectively and uniformly in the Community [now Union]. Council Regulation No. 17 of 6th February 1962,[50] First Regulation implementing Articles 81 and 82 of the Treaty [now Articles 101 and 102 TFEU], has allowed a Community competition policy to develop that has helped to disseminate a competition culture within the Community. In the light of experience, however, that Regulation should now be replaced by legislation designed to meet the challenges of an integrated market and a future enlargement of the Community [now Union].

(2) In particular, there is a need to rethink the arrangements for applying the exception from the prohibition on agreements, which restrict competition, laid down in Article 81(3) of the Treaty. Under Article 83(2)(b) of the Treaty, account must be taken in this regard of the need to ensure effective supervision, on the one hand, and to simplify administration to the greatest possible extent, on the other.

(3) The centralised scheme set up by Regulation No 17 no longer secures a balance between those two objectives. It hampers application of the Community competition rules by the courts and competition authorities of the Member States, and the system of notification it involves prevents the Commission from concentrating its resources on curbing the most serious infringements. It also imposes considerable costs on undertakings.

(4) The present system should therefore be replaced by a directly applicable exception system in which the competition authorities and courts of the Member States have the power to apply not only Article 81(1) and Article 82 of the Treaty [now Article 101(1) and Article 101(2) TFEU], which have direct applicability by virtue of the case-law of the Court of Justice of the European Communities, but also Article 81(3) of the Treaty [now Article 101(3) TFEU].

(5) In order to ensure an effective enforcement of the Community competition rules and at the same time the respect of fundamental rights of defence, this Regulation should regulate the burden of proof under Articles 81 and 82 of the Treaty. It should be for the party or the authority alleging an infringement of Article 81(1) and Article 82 of the Treaty [now Articles 101 and 102 TFEU] to prove the existence thereof to the required legal standard. It should be for the undertaking or association of undertakings invoking the benefit of a defence against a finding of an infringement to demonstrate to the required legal standard that the conditions for applying such defence are satisfied. This Regulation affects neither national rules on the standard of proof nor obligations of competition authorities and courts of the Member States to ascertain the relevant facts of a case, provided that such rules and obligations are compatible with general principles of Community law.

---

50 OJ 13 21.02.1962 p. 204.

(6) In order to ensure that the Community competition rules are applied effectively, the competition authorities of the Member States should be associated more closely with their application. To this end, they should be empowered to apply Community [now Union] law.

(7) National courts have an essential part to play in applying the Community competition rules. When deciding disputes between private individuals, they protect the subjective rights under Community law, for example by awarding damages to the victims of infringements. The role of the national courts here complements that of the competition authorities of the Member States. They should therefore be allowed to apply Articles 81 and 82 of the Treaty [now Articles 101 and 102 TFEU] in full.

EXPLAINING THE LAW

THE RELATIONSHIP BETWEEN NATIONAL LAW AND EU COMPETITION LAW

The Member States are allowed to impose stricter competition law requirements in their own legal systems than those required by EU competition law. Recital 8 of Regulation 1/2003 gives an example of this: national competition law may restrict unilateral conduct that would be permitted under Article 101, because Article 101 only covers coordinated behaviours between more than one undertaking. The specific examples it gives are: (i) abusive behaviours toward economically dependent undertakings (which would not be caught by Article 102 TFEU either unless the undertaking acting abusively was in a dominant position) and (ii) criminal sanctions imposed at national level that are not required by or related to EU law.

However, the same recital goes on to explain that if EU law specifically exempts a certain market behaviour under Article 101(3) TFEU, then stricter national rules may not prohibit it. This relationship with national competition law is simply a reflection of the general concepts of supremacy of EU law and of the competences of the EU: national law is only excluded when EU law is competent on a particular matter: when the EU is competent relating to a particular matter, national law contrary to EU law must be disapplied by national courts. Recital 9 sets out that national competition legislation may pursue other objectives not encompassed by (EU) competition law.

As regards enforcement, the Commission is empowered to step in and enforce competition law where national competition authorities are already exercising competence or could so: in this situation, national authorities are relieved of their competence.[51]

---

51 Regulation 1/2003 recital 17.

Summary of main secondary legislation on enforcement of competition law:

1962	Regulation 17/62[52]	Made explicit provision for enforcement of EEC competition law – provided for notification of agreements etc. to, and negative clearance of them, by Commission, as well as for investigation by Commission and imposition of fines
1968	Regulation 1017/68[53]	Applied rules of competition law to transport by rail, road and inland waterway
1971	Regulation 2821/71[54]	Exempted from notification to the Commission agreements etc. related to (a) the application of standards and types; (b) joint research and development; (c) specialisation in the manufacture of products, including agreements necessary for achieving this
1974	Regulation 2988/74[55]	Regulated limitation periods for enforcement of competition law by the Commission
1986	Regulation 4056/86[56]	Applied rules on competition law to maritime transport, especially regarding exemptions from competition law, such as loyalty arrangements
1987	Regulation 3975/87[57]	Applied competition law rules to the air sector
1987	Regulation 3976/87[58]	Exempted certain agreements etc. in the air transport sector from competition law, where the agreements concerned: – the allocation of seat capacity and the coordination of timetables; – consultations on tariffs; – certain agreements on joint operation of new services; – slot allocation in airports; computer reservation systems

52 OJ 13 21.02.1962 p. 204. (now superseded).
53 OJ L 175 23.7.1968 p. 1.
54 OJ L 285 29.12.1971 p. 49.
55 OJ L 319 29.11.1974 p. 1.
56 OJ L 378 31.12.1986 p. 4.
57 OJ L 374 31.12.1987 p. 1.
58 OJ L 374 31.12.1987 p. 9.

1991	Regulation 1534/91[59]	Exempted agreements etc. in the insurance sector, where the agreements concerned: (a) the establishment of common risk premium tariffs based on collectively ascertained statistics or the number of claims; (b) the establishment of common standard policy conditions; (c) the common coverage of certain types of risks; (d) the settlement of claims; (e) the testing and acceptance of security devices; (f) registers of, and information on, aggravated risks, provided that the keeping of these registers and the handling of this information is carried out subject to the proper protection of confidentiality
1992	Regulation 479/92[60]	Provided for exemptions to be made by the Commission under [now Article 101(3) TFEU] for agreements between shipping liner companies
1999	Regulation 1216/99[61]	Exempted vertical agreements concerning trade marks and the protection of intellectual property
2003	Regulation 1/2003 updates, consolidates and/or replaces previous legislation.	Apart from its consolidating effect, the main difference this made was to achieve a de-centralisation of enforcement of EU competition law (see below)

Summary of key provisions of Regulation 1/2003:

Article	Content	Significance
Article 1	**Application of Articles 101 and 102 TFEU** – Sets out that agreements etc. that contravene Articles 101(1) and 102 shall be prohibited without a prior decision being necessary, conversely, agreements etc. that satisfy Article 101(3) shall be lawful	Makes it clear that Articles 101 and 102 TFEU are to be directly effective and do not require national implementing decisions in particular cases

---

59 OJ L 143 7.6.1991 p. 1.
60 OJ L 055 29.02.1992 p. 3.
61 OJ L 148 15.6.1999 p. 5.

Article 2	**Burden of proof** – Sets out that a party alleging infringement of Articles 101 or 102 TFEU must prove it	This simply reflects a standard principle of evidence across the Member States, what matters in practice is what must be proven, which has previously been established in case law, although even now aspects remain unclear (see explanatory box below)
Article 3	**Relationship between Articles 101 and 102 TFEU and national competition laws** – Provides that: – When <u>national competition authorities apply national competition law, they shall also apply Articles 101 and 102 TFEU</u> if the subject matter affects trade between Member States (para. 1); – The application of national competition law <u>shall not permit agreements etc. prohibited under Article 101(1) TFEU nor prohibit agreements etc. permitted under Article 101(3)</u>; – The <u>Member States may apply their own merger rules and also pursue objectives</u> in national competition law other than those in Articles 101 and 102 TFEU	Regulates the relations between national law and EU competition law in a straightforward way by applying the supremacy doctrine: what EU law permits, national law must permit, and what EU law prohibits, national law must prohibit. However, this approach does not apply to merger control, which only later became a part of EU competition law as it is not Treaty-based
Article 4	**Powers of the Commission** – Provides that the Commission shall have what powers are set out in Regulation 1/2003	Reflects the fact that the enforcement of competition law is not dealt with in the Treaty
Article 5	**Powers of the competition authorities of the Member States** – Provides that national competition authorities shall have the power to apply Articles 101 and 102 TFEU in individual cases to requiring that an infringement be brought to an end, order interim measures, accept commitments, impose fines or penalties	This facilitates the direct effect of Articles 101 and 102 by de-centralising enforcement of the totality of both articles to national competition authorities

Article 6	**Powers of national courts** – Provides that national courts are to apply Articles 101 and 102 TFEU	This clearly establishes the direct effect of Articles 101 and 102
Article 7	**Finding and termination of infringement** – Provides that the Commission may of its own initiative or upon a complaint from a legal person or the Member States order the termination of an infringement by requiring either behavioural *or structural changes* and, further, that structural changes should only be ordered where they are necessary or less burdensome	This makes clear that the Commission's powers of enforcement remain, not withstanding de-centralisation. The provision on *structural changes*[62] is new compared to Regulation 17/62
Article 8	**Interim measures** – Provides that the Commission may order interim measures once a *prima facie* case is made out	This is a broadly framed power: the nature of the interim measures is not limited, nor is their duration (other than that they must be for a specified, but renewable, period)
Article 9	**Commitments** – Provides that the Commission may accept commitments as an alternative to a sanction	Commitments allow a non-contentious termination of proceedings against an undertaking. They do not amount to a finding of innocence and the undertakings do not waive their right of appeal. Commitments are not meant to be used where the Commission would otherwise impose a fine (Recital 13) (So this distinguishes Article 9 commitments from the settlement procedure, see below)

---

62 Under recital 12 of the regulation, the use of structural changes is limited to situations where there is a substantial risk of a lasting or repeated infringement that derives from the very 'structure of the undertaking' and where 'there is no equally effective behavioural remedy or where any equally effective behavioural remedy would be more burdensome for the undertaking'.

Article 10	**Finding of inapplicability** – Provides that the <u>Commission has the power not to apply Article 101 or 102 TFEU</u> when the conditions in the articles are not met	This provision is almost unnecessary, since it is inherent in any power that it need not be exercised when the conditions for its valid application do not exist
Article 11	**Cooperation between the Commission and the competition authorities of the Member States** – Provides that the competition authorities of the Member States will <u>inform the Commission</u> of their investigations and decisions and <u>the Commission will transmit to the Member States</u> the most important documents from its proceedings + Article 11(6) provides that the initiation by the Commission of proceedings shall relieve <u>national competition authorities</u> of their competence to apply Articles 101–102 TFEU and that the Commission will only do so after consulting with that national competition authority	Sets out a cooperative, 'federal' relationship between the Commission and national competition authorities, while establishing that the Commission has ultimate enforcement authority
Article 12	**Exchange of information** – Provides that: – the Commission and national competition authorities may <u>exchange all relevant information</u> between each other, – the information shall i. be used only regarding Articles 101 and 102 TFEU, ii. comply with national procedural rights of the defence, and iii. may not be used for custodial sanctions	Provides a wide-ranging right to transfer information between the Commission and Member States, but restricts its use in proceedings to comply with national law
Article 13	**Suspension or termination of proceedings** – Provides that the existence of proceedings before another competition authority is grounds for a national competition authority or the Commission to terminate a second proceeding	Provides a way to avoid duplication, but it is a discretionary power (see also Article 116 below)
Article 14	**Advisory Committee** – Provides that the Commission shall exercise its authority under Articles 7, 8, 9, 10, 23, 24(1), 29(1), i.e. in particular cases, <u>only after consulting either an Advisory Committee</u> consisting of the representatives of the Member States	The Commission is not bound to follow the Opinion of the Advisory Committee on a particular case, although Article 14(5) states that it must take 'utmost

	(usually of the competition authorities of the Member States)	account; of the Committee's opinion – this is another way of institutionalising the federal nature of EU competition law
Article 15	**Cooperation with national courts** – Provides that national courts: – may request information from the Commission, – must forward judgments on competition law to the Commission, – must accept written observations from national competition authorities and the Commission in proceedings, and – may permit oral observations from the same parties	This is a straightforward procedural facilitation of enforcement by national courts
Article 16	**Uniform application of Union competition law** – Provides that national courts or competition authorities <u>may not adopt decisions contrary to Commission</u> decisions under Articles 101 or 102 TFEU	This reflects the doctrine of the supremacy of EU law
Article 17	**Investigations into sectors of the economy and into types of agreements** – Provides that where circumstances restrict or distort trade within the common market, the Commission may: – <u>request relevant information</u> from undertakings – <u>publish reports concerning particular sectors or across sectors</u>	Obtaining information on market practice is necessary for the Commission to carry out its enforcement role, the power to publish reports though applies to sectors of the economy rather than particular undertakings
Article 18	**Requests for information** – Provides that the Commission: – may require <u>provision of necessary information</u> to carry out its duties, – shall state the legal basis and the purpose of the request, specify the required information, and fix i. the time-limit and ii. the penalties under Article 23 for supplying incorrect or misleading information	This provides a coercive power for the Commission to obtain information regarding its powers generally under the Regulation, including regarding particular undertakings

Article 19	**Power to take statements** – Provides that the <u>Commission may take statements</u> from natural or legal persons in undertakings, accompanied by representatives of national competition authorities if the latter request this	This is a necessary and basic power for conducting any investigation
Article 20	**The Commission's powers of inspection** – Provides (in para. 1) the Commission may <u>conduct all necessary inspections of undertakings</u>: (a) to enter any premises, land and means of transport; (b) to examine the books and other records in any form related to the business; (c) to copy or extract from such books or records; (d) to seal any business premises and books or records; (e) to ask for explanations on facts or documents and record the answers. Commission officials shall: – produce their authorisation and inform national competition authorities in advance (para. 2), – inform the undertakings themselves, who must comply, but who have the right to review before the Court of Justice (para. 3) National authorities are to assist the Commission with authorising inspections under national law (paras. 5–8)	The Commission is given wide-ranging powers of investigation, which touch on key constitutional rights, such as the right to property and privacy. This is another provision that can be described as 'quasi-criminal' and is the basis for so-called 'dawn raids'. Concerning confidentiality of records on the basis of legal privilege, case law indicates that this does not apply to in-house legal advice.[63]
Article 21	**Inspection of other Premises** – Provides that if a <u>reasonable suspicion exists that books or other records that may be relevant to prove a *serious* violation of Articles 101 or 102 TFEU</u> are being kept in any other	Provides for formal criteria in the execution of quite far-reaching inspection powers (trigger of reasonable suspicion and approval by

---

63 See Case 155/79 *AM and S Europe v Commission* [1982] ECR 1575; Case T–125/03 (R) *AKZO Nobel Chemicals Ltd v Commission* [2003] ECR II–4771.

premises, <u>including the homes of staff of undertakings, the Commission can order an inspection</u> of the premises with <u>approval of national courts</u>, but the Commission decision shall specify:
- the subject matter and purpose of the inspection,
- the date on which it is to begin, and
- indicate the right to have the decision reviewed by the Court of Justice.

In granting authorisation, national courts may not question the necessity of inspection (lawfulness being subject to review by the Court of Justice only)

national courts) for serious violations, and review of legality by Court of Justice

Article 22	**Investigations by competition authorities of Member States** – Provides that <u>the Member States may carry out, according to their own national law, inspections requested</u> by other Member States relating to Articles 101 and 121, and shall carry out such inspections requested by the Commission	Balances the ultimate enforcement primacy of the Commission with national procedural autonomy and facilitates cooperation between Member States
Article 23	**Fines** – Provides that the Commission <u>may impose fines of up to 1 per cent of preceding year's business turnover</u> for violation of procedural requirements during investigation (para. 1) or up to 10 per cent for actual infringement of Article 101 or Article 102 TFEU or a violation under Article 9 of Regulation 1/2003 (para. 3), and for fines on associations of undertakings (para. 4)	Although para. 5 states that fines shall not be criminal in nature, they can be considered to be quasi-criminal in having a punitive rationale. This raises the issue of the adequacy of procedural protections to the defence, including the issue of the onus of proof (see further below)
Article 24	**Periodic penalty payments** – Provides that the Commission may impose on undertakings <u>periodic penalty payments</u> not exceeding 5 per cent of the average daily turnover in the preceding business year per day, in order to compel compliance with the material or procedural requirements of EU competition law	Supplements Article 23

Article 25	**Limitation periods for the imposition of penalties** – Provides that the powers conferred on the Commission by Articles 23 and 24, concerning fines, are subject to <u>limitation periods</u>: (a) 3 years for infringements concerning requests for information or inspections; (b) 5 years in the case of all other infringements, but that the limitation period stops running upon any action taken by the Commission or national competition authorities for investigation or proceedings	The limitation periods give considerable flexibility to the EU institutions, both under Articles 25 and 26
Article 26	**Limitation period for the enforcement of penalties** – Provides that the power of the Commission to enforce decisions under Articles 23 and 24 are subject to <u>a limitation period of 5 years</u>, but this interrupted by any decision concerning variation of the fine or any enforcement action by the Commission or the Member States	As per above
Article 27	**Hearing of the parties, complainants and others** – The key paragraph is para. 2: 'The <u>rights of defence</u> of the parties concerned shall be fully respected in the proceedings. They shall be entitled to have <u>access to the Commission's file</u>, subject to the legitimate interest of undertakings in the protection of their <u>business secrets</u>. The right of access to the file shall not extend to <u>confidential information and internal documents of the Commission or the competition authorities of the Member States</u>. In particular, the right of access shall not extend to correspondence between the Commission and the competition authorities of the Member States, or between the latter, including documents drawn up pursuant to Articles 11 and 14. Nothing in this paragraph shall prevent the Commission from disclosing and using information necessary to prove an infringement.'	This provision clearly seeks to provide procedural rights for suspected undertakings. Several aspects are not addressed, however: – Burden of proof, – Any requirement for an oral hearing, – Scope of confidentiality exception

Article 28	**Professional secrecy** – Provides that in general information shall <u>only be used by national or EU authorities for the purpose of which it was obtained</u> and that information of the kind covered by professional secrecy shall not be disclosed	This addresses a point not included in Article 28 above, but the scope of professional secrecy is undefined
Article 29	**Withdrawal in individual cases** – Provides that either the Commission or a national competition authority can <u>withdraw an exemption Regulation</u> granted under Article 101(3) Article 101(3) is being breached	Contributes to the de-centralisation of enforcement by granting this authority to both the Commission and national competition authorities
Article 30	**Publication of decisions** – Provides that the Commission shall publish the decisions, which it takes pursuant to Articles 7 to 10, 23 and 24	Contributes to the building up of a jurisprudence of Commission decisions. As with Articles 27–28, the scope of confidentiality/ secrecy is not defined
Article 31	**Review by the Court of Justice** – Provides that the Court of Justice shall have <u>unlimited jurisdiction to review decisions whereby the Commission has fixed a fine or periodic penalty payment</u> and that it may cancel, reduce or increase this	Consistent with the general jurisdiction of the Court of Justice under Article 263 TFEU
Article 32	**Exclusions** – Provides for some <u>specific exclusions</u> relating to international tramp vessels, maritime transport services internal to the Member States, air transport between the EU and third countries	These are of limited scope
Article 33	**Implementing provisions**	
Article 34	**Transitional provisions**	
Article 35	**Designation of competition authorities of the Member States** – Provides that <u>the Member States may designate the appropriate national authorities</u> under the Regulation, subject to the powers of the Commission and Court of Justice	Confirms principle of national procedural autonomy subject to the specific powers of the Commission and Court of Justice
Articles 36–43	**Amendment of existing legislation**	Most of the amended legislation is included in the summary table above

** *Note that the relationship between appeals to the CAT and the judicial review jurisdiction of the High Court is quite compli-cated, the chart is indicative only*

National Enforcement of EU Competition Law in UK

National Competition Authority (NCA) – Competition and Mergers Authority (CMA) in UK

↓

Investigation
(*Van Gend en Loos* and Competition Act 1998)

↓

Powers of Investigation
(Chapter III, Competition Act 1998)

↓

Fine/Order by NCA/CMA

↓   ↓

Appeal to Competition Appeals Tribunal (CAT) and/or **Damages action at CAT**
(Competition Act 1998, s. 47A)

↓   ↓

Full Review on the Merits   **Judicial Review Procedure**
(Competition Act 1998, Sch. 8)   (Enterprise Act 2002, s. 120 regarding mergers)

↓   ↓

Remedies under Schedule 8, s. 3(2)   Judicial review remedies

↓

↑ **Possible preliminary reference (Article 267 TFEU):**

↵ Outcome goes back to national court/tribunal

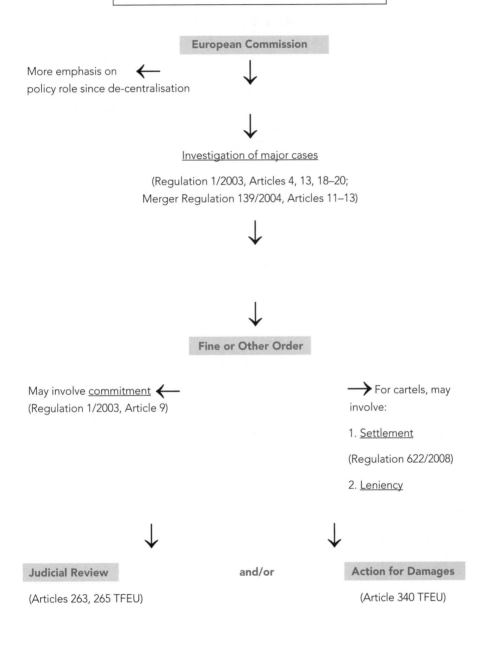

Enforcement of Competition Law at EU Level

European Commission

More emphasis on
policy role since de-centralisation ←

Investigation of major cases

(Regulation 1/2003, Articles 4, 13, 18–20;
Merger Regulation 139/2004, Articles 11–13)

Fine or Other Order

May involve <u>commitment</u> ←
(Regulation 1/2003, Article 9)

→ For cartels, may
involve:

1. <u>Settlement</u>

(Regulation 622/2008)

2. <u>Leniency</u>

Judicial Review

(Articles 263, 265 TFEU)

and/or

Action for Damages

(Article 340 TFEU)

EXPLAINING THE LAW

THE BURDEN OF PROOF AND DEFENCE RIGHTS IN COMPETITION CASES

Article 2 of Regulation 1/2003 states that the burden of proving a violation of Articles 101 or 102 TFEU shall rest with the party claiming the violation exists. Even more than 50 years after the establishment of the EU, some doubts arise from the case law as to the scope of this burden. Certainly, the basic principle is clear that the party alleging the violation must prove it. However, what is less clear is the extent of the duty across the spectrum of competition cases, including as regards a shift in the onus of proof, once the party claiming a violation sets out a prima facie case to that effect.

In UK law, there are two alternative burdens of proof: the civil burden of the 'balance of probabilities' and the criminal burden of 'beyond a reasonable doubt'. In general, the burden in competition cases is closest to the idea of the balance of probabilities. However, in cases where fines have been imposed, some case law indicates a stricter standard close to the criminal burden of beyond a reasonable doubt, if not quite that exacting.[64]

In merger cases, in particular, the approach of the EU courts is to consider that the burden of proof shifts to the defence to establish something like a prima facie defence once the prosecution has itself established a prima facie case of breach, whereupon the prosecution must establish that the defence is not valid.[65]

The burden of proof issue connects to the broader issue of defence rights in competition proceedings. Criticism is made of the lack of independence of the decision on a fine from the enforcement authority (the Commission investigates and punishes) and the absence of a full merits review by the Court of Justice.[66] In defence of the current enforcement system, it can be argued that a composite structure whereby administrative decision-making by the Commission is subject to independent judicial review satisfies the requirements of Article 6(1) ECHR.[67]

---

64 See e.g. Case T–1/89 *Rhône-Poulenc SA v Commission* [1991] ECR II–867 at 954. For discussion see Schweitzer (n 49) 13–16.

65 See e.g. Case T–201/04 *Microsoft v Commission* [2007] ECR II–3601 paras 688 and 1144.

66 See e.g. J Killick, P Berghe 'This is not the time to be tinkering with Regulation 1/2003 – It is time for fundamental reform – Europe should have change we can believe in' (2010) 6(2) *Competition Law Review* 259–85.

67 Schweitzer (n 49) 3–4, citing A Andreangeli *EU Competition Enforcement and Human Rights* (Edward Elgar 2008) 53; M Poustie 'The rule of law or the rule of lawyers? *Alconbury*, Article 6(1) and the role of the courts in administrative decision-making' (2001) 6 *European Human Rights Law Review* 657–76 at 663.

KEY LEARNING POINT

LETTERS OF GUIDANCE

The Commission has said that it will issue what are called 'letters of guidance',[68] which are similar to comfort letters – *but* these letters of guidance will only be issued in cases involving novel or especially complex points of law, whereas comfort letters were issued as a matter of routine by the Commission in many competition cases.

As with comfort letters, these letters of guidance are informal only and not legally binding; they are simply a way of letting people know the Commission's opinion on something. Ultimately, it is up to the ECJ to decide if the Commission's opinion in such a letter, in a given case, is correct.[69]

14.6.2 DECENTRALISING ENFORCEMENT – NATIONAL COMPETITION LAW

With the decentralisation of EU competition law, it now has a more federal nature, contrasting with the previous centralised, unitary character at EU level. National competition authorities are now the primary enforcers of EU competition law, leaving large and novel cases for the European Commission. The detail of how this works is set out in Regulation 1/2003, as set out above. The most important provision is Article 3 governing the relationship between national competition law and EU competition law:

– under Article 3(1), national courts must apply EU competition law wherever it is relevant, after which, additionally
– under Article 3(2), stricter national rules may be applied, but not if they conflict with Article 101(3) on exemptions to Article 101(1) (there are no exemptions under Article 102 TFEU, so there is no need to apply a similar approach there (see the next two chapters).

14.7 THE *DE MINIMIS* PRINCIPLE AND THE COMMISSION NOTICE ON AGREEMENTS OF MINOR IMPORTANCE

In its case law, the Commission developed the doctrine that an agreement or concerted practice will not be caught by Article 101(1) TFEU if it does not have an appreciable impact on competition or inter-state trade, even though technically it does represent a

---

68 OJ C101, 27.4.2004 at 78.
69 See http://eur-lex.europa.eu/legal-content/EN/TXT/?qid=1427993876426&uri-URISERV:I26112 (accessed 2 April 2015).

breach of Article 101(1) TFEU. This is known as the *de minimis* doctrine or rule and was established in *Völk v Vervaecke*.[70]

The Commission formalised this practice by developing specific criteria for when EU competition law would not be enforced (i.e. even though technically there was a breach of Article 101(1) TFEU): the Commission Notice on agreements of minor importance which do not appreciably restrict competition under Article 101(1) TFEU. This involves a *de minimis* presumption in that restrictive agreements will be exempt from Article 101 TFEU if any of the following apply:[71]

– the parties' market share does not exceed 10 per cent for horizontal agreements
– the parties' market share does not exceed 15 per cent for vertical agreements.

The threshold is reduced to 5 per cent where there are cumulative effects from several such agreements by different suppliers and distributors (referred to as cumulative foreclosure effect).

KEY LEARNING POINT

RESTRICTIONS BY OBJECT NOT SUBJECT TO *DE MINIMIS* PRINCIPLE
The Commission Notice does not apply to agreements that have as their object the restrictions of competition.[72] In other words, deliberate attempts to restrict or distort competition are automatically void, irrespective of whether they succeed or not. We will look further at the distinction between object and effect of cartel-like behaviours in the next chapter.

The size of market share is a partly distinct issue to the issue of affecting trade between Member States, but the smaller the breach in terms of market size, the less likely a breach may affect trade between Member States. The Commission has issued a separate Commission Notice – *Guidelines on the effect on trade concept*.[73] This sets a threshold combination of a 5 per cent market share threshold and a €40 million turnover for effect on trade between Member States; below this level, agreements (including those with the object of restricting or distorting trade) do not fall within Article 101 TFEU. In addition, in relation to small and medium-sized enterprises, the Commission is more lenient, as made explicit in the previous Notice on Agreements of Minor Importance:

. . . agreements between small and medium-sized undertakings, as defined in the Annex to Commission Recommendation 96/280/EC(3), are rarely capable of

70 Case 5/69 *Völk v Vervaecke* [1969] ECR 295. More recently see Case C–226/11 *Expedia*, not yet reported paras 16 and 17.
71 Brussels (25 June 2014) COM(2014) 4136 final.
72 Ibid para 13.
73 Commission Notice Guidelines on the effect on trade concept contained in arts 81 and 82 [now arts 101 and 102 TFEU] of the Treaty OJ C 101 27.4.2004 p. 81 paras 44–57.

appreciably affecting trade between Member States. Small and medium-sized undertakings are currently defined in that recommendation as undertakings which have fewer than 250 employees and have either an annual turnover not exceeding EUR 40 million or an annual balance-sheet total not exceeding EUR 27 million.[74]

The *de minimis* principle reflects a practical need to prioritise enforcement: restrictions on competition that do not have a significant impact are not worth the resources of enforcing against them. With the decentralisation of competition law, national competition authorities can, of course, choose to enforce below these thresholds within their own jurisdiction.

The Merger Regulation also adopts a *de minimis* principle, where the market share of the undertakings concerned does not exceed 25 per cent either in the common market or in a substantial part of it.[75]

14.8 SETTLEMENT AND LENIENCY PROCEDURES

14.8.1 LENIENCY POLICY WITH CARTELS

The leniency policy offers companies involved in a cartel and that voluntarily report their involvement to the Commission either total immunity from fines or a reduction of fines that the Commission would have otherwise imposed on them.[76] It is a way for the Commission to induce greater cooperation and, therefore, spare the Commission's limited enforcement resources.

To obtain total immunity under the leniency policy, a company that participated in a cartel must be the first one to inform the Commission of an undetected cartel by providing enough information to allow the Commission to launch an inspection at the premises of the companies allegedly involved in the cartel. If the Commission already has enough information to launch an inspection or has already undertaken one, the company must provide evidence that permits the Commission to prove the cartel infringement. In any case, the company must also fully cooperate with the Commission by providing it with all the evidence in its possession and immediately ending the infringement. It only applies where the undertaking seeking to benefit from it did not coerce the involvement of any party in the cartel.

---

74 Commission Notice on agreements of minor importance which do not appreciably restrict competition under art 81(1) of the Treaty establishing the European Community (*de minimis*) OJ C 368 22.12.2001 p. 13.

75 Merger Regulation 2004 recital 32.

76 See Commission Notice on Immunity from fines and reduction of fines in cartel cases OJ C 298 8.12.2006 p. 17.

Companies not qualifying for immunity may get a reduction of fines if they provide evidence that represents 'significant added value' to what the Commission already possesses and have stopped their participation in the cartel. Evidence is considered to be of a 'significant added value' for the Commission when it strengthens its ability to prove the infringement. The first company benefiting gets a 30–50 per cent reduction, the second a 20–30 per cent and subsequent companies up to 20 per cent.

14.8.2 SETTLEMENT WITH CARTELS

The Commission introduced a 'settlement procedure' in 2004, amended in 2008, to achieve procedural efficiency in fighting cartels.[77] The procedure is that where parties are prepared to acknowledge their participation in the cartels, the Commission has the discretion to disclose to them a statement of objections, i.e. an indication of the Commission's decision against the undertakings. On that basis, the parties can submit settlement submissions in return for a reduced penalty.

The outcome is 'cease and desist', so there is an avoidance to some extent of fines or penalties. It differs from leniency (which is more like plea bargaining) in that the Commission has to show the parties that it has sufficient evidence to bring a final decision, and must send a statement of objections.

14.9 UK ENFORCEMENT OF EU COMPETITION LAW

The UK had introduced some elements of regulation of competition prior to joining the EU, but membership resulted in a much more systematic approach. As with the other Member States, national competition authorities had a less central role owing to (now) Article 101(3) TFEU not having direct effect. With the implementation of Regulation 1/2003, UK competition authorities are now centrally involved in enforcement of EU competition law in the UK.

Regulation of competition first began with the common law doctrine of restraint of trade, developed in the early case of *Dyer*.[78] This is a doctrine in the context of employment contracts. The effect of the doctrine is to limit the entitlement of an employer, by contract with the employee, to restrict the employment options of the employee after the employee leaves his or her current job, e.g. a restriction on employees working with any competitors for a period of time after leaving.

---

77 Commission Regulation 622/2008/EC amending Regulation 773/2004/EC, as regards the conduct of settlement procedures in cartel cases OJ L 171 1.7.2008 p. 3; Commission Notice on the conduct of settlement procedures in view of the adoption of Decisions pursuant to Article 7 and Article 23 of Council Regulation 1/2003/EC in cartel cases OJ C 167 2.7.2008 p. 1.

78 (1414) 2 Hen V fol 5 pl 26.

The first legislation on competition law in the UK was the Monopolies and Restrictive Practices (Inquiry and Control) Act 1948, which provided for monopolies to be subject to some public control through the work of the Monopolies Commission (MC). The Restrictive Trade Practices Act 1956 provided that the legality of certain types of trade practices (including exclusive dealing,[79] collective boycotts, aggregated rebates, collective resale price maintenance,[80] and information agreements[81]) depended on them being in the public interest, and they had to be registered.

The Monopolies and Mergers Act 1965 established a system of merger control, extending the role of the MC to address this aspect of competition (making the UK only the second jurisdiction to do so by that date[82]). They were presumed to be unlawful as determined by the Restrictive Practices Court (a branch of the High Court). The Fair Trading Act 1973 changed the title of the MC to the Monopolies and Mergers Commission (MMC), whose task was to investigate mergers referred to it, but approval or otherwise of mergers was for the Secretary of State. The Fair Trading Act (also of 1973) established the Director General of Fair Trading as head of the Office of Fair Trading (OFT), with the task of reviewing commercial activities with regard to fair trading practice, including to assist the MMC.

The Competition Act 1998, which came into force in 2000, established a 'comprehensive modern statutory competition policy as a legal regime, fully separate from the realm of politics, with a strong institutional and legal framework for public enforcement'.[83] The 1998 Act is based on EU competition rules. Chapter I of the Act incorporates Article 101 TFEU, and Chapter II incorporates Article 102 TFEU.

Section 45 replaced the MMC with a Competition Commission, a non-departmental public body to conduct in-depth inquiries into mergers and regulated industries, when requested by the OFT or the Secretary of State or another regulatory body. The Enterprise Act 2002 further developed the competition framework in the UK:

– modified the powers of the OFT, by making it more independent
– established a criminal 'cartel offence', consisting of a dishonest agreement that two or more undertakings will engage in a horizontal hard-core cartel (price-fixing arrangements, arrangements limiting supply or production, market-sharing arrangements or bid-rigging arrangements) (the Act removed the requirement of dishonesty; it now only needs to be a knowing agreement)[84]

....

79 Exclusive dealing refers to an agreement between two undertakings or business to deal exclusively in one of the businesses products, e.g. a car dealer agreeing with the manufacturer to sell only new cars produced by that man-ufacturer.

80 Resale Prices Act 1964. For a relatively early English work in the field of competition law see R Wilberforce, A Campbell and N Elles *The Law of Restrictive Practices and Monopolies* (2nd edn Sweet and Maxwell 1966).

81 Restrictive Trade Practices Act 1968 and see Restrictive Trade Practices Order 1969 (SI 1969/1842).

82 A Scott *Merger Control in the UK* (Oxford University Press 2006) 3.

83 Schweitzer (n 49) 36.

84 Enterprise Act 2002 ss 188–89.

– established a competition disqualification order (CDO), under which a person can be prohibited from acting as a company director due to breaking competition rules.[85]

The most recent legislation is the Enterprise and Regulatory Reform Act 2013, which combines the functions of the OFT and the Competition Commission into a new Competition and Markets Authority (CMA) (while responsibility for credit institutions is transferred to a newly created Financial Conduct Authority). The responsibilities of the CMA are:

– investigating mergers which could restrict competition
– conducting market studies and investigations in markets where there may be competition and consumer problems
– investigating where there may be breaches of UK or EU prohibitions against anti-competitive agreements and abuses of dominant positions
– bringing criminal proceedings against individuals who commit the cartel offence
– enforcing consumer protection legislation to tackle practices and market conditions that make it difficult for consumers to exercise choice
– cooperating with sector regulators and encouraging them to use their competition powers
– considering regulatory references and appeals.[86]

The main competition law powers of the CMA are now:

– to conduct compulsory interviews[87]
– to obtain documents[88]
– to enter premises and search with or without a warrant[89]
– to impose interim measures[90]
– to impose civil financial penalties for failure to comply with investigatory powers.[91]

The Secretary of State can impose time limits in relation to the conduct of antitrust investigations and the making of antitrust infringement decisions by the CMA.[92]

---

85 Section 9A of the Company Directors Disqualification Act 1986 as amended by s 204 of the Enterprise Act 2002.
86 Enterprise and Regulatory Reform Act 2013 Part III, amending the Enterprise Act 2002.
87 Section 26A of the Competition Act 1998, as amended by s 39 of the Enterprise and Regulatory Reform Act 2013.
88 Section 26 Competition Act 1998.
89 Without a warrant, under s 27 of the Competition Act 1998, two days' notice must be given; with a warrant, under s 28 of the 1998 Act, there is no notice requirement (this is the legal basis for so-called 'dawn raids'). The Commission has this power under art 20 of Regulation 1/2003.
90 Section 35 of the Competition Act 1998. See also s 43 of the Enterprise and Regulatory Reform Act 2013.
91 Section 36 of the Competition Act 1998, as amended by s 44 of the Enterprise and Regulatory Reform Act 2013.
92 Section 45 of the Enterprise and Regulatory Reform Act 2013.

Two ways exist to challenge a decision of the CMA:

(1) appeals under the Competition Act 1998 on the merits
(2) judicial review.

Appeals under the Competition Act allow the Competition Appeals Tribunal (CAT), which consists of a lawyer (usually a High Court judge) and two subject experts, to rehear in full and to retake the original decision of the CMA (or to remit the matter to the CMA to reconsider).[93] Under judicial review proceedings, which are also heard by the CAT (rather than the regular High Court), the normal grounds of judicial review apply, so this is not a rehearing on the merits.[94]

14.10 EXTRA-TERRITORIAL SCOPE OF EU COMPETITION LAW AND ITS INTERNATIONAL DIMENSION

14.10.1 EXTRA-TERRITORIALITY OF EU COMPETITION LAW

The extra-territorial dimension of EU competition law has become increasingly important, and this reflects the greater international profile the EU possesses in light of developments resulting from the *ERTA* (see Chapter 7) doctrine of parallelism and pre-emption in external relations.

KEY LEARNING POINT
....

EXTRA-TERRITORIAL JURISDICTION AND COMPETITION LAW
Extra-territorial jurisdiction is the capacity of a state to claim jurisdiction over events occurring outside its territory. It typically arises in a criminal law context. There are several principles of jurisdiction in international law as to when a state can claim jurisdiction over events occurring outside its territory. These include the active personality principle (where the perpetrator of a legal wrong is a citizen of a state, but the legal wrong occurs outside the state's territory), the passive personality principle (where the victim is a citizen or national of the State asserting jurisdiction) and the effects doctrine (where the victim of a legal wrong is a citizen of a state, but the legal wrong occurs outside the state's territory). In competition law, the effects doctrine is typically the basis for extra-territorial jurisdiction.

....

93 Schedule 8 of the Competition Act 1998.
94 Enterprise Act 2002 s 120.

Essentially, parallelism is the doctrine that where the Member States have adopted common policies internally within the exclusive competence of the EU, the EU enjoys a parallel external competence that pre-empts the Member States engaging in international relations regarding the same matter. Extra-territorial jurisdiction in competition law allows the EU the freedom, without intervention by individual Member States (due to parallelism), to assert competition jurisdiction extra-territorially.

Competition law is not a completely exclusive EU competence, in that Member States are allowed to have additional national laws that are stricter than EU law (except for practices exempted under Article 103 TFEU). This national competence is residual and marginal: most competition matters are exclusively for EU competence. For example, according to the terms of reference of the Dialogue between the EU and China on competition (see below), the Commission Directorate General Competition functions as the sole agent from the EU side, to oversee the dialogue with China.

The European Commission has exercised extra-territorial jurisdiction in a number of high-profile cases in recent years. The Court of Justice confirmed that the EU could exercise such jurisdiction in the *Wood Pulp* cartel cases, where it set out an implementation doctrine whereby it is enough for undertakings to see within the EU for EU competition law to apply:

> . . . if the applicability of prohibitions laid down under competition law were made to depend on the place where the agreement . . . was formed, the result would obviously be to give undertakings an easy means of evading these prohibitions. The decisive factor is therefore the place where it is implemented.[95]

14.10.2 INTERNATIONAL COOPERATION IN COMPETITION LAW

The EU engages in both bilateral and multilateral cooperation in competition law and policy.[96] The importance of this cooperation results from the inter-connectedness of markets and existence of cross-border anti-competitive behaviour.[97] First, candidate countries for EU accession are generally bound to seek to achieve the implementation of EU law as a result of association agreements. This includes implementation of EU competition law.

In addition, EU competition law has been introduced to Iceland, Liechtenstein and Norway, through the European Economic Association (EEA). Further, memoranda of

---

95 Joined Cases C–89/85, C–104/85, C–114/85, C–116 &117/85 and C–125–129/85 *Wood Pulp* [1993] ECR 1307 para 16.
96 See generally M Dabbah *International and Comparative Competition Law* (Cambridge University Press 2010) 198–226.
97 Q Wu 'EU–China competition dialogue: a new step in the internationalisation of EU competition law' (2012) 18(3) *European Law Journal* 461–77 at 461. See also generally F Snyder *The EU, the WTO and China, Legal Pluralism and International Trade Regulation* (Hart Publishing 2011).

understanding and more formal and specific cooperation agreements in competition law (called dedicated agreements) are signed with other countries.

EXPLAINING THE LAW

THE INFLUENCE OF EU COMPETITION LAW INTERNATIONALLY

For example, the EU has had a formalised 'dialogue' with China on competition law since 2004.[98] This is the first example of the institutionalising of a dialogue or relationship in this way, in order to influence trade relations with a major trading partner. Further, as a result of the doctrine of parallelism, the EU represents the interests of the Member States at the World Trade Organization (WTO).

In the area of competition law, the WTO is not as developed as 'pure trade law' (customs barriers and especially non-customs barriers to trade in goods and services). This is largely due to a lack of consensus on how an international competition law would apply, especially disagreements between less developed and more developed. The EU's attempt to introduce minimum rules on harmonising competition did suffer a setback at the WTO Doha Round (the current round of WTO trade negotiations, which has been ongoing since 2001), the proposal was dropped from the WTO agenda in 2004 (the US and a coalition of developing countries opposed the initiative). Developing countries are reluctant to develop an international competition law primarily because they wish to maintain a degree of protection over national industries until they have developed further (thus any settlement may need to address transitional issues of development before being accepted).[99]

EU competition law has been influential on the Organisation for Economic Cooperation and Development (OECD) Best Practice and Recommendations on Competition Law,[100] and the United Nations' Conference on Trade and Development (UNCTAD) Set of Multilaterally Agreed Equitable Principles and Rules for the Control of Restrictive Practices.[101]

---

98 Terms of Reference for EU–China Competition Dialogue under an agreement between the Ministry of Commerce of China and the Directorate General for Competition of European Commission http://ec.europa.eu/competition/international/bilateral/cn2b_en.pdf (last accessed 21 January 2015).

99 US opposition was more due to a belief that a fully internationalised legal regime of competition law is not necessary and that convergence and cooperation can occur more spontaneously. See D Gerber 'The US–European conflict over the globalisation of antitrust law: a legal experience perspective' (1999) 34 *New England Law Review* 123–43 at 130–35.

100 See http://www.oecd.org/daf/competition/recommendations.htm (last accessed 21 January 2015).

101 Adopted by the United Nations General Assembly in Resolution 35/63 (December 1980) www.unctad.org/en/docs/tdrbpconf10r2.en.pdf (last accessed 21 January 2015). An updated draft was proposed in 2000 http://unctad.org/en/docs/tdrbpconf5d7.en.pdf (last accessed 21 January 2015).

The EU was also one of the original 14 parties in the US initiative of establishing an international competition network (ICN) for informal dialogue and cooperation between competition authorities.[102]

14.11 CONCLUSION

Competition law has always been a central element of the common market and European integration. The main developments in this field since the beginnings of European integration and cooperation have been in enforcement, which has become more decentralised, together with the emergence of a body of jurisprudence and practices from the EU institutions and the development of case law and secondary legislation on mergers. Decentralisation reflected a maturing of EU competition law and the development of a consistent body of principles. Compared with other areas of EU law, there has been less activism in this field from the Court of Justice and the Commission, because the key elements are already included in Articles 101, 102 and 107–109 TFEU.

This maturing is reflected in the influence EU competition law has had internationally, albeit that international law of competition has been slow to emerge from the WTO. Relating as it does to the original core idea of a common market, this area has been less politically controversial than other fields of EU integration. Competition law has obvious benefits for consumers in particular, by reducing the price of products and increasing quality and choice, but also for undertakings seeking to enter or grow in a market.

POINTS TO REVIEW

–   Several aims have been proposed for regulating free markets through competition or anti-trust law? The primary aim is consumer welfare, by increasing consumer choice and minimising the extent to which producers of goods can take advantage of limited supplies. An associated effect is the enablement of greater access to a market by different undertakings. Quite often, in a situation of perfect competition where there is a wide range of undertakings supplying a good or service, the interests of consumers and business may coincide (in that both consumers and new businesses benefit when it is easier for new business to enter a market and compete), but this is not always so.

–   Competition law aims to ensure that businesses do not cooperate to reduce natural competitive behaviour in the market to the detriment of consumers, e.g. by fixing

102 See www.internationalcompetitionnetwork.org (last accessed 21 January 2015).

prices at a level higher than is needed to maintain a profit (cartel behaviour). Another scenario is the emergence of oligopolistic or near monopolistic undertakings, who can control the market without fear of competition from other businesses (Marxist theory suggests capitalism inevitably results in monopoly). Preventing cartel-like behaviour, in the EU under Article 101 TFEU, and monopolies or over-dominance, in the EU under Article 102 TFEU, are two of the main strategies of EU competition law.

— In addition to laws directed at cartels and monopolistic-like scenarios, EU competition law also targets mergers that might result in over-dominance or monopolies ('merger control'), as well as state subsidies (state aid) designed to protect national industries from competition from foreign goods or services. Merger control is governed by secondary legislation, while Article 107–109 TFEU deal with state aid.

— A range of typical behaviours are considered harmful to competition in the market. Under the per se approach, these behaviours are defined in advance, e.g. price fixing, limiting production, dividing markets geographically. Under a rule of reason approach, the effects of any behaviour are examined, rather than defining anti-competitive behaviour by type in advance. EU competition law adopts both approaches.

— A distinct feature of competition law in the EU compared to competition or anti-trust law in other systems is its concern with a single market across national borders. Thus, behaviour that may not be harmful to consumers or undertakings in practice may still be prohibited, e.g. division of a market territorially.

— EU competition law was, for the first decades enforced centrally by the European Commission. The Court of Justice did not consider what is now Article 101(3) TFEU to have direct effect; enforcement was not dealt with at treaty level in the treaties, and so it was addressed by secondary legislation instead. Regulation 1/2003 provided for the decentralisation of enforcement, by enabling the direct effect of Article 101(3) TFEU. Other developments in enforcement are the leniency and settlement procedures for cartels under Article 101 TFEU.

— Member States have remaining competence in the sphere of competition law in that behaviours not regulated at EU level can still be regulated by national law, for example, unilateral conduct (which is not covered under Article 101 TFEU and so long as it is not an abuse of a dominant position contrary to Article 102 TFEU).

— As EU competition law has matured to form a stable and successful body of law, it increasingly has international influence. This is partly due to the assertion of extra-territorial jurisdiction by the EU in enforcing EU competition law, and partly due to the influence EU law has on the development of competition law in other jurisdictions, for example, China.

CHAPTER GLOSSARY

Anti-trust is the term used in the US, largely for historical reasons, to describe competition law. The reason it is used is that in the nineteenth century, corporations had a practice of buying shares in other corporations, through the vehicle or means of a 'trust'. A trust is a legal relationship whereby the owner of a property interest holds it on trust for, i.e. for the benefit of, another party. In this way, trusts were used by firms to acquire influence and control in other corporations and to try dominate or control the market in that way.

Block exemption refers to a formal legislative decision by the Commission that certain practices are compatible with EU competition law. These generally concern Article 101 TFEU. For example, a block exemption has been issued concerning vertical restraints.

Capitalism refers to the operation of a free market economy, in which the state has a minimal or limited role.

Cartel refers to a group of undertakings or enterprises cooperating or colluding in the market place, usually to limit completion for their own interests and profits.

Comfort letter refers to an informal letter previously sent by the Commission to undertakings with an assurance that the Commission would not take enforcement action against certain market activity. Although these were not legally binding, in practice they provided a degree of legal certainty for undertakings receiving them and could be generally relied on.

Cumulative foreclosure effect refers to cumulative effects from several agreements (either horizontal or vertical) by different suppliers and distributors, the effect of which is to restrict market access or share for competing undertakings.

Dedicated agreement refers to memoranda of understanding and more formal and specific cooperation agreements in competition law signed between the EU and third countries.

Demand refers to the extent of the desire of consumers of a good or service to purchase or access that good or service.

De minimis principle refers to the practice of the EU institutions to not enforce EU competition law to agreements, and concerted practices that only negligibly affect competition, even though they are technically contrary to competition law. These are referred to as agreements of minor importance.

Effects doctrine refers to the exercise of the jurisdiction of a state (either civilly or criminally) over activities that occurred outside its territory, but which produced effects within its territory.

European Economic Area (EEA) refers to an international organisation in Europe consisting of the Member States of the EU and of Norway, Iceland and Liechtenstein, the purpose of which is to enable participation in the internal market by the latter three countries.

Extraterritorial jurisdiction refers to the exercise by a state of jurisdiction over events occurring outside its territory. In the context of competition, the main type of extraterritorial jurisdiction is effects-based.

Leniency policy refers to the practice of the Commission to reduce fines and penalties for undertakings that cooperate in the enforcement of Article 101 TFEU by revealing evidence of a cartel.

Letters of guidance refers to guidance issued by the Commission concerning its approach to novel or important issues of competition law under Articles 101 and 102 TFEU.

Luxury good refers to a good that consumers do not consider essential to buy or own.

Market refers to the existence of commercial activity in a particular area (geographical market) or regarding a particular product or products (product market).

Market power refers to capacity of an undertaking (or of a buyer) to act independently of its competitors or consumers (or of producers in the case of buying power).

Market share refers to the proportion of the overall market in a good possessed by an undertaking in the market.

Marxist-socialist refers to the theory of society proposed by Karl Marx, according to which society is governed by material laws that lead to the domination of the working class by monopolistic capitalists.

Monopoly refers to a position of 100 per cent market share in a market of an undertaking.

Oligopoly refers to a market in a particular good or product in which a small number of firms have large market shares.

Ordoliberalism refers to a school of thought that, in the context of competition law, sees the achievement of economic freedom for individuals as the most important goal.

Organisation for Economic Cooperation and Development (OECD) is an inter-governmental organisation in Europe, in which almost all European countries have membership, and which seeks to provide standards and expertise in the matter of economic development, including standards regarding competition law.

Restraint of trade is an expression used in US competition law that refers to practices in the marketplace by undertakings or enterprises that restrict competition. In UK law, it generally means a clause in a contract preventing a person from trading in a particular market.

Settlement procedure refers to a method of resolving cartel disputes more quickly whereby the Commission discloses its case to the undertaking concerned, who then can decide to accept the Commission's in return for a reduced penalty.

Sherman Act refers to the Sherman Anti-Trust Act 1890 of the United States, which was the first modern legislation on competition law. It is mainly directed at cartel-like behaviour.

Supply refers to the actual or potential availability of a product or service in a particular market.

Undertaking refers to a fully or partially commercial business or enter-

prise that is subject to EU competition law.

United Nations Conference on Trade and Development is a UN body aimed at encouraging the Member States of the UN to cooperate in trade and development issues. The first conference was held in 1964.

TAKING THINGS FURTHER

K J Cseres *Competition Law and Consumer Protection* (Kluwer Law International 2005) This monograph studies a key general issue of EU competition law, namely, its underlying purpose and the relative importance of consumer protection compared with other goals, such as assisting enterprise and furthering integration.

Y Karagiannis 'The causes and consequences of collegial implementation of competition law' (2013) 19(5) *European Law Journal* 682–704 This examines the effectiveness of the collegiate structure of the European Commission in the context of competition law enforcement.

A Papadopoulos *The International Dimension of EU Competition Law and Policy* (Cambridge University Press 2011) This is a detailed study of the international aspects of EU competition law, including coverage of bilateral and multilateral agreements on competition law involving the EU and its role in international negotiations related to competition law.

E Szyszczak *The Regulation of the State in Competitive Markets in the EU* (Hart 2007) This work focuses on the impact of EU competition law on the role of the state at national level, taking a doctrinal rather than a fully comparative approach.

Q Wu 'EU–China competition dialogue: a new Step in the internationalisation of EU competition law' (2012) 18(3) *European Law Journal* 461–77 This article looks at the internationalisation of EU competition law and its characteristics. It examines the dialogue on competition law that the EU has with China and how the EU has influenced China's competition law norms and is one of the most specific studies to date of this type.

CHAPTER 15
COMPETITION LAW:
ARTICLE 101 TFEU

This chapter examines the first aspect of regulation of competition in the EU, a prohibition on agreements and concerted practices or 'cartel-like' behaviour. Article 101 TFEU is concerned with attempts by more than one business enterprise (or 'undertaking') to restrict freedom of competition in a way that protects the businesses involved to the disadvantage of consumers. The term 'cartel' is commonly used to describe this situation. The key elements in this area of the law are contained in the TFEU itself, although the case law of the Court of Justice interpreting these provisions is also very important. Most of this chapter is taken up with a step-by-step discussion of the successive elements of Article 101 TFEU.

AS YOU READ . . .

The key questions that will be answered in this chapter are as follows:

– What is the aim of Article 101 TFEU?

– What are the key definitions of terms in Article 101 TFEU?

– How broad is the scope of Article 101 TFEU? Can it apply, for example, to activities such as sports, which have a partly economic and partly non-economic dimension?

– What kinds of behaviour does Article 101 TFEU prohibit? To what extent does a rule of reason apply as opposed to a per se approach to the question of prohibited behaviour?

– To what extent does Article 101 TFEU protect businesses or consumers?

– What derogations are permitted under Article 101 TFEU and how are they applied?

15.1 INTRODUCTION

The phenomenon of cartels is the target of Article 101 TFEU. Cartels or cartel-like behaviour involves firms who should be competing with each other actually agreeing to restrict competition in a way that is mutually beneficial to those firms, but puts consumers in a less advantageous position than they would otherwise be. Since the development of the modern law of competition, cartels have been one of its main targets.

An example can illustrate the way in which cartels operate to the advantage of business and to the disadvantage of consumers. In many countries, large supermarkets make up a large portion of the market in grocery goods. Owing to their size, large supermarkets can generally sell the most common consumer goods at lower prices than smaller grocery stores. This is because the size of large supermarkets allows them to benefit from what economists call 'economies of scale'.

Because supermarkets sell more goods, the costs they incur for each good is less than that of smaller retailers. For example, generally, relative to the number of goods sold, large supermarkets have fewer staff than do smaller grocery stores. This allows supermarkets to sell their goods at cheaper prices. Suppose, however, that supermarkets all agree not to sell bread and milk below a certain price, even though their cost base would allow them to sell below that price and still make a profit. Supermarkets might agree to do this because they know these are essential items and consumers will buy them in any case. This is an example of an agreement or concerted practice to improve the profits of business that should be competing more freely. It is this kind of behaviour that Article 101 TFEU seeks to regulate and prevent.

This sort of situation has become very relevant in the UK energy sector, which has an oligopolistic market structure. In response to political controversy over high household energy bills in 2013, the Office of Gas and Electricity Market (Ofgem) in 2014 announced it was referring the household energy sector to the Competition and Markets Authority (CMA) for an inquiry into possible anti-competitive practice in the sector:

> The recent assessment of the energy market, prepared by Ofgem with the Office of Fair Trading (OFT) and CMA, showed that competition isn't working as well as it should for consumers. It showed increasing distrust of energy suppliers, uncertainty about the relationship between the supply businesses and the generation arms of the six largest suppliers, and rising profits with no clear evidence of suppliers reducing their own costs or becoming better at meeting customer expectations.[1]

---

1   Ofgem Press Release 'Ofgem refers the energy market for a full competition investigation' (26 June 2014) https://www.ofgem.gov.uk/press-releases/ofgem-refers-energy-market-full-competition-investigation (accessed 3 April 2015).

CARTELS AND COORDINATED BEHAVIOUR

In the example just given, supermarkets that should be competing are agreeing not to compete below a certain price level. This is an example of cartel-like behaviour, which involves coordination of behaviour by businesses in an attempt to limit competition to their mutual benefit (usually to the detriment of consumers).

15.2 THE DIRECT EFFECT OF ARTICLE 101 TFEU

In the early 1970s, the ECJ declared that (now) Article 101(1) TFEU, but *not* Article 101(2)–(3), was directly effective. In *Anne Marty SA v Estée Lauder*, the Court of Justice stated:

> As the Court held in its judgment of 30 January 1974 in Case 127/73, *BRT v SABAM* [1974] ECR 51, since the prohibitions contained in Articles 85(1) and 86 [now Article 101(1) and 102 TFEU] tend by their very nature to produce direct effects in relations between individuals, those Articles create direct rights in respect of the individuals concerned which the national courts must safeguard, to deny, by virtue of Article 9 of Regulation No. 17, the national court's jurisdiction to afford that safeguard would mean depriving the individuals of rights which they hold under the Treaty itself. It follows that the initiation by the Commission of a procedure under Articles 2, 3 or 6 of that Regulation cannot exempt a national court before which the direct effect of Article 85(1) is pleaded from giving judgment.[2]

EXPLAINING THE LAW

WHY ONLY THE FIRST PARAGRAPH OF (NOW) ARTICLE 101 TFEU HAD DIRECT EFFECT INITIALLY

The rationale behind the approach of the Court of Justice of only recognising the direct effect of the first paragraph was that the second and third paragraphs did not satisfy the clarity and unconditionality required for direct effect. This is because they are quite abstractly phrased and for that reason not precise enough. For example, paragraph 3 creates a category of derogation for cartel-like behaviour that 'contributes to improving the production or distribution of goods or to promoting technical or economic progress, while allowing consumers a fair share of the resulting benefit'. These elements are very open and tend to pose as many questions as they answer, e.g. what constitutes economic progress.

---

2   Case 37/79 *Anne Marty SA v Estée Lauder* [1980] ECR 2481 para 13.

As we saw in the previous chapter, Article 101(2)–(3) TFEU has become directly effective since Regulation 1/2003 came into effect, as the Regulation has allowed the fulfilment of the conditions of direct effect. In practice, what this means is that national courts can now more fully enforce EU competition law. This has resulted in a decentralisation of the enforcement of EU competition law to national level, whereas previously EU competition law was enforced directly by the Commission.

15.3 THE ELEMENTS OF ARTICLE 101 TFEU

KEY LEARNING POINT

APPLYING ARTICLE 101 TFEU THROUGH A SEQUENTIAL ANALYSIS OF THE DIFFERENT ELEMENTS IN IT

The essential elements of the regulation of cartels and cartel-like behaviour are contained in Article 101 TFEU itself. Unlike other areas of EU law (and unlike EU law on merger control), the Court of Justice has not developed fundamentally new points, although it has, characteristically, broadly interpreted the specific provisions in (now) Article 101 TFEU.

15.3.1 DEFINITION OF 'UNDERTAKINGS'

The competition law rules in Article 101 TFEU generally only apply to an 'undertaking' in the marketplace, the phrase used in the Treaty to convey the idea of an enterprise or business. The approach to interpretation by the ECJ of this term is, therefore, important in determining the scope of effect of EU competition law.

KEY LEARNING POINT

THE DEFINITION OF 'UNDERTAKING'

The ECJ has adopted a wide and flexible approach to the definition of 'undertaking'. It includes both natural and legal persons (a legal person is a company or other entity with a legal personality) who or that engage in an economic or commercial activity, regardless of its legal basis or the way it is financed. A rule of thumb would be that the entity or business must be operating on a 'for profit' basis.

As noted in the previous chapter, due to its central role in the enforcement of competition law in the first decades of what is now the EU, Commission decisions on competition matters have a status similar to case law. *Polypropylene Cartel v ICI* [3] is an example, adopting the broad formula of the meaning of undertaking as including

---

3   Commission Decision 86/398/EEC OJ L 230 18.08.1986 p. 1. Similarly see the ECJ decision in C–41/90 *Höfner v Elser* [1990] ECR I–1979 para 21.

any entity engaged in *economic* or *commercial* activity. A range of case law illustrates the definition. In *Pucet v Assurances General de France*, the ECJ held that sickness funds that are part of a social security system are not an 'undertaking'. The Court stated:

> 18. Sickness funds, and the organizations involved in the management of the public social security system, fulfil an exclusively social function. That activity is based on the principle of national solidarity and is entirely non-profit-making. The benefits paid are statutory benefits bearing no relation to the amount of the contributions.[4]

Similarly, in *SAT v Eurocontrol*, it was held that Eurocontrol, which has a public function to regulate air space in Europe, is not an undertaking within the meaning of (now) Article 101 TFEU; it does not operate on a for-profit basis.[5] A further example is *Diego Cali v SEPG*, where a body performing 'a task in the public interest which forms part of the essential functions of the State as regards protection of the environment in maritime areas' was found not to be an undertaking.[6] These are all examples of entities not included, but not-for-profit social functions are the only real category of entity excluded. Other examples in this category would be charities.

David Meca-Medina and Igor Majcen v Commission illustrates how broad the definition of 'undertaking' is.[7] This applied the *Wouters* case to a sporting context (on the *Wouters* case, see further below). The Court of Justice held that sport could come under treaty rules on competition law if it otherwise satisfied the conditions of Articles 101 or 102 TFEU. The Court accepted the common ground of the parties to the case that the International Olympic Committee was an undertaking, having first noted that sport was included within free movement when it was carried out on a professional or semi-professional basis.

On the facts, it was held that the legitimate objective of preventing doping could justify a restriction on competing when scientific evidence supported the banning of certain substance above certain levels that could also be produced naturally in the body. The Court stated that sport was not an exception to competition law, but that the characteristics could be taken into account under Article 101 TFEU.

15.3.2 DEFINITION OF 'AGREEMENTS': HORIZONTAL AND VERTICAL

KEY LEARNING POINT

THE DEFINITION OF 'AGREEMENT'
Both the Commission and the ECJ have taken an expansive view of what is an agreement, to the extent that it overlaps with the more generic or less specific expression 'concerted practice'. An informal 'gentleman's agreement' is included.

---

4   Case C–159/91 *Pucet v Assurances General de France* [1993] ECR I–637 para 18.
5   Case C–364/92 *SAT v Eurocontrol* [1994] I–43.
6   Case C–343/95 *Diego Cali v SEPG* [1997] ECR I–1547.
7   Case C–519/04 P *David Meca-Medina and Igor Majcen v Commission* [2006] ECR I–6991.

In *Polypropylene Cartel v ICI*, the Commission decided that an oral agreement that is not legally binding and that entails no sanctions in the event of its breach is still an agreement under Article 101 TFEU.[8] In *ACF Chemiefarma (aka Boehringer Mannheim) v Commission (Quinine Cartel)*, the ECJ interpreted agreement broadly to cover both formal agreements and a 'gentleman's agreement' or mutual understanding. This involved the parties mutually declaring themselves to be bound by the informal agreement. It was a faithful expression of a joint intention, although its existence in writing did not cover all of the relevant period when it existed.[9]

15.3.3 DEFINITION OF 'DECISIONS BY ASSOCIATIONS OF UNDERTAKINGS'

KEY LEARNING POINT

DEFINITION OF 'DECISIONS BY ASSOCIATIONS OF UNDERTAKINGS'

The expression 'decisions by associations of undertakings' is also broadly interpreted and can include simply advice from a trade or professional association to individual undertakings who are members of it.

An example is *IAZ International Belgium v Commission*, which involved advice from trade association recommending members not to connect customers' dishwashers to mains unless machines had technical standards label from the association of dishwasher manufacturers.[10]

15.3.4 DEFINITION OF 'CONCERTED PRACTICE'

KEY LEARNING POINT

DEFINITION OF 'CONCERTED PRACTICE'

This has also been interpreted broadly with the result that it encompasses agreements as well: when EU competition law is being enforced against a firm/undertaking, the practice is to refer to agreements and or concerted practices together. The idea of a 'conspiracy' can capture some of the character of concerted practices: subtler coordination of behaviours for the purpose of restricting competition, without openly acknowledging what is occurring, i.e. a secretive collusion.

---

8 Commission Decision 86/398 (n3).
9 Joined Cases 41, 44, 45/69 *ACF Chemiefarma (aka Boehringer Mannheim) v Commission (Quinine Cartel)* [1970] ECR 661 paras 28–29.
10 Case 96/82 *IAZ International Belgium v Commission* [1983] ECR 3369.

DISTINGUISHING PARALLEL BEHAVIOUR FROM 'CONCERTED PRACTICE'

One of the issues that arises here is how to distinguish a concerted practice, which implies some sort of deliberate coordination, from the natural behaviour of the market place. This problem arises in particular in the context of oligopolistic markets, where competitors will tend to be in close competition and as a result follow or copy each other's behaviour to an extent. In other words, in an oligopoly, undertakings naturally engage in 'parallel behaviour', e.g. if one firm reduces prices or keeps prices at a certain level, others might closely follow in order not to become anti-competitive themselves. The leading case is *ICI v Commission*, where the ECJ adopted an approach that makes expert economic evidence of decisive importance in distinguishing between normal, economically healthy competitive behaviour in an oligopoly and anti-competitive concerted practices.

ICI v Commission concerned the dyestuffs industry where a small number of firms alerted each other to price increases by announcing them in advance. The ECJ held that this amounted to a concerted practice and emphasised that concerted practices depart from the 'normal conditions of the market with regard to the nature of the product, the size and number of the undertakings, and the volume of the market'.[11] Similarly, in *Suiker Unie v Commission*, an informal agreement by sugar producers to stay out of each other's 'territory' was found to be a concerted practice and not normal or natural market behaviour.[12]

PROVING 'CONCERTATION' AS OPPOSED TO PARALLEL BEHAVIOUR

The ECJ has been careful not to put undertakings in a position where ambiguous behaviour could end up with a finding of a violation of Article 101 TFEU. In *Ahlström v Commission (Wood Pulp)*, the ECJ held that there must be 'a firm precise and consistent body of evidence' pointing to the existence of a concerted practice and that parallel conduct cannot be regarded as proof of concertation unless concertation constituted the only plausible explanation for the conduct.[13] The burden of proof rest with the Commission (or national enforcement authorities)

---

11 Case 48/69 *ICI v Commission* [1972] ECR 619 para 66.
12 Case 4/73 *Suiker Unie v Commission* [1975] ECR 1663.
13 Joined Cases 89, 104, 114, 116–17, 125–9/85 *Ahlström v Commission (Wood Pulp)* [1993] ECR I–1307.

to establish that behaviour does amount to a concerted practice (as opposed to parallel behaviour). The facts concerned alleged concerted practices by a large number of producers of wood pulp. The explanation given for the use of a quarterly cycle was that it resulted from a compromise between the paper manufacturers' desire for a degree of foreseeability as regards the price of pulp and the producers' desire not to miss any opportunities to make a profit in the event of a strengthening of the market. In its judgment finding that there was not a concerted practice, the Court emphasised the expert economic evidence that the behaviour resulted from an oligopolistic market structure.[14]

The Court's conclusions are worth quoting in full as they set out clearly the application of these principles to the facts of the case:

126. Following that analysis, it must be stated that, in this case, concertation is not the only plausible explanation for the parallel conduct. To begin with, the system of price announcements may be regarded as constituting a rational response to the fact that the pulp market constituted a long-term market and to the need felt by both buyers and sellers to limit commercial risks. Further, the similarity in the dates of price announcements may be regarded as a direct result of the high degree of market transparency, which does not have to be described as artificial. Finally, the parallelism of prices and the price trends may be satisfactorily explained by the oligopolistic tendencies of the market and by the specific circumstances prevailing in certain periods. Accordingly, the parallel conduct established by the Commission does not constitute evidence of concertation.

127. In the absence of a firm, precise and consistent body of evidence, it must be held that concertation regarding announced prices has not been established by the Commission. Article 1(1) of the contested decision must therefore be annulled.

EXPLAINING THE LAW

'AGREEMENTS', 'DECISIONS OF ASSOCIATIONS OF UNDERTAKINGS', AND 'CONCERTED PRACTICES' ARE NOT MUTUALLY EXCLUSIVE

It is important to note that three categories above – agreements, decisions of associations of undertakings, and concerted practices – are not mutually exclusive, they are overlapping. Thus a gentleman's agreement is close to the idea of concerted practices. The Court of Justice acknowledged this in *Anic*,

----

14 Ibid paras 101 ff.

when it noted that patterns of conduct could be manifestations of a single infringement.[15] As a corollary, a unilateral decision of a single undertaking cannot fall under Article 101 TFEU.[16]

The recent case of *Kone and Others* (a preliminary reference from Austria)[17] illustrates the many different ways in which cartels can operate. It dealt with the question of the extent to which cartel-like behaviour was present in tendering for a bid. It concerned an arrangement between four undertakings in the elevators and escalators sector. The four firms were participants in the market for the production, installation and servicing of elevators and escalators. The collusion between them involved coordinating their bids to a tender (normally they would be competing with each other in the tender market), with a view to determining in advance between them who would win and on what conditions, mainly concerning the price. The case involved a claim for compensation by the professional buyers who normally issued these tenders. The professional buyers claimed damages for the 'supra-competitive price', i.e. the artificially inflated price agreed as part of the cartel.

15.3.5 DEFINITION OF 'MAY AFFECT TRADE BETWEEN MEMBER STATES'

A broad approach has been taken to this, and it is not difficult to establish that an agreement or concerted practice may affect trade between Member States.

KEY LEARNING POINT

....

LOW THRESHOLD OF 'MAY AFFECT TRADE BETWEEN MEMBER STATES'

In order to show that the behaviour of an undertaking may affect trade between 'Member States', case law has suggested it is enough to show there is some potential effect on trade between Member States. In other words, a current impact on trade does not need to be shown, it is enough to identify a plausible hypothetical situation or possibility. This is not difficult to do, since any limitation on trade that on the face of it that seems currently to be purely internal might inhibit the development of *future* competition between the Member States. The *STM* case, quoted next, set out the standard test.

....

15 Case C–49/92P *Commission v Anic Partecipazioni SpA* [1999] ECR I–4125.
16 Case T–41/96 *Bayer AG v Commission* [2000] ECR II–3383.
17 Case C–557/12 *Kone and Ors*, judgment of 5 June 2014.

In *STM*, the ECJ held that the test was whether it was possible to:

> ... foresee with a sufficient degree of probability on the basis of a set of objective
> factors of law or of fact that the agreement in question may have an influence, direct
> or indirect, actual or potential, on the pattern of trade between Member States.
> In that respect, it is necessary to consider in particular whether the agreement is
> capable of bringing about a partitioning of the market in certain products between
> Member States.[18]

The language of the Court in *STM* also indicates the broad approach, the Court at one
point formulating the test as (the language is reminiscent of the *Dassonville* formula in
free movement of goods) '. . . it is to be feared that it might have an influence, direct or
indirect . . .'.[19]

Other case law illustrates how easy it is to satisfy this test. *Vereniging van
Cementhandelaren v Commission* concerned the activities of a cartel confined to
trade within the Netherlands. The Court determined that where the agreement
complained of extended over the whole of the territory of a Member State, of its
nature it could impact on trade between Member States by deterring entrants from
other Member States.[20]

Brasserie de Haecht SA v Wilkin & Wilkin was a preliminary reference from the
Netherlands in which a brewery contracted to furnish the defendant's cafe and
grant loans.[21] Here the Court used a similarly open formula: it is necessary that the
agreement or concerted practice appear[s] to be capable of having some influence,
direct or indirect on trade between Member States or being conducive to a
partitioning of the market and of hampering the economic interpenetration sought
by the Treaty.[22]

In other words, any future possible indirect impact on the facilitation of trade across
borders is enough: it seems clear that this can be a hypothetical (or 'potential', as the
Court says in some of its case law) effect. On the specific question referred, the ECJ
stated that an agreement by an undertaking to obtain supplies exclusively from one
other undertaking was not necessarily contrary to (now) Article 101 TFEU, but could
affect trade between Member States.

....

18 Case 56/65 *STM* [1966] ECR 235 at 249–50.
19 Ibid at 250. The facts concerned a clause about exclusive sale (it was a preliminary reference, so the Court of
   Justice did not go into the facts of the case, instead answering the legal question in the abstract about the legality
   of exclusive sale clause and referring the case back to the French court to apply the ruling to the facts).
20 Case 8/72 *Vereniging van Cementhandelaren v Commission* [1972] ECR 977 paras 29–30.
21 Case 23/67 *Brasserie de Haecht SA v Wilkin & Wilkin* [1967] ECR 407.
22 Ibid 415.

KEY LEARNING POINT

UNDERTAKINGS MAY BE BASED IN THIRD COUNTRIES

Article 101 TFEU applies to any undertaking trading within the EU even those based in third countries. For example, *Ahlström v Commission* concerned a concerted practice on price fixing by producers of wood pulp in Finland and Sweden (prior to their joining the EU in 1995), and Canada.[23] It was enough for the undertakings to be selling products in the EU to be subject to EU law.

ANALYSING THE LAW

INTRA-STATE AND INTER-STATE IMPACT OF COMPETITION LAW AND THE 'APPRECIABLE IMPACT' THRESHOLD IN THE CONTEXT OF NATIONAL COMPETENCES

The very wide, flexible approach of the ECJ to the requirement for an effect on trade between Member States has a significant consequence for national competences in competition law. The approach of EU law effectively supplants almost all remaining competence of the Member States in the regulation of competition. Since it is very hard to say that anti-competitive practices at national level could never potentially impact trade between Member States, it is very hard to say that any question of cartel-like behaviour at national level is excluded from EU law and is governed solely by national law. As a result, most Member States have simply applied EU competition law rules as national rules also.[24] This has also facilitated the decentralisation of the enforcement of EU competition law.

Recognising the potential impact on national competences through such a broader approach, in its well known judgment in *Tobacco Advertising*, the ECJ suggested Community/Union competence was only engaged when practices at national level had an appreciable impact on competition. In other words, it set a threshold that had to be met before the EU has competence. As the Court rightly pointed out, in the absence of such a threshold, the powers of the Community legislature would be practically unlimited.[25] This case is examined in more detail in Chapter 7 on competences. However, a difficulty that remains in this context, from a competence perspective, is that the ECJ has not paid much attention to the existence of this threshold in subsequent case law.

---

23 Joined Cases 89, 104, 114, 116–17, 125–9/85 *Ahlström v Commission* [1993] ECR I–1307. See also e.g. Case 48/69 *ICI v Commission* [1972] ECR 619.

24 See e.g. K J Cseres 'The impact of Regulation 1/2003 in the new Member States' (2010) 6(2) *Competition Law Review* 145–282.

25 Case 376/98 *Germany v Parliament* [2000] ECR I–8419 (*Tobacco Advertising*) paras 106–107.

15.3.6 DEFINITION OF 'OBJECT OR EFFECT' OF RESTRICTING COMPETITION

> KEY LEARNING POINT
> ....
>
> ### OBJECT OR EFFECT OF RESTRICTING COMPETITION
>
> It is enough for an agreement or concerted practice to have either the object or the effect of restricting competition (i.e. 'or' here is to be read disjunctively, rather than conjunctively). In other words, if an agreement has the object of restricting competition, there is no need to examine its effects, and vice versa.[26] A range of case law illustrates this basic point, although the theory behind it is one of the main issues of debate surrounding Article 101 TFEU. The Court of Justice expressed the rationale of object-based restrictions on competition in the following passage:
>
> > . . . the distinction between infringements by object and infringements by effect arises from the fact that certain forms of collusion between undertakings can be regarded, by their very nature, as being injurious to the proper functioning of normal competition.[27]

STM is a leading authority that it is enough to show either the object or effect of an undertaking's behaviour is restrictive of competition. The passage from the judgment is, however, somewhat unfortunate in its wording:

> The fact that these are not cumulative criteria but alternative requirements indicated by the conjunction 'or', leads first to the need to consider the precise purpose of the agreement, in the economic context in which it is to be applied. This interference with competition referred to in [then] Article 85(1) must result from all or some of the clauses of the agreement itself. Where, however, an analysis of the said clauses does not reveal the effect on competition to be sufficiently deleterious, the consequences of the agreement should then be considered and for it to be caught by the prohibition it is then necessary to find that those factors are present which show that competition has in fact been prevented or restricted or distorted to an appreciable extent.[28]

Here the Court moves from discussing the 'effect' *of the object* to the effect in terms of consequences, which is a confusion of terminology, since 'effect' is used also in relation to the object. The point of the passage might be better conveyed by using 'nature' or 'character' as a synonym for 'object'. The rationale behind treating certain kinds of agreement as by their 'object', 'character' or 'nature' as anti-competitive is that economists agree on these kinds of agreement having a harmful effect on competition per se, i.e. without examining their actual effects. Sales or production quotas are an example.[29]

....

26 For example Joined Cases 56 & 58/64 *Etablissements Consten SA and Grundigverkaufs-GmbH v Commission* [1966] ECR 342; Joined Cases C–101 & 110/07 P *Coop de France Bétail et Viande v Commission* [2008] ECR I–10193 para 87.

27 Case C–209/07 *Competition Authority v Beef Industry Development Society and Barry Brothers* [2008] ECR I–8637 para 17.

28 Case 56/65 *STM* [1966] ECR 235 at 249.

29 D Bailey 'Restriction of competition by object under Article 101 TFEU' (2012) 49 *Common Market Law Review* 559–600 at 563.

In *Consten and Grundig*, the Court made clear a practical consequence for the Court's procedure of this approach. Once it is established that the object of behaviour is to restrict, there is no need to produce evidence of its actual effects:

> Besides, for the purpose of applying Article 85(1), there is no need to take account of the concrete effects of an agreement once it appears that it has as its object the prevention, restriction or distortion of competition.[30]

15.3.7 'PER SE' VERSUS 'RULE OF REASON' APPROACH TO INTERPRETING 'OBJECT OR EFFECT' UNDER ARTICLE 101 TFEU

ANALYSING THE LAW

OBJECT OR EFFECT OF RESTRICTING COMPETITION
One of the more general issues that arises with Article 101 TFEU is whether it is better to attempt an exhaustive definition of different types or categories of agreement that will fall foul of the Article (a 'per se' approach), or whether it is best to look at each agreement or concerted practice and its economic effects on a case-by-case basis (the latter approach is sometimes referred to as the 'Rule of Reason').[31] Article 101 itself by referring to object or effect leaves this issue open. In practice, whether or not a type of agreement or cartel-like behaviour has its object the restriction of competition tends to reduce to a discussion of the nature or character of certain agreements or behaviours as inherently anti-competitive. Much case law simply focuses on effects, as is allowed under Article 101, yet is clear that object-based analysis is also included in the article. The rationale for holding agreements or behaviours as restrictive of competition by object is: first, some agreements are by their nature anti-competitive; second, prior definition (as opposed to effects-based analysis) achieves legal certainty and analytical clarity. The approach of Article 101 is mixed: categories (a)–(e) in Article 101(1) TFEU adopted an object-based or per se approach, but the provision leaves open effects-based analysis, i.e. (a)–(e) are not meant to be exhaustive (this is indicated by the phrase 'including' and the earlier reference to effects in Article 101(1)).

In other words, while agreements or concerted practices that fall within one of sub-paragraphs (a)–(e) of Article 101(1) TFEU or that obviously have the object of restricting competition will generally, by definition, be contrary to Article 101(1) (i.e. the 'per se' approach), *other* agreements or concerted practices (i.e. not included in the list) that have the effect of restricting competition are also prohibited. This is established

....

30 Cases 56 & 58/64 *Consten and Grundig* [1966] ECR 299 at 342.

31 The Court of First Instance rejected the concept of a rule of reason in Case T–112/99 *M6 and Others v Commission* [2001] ECR II–2459, but whatever terminology is used, once effects–based analysis is applied, then the concept seems broadly applicable.

by expert economic analysis on the specific facts of each case, and this is sometimes called a 'rule of reason' approach.

Remia BV v Commission[32] is an example of a case where the ECJ seemed to adopt a Rule of Reason approach. It involved clauses in an agreement for the sale of an undertaking provided that the vendor would not engage in competition subsequently with the purchaser (a type of 'restraint of trade'[33] clause). This was necessary to give effect to the sale, since an assessment of the market conditions indicated that otherwise the vendor with his specialist knowledge of the transferred undertaking could simply win back the custom from the purchaser of the undertaking. The ECJ held this was not necessarily contrary to Article 101 TFEU, so long as it was limited in time or scope, but clearly this means it could have been.

Reflecting the background context of European integration, the Court of Justice tends to treat agreements that restrict cross-border competition as anti-competitive by object, without looking into the actual economic effects. An example is *Football Association Premier League v QC Leisure*, which involved territorial exclusivity of licences to broadcast live Premier League football matches.

The Court concluded on this point that, where a licensing agreement is designed to prohibit or limit the cross-border provision of broadcasting services: 'it is deemed to have as its object the restriction of competition, unless other circumstances falling within its economic and legal context justify the finding that such an agreement is not liable to impair competition'.[34] Another way of expressing this is to say that the agreement was prohibited by object under Article 101(1) TFEU, but might be justified under Article 101(3) TFEU. On the facts, the Court found that Article 101(3) could not save the agreement.

EXPLAINING THE LAW

THE OVERLAP BETWEEN EFFECTS-BASED ANALYSIS UNDER ARTICLE 101(1) AND ARTICLE 101(3) TFEU

A similar issue arises in reverse form under Article 101(3) TFEU, concerning exemptions, in that Article 101(3) exempts agreements that can be shown to be economically beneficial, which is a kind of effects-based economic analysis: there the approach has similarly been a mixture of a *per se* approach (e.g. Block Exemptions under Article 81(3)) and a Rule of Reason. We will look at this further below.

---

32 Case 42/84 *Remia BV v Commission* [1985] ECR 2545.

33 A restraint of trade clause is a clause or provision in a commercial or employment contract limiting competition. It is typically found in employment contracts where employment involves high levels of technical skill and research: a contract may prohibit an employee working for competing firms after leaving, for a certain period of time, in order to prevent competitors gaining access to sensitive information.

34 Joined Cases C–403 & 429/08 *Football Association Premier League Ltd. v QC Leisure*, [2011] ECR I–09083 para 140.

15.3.8 VERTICAL RESTRAINTS/AGREEMENTS

It is a matter of some dispute amongst economists as to whether vertical restraints are anti-competitive or in fact help and improve competition by increasing efficiency (for example, exclusive dealership agreements between car manufacturers and garage owners selling cars can be useful as retailers develop a relationship with the manufacturer, which can, for example, improve after-sale service).

In general, vertical restraints/agreements in EU law are permitted, so long as they do not establish exclusive territorial protection, i.e. absolutely divide up the common or internal market territorially. The particular character of vertical agreements is acknowledged by the ECJ in *Pierre Fabre*, where the Court stated that a vertical agreement containing a *prima facie* object restriction may be exonerated by an objective justification.[35] The following passages illustrate the approach of the Court:

> 39. As regards agreements constituting a selective distribution system, the Court has already stated that such agreements necessarily affect competition in the common market (Case 107/82 *AEG Telefunken v Commission* [1983] ECR 3151, paragraph 33). Such agreements are to be considered, in the absence of objective justification, as 'restrictions by object'.

> 40. However, it has always been recognised in the case-law of the Court that there are legitimate requirements, such as the maintenance of a specialist trade capable of providing specific services as regards high-quality and high-technology products, which may justify a reduction of price competition in favour of competition relating to factors other than price. Systems of selective distribution, in so far as they aim at the attainment of a legitimate goal capable of improving competition in relation to factors other than price, therefore constitute an element of competition which is in conformity with Article 101(1) TFEU (*AEG Telefunken v Commission*, paragraph 33).

> 41. In that regard, the Court has already pointed out that the organisation of such a network is not prohibited by Article 101(1) TFEU, to the extent that resellers are chosen on the basis of objective criteria of a qualitative nature, laid down uniformly for all potential resellers and not applied in a discriminatory fashion, that the characteristics of the product in question necessitate such a network in order to preserve its quality and ensure its proper use and, finally, that the criteria laid down do not go beyond what is necessary (Case 26/76 *Metro SB Großmärkte v Commission* [1977] ECR 1875, paragraph 20, and Case 31/80 *L'Oréal* [1980] ECR 3775, paragraphs 15 and 16).

....

35 Case C–439/09 *Pierre Fabre Dermo-Cosmétique SAS v Président de l'Autorité de la concurrence and Ministre de l'Économie, de l'Industrie et de l'Emploi*, [2011] ECR I–9419 paras 39–47.

From the above passages, the Court does not clearly distinguish justification as arising under Article 101(1) or Article 101(3), and this is sometimes the case in its other judgments. The Court refers to selective distribution agreements (i.e. agreements between a producer and retailers that only those retailers would supply a product to the market) as being a restriction by object (though they may be justified). All the more so, therefore, are *exclusive* distribution agreements (i.e. an agreement between a producer and a retailer that the retailer would be the *only* supplier of a product to the market).

ANALYSING THE LAW

WHY ARE EXCLUSIVE DISTRIBUTION AGREEMENTS ABSOLUTELY PROHIBITED?

In *Consten and Grundig*,[36] the Court of Justice seemed to suggest that exclusive distribution agreements are not capable of justification, in other words, they are absolutely prohibited, irrespective of any possible economic effects it might produce. However, even exclusive distribution agreements may have economically beneficial effects or justification, e.g. they may be necessary to persuade a distributor to market a new product or to market an existing product in a new area. The approach of the Court can be seen to be motivated as much by integration as competition per se, since an analysis based purely on economics would leave open the possibility of justification.

Regarding selective distribution agreements, although these are capable of justification in the approach of the Court, it has emphasised that the justification must be genuine and objective. An example is *Metro v Commission*, where the ECJ accepted that selective distribution agreements were not always contrary to (now) Article 101 TFEU in the market for high quality and technically advanced consumer durables, so long as the distributors were chosen by objective criteria of a qualitative nature relating to their technical qualification or the suitability of their premises, and so long as these criteria were applied uniformly and in a non-discriminatory way.[37]

The facts related to electronic devices for the leisure market, these devices were expensive, but in demand because of their quality. The Court noted that the advantages of selective distribution in this kind of market could relate to adaption to the peculiar characteristics of particular producers or the requirements of consumers.[38]

....

36 Cases 56, 58/64 *Consten and Grundig* [1966] ECR 299, 343.
37 Case 26/76 *Metro v Commission* [1977] ECR 1875 para 20.
38 Ibid para 20.

In *BMW v ALD Autoleasing*, however, the Court made clear that neither may selective distribution agreements confer *absolute territorial protection*.[39] The Court held that (now) Article 101 TFEU must be interpreted as meaning that it prevents a motor vehicle manufacturer from selling its vehicles through a selective distribution system whereby it agrees with its authorised dealers that they will not deliver vehicles to independent leasing companies where those companies lease, without selling, the vehicles to lessees residing outside the contract territory of the dealer.[40]

This kind of arrangement means that the dealer is agreeing not to extend his selling outside his own particular area. The Court's rationale was that this kind of agreement established absolute territorial protection despite the presence of several distributors, by dividing up the market geographically through a prohibition on down-stream transactions, i.e. transactions later on, after initial distribution.[41]

15.3.9 CASE LAW ON THE INDIVIDUAL CATEGORIES (A)–(E) OF ARTICLE 101(1) TFEU

Case law illustrates the application of the specific categories in Article 101(1) TFEU, and we will look briefly at these in turn.

15.3.9.1 (A) 'FIX PURCHASE PRICE . . . TRADING CONDITIONS'

Whilst fixing prices or pricing conditions is a classic example of limiting competition, in *Metro v Commission*, the ECJ recognised that maintaining a certain price level may not be to discourage competition, but simply in order to retain the viability of production and sale of a good.[42] Here, the Court noted that:

> For specialist wholesalers and retailers the desire to maintain a certain price level, which corresponds to the desire to preserve, in the interests of consumers, the possibility of the continued existence of this channel of distribution in conjunction with new methods of distribution based on a different type of competition policy, forms one of the objectives which may be pursued without necessarily falling under the prohibition contained in [now Article 101(1) TFEU] and, if it does fall thereunder, either wholly or in part, coming within the framework of [now Article 101(3) TFEU].

In *Hennessy-Henkell*, the Commission found that setting both *minimum* and *maximum* prices in order to prevent parallel imports was in breach of Article 101 TFEU.[43]

....

39 Case C–70/93 *BMW v ALD Autoleasing* [1995] ECR I–3439.
40 Ibid para 22.
41 Ibid para 19.
42 Case 26/76 *Metro v Commission* [1977] ECR 1875 para 21.
43 Commission Decision 80/1333/EEC OJ L 383 31.22.1980 p. 1.

15.3.9.2 (B) 'LIMIT OR CONTROL PRODUCTION, MARKETS, INVESTMENT ETC'

In *ACF Chemiefarma (aka Boehringer Mannheim) v Commission (Quinine Cartel)*, the ECJ found that allocating production quotas complemented a common pricing policy and was contrary to (now) Article 101(1) TFEU.[44] Case law on this category also illustrates the roles horizontal and vertical agreements can play. *Suiker Unie v Commission*, discussed above, involved an agreement between sugar producers to establish territories and that each would stick to their own territory. *Consten and Grundig*, discussed above, is an example of a prohibited horizontal agreement offering an exclusive right to distribute within a Member State.

15.3.9.3 (C) 'SHARE MARKETS ETC'

Quinine Cartel, discussed above, involved a gentleman's agreement between undertakings to share domestic markets and to fix prices. The *Suiker Unie* and *Consten and Grundig* cases are also examples under this category.

15.3.9.4 (D) 'APPLY DISSIMILAR CONDITIONS TO EQUIVALENT TRANSACTIONS . . .'

JAZ International Belgium illustrates this category.[45] It concerned a requirement imposed by a Belgian trade association that only washing machines and dryers that had a certificate of conformity with Belgian standards could be installed in Belgium and that only the trade association was entitled to deliver certificates of conformity.

15.3.9.5 (E) 'MAKE THE CONCLUSION OF CONTRACTS SUBJECT TO ACCEPTANCE BY THE OTHER PARTIES OF SUPPLEMENTARY OBLIGATIONS WHICH, BY THEIR NATURE OR ACCORDING TO COMMERCIAL USAGE, HAVE NO CONNECTION WITH THE SUBJECT OF SUCH CONTRACTS'

In *Vaessen/Morris*, the Commission condemned a clause that required a licensee to buy from the patentee not only a patented device for packing sausage meat into a casting to create *sauccissons de Boulogne* but also the casting itself.[46]

KEY CASE *THE WOUTERS CASE*

In this case, the ECJ appeared to balance non-competition objectives with the anti-competitive effects of an agreement or concerted practice, and on balance, concluded that a rule of the Dutch Bar Council that prohibited lawyers from entering into partnership with non-lawyers did not infringe Article 101(1) TFEU.[47] The case is significant especially because the ECJ appeared to take into account the exceptions/derogations to Article 101(3) in Article 101(1) itself, rather than

---

44 Joined Cases 41, 44 & 45/69 *ACF Chemiefarma (aka Boehringer Mannheim) v Commission (Quinine Cartel)* [1970] ECR 661.

45 Case 96/82 *JAZ International Belgium* [1983] ECR 3369.

46 *Vaessen/Morris* (Commission Decision 79/86) [1979] 1 CMLR 511.

47 Case C–309/99 *Wouters v Algemene Raad van de Nederlandsche Orde van Advocaten* [2002] ECR I–1577.

separately under Article 101(3) TFEU, whereas Article 101(3) TFEU is where the exception/derogations are formally set out. The Court stated:

> However, not every agreement between undertakings or any decision of an association of undertakings which restricts the freedom of action of the parties or of one of them necessarily falls within the prohibition laid down in Article [101(1)] of the Treaty. For the purposes of the application of that provision to a particular case, account must first of all be taken of the overall context in which the decision of the association of undertakings was taken or produces its effects. More particularly, account must be taken of its objectives, which are here connected with the need to make rules relating to organisation, qualifications, professional ethics, supervision and liability, in order to ensure that the ultimate consumers of legal services and the sound administration of justice are provided with the necessary guarantees in relation to integrity and experience . . . It has then to be considered whether the consequential effects restrictive of competition are inherent in the pursuit of those objectives.[48]

ANALYSING THE LAW

WHY WAS THE LEGAL PROFESSION TREATED DIFFERENTLY IN *WOUTERS*?

It may be that the case was motivated by a sense of identity by the Court with the traditions of legal professions (in which case the judgment might be criticised as recognising 'special pleading'). Generally, it leaves open the possibility the Court make an exception for individual professions based on their idiosyncratic characteristics and that non-economic considerations can arise under Article 101.

15.4 RESTRICTIVE AGREEMENTS THAT ARE NOT ANTI-COMPETITIVE: EXCEPTIONS OR DEROGATIONS UNDER ARTICLE 101(3) TFEU

15.4.1 OVERVIEW

Not all restrictive practices are designed to prevent, restrict or distort competition. Some have beneficial effects on competition, such as by encouraging new entrants to a market. Agreements such as this are approved under Article 101(3) TFEU. The same issue

---

48 Ibid para 97.

arises here as arose under Article 101(1) above in distinguishing between the object and effect of agreements. Can certain types of agreement be said, in advance as a matter of categorisation, to have an object or character that is not harmful to competition? Or is it always necessary to look at the effects?

We saw above how under Article 101(1) there is a mixed approach: some kinds of agreements are considered to be by object contrary to competition, for other agreements it is a matter of looking at the actual economic effects they have. The same applies under Article 101(3) TFEU. Some agreements are given a block exemption by secondary legislation, meaning such agreements are automatically valid under Article 101(3).

The preamble to Council Regulation 19/6534 provides that the Commission may adopt a block exemption regulation 'after sufficient experience has been gained in the light of individual decisions', enabling it to define categories of agreements falling within Article 101(3)[49] (we will look at block exemptions further below). For agreements not subject to a block exemption, an effects–based analysis is adopted.

STM is a leading authority setting out factors considered by the ECJ in deciding whether agreements are economically justifiable regarding:

- the necessity for penetration of a new area by an undertaking
- the nature and quantity of the products covered
- the position and importance of both parties in the market for the products concerned
- the extent to which the agreement is an isolated one or is positioned within a series of agreements
- the opportunities for other commercial competitors in the same products through parallel re-exportation and importation.[50]

To satisfy Article 101(3), all of the elements must generally be demonstrated by the undertaking.[51] *Piau v Commission* is an example of where (now) Article 103(3) was successfully invoked by undertakings.[52] It involved a requirement by the Fédération Internationale de Football Association (FIFA) that football agents have a licence (this fell under the category of 'decisions of associations of undertakings'). The CFI held it to be a barrier to access to economic activity and so within the scope of Article 101(1), but that it could be justified by the need to regulate the profession of agents, which was not otherwise regulated, in the interests of ethical standards and the welfare of players. The ECJ upheld the judgment.

....

49 Council Regulation 19/65/EEC OJ L 36 06.03.1965 p. 533, as amended by Council Regulation 1215/99 OJ L 148 15.06.1999 p. 1.
50 Case 56/65 *STM* [1966] ECR 235 at 250.
51 Commission Decision 73/323 *Prym-Werke* [1973] CMLR D250, [1981] 2 CMLR 217.
52 Case C–171/05P *Piau v Commission* [2005] ECR II–209.

Some authority exists also that public-interest considerations other than purely economic ones can be taken into account under Article 101(3) TFEU. For example, in *Métropole Télévision SA v Commission*, the CFI stated:

> Admittedly, in the context of an overall assessment, the Commission is entitled to base itself on considerations connected with the pursuit of the public interest in order to grant an exemption under Article [now 101(3)]. However, in the present case it should have shown that such considerations required exclusivity of rights to transmit sports events, which the Decision authorises for the benefit of members of EBU, and that that exclusivity was indispensable in order to allow them a fair return on their investments.[53]

On the facts, the Court found the Commission had erred in accepting a scheme by the European Broadcasting Union limiting retransmission of sports events.

KEY LEARNING POINT

....

ANY AGREEMENT, DECISION BY AN ASSOCIATION OF UNDERTAKINGS, OR CONCERTED PRACTICE CAN COME UNDER ARTICLE 101(3) TFEU

In principle, any kind of agreement, decision by an association of undertakings, or concerted practice can come under Article 101(3) TFEU. Thus, even agreements etc. that are per se unlawful or are by object anti-competitive can be justified.[54]

15.4.2 INDIVIDUAL AND BLOCK EXEMPTIONS

In the past, the Commission has had the power to grant both individual exemptions and block exemptions.

KEY LEARNING POINT

....

INDIVIDUAL AND BLOCK EXEMPTIONS

An *individual exemption* was a formal, legally binding document from the Commission stating that in its view, a particular agreement or concerted practice by given undertakings was not contrary to Article 101 TFEU. With the decentralisation of the enforcement of competition law (see Chapter 14), these are no longer issued. A *block exemption* (which are still in force) is a formal, legally binding statement from the Commission exempting a particular class or defined type of agreement from the effects of Article 101(1)–(2) TFEU.

....

53 Joined Cases T–528, 542, 543 & 546/93 *Métropole Télévision SA v Commission* [1996] ECR II–649 para 118.
54 Case T–17/93 *Matra Hachette v Commission* [1994] ECR II–595 para 85.

> Block exemptions have been issued to cover specialisation agreements,[55]
> research and development agreements,[56] and vertical restraints.[57] As we have
> seen, vertical restraints are generally considered less restrictive of competition,
> and the block exemption on them is an important category of exception to
> Article 101(1). It lists certain 'hard-core' restrictions that vertical restraints may not
> engage in,[58] as well as three other practices that are prohibited,[59] but otherwise
> all vertical restraints not involving more than 30 per cent of the market are
> exempted.

The above block exemptions are general, in applying to categories of agreement across
different economic or business sectors. The Commission can also issue block exemptions
particular to an industry. One of the most important sector-specific block exemptions
is Commission 461/2010 on the application of Article 101(3) TFEU to categories of
vertical agreements and concerted practices in the motor vehicle sector, which extended
a previous block exemption on the motor industry for three years before this industry
comes under the general block exemption on vertical restraints.[60] The advantages of
motor dealerships, for example, are obvious: they allow dealers to build up expertise in
a particular category or make of cars and therefore allow for better after-sales and repair
services.

15.4.3 THE *DE MINIMIS* PRINCIPLE AND COMMISSION NOTICE ON AGREEMENTS OF MINOR IMPORTANCE

In its enforcement practice, the Commission developed the doctrine that an agreement
or concerted practice will not be caught by Article 101(1) TFEU if it does not have an
appreciable impact on competition or inter-state trade, even though technically it does
represent a breach of Article 101(1) TFEU. This is known as the *de minimis* doctrine or
rule and was accepted by the Court of Justice in *Völk v Vervaecke*.[61]

The Commission formalised this practice by developing specific criteria for when EU
competition law would not be enforced, even though technically there was a breach

....

55 Specialisation Agreements (Commission) Regulation 1218/2010/EU OJ L 335 18.12.2010 p. 43.

56 Research and Development Agreements (Commission) Regulation No 1217/2010 OJ L 335 18.12.2010 p. 36.

57 Vertical Supply and Distribution Agreement (Commission) Regulation No 330/2010 OJ L 102 23.04.2010 p. 1.

58 These concern resale price maintenance, territorial restrictions, selective distribution agreements affecting either
   end users or other distributers and supply of spare parts.

59 Non-compete obligations during a contract, non-compete obligations after a contract and the exclusion of
   specific brands from selective distribution agreements.

60 Commission Regulation 461/2010/EU on the Application of article 101(3) of the Treaty on the Functioning of
   the European Union to categories of vertical agreements and concerted practices in the motor vehicle sector OJ
   L 129 28.05.2010 p. 52 http://ec.europa.eu/competition/sectors/motor_vehicles/legislation/legislation.html
   (last accessed 21 January 2015). See S M Colino 'Recent changes in the regulation of motor vehicle distribution
   in Europe: questioning the logic of sector-specific rules for the car industry' (2010) 6(2) *Competition Law Review*
   203–24.

61 Case 5/69 *Völk v Vervaecke* [1969] ECR 295.

of Article 101(1) TFEU, in its Notice on agreements of minor importance which do not appreciably restrict competition under (then) Article 81(1) ECT.[62] This set out a *de minimis* presumption in that restrictive agreements will be exempt from Article 81 ECT (now Article 101 TFEU) if any of the following apply:

- the parties' market share does not exceed 10 per cent for horizontal agreements
- the parties' market share does not exceed 15 per cent for vertical agreements.

In particular, in relation to small and medium-sized enterprises, the Commission has been more lenient:

> agreements between small and medium-sized undertakings, as defined in the Annex to Commission Recommendation 96/280/EC(3), are rarely capable of appreciably affecting trade between Member States. Small and medium-sized undertakings are currently defined in that recommendation as undertakings which have fewer than 250 employees and have either an annual turnover not exceeding EUR 40 million or an annual balance-sheet total not exceeding EUR 27 million.[63]

In June 2014, the Commission issued an updated *de minimis* notice (the thresholds remained the same).[64] This was prompted, in particular, by the *Expedia* case.[65]

KEY CASE EXPEDIA

In effect, the judgment in *Expedia* excluded the *de minimis* principle regarding object restrictions on competition, in that the ECJ stated that an agreement that may affect trade between Member States and that has an anti-competitive object (i.e. object restrictions discussed above) constitutes by its nature and independently of any concrete effects that it may have, an appreciable restriction on competition.[66]

The Revised Notice reflects the judgment in *Expedia* by excluding agreements by object from its scope.[67] Another significant change in the revised Notice is that it clarifies that it does not apply to any hard-core restrictions identified in future block exemption

---

62 Commission Notice on agreements of minor importance which do not appreciably restrict competition under art 81(1) ECT OJ C 368 22.12.2001 p. 1.

63 Ibid para 3.

64 European Commission Notice on Agreements of minor importance (Revised Notice) OJ C 291, 30.08.2014 p. 1.

65 Case C–226/11 *Expedia*, judgment of 6 September 2012.

66 Ibid para 37.

67 Revised Notice paras 2, 13.

regulations.[68] The Revised Notice was accompanied by a Staff Working Document,[69] which gave examples of agreements now excluded from the *de minimis* principle, e.g. a restriction on where or to whom a buyer of a product may sell it to consumers[70] or restrictions on the supplier's ability to place its trade mark or logo effectively and in an easily visible manner on the components supplied or on spare parts.[71]

15.5 CONCLUSION

Article 101 TFEU governs one of the three core aspects of competition law: cartel-like behaviour. It does so comprehensively, in that as well as listing certain categories of behaviour as automatically prohibited, it also leaves open the possibility for other behaviours to be caught. These other behaviours, not classified by type, are subject to expert economic analysis. The Court of Justice has not played as decisive a role in this area of law, because the fundamental provisions are already contained in the treaties. Understanding this area of the law is really a matter of going through the elements of Article 101 TFEU step-by-step. However, the Court has broadly interpreted the provisions and its case is important for understanding the elements of Article 101.

APPLYING THE LAW

SAMPLE PROBLEM QUESTION AND OUTLINE ANSWER

Problem
Vision Opticals is a company based in England that manufactures highly specialised equipment used by opticians and has a significant market share both in the UK and France. The company has recently signed an agreement with a distribution company in France, Clin d'Oeil. The agreement contains the following provisions:

(i) Clin d'Oeil will have exclusive distribution rights of all Vision Opticals' products in France

---

68 Ibid para 13.
69 European Commission *Guidance on Restrictions of Competition 'by Object' for the Purpose of Defining which Agreements May Benefit from the* De Minimis *Notice* Brussels (25 June 2014) SWD(2014) 198 final. The term 'hard core' is not used in the treaties, and the Court has held that the use of it in Commission block exemptions may not of itself necessarily determine whether an agreement has the object or effect of restricting competition: see the Opinion of Advocate General Mazák in Case C–439/09 *Pierre Fabre v President de l'Autorité de la Concurrence* [2011] ECR I–9419 para 29.
70 European Commission *Guidance on* De Minimis *Notice* ibid p. 13.
71 Ibid p. 16.

(ii) Clin d'Oeil will not supply Vision Opticals' products to any opticians or distributors outside of France

(iii) Clin d'Oeil sales representatives can only sell Vision Opticals' products after attending a week-long residential course in England run by Ophthalmic Opticals at a cost of £3000 per person, the cost being met by Clin d'Oeil

(iv) Clin d'Oeil is also required to distribute a range of skin cosmetics manufactured by Optimum Facial Care, a subsidiary of Vision Opticals

(v) Vision Opticals recently sent a press release to the UK trade journal *Opticians' News* announcing that it would be increasing wholesale prices on its range of products. Within a few days of publication a rival company in the UK market, Clear Eyecare, increased the prices of comparable products to match those in Vision Opticals' Optimum Facial Care range. Six months earlier Vision Opticals had increased its prices a week after publication of a similar story about Clear Eyecare products

(vi) As well as producing specialised equipment used by opticians, Vision Opticals produces low-cost glasses and contact lenses. It has a market share of 38 per cent in the market in low-cost glasses and contact lenses. The next biggest competitor has a share of 9 per cent. Vision Opticals enters into a distribution agreement with Beets pharmaceutical chain whereby Beets agrees to stock and advertise all of Vision Opticals' low-cost glasses and contact lens products, whilst Vision Opticals agrees that it will only supply its low-cost products to Beets in England and Wales. In Scotland, where Beets has fewer pharmacy outlets, Vision Opticals agrees to distribute its goods to Beets at a lower price than Vision Opticals charges to other pharmacy and optician outlets.

Advise:

(a) whether any of these companies has breached Article 101 TFEU [50 per cent], and

(b) whether Vision Opticals has breached Article 102 TFEU [30 per cent], and

(c) what requirements or sanctions the Commission could impose regarding any breaches [20 per cent of marks for the question].

Outline answer
You should note firstly that the problem raises issues under both Article 101 TFEU and Article 102 TFEU. Here, we will look just at the Article 101 aspect, the next chapter will provide an outline to the Article 102 aspect of the question.

Answers should first outline the scope of Article 101 TFEU as capturing agreements or concerted practices between undertakings and decisions by associations of undertakings that have the effect of restricting or distorting competition, including in the ways specific in (a)–(e) of Article 101(1). Answers should systematically work through the elements of Article 101(1):

- status as undertaking (if engages in economic activity, e.g. *Polypropylene Cartel*)
- existence of an agreement (e.g. *Mannesmann, Chemiefarma*) (identification of it as a vertical agreement is more relevant to considering Article 101(3) TFEU)
- that could affect trade between MS (e.g. *STM*)
- that has object or effect of restricting competition: *Consten and Grundig*, the facts of which are especially relevant to the problem as it involved an exclusive distribution agreement that established absolute territorial protection. Even though vertical agreements are less likely to be contrary to Article 101 TFEU, where they establish such protection, they are prohibited
- anti-competitive effects: identify rule of reason versus exhaustive definition, Article 101(1) (a)–(e) not exhaustive as indicated by including, suggesting rule of reasons of practices outside of (a)–(e):
  - here (i) and (ii) in the question seeks to limit or control market territorially (i.e. *Consten and Grundig*)
  - (iii) and (iv) relate to Article 101(e) (e.g. Commission Decision *Vaessen/Morris*) and discuss how to apply it.

The relevance of Article 101(3) TFEU can then be assessed. *STM* lists the conditions, but because absolute territorial protection here, not really applicable. The *de minimis* principle and block exemptions on specialisation and research and development should also be mentioned in a comprehensive answer, although we are not given enough information to assess their application.

Paragraph (v) concerns the distinction between parallel behaviours in an oligopolistic market and agreement, decisions or concerted practices contrary to Article 101(1) TFEU. A leading case is *Ahlström v Commission (Wood Pulp)*, whereby parallel conduct cannot be regarded as proof of concertation unless concertation constituted the only plausible explanation for the conduct.

Paragraph (vi) concerns an exclusive distribution agreement; these are generally prohibited.

The final part of the question concerns Commission powers, namely:
- issuing decisions requiring changes in practices by undertakings found to be in violation of Articles 101 or 102 TFEU (Article 7 of Regulation 1/2003), adopt interim measures (Article 8 of the Regulation) and require commitments (Article 9 of the Regulation)
- issuing fines and periodic penalty payments (under Articles 23 and 24 of Regulation 1/2003).

See further the end of the next chapter for an outline answer to the Article 102 TFEU aspect of the question.

POINTS TO REVIEW

- Article 101 TFEU is concerned with regulating the conduct of cartels in the internal market: it prohibits behaviours by more than one undertaking intended to limit the effects of competition for all of the involved undertaking to their advantage and the disadvantage of consumers.

- The Court of Justice has broadly interpreted the provisions of Article 101, for example the definitions of 'undertaking' and of 'agreement', 'decisions of associations of undertakings', and 'concerted practice'.

- Article 101(1) TFEU prohibits practices that have either their object or effect the restriction of competition. It is not necessary to show both the object and effect is restrictive, one or other is enough. This means that by classifying certain behaviours as being by object anti-competitive, there is no need to engage in an economic analysis of their effects, since they are automatically contrary to Article 101(1).

- Article 101(1) TFEU contains a list of prohibited behaviours for undertakings, and they can be taken as behaviours that can be classified as by object being contrary to Article 101(1). However, the list is not exhaustive and other behaviours by undertakings can also be caught. In this case, an effects-based economic analysis is needed. The latter approach is sometimes called a 'Rule of Reason'.

- Article 103(3) creates an open-ended category of exception for cartel-like behaviour that is economically beneficial. A similar type of rule-of-reason analysis applies here.

CHAPTER GLOSSARY

Association of undertakings refers to trade associations or professional organisations. Decisions taken at the level of the association, which influence the behaviour of individual member enterprises, are also caught by Article 101 TFEU.

Block exemption refers to a formal legal document issued by the Commission acknowledging that a certain category of agreement or concerted practice is not contrary to EU competition law. The main block exemption now relates to

vertical agreements in the motor industry between car or vehicle manufacturers and dealerships.

Cartel refers to a group of business enterprises coordinating their behaviour in the market (i.e. colluding) so as to limit freedom of competition.

Concerted practice refers to coordinated behaviour between undertakings or business enterprises in the market place, which stops short of being an agreement, but which nonetheless does involve a degree of coordination. There is overlap between the idea of a 'gentleman's agreement' and a concerted practice.

Object or effect in the context of competition law refers respectively to the ideas that certain business practices have as their purpose the restriction of competition or alternatively have not this purpose (object), but nonetheless have this effect. Either is enough for Article 102 TFEU to apply.

Oligopoly refers to a market in which there are a small number of undertakings competing.

Parallel behaviour refers to behaviour in an oligopolistic market in particular, where undertakings tend to adopt similar product, pricing or sales policies in order not to be under-cut by competitors.

Parallel behaviour is considered to reflect natural competitive forces.

Restraint of trade means a clause or provision in a commercial or employment contract limiting competition. It is typically found in employment contracts where employment involves high levels of technical skill and research: a contract may prohibit an employee working for competing firms after leaving, for a certain period of time, in order to prevent competitors gaining access to sensitive information.

Undertaking means a business or commercial enterprise in a marketplace.

Vertical restraint/agreement refers to an agreement between undertakings at different stages of the process of production and sale of goods or services, e.g. between a manufacturer and retailers selling that manufacturer's products.

TAKING THINGS FURTHER

D Bailey 'Restriction of competition by object under Article 101 TFEU' (2012) 49 *Common Market Law Review* 559–600 This article looks in detail at the significance in Article 101 TFEU of practices that have as alternatives the object or effect of restricting competition, examining in particular, anti-competitive objectives, since in this case anti-competitive effects do not have to be proven. Among the issues discussed are whether particular types of objective or effect should be automatically considered contrary to Article 101, or whether it is preferable to have a more open-ended test.

M Colino *Competition Law of the EU and UK* (7th edn Oxford University Press 2011) This book has the advantage of comprehensive coverage of EU competition law at EU level and of competition law and enforcement in the UK and explains fully the relationship between them, as well as covering economic theory underlying competition law.

C Petrucci 'Parallel trade of pharmaceutical products' (2010) 35 *European Law Review* 275–86 This article looks at the decision of the Court of Justice in *GlaxoSmithKline Ltd v Commission*, which interprets the concept of restriction by object of competition. The article discusses the role that consumer welfare plays in competition law.

R Whish, D Bailey *Competition Law* (7th edn Oxford University Press 2012) This comprehensive and clearly written textbook on EU and UK competition law looks in depth at Article 101 TFEU, in particular; see Chapter 3 (overview), Chapter 4 (Article 101(3)), Chapter 13 (horizontal cartel agreements), Chapter 14 (horizontal oligopoly, tacit collusion, and collective dominance), Chapter 15 (horizontal cooperation agreements) and Chapter 16 (vertical agreements).

CHAPTER 16
COMPETITION LAW: ARTICLE 102 TFEU

This chapter examines the second main aspect of regulation of competition in the EU, the regulation of the behaviour of 'dominant' firms. Article 102 TFEU seeks to regulate the market behaviour of firms who have acquired a dominant presence in the market, in order to prevent such firms from using their dominance to restrict competition. As with Article 101 TFEU, Article 102 TFEU contains all the essential elements of the law. In essence, once a firm is in a dominant position in a particular market, it is subject to stricter regulation and may not engage in certain behaviours that would otherwise be open to it. What is restricted is quite similar to the restrictions on cartels under Article 101. Key elements to define from the Article are, therefore, the 'market', since firms are only dominant in relation to a particular market, and 'dominance'.

AS YOU READ . . .

The key questions that will be answered in this chapter are as follows:

– What is the aim of Article 102 TFEU?

– What are the key definitions of terms in Article 102 TFEU? In particular, how are distinct markets determined and defined?

– What kinds of behaviours does Article 102 TFEU prohibit? To what extent does a rule of reason apply as opposed to a 'per se' approach to the question of prohibited behaviour?

– To what extent does Article 102 TFEU protect businesses or consumers?

– What are the limitations of or criticisms that might be made of the scope of Article 102 TFEU?

16.1 INTRODUCTION

As with Article 101 TFEU, the easiest way to approach Article 102 TFEU is to systematically identify each element of the Article. Whereas Article 101 TFEU is concerned with one or more undertaking acting collusively, Article 102 TFEU is concerned with a single undertaking in a dominant position (there is some possibility of overlap between Articles 101 and 102 TFEU, which is dealt with at the end of this chapter).

It is not the mere fact of a dominant position, but its *abuse* that involves a breach of Article 102 TFEU. Firms/undertakings in a dominant position have particular responsibilities to the market and must be more careful than firms that are not dominant (plus, in the *Continental Can* judgment, see further below, the ECJ seemed to suggest that a merger between two firms might of itself involve abuse.

> KEY LEARNING POINT
> ....
>
> ### A PROHIBITION ON ABUSE OF A DOMINANT POSITION BY AN UNDERTAKING
> It is not unlawful for undertakings to be in a dominant position; what is unlawful is the abuse of this position. Undertaking has the same meaning under Articles 101 and 102 TFEU.[1]

16.2 DIRECT EFFECT OF ARTICLE 102 TFEU

> MAKING CONNECTIONS
> + + + + + + + + + + + + + + + + +
>
> ### ALL OF ARTICLE 102 TFEU IS DIRECTLY EFFECTIVE
> As with Article 101 TFEU, Article 102 TFEU has direct effect. In addition, under Article 102, there are no exemptions (there is only one paragraph to the Article), so there was no issue with part of Article 102 being directly effective and part of it not being so, as there was with Article (now) 101 TFEU.

In *Tetra Pak Rausing*, the CFI noted (regarding then Article 86 EEC Treaty, now Article 101 TFEU):

> On this question, the Court finds a consistent line of case-law to the effect that 'the prohibitions of Article 86 have a direct effect and confer on interested parties

---

1 See e.g. Case T–319/99 *FENIN v Commission* [2003] ECR II–357, on appeal Case C–205/03 P *FENIN v Commission* [2006] ECR I–6295 (concerning the Spanish Health Service).

rights which the national courts must safeguard' (Case 155/73 *Sacchi* [1974] ECR 409, paragraph 18; see also Case 127/73 *BRT v Sabam*, cited above, paragraph 16, and Case 66/86 *Ahmed Saeed*, cited above, paragraph 32 *in fine*). If Community law allows Article 86 to be applied in respect of an agreement exempt under Article 85(3), there is nothing to justify limiting the power of national courts to apply Article 86 on the ground that the practice in question has been granted exemption under Article 85(3).[2]

16.3 DEFINITION OF 'MARKET'

The term 'market' is not defined in Article 102 TFEU, so it has been up to the ECJ to determine a definition. Dominance exists not in an abstract way, but in relation to a particular market.

KEY LEARNING POINT

DEFINITION OF THE MARKET
The ECJ tends to look at three aspects or dimensions in defining the market: the product market, the geographical market and the temporal market. The product market is the most important test.

16.3.1 PRODUCT MARKET

The essential idea with defining a market by product is that of the interchangeability of products. If products are considered interchangeable by consumers, they are considered to be in the same market.

EXPLAINING THE LAW

INTERCHANGEABILITY OF GOODS AND THE PRODUCT MARKET
To say that goods are interchangeable means that they are treated as substitutes or alternatives to each other by consumers. Consumers would generally consider buying either of the products and would make a decision based on price or quality or attractiveness. In other words, the products are similar. For example, small cars from different car manufacturers are in the same product market with each other. But they would not be in the same product market as very big cars, because consumers do not treat small cars and big cars as substitutes.

---

2   Case T–51/89 *Tetra Pak Rausing SA v Commission* [1990] ECR II–309 para 42.

The leading authority on product interchangeability is *United Brands Co.*[3] The facts involved bananas: were bananas in the same market as other fruit? The ECJ looked in particular to physical characteristics, taste, seedlessness, softness, and also referred to easy handling and year-round availability. On the basis of this, it concluded that bananas were only substitutable or interchangeable with other fruit to a limited degree, and so bananas were in a separate market relative to fruit. In *Banden-Industrie Michelin*, the issue was whether car tyres and large-vehicle tyres were interchangeable.[4]

The Court of Justice found that they were not, a ruling that is easy to understand in terms of interchangeability: large tyres cannot be substituted for small tyres. *Hugin* illustrates well the importance of the definition of the market.[5] In this case, Hugin was just one of several undertakings in the market for cash registers, which was described as very competitive, and Hugin was described as only having a small share in it. However, when the market was more narrowly defined to relate only to spare parts for Hugin machines, which Hugin supplied to providers of repair services for cash machines, Hugin was found to be in a monopoly.[6]

KEY LEARNING POINT

DIFFERENT USES FOR THE SAME PRODUCT AND INTERCHANGEABILITY

In *Hoffmann-La Roche*, the facts concerned different kinds of vitamins, where the ECJ noted that the same product may have several different uses and could be in separate markets. In other words, interchangeability needs to be carefully analysed with respect to the use of a product and substitutability for specific, different uses.

> If a product could be used for different purposes and if these different uses are in accordance with economic needs, which are themselves also different, there are good grounds for accepting that this product may, according to the circumstances belong to separate markets which may present specific features which differ from the standpoint both of the structure and of the conditions of competition.

> However, this finding does not justify the conclusion that such a product together with all the other products which can replace it as far as concerns the various uses to which it may be put and with which it may compete, forms one single market.

> The concept of the relevant market in fact implies that there can be effective competition between the products which form part of it and this presupposes that there is a sufficient degree of interchangeability between all products forming part of the same market in so far as a specific use of such products is concerned.

---

3 Case 27/76 *United Brands Company and United Brands Continentaal BV v Commission* [1978] ECR 207.
4 Case 322/81 *Nederlandsche Banden-Industrie Michelin v Commission* [1983] ECR 3461.
5 Case 22/78 *Hugin v Commission* [1979] ECR 1869.
6 Ibid paras 3–8.

There was no such interchangeability, at any rate during the period under consideration, between all the vitamins of each of the groups C and E and all the products which, according to the circumstances, may be substituted for one or other of these group of vitamins for technological uses which are themselves extremely varied.[7]

KEY LEARNING POINT

THE DIFFERENCE BETWEEN SUPPLY-SIDE AND DEMAND-SIDE SUBSTITUTABILITY

Substitutability can be looked at either from the point of view of demand or of supply. Goods are substitutable from the point of view of demand if consumers will switch easily from good A to good B when the price of good A goes up and becomes uncompetitive relative to good B. Good B then is an easy alternative to good A for consumers. Supply-side substitutability has to do with the ease of alternative suppliers of a good coming into the market and competing.

For example, company A may manufacture good A, which is very popular with consumers owing to its quality and low price. Suppose company A then raises the price. Alternative suppliers then have an opportunity to compete more effectively if they do not set prices as high as company A. The ease with which alternative suppliers can get into the market and offer a competing good to good A is referred to as supply-side substitutability. We will look below at how the Commission Notice on the Definition of the Relevant Market uses these ideas in deciding what the market is.

In order to provide more clarity, the Commission issued a notice in 1997 setting out its view of the main elements of the legal test to define the market. Although this notice is not legislative in nature, it is considered to be authoritative: see Commission Notice on the Definition of the Relevant Market.[8] The purpose of identifying a market is 'to determine whether there are actual competitors which are capable of constraining the behaviour of the firms in question and to assess the degree of real competition on the market'.[9]

EXPLAINING THE LAW

THE COMMISSION NOTICE ON THE DEFINITION OF THE RELEVANT MARKET

The Commission's approach is to focus on: (1) the physical characteristics of products and (2) cross-elasticity of demand. The Commission carries out a detailed analysis based on the idea of substitutability. Initially, it will look at the

---

7   Case 85/76 *Hoffmann-La Roche v Commission* [1979] ECR 461 para 28.

8   OJ C 372 09.12.1997 p. 5.

9   Ibid para 2.

physical characteristics of products to get a rough idea of possible substitutability and then carry out a more in-depth economic analysis. To be in a competitive market, firms must have to deal with demand substitution, i.e. can consumers change from one product to another, and supply substitution, i.e. can competing undertakings easily enter the market.

The two together make up what economists call cross-elasticity of demand: when the demand for a product goes down, e.g. typically because of a price increase, demand for competing products correspondingly goes up because they are readily available and are more competitive. A market is competitive if customers can choose between products with similar characteristics and if there are not insurmountable obstacles to supplying products or services on a given market. The final aspect is to look at the cross-border implications, but this is quite easy to establish as plausible *potential* obstacles are enough for Article 102 TFEU to be engaged, as with Article 101 TFEU.

16.3.2 GEOGRAPHICAL MARKET

Geography may affect substitutability. Generally the entire EU is taken as the geographical market, unless transport costs or other technical or practical reasons make wide distribution problematic. The geographic market is the territory within which goods can be sold. We have seen how the Court treats potential effects on competition as engaging Articles 101 and 102 TFEU, and this can be related to the approach of treating the geographic market as the whole of the EU. With modern transport, it is generally easy to envisage the whole of the EU as potentially part of the same market. However, it may be that in practice, it is difficult for suppliers readily to switch supply of goods to a particular area.

Thus, while the Court always has a background conception of the entire EU as the market, in reality, market conditions of supply may mean that goods are not in the same market if they cannot easily be transported in order to be in competition with each other. Transportation (e.g. costs, length of time) and the easy flow of trade are important considerations. Other factors are also relevant to ease of supply; for instance, is it necessary to have a local outlet or office? The same also works as regards demand: if consumers cannot easily switch to products sold in another area, that other area might not be considered to be in the same market. The Commission defines the geographic market as follows:

The relevant geographic market comprises the area in which the undertakings concerned are involved in the supply and demand of products or services, in which the conditions of competition are sufficiently homogeneous and which can be distinguished from neighbouring areas because the conditions of competition are appreciably different in those areas.[10]

Relatively little case law is taken up with defining the geographic market.[11] This may be because it is normally considered on an intuitive or common sense basis and because it is not disputed by the parties, as well as by the ease of transporting goods and services given the free movement principles.[12] However, it has been addressed to some extent. One of the points emphasised by the case law is that for goods to be considered within the same geographical market, the market conditions in the geographical area must be sufficiently homogeneous. In *United Brands*, the Court stated:

> The opportunities for competition under Article 86 [EEC Treaty, now Article 102 TFEU] of the Treaty must be considered . . . with reference to a clearly defined geographic area in which it is marketed and where the conditions of competition are sufficiently homogeneous for the effect of the economic power of the undertaking concerned to be able to be evaluated.[13]

KEY LEARNING POINT

HOMOGENEOUS CONDITIONS

Although the Court emphasised the importance of homogeneous market conditions within a defined geographic area for it to constitute a market, in *Deutsch Bahn* it noted that these conditions did not have to be exactly the same:

> . . . the definition of the geographical market does not require the objective conditions of competition between traders to be perfectly homogeneous. It is sufficient if they are 'similar' or 'sufficiently homogeneous' and, accordingly, only areas in which the objective conditions of competition are heterogeneous may not be considered to constitute a uniform market.[14]

A notable difference between Articles 101 and 102 TFEU concerns this issue of the geographic scope of the undertakings and their activities.

---

10 Ibid para 8.

11 See also D Hildebrand *The Role of Economic Analysis in the EC Competition Rules* (2nd edn Kluwer Law International 2002) 303.

12 In *Michelin I* the Court of Justice took a narrow definition of the geographic market, the Netherlands, without really considering issue as transport costs to other areas: see Case 322/81 *Nederlandsche Banden-Industrie Michelin v Commission* [1983] ECR 3461.

13 Case 27/76 *United Brands Company and United Brands Continentaal BV v Commission* [1978] ECR 207 para 11.

14 Case T–229/94 *Deutsche Bahn AG v Commission* [1997] ECR II–1689 para 92. See also Case 27/76 *United Brands v Commission* [1978] ECR 207 paras 11, 53 and Case C–333/94 P *Tetra Pak International SA v Commission (Tetra Pak II)* [1996] ECR I-5951 paras 91–92.

EXPLAINING THE LAW

COMPARING ARTICLE 101 TFEU AND ARTICLE 102 TFEU IN THE CONTEXT OF THE GEOGRAPHIC MARKET

We have seen how, in order to show that the behaviour of an undertaking may affect trade between 'Member States', case law has suggested it is enough to show there is *some potential* effect on trade between Member States, which is quite a low threshold to satisfy. In contrast, in *United Brands*, the Court indicated that, to be in a dominant position, an undertaking should be operating within a substantial portion of the common market. This is a more exacting standard. It reflects that, as we will see further below, Article 102 is quite onerous in placing additional burdens on an individual firm in that it restricts certain market behaviours that would otherwise be open to the firm or undertaking. However, the case law is not consistent in this respect. Some cases have been content to treat national markets as constituting a market within which dominance can take place, such as *Michelin I* (concerning the sale of tyres in the Netherlands) and *British Telecommunications* (concerning telecommunications services).[15]

In *United Brands*, the Court found that the Commission was right to exclude three Member States from the geographic market because the conditions for the sale of the bananas in those markets were different from each other.[16]

16.3.3 TEMPORAL MARKET

For some products, especially food products, the market may vary over time. The easiest example relates to fruit, some of which only grow at certain times of the year. Sometimes, technology can mitigate a seasonal production cycle: food can be stored so that it is relatively easily available all year round. This is often the case, given modern technology. However, the interplay or geography with seasonal factors can restrict a market. It may not be profitable to go to the trouble and expense of preserving or registering foodstuffs and in some cases it may not be possible.

As with product characteristics and geography, the key idea is substitutability: does time affect substitutability? This will be a matter for expert economic or other evidence in each case to determine. It does not arise much in practice, where it tends to be considered peripheral. In *United Brands*, for example, the Commission and Court conceived of the market in bananas as year-round, even though there was some evidence in the case that supply peaked at certain times of the year.[17] In *Hoffmann-La Roche*, the Court of Justice noted that interchangeability did not vary in the period under

---

15 Case No IV/29.877 *British Telecommunications* OJ L 360 21.12.1982 p. 36.
16 Case 27/76 *United Brands* [1978] ECR 207 paras 46–56.
17 Ibid paras 16–26.

consideration, suggesting that a variation over time *could* affect interchangeability and thus market definition.[18]

16.4 THE DEFINITION OF DOMINANCE

After the market has been defined and determined, the next step is to determine *whether dominance exists in the market.*

KEY LEARNING POINT

THE ESSENCE OF DOMINANCE IS INDEPENDENCE FROM COMPETITORS

The basic legal test or idea the ECJ has developed as to what dominance involves is whether the market position enjoyed by an undertaking allows it 'to prevent effective competition and to behave to an appreciable extent independently of competitors, customers, and consumers', as it stated in *United Brands*.[19] The Court described the capacity to dominate in the longer term, even if temporary competitive pressures do exist, or to fix prices, i.e. without having to be concerned about what competitors do as the essence of dominance.[20]

Dominance, therefore, means an undertaking does not need to pay very much attention to the behaviour of competitors; it can simply carry on its pricing, selling or product policies more or less as it wishes. The ECJ has developed a number of principles to elaborate or complement this idea of independence from competitors:

1. The dominant firm/undertaking does not have to be in a position to eliminate all competition, which would result in a monopoly situation. For example, in *Hoffmann-La Roche*, the Court noted that it may have been in a position to eliminate 'some of' its competitors.[21]
2. A statutory monopoly does not give immunity from Article 102 TFEU, as seen in *Italy v Commission*.[22]
3. Two factors tend to be considered as indicative of dominance, namely market share and barriers to market entry.

16.4.1 MARKET SHARE

There is no absolute rule about what percentage or fraction of a market enjoyed by an undertaking means it is dominant, but a 40 per cent or higher market share means an

---

18 Case 85/76 *Hoffmann-La Roche* [1979] ECR 461 para 28.
19 Case 27/76, *United Brands* [1978] ECR 207 para 65.
20 Ibid para 125.
21 Case 85/76 *Hoffmann-La Roche* [1979] ECR 461 para 55.
22 Case 41/83 *Italy v Commission* [1985] ECR 873.

undertaking is likely to be dominant. In *United Brands*, 40–45 per cent in conjunction with other factors amounted to dominance. These other factors included, most importantly, the number and size of competitors[23] and the relatively small size of the next biggest competitor, who only had a 16 per cent share. The smaller the share of the nearest competitors, the more likely an undertaking is to be in a dominant position.

In *AKZO*, the Court noted that the existence of a very large market share itself by one undertaking was itself evidence of dominance. On the facts, it held that a 50 per cent share in the market for organic peroxides was such a very large share.[24] In *British Airways v Commission*, British Airways had 39.7 per cent of the UK market, whereas its nearest rival Virgin had only 5.5 per cent. The relatively small size of its nearest competitor contributed to the finding that BA was in a dominant position.[25]

KEY CASE *THE AKZO PRESUMPTION*

In *AKZO*, the Court of Justice indicated that a firm with a 50 per cent or more market share will automatically be considered dominant, or at least that the firm must prove that it is not. This approach was also applied in *Hilti AG v Commission*.[26]

16.4.2 BARRIERS TO MARKET ENTRY

This is somewhat controversial as an aspect of market definition, as sometimes barriers to market entry may indicate the superior efficiency of an existing operator, rather than any illicit market dominance or behaviour. *Hoffmann-La Roche* concerned the market in vitamins. The ECJ referred to highly developed sales networks and technological leads of allegedly dominant undertakings as contributing to dominance.[27] The more of these types of barriers to market entry for other undertakings there are, the more likely it is an existing undertaking will be found to be in a dominant position.

EXPLAINING THE LAW

THE SPECIAL CASE OF A MONOPOLY FIRM IN ONE MARKET AND ITS SHARE IN ASSOCIATED MARKETS

A special situation arises where a firm is in a near-monopoly position in one market, and is also a competitor in closely associated markets. In this situation, in the latter markets, even though these can be defined as separate markets,

---

23 Case 27/76 *United Brands* [1978] ECR 207 para 110.
24 Case 62/86 *AKZO v Commission* [1991] ECR I–3359 para 60.
25 Case T–219/99 *British Airways v Commission* [2003] ECR II–5917 paras 211–19.
26 Case T–3089 *Hilti AG v Commission* [1991] ECR II–1439.
27 Case 85/76 *Hoffmann-La Roche* [1979] ECR 461 para 48.

the undertaking will be under the same obligations as if it were in a dominant position. In *Tetra Pak*, it was found that:

> An undertaking which enjoys a quasi-monopoly on certain markets and a leading position on distinct, though closely associated, markets is placed in a situation comparable to that of holding a dominant position on those markets as a whole. Conduct by such an undertaking on those distinct markets which is alleged to be abusive may therefore be covered by Article 86 [now 101] of the Treaty without any need to show that it is dominant on them.[28]

Tetra Pak coordinated the policy of a group of companies specialising in equipment for the packaging of liquid or semi-liquid food products in cartons, with its activities covering both the aseptic and the non-aseptic packaging sectors. One of the main issues was the existence of aseptic and non-aseptic sectors and whether the packaging of milk, the packaging of dairy products other than milk and the packaging of non-dairy products were separate markets. The ECJ concluded:

> Accordingly, the Court of First Instance was right to accept the application of Article 86 of the Treaty in this case, given that the quasi-monopoly enjoyed by Tetra Pak on the aseptic markets and its leading position on the distinct, though closely associated, non-aseptic markets placed it in a situation comparable to that of holding a dominant position on the markets in question as a whole.[29]

16.5 THE DEFINITION OF 'ABUSE' OF A DOMINANT POSITION

EXPLAINING THE LAW

THE ABUSE OF DOMINANCE, NOT DOMINANCE ITSELF, IS UNLAWFUL UNDER ARTICLE 102 TFEU

The essential idea here is that it is not dominance per se, but its abuse, which violates Article 102 TFEU. The position is that once a firm is in a dominant position, its freedom of manoeuvre in the marketplace is limited by competition law and it may not engage in the specific categories of behaviour identified in

---

28 Case C–333/94 P *Tetra Pak International SA v Commission* [1996] ECR I–5951, from the headnote and see paras 27–30.

29 Ibid para 31.

Article 102 TFEU (a)–(d). Another way of putting this is that once a firm is in a position of dominance, competition law imposes additional responsibilities on it. In *Michelin v Commission*, the Court of Justice observed that a dominant firm 'has a special responsibility not to allow its conduct to impair undistorted competition on the common market'.[30] It may not engage in certain behaviours that, if it were not dominant, it could do as part of normal free market conditions. These behaviours are listed in paragraphs (a)–(d) of Article 102 TFEU, and they are similar to the behaviours prohibited under Article 101 in the context of cartels.

However, it is also worth noting that the more dominant a firm is, the more likely it is to be found to have abused its dominance. This is sometimes referred to as 'super dominance' or, as one Advocate General put it, a firm may enjoy 'a position of dominance approaching a monopoly'.[31] In *Compagnie Maritime Belge Transports SA v Commission*, the ECJ found that selective cost-cutting was abusive in the context of a firm with over 90 per cent of the market, but left open the possibility that such a practice might not be abusive on different facts.[32]

We will now look at the prohibited behaviours in paragraphs (a)–(d) of Article 102 TFEU. As with Article 101(1) TFEU, the specific behaviours listed are not exhaustive, i.e. there is a mixture of per se and rule of reason approaches here too.[33] The ECJ has observed that:

In order to determine whether a dominant undertaking has abused its dominant position by its pricing practices, it is necessary to consider all the circumstances and to examine whether those practices tend to remove or restrict the buyer's freedom as regards choice of sources of supply, to bar competitors from access to the market, to apply dissimilar conditions to equivalent transactions with other trading parties, thereby placing them at a competitive disadvantage, or to strengthen the dominant position by distorting competition (see, to that effect, *Deutsche Telekom v Commission*, paragraph 175 and case-law cited).[34]

16.5.1 '(A) IMPOSING UNFAIR PURCHASE OR SELLING PRICES'

United Brands is an example of price discrimination, where United Brands charged different prices for bananas in different Member States.[35] In *Hoffmann-La Roche*, the

---

30 Case 322/81 *Nederlandsche Banden-Industrie Michelin v Commission* [1983] ECR 3461 para 57. See also e.g. Case C–202/07 P *France Télécom v Commission* [2009] ECR I–2369 para 105 and case law cited.
31 Advocate General Fennelly in Case C–395/96 P *Compagnie Maritime Belge Transports SA v Commission* [2000] ECR I–1365, at para 136 of his Opinion.
32 Ibid, judgment of the Court of Justice at paras 118–19.
33 Case C–333/94 P *Tetra Pak v Commission* [1996] ECR I–5951 para 37.
34 Case C-209/10 *Post Danmark A/S v Konkurrencerådet* [2012] ECR I-0000 para 26.
35 Case 27/76 *United Brands* [1978] ECR 207 paras 209–33.

ECJ held that a dominant firm abuses its position where rebates/reductions are given in return for customers agreeing to continue to purchase a product for all or most of their relevant requirements.[36]

The Court noted that a fidelity rebate, unlike a quantity rebate related solely to the amount of a product purchased, is designed through the granting of a financial advantage to prevent customers from obtaining their supplies from competitors.[37] In *AKZO*, the ECJ found to be prohibited predatory pricing, whereby a dominant firm reduces prices to a level that competitors cannot match in order to eliminate competition.[38]

16.5.2 '(B) LIMITING PRODUCTION, MARKETS OR TECHNICAL DEVELOPMENT'

Suiker Unie is an example of prohibited restrictions on exports through a system of national quotas.[39]

MAKING CONNECTIONS
+ + + + + + + + + + + + + + + + +

THE LINK BETWEEN INTELLECTUAL PROPERTY LAW AND COMPETITION LAW

Competition law interacts with intellectual property (IP) law in the context of category (b). By means of Article 102 TFEU, the Commission in effect forced the compulsory licensing of intellectual property rights in the case of *Microsoft*.[40] IP falls into natural conflict with competition law by creating fixed-term monopolies protected by patents and copyright. In Microsoft's case, its refusal to supply its IP-protected interoperability codes (although the result of expensive investment) was regarded by the Commission as maintaining Microsoft's virtual monopoly power, by preventing competition in adjacent operating system markets. While encouraging competition, interference in those IP rights by competition law can be seen as 'damaging the incentives for future investment in research and development, as well as constituting a fundamental interference with private parties' freedom to dispose of their property as they wish'.[41]

---

36 Case 85/76 *Hoffmann-La Roche* [1979] ECR 461 para 89.

37 Ibid para 90. See also Joined Cases 40–48, 50, 54–56, 111, 113 & 114/73 *Suiker Unie UA and Others v Commission* [1975] ECR 1663 paras 506–13 and, more recently, Case C–549/10 P *Tomra v Commission*, judgment of 19 April 2012 paras 62–65.

38 Case 62/86 *AKZO Chemie BV v Commission* [1991] ECR I-3359 paras 98–103, referring to 'unreasonably low prices'.

39 Joined Cases 40–48, 50, 54–56, 111, 113 & 114/73 *Suiker Unie UA and Others v Commission* [1975] ECR 1663 paras 14–17.

40 Case T–201/04 *Microsoft* [2007] ECR II–3601 para 643.

41 A Stephan 'Editorial: reforming EU competition law' (2010) 6(2) *Competition Law Review* 139–43 at 141.

16.5.3 '(C) APPLYING DISSIMILAR CONDITIONS TO EQUIVALENT TRANSACTIONS WITH OTHER TRADING PARTIES, THEREBY PLACING THEM AT A COMPETITIVE DISADVANTAGE'

In *United Brands*, the ECJ held that a dominant firm cannot stop supplying a long-standing customer who abides by regular commercial practice, if orders placed are in no way out of the ordinary, and that self-protection by a dominant firm must be proportionate.[42] BPB Industries applied the above principle to new customers.[43] A fidelity rebate falls under this category, in that two customers are paying different prices for the same product depending on whether they obtain their supply exclusively from the same supplier or have more than one supplier.[44]

Commercial Solvents v Commission involved a refusal to supply competitors, creating a risk that they would go out of business.[45] The ECJ judgment was broadly framed so as to include a refusal to supply based on a desire by the dominant firm to integrate vertically down into the finished product market.[46] This case is an example of a judgment protecting competitors in the first instance, rather than simply consumers.

However, other case law indicates that only exceptionally would a dominant firm be required to deal with direct rivals under Article 102 TFEU,[47] and the case law has left somewhat open the exact scope of the responsibilities of dominant firms in this regard.[48] In *Oscar Bronner*, a newspaper publisher that operated the only home delivery scheme for newspapers in Austria was found not to have abused its dominant position in refusing to include in its service the papers of a competing newspaper publisher.[49]

16.5.4 '(D) IMPOSING SUPPLEMENTARY OBLIGATIONS UNRELATED TO THE TRANSACTION'

This ground involves an undertaking inserting a clause in a contract or insisting on preconditions before completing a transaction, when these conditions are not required by the transaction. This is sometimes called tying or bundling. An example is *Microsoft*, where consumers are unable to acquire the Windows client PC operating system without simultaneously acquiring Windows Media Player.[50] In *Microsoft*, the Court found that the Commission was correct that this involved a foreclosure effect on competition, i.e. it made it less likely that competition would develop.[51]

---

42 Case 27/76 *United Brands* [1978] ECR 207 para 182.
43 Case T–65/89 *BPB Industries* [1993] ECR II–389.
44 Case 85/76 *Hoffmann-La Roche* [1979] ECR 461 para 90.
45 Cases 6 & 7/73 *Commercial Solvents v Commission* [1974] ECR 223.
46 Ibid paras 23–25.
47 See e.g. case C–14/01 *IMS Health GmbH and Co OMG v NDC Health GmbH & Co GH* [2004] ECR I–4059.
48 I Colomo 'Exclusionary discrimination under Article 102 TFEU' (2014) 51 *Common Market Law Review* 141–64.
49 Case C–7/97 *Oscar Bronner GmbH & Co KG v Mediaprint* [1998] ECR I–7791.
50 Case T–201/04 *Microsoft* [2007] ECR II–3601 para 961.
51 Ibid paras 868, 1038–51.

ANALYSING THE LAW

PER SE VERSUS THE RULE OF REASON APPROACHES
UNDER ARTICLE 102 TFEU

As with Article 101 TFEU, the issue arises whether it is appropriate to look at
the effects of the behaviour of a dominant firm or to consider certain categories
of behaviour as automatically abusive, irrespective of effects. To an extent,
categories (a)–(d) are per se categorisations. However, they are also somewhat
abstract, or at least open to interpretation, and this leaves room for more effects-
based analysis or 'rule of reason'. The Commission has recently sought to refocus
the application of Article 102 TFEU to a more effects-oriented economic analysis
concerning what are called 'exclusionary abuses'.[52]

The concept of anti-competitive 'foreclosure' has also developed. This is conduct
that is likely to prevent competition developing, by an objective assessment,
rather than merely the intention of the undertakings concerned.[53] Thus bundling
or tying might not be imposed, but a practice of bundling or tying on an
economic assessment can make effective competition less likely. *AstraZeneca*
involved an attempt by a pharmaceutical company to prevent the emergence
of competing generic medicine products by misrepresentations to patent
offices and national courts and by a strategic implementation of the regulatory
framework, behaviours that are not caught in Article 102(a)–(d) TFEU. The Court
held that Article 102 prohibited a dominant undertaking from eliminating a
competitor and thereby strengthening its position by using methods other than
those which come within the scope what it called 'competition on the merits'.[54]

These are abuses targeting competitors (rather than 'exploitative abuses' relating
to consumers) and aim at excluding other competitors. However, the ECJ
has adopted a per se approach here too when it considers it appropriate, for
example, concerning so-called price squeezes or predatory pricing arrangements,
which the Court considers automatically a category of abuse.[55] This is the selling
of products by a dominant firm at prices that will make competing unprofitable
for competitor undertakings, who then exit the market, allowing the dominant
firm to become even more dominant and increase prices much more freely
without fear of substantial competition any more.

---

52 Guidance on the Commission Enforcement Priorities in Applying [Article 102 TFEU] to Abusive Exclusionary
   Conduct by Dominant Undertakings OJ C 45 24.2.2009 p. 7.
53 Case C–549/10 P *Tomra*, judgment of 19 April 2012 para 24.
54 Ibid para 75, citing Case 62/866 *AKZO v Commission* [1991] ECR I–3359 para 70 and Case C–202/07 P *France
   Télécom v Commission* [2009] ECR I–2369 para 106. See also Case 549/10 P *Tomra*, (n 53) para 42.
55 Case C–52/09 *Konkurrensverket v TeliaSonera Sverige AB* [2011] ECR I–527. See the clear discussion in A Kaczorowska *European Union Law* (3rd edn Routledge 2013) 831–32, 851–57.

16.6 OBJECTIVE JUSTIFICATION UNDER ARTICLE 102 TFEU

No equivalent to Article 101(3) TFEU is found in Article 102 TFEU, raising the question of whether practices found to be contrary to Article 102 TFEU can be considered justified. The ECJ has developed to some extent a concept of 'objective justification' under Article 102. For example, in *Tetra Pak II*, the Court observed that even where tied sales of two products are in accordance with commercial usage, such sales may still constitute abuse within the meaning of Article 82 EC (now Article 102 TFEU) unless they are objectively justified.[56]

KEY CASE *THE* POST DANMARK *CASE AND THE TEST FOR
OBJECTIVE JUSTIFICATION UNDER ARTICLE 102 TFEU*

In *Post Danmark*,[57] the ECJ went on to set out a test for 'objective justification' under Article 102 TFEU. The facts related to the market in the distribution of unaddressed mail in Denmark, which was completely liberalised and not subject to legislation.

At the material time, Post Danmark enjoyed a monopoly in the delivery of addressed letters and parcels not exceeding a certain weight, which, on account of the sole right of distribution, was allied with a universal service obligation to deliver addressed mail under that weight. For that purpose, Post Danmark had a network that covered the national territory in its entirety and that was also used for the distribution of unaddressed mail. Post Danmark succeeded in winning customers in the unaddressed mail sector from Forbruger-Kontakt, whose chief business was in the unaddressed mail sector and which had created a distribution network covering almost the entire national territory, chiefly through the acquisition of smaller distribution undertakings.

The Danish competition authority, Konkurrencerådet, received a complaint made by Forbruger-Kontakt, and held that Post Danmark had abused its dominant position on the Danish market for the distribution of unaddressed mail, practising a targeted policy of reductions designed to ensure its customers' loyalty, by, first, not putting its customers on an equal footing in terms of rates and rebates (which the Konkurrencerådet called 'secondary-line price discrimination') and, secondly, charging Forbruger-Kontakt's former customers rates different from those it charged its own pre-existing customers without being able to justify those significant differences in its rate and rebate conditions by considerations relating to its costs (a practice described by the Konkurrencerådet as 'primary-line price discrimination').[58]

---

56 Case C–333/94 P *Tetra Pak International SA v Commission* [1996] ECR I-5951 para 37.
57 Case C–209/10 *Post Danmark A/S v Konkurrencerådet* [2012] ECR I–0000, judgment of 27 March 2012.
58 Ibid paras 3–8.

The Konkurrenceankenævnet (competition appeals tribunal) upheld the Konkurrencerådet's decision. Both found that that there was no abuse of a dominant position as a result of predatory pricing and, on the other, that there was such abuse by reason of the policy of 'secondary-line price discrimination' with respect to Post Danmark's customers other than the SuperBest, Spar and Coop groups.[59]

The decisions concerning an abuse of a dominant position by means of selectively low prices applied to those groups were challenged by Post Danmark before the courts, which resulted in a preliminary reference. Post Danmark argued that the prices offered to the Coop group may be considered to amount to abuse only if an intention to drive a competitor from the market can be established.[60]

The ECJ noted that not every exclusionary effect is necessarily detrimental to competition in that competition on the merits may, by definition, lead to the departure from the market or the marginalisation of competitors that are less efficient and so less attractive to consumers from the point of view of, among other things, price, choice, quality or innovation.[61]

The ECJ also noted that price discrimination by a dominant undertaking was not necessarily abusive.[62] After an analysis of costs issues, the Court stated that, to the extent that a dominant undertaking sets its prices at a level covering the great bulk of the costs attributable to the supply of the goods or services in question, it will, as a general rule, be possible for a competitor as efficient as that undertaking to compete with those prices without suffering losses that are unsustainable in the long term.[63]

In deciding that the issues of fact specific to the case were for the national court, the ECJ went on to set out a test for 'objective justification' under Article 102 TFEU that is quite similar to that provided for in Article 101(3) TFEU:

> 40. If the court making the reference, after carrying out that assessment, should nevertheless make a finding of anti-competitive effects due to Post Danmark's actions, it should be recalled that it is open to a dominant undertaking to provide justification for behaviour that is liable to be caught by the prohibition under Article 82 EC (see, to this effect, Case 27/76 *United Brands and United Brands Continentaal v Commission* [1978] ECR 207, paragraph 184; Joined Cases C–241/91 P and C–242/91 P *RTE and ITP* v *Commission* [1995] ECR I–743, paragraphs 54 and 55; and *TeliaSonera Sverige*, paragraphs 31 and 75).

---

59 Ibid para 14.
60 Case C–62/86 *AKZO v Commission* [1991] ECR I-3359.
61 Case C–333/94 P *Tetra Pak International SA v Commission* [1996] ECR I-5951 para 22.
62 Ibid para 30.
63 Ibid para 38.

41. In particular, such an undertaking may demonstrate, for that purpose, either that its conduct is objectively necessary (see, to that effect, Case 311/84 *CBEM* [1985] ECR 3261, paragraph 27), or that the exclusionary effect produced may be counterbalanced, outweighed even, by advantages in terms of efficiency that also benefit consumers (Case C–95/04 P *British Airways v Commission* [2007] ECR I–2331, paragraph 86, and *TeliaSonera Sverige*, paragraph 76).

42. In that last regard, it is for the dominant undertaking to show that the efficiency gains likely to result from the conduct under consideration counteract any likely negative effects on competition and consumer welfare in the affected markets, that those gains have been, or are likely to be, brought about as a result of that conduct, that such conduct is necessary for the achievement of those gains in efficiency and that it does not eliminate effective competition, by removing all or most existing sources of actual or potential competition.

16.7 'UNDERTAKINGS' AND OLIGOPOLY AND THE RELATIONSHIP OR OVERLAP BETWEEN ARTICLES 101 AND 102 TFEU

Although the application of Articles 101 TFEU and 102 TFEU is usually different in that Article 101 TFEU is concerned with more than one undertaking, whereas Article 102 is concerned with one dominant undertaking, there may be overlap between the two provisions. This is illustrated, for example, by *DIP SpA v Commune di Bassano del Grappa*, where the Court of Justice found that there may be collective dominance where undertakings are linked in such a way that they adopt the same conduct in the market.[64]

Undertakings behaving like this are acting like a single undertaking. Generally, it seems that what will be caught by Article 102 TFEU that is not covered by Article 101 TFEU is non-collusive behaviour that restricts competition, although it may be hard here to distinguish between an uncompetitive market structure where there is collective dominance and parallel behaviour in an oligopoly: it is a question of degree, of how closely intertwined the behaviour is. This point can be illustrated with the example of mergers.

> KEY LEARNING POINT
>
> **MERGERS, A 'RULE OF REASON' AND ABUSE OF A DOMINANT POSITION**
> Generally speaking, mergers can be dealt with as a separate topic and are subject to specific secondary legislation, which we have looked at briefly in

---

64 Case C–140/94 *DIP SpA v Commune di Bassano del Grappa* [1995] ECR I–3527.

Chapter 14. However, in *Continental Can*, the ECJ seemed to consider that a merger could of itself, where it altered the competitive structure of the market place, be considered abuse. The ECJ thereby seemed to equate dominance itself with abuse, at least in this particular context. The approach of the Court was that categories (a)–(d) were not exhaustive, and a merger of itself could be abusive. The Commission has also adopted a more effects-based approach in its assessments under Article 102.[65]

Continental Can[66] involved a merger, which was substantial enough to raise the issue of the structure of the market. The facts concerned the purchase of 80 per cent of one undertaking by a subsidiary of Continental Can, with the result that competition was virtually eliminated.[67] The ECJ referred to the spirit, general scheme and wording of Article 86 (later Article 82, now Article 102), and also to the system and objectives of the EC Treaty (a good example of teleological reasoning), and held clauses (a)–(d) in (now) Article 102 are not exhaustive and that the strengthening of a position of dominance through a merger may be abuse where it undermines the competitive structure of the market so as to practically eliminate competition.[68] This could be considered another example of 'super-dominance'.

It is also possible for a practice that would otherwise be exempt under Article 101(3) TFEU to breach Article 102,[69] although this is less likely where a block exemption now is applicable only where the market share involved is not above 30 per cent.

MAKING CONNECTIONS
+++++++++++++++++++
RELATING ARTICLE 101(3) TFEU AND ARTICLE 102 TFEU
Where there is a conflict between the application of Article 101(3) and Article 102 TFEU, Article 102 prevents the application of Article 101(3).[70]

16.8 CONCLUSION

Article 102 TFEU is addressed to single undertakings that have achieved a position of dominance in the market. It regulates the behaviour of firms defined as being in a dominant position, meaning that such firms cannot engage in certain behaviours that

---

65 Guidance on the Commission's enforcement priorities in applying Article 102 TFEU above.
66 Case 6/72 *Europemballage Corporation and Continental Can v Commission* [1973] ECR 215.
67 Ibid para 18.
68 Ibid para 25.
69 Case 37/79 *Anne Marty SA v Estée Lauder* [1980] ECR 2481 para 13; Case T–51/89 *Tetra Pak Rausing v Commission* [1990] ECR II–309.
70 Cases T–191/98 T–212/98 to T–214/98 *Atlantic Container Line v Commission* [2003] ECR II–3275.

would otherwise be open to them. Firms in a dominant position can thus be said to have special responsibilities in the marketplace. However, the behaviours that they are not allowed to engage in are not exhausted in the criteria (a)–(d) (restrictions similar to those placed on cartels under Article 101 TFEU); a rule of reason also applies, whereby behaviours that can foreclose competition will be caught. No exemptions are contained in the Article and, in that sense, it is more stringent than Article 101 TFEU, but the Court of Justice in some case law has been willing to accept 'objective justification'.

APPLYING THE LAW

SAMPLE PROBLEM QUESTION AND OUTLINE ANSWER
Problem
The problem question at the end of Chapter 15 includes elements that fall under Article 101 and Article 102 TFEU. Please reread this and try to identify the elements that come under Article 102.

Outline answer
Part vi of the problem concerns Article 102 TFEU:

- The first issue is the definition of the market. Answers should note the different elements of defining the market: product market (*United Brands*), geographical market (e.g. *Hilti*), temporal market (not really relevant on facts).
- Existence of a dominant position is the next element: market share is the most important element here (e.g. *United Brands*, *AKZO*), but barriers to entry are also an important consideration (*Hoffmann-La Roche*) (on the information given, Vision Opticals is probably in a dominant position in the market in low-cost glasses and contact lenses).
- It is not the existence of a dominant position that is unlawful, rather its abuse: here Article 102(b) (e.g. *Suiker Unie*), (d) (e.g. *United Brands, Commercial Solvents*).
- Better answers might note that the role of a market access test (e.g. *Hoffmann-La Roche*) under Article 102 TFEU moves away from a formalistic approach to look at actual market effects (although this does depend on economic analysis), as does the possibility of justification under Article 102 TFEU (e.g. *United Brands*).
- Prohibition on exclusive distribution agreements (e.g. *Consten and Grundig*) should also be mentioned, along with block exemptions.

POINTS TO REVIEW

- The aim of Article 102 TFEU is to prevent dominant firms or undertakings from acting independently of competition.

- The key definitions in Article 102 TFEU are 'market', 'dominant position' and 'abuse'?

- A market refers to a category of goods in competition or interchangeable with each other and is defined primarily on the basis of similarity of product characteristics. A given market may also have geographic or temporal dimensions.

- Dominance is defined primarily with reference to the market share of an undertaking and barriers to market access for other undertakings.

- As with Article 101 TFEU, a distinction can be drawn between a 'per se' approach or a rule of reason. Both apply under Article 102 TFEU. Categories (a)–(d) in Article 102 are per se abuses, but an effects-based economic analysis can capture other types of abuses that allow a dominant firm to act independently of competitors.

- Article 102 TFEU is intended to capture both exclusionary abuses and exploitative abuses, as is clear from the variety of behaviour captured in (a)–(d) of Article 102 TFEU.

- As Article 102 TFEU does not allow for exceptions, its scope appears very broad. One criticism that might be made of it as it has been applied in EU law is that barriers to market entry are too easily considered evidence of dominance, when such barriers may simply reflect the technological superiority of an existing undertaking. However, the development in case law of a category of exception or objective justification may address over-breadth in the scope of Article 102 TFEU.

CHAPTER GLOSSARY

Abuse refers to behaviours that a firm or undertaking in a dominant position in the marketplace may not engage in under Article 102 TFEU.

Barrier to access refers to a factor in the marketplace that makes it difficult for a new firm to enter.

Dominant position refers to the position of a firm in the marketplace that allows it to an appreciable extent to act independently of its competitors, especially in the longer term, although it may be subject to competitive pressures temporarily. See also 'super-dominance' below.

Exclusionary abuses refers to practices by a dominant firm targeting in the first instance competitors, rather than consumers.

Exploitative abuses refers to practices by a dominant firm targeting consumers, rather than competitors.

Geographic market refers to an aspect of the definition of the market in particular products. It concerns the existence of similar or homogeneous conditions over territory: a market is considered to exist for a given product over territory within which market conditions are broadly similar.

Market is the term used to describe a category of goods in competition with each other.

Product market refers to the categorisation of products as being in competition with each other on the basis of the similarity of the products, their composition and characteristics.

Substitutability of demand refers to the effect on demand for a product of a price increase and the ability of consumers to switch to other products as an alternative.

Substitutability of supply refers to the ability of suppliers to switch to the supply of alternative products, or the ability of competing suppliers to enter a market in a given product.

Super-dominance refers to a position of dominance of a single undertaking that is so strong that the undertaking is approaching being in a monopoly.

Temporal market means the susceptibility of a given market in goods to change based on time or seasonal factors.

TAKING THINGS FURTHER

A Llorens 'The role of objective justification and efficiencies in the application of Article 82 EC' (2007) 44 *Common Market Law Review* 1727–61 This article discusses the extent to which Article 102 TFEU can accommodate justification of practices, which includes the issue of a rule of reason (remember there are no formal derogations or exceptions under Article 102).

A Andreangeli 'Interoperability as an "essential facility" in the *Microsoft* case: encouraging competition or stifling innovation' (2009) 34 *European Law Review* 584 This article looks at the role that new technology plays in the responsibilities of a firm in a dominant position and whether the responsibilities imposed by Article 102 TFEU are too burdensome, with the result that they may inhibit innovation.

F Dethmers, H Engelen 'Fines under Article 102 of the Treaty on the Functioning of the European Union' (2011) 2 *European Competition Law Review* 86–98 This article looks in detail at the approach of the Commission to sanctions and fines for breaches of Article 102 TFEU, noting the tension between a restriction by object approach and a per se approach in the practice of the Commission.

R Whish, D Bailey *Competition Law* (7th edn Oxford University Press 2012) This comprehensive and clearly written textbook on EU and UK competition law looks in depth at Article 102 TFEU. In particular see Chapter 5 (overview), Chapter 17 (abuse of dominance through non-pricing practices) and Chapter 18 (abuse of dominance through pricing practices).

CHAPTER 17
ECONOMIC AND MONETARY UNION

This chapter examines perhaps the most topical and controversial aspect of the EU, Economic and Monetary Union or EMU. This is one of the more recent developments in the process of European integration, although it was perhaps anticipated to at least some extent from the beginning. Some elements of the original treaties were relevant to EMU, but it became a more central part of the 'European project' from the Single European Act 1986 onwards. The culmination of it came with the adoption of the Euro currency in 2001. To some extent, there has been a sense of inevitability about European integration, but the crisis in the Eurozone and the adoption of two treaties, strictly speaking, outside the EU Treaty framework by 25 of the Member States in response has exposed the underlying tensions between the economic idea of EMU and its political implications. This remains one of the most controversial and contested aspects of EU law and of EU integration.

AS YOU READ . . .

The key questions that will be answered in this chapter are as follows:

— What does Economic and Monetary Union (EMU) add to the common or internal market?

— What has been the course of development of EMU?

— To what extent is EMU an example of differentiated integration? What are the obligations and criteria of membership of the Eurozone?

— What are the advantages and disadvantages of joining the Eurozone? Why have only some Member States done so?

— What has been the impact of the Eurozone crisis on EMU overall? How have the Member States reacted?

— What are the prospects for EMU?

17.1 INTRODUCTION

EMU has perhaps been the most controversial aspect of EU cooperation to date, at least with the emergence of the crisis of excess debt in the Eurozone in 2008 and subsequent years. EMU can be seen as a logical continuation of the common market principle: it extends it to monetary (currency and money supply) matters. EMU is a good example of the incremental method that has become characteristic of European integration. It proceeded in three stages, by smaller steps, gradually culminating in the adoption of the Euro currency from 1999 onwards, with the currency actually being introduced in 2001.

The ultimate pathway of EMU and its link with broader economic coordination remains very much contested and controversial. For some, the Eurozone crisis showed the need for further economic coordination, at a fiscal level of taxation and spending in the Member States. People with this perspective have started to talk about a 'fiscal union', in which the Member States agree common tax and spending policies as a way of ensuring stability of the single currency. For others, the crisis illustrates the problems of pushing for economic integration, without a convergence of standards within Member State economies and the necessary sense of political and loyalty and identity to accompany it.

KEY LEARNING POINT

THE LINK BETWEEN ECONOMIC AND MONETARY POLICY IN THE EU

The method of EMU has been described as 'asymmetric',[1] because the Member States retain primary power over economic policy, including fiscal policy subject to the limits of the Stability and Growth Pact (SGP), while the EU has responsibility for monetary policy. Economic and monetary policy are closely related: Member States' fiscal or spending discipline, an important part of national economic policy, is considered to be vital for price stability (i.e. the value of a currency and the level of inflation), which is the primary objective of monetary policy according to Article 119(2) TFEU. Overall, the EU response to the Eurozone crisis has been to entrench the requirement of the SGP as regards budget deficits legally, thus bringing this important aspect of fiscal policy within EU competence.

At a practical economic level, it can be difficult to sustain a common currency without fiscal coordination to go with it. This is because of the interaction of monetary and fiscal policy. Monetary policy can complement and address problems in fiscal policy. For example, devaluation of a currency can help stimulate the growth of exports by making a country's goods cheaper. This policy option was not open to Greece, for example, in addressing its economic recession during the Eurozone crisis. Interest rates, which

---

1   F Amtenbrink, J de Haan 'Economic governance in the European Union: fiscal policy discipline versus flexibility' (2003) 40 *Common Market Law Review* 1075–1106 at 1078.

are usually the function of central banks, are also important tools of addressing current economic conditions in a country.

Raising interest rates has the effect of 'cooling down' an economy, encouraging savings and making borrowing more expensive. Lowering interest rates has the opposite effect. In the Eurozone, interest rates are set for all the economies at the same rate, irrespective of the different economic conditions prevailing in each of the Eurozone Member States. Membership of a single currency, therefore, limits the capacity of individual countries to respond to their specific economic situation. Advantages of a single currency are that it leads to greater monetary stability, reduces currency speculation and facilitates a single market.

KEY LEARNING POINT

DEGREES OF EMU
EMU is now associated with the adoption of the Euro currency, but it is a broader process involving convergence of monetary policy to varying degrees. While the adoption of the Euro is the most important element of its culmination, those countries that have not adopted the Euro also participate in EMU to a lesser extent through fiscal discipline and stable monetary policy.

17.2 THE EVOLUTION AND STAGES OF EMU

The process of EMU was planned from the beginning to take place in several stages. It required in the first place stability in the exchange rates between Member States, and the culmination of the process has been the adoption of the Euro currency.

MAKING CONNECTIONS
+ + + + + + + + + + + + + + + + +

THE CONNECTION BETWEEN EMU AND FREE MOVEMENT OF CAPITAL AND PAYMENTS
The complete liberalisation of exchange controls and the completion of free movement of capital and payments that resulted was a first step in EMU. This allowed the EU to be treated as a single currency area later on when a single currency was actually adopted, when it would not be possible for exchange controls to apply. It is characteristic of a single national economy that payments can be made for goods and services without the mere fact of a movement of capital within the national economy to pay for them giving rise to any charge or tax. The logic of the first stage of EMU was to achieve this single geographical or territorial space for the movement of money, even when different currencies still existed.

Prior to formal introduction of EMU by the Treaty of Maastricht in 1992, in Article 3a ECT, the Member States informally cooperated in monetary policy from the early 1970s and established a European Exchange Rate Mechanism (ERM) as part of a European Monetary System (EMS) from 1979, although the UK did not join until it did so reluctantly in 1990.

This also involved the introduction of the European Currency Unit (ECU), a basket of the Community's currencies, which would be used as the denominator for fixing exchange rates and financial support mechanisms. Finally, in December 1978, the European Council meeting in Brussels agreed to set up the EMS, as a system of 'fixed but adjustable' exchange rates. The aim was to ensure there were not wide fluctuations in the values of the currencies relative to each other, which would in turn contribute to overall economic stability and facilitate free movement.[2]

The German *Deutschsmark* emerged as the benchmark currency. It proved difficult to maintain the agreed maximum fluctuation rate between the currencies, since exchange rate values are intertwined with many aspects of an economy, especially inflation rates and exchange rates, which differ within each Member State. This eventually led to the UK and Italy leaving in 1992 and an agreement for a wider band of fluctuation of 15 per cent in 1993. EMS was overtaken by ERM II.

EXPLAINING THE LAW

STAGES OF EMU

Stage	Member States	Main Elements
European Monetary System (EMS) – Precursor to EMU (1979–1998)	All then EEC Member States except UK, UK joined 1990 and left 1992, Italy left 1992	European exchange rate mechanism limiting fluctuation to 2.25% or maximum of 6% (changed to 15% 1993)
EMU I (June 1990– December 1993)	All	– Abolition of exchange controls – Adoption of criteria of economic convergence in Treaty of Maastricht, e.g. i. maximum current budget deficit of 3% of GDP and maximum overall debt of 60% of GDP;[3] ii. inflation;[4]

---

2 J Kelly 'The Irish pound: from origins to EMU' (2003) *Irish Central Bank Quarterly Bulletin* 89–115 at 96–97.

3 Article 1 of Protocol to TEU on Excessive Debit Procedure, defining terms in Article 104c(2) Treaty establishing the European Community (ECT). Article 3 of the Protocol made the Member State governments responsible for enforcing it, thus implementation was purely political. This contrasts sharply with the recent jurisdiction given to the Court of Justice.

4 Article 1 of Protocol to TEU on convergence criteria referred to in Article 109j of the ECT.

		iii. maximum exchange rate fluctuation under the European Exchange Rate Mechanism;[5] and interest rates[6]
EMU II (January 1994– December 1998)	All	– European Monetary Institute established in 1994 as forerunner to European Central Bank established in 1998 – Stability and Growth Pact agreed in 1997 – Decision on which MSs to adopt Euro currency – Fulfil criteria for 2 years
EMU III 1999–to date	Austria, Belgium, Finland, France, Germany, Ireland, Italy, Luxembourg, Netherlands, Portugal, Spain as first 11 States (see further in box below)	– Euro currency coins and notes introduced in 2002 – Adoption of secondary legislation to strengthen SGP (so-called 'six-pack' and 'two-pack' in 2011)
Fiscal Compact (FC) and ESM Treaty (2012)	All except UK and Czech Republic ratified the FC, but only applicable to Eurozone Member States	– Prohibition on national budget deficits – Deficit correction procedure + – Jurisdiction of ECJ – European Stability Mechanism Fund

The Euro has now been adopted by 18 Member States. Since the emergence of the crisis in the Eurozone, which is further discussed below, public support for adopting the Euro has declined dramatically.

KEY LEARNING POINT

....

MEMBER STATES WHO HAVE ADOPTED THE EURO AS OF 2014
The following Member States have adopted the Euro as of January 2014: Austria, Belgium, Cyprus, Estonia, Finland, France, Germany, Greece, Ireland, Italy, Latvia, Luxembourg, Malta, the Netherlands, Portugal, Slovenia, Slovakia and Spain.

....

5   Article 3 of Protocol to TEU on convergence criteria referred to in Article 109j of the ECT.
6   Ibid.

The following Member States have committed to joining, but have not completed EMU II: Bulgaria, Croatia, Czech Republic, Hungary, Lithuania (which joined on 1 January 2015), Poland, Romania, Sweden.

The following Member States have opt-outs: the United Kingdom and Denmark.

In Sweden, for example, support for joining was generally above 40 per cent throughout much of the first half of the 2000s. Adoption was defeated in a referendum in 2003, with 55.9 per cent voting no. Now, large majorities, up to 80 per cent, of public opinion oppose entry in polling.[7]

EXPLAINING THE LAW

EMU AS AN EXAMPLE OF FLEXIBLE COOPERATION

The differing degrees of involvement by the Member States in the process of EMU is the most prominent example of differentiated or flexible cooperation in the EU. The United Kingdom and Denmark have secured opt-outs from the third stage of EMU, through Protocols to the treaties. Whilst the other Member States not currently in the Euro have committed to joining it in the treaties, in reality, they have a discretion about doing so simply by deliberately not fulfilling the criteria for entry to the Euro. For example, to take Sweden, it has not joined ERM II and it does this by allowing its currency to fluctuate beyond the range of + or – 2.25 per cent.

The Stability and Growth Pact was one of the most contentious elements of EMU III. This was because it required quite strict fiscal discipline by the Member States involved, with a limit on budget deficits. This had major implications for the overall management of Member State economies, including the amount of financing available for social protection by Member State governments. This involves the very political question of the role of government in redistributing wealth and in social protection, which remains within national competences.

EXPLAINING THE LAW

THE STABILITY AND GROWTH PACT (SGP) TODAY

The Stability and Growth Pact was agreed in the 1990s as part of EMU II. It was provided for by the Treaty of Maastricht[8] and later elaborated upon in

---

7 See Central Statistics Bureau of Sweden http://www.scb.se/sv_/Hitta-statistik/Statistik-efter-amne/Demokrati/ Partisympatier/Partisympatiundersokningen-PSU-/12436/12443/Behallare-for-Press/368252 (last accessed 20 January 2015).

8 Article 1 of Protocol to TEU on Excessive Debit Procedure, defining terms in Article 104c(2) Treaty establishing the European Community (ECT). Article 3 of the Protocol made the Member State governments responsible for enforcing it, thus implementation was purely political. This contrasts sharply with the recent jurisdiction given to the Court of Justice.

two regulations.[9] It sets out an excessive deficit procedure (EDP). The excess deficit rule is now in Article 126 TFEU. This involved an oversight role for the Commission, which could issue recommendations about correcting national deficits. It was later reformed to include an automatic fine for ignoring the excess deficit rules. For the Euro Member States, the Fiscal Compact (a new treaty, discussed below), has largely replaced the previous SGP rules. The Fiscal Compact adds important new elements, prohibiting deficits and providing for ECJ jurisdiction. The UK has had an opt-out from the excess deficit procedure so long as it does not join the Euro.[10] The SGP sets a maximum of 3 per cent for a budget deficit and 60 per cent for public debt.

Each year, all EU Member States must submit a compliance report on the SGP for scrutiny by the European Commission and the Council (of Ministers), relating to the current fiscal position of the Member State and its projected position over the following three years. These reports are called 'stability programmes' for Eurozone Member States and 'convergence programmes' for non-Eurozone Member States.

After the reform of the SGP in 2005, these programmes have also included the Medium-term Budgetary Objectives (MTOs), being individually calculated for each Member State as the medium-term sustainable average-limit for the country's structural deficit. This was a forerunner of the more developed EDP in the Fiscal Compact.

▌ KEY LEARNING POINT
....

THE EXCESSIVE DEFICIT PROCEDURE (EDP) IN ARTICLE 126 TFEU AS DEVELOPED BY THE FISCAL COMPACT

If the EU Member States do not comply with both the deficit limit (i.e. annual budget deficit) and the debt limit (i.e. overall national debt limit), the EDP applies, which sets out an adjustment path towards correcting an excessive deficit. Under Article 126 TFEU, the Council decides on the basis of a Commission recommendation. A more comprehensive approach to the EDP for Eurozone Member States is contained in the Fiscal Compact, see further below. The Fiscal Compact provides more comprehensively for the Member State to reach a Medium-Term Budgetary Objective (MTO). The MTO is a target to be reached for reducing the deficit within a defined time limit.

---

9 Council Regulation 1466/97/EC on the strengthening of the surveillance of budgetary positions and the surveillance and coordination of economic policies OJ L 209 2.8.1997 p. 1; Council Regulation 1467/97/EC on speeding up and clarifying the implementation of the excessive deficit procedure, OJ L 209 2.8.1997 p. 6.

10 Protocol on certain provisions relating to the United Kingdom of Great Britain and Northern Ireland (1992), annexed to the ECT.

17.3 THE EUROZONE CRISIS AND THE RESPONSE OF THE MEMBER STATES

17.3.1 INTRODUCTION

The crisis in the world economy and the related crisis in the Eurozone in the late 2000s have posed perhaps the greatest challenge to the 'project' of European integration to date. The most immediate cause of the crisis regarding the Euro currency was over-indebtedness in the economies of several Eurozone states, particularly Southern European states and Ireland. In Southern European countries, governments had considerably exceeded the budget deficit maximum initially allowed under EMU III rules, although France, Germany and Portugal were the first to breach it.[11] A number of Member State governments were unable to meet their debt repayments when the global economy collapsed into recession.

A related problem was that consumption in Eurozone economies expanded greatly, fuelled by either low taxes allowed by government deficits or the easy availability of credit owing to excess borrowing between banking systems across the Member States. The latter was particularly the case in Ireland, whose banks borrowed heavily on the inter-bank loan market, especially from German banks. Irish banks then made credit too easily available for businesses and consumers, e.g. by requiring only a minimum deposit from the lender.

Excess availability of credit should be addressed by the central banks of the Member States, but many of these failed to carry out their functions effectively.[12] Similarly, the ECB could have sounded an alarm about the pattern of excess inter-bank lending between Member State economies, but it too failed to do so.[13]

17.3.2 RESPONSE AT THE LEVEL OF SECONDARY LEGISLATION: 'SIX-PACK' AND 'TWO-PACK'

In October 2010, a task force chaired by the then President of the Council (of Ministers) Herman van Rompuy, called for greater fiscal discipline within the Euro area.[14] The so-called 'six-pack' of five Regulations and one Directive included were adopted to strengthen the existing fiscal discipline procedure. This six-pack was based on the existing treaty provisions. They set out more specific objectives: avoiding a GDP deficit

---

11 'Europe's Stability and Growth Pact: loosening those bonds' *The Economist* (17 July 2003).

12 Even the normally apolitical President of Ireland, then Mary McAleese, felt free to point this out: 'Irish President Mary McAleese's astonishing attack over slump' *The Belfast Telegraph* (11 September 2010).

13 See the speech by former Irish Taoiseach (Prime Minister) John Bruton, also formerly EU Ambassador to the USA, at the London School of Economics 'The economic future of the European Union' (7 March 2011) http://www.lse.ac.uk/assets/richmedia/channels/publicLecturesAndEvents/transcripts/20110307_1830_the EconomicFutureOfTheEuropeanUnion_tr.pdf (last accessed 20 January 2015).

14 Strengthening Economic Governance in the EU: Report of the Task Force on the European Council (October 2010) www.consilium.europa.eu/uedocs/cms_data/docs/pressdata/en/ec/117236.pdf (last accessed 21 January 2015).

higher than 3 per cent, bringing total debt below 60 per cent of the GDP, having more balanced budgets by avoiding 'macro–economic imbalances' (e.g. avoiding large trade deficits, where a country imports much more than it exports and which can reduce economic growth).

The six-pack amounts to a more comprehensive version of the SGP, providing for greater fiscal discipline. In particular, it provides for more comprehensive enforcement, through a strengthened EDP and a new EIP (the purpose of the latter being to detect and correct underlying problems that might prevent achievement of the SGP targets for government deficits and debt). More critically, this package can be seen as a restriction of the fiscal flexibility open to national governments in the Eurozone. The primary criticism has been that it is biased in favour of deficit reduction and that this has reduced the capacity of Eurozone Member States to stimulate economic growth. Borrowing in order to have funds to stimulate economic growth can be more cost-effective in the long run. This is especially the case with borrowing for capital expenditure, i.e. the building of infrastructure or economic resources that provide a basis for further economic growth.

The six-pack does not change budgetary or fiscal objectives of the SGP, but it establishes a system of sanctions for its breach. Previously, no sanctions applied, and it was not unusual for the Member States to breach the SGP. Examples are France and Germany, which both broke the SGP in 2003, leading to a 2005 agreement to be somewhat more flexible with the SGP.[15]

KEY LEARNING POINT

THE SIX-PACK, THE TFEU AND THE TWO INTERGOVERNMENTAL TREATIES

The six-pack is intended to reinforce the multilateral surveillance procedure (a kind of early warning mechanism) in Article 121 TFEU and the excessive deficit procedure (EDP) in Article 126 TFEU. The six-pack has been adopted under Article 121(6) TFEU alone or combined with Article 136 TFEU[16] and Article 126(14) TFEU.[17] The rationale for the Fiscal Compact[18] and the ESM Treaty,[19] adopted subsequently to the six-pack, is that the SGP and six-pack was considered to need strengthening in the support given to them in national law, which required national constitutional change, and to provide a legal basis for the granting of financial assistance to Euro Member States. Adopting the content of the six-pack

---

15 E.g. through more differentiation of medium–term budgetary objectives: see Regulation 1055/05/EC OJ L 174 7.7.2005 p. 1 and Regulation 1056/05 OJ L 174 7.7.2005 p. 5.

16 Article 136 TFEU, in Chapter IV on measures specific to the Eurozone Member States, provides that the Eurozone Member States may adopt additional measures relating to budgetary discipline and economic policy.

17 Article 126(14) TFEU provides that the Council shall, acting unanimously in accordance with a special legislative procedure and after consulting the European Parliament and the European Central Bank adopt the appropriate provisions to replace the Protocol on the excessive deficit procedure annexed to the treaties.

18 Treaty on Stability, Coordination and Governance in the Economic and Monetary Union, Brussels, 2nd March 2011.

19 Treaty Establishing the European Stability Mechanism OJ L 91 6.4.2011 p. 1 (signed at the European Council Meeting of 2 March 2012, signed by Hungary on 25 March 2012).

in the form of secondary legislation had the advantage of being achievable more quickly, compared with treaty amendment. Although under the EDP already provided for in the Treaty, the Council may impose sanctions including, for example, non-interest-bearing deposits and fines, the Member States were reluctant to make use of this provision. The six-pack seeks to strengthen enforcement.

For example, under the six-pack, when a Member State in the Eurozone fails to comply with an EDP by failing to eliminate its deficit, an interest-bearing deposit equalling 0.2 per cent of GDP is due. If non-compliance continues, the deposit is treated as a fine. Further, automatic sanctions are triggered based on a different voting procedure in the Council, i.e. reverse majority voting. If a Member State in the Eurozone is reported to have provided false data, an additional fine may be imposed. As background to this, claims had been made against Greece that it had under-stated the extent of government borrowing.[20]

The elements of the six-pack are as follows:

1. *Regulation 1175/2011*,[21] amending Regulation 1466/97,[22] on the strengthening of the surveillance of budgetary positions and the surveillance and coordination of economic policies. It takes effect in all the Member States, although some provisions apply only to Eurozone countries or non-Eurozone countries. **It aims to monitor and coordinate Member States' budgetary policies, by a preventive mechanism to ensure budgetary discipline by the Member States**. It was adopted under Article 121(6) TFEU. Article 1 states that the Regulation sets out the rules covering the content, the submission, the examination and the monitoring of stability programmes and convergence programmes as part of multilateral surveillance by the Council and the Commission so as to prevent, at an early stage, the occurrence of excessive general government deficits and to promote the surveillance and coordination of economic policies thereby supporting the achievement of the Union's objectives for growth and employment. The Regulation provides for a European Semester at the start of each year to assist Member States to adopt budgetary policies within the criteria of the SGP (Section 1A). Member States submit to the Commission stability programmes (for Member States in the Eurozone) (Articles 3–4) and convergence programmes (for Member States outside the Eurozone) (Articles 7–8) in which they adopt medium-term budgetary objectives (the latter are provided for under Article 2a and are for a period of three years). These programmes are assessed by the Commission and are the subject of specific Council recommendations for each Member State. The **European Semester** is a six-month period. At the start of the Semester, the Council identify the key economic challenges and provides Member States with strategic policy guidelines. At the end of the European Semester, the Council sends recommendations to each Member

---

20 See, e.g. M Saragosa 'Greece warned on false Euro data' (1 December 2004) http://news.bbc.co.uk/1/hi/business/4058327.stm (last accessed 21 January 2015).
21 OJ L 306 23.11.2011 p. 12.
22 OJ L 209 2.8.1997 p. 1.

State (Articles 6(2) and 10(2)) and, based on the opinions of the Commission and the Economic and Financial Committee (Article 5),[23] makes known its assessments before Member States draw up their final budgets for the following year. If the Commission identifies a significant divergence from the medium-term budgetary objective or from the adjustment path that should lead to that objective being achieved, it is to address recommendations to the Member State to avoid an excessive deficit (Articles 6 and 10). This is the **early warning mechanism**, provided for under Article 121(4) TFEU.

2. *Regulation 1173/2011*[24] on the effective enforcement of budgetary surveillance in the Euro area and applies to the Eurozone only. It was adopted under Article 136 TFEU in combination with Article 121(6) TFEU. It supplements Article 126 TFEU. Article 1 states that the Regulation **sets out a system of sanctions for enhancing the enforcement of the preventive and corrective parts of the SGP in the Eurozone**. Article 6(1) states that if the Council, acting under Article 126(8) TFEU, decides that a Member State has not taken effective action to correct its excessive deficit, the Commission shall, within 20 days of that decision, recommend that the Council, by a further decision, impose a fine, amounting to 0.2 per cent of the Member State's GDP in the preceding year. Article 6(2) provides for reverse majority voting, stating that the decision imposing a fine shall be deemed to be adopted by the Council unless it decides by a qualified majority to reject the Commission's recommendation within 10 days of the Commission's adoption thereof.

3. *Regulation 1177/2011*,[25] amending Regulation 1467/97,[26] on speeding up and clarifying the implementation of the excessive deficit procedure established under Article 126 TFEU. It was adopted under Article 126(14) TFEU and applies to all Member States. Article 1 states its purpose as laying down the provisions for **speeding up and clarifying the excessive deficit procedure** (EDP), where compliance with the budgetary discipline is examined on the basis of the government deficit and government debt criteria. Article 2(4) states that the Council recommendation made in accordance with Article 126(7) TFEU shall establish a maximum deadline of six months for effective action to be taken by the Member State concerned. Articles 11–16 specify the operation of fines under Article 126(11) TFEU.

---

23 Article 126(4) TFEU provides that the Economic and Financial Committee will formulate an opinion of the Commission's report on a Member State having an excessive deficit: Council Decision 98/743/EC on the detailed provisions concerning the composition of the Economic and Financial Committee OJ L 358 31.12.1998 p. 109, in Article 1, provides that each Member State shall appoint two members (and may appoint two alternate members) and, under Article 2, these members are to possess outstanding competence in the economic and financial field. The role of the Economic and Financial Committee might be considered a variation of comitology. It is a way for the Member States to supplement the advisory role of the Commission with their own experts.
24 OJ L 306, 23.11.2011 p. 1.
25 OJ L 306, 23.11.2011 p. 33.
26 OJ L 209 2.8.1997 p. 1.

4. *Directive 2011/85*[27] on requirements for budgetary frameworks of the Member States. The Directive is to be implemented by all EU Member States no later than 31 December 2013. It was adopted under Article 126(14)(3) TFEU. Article 1 states that the Directive lays down detailed rules concerning the characteristics of the budgetary frameworks of the Member States. Those rules are considered necessary to ensure Member States' compliance with obligations under the TFEU to avoid excessive government deficits i.e. to implement the SGP. It addresses forecasting, statistical data and a medium-term budgetary framework.

5. *Regulation 1176/2011*[28] on the prevention and correction of macroeconomic imbalances. It was adopted under Article 121(6) TFEU. The Regulation **lays out the details of the macroeconomic imbalance surveillance procedure and covers all EU Member States**. Recital 1 sets out the context in stating that the coordination of the economic policies of the Member States within the Union should be developed in the context of the broad economic policy guidelines and the employment guidelines, as provided for by the TFEU, and should entail compliance with the guiding principles of stable prices, sound and sustainable public finances and monetary conditions and a sustainable balance of payments. Article 2 defines imbalance as any trend giving rise to macroeconomic developments which are adversely affecting, or have the potential adversely to affect, the proper functioning of the economy of a Member State or of the economic and monetary union, or of the Union as a whole, while 'excessive imbalances' means severe imbalances, including imbalances that jeopardise or risks jeopardising the proper functioning of the economic and monetary union. This is **a much broader term, thus, than excessive deficits under the SGP**. Article 3 establishes an alert mechanism to facilitate the early identification and the monitoring of imbalances, under an **excessive imbalance procedure** (EIP). Article 4 sets out the workings of a scoreboard comprising a set of indicators to facilitate early identification and monitoring of imbalances. Article 5 provides for in-depth review of the risk of imbalances in individual Member States to be undertaken by the Commission. Article 6 provides for the Council, on a recommendation from the Commission, to address the necessary recommendations to the Member State concerned, in accordance with the procedure set out in Article 121(2) TFEU, on the basis of the in-depth review referred to in Article 5, if the Commission considers that a Member State is experiencing imbalances. Article 7(2) provides that the Council, on a recommendation from the Commission, may, in accordance with Article 121(4) TFEU, adopt a recommendation establishing the existence of an excessive imbalance and recommending that the Member State concerned take corrective action. Articles 8–10 address the detail of the 'corrective action plan' process. Article 11 provides that the Council, on a recommendation from the Commission, shall abrogate recommendations issued under Articles 7, 8 or 10 as soon as it considers that the Member State concerned is no longer affected by excessive imbalances as outlined in the recommendation referred to in Article 7(2).

---

27 Ibid at 41.
28 Ibid at 25.

6. *Regulation 1174/2011*[29] on enforcement action to correct excessive macroeconomic imbalances in the Eurozone. This Regulation complements Regulation 1176/2011 and provides for sanctions and other procedures for enforcement of the 'corrective action plan'. It responds to the EIP recommendation from the Council.

KEY LEARNING POINT

APPLICATION OF THE SIX-PACK TO THE EUROZONE AND NON-EUROZONE

Of the six-pack, the rules on sanctions, Regulation 1173/2011 and Regulation 1174/2011 apply to the Eurozone only.

The six-pack entered into force on 13 December 2011. The six-pack was a forerunner to a new treaty, the Fiscal Compact (the Treaty on Stability Coordination and Governance in the Economic and Monetary Union), which was intended to strengthen further the framework of fiscal control and discipline for Eurozone Member States. The Treaty was originally meant to form part of EU law, but initially the United Kingdom and then the Czech Republic refused to ratify it. This is discussed further below.

Two further Regulations, the so-called two-pack, were introduced in late 2011, providing for additional 'economic surveillance', especially concerning the excessive imbalance procedure or EIP, and only applicable to the Eurozone Member States.[30] They came into effect on 28 May 2013. They are closely related to Articles 5 and 6, in particular, of the Fiscal Compact.

Regulation 473/2013[31] on common provisions for monitoring and assessing draft budgetary plans and ensuring the correction of excessive deficits of the Member States in the Euro area. It was adopted under Article 136 TFEU in combination with Article 121(6) TFEU. Article 1 states that the Regulation sets out provisions for enhanced monitoring of budgetary policies in the Eurozone and for ensuring that national budgets are consistent with the economic policy guidance issued in the context of the SGP and the European Semester for economic policy coordination. *If the Eurozone Member State is not involved in an EDP, the Regulation creates an additional monitoring requirement for the Member State to submit its draft fiscal budget for the upcoming year to the European Commission*, no later than 15 October, for the Commission to assess and give an opinion before the draft budget is debated and voted for in the national Parliament. In addition it *provides for Economic Partnership Programmes* for Member States in an EDP, whereby

---

29 Ibid at 8.
30 European Commission MEMO/11/822 (23 November 2011) http://europa.eu/rapid/press-release_MEMO-11-822_en.htm?locale=en (last accessed 21 January 2015).
31 OJ L 140 27.05.2013 p. 11.

the Member State describes the policy measures and structural reforms that are needed to ensure an effective and lasting correction of the excessive deficit, as a development of its national reform programme and its stability programme, taking into account relevant Council recommendations. The Council may replace an Economic Partnership Programme with a corrective action plan under Regulation 1176/2011.

Regulation 472/2013[32] on the strengthening of economic and budgetary surveillance of Member States in the Euro area experiencing or threatened with serious difficulties with respect to their financial stability: Applies to those Member States **subject to an EDP who are also subject to a 'macroeconomic adjustment programme' under the Regulation, imposing increased reporting requirements**. It was adopted under Article 136 TFEU in combination with Article 121(6) TFEU. The Regulation **provides for a macroeconomic adjustment programme to build on and substitute any economic partnership programme** under Regulation 473/2011 and which shall include annual budgetary targets. Regulation 472/2013 will not apply for a Member State without an open EIP receiving macroeconomic financial assistance only in the form of an undrawn 'Precautionary Conditioned Credit Line', i.e. who have been given the possibility of credit, but who have not yet used it.

The two-pack overlaps with elements of the Fiscal Compact or FC, especially Articles 5 and 6 of the FC, e.g. incorporating fiscal rules into national law, preparing economic partnership programmes, and coordinating with other Member States on an *ex ante* basis debt issuance programmes.

Summary of Six-Pack:

Regulation 1175/2011 amending Council Regulation (EC) No 1466/97 on the strengthening of the surveillance of budgetary positions and the surveillance and coordination of economic policies	Legal basis of Article 121(6) TFEU, amends Regulation 1466/96	Aims to monitor and coordinate Member States' budgetary policies, by a preventive mechanism to ensure budgetary discipline by the Member States called the European Semester
Regulation 1173/2011 on the effective enforcement of budgetary surveillance in the Euro area	Legal basis of Article 136 TFEU in combination with Article 121(6) TFEU	Sets out a system of sanctions for enhancing the enforcement of the preventive and corrective parts of the SGP in the Eurozone

32 Ibid at 1.

Regulation 1177/2011 amending Regulation (EC) No 1467/97 on speeding up and clarifying the implementation of the excessive deficit procedure	Legal basis of Article 126(14) TFEU (which requires unanimity in the Council, after consulting EP and ECB)	Aims to speed up and clarify the implementation of the excessive deficit procedure established under Article 126 TFEU
Directive 2011/85 on requirements for budgetary frameworks of the Member States	Legal basis of Article 126(14) TFEU	Sets out requirements for national budgetary frameworks to ensure Member States' compliance with the TFEU to avoiding excessive deficits and addresses forecasting, statistical data, and a medium-term budgetary framework
Regulation 1176/2011 on the prevention and correction of macroeconomic imbalances	Legal basis of Article 121(6) TFEU	Aims to prevent and correct 'macroeconomic imbalances', which is any trend giving rise to macroeconomic developments which are adversely affecting, or have the potential adversely to affect, the proper functioning of the economy of a Member State or of the economic and monetary union, or of the Union as a whole. It provides for the adoption of 'corrective action plan' by Member States experiencing a macroeconomic imbalance

Summary of Two-Pack – Applicable only to the Eurozone Member States:

Regulation 473/2013 on common provisions for monitoring and assessing draft budgetary plans and ensuring the correction of excessive deficit of the Member States in the Euro area	Legal basis of Article 136 TFEU in combination with Article 121(6) TFEU	Sets out provisions for enhanced monitoring of budgetary policies in the Eurozone (i.e. it deals with the monitoring process leading up to an EDP in the Eurozone) and for ensuring that national budgets are consistent with the economic policy guidance issued in the context of the SGP and the European Semester for economic policy coordination, as well as setting out some further provisions relating to the EDP
Regulation 1174/2011 on enforcement measures to correct excessive macroeconomic imbalances in the Euro area	Legal basis of Article 136 TFEU in combination with Article 121(6) TFEU	This Regulation complements Regulation 1176/2011 and provides for sanctions and other procedures for enforcement of the corrective action plan
Regulation 472/2013 on the strengthening of economic and budgetary surveillance of Member States in the Euro area experiencing or threatened with serious difficulties with respect to their financial stability	Legal basis of Article 136 TFEU in combination with Article 121(6) TFEU	Provides for a macroeconomic adjustment programme to build on and substitute any economic partnership programme under Regulation 473/2011 and which shall include annual budgetary targets

KEY LEARNING POINT

REVERSE MAJORITY VOTING UNDER THE SIX-PACK

Under the six-pack, a new reverse majority voting (RMV) procedure applies in the Council. RMV means that a decision shall be deemed to be adopted by the Council unless it is decided by a qualified majority to reject the Commission's recommendation within 10 days of the Commission's adoption. This weakens the power of the Council relative to the Commission. Doubts have been raised about whether there is a treaty basis for it.[33]

---

33 See the thorough appraisal in R Palmstorfer 'The reverse majority voting under the "six-pack": a bad turn for the Union' (2014) 20(2) *European Law Journal* 186–203.

Economic Governance in the EU

- Stability and Growth Pact (SGP):   - SGP:

Article 121 TFEU – Early warning mechanism

Article 126 TFEU – Excessive deficit procedure

- New enforcement: - New enforcement:

i. Six-pack and Two-pack   Six-pack, but not the

sanctions or Regulation

1173/2011 and Regulation

1174/2011

ii. FC and ESM Treaty

Summarising differences:

• FC and ESM Treaty apply to Eurozone Member States only

• The rules on sanctions in the six-pack only apply to the non-Eurozone Member States, as do Regulations 1173/2011 and 1174/2011

• The two-pack only applies to the Eurozone

Another significant initiative of secondary legislation is the European Financial Stabilisation Mechanism (EFSM), established by means of Council Regulation (EU) No 407/2010.[34] Article 1 explains its aim and scope as, with a view to preserving the financial stability of the EU, to establish the conditions and procedures under which Union financial assistance may be granted to a Member State which is experiencing, or is seriously threatened with, a severe economic or financial disturbance caused by exceptional occurrences beyond its control, taking into account the possible application of the existing facility providing medium-term financial assistance for non-Euro-area Member States' balances of payments, as established by Regulation (EC) No 332/2002.[35]

---

34 Council Regulation 407/2010/EU establishing a European financial stabilisation mechanism OJ L 118, 12.05.2010 p. 1.
35 Regulation 332/2002/EC OJ L 53, 23.02.2002 p. 1.

Article 2 states that Union financial assistance for the purposes of this Regulation shall take the form of a loan or of a credit line granted to the Member State concerned. The Commission can borrow in financial markets on behalf of the Union, and then loan it to the Member State, as a type of EU budget guarantee. The EFSM was a precursor to the ESM Treaty (see below).

Although not in the form of secondary legislation, a related development is the possible use of outright monetary transactions (OMTs) by the ECB.[36] This is a process whereby the ECB buys the bonds of Eurozone Member States in order to strengthen the credit rating of the Member State. At the time of writing, the German Federal Constitutional Court has made a preliminary reference to the ECJ on the compatibility of this procedure with the TFEU.[37] On the face of it, OMTs seem potentially contrary to Article 123(1) TFEU prohibiting the ECB from purchasing the debt of Member States:

> Overdraft facilities or any other type of credit facility with the European Central Bank or with the central banks of the Member States (hereinafter referred to as 'national central banks') in favour of Union institutions, bodies, offices or agencies, central governments, regional, local or other public authorities, other bodies governed by public law, or public undertakings of Member States shall be prohibited, as shall the purchase directly from them by the European Central Bank or national central banks of debt instruments.

KEY LEARNING POINT
....

THE TWO NEW 'INTERGOVERNMENTAL' TREATIES
The Member States responded to the crisis in the Eurozone by the adoption of two new treaties designed to ensure stricter adherence to budgetary discipline in the countries of the Eurozone. A remarkable feature of these treaties is that they were ratified by only 25 of the then 27 Member States. UK Prime Minister David Cameron refused to agree to the first of the two new treaties, the first time a head of government has voted against a proposed treaty. Later, the Czech Republic refused to ratify it also. As a result, the Fiscal Compact is not technically an EU Treaty, while the ESM has been adopted as a Treaty amendment under Article 136 TFEU, as we saw in Chapter 3.

17.3.3 TREATY ON STABILITY, COORDINATION AND GOVERNANCE IN THE ECONOMIC AND MONETARY UNION (FISCAL COMPACT) 2011

The UK and the Czech Republic have opted out of this Treaty. As discussed in Chapter 3, the Treaty prevents Member States having a budget deficit and from allowing their national debt to exceed 60 per cent of GDP. Prior to this, the non-binding guidelines permitted an annual budget deficit of 3 per cent. Very importantly, in

---

36 OMT Decision of the Governing Council of the European Central Bank of 6 September 2012.
37 Orders of 17 December 2013 and of 14 January 2014, 2 BvR 1390/12 (partly separated as 2 BvR 2728/13), 2 BvR 1421/12 (partly separated as 2 BvR 2729/13), 2 BvR 1438/12 (partly separated as 2 BvR 2730/13), 2 BvR 1439/12, 2 BvR 1440/12, 2 BvR 1824/12 (partly separated as 2 BvR 2731/13), 2 BvE 6/12 (partly separated as 2 BvE 13/13).

Article 8 it gives the ECJ jurisdiction to rule on the compliance of Member States with this provision. This represents a kind of constitutionalisation of a prohibition on budget deficits in the Member States of the Eurozone.

ANALYSING THE LAW

CONSTITUTIONALISING A PROHIBITION ON BUDGET DEFICITS

The effective constitutionalisation of a ban on national budget deficit is one of the consequences of the Fiscal Compact for Member States of the Eurozone. This is quite remarkable compared to the regulation of budgetary issues at national level. Most commonly, budgets are considered non-justiciable and as being for the political branch to determine. In UK public law, for example, the allocation of government resources is not subject to judicial review.[38] Similarly, the Irish Constitution makes clear that the social and economic policy aspirations of the State are not subject to constitutional review.[39]

Article 3 FC envisages a correction mechanism for current budget deficits to apply in an anticipatory way, i.e. if there are significant observed deviations from the medium-term objective for the current budget deficit or the *adjustment path* towards it. However, as we saw in Chapter 3, Article 7 allows the Member States acting by qualified majority to reverse any budget corrections mandated by the Commission.

17.3.4 TREATY ESTABLISHING THE EUROPEAN STABILITY MECHANISM 2012

Only Eurozone Member States have adopted this treaty. The purpose of the ESM is to provide financial assistance in the framework of a macroeconomic adjustment programme, mainly by purchasing Member States' debt in primary and secondary markets, for Member States of the Eurozone. It can also provide loans of up to 500 billion Euros at borrowing rates as low as 3 per cent. Avoiding the need of referendums in some of the Member States, such as Ireland, the European Council was able to amend the treaties to achieve this using Article 48(6) TEU, which allows it to make amendments to Part III of the TFEU acting by unanimity.[40]

A paragraph added to Article 136 TFEU authorised the establishment of the ESM under EU law. It states that the enactment and entry into force of the regulations require the Council's adoption in agreement with the European Parliament, subject to a qualified majority of the Eurozone Member States.

---

38 *R v Cambridge Health Authority, ex parte B* [1995] 1 WLR 898, concerning resources in the National Health Service.

39 Article 45 of the Constitution of Ireland (Bunracht na hÉireann), on Directive Principles of Social Policy, which are non-justiciable.

40 European Council Decision 2011/199 amending Article 136 TFEU with regard to a stability mechanism for Member States whose currency is the Euro OJ L 06.04.2011 p. 1.

KEY LEARNING POINT

THE RELATIONSHIP BETWEEN THE FISCAL COMPACT
AND ESM TREATY

This Treaty (ESM Treaty) supplements the Fiscal Compact (FC). The ESM Treaty
will help finance 'bailouts' of Eurozone countries in danger of defaulting on their
national debt repayments.

It came into force when Member States representing 90 per cent of its capital ratified
it.[41] The Member States are to make proportionate contributions.[42]

ANALYSING THE LAW

THE *PRINGLE* CASE

The *Pringle* case concerned the legal basis of the ESM Treaty, it was a
preliminary reference from the Supreme Court of Ireland.[43] The Treaty was
adopted under Article 136 TFEU, which provides for measures to be adopted
specific to Euro Member States. Member States acting in the European Council
in the Eurozone[44] on the basis of the simplified revision procedure under Article
48(6) TEU on the internal market, which falls under Part III TFEU, inserted a
paragraph 3 in Article 136 TFEU establishing a stability mechanism. Specifically,
the amendment provides that the Member States whose currency is the Euro,
may establish a mechanism such as the European Stability Mechanism (ESM) so
long as that mechanism is only activated when indispensable to safeguarding
the stability of the Euro area as a whole, and only if the financial assistance is
made subject to strict conditionality. The ECJ concluded that the ESM Treaty
did not fall under monetary policy under Part I TFEU, that it came under the
internal market competence (meaning it was legitimate for the Member States
to use Article 48(6) in this way). This is a good example of the *lex specialis*
of monetary policy being side-stepped by the more general internal market
competence. It would have been politically undesirable for the Member States'
use of the revision clause to be declared unlawful, which helps explain the
flexible approach of the ECJ, but the Court is typically willing to depart from
stricter notions of interpretative restraints, in order to enhance integration.
The Court declared that the treaty was not concerned with price stability, but
with addressing the financing requirements of the Euro Member States. Price
stability is, however, just one aspect of monetary policy, and the financing

---

41 Article 48 ESM Treaty.

42 Articles 2(3) and 8(5) ESM Treaty.

43 Case C–370/12 *Thomas Pringle v Government of Ireland, Ireland and The Attorney General*, judgment of 27 November 2012.

44 European Council Decision 2011/199/EU amending Article 136 TFEU with regard to a stability mechanism
   for Member States whose currency is the Euro OJ L 91 06.04.2011 p. 1.

requirements related to the maintenance of the currency, so the Court's reasoning is not absolutely persuasive on this point.

96. Under Articles 3 and 12(1) of the ESM Treaty, it is not the purpose of the ESM to maintain price stability, but rather to meet the financing requirements of ESM Members, namely Member States whose currency is the Euro, who are experiencing or are threatened by severe financing problems, if indispensable to safeguard the financial stability of the Euro area as a whole and of its Member States. To that end, the ESM is not entitled either to set the key interest rates for the Euro area or to issue Euro currency, while the financial assistance which the ESM grants must be entirely funded – the provisions of Article 123(1) TFEU being respected – from paid-in capital or by the issue of financial instruments, as provided for in Article 3 of the ESM Treaty.

97 As is apparent from paragraph 56 of this judgment, any effect of the activities of the ESM on price stability is not such as to call into question that finding. Even if the activities of the ESM might influence the rate of inflation, such an influence would constitute only the indirect consequence of the economic policy measures adopted.

98 It follows from the foregoing that Articles 3(1)(c) TFEU and 127 TFEU do not preclude either the conclusion by the Member States whose currency is the Euro of an agreement such as the ESM Treaty or their ratification of it.[45]

The Court further found that (1) the ESM Treaty did not affect common policies adopted by all the EU Member States under the TEU or TFEU, thus meaning that it was not contrary to the *ERTA* doctrine on parallelism (on the latter, see further Chapter 7) and (2) did not alter the TFEU through creating a new system of economic coordination.[46]

17.3.5 THE BANKING UNION

The next major step that the Eurozone countries took was the adoption of a common mechanism for bailing out banks in financial difficulty. The inability of national banks to repay debt was one of the main reasons for the crisis in several Eurozone countries, especially Ireland. The Irish Government, for example, felt it was necessary to give a state guarantee of several Irish banks that had over-lent and were unable to finance their ongoing operations due to the sheer amount of bad debts that occurred following the

---

45 Case C–370/12 *Thomas Pringle* (n 43) paras 96–98.

46 Ibid paras 99–122. See further V Borger 'The ESM and the European Court's predicament in *Pringle*' (2013) 14 *German Law Journal* 113–40; P-A Van Malleghem '*Pringle:* a paradigm shift in the European Union's monetary constitution' (2013) 14 *German Law Journal* 141–68.

global recession. Irish banks had borrowed money on the inter-bank market in order to lend an unsustainably large amount in the Irish economy. Bad debts now experienced by the banks meant they could not pay back their own creditors.

The view of the Irish Government was that if the state did not guarantee the financial viability of banks, the Irish banking system might have collapsed, with disastrous consequences for all aspects of the Irish economy. By taking over bad debts, the Irish Government greatly increased its own indebtedness.

Member States are currently negotiating the creation of a Eurozone Single Resolution Mechanism (SRM), with the power to close failing banks, combined with a new financial supervisor or regulator for the Eurozone, called the European Banking Authority (EBA), under the auspices of the European Central Bank (ECB). The adoption of the EBA involves transferring prudential supervision from national competences to EU competence for Eurozone Member States. It was agreed through two Regulations in October 2013.[47]

KEY LEARNING POINT

MEMBER STATES AND THE BANKING UNION
The Regulations establishing the Banking Union were adopted under Article 127(6) TFEU, which provides a legal basis to transfer competence to the ECB for prudential supervision in the Eurozone. The provision had not been used previously. All Member States have signed up to the Banking Union, which was created using pre-existing Treaty provisions and did not necessitate a Treaty amendment.

One of the major features of the proposed banking union is a common fund to 'bail out' banks in trouble at national level, which will in turn mean national governments do not have to take over their own bad banks and thereby destabilise national finances. The fund will be built up by Member State through contributions over a ten-year period to 2025, which in turn would be financed by bank levies.

The Member States have agreed the outline of this proposal, but it is more controversial than establishing the EBA (a dispute has arisen about the legislative method that should be used and whether the ordinary legislative method, which would involve the European Parliament as co-legislator, is legally required). The proposal currently allows the Council (of Ministers) to block decisions under the SRM by a simple majority.

---

47 Council Regulation 1024/2013/EU conferring specific tasks on the European Central Bank concerning policies relating to prudential supervision of credit institutions, OJ 2013 L 287 29.10.2013 p. 63; Council Regulation 1022/2013/EU amending Regulation 1093/2010/EU establishing a European Supervisory Authority (European Banking Authority) as regards the conferral of specific tasks on the European Central Bank pursuant to Council Regulation 1024/2013/EU OJ L 287 29.10.2013 p. 5.

Some Member States, especially Germany, wish to satisfy their domestic electorate by avoiding a sharing or mutualisation of banking debt, which is one of the issues currently being negotiated by the Member States.

17.4 PROSPECTS FOR EMU

Advocates of increased European integration, with perhaps the eventual emergence of a federal European 'super State', have seen in the Euro crisis a rationale to deepen integration to include fiscal policy. Fiscal policy concerns government spending and taxation. For example, Ireland was encouraged to surrender its competence in corporate taxation as a term for EU help in deadline with the problem of excess government debt. Ireland refused, with a consensus of Irish politicians, both governmental and opposition, rejecting the attempt led by then French President Sarkozy. This is an example of how the crisis in the Eurozone raises questions about the very nature of the EU and whether it represents an inevitable move towards statehood.

ANALYSING THE LAW

THE FUTURE OF EMU

With the adoption of the Fiscal Compact and ESM Treaty, the EU took the first major steps towards addressing the problem of over-indebtedness. This was not the only possible solution. Some suggested that Southern European countries should be allowed to enter into an orderly exit from the Eurozone and to revert to their own currencies.[48] This would allow these countries to set their currency at a level that would make their exports competitive, i.e. to reduce the value of their currency, making their goods cheaper when purchased by other currencies, and thus more competitive. Such re-valuation of a currency is possible for a country with its own currency, but is not of course possible for a country in a joint currency with 17 other countries: a single valuation applies to all.

Critics of the way in which the Euro was adopted (and not necessarily of the principle of single currency) pointed out that it was a mistake to think very different economies could be all joined up through a single currency, as if their economies would automatically converge as a result.[49] In the end, rescue packages and budget deficit reduction programmes were adopted to keep all countries within the Eurozone, although with considerable political and social consequences. In

48 See e.g. 'IMF chief raises possibility of Greece's "orderly exit" from eurozone' *Financial Post* (15 May 2012) http://business.financialpost.com/2012/05/15/imf-chief-raises-possibility-of-greeces-orderly-exit-from-eurozone/ (last accessed 20 January 2015).

49 See e.g. 'The ticking Euro bomb: how a good idea became a tragedy' *Der Spiegel* (5 October 2011) http://www.spiegel.de/international/europe/the-ticking-euro-bomb-how-a-good-idea-became-a-tragedy-a-790138-3.html (last accessed 20 January 2015).

Greece and Portugal, for example, sustained public protests took place at the deflationary effects that these deficit reduction programmes produced, which contributed to very high unemployment rates.

The impact of all of this on the standing of the EU has been very considerable. With the programme of structural funds that characterised the earlier years of what is now the EU, the organisation gained support from the populations of Member States as a cause of economic growth and prosperity. With the crisis in the Eurozone, drastic budgetary cuts, and the economic inflexibility of 17–18 countries' economies being tied to a single exchange rate, the populations of EU Member States, especially those who have suffered the most economically and socially, have come to associate the EU with economic stagnation and social problems in a way that has never occurred before in the history of the EU.

17.5 CONCLUSION

EMU represents the most intense degree of European integration. It has proceeded gradually from the 1970s through European Monetary System followed by the European Exchange Rate Mechanism (ERM) from 1979, it became formalised in the treaties with the Treaty of Maastricht in 1992. From the beginning, the UK was a reluctant participant, joining the ERM in 1990 and leaving two years later. This has remained the case, with the UK and Denmark being the two Member States of 28 with a full opt-out from EMU.

However, nine Member States have yet to fulfil the criteria for ERM II, which they have the legal option not to do if they so elect. With the severe crisis in the Eurozone in the late 2000s creating doubts about the viability of a single currency across diverse economies, it is likely that the pace of accession to the Euro will slow. The current Member States of the EU are negotiating the Banking Union, but plans for deeper fiscal integration remain too controversial politically to be progressed at the time of writing.

POINTS TO REVIEW

– Economic and Monetary Union (EMU) adds an important new dimension to the common market: harmonisation in the sphere of currency, money supply and bank interest rates.

– EMU began outside the treaties with the European Monetary System (EMS) and Exchange Rate Mechanism (ERM) of the 1970s and was introduced at treaty level with a three-stage process: EMU I, EMU II and EMU III. Completion of convergence criteria in EMU II leads to full participation in EMU III, which is the adoption of the Euro.

– 26 of the 28 Member States have committed at treaty level to joining the Euro while the UK and Denmark have opt-outs. So far 18 Member States have joined. The other eight who do not have opt-outs can in practice postpone joining for as long as they wish by simply not fulfilling, as a matter of policy, the criteria of EMU II.

– The chief benefits of the single currency are the facilitation of trade across borders and stability in monetary matters across the Member States.

– The disadvantages of the Euro have become manifest in the Euro crisis. The biggest disadvantage is inflexibility in currency valuation and interest rates, as all the participating economies, regardless of their different stages of economic development and different strengths and weaknesses, are all tied to the same monetary conditions. This makes it difficult for indebted Eurozone Member States to overcome their indebtedness.

– The Member States have responded, initially with secondary legislation in the form primarily of the so-called 'six-pack' and 'twin-pack', and then with the Fiscal Compact and European Stability Mechanism treaties agreed by 25 of the Member States, to prohibit budget deficits and establish a European-wide fund to help Member State governments in financial difficulty. In addition, European-wide supervision of banking is being negotiated.

– The longer-term prospects for EMU remain uncertain. Some argue for fiscal coordination and government in the Eurozone, but this is resisted as impractical for very diverse countries who do not share sufficiently a sense of political identity.

CHAPTER GLOSSARY

Banking union refers to the adoption by Member States who use the Euro currency of a system of prudential supervision of banks at European level. At the time of writing, it is still in the negotiation stage.

Convergence programme is the equivalent for non-Eurozone Member States of stability programmes (see below) for Eurozone Member States.

Copenhagen criteria are the criteria adopted at meeting of the European Council in Copenhagen in June 1993 that must be satisfied by Member States wishing to join the EU, and they include the criteria for EMU.

Corrective action plan is a programme of economic policy adjustment a Eurozone Member State may have to adopt under one of the six-pack Regulations as a result of a macroeconomic imbalance.

Economic and Financial Committee (EFC) under Article 126(4) TFEU is to formulate an opinion of the Commission's report on a Member State having an excessive deficit.

Economic and Monetary Union (EMU) refers to the process of convergence of the monetary policies and more generally of the economies of the Member States of the EU. It was developed in three main stages, EMU I, II and III.

European Banking Authority (EBA) refers to a new system of supervision of banks throughout the Eurozone. Its task is prudential supervision of banks in Eurozone Member States.

European Currency Unit (ECU) was a notional currency unit adopted in 1979 as part of EMS based on a basket of the Community's currencies, which would be used as the denominator for fixing exchange rates and financial support mechanisms.

European Monetary System (EMS) refers to the informal (in the sense that it was not set out in the treaties) system of exchange rate control agreed between the Member States from the 1970s onwards. It was superseded by ERM II in the 1990s.

European Semester is a six-month semester at the start of each year to assist Member States adopt budgetary policies within the criteria of the SGP.

European Stability Mechanism (ESM) refers to a fund established by the European Stability Mechanism Treaty 2012 to help finance 'bailouts' of Eurozone

countries in danger of defaulting on their national debt repayments.

Eurozone refers to countries that have completed Stage III of EMU, which means they have joined the Euro currency.

Excessive deficit procedure (EDP) is the procedure followed under Article 126 TFEU, supplemented by secondary legislation, when a Member State has a budget deficit in excess of the SGP maximum.

Excessive imbalance procedure (EIP) is the procedure followed under Regulation 1176/2011 relating to severe macroeconomic imbalances e.g. a severe trade imbalance, including imbalances that jeopardise or risks jeopardising the proper functioning of the economic and monetary union.

Exchange Rate Mechanism (ERM) refers to the system adopted from 1979 by which Member States of the then EEC agreed to a narrow range of fluctuation in the value of their currencies relative to each other, as a preparatory process to the introduction of the Euro. It was divided into stages, with the adoption of the Euro being the final stage or 'ERM III'.

Fiscal Compact is the shorthand name for the Treaty on Stability, Coordination and Governance in the Economic and Monetary Union 2011. Its purpose is to strengthen control of budget deficits in Eurozone Member States.

Fiscal policy refers to government policy on taxation and spending.

Macroeconomic adjustment programme is part of Regulation 472/2013 to build on and substitute any economic partnership programme under Regulation 473/2013 and which shall include annual budgetary targets.

Macro-economic imbalance is any trend giving rise to macroeconomic developments which are adversely affecting, or have the potential adversely to affect, the proper functioning of the economy of a Member State or of the economic and monetary union, or of the Union as a whole (e.g. a trade imbalance).

Medium-term Budgetary Objectives relate to the medium term budgetary targets of the Member States under the SGP. These were introduced in 2005.

Monetary policy refers to the practices and rules on a currency and money supply in a given economy.

Outright monetary transactions (OMTs) is a process whereby the ECB buys the bonds of Eurozone Member States in order to strengthen the credit rating of the Member State.

Prudential supervision refers to control by a central bank of the lending and credit policies of retail and commercial banks within an economy. Prudential supervision is intended to prevent banks over-lending, with a risk that banks will

be over-exposed to bad debts, or that too much lending creates excessive inflationary effects.

Single resolution mechanism (SRM) refers to the adoption by Member States of the EU of a European fund to support financially troubled banks in the EU.

Single Supervisory Mechanism (SSM) refers to a new system of supervision of banks throughout the Eurozone. Its task is prudential supervision of banks in Eurozone Member States. It will be headed by the European Banking Authority, acting under the European Central Bank.

Stability and Growth Pact (SGP) refers to an agreement adopted in the 1990s as part of ERM II to limit national budget deficits. For Eurozone Member States, it has been superseded by the Fiscal Compact.

Stability programme is an annual compliance report by Eurozone Member States on the SGP for scrutiny and evaluation of the European Commission and the Council (of Ministers), relating to the current fiscal position of the Member State and its projected position over the following three years. These reports are called 'convergence programmes' for non-Eurozone Member States.

TAKING THINGS FURTHER

A de Streel 'The evolution of the EU economic Governance since the Treaty of Maastricht: an unfinished task' (2013) 13(3) *Maastricht Journal of European and Comparative Law* 336 This article overviews the whole process of EMU at treaty level, since it was first introduced at the Treaty of Maastricht in 1992 and includes an assessment of options for the future.

J. Bruton, 'The economic future of the European Union' (7 March 2011)
http://www.lse.ac.uk/assets/richmedia/channels/publicLecturesAndEvents/
transcripts/20110307_1830_theEconomicFutureOfTheEuropeanUnion_tr.pdf (last
accessed 21 January 2015) This speech by a former Irish Prime Minister and former EU
Ambassador to Washington DC examines the Euro crisis, its cause and the benefits of
the Euro that nonetheless can be identified.

A De Gregorio Merion 'Legal development in the Economic and Monetary Union
during the debt crisis' (2014) 49 Common Market Law Review 1613–46 This article
looks at the legal framework for the EU to provide financial assistance to the Member
States.

C Hoffman 'A legal analysis of the Eurozone crisis' (2013) 18 Fordham Journal
of Corporate Law 519–64 This article analyses the limits of intergovernmental
cooperation by 26 of the Member States of the EU in combating the Eurozone crisis.

P Leino, J. Salminen 'The Euro crisis and its constitutional consequences for Finland:
is there room for national politics in EU decision-making?' (2013) 9(3) European
Constitutional Law Review 451–79 This article examines how Eurozone membership
is accommodated constitutionally in Finland and how the Eurozone crisis has created
a new level of debate in Finland on the benefits of the EU, compared with a previous
national consensus.

R Lastra, J-V Louis 'European Economic and Monetary Union: history, trends and
prospects' (2013) 32 Yearbook of European Law 1–150 (2013) This almost book-
length article provides a detailed overview of the process of EMU from beginning to
date.

CHAPTER 18
SOCIAL EUROPE

This chapter examines the role of the EU in social policy matters. The term social policy is broad and in a national context refers to a wide spectrum of matters, including social welfare, labour law, equality concerns, and integration of citizens into society. In the Communities originally, the main distinctly 'social' concern was the requirement for equal pay for equal work for men and women (including the question of pensions), i.e. gender equality. With the Single European Act 1986, the Treaty basis for social policy started to expand, culminating in the 'Social Charter' in the Treaty of Maastricht, from which the UK opted out initially. To some extent, the Treaty of Lisbon has clarified and extended the scope of EU competences in the social sphere, but Member State competence remains dominant for the most part. Following an overview of the Treaty of Lisbon provisions on social competence, this chapter will look at the issues typically considered 'social' in an EU context, namely, gender equality and aspects of labour law. It will also examine entitlements to healthcare related to EU law. Healthcare does not fall within the sections of the treaties specifically on social competence, rather they arise mostly as part of the internal market, but healthcare issues illustrate well how it can be difficult to separate out specific categories of competence from the general competences associated with the internal market in light of how the Court of Justice generally addresses competence issues. The chapter concludes by noting the overlap of competences between the Council of Europe and the EU in social matters, particularly regarding the Council of Europe's European Social Charter 1961.

AS YOU READ . . .

The key questions that will be answered in this chapter are as follows:

— What is the scope of EU competences in social matters? How have these competences developed over time?

— How did gender equality play a key role from the early period of the Communities to today?

– What is the scope of EU labour law? Why has this been particularly controversial, e.g. concerning the working-time directive or trade union rights?

– How does social competence of the EU interact with other competences, especially the general internal market competences?

– What is the approach of the Court of Justice in this sphere?

– How do the roles of the EU and Council of Europe interact in social matters? How does the EU Charter of Fundamental Rights affect EU social policy and law?

– How might EU competence in social matters develop in the future?

18.1 INTRODUCTION

This chapter examines the role of the EU in social policy matters. In the Communities originally, the main distinctly 'social' concern was the requirement for equal pay for equal work for men and women (including the question of pensions), i.e. gender equality. With the Single European Act 1986, the treaty basis for social policy started to expand, culminating in the 'Social Charter' in the Treaty of Maastricht, from which the UK opted out initially.

To some extent, the Treaty of Lisbon has clarified and extended somewhat the scope of EU competences in the social sphere. A more social dimension of European integration is seen as a counterbalance to the principles of free movement and undistorted competition, which are more associated with a liberal economic philosophy to promote enterprise and economic growth. A 'social Europe' is concerned with the welfare of workers and citizens independently of economic growth. The importance of a social concern raises the issue of the values permeating European integration.

The presentation of the project of a common market in the first period of integration could suggest an essentially technical project to achieve liberalisation of trade and freedom of competition, although there were some limited social elements. However, economic choices are a part of and involve choices about social and political trade-offs: 'The creation of the internal market is not a value-neutral technical project that can be left to the experts to manage, but must be an object of wider debate and contestation'.[1] As European integration continues, the balance between economic growth and integration and social equity is more and more debated.

....

1   J Snell 'The internal market and the philosophies of market integration' in C Barnard, S Peers (eds) *European Union Law* (Oxford University Press 2014) 307.

Joerges and Rödl have described 'Social Europe' as 'the ensemble of European social and labour law and policy and social rights . . . A wide and opaque field of such complexity that generalists in European law . . . tend to shy away from'.[2] The coverage in this chapter is necessarily selective, but it does seek to give an overview of the main ways in which the EU has competence in and influence social policy in the Member States.

Following an overview of the Treaty of Lisbon provisions on social competence, this chapter will look at the issues typically considered 'social' in an EU context, namely, gender equality and aspects of labour law. It will also examine entitlements to healthcare related to EU law. Healthcare does not fall within the sections of the treaties specifically on social competence; rather, it arises mostly as part of the internal market, along with a complementary competence in public health. Healthcare issues illustrate well how it can be difficult to separate out specific categories of competence from the general competences associated with the internal market in light of how the Court of Justice generally addresses competence issues.

The chapter concludes by analysing the overlap of competences between the Council of Europe and the EU in social matters, particularly regarding the Council of Europe's European Social Charter 1961 (revised in 1996).

> ### KEY LEARNING POINT
> ....
>
> ### THE MEANING OF THE TERM 'SOCIAL'
> The term social policy is broad and in a national context refers to a wide spectrum of matters, including social welfare, labour law, equality concerns, and integration of citizens into society.

18.2 THE DEVELOPMENT AND CURRENT SCOPE OF EU COMPETENCES IN SOCIAL MATTERS

18.2.1 INTRODUCTION: THE EARLY PERIOD

The founding treaties of the European Communities – European Coal and Steel Community (ECSC) Treaty, the European Atomic Energy Community (EURATOM) Treaty, and the European Economic Community (EEC) Treaty – were essentially economic in nature and were not understood as being essentially about 'social matters'. At that time, social matters were largely within the sphere of the Council of Europe, which adopted the European Social Charter in 1961 (see further below).

....

2   C Joerges, F Rödl 'Informal politics, formalised law and the "social deficit" of European integration: reflections after the judgments of the ECJ in *Viking* and *Laval*' (2009) 15(1) *European Law Journal* 1–19 at 1–2.

The key social provision in the context of the EEC Treaty was in Article 119 EEC Treaty, which provided for an equal pay for equal work principle. This played an especially important role in the development of the Communities, because it achieved equality for women in an important regard in the workplace that was still far from being achieved within the Member States. The Communities in their first phase thus became associated with a decisive social progression for women. The Communities were not the first to introduce equal pay for women,[3] which was included in the treaty at the behest of France, as France was concerned that its better protection of pay for women would put it at a competitive disadvantage.[4] However, as a consequence, the principle spread throughout the Member States more quickly than it might otherwise have done.

A number of other social elements did, albeit not very prominently, feature as part of the original treaties. These were the result to some extent of French concerns that its relatively high social costs would undermine its competiveness in an open common market.[5] In addition to the equal pay provision, the EEC Treaty referred, for example, to the need to harmonise working conditions and standards of living for workers.[6]

Title III of the EEC Treaty was entitled 'Social Policy' and contained in Chapter I some general provisions on cooperation in social matters such as employment law and social security,[7] as well as specific provisions on equal pay for equal work,[8] and equivalence between paid holiday schemes.[9] Chapter II established a European Social Fund (ESF), with the quite open task of 'rendering the employment of workers easier and of increasing their geographical and occupational mobility within the Community'.[10] The ESF has been used primarily as a vehicle for development assistance and is part of the EU's structural funds. At first, it focused on managing the migration of workers within Europe. Later, combating unemployment became more important in its activities.

Two other bodies established under the EEC Treaty were the Economic and Social Committee and the European Investment Bank. The Economic and Social Committee had the task of advising the Council and Commission.[11]

....

3 I am grateful to Dr Leanne O'Leary for pointing this out to me.

4 S Burri, S Prechal *EU Gender Equality Law 2010* (European Network of Experts in the Field of Gender Equality 2011) 2.

5 Snell in Barnard and Peers (eds) (n 1) 308.

6 The preamble to the Treaty of Rome included as follows:'. . . AFFIRMING as the essential objective of their efforts the constant improvement of the living and working conditions of their peoples . . .'. See also art 117 EEC Treaty.

7 Ibid art 118.

8 Ibid art 119.

9 Ibid art 120.

10 Ibid arts 123–127.

11 Ibid art 4. See also arts 43, 47, 49, 54, 63, 79, 83, 100, 118, 121, 127, 128, and 242 (concerning consultation) and specifically on the Economic and Social Committee arts 193–98 EEC Treaty. Today, see in particular arts 301–304 TFEU, but numerous other Articles provide for consultation of the Economic and Social Committee.

18.2.2 THE SEA, THE MAASTRICHT TREATY AND THE UK OPT-OUT FROM THE SOCIAL CHARTER

The SEA added two elements to the social dimension of the treaty. Article 118a EEC Treaty as inserted by Article 21 SEA provided a legal basis for Community legislation to adopt directives to improve, especially in the working environment, the health and safety of workers. Article 118b EEC Treaty as inserted by Article 22 contained a relatively weak provision regarding dialogue between management and labour. Apart from these treaty provisions, several other legal instruments are relevant to social policy.

EXPLAINING THE LAW

OVERLAPPING INSTRUMENTS AND TERMINOLOGY AND UK OPT-OUTS

In 1989, 11 of the then 12 Member States adopted the Charter of Fundamental Social Rights of Workers ('Social Charter 1989').[12] The UK opted out and continued this opt-out when the content of the 1989 Charter was largely included as a 'chapter' of the Maastricht Treaty, or to be more precise, in the form of a Protocol to the Maastricht Treaty having been agreed by 11 of the Member States in December 1991.[13] The terminology can be confusing. The Social Charter 1989 signed by 11 of the then 12 Community Member States is different to the Council of Europe Social Charter of 1961 (later amended, see further below).[14]

The Social Charter 1989 is quite general and is merely declaratory. These instruments are also not to be confused with the later EU Charter of Fundamental Rights,[15] discussed in Chapter 8. Both the Council of Europe Social Charter 1961 and the Social Charter of 1989 are now referred to in Article 151 TFEU.[16] The incoming Labour Government of 1997 ended the UK opt-out from the social chapter of the Maastricht Treaty. Since then, the EU Charter of Fundamental Rights has been adopted. It is inclusive enough to cover most of the content of previous Social Charters (see further below). However, the UK, with the same Labour Government, has been careful to qualify its acceptance of the EU Charter of Fundamental Rights in this regard. The Treaty of Lisbon includes a Protocol regarding Poland and the UK.[17]

Article 1(1) of the Protocol provides that the EU Charter of Fundamental Rights does not extend the ability of the Court of Justice, or any court or tribunal of

---

12 9 December 1989, COM (89) 471 final.
13 See generally, e.g. J Lourie 'The Social Charter' House of Commons Research Paper 97/102 (1997).
14 ETS No 35. See further below section 18.7 below.
15 OJ C 326 26.10.2012 p. 391.
16 Article 151 TFEU.
17 Protocol 30 on the application of Charter of Fundamental Rights of the EU to Poland and the UK.

Poland or the UK, to find that the laws, practices or action of Poland or the UK are inconsistent with the fundamental rights, freedoms and principles that it reaffirms, while Article 1(2) then states that, in particular, and for the avoidance of doubt, nothing in Title IV of the Charter on economic and social rights creates justiciable rights applicable to Poland or the UK except in so far as Poland or the UK has provided for such rights in its national law.

The main provisions of the Social Charter of 1989 concerned:

- freedom of movement (Articles 1–3)
- employment and remuneration (Articles 4–6)
- improvement of living and working conditions (Articles 7–9)
- social protection (Article 10)
- freedom of association and collective bargaining (Articles 11–14)
- vocational training (Article 15)
- equal treatment for men and women (Article 16)
- information and consultation for workers (Articles 17–18)
- health protection and safety at the workplace (Article 19)
- protection of children and adolescents (Articles 20–23)
- elderly persons (Articles 24–25)
- disabled persons (Article 26)
- Member States' action (implementation) (Articles 27–30).

Most of these provisions are now also reflected in the EU Charter of Fundamental Rights,[18] see further below in section 18.9.

18.2.3 DEVELOPMENTS FROM MAASTRICHT TO LISBON

The Treaty of Lisbon commits the EU to the goal of a social market economy, a slogan that suggests a balance between purely economic goals and social concerns. Apart from treaty provisions, the case law of the Court of Justice developing free movement, in particular, had an important dimension from a social point of view. In *Cassis de Dijon*,[19] the Court effected an important shift in the approach to market integration by developing the principle of mutual recognition, as an alternative to harmonisation. As discussed in Chapter 10, the mutual recognition principle requires the Member States to accept each other's regulatory standards. This avoids the need for harmonisation of standards.

However, mutual recognition opens up the possibility for regulatory competition. A Member State that has lesser social protection for workers may become more competitive

---

18 See n 15.
19 Case 120/78 *Cassis de Dijon* [1979] ECR 649.

because its labour costs are lower. This can create pressure on other Member States to reduce labour costs by lowering social protection, in order to be competitive.[20] This is quite dramatically apparent from the recent *Viking* and *Laval* cases, discussed further below.

18.2.4 SOCIAL PROVISIONS OF THE TREATY OF LISBON

Title X TFEU sets out social policy in Articles 151–161 TFEU, which are summarised in the table below.

Article 151	Paragraph 1 states that the EU and the Member States, having in mind fundamental social rights such as those set out in the European Social Charter signed at Turin on 18 October 1961 and in the 1989 Community Charter of the Fundamental Social Rights of Workers, shall have as their objectives the promotion of employment, improved living and working conditions, so as to make possible their harmonisation while the improvement is being maintained, proper social protection, dialogue between management and labour, the development of human resources with a view to lasting high employment and the combating of exclusion.	Compared to the original treaty provision, this brings social policy within the domain of harmonisation in principle, but without there being any obligation to that effect, the Member States are to have harmonisation as an objective. This leaves the initiative in this field to the political branch, namely, the Commission, Council, and the Parliament. Limited progress to harmonisation has been made to date, largely because of quite different models of social policy across the Member States.
Article 152	Provides that the Union recognises and promotes the role of the social partners at its level, taking into account the diversity of national systems. It shall facilitate dialogue between the social partners, respecting their autonomy.	This gives the EU a quite limited competence to engage with civic society, such as trade unions, in the Member States, without any power to harmonise.
Article 153	The first paragraph of this provision provides that the Union shall support and complement the activities of the Member States in the following fields: (a) improvement in particular of the working environment to protect workers' health and safety;	Although at first glance this Article assigns a wide range of policy competences to the EU in (a)–(k), the remainder of the Article is hedged with qualifications of the

20 See e.g. Snell in Barnard and Peers (eds) (n 1) 311.

(b) working conditions;

(c) social security and social protection of workers;

(d) protection of workers where their employment contract is terminated;

(e) the information and consultation of workers;

(f) representation and collective defence of the interests of workers and employers, including co-determination, subject to paragraph 5;

(g) conditions of employment for third-country nationals legally residing in Union territory;

(h) the integration of persons excluded from the labour market, without prejudice to Article 166;

(i) equality between men and women with regard to labour market opportunities and treatment at work;

(j) the combating of social exclusion;

(k) the modernisation of social protection systems without prejudice to point (c). Measures related to 1(c), (d), (f) and (g) must be adopted by unanimity.

The second paragraph provides that the Member States shall (a) adopt measures to encourage cooperation in what could be termed knowledge exchange, excluding harmonisation, and (b) minimal guidelines for implementation, by means of directives.

The fourth paragraph states that the Member States (a) shall not be affected in defining the fundamental principles of their social security systems and must not significantly affect the financial equilibrium thereof and (b) may adopt higher standards of protection.

The fifth paragraph states that the Article shall not apply to pay, the right of association, the right to strike or the right to impose lock-outs.

limited competences of the EU. The EU may adopt only measures to encourage (not mandate) the achievement of policy or may adopt minimal measures for implementation.

The fourth and fifth paragraphs are express reservations of Member State competence (but as noted elsewhere in this chapter, the Court of Justice has circumvented the apparent exclusion of strikes from the Treaty).

Article 154	This paragraph provides that the Commission shall have the task of promoting the consultation of management and labour at Union level and shall take any relevant measure to facilitate their dialogue by ensuring balanced support for the parties.	This paragraph is unremarkable, it provides for the policy-making role that the Commission generally enjoys and is framed in non-binding terms.
Article 155	This provides that should management and labour so desire, the dialogue between them at Union level may lead to contractual relations, including agreements. In addition, the Council may adopt implementing decisions by unanimity, on a proposal from the Commission and having informed the European Parliament.	This provision is consistent with a secondary role for the EU in social policy, leaving the initiative up to social partners and providing for a legislative competence in implementation only. It might be described as a 'soft law' role. Nonetheless, it leaves scope for the Commission and Council to provide stimulus and initiative in this field.
Article 156	This provides in paragraph 1 that with a view to achieving the objectives of Article 151 and without prejudice to the other provisions of the treaties, the Commission shall encourage cooperation between the Member States and facilitate the coordination of their action in all social policy fields under this Chapter, particularly in matters relating to: – employment, – labour law and working conditions, – basic and advanced vocational training, – social security, – prevention of occupational accidents and diseases, – occupational hygiene, – the right of association and collective bargaining between employers and workers.	Again this provision may seem like a quite broad competence clause for the EU in terms of the subject matter covered, but the rest of the Article confines the Commission role to soft law actions in the form of 'making studies, delivering opinions and arranging consultations both on problems arising at national level and on those of concern to international organisations, in particular initiatives aiming at the establishment of guidelines and indicators, the organisation of exchange of best practice, and the preparation of the necessary elements for periodic monitoring and evaluation'.

Article 157	This provides for equal pay for equal work, discussed in more detail below.	Historically, this had been a very important provision, being in the treaties from the beginning and bringing about one of the most dramatic results of membership of what is now the Union. One of the main issues surrounding its interpretation concerns the meaning of pay: does it include pensions? The Court of Justice determined that it did, which prompted a reaction from the Member States, discussed in more detail below.
Article 158	Provides that the Member States shall endeavour to maintain the existing equivalence between paid holiday schemes.	This provision has been in the treaties from the beginning. Perhaps surprisingly, it is still expressed in aspirational, rather than mandatory terms; on the other hand, this reflects the marked divergences in labour law and practice between the Member States.
Article 159	This Article provides that the Commission shall draw up a report each year on progress in achieving the objectives of Article 151, including the demographic situation in the Union. It shall forward the report to the European Parliament, the Council and the Economic and Social Committee.	This Article is self-explanatory.
Article 160	This Article provides that the Council, acting by a simple majority after consulting the European Parliament, shall establish a Social Protection Committee with advisory status to promote cooperation on social protection policies between Member States and with the Commission.	The Committee's work is quite broad-ranging, going beyond conditions of work. Its thematic reports to date concern: pension adequacy, child poverty and wellbeing, social services of general interest, and long-term care.

| **Article 161** | This Article provides that (1) the Commission shall include a separate chapter on social developments within the Union in its annual report to the European Parliament and (2) that the European Parliament may invite the Commission to draw up reports on any particular problems concerning social conditions. | This Article is self-explanatory. |

18.3 SOCIAL SECURITY

Social security was not generally a part of EU activity. Only workers or family members are entitled to claim full social security, comparable with nationals of the host Member State. Article 48 TFEU now provides as follows:

ARTICLE 48 TFEU

The European Parliament and the Council shall, acting in accordance with the ordinary legislative procedure, adopt such measures in the field of social security as are necessary to provide freedom of movement for workers; to this end, they shall make arrangements to secure for employed and self-employed migrant workers and their dependants . . .

KEY LEARNING POINT

'SOCIAL SECURITY' VERSUS 'SOCIAL ASSISTANCE'
A distinction is sometimes drawn between social security and social assistance. Social security refers to the benefits the State will confer on a citizen as result of social insurance payments or taxes paid by the individual in the past while he or she worked, i.e. social security refers to a contributory benefit.[21] Social assistance, on the other hand, is sometimes used to describe benefits that are paid by the state, irrespective of contributions, i.e. non-contributory benefits.

---

21 D Sindbjerg Martinsen 'Social security regulation in the EU: the de-territorialisation of welfare?' in G de Búrca (ed) *EU Law and the Welfare State: In Search of Solidarity* (Oxford University Press 2005) 91–92 (and generally, for an albeit somewhat inaccessible overview of the topic).

A number of secondary instruments were passed in this field, including Council Regulation 1408/71/EEC on the application of social security schemes to employed persons and their families moving within the Community[22] and Council Regulation 574/72/EEC fixing the procedure for implementing Regulation 1408/71/EEC on the coordination of social security schemes for persons moving within the Community.

The most recent principal legislation is Regulation 883/2004 on the coordination of social security systems of the Member States, which replaces Regulation 1408/71.[23] This tends to confirm the entitlement of workers and service providers to benefit from social security, in proportion to the amount they have contributed. The recitals to the Regulation 883/2004 set out its general context:

> (7) Due to the major differences existing between national legislation in terms of the persons covered, it is preferable to lay down the principle that this Regulation is to apply to nationals of a Member State, stateless persons and refugees resident in the territory of a Member State who are or have been subject to the social security legislation of one or more Member States, as well as to the members of their families and to their survivors.

> (8) The general principle of equal treatment is of particular importance for workers who do not reside in the Member State of their employment, including frontier workers.

> . . .

> (10) However, the principle of treating certain facts or events occurring in the territory of another Member State as if they had taken place in the territory of the Member State whose legislation is applicable should not interfere with the principle of aggregating periods of insurance, employment, self-employment or residence completed under the legislation of another Member State with those completed under the legislation of the competent Member State. Periods completed under the legislation of another Member State should therefore be taken into account solely by applying the principle of aggregation of periods.

Thus, the regulation seeks to ensure that only the current Member State of an EU citizen's employment is paying social security to a person and that that person's previous social security contributions in other Member States are taken into account. Overall, Regulation 883/2004 seeks to simplify the rules.

Regulation 592/2008 on the implementation of social security measures[24] amends the annexes to Regulation 1408/71 so as to take account of changes in national legislation. EU law does not harmonise; rather, it coordinates the social security schemes

....

22 OJ L 149 05.07.1971 p. 2.
23 OJ L 166 30.04.2004 p. 1. However, Regulation 1408/71 remains in force for certain limited purposes of certain acts, e.g. it remains valid regarding the content of Council Regulation 859/2003 (OJ L 124 20.05.2003 p. 36) for nationals of third countries who are not already covered by those provisions solely on the ground of their nationality.
24 OJ L 177 4.7.2008 p. 1.

of EU Member States. Member States can determine the details of their own social security systems, including which benefits shall be provided, the conditions of eligibility and the value of these benefits, as long as they accept the basic principle of equality of treatment and non-discrimination in how employees and the self-employed from other Member States are treated.

> ### KEY LEARNING POINT
>
> #### COORDINATION OF SOCIAL SECURITY
> The general approach of the Regulations is that a worker is subject to the legislation of only one Member State and to avoid overlapping social security payments by more than one Member State (Article 10 of Regulation 883/2004).

The main principle is that social security is paid by the Member State in which the person concerned pursues his activity as an employed or self-employed person,[25] according to the social security regime of that Member State. The regulation applies to certain benefits, whether contributory or non-contributory (so there is overlap with what might strictly be called social assistance) in the following categories:

(a) sickness benefits
(b) maternity and equivalent paternity benefits
(c) invalidity benefits
(d) old-age benefits
(e) survivors' benefits
(f) benefits in respect of accidents at work and occupational diseases
(g) death grants
(h) unemployment benefits
(i) pre-retirement benefits
(j) family benefits.

Articles 5 and 6 set out a principle of equal treatment of benefits, income facts or events and aggregation of them. What this means is that the 'competent Member State', i.e. the Member State where the worker is currently employed, must take into account the same previous facts as it considers relevant to acquiring social security of its own citizens working in that Member State where those facts have occurred in another Member State for a worker now working in the competent Member State.

The situation where an EU citizen is working in one Member State, but living in another, is also dealt with.[26] The following general rules apply:

---

25 Regulation 883/2004, recital 17 and see arts 17–19 for more detail.
26 Ibid recital 35. The regulation also applies to stateless persons and refugees: see art 2. Thus, it is an unusual example of EU law conferring benefits on non-EU citizens other than in the context of family relations between an EU citizen and a third-country national.

- a person employed in the territory of a Member State is subject to the legislation of that state;
- a person employed on board a vessel flying the flag of a Member State is subject to the legislation of that state;
- civil servants are subject to the legislation of the Member State to which the administration employing them is subject;
- a worker called up or recalled for service in the armed forces or for civilian service of a Member State retains the status of worker and is subject to the legislation of that state;
- retired persons are subject to the laws of the Member State in which they reside.[27]

Regulation 883/2004 is very detailed and quite technical. Title III contains specific rules about each different type of benefit listed above.

MAKING CONNECTIONS
+ + + + + + + + + + + + + + + + +

THE RELATIONSHIP BETWEEN REGULATION 883/2004 AND ARTICLE 7(2) OF REGULATION 492/2011

Regulation 883/2004 and Article 7(2) of Regulation 492/2011 overlap in terms of the subject matter they deal with – 'social security' under Regulation 883/2004 could be viewed as a sub-category of the 'social and tax advantages' guaranteed to workers under Article 7(2). However, Regulation 883/2004 deals with a more specific and slightly different aspect of the issue: it is concerned with taking into account social security contributions (or 'credit', since non-contributory social security is also included) paid or gained by a worker in a Member State where previously the worker was employed and paying social security in the Member State where the worker is currently employed. One way of putting it is that Article 7(2) is concerned with current social advantages more broadly, Regulation 883/2004 is concerned with previous social security contributions from another Member State being taken into account in the current Member State, so that there is no overlapping payments between or by the two Member States (Article 10 of Regulation 883/2004). Article 4 of Regulation 883/2004 repeats the general principle of equal treatment with a Member State's own nationals, regarding social security benefits, contained in Article 7(2) of Regulation 492/2011 regarding social and tax advantages more generally.

....

27 Regulation 883/2004 art 11. Regulation 883/2004 does not contain a definition of a worker, but under Regulation 1408/71 art 1, a worker is defined as a person who is insured, compulsorily or on an optional continued basis, on the basis of social security contributions.

18.4 GENDER EQUALITY

18.4.1 INTRODUCTION

Article 119 EEC Treaty was one of the most important provisions of the original treaties, in the sense that it had quite a profound effect, at least in some Member States. It transformed the role and rights of women in countries that required women to leave public service jobs when they married, for example, in Ireland and Portugal. Some of the cases on Article 119 were also important because the Court of Justice took the opportunity to develop the doctrine of direct effect.

These cases could be seen to have been astutely chosen by the Court, because at the same time as doing something that seemed clearly desirable as an important measure of social justice, the Court was also developing the constitutional framework of the treaties (the social justice dimension could be seen as a vehicle to help legitimate the latter). It was by attributing direct effect to Article 119 that the Court was able to make this important contribution to gender equality, even if from a specifically legal point of view, the doctrine of direct effect was clearly an example of judicial activism.

The general principle of gender equality has now become widely accepted throughout the EU, and it is now expressed in Articles 21 and 23 of the EU Charter of Fundamental Rights. Significant issues arise in practice in achieving gender equality, related to pregnancy, for example. Both the Union legislature and the Court of Justice have played a role in the context of maternity care rights, although in this field the legislature has been consistently active.

18.4.2 CASE LAW

The Court has played an important role not in establishing a principle of equality of treatment, which was set out in the treaty, but in broadly interpreting it and in strengthening the institutional structure of the EU in this area and its own capacity to influence the law. In *Defrenne v Belgian State (Defrenne I)*, the Court found that Article 119 EEC Treaty (now Article 157 TFEU) was horizontally directly effective, the first time the Court did so regarding a treaty article (SABENA was a company and not the state, although it was state-owned).[28]

The decision to give a prospective ruling later in the case of *Defrenne v SABENA (Defrenne II)*, recognised the novelty of the Court's ruling in *Defrenne I* that Article 119 had such horizontal direct effect (where the doctrine of direct effect was applied to the equal pay principle).[29] In *Defrenne v SABENA (Defrenne III)*, the Court recognised

....

28 Case 80/70 *Defrenne v Belgian State (Defrenne I)* [1971] ECR I–445.
29 Case 43/75 *Defrenne v SABENA (Defrenne II)* [1976] ECR 455.

equality as 'a general principle of Community law'.[30] The result was that the Court applied the principle of equality across any context of EU law, without having to rely on a specific treaty provision such as Article 119 EEC Treaty. *Defrenne III* defined equality as a general principle of Community law.

This approach paved the way for *Barber v Guardian Royal Exchange Assurance Group*, in which the Court broadly interpreted 'pay'[31] so that pension entitlements fell within now Article 157 TFEU on equal pay for equal work. Unlike in *Defrenne II*, the Court did not declare its ruling to be prospective only. This created very considerable financial implications for the Member States, as they would have had to backdate equality of pension entitlements to the moment of joining the then Communities. The Member States responded by amending the treaty so as to clarify that *Barber* was to have prospective effect only, through the 'Barber Protocol' to the Treaty of Maastricht.

KEY LEARNING POINT

THE BARBER PROTOCOL
The Barber Protocol to the Treaty of Maastricht is one of the few instances where the Member States have reversed or partly reversed the effects of an ECJ ruling. In this case, the Member States were reversing an interpretation of the Treaty, which meant that they had to do so by Treaty amendment, secondary legislation would not have been sufficient. The difficulty of achieving consensus amongst all the Member States is one of the main reasons such treaty amendments are so rare.

18.4.3 SECONDARY LEGISLATION

The legislature of the EU has been consistently active in this field. It has gradually extended equal treatment to cover almost all aspects of work, employed or self-employed, and relating it to pensions and social security, although levels of social security are a matter for each Member State. The following table summarises the main instruments to date.

Legislation	Summary of content	Comment
Equal Pay Directive 75/117/EEC[32]	Article 1 provides that the principle of 'principle of equal pay' in (now) Article 157 TFEU means 'for the same work or for work to which equal value is attributed, the elimination of all discrimination	Although the basic provision on equal pay is in the Treaty, this specifies it and clarifies its scope of application. Replaced by Directive 2006/54.

30 Case 149/77 *Defrenne v SABENA (Defrenne III)* [1978] ECR 1365.
31 Case C–262/88 *Barber v Guardian Royal Exchange Assurance Group* [1990] ECR I–1889.
32 OJ L 45 19.2.1975 p. 19.

on grounds of sex with regard
to all aspects and conditions of
remuneration'. Article 2 requires
Member States to ensure that the
national legislation give effect to
this principle and Article 3 that
they provide a mechanism for
redress where the principle has
been violated. Under Article 5,
Member States must protect
employees from victimisation by
employers for taking action to
enforce the principle.

Equal Treatment Directive 76/207/ EEC[33]	On the implementation of the principle of equal treatment for men and women as regards access to employment, vocational training and promotion, and working conditions.	Replaced by Directive 2006/54.
Social Security Directive 79/7/EEC[34]	On the progressive implementation of the principle of equal treatment for men and women in matters of social security. Article 3 states that the Directive shall apply to: (a) statutory schemes which provide protection against the following risks: – sickness, – invalidity, – old age, – accidents at work and occupational diseases, – unemployment; (b) social assistance, in so far as it is intended to supplement or replace the schemes referred to in (a). Under Article 7, old-age benefits are generally excluded.	The difference between social security and social assistance under s. 3(b) relates to contribution-based benefits. This Directive is a necessary complement to the Directive on equal pay.

33 OJ L 39 14.2.1976 p. 40.
34 OJ L 6 10.1.1979 p. 24.

Occupational Pensions Directive 86/378/EEC[35]	Among the prohibitions in this Directive are the setting of different retirement ages.	Represents the gradual extension of equal treatment pension entitlements. Replaced by Directive 2006/54.
Pregnant and Breastfeeding Workers Directive 92/85/EC[36]	Article 3 provides that a set of guidelines detail the assessment of the chemical, physical and biological agents and industrial processes considered dangerous for the health and safety of pregnant women or women who have just given birth and are breastfeeding and Article 4 that employers assess the risks faced by women due to pregnancy. The Directive also includes provision on maternity leave (14 weeks is a minimum under Article 8), and night work (Article 7).	Seeks to ensure that pregnancy has a minimal effect on women's capacity to work.
Part-time Workers Directive 97/81/EC[37]	The purpose of the Directive is to eliminate discrimination against part-time workers and to improve the quality of part-time work.	This applies equally to men and women, but historically women have been more likely to occupy part-time jobs.
Equal Treatment Directive 2000/78/EC[38]	Equal treatment in employment and occupation, based on now Article 19 TFEU, laying down a general framework for combatting discrimination on grounds of religion or belief, disability, age, or sexual orientation.	Not directly related to gender, but women (and men) in one of the protected categories may benefit.
Equal Treatment Directive 2000/43/EC[39]	Equal treatment irrespective of racial or ethnic origin, based on now Article 19 TFEU.	Not directly related to gender, but women (and men) in one of the protected categories may benefit.

35 OJ L 51 20.2.1987 p. 56.
36 OJ L 348 28.11.1992 p. 1.
37 OJ L 14 20.1.1998 p. 9.
38 OJ L 303 02.12.2000 p. 16.
39 OJ L 180 19.7.2000 p. 22.

Equal Treatment Directive 2004/113/EC[40]	Equal treatment between men and women in access to and supply of goods and services, adopted under now Article 19 TFEU. Applies to both direct and indirect discrimination (Article 4), though positive discrimination in favour of women is permitted (Article 6).	Until this Directive, EU action on gender equality had been largely directed at the more regulated context of employment. However, discrimination can occur in any commercial context. Some contexts are particularly difficult to regulate, and the content of media and advertising and education have been excluded from the Directive (Article 3).
Directive 2006/54/EC[41]	Consolidating Directive, recasting and updating Directives 75/117, 76/207, 86/378, and 97/80.[42] Includes, for example, provisions reflecting case law from the Court of Justice that gender equality also applies to gender re-assignment.[43] Among new elements, it provides that associations, organisations and other legal entities should also be empowered to engage in proceedings, as the Member States so determine, either on behalf or in support of a complainant, under Recital 32. It also provides detailed rules on occupational pension schemes, in Articles 5–13.	Most of the law on gender equality is now contained in or affected by this Directive, including, for example, sexual harassment. This is considered a type of discrimination and is prohibited on that basis (Article 2).
Parental Leave Directive 2010/18/EU[44]	Extends the period of parental leave to four months and applies it to both men and women, but leaves it to Member States to determine salary or social security payments during this period.	This is an example of men benefiting from gender equality law relative to previously less favourable treatment. The Directive replaces Directive 93/34 on

40 OJ L 373 21.12.2004 p. 37.
41 OJ L 204 26.7.2006 p. 23.
42 Council Directive 97/80/EC of 15 December 1997 on the burden of proof in cases of discrimination based on sex, OJ L 225 12.8.1986 p. 40.
43 See, e.g. Case C–423/04 *Sarah Margaret Richards v Secretary of State for Work and Pensions* [2006] ECR I–3585.
44 OJ L 68 18.3.2010 p. 13.

		parental leave, which had provided for a three-month period of parental leave for men and women.[45]
Equal Treatment Directive 2010/41/EU[46]	On equal treatment between self-employed men and women. Article 4 establishes a general principle of equal treatment, while subsequent articles deal with more specific points. For example, Article 6 provides the Member States should ensure it is no more restrictive for spouses to establish a company than others to do so. Article 8 provides that the Member States shall take the necessary measures to ensure that female self-employed workers and female spouses and life partners referred to in Article 2 may, in accordance with national law, be granted a sufficient maternity allowance enabling interruptions in their occupational activity owing to pregnancy or motherhood for at least 14 weeks.	This Directive revises Directive 86/613/EEC[47] in order to safeguard the rights related to motherhood and fatherhood of self-employed workers and their helping spouses.

18.5 LABOUR LAW

18.5.1 TREATY PROVISIONS ON LABOUR LAW

As well as the historically important equal pay provision discussed above, the treaty has a number of articles specifically on employment, in Title IX TFEU (Articles 145–150 TFEU). They are summarised in the following table:

---

45 Council Directive 96/34/EC of 3 June 1996 on the framework agreement on parental leave concluded by UNICE, CEEP and the ETUC, OJ L 145 19.6.1996 p. 4.
46 OJ L 180 15.07.2010 p. 1.
47 OJ L 359 19.12.1986 p. 56.

Summary of Treaty provisions on labour law

Article	Content	Significance
Article 145 TFEU	Provides that Member States and the Union shall, in accordance with this Title, work towards developing a coordinated strategy for employment and particularly for promoting a skilled, trained and adaptable workforce and labour markets responsive to economic change with a view to achieving the objectives defined in Article 3 TEU	This provision is a general exhortation to cooperate in the field of employment law
Article 146 TFEU	Provides that the Member States, shall (1) act under Article 145 in a way consistent with the broad guidelines of the economic policies of the Member States and of the Union and (2) regard promoting employment as a matter of common concern and shall coordinate their action in this respect within the Council	Like the previous provision, this is a general exhortation to cooperate, but it does specify that Member States must at least take into account the economic concerns of other Member States and overall EU policy
Article 147 TFEU	The main element requires the Union to contribute to a high level of employment by encouraging cooperation between Member States and by supporting and, if necessary, complementing their action and in doing so, the competences of the Member States shall be respected	Makes clear that the Member States have primary competence in the employment field
Article 148 TFEU	Contains detailed rules on the roles of the European Council, the Commission, and the Council as well as the Economic and Social Committee, the Committee of the Regions, and the Employment Committee. The European Council is to adopt conclusions on the employment situation, which the Commission is then to use, following consultation with the various committees, as a basis for guidelines that the Member States	The EU institutions do not have the power to adopt binding legislation, but they can set the agenda for employment through the procedure for adopting guidelines

are to take into account, for the Council to adopt

Article 149 TFEU	Provides that the Council and the Parliament, following the ordinary legislative procedure, and after consultation with the Economic and Social Committee and the Committee of the Regions, may adopt incentive measures involving initiatives aimed at developing exchanges of information and best practices, providing comparative analysis and advice as well as promoting innovative approaches and evaluating experiences, in particular by recourse to pilot projects	This reflects a 'soft law' approach to encourage cooperation between the Member States in terms of practical initiatives and policy approaches
Article 150 TFEU	Provides that the Council, acting by a simple majority after consulting the European Parliament, shall establish an Employment Committee with advisory status to promote coordination between Member States on employment and labour market policies. Each Member State and the Commission are to appoint two members of the Committee	This is another example of a 'soft law' approach to employment as an economic issue

18.5.2 THE RELATIONSHIP BETWEEN LABOUR LAW AND OTHER ASPECTS OF EU LAW

ANALYSING THE LAW

THE *VIKING* AND *LAVAL* CASES AND DIFFERENT APPROACHES TO THE ECONOMIC AND SOCIAL CONSTITUTIONS OF THE EU

Recently, the decisions in *Viking* and *Laval*[48] provided the opportunity for the ECJ to clarify the status of trade union-related rights relative to the free movement principles. The *Laval* and *Viking* judgments suggest ambivalence as to the

---

48 Case C–438/05 *The International Transport Workers' Federation and The Finnish Seamen's Union v Viking Line ABP and OÜ Viking Line Eesti* [2007] ECR I–10779; Case C–341/05 *Laval un Partneri Ltd v Svenska Byggnadsarbetareföbundet* [2007] ECR I–11767.

exact normative status of traditional human rights compared with the economic freedoms in the EU legal order. The cases concerned the relationship between free movement and the right to strike as protected in national laws. Despite the specific exclusion of the right to strike from the social competence of the Union by then Article 137(5) ECT (now Article 153(5) TFEU), the ECJ held that national rules permitting strikes where such strikes have the effect of being an inhibition to the posting of workers from one Member State to another were contrary to Community law.[49] This could be considered as simply a limitation on the right to strike, and as such unremarkable given that few rights are absolute.[50]

However, it was more significant in its broad scope, in entirely excluding strikes in this situation, and in subordinating the right to strike to free market freedoms, despite the saving clause for strikes in the Treaty. From a human rights angle, it seems hard to reconcile the decision in *Viking* and *Laval* with any of the provisions of the EU Charter of Fundamental Rights, although this may partly be because the EU Charter of Fundamental Rights was only soft law at the time of the judgments. Whereas the Charter seems not to accord the right to freedom to choose an occupation and right to engage in work (applicable to any EU citizen in any Member State) (Article 15) and the freedom to conduct a business (Article 16) any pre-eminent status and to establish the priority of national law on the right to strike, the ECJ in *Laval* and *Viking* seemed to suggest that free movement principles trumped any national rules on the right to strike.[51]

Some presumptive priority for the right to strike seems justified given the reserve of competence in this area to the Member States, but also because there is no obvious or compelling reason articulated in the case law as to why workers' rights should be subordinated to free movement of businesses. The priority of other rights over the economic freedoms could be achieved, for example, by requiring that only a very substantial impairment of free movement could call into question (e.g. if all of the ports of Member States were blockaded, as opposed to a single business) rights reserved to national sovereignty.

---

49 Case C–438/05, *Viking* [2007] ECR I–10779 paras 39–40; Case C–341/05, *Laval* [2007] ECR I–11767 paras 87–88. There was no general discussion of human rights in either judgment, although various sources were referred to on the right to strike, which was described as a fundamental right (*Viking*, ibid, paras 43–44; *Laval*, ibid paras 90–91). Article 11 ECHR provides for a right to join a trade union for the protection of a person's interests. Article 28 of the EU Charter of Fundamental Rights explicitly protects the right to strike. See also A Hinarejos 'Laval and Viking: The right to collective action versus EU fundamental freedoms' (2008) 8(4) *Human Rights Law Review* 714–29 at 728, noting that the judgments come close to establishing a hierarchy where the economic fundamental freedoms are placed higher than the right to collective action.

50 See N Reich 'Free movement v Social rights in an enlarged union: the *Laval* and *Viking* cases before the ECJ' (2008) 9(2) *German Law Journal* 125–61 at 155.

51 Article 52.3 of the Charter seems to work in the opposite direction to other provisions of the Charter in permitting a very broad category of limits on rights based on 'the general interest'.

As is often the case, the issue is about balancing rights, a point that could have been more thoroughly articulated and addressed in the judgments, along with the issue of how to reconcile the judgments with Article 153(5) TFEU. As the judgment stands, it is difficult to conceptualise the limits of Union competence now in labour and employment law.[52] The effect of the ECJ decision in *Laval* was to prevent Sweden from permitting trade union action in order to pressure an employer to provide a minimum wage greater than that provided for by Community secondary legislation,[53] which does not obviously seem to entail a substantial impairment of free movement in general, although this seems open to argument on the facts, at least as to the potential impact of the strikes on the companies involved.[54]

The reasoning in the *Albany*[55] case on competition, rather than free movement, can be contrasted with that in *Viking* and *Laval* concerning the exclusion of strikes or collective action from the scope of the common or internal market, i.e. from a competence point of view. In *Albany*, the provisions of a collective agreement negotiated during bargaining between management and labour were found to be exempt from the competition law provisions. Advocate General Maduro in *Viking* sought to distinguish the reasoning of the ECJ in *Albany*:

> Moreover, the underlying concern in *Albany* appears to have been to avoid a possible contradiction in the Treaty. The Treaty encourages social dialogue leading to the conclusion of collective agreements on working conditions and wages. However, this objective would be seriously undermined if the Treaty were, at the same time, to prohibit such agreements by reason of their inherent effects on competition. Accordingly, collective agreements must enjoy a 'limited antitrust immunity'. By contrast, the Treaty provisions on freedom of movement present no such risk of contradiction, since, as I pointed out above, these provisions can be reconciled with social policy objectives.

....

52 Criticising the vagueness of the ECJ criteria in *Laval* and *Viking*, see R Zahn 'The *Viking* and *Laval* cases in the context of European enlargement' (2008) 3 *Web Journal of Current Legal Issues* (2008).

53 Case C–341/05, *Laval* [2007] ECR I–11767 para 70.

54 In Case C–341/05, *Laval* [2007] ECR I–11767, the ECJ held that free movement principles might legitimately be restricted by the fundamental right to strike (para 57), but that '. . . however, as regards the specific obligations, linked to signature of the collective agreement for the building sector, which the trade unions seek to impose on undertakings established in other Member States by way of collective action such as that at issue in the case in the main proceedings, the obstacle which that collective actions forms cannot be justified with regard to such an objective' (para 108). Compared to *Viking*, the ECJ decision in *Laval* seems to leave national courts with less autonomy or discretion in balancing the free movement principle with legitimate exceptions (e.g. compare para 65 in *Viking*).

55 Case C–67/96 *Albany* [1999] ECR I–5751 paras 59–64. The facts concerned a collective agreement between organisations representing employers and workers setting up a sectoral pension fund to which affiliation was made compulsory.

The difference identified between the scope of the competition and free movement principles here relates to competence: is the right to strike wholly a matter for the Member States? *Viking* and *Laval* suggest not, whereas *Albany* is more sensitive to competence issue, suggesting strikes are not within the internal market. Partly, this appears to be because the bringing of strikes or collective action within the competition principle was considered to automatically render them unlawful, whereas the scope for exceptions under free movement is more flexible. However, this reasoning in *Albany* would be more persuasive if Article 81 EC Treaty (now Article 101 TFEU) on competition competence had permitted of no exception, whereas it does provide for exceptions relating to, inter alia, 'improving the production or distribution of goods or to promoting technical or economic progress' (Article 101(3) TFEU). The right to strike could be considered to come within the concept of economic progress, since it relates to the welfare of workers which could be considered a prerequisite for such progress.[56]

Joerges & Rödl have recently argued that supranational conflict of laws provides a framework for understanding the EU legal system. Their approach is a broad contextual account of EU law and constitutionalism, and it shows the potential for 'conflict' as a lens for analysing the dynamics of EU law. On *Laval* and *Viking*, they note the fundamental character of the conflict between the economic freedoms envisaged in the treaties and the national constitutional orders:

> . . . [European particularity] was underlined at the beginning, namely the sectoral decoupling of the social from the economic constitution – and the difficulties involved in the establishment of a European *Sozialstaat*. The ECJ's argument implies that European economic freedoms, rhetorically tamed only by an unspecified social dimension of the Union, trump the labour and social constitution (*Arbeits* and *Sozialverfassung*) of a Member State. In view of the obstacles to the establishment of a comprehensive European welfare state, the respect for the common European legacy of *Sozialstaatlichkeit* seems to require both the acceptance of European diversity and judicial self-restraint whenever European economic freedoms come into conflict with national welfare state traditions. . . . [The ECJ] is not legitimised to reorganise the interdependence of Europe's social and economic constitutions, let alone replace the variety of European social models with a uniform Hayekian *Rechtsstaat*.[57]

---

56 For a broad view as to the scope of (ex) art 81 EC Treaty (now Article 101 TFEU), suggesting that factors other than purely economic in the narrow sense should be considered relevant, see R Whish *Competition Law* (5th edn Butterworths 2003) 152–55.

57 Joerges and Rödl (n 2) 18. 'Hayekian' is a reference to the Austrian economist and political theorist Friedrich Hayek (1899–1992), who believed in economic freedom under the rule of law as essential to political freedom.

18.6 HEALTHCARE IN THE EU

18.6.1 TREATY PROVISIONS ON HEALTH

Article 35 of the EU Charter of Fundamental Rights of the European Union[58] acknowledges provision of healthcare as a fundamental right, but this is an area in which the EU has quite limited competence. The Lisbon Treaty provided for a partial, shared competence of the EU in health. Article 4(2) TFEU provides that the EU shall have shared competence in '. . . (k) common safety concerns in public health matters, for the aspects defined in this Treaty'. Article 6 TFEU, which sets out the complementary competences of the EU ('support, coordinate or supplement the actions of the Member States'), provides that the EU has such competence '(a) protection and improvement of human health'. Article 99 TFEU contains a very general clause that:

ARTICLE 99 TFEU

In defining and implementing its policies and activities, the Union shall take into account requirements linked to the promotion of a high level of employment, the guarantee of adequate social protection, the fight against social exclusion, and a high level of education, training and protection of human health.

The reference to 'protection of human health' can be considered broadly to include almost any aspect of healthcare, but the 'take into account requirements' suggests only what can be considered necessities, i.e. matters that are not subject to much policy disagreement.

In addition, the provisions in the TFEU on derogations from the movement principles include a public health derogation, such as Article 45(3) on free movement of workers. This is, however, quite strictly interpreted, and it requires the presence or threat of disease of epidemic potential for the derogation to be applied.[59] Further, Article 114(3) TFEU provides that if the Member States use the harmonising provision in Article 114(1) TFEU to achieve an objective of the internal market and this concerns health (or safety, environmental protection and consumer protection), the Commission in its proposals will take as a base a high level of protection, taking account in particular of any new development based on scientific facts. Article 114(8) TFEU provides that if a Member State raises a specific problem on public health in a field subject to prior harmonisation measures, it shall alert the Commission, which shall immediately examine whether to propose appropriate measures to the Council.

---

58 See above n 15, Article 35 states: Everyone has the right of access to preventive health care and the right to benefit from medical treatment under the conditions established by national laws and practices. A high level of human health protection shall be ensured in the definition and implementation of all Union policies and activities.

59 Directive 2004/38 on the right of citizens of the Union and their family members to move and reside freely within the territory of the Member States, OJ L 1458 30.04.2004 p. 77, art 29.

Article 153(1) TFEU provides that with a view to achieving the objectives of Article 151 TFEU on EU social policy, the EU shall support and complement the activities of the Member States in a number of fields, including (a) improvement in particular of the working environment to protect workers' health and safety.

The most specific treaty provision on health is Article 168 TFEU, which provides:

ARTICLE 168 TFEU

1. A high level of human health protection shall be ensured in the definition and implementation of all Union policies and activities.

Union action, which shall complement national policies, shall be directed towards improving public health, preventing physical and mental illness and diseases, and obviating sources of danger to physical and mental health. Such action shall cover the fight against the major health scourges, by promoting research into their causes, their transmission and their prevention, as well as health information and education, and monitoring, early warning of and combating serious cross-border threats to health.

The Union shall complement the Member States' action in reducing drugs-related health damage, including information and prevention.

2. The Union shall encourage cooperation between the Member States in the areas referred to in this Article and, if necessary, lend support to their action. It shall in particular encourage cooperation between the Member States to improve the complementarity of their health services in cross-border areas.

Member States shall, in liaison with the Commission, coordinate among themselves their policies and programmes in the areas referred to in paragraph 1. The Commission may, in close contact with the Member States, take any useful initiative to promote such coordination, in particular initiatives aiming at the establishment of guidelines and indicators, the organisation of exchange of best practice, and the preparation of the necessary elements for periodic monitoring and evaluation. The European Parliament shall be kept fully informed.

3. The Union and the Member States shall foster cooperation with third countries and the competent international organisations in the sphere of public health.

4. By way of derogation from Article 2(5) and Article 6(a) and in accordance with Article 4(2)(k) the European Parliament and the Council, acting in accordance with the ordinary legislative procedure and after consulting the Economic and Social Committee and the Committee of the Regions, shall contribute to the

achievement of the objectives referred to in this Article through adopting in order to meet common safety concerns:

(a) measures setting high standards of quality and safety of organs and substances of human origin, blood and blood derivatives; these measures shall not prevent any Member State from maintaining or introducing more stringent protective measures;

(b) measures in the veterinary and phytosanitary fields which have as their direct objective the protection of public health;

(c) measures setting high standards of quality and safety for medicinal products and devices for medical use.

5. The European Parliament and the Council, acting in accordance with the ordinary legislative procedure and after consulting the Economic and Social Committee and the Committee of the Regions, may also adopt incentive measures designed to protect and improve human health and in particular to combat the major cross-border health scourges, measures concerning monitoring, early warning of and combating serious cross-border threats to health, and measures which have as their direct objective the protection of public health regarding tobacco and the abuse of alcohol, excluding any harmonisation of the laws and regulations of the Member States.

6. The Council, on a proposal from the Commission, may also adopt recommendations for the purposes set out in this Article.

7. Union action shall respect the responsibilities of the Member States for the definition of their health policy and for the organisation and delivery of health services and medical care. The responsibilities of the Member States shall include the management of health services and medical care and the allocation of the resources assigned to them. The measures referred to in paragraph 4(a) shall not affect national provisions on the donation or medical use of organs and blood.

Article 168 TFEU is carefully phrased also as to attribute a secondary or limited competence to the EU in public health matters. This is clear, in particular, from Article 168(7) TFEU concerning respect for the responsibilities of the Member States defining health policy and providing for health care. The ordinary legislative procedure applies, under Article 168(4)–(5) TFEU, but legislation is limited to establishing health standards in goods and products associated with healthcare or to incentive measures. The reluctance to extend EU competence in healthcare is also reflected in the exclusion from the scope of the Services Directive of healthcare, relatively modest though the Services Directive eventually turned out to be with the dropping of the country of origin principle (see Chapter 12).

KEY CASE TOBACCO ADVERTISING

The predecessor provision in the EC Treaty to Article 168 TFEU was the subject of the first judgment of the Court of Justice invalidating legislation passed by the EU legislature. In *Tobacco Advertising*, the Court held that:

77. The first indent of Article 129(4) of the Treaty [now Article 168 TFEU] excludes any harmonisation of laws and regulations of the Member States designed to protect and improve human health.

78. But that provision does not mean that harmonising measures adopted on the basis of other provisions of the Treaty cannot have any impact on the protection of human health. Indeed, the third paragraph of Article 129(1) provides that health requirements are to form a constituent part of the Community's other policies.

79. Other articles of the Treaty may not, however, be used as a legal basis in order to circumvent the express exclusion of harmonisation laid down in Article 129(4) of the Treaty.[60]

The result is that the health provision should be used when the 'centre of gravity' of a proposed legislation concerns health. Under this test, a measure having a twofold aim or twofold component has as a legal basis that of the main aim or component; where a measure has several objectives, without one being incidental to the other, the measure could exceptionally be based on more than one legal basis.[61]

A range of quite technical and specific legislative acts have been adopted pursuant to (now) Article 168 TFEU. For example, Directive 2002/98/EC setting standards of quality and safety for the collection, testing, processing, storage and distribution of human blood and blood components and amending Directive 2001/83/EC.[62]

18.6.2 HEALTH AS A DIMENSION OF FREEDOM OF MOVEMENT

One of the challenging aspects of EU competence is the relationship between general competences and specific competences. While health is dealt with most specifically in

---

60 This reasoning is in sharp contrast with that which prevailed in *Laval* and *Viking*, discussed further above.
61 See generally ch 7 on competences.
62 Directive 2002/98/EC setting standards of quality and safety for the collection, testing, processing, storage and distribution of human blood and blood components and amending Directive 2001/83/EC OJ L 33 8.2.2003 p. 30. This has been amended by Regulation 596/2009/EC of the European Parliament and of the Council adapting a number of instruments subject to the procedure referred to in art 251 of the Treaty to Council Decision 1999/468/EC with regard to the regulatory procedure with scrutiny – Adaptation to the regulatory procedure with scrutiny – Part Four, OJ L 188 18.7.2009 p. 14.

Article 168 TFEU, as noted above, health could be relevant to a harmonising measure to achieve the internal market under Article 114 TFEU.

> MAKING CONNECTIONS
> +++++++++++++++++
> ### HEALTHCARE AND SERVICES
> Of more significance in practice is the fact that healthcare satisfies the definition of a service and thus falls within the scope of freedom of movement of services and of establishment. Thus, both the provision of health and the benefit of health care come within free movement.

Gekiere and others have explained the overall context in which this occurs very well:

> Mainly spurred on by the jurisprudence of the European Court of Justice (the Court) and the action undertaken by the European Commission, the application of these two principles has gradually made its way into national health systems and has extended far beyond the specific cases of patient and provider mobility. This trend is followed with suspicion by many policy-makers and actors. They mainly fear the deregulatory effect that is likely to cripple steering instruments and may conflict with the specific objectives pursued by national health policy and its important challenges. Most policy actors also point to the legal uncertainty created by the internal market logic and its inequitable consequences. The political debate, which culminated in the exclusion of health services from the Services Directive, looks at how free movement principles can be reconciled with health policy objectives, and how an acceptable balance can be found between respecting free movement principles and the need to regulate and steer the health sector (footnotes omitted).[63]

As examined in Chapter 12, a service under EU law is the carrying out of some task on a commercial basis, other than the sale of goods. Although healthcare might be thought to have a specificity that distinguishes it from other goods, given its status as an essential service and one in which Member States have traditionally been very involved according to their distinct national traditions,[64] healthcare generally fits within this definition, since in most Member States in the UK, healthcare is provided in return for a fee. Even in a system like the National Health Service in the UK, which is available universally free of charge, most recipients contribute in the form of taxation and social insurance contributions when they are working.

----

63 W Gekiere, R Baeten and W Palm 'Free movement of services in the EU and healthcare' in E Mossiolos, G Permanand, R Baeten and T K Hervey (eds) *Health Systems Governance in Europe: The Role of European Union Law and Policy* (Cambridge University Press 2010) 461–62.
64 See Opinion of the Advocate General Tesauro in Case C–120/95 *Decker v Caisse de Maladie des Employés Privés* [1998] ECR I–1831, referring to the perception of healthcare as 'an island beyond the reach of Community rules' (at para 17).

There are several ways in which healthcare falls within free movement of services.[65] Recipients of healthcare services have a right to travel from one Member State to another Member State to receive them under Article 56 TFEU. Providers of healthcare services have a right to establish themselves to do so in another Member State under Article 49 TFEU.

KEY CASE DECKER

Decker was amongst the first cases in which healthcare was subjected to freedom of movement principles.[66] Decker was a Luxembourg national who purchased a pair of spectacles in Belgium on prescription from an ophthalmologist established in Luxembourg. He then applied to the applicable social security fund for a contribution toward the cost, but the fund refused to make the flat rate payment to Decker on the ground that the spectacles had been purchased abroad without prior authorisation. By analogy with its case law on free movement of goods, under which the Court had held that measures adopted by Member States in social security matters that may affect the marketing of medical products and indirectly influence the possibilities of importing those products are subject to the treaty rules on the free movement of goods,[67] the Court held the fact that the national rules at issue in the main proceedings fall within the sphere of social security cannot exclude the application of freedom of movement of services.[68]

The Court of Justice has further confirmed in *Watts* that healthcare falls within freedom of movement of services irrespective of how it is financed:

> Article 49 EC applies where a patient . . . receives medical services in a hospital environment for consideration in a Member State other than her State of residence, regardless of the way in which the national system with which that person is registered and from which reimbursement of the cost of those services is subsequently sought operates.[69]

---

65 This chapter does not cover free movement of service applied to health insurance, as this is not really fundamentally different to insurance in general on the basis of relating to healthcare. For discussion of this, see W Palm, I A Glinos 'Enabling patient mobility in the EU: between free movement and coordination' in Gekiere and others in Mossiolos and others (eds) (n 63).

66 See also Case C–158/96 *Kohll v Union des Caisses de Maladie* [1998] ECR I–1931.

67 Case 238/82 *Duphar and Others v Netherlands* [1984] ECR 523.

68 Case C–120/95 *Decker* [1998] ECR I–1831 paras 24–25. The case law has not tended to deal with the free provision of healthcare in the home Member State, which is less obviously subject to freedom of movement since it is less 'economic' in nature. For this reason, the Court has been less willing to subject healthcare to competition rules. See e.g. Case C–205/03 *FENIN* [2006] ECR I–6295 and Gekiere and others in Mossiolos and others (eds) (n 63) 467.

69 Case C–372/04 *Watts* [2006] ECR I–4325 para 90.

Given the very broad interpretation of the free movement principles by the Court of Justice as encompassing any obstacles to free movement, 'almost any regulatory or institutional aspect of health care provision can be challenged' as such a potential obstacle to free movement.[70] The result is that when health service providers are established in a Member State and lawfully provide services similar to the ones that they plan to provide abroad, they consequently acquire a right to provide their services in other Member States. An example is *Commission v France*, where the Court found against a French rule that in order to get a licence to provide biomedical laboratory service, the service provider had to have a seat in France.[71]

MAKING CONNECTIONS
+++++++++++++++++++

HEALTHCARE AND ESTABLISHMENT

The broad approach to non-discriminatory obstacles can be considered less applicable to freedom of establishment, since it is accepted under the Treaty that national regulations may apply to establishment as opposed to services.[72] However, the Court has gradually shown a greater willingness to apply the logic of non-discriminatory obstacles to establishment as well. For example, it has found to be unlawful national rules reserving the ownership of pharmacies for pharmacists or legal entities consisting of pharmacists.[73]

Given this tendency, the approach of the Court to justifications for national refusal contrary to free movement becomes more important.[74]

MAKING CONNECTIONS
+++++++++++++++++++

DEROGATIONS IN THE CONTEXT OF HEALTHCARE AS SERVICES OR ESTABLISHMENT

As in other areas of free movement, the Court is open to justifications in its caselaw on grounds of public policy (except for direct discrimination, which is only justifiable under the derogations in the treaty) subject to the tests of non-discrimination, necessity and proportionality.

Examples are *MacQuen* and *Gräbner*, which concerned national provisions reserving the exercise of certain medical activities to physicians, which were found to be justified to

---

70 Ibid, 463. See, e.g. Case C–76/90, *Säger v Dennemeyer* [1991] ECR I–4221 para 12.
71 Case C–496/01 *Commission v France* [2004] ECR I–2351 para 91.
72 Case 221/85 *Commission v Belgium* [1987] ECR 719 para 9.
73 Case C–531/06 *Commission v Italy* [2009] ECR I–4102.
74 See Gekiere and others in Mossiolos and others (eds) (n 63) 477 ff.

protect public health.[75] In *Watts*, the Court accepted that the needs of hospital planning, including planning for costs, could justify limitations on freedom of movement.[76]

The case of *Commission v Greece* illustrates the application of proportionality. The Court held that a prohibition on qualified opticians from operating more than one optician's shop was not justified, since less restrictive measures such as 'requiring the presence of qualified, salaried opticians or associates in each optician's shop, rules concerning civil liability and rules requiring professional indemnity insurance' could equally achieve the objective of protecting public health.[77]

18.6.3 LEGISLATIVE PROPOSALS

In 2011, the Member States adopted Directive 2011/24/EU on the application of patients' rights in cross-border healthcare.[78] Recital 2 states that Article 114 TFEU is the appropriate legal basis since the majority of the provisions of the Directive aim to improve the functioning of the internal market and the free movement of goods, persons and services, and notes that Article 114(3) TFEU explicitly requires that, in achieving harmonisation, a high level of protection of human health is to be guaranteed, taking account in particular of any new development based on scientific facts. Recital 4 notes that the Member States retain responsibility for providing safe, high quality, efficient and quantitatively adequate healthcare to citizens on their territory, while Recital 5 notes a set of operating principles that are shared by health systems throughout the Union.

The Directive is quite specifically focused on patients' practical rights as regards equal treatment on grounds of nationality and reimbursement across borders, as well as, for example, mutual recognition of prescriptions, as opposed to more generic provisions that might have opened up healthcare to more intrusive 'free movement' regulation.

18.7 INTERACTION OF THE COMPETENCE OF THE EU AND OF THE COUNCIL OF EUROPE IN SOCIAL MATTERS

Many of the matters covered in this chapter as falling under EU law are also regulated by the Council of Europe's European Social Charter, which was first adopted in 1961[79] and revised in 1996.[80] As part of the Council of Europe system, cooperation between

....

75 Case C–8/96 *MacQuen* [2001] ECR I–837; and Case C–294/00 *Deutsche Paracelsus Schulen v Gräbner* [2002] ECR I–6515.

76 See Case C–372/04 *Watts* [2006] ECR I–4325 para 109; Case C–385/99, *Müller-Fauré* [2003] ECR I–4509 paras 79–80.

77 OJ L88 04.04.2011 p. 45.

78 OJ L 88 04.04.2011 p. 45.

79 ETS No 35.

80 ETS No 168.

countries is largely voluntary in character, although there is a monitoring mechanism for its Social Charter in the form of the European Committee of Social Rights. The European Social Charter is intended to establish basic rights in the context of citizens' social wellbeing. It is mainly concerned with economic-related matters, especially work.

The main difference with EU law, apart from its more voluntary character, is that the European Social Charter is primarily concerned with how states deal with their own citizens, whereas EU law is primarily concerned that states treat citizens from other Member States in the same way as they treat their own nationals. The European Social Charter does not create any rights for those who do already have the right to work in a state.[81]

In the following table, the rights established under the European Social Charter are listed, alongside the closest equivalents in the EU. Rather than establishing such basic rights as a right to work, the closest equivalent in EU law tends to assume the right exists and applies a principle of non-discrimination.

Summary of the Council of Europe's 'European Social Charter'

Article	Content	Closest equivalent in the EU
Article 1	The right to work	Article 45 TFEU
Article 2	The right to just conditions of work	Regulation 883/2004 and especially Regulation 492/2011
Article 3	The right to safe and healthy working conditions	Various Directives adopted under Article 153 TFEU, e.g. European Framework Directive on Safety and Health at Work (Directive 89/391 EEC)[82]
Article 4	The right to fair remuneration	Article 157 TFEU
Article 5	The right to organise	Article 12 EU Charter of Fundamental Rights, Article 163 TFEU
Article 6	The right to bargain collectively	As for Article 5
Article 7	The right of children and young persons to protection	Article 32 of the EU Charter of Fundamental Rights

81 Appendix to the Social Charter (Revised), Scope of the Revised European Charter in Terms of Persons Protected, Note 1.

82 OJ L 183 29.6.1989 p. 1 (later amended).

Article 8	The right of employed women to protection of maternity	Directive 2006/54/EC (on the implementation of the principle of equal opportunities and equal treatment of men and women in matters of employment and occupation (recast)); Directive 2010/18 (parental leave); Directive 92/85 (Pregnant and Breastfeeding Workers)
Article 9	The right to vocational guidance	Article 29 of the EU Charter of Fundamental Rights
Article 10	The right to vocational training	Article 14(1) of the EU Charter of Fundamental Rights; Articles 7(3) & 10 of Regulation 492/2011
Article 11	The right to protection of health	Articles 31 & 35 of the EU Charter of Fundamental Rights, Directive 883/2004, Regulation 492/2011 (Article 7)
Article 12	The right to social security	Article 34 of the EU Charter of Fundamental Rights; Directive 883/2004, Regulation 492/2011 (Article 7)
Article 13	The right to social and medical assistance	Articles 34 & 35 of the EU Charter of Fundamental Rights
Article 14	The right to benefit from social welfare services	Directive 883/2004, Regulation 492/2011 (Article 7)
Article 15	The right of persons with disabilities to independence, social integration and participation in the life of the community	Articles 21 & 26 of the EU Charter of Fundamental Rights, Directive 2000/78 (equal treatment in employment and occupation, including on grounds of disability)
Article 16	The right of the family to social, legal, and economic protection	Article 33 of the EU Charter of Fundamental Rights, Regulation 492/2011 (Article 7), Directive 2004/38
Article 17	The right of children and young persons to social, legal and economic protection	Article 24 of the EU Charter of Fundamental Rights
Article 18	The right to engage in a gainful occupation in the territory of other Parties	Articles 45–62 TFEU, Regulation 492/2011, Directive 2004/38

Article 19	The right of migrant workers and their families to assistance and protection	Regulation 492/2011, Directive 2004/38, citizenship case law
Article 20	The right to equal opportunities and equal treatment in matters of employment and occupation without discrimination on the grounds of sex	Articles 8, 10, 19 & 157 TFEU; Directive 75/1 (equal pay); Directive 76/207 (equal treatment); Directive 79/7 (social security); Directive 86 (occupational pensions); Directive 2004/113 (equal treatment between men and women in access to and supply of goods and services); Directive 2006/54/EC (on the implementation of the principle of equal opportunities and equal treatment of men and women in matters of employment and occupation (recast)); Directive 2010/18 (parental leave); Directive 2010/41 (on equal treatment between self-employed men and women)
Article 21	Right of workers to information and consultation	Article 153(1)(e)-(f) TFEU
Article 22	The right to take part in the determination and improvement of working conditions and environment	As for Article 5
Article 23	The right of elderly persons to social protection	Articles 21, 25, 34 of the EU Charter of Fundamental Rights; Directive 2000/78/EC (equal treatment in employment and occupation on grounds including age); Case 114/04, *Mangold v Helm* [2005] ECR 9981
Article 24	The right to protection in cases of termination of employment	Article 7 of Regulation 492/2011; Articles 3, 6 & 11 of Directive 2000/78
Article 25	The right of workers to protection during insolvency of their employer	Directive 2008/94 (on the protection of employees in the event of the insolvency of their employer)[83]
Article 26	The right to dignity at work	Article 31 of the EU Charter of Fundamental Rights
Article 27	The right of workers with family responsibilities to equal opportunities and treatment	Directive 92/85 (Pregnant and Breastfeeding Workers), Directive 2010/18 (parental leave)

83 OJ L 283 28.10.2008 p. 36.

Article 28	The right of workers' representatives to protection in the undertaking and facilities to be accorded to them	As for Article 5
Article 29	The right to information and consultation in collective redundancy	Articles 2 & 3 of Directive 98/59 on the approximation of the laws of the Member States relating to collective redundancies[84]
Article 30	The right to protection against poverty and social exclusion	Article 34(3) of the EU Charter of Fundamental Rights
Article 31	The right to housing	As for Article 30

The content of the two additional protocols is not included in the table. The first Additional Protocol to the European Social Charter dealt with equal opportunities in the workplace, the right of workers to information and consultation, the right to take part in the determination and improvement of working conditions and the right of elderly persons to social protection.[85] The second additional protocol or the Protocol Amending the Social Charter enhanced the supervision procedure.[86]

18.8 THE SAGA OF THE WORKING TIME DIRECTIVES

The exercise by the EU of competence in the matter of working time in employment has been one of the most controversial aspects of EU social policy, especially in the UK. A series of successive directives have been adopted on the topic. They regulate the maximum number of working hours in a week, as an 'offshoot' of EU competence concerning the free movement of workers. The legal basis for the directives, however, is Article 153 TFEU (ex Article 127 ECT), which provides that the EU has a complementary competence in, inter alia, (a) improvement in particular of the working environment to protect workers' health and safety and (b) working conditions.

These Working Time Directives have been controversial because they impact on the flexibility of the labour market. The more rigid rules on maximum working hours are, the more restricted businesses are in asking for long hours in return for higher

---

84 OJ L 225 12.8.1998 p. 16.
85 ETS No 128.
86 ETS No 142.

pay in order to compete more effectively with countries (such as the US, which has very flexible labour laws from an employer's perspective, and developing countries, which have lower labour costs) where employers are not burdened by such limitations on how much work they can ask of their existing employees. The consequence for EU businesses is that they may have to hire new employees, rather than ask existing employees to work longer, and the former is a more expensive option.

The following are the main provisions of the most recent Working Time Directive 2003/88/EC:[87]

- rest time of at least 11 consecutive hours per 24 hours (Article 3), at least every six hours of work (Article 4), weekly rest period of at least 24 hours (Article 5)
- maximum working hours per week of 48 hours for each week period (Article 6)
- minimum number of paid annual leave of at least four weeks per year (Article 7)
- derogations are provided for in certain categories and situations under Articles 17–20, e.g. doctors (Article 17(5)) and collective agreements (Article 18).

ANALYSING THE LAW

CONTROVERSY OVER THE WORKING TIME DIRECTIVE[88]

Very different approaches to the regulation of labour markets exist between the Member States. France has what can be described as a *dirigiste* (French for 'directory' or interventionist) approach to labour law: it is highly interventionist and has an extensive range of social protections for employees. The UK, especially since the conflict between the Thatcher government of the 1980s and trade unions over privatisation and more flexible working conditions, has a less interventionist approach, which can enhance the competitiveness of UK firms, giving them more flexibility about how much work they ask of existing employees. Thus, France and the UK are at different ends of this spectrum: France tends toward considerable state regulation and protection for workers; the UK tends towards a more pro-enterprise regime.

UK governments, more so those in which the Conservative Party is dominant, have objected to the directive's restriction of employers' freedom of enterprise

---

87 Directive 2003/88/EC of the European Parliament and of the Council of 4 November 2003 concerning certain aspects of the organisation of working time, OJ L 299 18.11.2003 p. 9. The previous versions were Council Directive 93/104/EC concerning certain aspects of the organisation of working time OJ L 307 13.12.1993 p. 18, which was amended by Directive 2000/34/EC 2000 amending Council Directive 93/104/EC concerning certain aspects of the organisation of working time to cover sectors and activities excluded from that Directive, OJ L 195 1.8.2000 p. 41.

88 See further D Dimitrakopoulos, 'Debates over the EU's Working Time Directive epitomise the conflict between neo-liberal and centre-left visions of Europe', http://blogs.lse.ac.uk/europpblog/2013/04/24/debates-over-the-eus-working-time-directive-epitomise-the-conflict-between-neo-liberal-and-centre-left-visions-of-europe/ (last accessed 21 January 2015).

as harmful to economic growth. When the directive was first proposed, the UK brought an annulment action, but it did not succeed before the Court of Justice:[89]

> There is nothing in the wording of Article 118a to indicate that the concepts of 'working environment', 'safety' and 'health' as used in that provision should, in the absence of other indications, be interpreted restrictively, and not as embracing all factors, physical or otherwise, capable of affecting the health and safety of the worker in his working environment, including in particular certain aspects of the organization of working time.

'Working environment' is given a broad interpretation here, characteristic of the ECJ. Many might consider the environment to relate to the physical conditions of work, rather than the actual amount of working time.

18.9 FUTURE OF EU SOCIAL LAW AND POLICY

Since the economic crisis, most major reform proposals for the EU have focused on economic policy. Member States have adopted the inter-governmental European Stability Mechanism Treaty and Fiscal Compact, as well as the so-called six-pack and two-pack of associated secondary legislation (see Chapter 17). Indeed, one of the critiques of the EU that has emerged from the economic crisis is that the EU response has been a narrow, technical one focused on deficit reduction to the exclusion of a broader vision of Europe with a social dimension focused on the welfare and prospects of ordinary citizens, rather than economic and political elites.

Critics of the austerity that has been adopted to curb national budget deficits, seen as central to the crisis of confidence in the Euro currency, claim it is creating social hardship through increased unemployment and lower spending power for citizens as wages and government and consumer spending contract. The economic crisis does not bode well, in that context, for a convergence of views on social policy. Rather, it seems to have merely highlighted the sharp differences in political vision to be found in European politics between the economic 'right', determined to push through austerity regardless of the social costs (including European integrationists, who have seized upon the crisis as the latest opportunity to enhanced EU powers over national fiscal policy) and the economic left, who see austerity as exemplifying a narrow, socially irresponsible economic focus.

Moreover, critics of austerity argue that it actually worsens the deficit situation by depressing economies and inhibiting the growth that would enable governments to

....
89 Case C–84/94 *United Kingdom of Great Britain and Northern Ireland v Council* [1996] ECR I–5755 para 15.

reduce deficits by benefiting from the extra taxes and wages that accompany economic development. For example, it is widely agreed that capital and infrastructure investment by governments can be economically beneficial in the long-run, even if financed by deficits in the short to medium term.

At the time of writing, the French Government presented its resignation to President Hollande because of sharp disagreements amongst the ruling socialist party over the decision to adopt a path of deficit reduction through austerity.[90] The cleavage of opinion that was apparent in the debate over *Viking* and *Laval* represents itself in more dramatic form here.

18.10 CONCLUSION

As the crisis in the Eurozone has dramatically demonstrated, different visions of the EU place different emphasis on the economic and social aspects of integration. The EU has always had an only limited competence in social matters, but nonetheless the Treaty has some important provisions on equal pay for equal work and the legal basis, for example, for Working Time Directive. The EU has a partial, shared competence in public health as specified in the Treaty, but also aspects of healthcare come within the internal market as a provision of a service. It remains to be seen what convergence of views on social policy might develop to allow for more integration in this sphere. The economic crisis, however, has tended to reinforce views that the EU has a somewhat unbalanced approach that is more concerned with economic data and profiling, and less with the concrete social reality of EU citizens, despite past achievements, for example, in gender equality. In the social sphere, in particular, it may be best to think of looser 'cooperation' rather than a more loaded concept of integration, the latter implying greater harmonisation of standards and approaches.

POINTS TO REVIEW

– The scope of EU competences in social matters has developed incrementally over time, albeit that it is still quite limited. Initially, the treaty provisions were either largely aspirational or limited in character, such as Article 119 EEC Treaty on equal pay for men and women.

– Gender equality played a key role from the early period of the Communities because of the provision of equal pay for equal work. This had a transformational impact in some of the Member States and contributed to the sense of legitimation of the Communities in their early period.

....

90 'France rejects rebel minister Montebourg from Cabinet' *Reuters,com* (25 August 2014); see also M Blyth, 'Austerity as ideology: a reply to my critics' (2013) 11 *Comparative European Politics* 737–51.

- Apart from the principle of equal pay for equal work, EU labour law extends to the application of free movement principles in the workplace (based on the principle of non-discrimination on grounds of nationality). Among the more controversial EU policies, at least in the UK, has been the Working Time Directive.

- Social competence of the EU interacts with other competences, especially the general internal market competences. As technically a service, healthcare came within EU free movement competence irrespective of specific provisions on healthcare. The approach of the Court of Justice in this sphere reflects its approach to free movement of services and of establishment: non-discriminatory obstacles to the provisions of services falls within the scope of the treaties.

- Primarily, EU law is concerned with the right to receive healthcare or to travel to receive it or provide it. EU competence in healthcare as provided for specifically in the Treaty is shared with the Member States only in public health matters.

- The roles of the EU and Council of Europe interact in social matters in that the Council of Europe has adopted measures that overlap with EU measures concerning social policy. However, as the Council of Europe represents a typical, voluntary system of international cooperation, meaning that any conflict with EU law in national legal systems is resolved in favour of EU law.

- The crisis in the Eurozone has tended to reinforce an image of the EU as more about economics than social wellbeing. The two aspects of integration are, of course, tightly interwoven. For now, the Member States retain primary competence in the social sphere.

CHAPTER GLOSSARY

Charter of Fundamental Rights of Workers refers to a document agreed in 1989 between 11 of the 12 Member States of what is now the EU. It is sometimes shortened to 'Social Charter', but is separate to the European Social Charter of 1961 of the Council of Europe.

Economic and Social Committee refers to an advisory body established under Article 300 TFEU to assist the Commission and Council in economic and social policy.

Employment Committee is an advisory body under Article 150 TFEU to assist the Commission and Council with their decision-making on employment issues.

Equal pay for equal work refers to a provision in the EEC Treaty, Article 119 (now Article 157 TFEU), concerning equal pay for equal work applied to gender.

European Committee of Social Rights monitors compliance with the (Council of Europe) European Social Charter by the contracting states.

European Social Charter refers to a Council of Europe Treaty adopted in 1961 and revised in 1996. The European Committee of Social Rights is the monitoring body for the Charter.

Services of the general interest refers to the broad category of public policy, in the context of the internal market principles of freedom of movement, justifying a limitation on free movement.

Social chapter refers to a Protocol to the Maastricht Treaty on social policy, agreed between 11 of the then Member States.

Working Time Directive refers to a Directive of the EU concerning the maximum number of working hours employees must perform.

TAKING THINGS FURTHER

G de Búrca (ed) *EU Law and the Welfare State* (Oxford University Press 2005) This collection of essays looks at various aspects of EU social law and policy from the perspective of law, political science, and social policy. It examines: welfare as an aspect of citizenship, social security regulation, health law and policy, welfare aspects of competition law, and governance of welfare issues.

J Shaw, J Hunt and C Wallace *The Economic and Social Law of the European Union* (Palgrave 2007) One of the few textbooks to concentrate on social aspects of the EU (although it now predates Lisbon).

C Joerges, F Rödl 'Informal politics, formalised law and the "social deficit" of European integration: reflections after the judgments of the ECJ in *Viking* and *Laval*' (2009) 15(1) *European Law Journal* 1–19 This article takes an analytical look at the significance of ECJ case law bringing trade union activity within the scope of free movement principles and analyses implications for different views of the European polity.

D O'Keeffe 'The uneasy progress of European social policy' (1996) 2 *Columbia Journal of European Law* 241 Although now quite dated, this article has interesting background information on the development of EU social policy.

European Labour Law Journal is a specialist journal on labour law aspects of the EU. See http://www.ellj.eu/content_page.aspx?contentId=109 (last accessed 21 January 2015).

INDEX